TALL WALLS
AND
HIGH FENCES

OFFICERS AND OFFENDERS,
THE TEXAS PRISON STORY

BOB ALEXANDER AND RICHARD K. ALFORD
FOREWORD BY BILL STEPHENS, DIRECTOR, TEXAS PRISON MUSEUM

Number 12 in the North Texas Crime and Criminal Justice Series

University of North Texas Press
Denton, Texas

10 9 8 7 6 5 4 3 2 1

Permissions:
University of North Texas Press
1155 Union Circle #311336
Denton, TX 76203-5017

The paper used in this book meets the minimum requirements of the American National Standard for Permanence of Paper for Printed Library Materials, z39.48.1984. Binding materials have been chosen for durability.

Library of Congress Cataloging-in-Publication Data

Names: Alexander, Bob, 1943- author. | Alford, Richard K., 1968- author. | Stephens, Bill (William L.), writer of foreword.
Title: Tall walls and high fences : officers and offenders, the Texas prison story / by Bob Alexander and Richard K. Alford ; foreword by Bill Stephens, Director, Texas Prison Museum.
Other titles: North Texas crime and criminal justice series ; no. 12.
Description: Denton, Texas : University of North Texas Press, [2020] | Series: North Texas crime and criminal justice series ; number 12 | Includes bibliographical references and index.
Identifiers: LCCN 2020021092 | ISBN 9781574418071 (cloth) | ISBN 9781574418163 (ebook)
Subjects: LCSH: Texas Prison System--History. | Prisons--Texas--History. | Prison administration--Texas--History. | Correctional personnel--Texas--Biography--Anecdotes. | Prisoners--Texas--Biography--Anecdotes.
Classification: LCC HV9475.T4 A54 2020 | DDC 365/.9764--dc23
LC record available at https://lccn.loc.gov/2020021092

The electronic edition of this book was made possible by the support of the Vick Family Foundation.

Cover and text design by Rose Design

This book is respectfully dedicated
to the
Past, Present, and Future
Men and Women
of
The Texas Department of Criminal Justice
Correctional Institutions Division

"Know You Have Not and Never Will Be Forgotten"

Contents

Foreword

THE PRISON SYSTEM IN TEXAS has held many names/titles through the years: The Texas Penitentiary, The Texas Prison System, The Texas Department of Corrections (TDC), and more recently, The Texas Department of Criminal Justice (TDCJ). The current TDCJ encompasses most of the operations of the criminal justice system (post-adjudication) to include probation, parole, and prison. The prison division within the TDCJ has taken the names of Institutional Division and/or Correctional Institutions Division, merely fancy titles for "running prisons." I will keep it simple and hereafter refer to it as the Prison System.

Also, multiple terms have been used though the years when addressing those persons convicted and sentenced to serve time in prison. Convict, thief, inmate, offender, resident, and client have been used at one time or another. I will use inmate.

The authors of this book have chronicled many of the significant events related to the Prison System. It would be impossible to write about every episode which occurred in a history which now exceeds 170 years. There have been hundreds of thousands, if not more, folks that have been involved in the prison business in Texas. The employees, inmates, public officials, private industry representatives, and volunteers have all entered these secure facilities and experienced a different world.

It has been said many times that the culture of the prisons is a microcosm of society. My experience, for the most part, has supported this notion. From the early years of the Prison System to today, for the public and their elected officials, along with some forward-thinking prison administrators, there has been one common pursuit—Reform.

The core mission of the Prison System through the years which has held fast is public safety. However, ideas of reform have been presented in many diverse ways. In the early years, isolation and separation from society was believed to be the best way to change a man's behavior. Some believed that simply by being left alone, it would cause the inmate to feel remorseful or guilty for their transgressions. Later, hard labor was demanded from the inmate population. Gradually, significant changes occurred which allowed inmates to congregate for meals, recreation, and religious services. By the end of the 1940s general education courses, counseling, visitation, music, intramural sports to include rodeo were occurring frequently. Mechanized farming, work skills, and college credits, were becoming the norm. Through the 1960s to today, a focus has been applied to establish systems of accountability either through the courts or legislative processes. By the time I began my career with the Texas Prison System all of these "Reforms" and many others were already in place, including oversight by a Federal Court. It is quite possible, even today, that there is someone, somewhere, making a pitch that we need some "Reform." While all of these measures impacted the inmates, the influences were just as significant for the front-line staff. Subsequent to a 35-year-career with the Texas Prison System, I have learned that "Reform" is an ever evolving quest.

A tremendous effort goes towards ensuring the custody, care, and treatment of the prison population. It is the responsibility of every staff member (security and non-security) to recognize that their actions have an effect on the successful reintegration of inmates into society. While every staff member may have a specific role, ensuring that staff, inmates, and the public are safe is accomplished through collaborative efforts of all parties.

Some years ago, the Texas Prison System was forced to deal with a massive and dangerous inmate gang problem. Inmate homicides and serious assaults were occurring at a never before seen rate. Possession of contraband was rampant. Inmate gangs were fighting for control. To combat this violence, the Administrative Segregation Plan was introduced. It required that offenders who exhibited assaultive behavior against staff and/or other inmates, those that were confirmed members of these violent gangs, and those who had demonstrated a desire to escape were placed in single cells and confined to that cell for 23 hours a day. Most services that were afforded to them prior to placements, were delivered cell side. Basically, it became a jail within the jail. Remarkably, the gangs gradually came under control and inmates realized that they didn't have to join a gang just to survive. The process of placement in Administrative Segregation was clearly spelled out and an avenue for release from Administrative Segregation was provided to the inmate as well. As the years have passed the practice of segregation has received a good deal of negative attention from a number of policy makers. However, segregating those inmates who are hurting staff and other inmates as well as making determined attempts to escape is good prison management.

The majority of inmates do not cause problems. They are there to "do their time and get out." There are a number of programs in the Prison System that are designed towards providing inmates opportunities for successful reentry into society. To be successful, these programs require an environment that is conducive to learning and change. The environment has to be safe, orderly, and productive. The job of the Correctional Officer can be complex at times. However, they must ensure custody and control of the inmate population at all times. Those inmates that are assaultive and tend to "buck the system" have to be moved out of the way so the programs can be successful. There are a few inmates that create chaos and havoc, regardless. This group of inmates makes the officers' jobs very challenging. The Correctional Officers must be diligent, professional, and have integrity.

Today's Correctional Officers are well-trained and held accountable for their actions. A significant amount of time and resources are allocated to equip an officer with interpersonal skills, communication abilities, crisis intervention techniques, and self-defense tactics. They are held to a Standard of Conduct that includes actions while on and/or off duty. There have been cases in which persons wearing the blue/gray had become corrupted or manipulated. However, there have been thousands and thousands and more, dedicated hard-working correctional professionals to wear the uniform of a Texas Prison Correctional Officer. The citizens of Texas should be—and can be—proud of these brave and resilient men and women. I am!

Unfortunately, this is not always the case. There is a sector of the public that stereotypes the Correctional Officer as an uneducated, tobacco chewing, redneck guard. More so, on television and the movies, the prison officials are portrayed as mean and corrupt. As always, it is the "bad ones" that make the news: And we all believe the news, right? On occasion one might read/hear about an outstanding accomplishment by a prison employee or a successful prison program, generally acclaiming a teacher, counselor, chaplain, or medical/mental health provider. But, let us not forget, it is the Correctional Officer that facilitates overall operations by providing an environment conducive to safety and positive change.

It is those men and women that daily walk the hallways, dining halls, inmate housing quarters, industrial plants, farms, medical departments, chapels, and rehabilitative programming areas that ensure everyone is safe. They are the true heroes. Their attention to duty, compassion for humanity and more importantly strength to "do the right thing," even when challenged in extremely dangerous circumstances, is what deserves recognition. After reading the manuscript for this book I believe the authors have done just that.

The modern-day officers, as well as those of the past, are presented with challenges and oppositions a number of times each day. A large number of them are assigned to facilities that are short-handed in which there is no immediate "back up." Their duties include searching inmates and their property, counting inmates (as little as seven times a day), controlling inmate movement, supervising inmate activities, and counseling inmates for rule infractions. They have to make sure inmates do not harm each other and prevent inmates from harming themselves.

While this book may not reach millions, maybe those blessed few who read it will have a better appreciation of what some employees have gone through. Not many of us grew up wanting to be a Correctional Officer. Life's circumstances, normally, dictated this career. Many of us found a tight knit and supportive group of men and women who believe in what we do. Many live paycheck to pay-check and supplement their low salary with overtime or other employment on their few days off. Stress levels are high. Family time is sacrificed. However, they continue to persevere. Not because they can't do anything else, it's because they do not want to let their coworkers down. They believe in the mission of the TDCJ.

Also deserving recognition are the 20,000 or so approved volunteers that assist TDCJ today within the rehabilitative and reentry programs. While the majority of these men and women assist with religious services or spiritual counseling, there are a number of them providing support to the education, life-skills training, substance abuse counseling, and mental health programs. Theses volunteers become mentors to the inmates and provide assistance post release from prison as well. The Prison System benefits greatly from this group of dedicated and purpose driven individuals. During staffing vacancies, the volunteers also provide continuity in programs. Some volunteers have become fulltime employees in theses areas. We should appreciate their efforts in trying to change hearts and minds.

Speaking of volunteers, it is important to also recognize a group of Correctional Officers who are making a difference by impacting the officers they work with. These officers receive no additional compensation for this responsibility. For the past several years TDCJ has struggled with recruiting and retaining proficient staff. The agency established a number of programs related to recruitment and retention of a quality staff. The policy that has been most impactful has been the establishment of a formal mentoring program. Tenured officers volunteer to become "Mentors." After a thorough vetting process, these experienced officers provide new recruits a "hands-on, front-line" resource for guidance on technical and practical issues of the job. But, more importantly, they furnish an example of how to properly deal with the combative or manipulative inmate. Wardens have noted that since the program began the retention rate of the "good ones," has increased. As a Warden with responsibility for a unit, one soon learns to appreciate their dedication to the mission of TDCJ.

I hope readers find this book as interesting as I did. It has been a privilege to work with the authors of this worthwhile project. The Texas Prison Museum was recently expanded. When finished, we will have a display honoring those dedicated men and women who lost their lives while protecting the citizens of Texas. I have always been amazed at the devotion, perseverance, and strength Texas Prison System employees have exhibited. They all know the dangers of their job but continue to provide safety to the citizens of the State of Texas with very little recognition. I am honored and humbled to have been a part of this family.

William L. "Bill" Stephens, TDCJ-CID Director, Ret.
Director, Texas Prison Museum
Huntsville, Texas

Preface and Acknowledgments

STRIKING THE RIGHT BALANCE BETWEEN inane political correctness and commonsense is not easy. Admittedly, then, surgically cutting to the underlying theme of this book is a tricky proposition. Pie-in-the-sky idealism may be a lofty and, yes, a particularly sought-after objective, but real world candor sometimes short-circuits the very best intentions of principled men and/or women. Certainly the Lone Star State penitentiary system provides the backdrop for diverse perspectives, besides spawning one helluva good story. Herein the voice of the typically unheard will be given a platform, one soundly structured atop concrete pillars of truths: Truths that might be downright uncomfortable for ensconced prisoners—as well as a smattering of state-paid prison employees. And those employees, as they enter the State of Texas workforce, make a meaningful pledge:

> I do solemnly swear that I will faithfully execute the duties of a Correctional Professional for the great State of Texas. Through Courage, I will provide public safety. Through Commitment I will promote positive change in offender behavior. With Perseverance and Integrity, I will not be corrupted; I will not be manipulated. I will not be distracted from the agency's mission. I will adhere to the laws of the State of Texas and this agency's Code of Ethics. I will embrace our Core Values as I enforce the rules and regulations of the Texas Department of Criminal Justice. So Help Me.

Too, it's not inappropriate to hypothesize that non-felons and persons not drawing penitentiary paychecks might tuck into their psyches a fresh, though certainly at times appalling appreciation of bona fide down-to-earth cellblock doings. The gritty sociological arena behind tall walls and high fences and electrically controlled steel gates and doors, perhaps, best typifies the dichotomy separating what ought to be and what is.

For the blameless layperson many perceptions about prisoners and prisons are misleadingly grounded in false-fronted back-lots and on sound-stages at Hollywood, theatrics promulgated to generate dollars, not constructively tutor the unacquainted about society's malefactors and/or correctively spotlight examples of institutional personnel's malfunctions. Too, and it's a surefire bet, seldom—seemingly never—in these manifestly fanciful and sometimes far-fetched celluloid productions is the overworked, underpaid, and undervalued prison employee graced with even an appreciative pat on the back.[1]

Auspiciously for most circumstances American citizens are constitutionally draped with unmistakable First Amendment protections regarding the uncensored exercise of free speech. Somewhat unfortunately, it may also be credibly argued, entertainment media wheel-horses therefore cleave unto themselves the leeway to sell their incredible versions of history, habitually with little or no emphasis on factuality.[2] Though many—if not most—of the gizmo-afflicted Millennial Generation are hardly familiar with Old West character Wyatt Barry Stapp Earp, for some aging Baby-Boomers his name is synonymous with sterling virtue and laudable courage. Thanks in large part to the television marketplace of days long past, Mr. Wyatt B.S. Earp sat at the pinnacle of many Philco viewers' beliefs regarding a frontier lawman's heroism and integrity and supposed six-shooter superiority. Never mind the fact that Earp is credited with custodial arrests for pimping at Peoria, never participated in a standalone gunfight, and with an assumed name desperately fled Arizona Territory ahead of lawfully drawn warrants demanding he answer for participation in murders near Tucson's railroad depot and in the wilds of Cochise County.[3] Sometimes evidence is troubling—deflating!

Glamorization of seedy and shady and sorry folks is a staple stratagem for profit-motivated movie moguls and talented scriptwriters. Outlaws Bonnie Parker and Clyde Barrow, though dead and long buried, were resurrected into folkloric status subsequent to release of their life-stories playing out before enthralled patrons looking up at 1967 Technicolor screens. Popcorn and passionate vicariousness are not strange bedfellows. Truth, though, is not pretty. Wholly tallying the thoroughly dead bodies left in the wake of Bonnie and Clyde's highly publicized crime-spree is not necessary, but mention of their partaking in a prison-break wherein an employee was fatally gunned down and the coldblooded Sunday morning murders of two unsuspecting Texas Highway Department Patrolmen near Grapevine in Tarrant County is diagnosis enough—they were not nice people.[4]

Thankfully, now, even with Hollywood's anticipated literary license to spice the true-life drama, the 2019 release of *The Highwaymen* starring actors Kevin Costner as Frank Hamer and Woody Harrelson as Maney Gault, is rather refreshing.[5] Each, at the time they lived, banked experience as Texas Rangers, and both were sure enough salty lawmen of note. In this updated film version rapt audiences are given a new and somewhat more accurate characterization of the iconic Depression Era hoodlums—one wearing long pants, the other a skirt—and each shy of any meaningful scruples. There too—with regards to the real-life viciousness of Clyde and Bonnie—are salient data for the prison piece in hand; a momentary sidebar is but fair. After behind-the-scenes wheeling and dealings by Sheriff Henderson Jordan, Bienville Parish (parish seat Arcadia), east of Shreveport, Louisiana, the death-trap had been set.[6] The second-rate robbers, though they were first-rate murderers of lawmen, had been sold out. The evil couple, using jargon of the day, "had been put on the spot." A pair of the half-dozen participants in the justified back-road gunning down of the Texas misfits hiding out in the Pelican State, were Frank Hamer and Maney Gault. At the time Bonnie and Clyde went under for keeps in their rolling Ford V-8 arsenal, the irrefutably gutsy and tenacious Hamer was answering to and drawing his monthly paycheck and per diem, not from the Lone Star State's legendary Rangers, but from the Texas Prison System.[7]

The above cited examples tend to make the point—hopefully. Lamentably it may be proffered that unless one actually banks first-hand ground-level experience some of their outlooks may be shaped and/or twisted by how the amusement industry shuffles spectators into stereotypically accepting what is not true. Though it's abhorrent to an older generation, at least for a detachment of younger people the day's happenings are funneled through the interpretative antics and comedy and political leanings of late-night television personalities. Sadly, in a day of fast-paced twenty-four-hour programming cycles, not just a few supposed newscast anchor-desk holders are masquerading as nonpartisan purveyors of the news, rather than admitting their advocacy for causes dear to their politically motivated heads and hearts. Within critical circles the debate rages white-hot: Have newsrooms morphed into venues for popular entertainment and mindlessness? Thankfully not all essayists and print media journalist have succumbed to idealism's ambiguities. An accomplished wordsmith and investigative reporter in a fascinating look-see into hard truths, *The Mexican Mafia*, figuratively fired his inked dead-shot with aplomb: "The real value of any book like this [one about gangs and prisons] is not determined by the interest, or lack of it, from the media gatekeepers who appoint themselves as the arbiters of what is significant or newsworthy. . . . [but] from the people who have invested the most skin in the game: the victims, the survivors, those who have turned away from crime and the people on the front lines who daily strap on ballistic vests to keep the rest of us safe."[8]

Bringing this notion to relevancy for the treatment in hand is uncomplicated and should not stand too much serious debate—if any. Though there are aberrations, in the vast majority of movie and television productions with a penitentiary setting—or as part of the colorful blood and thunder storyline—the prison wardens and their subordinate custodial staff are typecast to play the roles of less than admirable people. With regards to this drift, one only has to conjure unsettling memories of actor Strother Martin's character in the 1967 film classic *Cool Hand Luke* or Tommy Lee Jones's chilling prison warden portrayal in *Natural Born Killers*.

Featuring capable prison wardens in the parts of heroic protagonists is foreign to filmmakers' mindsets and predisposed messaging schematics. The fellow—usually no ladies—maintaining executive control of the institutional site is tyrannical at the bottom end of the scale and at the top end psychologically damaged with an inclination tilted toward blatant sadism and heartlessness. Characteristically the wholly unskilled prison workforce from entry-level through mid-level management for these fictional portrayals has been haphazardly recruited from a shallow and stagnant pool, one comprised solely of uncaring, undereducated, and unscrupulous misfits incapable of finding meaningful employment elsewhere.[9] Nothing is, of course, farther from the truth, but transference from the screen into the sub-consciousness of the unawares viewer is a phenomenon that is real.

There is another dynamic that, too, is real: The tendency to scapegoat policing and prison personnel for some of the ills parents and educators and theologians and therapeutic practitioners have been unable to mend through the eons of time—though all have no doubt given it a commendable and mighty try. And, of course, that's discounting the horde of glad-handing and back-slapping politicos that were straightaway reborn as experts in penology and penitentiary management the instant the polls closed, no matter their unmistakable naiveté and dearth of practical experience. Theorizing about cause and effect and problem resolution is surely apropos, even if categorical and consequential answers have truly remained, for the most part, quite elusive—uncomfortable as that might be. When all's said and done and all else fails, it's the exhausted and underpaid law enforcing and penological communities inheriting what America's broader society has proven incapable of fixing.

Perhaps at this point it is but apropos to highlight the truism. Quite articulately and accurately an ex-armed robber and former inmate and later credentialed PhD pulled the trigger on truth when authoring *Prisons in Turmoil*. Professor John Irwin identified the recurrent and inaccurate theme so common and, sometimes, accepted in sociological writings:

> When prisons are reproached for escapes, riots, and other forms
> of disorder among prisoners, the guard force receives the brunt

of the criticism. On the other hand, they are not rewarded for any accomplishments, not even prevention of escapes and maintenance of order. (The prison receives no attention when things are running smoothly.) Rewards for rehabilitative progress, if it is claimed, go to the treatment branch. The guards are only criticized or ignored.[10]

Compounding confusion with regards to actualities is the so-called enlightened focus on the prisoner and his/her writings and viewpoints. That they are rightfully entitled to pen their stories and postulate their opinions and propose their remedies is logically a straightforward no-brainer. On the other hand, circumspect analysis is not out of place but is occasionally brushed aside by a few well-intentioned academicians and a passel of pseudo-intellectuals and a pot full of agenda-driven chroniclers and correspondents. At this stage, quoting from but one, perhaps, makes the point. One doesn't even have to read between the lines if not romanced and artlessly seduced by prisoners' writings. Jack Henry Abbott, who had killed one inmate, wounded another, viciously assaulted a Correctional Officer with an improvised bludgeon, and escaped from a Maximum Security prison, feebly rationalized and wrote, *In the Belly of the Beast: Letters from Prison.* With a touch of herein-added emphasis, convict Jack Abbott, in trying to downplay reality, said: "I am at this moment thirty-seven years old. I have been free the sum total of nine and a half months. I have served many terms in solitary. . . . I would estimate that I have served a good fourteen or fifteen years in solitary. The only *serious* crime I have ever committed in *free society* was *bank robbery* during the time I was a fugitive."[11] Should we collectively applaud the author for committing only one serious crime outside an institutional setting? Are the other *less serious* felonies measured at a discounted rate?

Quite often, though, some of these journalistic prisoner musings from behind the high fences squared by tall guard towers are inordinately critical of the correctional staff overseeing their lawful confinement. Such should not be a shocker to folks owning a

Preface and Acknowledgments

modicum of commonsense and not blinded by maudlin presumptions about what real life should be like in a perfect universe, a place where everybody courteously smiles, behaves, and befriends their neighbors. No doubt, sometimes the prisoners' angst is legit and not contrived. Incontestably not all prison personnel are guiltless, either from the legal standpoint or ethically emancipated from adhering to guidelines carefully crafted into the three-ring Policy and Procedure Manuals. In the round, most *Homo sapiens* are not faultless, and a small percentage of prison personnel are purposefully choosing deceit and dishonesty over conscientious devotion to duty, dishonoring their fellow hardworking employees. Temptation to do wrong—whatever the lame excuse—is omnipresent. However, suggesting that upper-tier managerial prison administrators don't or won't cull the wrongdoers is a refutable misnomer. And herein it's but fair to also note, typically unless the crime is particularly egregious, the adjudicated perpetrator is seldom imprisoned for his/her criminality the first time around: Getting into prison is not necessarily as easy as the unfamiliar and uninformed honest citizen might presume.[12] Probated and plea-bargained reduced sentences and deferred adjudications are commonplace.

Perhaps inadvertently, even now in the twenty-first century, some scholarly treatments seem to speed-wash commonsense into an abyss of illogical conjecture. For one academic exercise the methodology was to personally interview ex-convicts, recording their remarks and synthesizing their first-person revelations about prison violence. According to the interviewing educator there was, at least for one subtopic, an identifiable commonality: All of the male ex-convicts held Correctional Officers in especially low regard, universally declaring they were, according to the educated analytic questioner, "lazy" and "dumb."[13] Such fallaciousness—on its face—begs for a coherent reply. With regards to "laziness" it must sensibly be noted that all of those scorned Correctional Officers were not unemployed and each one of them had real jobs. They weren't slothful enough to lie in bed till noon, waiting for neon lights and unguarded safes to beckon. With respect to being "dumb," at least for the inquiring professor's sampling and at that point in time, all of the Correctional Officers were, provably, at a minimum—honest and smart enough not to be imprisoned.

From a free-world (outside the tall walls and the high fences) notion there is, however, a bottom-line criminal justice truism. Indelicate as it seems to be, no matter how they might personally despise or journalistically denigrate or conversationally castigate their dutiful penitentiary guardians, the incarcerated convicts/inmates (absent appellate court reversals and/or pardons) are wholly unqualified to attain one of those jobs—even if they really wanted to. Inconvenient as that might be, that niggling bottom-line is ever there. Correctional staff guys and gals and big-time penitentiary administrators are not somehow automatically exempt from becoming some wayward convict's upset and forlorn cellmate, but assuredly it's not vice versa! For a number of reasons, real poor choices have embargoed penitentiary prisoners' chances of following in the workplace footsteps of that cadre of employees who they deride and/or detest. The irony is rich.

Poor though, at times is the tendency to try and connect two-sided theoretical issues to the ground-level prison employees: working folks far removed from the legislative remedies and/or administrative regulations promulgated elsewhere. With clumsy simplicity, sharply cutting to the nub, the employees are expected to faithfully do their jobs. Personnel, as human beings, are instilled with personal opinions, and that's okay. Those beliefs, however, cannot override fidelity to duty—that pledge backed by a sworn oath. Although insensitivity is not intended, by and large as a prison employee it's irrelevant what one thinks about some of the contentious and/or hot-button issues swamping penology. Someone expressively in favor of Capital Punishment is expected to do his/her job. An employee opposed to the idea of Capital Punishment is expected to do his/her job. Much the same can be said of today's dedicated law enforcement officers ordered to protect personnel and the physical plant at abortion clinics—regardless whether they are pro-life or pro-choice, their sworn oath was/is plain. For the prison setting, off-duty beer table and/or classroom arguments about the wisdom of certain rehabilitative programs or whether or not the absolute prohibition of tobacco products had unintended consequences or would there be any noticeable—and empirical—advantage were prisoners granted conjugal visits is just fine. Are mandatory sentences really a plus? Does proper application of the time-tested control model of Texas correctional management ensure order?[14] Do good grooming standards for prisoners and staff contribute to sound supervision and beget logical tranquility? What is fair and lawful punishment for assaultive behavior by incorrigible prisoners? Should prisoners work or lounge? First-rate leaders encourage provocative thinking. And good leaders—of which there are many in the Texas Department of Criminal Justice—make sure their twenty-four-and-seven shifts of Correctional Officers shed their personal feelings about controversial issues at the front gate.

Though on its surface the clearheaded assertion may seem callous, professionally and fair-minded Correctional Officers cannot and should not immerse themselves in the intricate issues revolving around a prisoner's actual *Guilt* or *Innocence*. Even an eminent professor doing firsthand research at Texas prisons overheard two involuntary residents bantering back and forth. Herein is part of what he noted the prisoners said:

> You ain't supposed to cop out to nothin'. If the judge catch you flyin' a kite you supposed to plead not guilty.—That's right. The facts of the business: you ain't *never* guilty.—That's right. Let 'em *find* you guilty. Sometimes a lie help you and sometimes a lie stick you. You know how it go.—Ol' buddy, you never tell the truth. You never do tell the truth. That's right. . . .[15]

Confinement in the penitentiary is a result of a courthouse conviction. Admittedly, from time to time, persons so convicted are ultimately exonerated—their forced stint in prison an awful example of unjust imprisonment—or worse! Wrongful convictions are wrong. Conversely, taking into account numbers ranging into the substantial thousands for the Lone Star State's prisoner population, the exonerations are statistically small, not irrelevant by any standard, but the troubling exceptions not the norm. However the dedicated and evenhanded Correctional Officer will do his or her best to ensure equality of managing those prisoners they are not only charged with protecting but mandated to safely and conscientiously control—interdicting any plans for an escape or riotous commotion or in-house murders. They are not prosecutors or defense lawyers or district judges or jurors—and none sit with authority on the Appellate Court's bench. As prison system employees they are but heirs to society's legislatively propagated and legally handed down decisions. Inside the tall walls and behind the high fences impartiality on the part of Correctional Officers is key. Within the unique penitentiary setting, *fair* but *firm* and *consistent* are pertinent watchwords of wisdom.

Owning up to the fact that today it's somewhat impolitic to tag someone sentenced to spend time in prison as a convict, nevertheless, one and all were convicted of one or more felonies. Though it may seem elementary to make mention, there is a stark difference separating jail-time and prison-time. Residents behind bars at county jailhouses may have yet to stand trial, having not been courtroom convicted of anything but being incapable of securing bail monies or convincing a magistrate their word to appear as directed would be as good as gold. Or they may be serving time post-adjudication of a criminal matter registering as a misdemeanor. On the other hand, in Texas there are State Jail Offenses with minimal sentences and State Jails. However, for this project the emphasis is penitentiary bound. A felony-ticket is requisite for entry and temporary or permanent residency at the Big House.[16] Colloquially—within the idiom of prison talk—there is an old saw: "Convicts" do their own time, whereas "Inmates" do everybody else's time.[17] Nowadays, due to the prevalence of bowing or curtsying before bewildering courts of political correctness, all overnight penitentiary residents are deferentially lumped into a singular sorting: politely they are classed as "Offenders." Sometimes the tag is further liberalized for the penitentiary prisoners in residency or back in the free-world under bureaucracy's supervision they become "Captives" or "Refugees" or "Clients," and for at least one professional penologist his involuntary wards of the Criminal Justice System were his "Customers." For this treatment no insensitivity is intended, though clarity is. Within the prison setting there is a not ill-defined line separating the keepers from the kept, the non-felons from the convicted. Readers, as it should be, are afforded the discretion to swap terminology as they see fit or deem appropriate. For *Tall Walls and High Fences*, however, the sharpest distinction will prevail.

The aforesaid distinction is presented as precursor for accepting a solid sociological certainty: "The walls and goals of prison do not make a neat or logical package."[18] Behind the tall walls and inside the high fences exists a different and unfamiliar world, one that would be scary and strange to the majority of everyday Texas working folks, those having not a clue about convicted lawbreakers and/or their custodial superintendents. Naiveté of the Texas free-world population would be exposed—nakedly so—as tenderfoot visitors traverse the penitentiary's threshold, the sound of locks' tumblers electrically disengaging before them and engaging behind them as each hesitant step carries them farther into the bowels of palpable uneasiness. The obligatory printed sign reminding them that there will be absolutely no negotiated free-pass for hostage-takers amplifies trepidation and, rightfully so; there are definitely no such ominous warnings posted at the neighborhood Wal-Mart.[19]

More than likely were he/she given ample opportunity the free-world visitor would be bewildered trying to literally grasp understandings of the linguistics—the seemingly foreign tongue casually spoken by prisoners and staff. As with most societal subsets a unique lingo cultivates over time, one wherein common words have multiple meanings and certain phrases had best be interpreted properly lest mix-ups be the gateway to confusion and/or chaos.[20] One of the simplest examples would be the word "picket." To the untutored free-world homeowner, groundskeeper, or gardener it would signify the wooden plank in an attractive white yard-fence. A cowboy or modern-day equestrian would tie their mount on a picket-line or drive a picket into the ground to secure the lead-rope attached to the horse's halter. Inside the penitentiary or at surrounding outside observation points, a picket equates to a fixed location, such as a guard tower or an especially secure inside room where employees keep a watchful eye on individual cells and/or dayrooms, while sitting before a panel of electronic switches, buttons, and buzzers. And most assuredly a "one-eyed Aggie" is not a college student or Texas A&M graduate with an eye-patch covering a sightless socket, but in prison talk it is a long-handled hoe used for agricultural weeding and chopping, performing the necessary fieldwork at gargantuan prison farms.[21] Though exactness will herein be temporarily shortstopped for a later full-throated clarification, it is guaranteed that the expression "catching a ride" does not mean a prisoner is hitchhiking or standing at the corner bus-stop. Rather than inclusion now, the vehicle carrying much of the in-house prison vernacular will roll as these pages unfurl.

And as these pages turn it will become patently clear that behind the tall walls and inside the high fences exists a captivating world within itself. There are kitchens and dining halls and laundries and mail rooms and infirmaries and barber chairs and libraries and classrooms and industrial workshops and handicraft rooms and commissary stores and sewage plants and basketball courts and baseball diamonds: Even the shortlist seemingly stretches *ad infinitum.*[22] There's little doubt that many city mayors and municipal managers would be dumbfounded were they handed keys to a prison and thrust into the day to day operation—at the same time never neglecting serious security concerns, by legislative designation and the public's expectation their primary duty. Problems incalculable! Though metaphorically speaking, sometimes a crew of imprisoned pirates may be involuntarily serving as deckhands, but the professional correctional staff is face to the wind, standing at the helm and navigating through the churning troubled seas of institutional and/or political squalls—with a weather-beaten sextant perpetually turned toward possibility of looming thunderheads and, maybe, a wicked and murderous mutiny.[23] Sailing these ships of state, truly, is fraught with peril.[24]

Part of that peril is predicated by prison reality: The residents have broken the law and, like the aforesaid Bonnie and Clyde, not all state and federal penitentiary tenants are nice people. Most judicious criminologists will not argue that: "Prison is a violent, stressful place with its own unique subculture and language."[25] A multi-term twenty-first-century inmate confirmed the worrying core truth: Prisons have always been a brewing hotbed for turmoil and violence.[26] Depression-era desperado Willie Sutton mockingly chided— *allegedly*—that he robbed banks because that's where the money was. With regards to the so-called enlightened and progressive milieu of correctional philosophy, an astute academician deftly dropped the hammer on actuality: "Most prison violence involves inmates assaulting each other. One reason is that violent men and men from violent subcultures live in prison," and particularly he noted that to a certain extent "violence behind the walls becomes acceptable behavior. . . ." Furthermore, he perceptively posits: "In prison, potential for violence is an asset. Prestige results if one can act tough when the situation is defined as calling for it. Those that lack the ability to muster a reaction of power or those who lack a reputation of being capable of violence are apt to be victimized."[27] Another researcher quite competently it seems, affirms: "In short the inmate social system is a reflection of the criminal subculture which exists outside the institution yet having similar value systems, roles, stratification systems and unwritten moral and behavioral codes."[28]

Even while parked on the Lone Star State's Death Row, conspiring prisoners recently plotted viciousness.[29] Although the headlines were marking an event outside Texas, in the same general timeframe this Preface is being written not just a few malicious prisoners at the maximum custody Lee Correctional Center in South Carolina wickedly ran amok with a devastating menu of meanness, one registering their appetites for bloodletting: Seven luckless prisoners were DRT (Dead Right There); seventeen more were suitably hospitalized.[30] Thankfully, no correctional staff members suffered the taste of sharpened cold steel. Despite the indelicate politically incorrect fundamental truths, a not insignificant number of penitentiary inhabitants are downright mean and downright dangerous, devoid of societal scruples or a reasonably functioning conscience; blood-spattered particulars are sometimes borne by resultant courtroom and/or plea-bargained state and/or federal Penal Code convictions. There is no feasible room for any misleading fuzziness. Sugarcoating otherwise would be fraudulent on its face.

A U.S. District Court Judge for the Eastern District of Texas acknowledged that, indeed, a number of Lone Star State prisoners were "aggressive and predatory" and if not supervised appropriately would be "free to do as they wish in the living areas, and their victims can be threatened, extorted, beaten, or raped, in the absence of protection from civilian personnel."[31] There is a flip side to the coin vis-à-vis risks. Prison personnel are exposed to mind-boggling madness. Some of their custodial charges are conscienceless, unpleasant as that may be for a few folks seduced by idealism's fantasies. Though not affiliated with a trial court, an incisive investigative journalist and talented writer, among other shocking instances, focused the burning spotlight on one incident wherein a hapless Texas prisoner was purposely set afire, then viciously stabbed by merciless and, unquestionably, thoroughly unremorseful inmates.[32] Beyond belief inmate ingenuity will affirm that prisons are not weaponless worlds. Resorting to the aforementioned jurist's haunting depiction—which will be more than solidly demonstrated as this treatment unravels— there are actually quite a few instances wherein that assemblage of civilian prison personnel, the staff, are themselves the vulnerable victims, "threatened, extorted, beaten, or raped" and sometimes even murdered by inmates predisposed with that federal court's primitively branded "aggressive and predatory" behavior.

Notwithstanding what some psychiatrists, psychologists, professors, sociologists, and sincere criminologists might hawk in classrooms or professional buildings, there has been no cessation of criminality nor is there a dearth of callous criminals—some quite coldhearted and ruthless. Statistically crime and incarceration rates ebb and flow, but never do they wash into nothingness. Collectively we might wish it ain't so, but it is! Unfortunately—at least to date—theoretical reasoning and its resultant applications have yet to eradicate the need for court-imposed sanctions regarding some folks and their criminal wrongdoings. Armchair solutions to big problems are commonplace but societal exigency—at the state and federal level—has yet not found sound justification for totally eliminating penitentiaries and not incarcerating miscreants, an unspecified percentage being the baddest of the bad. Correctional employees by virtue of their job step to the forefront trying to ensure that their charges safely do their time and remain where they are supposed to be at any given moment, which allows others of a more cerebral inclination to philosophically ponder and fervently debate the whys and wherefores of criminal justice—or injustice. Safe-space thinking with regards to correctional matters is fitting, but everyday prison personnel are seldom afforded such luxury.

Adding to that din, after politicians pontificate and educators elucidate and intellectuals illuminate and real reverends ruminate, while lay preachers are proselytizing, the bottom-line stays unmoved. And just as with the professionals previously cited in the preceding paragraphs, society's outlaws still deprecate and some few get nabbed, earning their passports guaranteeing Big House residency or Death Row placement. Significant sociological breakdowns are easy to spot, but problematical to repair. Americans—Texans—have yet to discover an alternative to incarceration. And, once again, when the supplementary social institutions and heavy thinkers have come up short, the nervy correctional employees by virtue of their job do what they are paid to do—safely secure the state's prison population behind tall walls and high fences—or try to. Fittingly a *Dallas Morning News* editorial writer had not been hoodwinked by hardcore reality:

> . . . Out of the limelight, prison guards and officials are the unsung heroes of the criminal justice system. . . . They must deal daily with many of the most violent, mentally unbalanced people in our society. And corrections officials do so with little appreciation or understanding of their roles. . . . An unexpected outbreak of violence can occur at any time. . . . Critics often scoff

at the rules and regulations in the prison system. But the measures are designed to assure the safety of everyone—inmate and
officer alike—in the thankless process of corrections. . . . Their
sacrifice should awaken the public to the fact that corrections officials merit much more appreciation and support than is usually
accorded.[33]

Regrettably and provably working within the prison setting is no
stress-free career. Several men and/or women, dozens, have made
the ultimate sacrifice, in the name of the state and for the sake of
mankind.[34] Especially in theoretically driven treatments, seldom are
the mentions of Correctional Officers being murdered in the line
of duty; much less they are rarely identified by name. Such neglect
seems an abysmal omission, an insufferable affront to common
decency. When workplace tragedy strikes—murder or rape or aggravated assault or an untimely and unforeseen accident—underpaid
colleagues collectively pass the hat, sadly hustling a little financial
aid for funerals and/or medical bills. Tearful recollections are flushed
into the past's abyss. Then it's back to work. Correctional folks are,
positively, unsung heroes and heroines of Texas' criminal justice system. This then is their story.

■ ■ ■

Thumbing pages to this point should have oriented the potential full-
bore reader to the truth. There is an editorial angle to the product
in hand. The heretofore often overlooked or forgotten Correctional
Officers—heroes and heroines—of the Texas Department of
Criminal Justice are at the forefront of this treatment—as they
are vanguards in the real world separating violators from the general public; sanctions imposed by the courts and endorsed by the
Texas citizenry at large. The correctional personnel—*per se*—didn't
imprison anyone.

With that in mind, it's also relevant to note this work, though
buttressed with written primary and secondary sourced endnotes, as
well as many first-person interviews, is purposefully designed for a

general audience readership. Even though the authors can rightfully bank years of personal and professional experience working within the modern-era Criminal Justice System, neither profess in any way to have squirreled away meaningful or conclusive answers that have thus far eluded well-intentioned academicians and a sampling of wannabe experts. Herein this book's underbelly is not to challenge or condemn or squabble about quandaries endemic to the practices of incarcerating or rehabilitation or orchestrating lawful executions in the name of the State of Texas. Straightforwardly, after turning the very last page, if John Q. or Jane Q. Public grasps a better understanding of the history of Texas penology and the Correctional Officers' lives behind tall walls and high fences, one of the primary focuses and justifications for this project will have been achieved. Secondly, it seems but right, too, in some small way to memorialize by name some of those dedicated prison employees, both security and civilian, who forfeited their lives while engaged in the hard work of confining, protecting, educating, and hopefully, improving the lives of the lawfully incarcerated.

With regard to the aforementioned subject the authors deferentially beg for understanding. Unfortunately, the saga in hand will enumerate the ultimate sacrifice made by not just a few employees. Mournfully, the list is far too long. There was, then, that prickly necessity for dealing with a looming inevitability: With a rich and fascinating and evolving and enlightened history now touching three separate centuries, would it be editorially feasible to narrate in full detail each and every Correctional Officer's on-duty death? Alas, the answer is no. Working in a world—through the course of time—with spooky horses, firearms, falling timber, electricity, tall towers, trap-doors, and ever speedier motor vehicles racing down the congested byways, leads to the predictable: Deadly accidents, too, are a part of the Texas Prison storyline. The fact a Correctional Officer lost his/her life in a highway wreck while on the job does not and should not diminish their or their family's poignant forfeit. So herein there may not be mention of speeding autos ramming into prisoner transport vans or Bluebird buses resting sideways in the bar-ditch or on the interstate's grassy medians; nevertheless the human losses were tragic and felt throughout the whole prison organization. Although it certainly may not be enough, with heartfelt respect we have included in Appendix A the listing of those whose earthly time ended too soon. With hat in hand, we mention their names and honor their sacrifice.

That said it's worthwhile to dutifully acknowledge that wholesale generalizations are messy. Certainly the entire Texas prison population is not plagued with brutal and psychotic inmates, all bent toward escape and/or murderous plots designed to sustain supremacy over incarcerated neighbors or nastily inculcate fear into the psyches of rival gang members. The convict doing his/her own time seldom catches any positive notice, while the malcontent recalcitrant and schemers wreak havoc, generating headlines—more often than not to the wholesale detriment of the rule-compliant prisoners.

Likewise just because Correctional Officers don the grey uniform trimmed in blue and swear allegiance, does not relieve them of fidelity to the law or conscientious loyalty to workplace brothers and sisters in the trenches with them. Correspondingly, no human subgroup is 100 percent uncorrupted, be they peace officers or bigwig executives or physicians or veterinarians or CPAs or loquacious lawyers or college professors with PhDs.[35] For *Tall Walls and High Fences*, as the endnotes will patently sustain, hard truths override any misplaced romanticism.

If there is need for a genteel disclaimer for the faint of heart let the reader be apprised, herein there will be no shying away from the truths, hard as they might be. What follows necessarily will be awash with deceitful gamesmanship and ingenuousness near unbelievable. Aside from an inexorable black-market economy, duplicity and betrayal are pandemic in prison surroundings. Snitching self-interest is supreme, regardless the chameleon denials of homeboys and gangsters and racially motivated supremacists, no matter the ethnic stripe. Treachery is ever-present. Whittling to the sharp point is easy, a truism brought home by a pair of prominent academicians: "Prisons are places of ultimate self-interest."[36] Even a notorious murderer, John Wesley Hardin, himself a long-term Texas penitentiary occupant, warily commented: "They say there is honor among thieves, but don't you believe it. There's not a word of truth in it. When they can't steal from anybody else, they steal from one another."[37] Seemingly little has changed with the passage of time. More than a hundred years later in a guide for families and friends of prison tenants, a convicted offender warned that new arrivals best not make their penitentiary debut wearing flashy jewelry or pricy footwear, else that much coveted property would be stolen by fellow prisoners—or might even lead to hassles more trying.[38]

Outfoxing the correctional staff or getting the goods on a guard is a real coup—a pathway to special favors and access to contraband by way of compromised integrity. Mentally blueprinted escape plots sometimes erupt into reality, from time to time with a deadly outcome. Truthfully, the real world is yet turning, but in the penitentiary setting it habitually spins on an axis of disingenuousness. Notwithstanding the very best intentions of a gaggle of gullible do-gooders and well-meaning reformers—those sleeping in free-world homes as darkness closes in—the potential for hazard takes no holiday. Appallingly, for this nonfiction assessment there will be no shortage of metaphorical mops to swab blood from the cellblock decks or in the farm field's turn-rows or genuine mops to sop real blood from the cells' floors, in the runs (passageways), and from the farm's plowed grounds and pastures. Surveillance cameras are not all seeing; there are blind-spots, locales pre-identified by merciless outlaws with evil plans—some with nothing to lose, wherein another life sentence without parole is pointless. Living life, surviving, within prison complexes can prove a gut-wrenching as well as a literal gut-cuttin' experience.

Most prisoners are in want of personal security and prison employees want to safely end their shift and go home. Survival is not a one-dimensional facet behind the tall walls and high fences. Although perhaps somewhat unfathomable, this uncorking story will also be regrettably replete with bloodhounds and chases and gunfights, deadly confrontations not necessarily buried in the too-distant past. There are twenty-first-century homicidal escapes. Trafficking in humans for sexual exploitation and/or slavery is not bizarre inside the Big House. Masturbation and murder will merit mention—as will the ferocious forcible rapes and passionate clandestine consensual trysts. The black-robed trial judge's gavel may have tapped, halting a prisoner's free-world residency, but even that jurist from the courtroom's bench could not and cannot curtail or handcuff raging hormones and urges bubbling forth from within. This book's content isn't pretty: Just real, nitty-gritty, but real.

Certainly also indisputable are the genial contributions of helpmates stepping to the forefront for this nonfiction project. Their unadulterated ability and loyalty to straightforwardness is not and should not be discounted.

First and foremost the authors deferentially wish to extend a warm and heartfelt "thank you" to William L. "Bill" Stephens, recently retired Director of the Texas Department of Criminal Justice—Correctional Institutions Division (TDCJ-CID) and currently Director of the marvelous Texas Prison Museum (TPM) on the northern outskirts of Huntsville, Texas. Selflessly and enthusiastically Bill graciously consented when asked to write a Foreword for this nonfiction narrative about the founding and evolution and everyday workings of the Lone Star State's prisons and its cadre of steadfast Correctional Officers. Bill Stephens is tenaciously committed to preserving and safeguarding the rich history of the multifaceted Texas prison story. And who better could write that Foreword than a professional at one time in charge of all Texas prisons? Aside from the privilege of being recipient of his Foreword for *Tall Walls and High Fences*, the appreciative authors readily acknowledge he was the go-to guy for answering sometimes thorny questions associated with Texas penitentiary administration. And, too, we would be remiss without a tip of the hat to the entire TPM staff for their cordial commitment to excellence; those efforts were significant lynchpins for making this treatment possible.

Also metaphorically leaning forward in the foxhole was Rick Miller, retired County Attorney for Bell County, a former Texas lawman, and an award-winning nonfiction writer of Old West doings and personalities. Absent any prompting or begging or bribing, when apprised of the rationale for the project in hand, Rick Miller at once recognized it as a worthwhile undertaking. He willingly sidelined his own endeavors so that he could contribute to telling the Texas prison narrative in the round—with particularly focused attention to primary source materials and crucial interpretations of both civil and criminal court actions. His tireless efforts and critical legal analyses are and were indispensible for trying to put this story right—in context and accurately. Rick Miller's conscientious participation should not be and is not unappreciated or undervalued. In short it seems an oversimplification, but the thanks are genuine.

Another indispensible helpmate was Michael J. Bailey, Curator, Brazoria County Historical Museum at Angleton, Texas. Brazoria County history and the Texas Prison story are interlocked. Highlighting history of one compels mention of the other, a fact, guaranteed by time and place. Thankfully, Mike Bailey is a master of both. His personal knowledge of area geography and its earliest human habitation is—in short—phenomenal. Honed by years of vigilant research and the ability to construe sociological impact of one on the other is—obviously—Mike Bailey's forte. In a nutshell he knows the places and the people. Most importantly, however, he wants to share that knowledge—as legit historians are want to do. A simple request to Mike Bailey for data about this or that phase of Brazoria County or its prison units history will, more often than not, result in an absolute avalanche of treasure. And that's what good researchers do, delve deeply and thoroughly and share what they've uncovered and/or discovered. Mike Bailey is a good researcher and a good friend—and, in the end, *Tall Walls and High Fences* is beneficiary.

Likewise two other *bueno amigos* stepped to the forefront when asked for help. Lending his expertise in locating arcane source materials was the stellar efforts of Dave Johnson, a nonfiction writer of renown and prominent authority on Texas and Southwest feuds of days long past. Dave's diligent pursuits added measurably—and positively—to the volume in hand. Equally, when a plea for assistance was tendered to Doug Dukes the response was quick and thorough, which would not be surprising to those who know him. A retired Lieutenant with the Austin PD and sitting TRHF&M Board Member, Doug Dukes is perhaps the consummate authority on weaponry of the Rangers, whether it was the era transitioning from saddles to sedans—or today. Correctional Officers—then or now—must be familiar with a wide array of tactical tools—and firearms are an integral component. Doug's contribution within this framework is and was insightful and impressive and informative. Dave and Doug earned their mention herein—and appreciatively so!

Another cadre of dedicated professionals unreservedly merit name specific acknowledgment: Joanna Rebecca Alford, TDCJ Training Sergeant; Ronald J. "Ron" Alford, TDCJ Major, Ret.; Carlos Beltran, Copy & Ship Resources, Waxahachie, TX; Raymond "Rusty" Bloxom, Research Librarian, Texas Ranger Hall of Fame & Museum (TRHF&M) Waco, TX; Lieutenant Jason Bobo, Company B, Texas Rangers; Donaly E. Brice, Author and Senior Archivist, Ret., Texas State Library and Archives, Austin, TX; Joshua Burson, Company C, Texas Rangers; Barry K. Caver, Capitan, Texas Rangers, Ret., and sitting TRHF&M Board Member; Matt Cawthon, Texas Rangers, Ret., and sitting TRHF&M Board Member; Leslie "Les" Cotton, Navarro County Sheriff, Ret.; Shelly A. Crittendon, Collections Manager, TRHF&M; Jack O. Dean, Texas Ranger Capitan and Western District of Texas U.S. Marshal, Ret., and sitting TRHF&M Board Member; Kyle Lynn Dean, Texas Ranger, Ret., and former TDCJ Correctional Officer; Lieutenant Antonio DeLuna, Company D, Texas Rangers; Kirby W. Dendy, Chief, Texas Rangers, Ret.; Ronnie Dean Dobbs, Arkansas Prison Administrator, Ret.; Samuel K. Dolan, Author and documentary producing Emmy Award recipient; Jan Devereaux, award-winning Author and TRHF&M Laureate; Kevin S. Fontenot, Folklore and Music Historian; Robert D. Garza, Jr., Texas Rangers, Ret.; West Gilbreath, Capitan, UNT Police Department and Author; Lon Bennett Glenn, Author and TDCJ Warden, Ret.; James R. "Chip" Gayle IV, Chief, Angleton ISD Police Department; District Judge J. Ray Gayle III and Nancy Gayle; Caroline Gnagy, Author and Musician;

Laura Greenwood, sitting TRHF&M Board Member and former TDCJ Correctional Officer; Charles H. Harris III, Ph.D., and award-winning Author; Pam Hobson, daughter of hostage Julia Standley; Byron Johnson, Director, TRHF&M; Joe King, former Brazoria County Sheriff; Mike Koch, Author and Parole Board Investigator, Ret.; Edward M. "Mike" Konczak, National Exploration and Research Agency; Audrey Ladd, Education Program Manager, TRHF&M; Josh Lehew, computer guru and technical troubleshooter; Kathryn M. Lloyd, Sales Manager, Texas A&M University Press; Frank Malinak, Assistant Chief, Texas Rangers, Ret. and TRHF&M Board Member; Reuben T. Mankin, Company B, Texas Rangers; Brenda Martin, TDCJ Clinical Corrections Associate, Ret.; Richard Martin, TDCJ Telecommunications Specialist; Bill Neal, former District Attorney and an award-winning author; Tom Norsworthy, Company A, Texas Rangers; Tony O'Hare, TDCJ Regional Director, Ret.; Bill O'Neal, past Texas State Historian and prolific award-winning author; Lea Anne Kindle Ousley, Correctional Officer, Ret.; Robert J. "Bob" Parker, TDCJ Regional Director, Ret.; Christine W. Rothenbush, Marketing, Promotions, & Development Coordinator, TRHF&M; George Ruth, Jr., TDCJ Captain, Ret.; Louis Ray Sadler, Ph.D., and award winning Author; Dr. Anthony S. "Tony" Sapienza, renowned collector of Western Memorabilia (photographs, documents, and firearms); Robert L. "Bob" Schwebel, D.V.M. and TDCJ contract veterinarian, Ret.; Tom Selleck former Assistant District Attorney, Brazoria County; Rachel Smith, Assistant Collections Manager, TRHF&M; Paul N. Spellman, Ph.D., Wharton County Junior College and award-winning author; Red Steagall, Western Entertainer and Television Personality; Christina Stopka, Deputy Director and Head, Armstrong Research Center, TRHF&M; Lieutenant James Thomas, Company F, Texas Rangers; David Turk, Historian, U.S. Marshals Service; Lieutenant George Turner, Texas Rangers, Ret.; Arthur Velasquez, TDCJ Warden, Ret.; Lieutenant Wende O. Wakeman, Company A, Texas Rangers; Teddy Weaver, Weaver Rodeo Company; H.L. "Hank" Whitman, Chief, Texas Rangers, Ret.; and Jim Willett, TDCJ Warden, Ret. and former TPM Director

Moreover it would be an oversight—an embarrassing omission—not to share a favorable comment with regards to the sterling efforts of the University of North Texas Press. The outfit's Director, Ron Chrisman, has carved an enviable notch with publication of serious studies not only of the Old West genre, but with Criminal Justice topics as well. Often the two subjects intertwine, presenting past and present sociological commentary of note. The relevancy of many UNT Press titles is undisputed. Moving the manuscript from UNT Press to the marketplace and bookshelf is no easy task, but is more than proficiently handled by the unparalleled work of Karen J. DeVinney, Ph.D., Assistant Director/Managing Editor, Bess Whitby, Marketing Manager, and Denise Crosswhite, Administrative Coordinator. Kudos all the way around!

1

"Punishment of the refractory"

SUDDENLY, DEAFENING GUNFIRE REVERBERATED throughout the Walker County courtroom. Assuredly the indescribable reek of freshly burnt charges of black-powder irritated nostrils flaring below minds sparked into out-and-out surprise. Wafts of blue smoke embargoed clear eyesight. Amid the profanity and pandemonium some few of the twenty to forty .36 and .44 caliber lead balls were finding their marks—tearing into flesh and/or channeling scratches fast filling with blood. The unfolding and emphatically dramatic gun-play was endemic of the day and the times. In the Lone Star State, resorting to six-shooter settlement was not an unusual method of problem resolution: Certainly it was unseemly in the courtroom, but for the most part Texans revered gunfighter grit. Even in legal and scholarly circles there was general acceptance of the "Texas Rule," the right to stand one's ground, no duty to retreat. Such was treasured doctrine. "Eventually the United States Supreme Court would speak approvingly of the Texas rule."[1] Unquestionably for this quick booming Walker County courthouse brouhaha the old-time Texas maxim, although admittedly somewhat clichéd, did and does have an eerie ring of genuine truth: "If God had intended for Texans to fight like cats and dogs, He'd givin' 'em claws and paws." On that eleventh day of January 1871, at Huntsville, the county seat, cap and ball six-shooters were ubiquitous; seemingly everyone had one

1

or two—or more. And most folks feared not, nor were they ashamed or disinclined to pull a trigger.

As best as can be determined, the genesis for the sizzling hubbub lay in the coldblooded murder of a transplant from Tennessee, Sam Jenkins, an elderly freedman. Two salient points merit mention. First, Sam Jenkins was a farm laborer involved in a heated dispute with Fred Parks regarding the division of crops—or the profits thereof. And, purportedly, Sam Jenkins was also a very vocal and very energetic member of the Union League, leading to one area resident characterizing him as "one of the leaders under 'Carpetbagism' rule," who "made himself obnoxious to white people generally."[2] Whether accurately or not, a newspaperman for the *Houston Daily Telegraph* graded Sam Jenkins somewhat unfavorably, declaring in part that he had "been the cause of a good deal of trouble wherever he has lived. . . ."[3] And, according to another accusation, Sam Jenkins "was one of a few insolent negroes [sic] who had insulted some young ladies on the street returning home from a shopping tour."[4] *¿Quién sabe?*[5] Therefore, with that said, it should come as no surprise Sam Jenkins was no friend of John (Joseph) Wright, Nathanial A. "Nat" Outlaw, and Jonathan M. Parish (possibly McParish), an openly rambunctious trio of Fred Parks's bosom buddies. On the outskirts of Huntsville town Sam Jenkins was physically assaulted and threatened that he best keep his damn mouth shut about his most severe and merciless beating with hardwood sticks. The thrashing was brutal, almost killing Sam Jenkins. Whatever he was, real good or real bad, Sam Jenkins was not at all disposed toward tucking tail like a whimpering dog and crawling under the front porch. He was stubborn. Coldly abusing Sam Jenkins was really foolish, if the perpetrators thought he would remain silent. Sam Jenkins had plenty to say, and the multi-racial Walker County Grand Jury was raring to go, all ears.[6] Although a number of blacks were sitting members of the Grand Jury, Sam Jenkins didn't earn undue credibility simply because he was a local man of color. After examining the available evidence and "giving the matter a very thorough investigation," the Grand Jury opted not to return any indictments.[7]

Shortly thereafter, three miles from Huntsville, Sam Jenkins was confronted and murdered, shot in the head and torso. He had been warned not to testify, naming names. The state's Reconstruction Governor, Edmund J. Davis, was not happy about the apparent lawlessness and lack of enthusiasm for ferreting out the guilty parties and hauling them before the bench of District Court Judge James Russell Burnett, 30th Judicial District of Texas. For his lackluster performance of duty, Sheriff William H. Stewart was removed from office.[8]

Captain Leander Harvey McNelly of the Texas State Police (not the Texas Rangers) was ordered to Walker County. The assignment was—on paper—simple. Captain L.H. McNelly was to unflaggingly bring the killer or killers of Sam Jenkins to bay and haul him/her or them into court. And this he did, taking into custody the aforementioned four, Parks, Outlaw, Wright, and Parish.[9] The stage, then, was set. High-drama was drawing near.

At the twenty-year-old brick courthouse, inside the upstairs courtroom, Captain McNelly was accompanied by three of his subordinate policemen, Joseph L. Martin, L.E. Dunn, and Thomas "Tom" Keesee. Captain McNelly's other two state-paid gendarmes, Val Lemmons and Hugh Pennington, were tactically positioned on the first floor at the stairwell. The defendants were represented by Huntsville attorneys, James M. Maxey, James A. Baker, and Lewis B. Hightower. Particularly, lawyer Maxey thought the prosecutorial mess was nothing less than a put-up job, "political prosecution."[10] In fact he would contend, publicly, that the "whole thing was fixed up in Austin and the dark room at the Penitentiary, where schemers met to plot the destruction of these young men."[11] The barrister's alluding to a terribly sinister plot cooked up inside the state penitentiary escaped sufficient clarity then—as it does now.[12] During the Preliminary Hearing, which lasted three full days, enough admissible evidence was presented by the District Attorney, William E. Horne, to persuade Judge Burnett that, indeed, ample Probable Cause existed for binding three of the defendants over for trial. They could have their day in court, but he would know where to find them when the docket was called. The prisoners were to be cagily jailed until then inside the Cedar Street (now Eleventh Street) lockup, a rather porous custodial facility in dreadful shape, one ripe for costly renovation. The fourth purposed/alleged murder defendant, Fred Parks, was set free, admissible and conclusive evidence of his culpability being in short supply, so thought the Honorable J.R. Burnett, the man with the say-so.[13]

The three defendants were not of a mind to be peacefully escorted to the decrepit calaboose. In a heartbeat it turned "Western" inside the Walker County courtroom. The trio may have been *alleged* murderers, but they were surefire each armed with a brace of Colt's six-shooters.[14] Bullets started flying. Captain McNelly and his policemen returned the compliment, severely wounding Parish in the right arm and Wright in the midsection and leg. "McNelly was also shot in the leg, and Keesee received a ball in the jaw that passed around the neck."[15] Downstairs, Policemen Lemmons and Pennington "were prevented from giving any assistance by confederates of the prisoners, who with pistols presented and cocked, were threatened with immediate death, if they attempted to move."[16] Outside on the dirt street the prisoners' pals and sympathizers had more arms and horses prepositioned for the getaway. Although wounded, Parish and Wright, amid the thunderous cheers of not just a few thrilled townsmen, "shooting off their pistols and yelling like savages. . . . made their escape from town."[17]

Upstairs in the courtroom, defendant Nat Outlaw remained Captain Leander McNelly's sole prisoner, though slightly wounded by friendly fire—from his cronies—which certainly proved not to be any too friendly! Captain McNelly and Judge Burnett were not blindsided by knotty real-time reality. District Judge Burnett was adamant about hammering his gavel on calmness: "The people must be taught that we live under a government of law, and not that of a mob."[18] Trying to safely hold Nat Outlaw in the local jailhouse would be problematic at best, disastrous at worst. Adopting the philosophy that sometimes it's better to beg forgiveness than ask for permission, rather shrewdly the Captain and the Judge acted first, and then

Governor E.J. Davis was notified. Judge Burnett explained the whys and wherefores to the Chief Executive:

> I ordered the prisoners to jail, but in view of its insecurity, Outlaw was taken to the penitentiary. Threats of his rescue were made last night, but no intention manifested of carrying them into execution. The penitentiary is strongly guarded and will not be successfully attacked. . . . In view of the utter insecurity of the county jail, I respectfully suggest that you order that the prisoners be placed in the State Penitentiary for safe-keeping. This has been done here by judicial officers, but I doubt whether such authority is granted to me, except perhaps in cases of emergency.[19]

Captain McNelly, though wounded, complying with orders and commonsense, ensconced his lone prisoner, an uninvited guest, in "the penitentiary for safe-keeping. It was surmised that no attempt would be made to rescue Outlaw while in the secure confines of the prison."[20] And much the same could be said about apprehending the other two fugitives in the wild and woolly snarls and tangled lairs of Walker County. Judge Burnett wasn't fooled—or foolish: "The two escaped prisoners are severely wounded, and they are still in this county, guarded by some thirty or forty of their friends, who are strongly armed, and say that they cannot be taken. There are a few lawless men about town and I learn threats have been made to assassinate me. One demonstration was made by ex-sheriff Stewart in this direction, the other night, and it is said he was supported by three or four men of like ilk. There are quite a number of citizens here who secretly oppose these outrages, but very few who openly denounce them."[21]

Reconstruction Governor Davis had a strong message for the folks of Walker County and he would follow through, declaring Martial Law: "Your communication of the twelfth inst. has been received, giving an account of the late riot at Huntsville. The matter you refer to, I have already heard something of by telegraph. I am preparing to regulate affairs in the county of Walker, as you will see shortly. I am fully satisfied with your course there as judge, and intend to sustain you."[22] Then he pitched in the kicker!

You are authorized to inform the citizens of Walker county, that these outrages that have taken place, will bring upon them severe expense and retributions as well as injury to the reputation and prosperity of the county.[23]

The citizens of Walker County—based on their alleged (and not so alleged) recklessness and lawlessness—found themselves suffering the imposition of Martial Law.[24] The impotency or virility of the declaration can and does deserve clearheaded deliberation, but one fact for this treatment stands unarguably clear: An outlaw named Outlaw was inside the tall walls, trying to take a peek at the Texas world passing by. The view was dismal—for the moment.

Though domiciled inside the state prison at Huntsville, Nat Outlaw's residency there would be short-lived. Following a tense trial before a Reconstruction Military Court, Nat Outlaw had been found culpable for Sam Jenkins's killing and sentenced, catching a nickel—five years to do.[25] In what can best be characterized as an utterly bizarre piece of jurisprudence, Texas Governor Edmund J. Davis did "remit the sentence passed upon said Outlaw by said court, and direct his discharge from the State Penitentiary." Musings of the Chief Executive were curious if not crazy. In the mind of Governor Davis, if Nat Outlaw was guilty he should have been hanged, "or if the evidence connecting him with the murder was not believed, [he] should have been altogether acquitted and discharged. . . ." Any compromise was, in his mind, harebrained. Of the judgment rendered by the Reconstruction Governor, a newspaper editor commented on the officially sanctioned proclamation freeing the overjoyed Nat Outlaw from custody: "Such a state paper as that would consign the Governor to an asylum for idiots, if presented to any disinterested jury. Such a piece of reasoning is entirely unique."[26] Not only were prisoners sentenced to hard time making a getaway, convicts already calling the Texas penitentiary their home away from home were jumping—the escapes running rampant. Hardcore Texans were not looking upon the Texas State Police with favor. At Huntsville it was alleged, "There are about ten State policemen lying around town, drawing eighty dollars a month, doing no good, not even in arresting escaped convicts." For many Texans it seemed that Reconstruction Governor Davis was at the penitentiary's back gate handing out pardons as quick as convicts could be processed and saunter across the prison's interior yard.[27]

The actual depth of security within the prison might stand debate—then or now—but collectively and early on, everyday Texans had felt the legit need for a penitentiary. When State Police Captain Leander Harvey McNelly hustled Nat Outlaw behind tall walls for safekeeping, the Lone Star State's storied penal institution had been in existence for slightly more than twenty years. From the birth, institutionally, her history is rich.

Frequently it's overlooked, but even before Texas Independence the Mexican state of *Coahuila y Tejas* by formalized legislation had given the okay for private interests, today's "venture capitalists," to construct and operate five colonial *carcels* to incarcerate wrongdoers. The criminals were to be separated from citizens who were inclined to abide by expected societal standards and obey the law. Even at that early date, aside from punishment and incarceration for his errant behavior, a prisoner was given an opportunity—compelled—to learn a legitimate trade in order that he could, upon completion of his sentence, "sustain himself by honest labor."[28] Predictably, in 1836 when and after Texans shed their affiliation with Mexico, any concept of Mexican penology went by the wayside. Dealing with law-breakers was now Texans' challenge.

There was a time-warp before Texans availed themselves of progressive thinking with regards to crime and punishment and incarcerating the lawless misfits among them. Other remedies were and had been in play—but it was no gentle game.

So open to criticism was the conduct of early-day sheriffs in their treatment of prisoners that courts frequently ordered the defendant whipped and turned loose on society. In those days many outlaws from the United States and Mexico fled to Texas, where enforcement of law and order soon became a serious problem. Texas resorted to harshness of punishment in an effort to cope with the situation.

"For murder, arson, rape, robbery or burglary, on conviction thereof, he shall receive death." So ran the stern words of the statute. For taking or stealing any "goods, chattels, money or articles of value under $20," the penalty was a fine not to exceed $1000, with or without the infliction of thirty-nine lashes. If the thief took anything of value of $20 or more, the penalty was restoration of the full value wrongfully taken, plus thirty-nine lashes on the bare back, plus branding of the right hand with the letter "T," for thief. Cattle or horse theft in those days called for restoration of full value to the rightful owner and thirty-nine lashes for the thief. Counterfeiting was a capital offense.[29]

Sociological evolution is seldom an overnight phenomenon. For Texans, the *public* whipping post had become passé and prisoners being trudged between Gonzales and San Antonio and Seguin were no longer chained to the "iron holding posts" strategically situated between towns. Citizens were relieved from furnishing food and security for the weary lawmen trying to catch forty winks while their pedestrian charges were chained to the posts like so many pet bears.[30] Enlightenment comes not from a sudden and supercharged bolt of lightning. Nevertheless, Texans had long been pondering the actual practically of a state penitentiary. There was a move underfoot to build an institution "to serve as an alternative to more barbaric practices of capital and corporal punishment for crimes. Penitentiary advocates hoped these facilities would rehabilitate offenders, making them productive members of society, while at the same time protecting citizens from danger."[31]

Situated not too far north of Harris County's seat of government, Houston, Walker County's geographical setting is pleasant and pretty. Primarily the landscape is heavily forested, but sufficient open meadows and vales in the Trinity and San Jacinto River watersheds, combined with an overall mild climate, allowed for a blossoming and booming agricultural community. Walker County was carved from Montgomery County during 1846, and formally organized on 18 July of that same year. The enchanting hamlet of Huntsville was chosen as its shiretown.

Though it is somewhat out of chronological sync, it's not inappropriate to make mention of the county's naming issue—and hot controversy. At birth Walker County was named after Robert John Walker, former Secretary of Treasury and a United States Senator. In his official capacity Robert Walker had sponsored a resolution acknowledging the independence of the Republic of Texas, and later was a strong advocate for folding Texas into the body of America's collection of states. Until the dawn of the Civil War, Robert John Walker was applauded in Texas. That changed! He sided with the Union, not the Confederacy. Rather than taking their revenge by renaming the county, on 10 December 1863 the Texas Legislature simply shifted to another designee to honor with the county's name. From that day forward—with due respect—Walker County would stand as the namesake of Samuel H. Walker, the celebrated Texas Ranger with a hefty Colt's six-shooting revolver named after him and the luminary who perished in the 1840s war with Mexico.[32]

Subsequent to the close of the conflict with Mexico and the newfound status of statehood, Texas legislators turned part of their attention to penology—the need for that state penitentiary. Heretofore maintaining custody of lawbreakers had been the bailiwick of local authorities, a responsibility of the elected sheriff and area taxpayers. The Texas population was mushrooming. By April 1848 the Lone Star's original twenty-three counties had grown exponentially, jumping to a grand total of seventy-eight.[33] Perhaps, for non-informed non-Texans, it's but relevant to mention that today the tally of Texas counties registers at 254, and correspondingly there are 254 men and/or women officially garnering the title as duly inaugurated sheriffs. Resultantly, then, even during that early timeframe (1848), there were seventy-eight sheriffs responsible for holding prisoners committing crimes in seventy-eight counties. Those seventy-eight sheriffs were officially tasked with overseeing their convicted prisoners, ensuring that those miscreants pulled their adjudicated time as determined by local judges or juries.[34] Rumblings about the possibility of a prison, one financed and operated by the state, were rampant.

After many fits and starts, over a period of several years, Statehouse legislators at last acted. Colloquially speaking it was a done deal with passage of carefully crafted enabling legislation on 13 March 1848.[35] Allowing the governor to appoint three commissioners, three directors, and a penitentiary superintendent, the long-sought process had begun. What would be a suitable site? The Act allowed for the purchase of up to 100 acres. That is, if the purchase price did not exceed $5.00 per acre.[36] The commissioners were tasked with finding that 100-acre plot, keeping in mind that it should be situated in a healthy clime and reasonably near a navigable body of water, allowing for the "importation of machinery, tools, [and] materials to be . . . manufactured, and for the transportation of articles made . . . by the convicts to a market."[37]

Although LaGrange in Fayette County was a contender, the commissioners finally gave the site selection nod to Huntsville.[38] Though historians are innately bent toward argument—which is not unsound—the real time bottom-line is unalterable. So, whether the then Texas Governor George Tyler Wood, a public figure and Mexican War veteran, pressured the commissioners to choose Huntsville due to his being a Sam Houston partisan is realistically moot. Or could the fact that Commissioner William Palmer had Walker County ties have weighed into the equation?[39] Regardless, Huntsville, with widespread community support, won the prize: the state's nascent penitentiary.[40] Basically once the site was determined, the actual formulation of plans, oversight of construction within legislative guidelines, and actual institutional operational management were left to the three appointed directors and the prison superintendant.

Abner Hugh Cook, politically well-placed and an eminent architect, was contracted to build the penitentiary, a thoughtfully designed facility with individual cells, common work quarters, and an adequate recreational yard—all completely surrounded by daunting tall perimeter walls.[41] Clearing the land and digging a well launched on 5 August 1848.[42] Actual building construction commenced ten days later on the fifteenth, roughly five months after the formalized legislative okay. The first building was a wooden jail-type structure.

Arrangements had to be made for prisoners before the somewhat massive project could be finished.[43]

Huntsville's penitentiary, scarcely a year later, was moderately ready and somewhat open for business. For the most part—and it's important—the kept had been kept busy: "Most of the convicts are engaged in the transaction of the building, the whole of which thus far have been done by them."[44] At first the finished design consisted of three custodial structures, the east, south, and west units. The first had eighty-eight cells, "including two dark cells or dungeons, for the "punishment of the refractory," the second, one hundred and forty-four individual cells, and the last with thirty-six cells specifically reserved for female Penal Code wrongdoers. The men's cells measured a width of five feet, a length of seven feet, and an overhead height of eight feet. The women's personal living quarters were one foot wider. Cell walls were mortared with "hard Texas brick," measuring two feet thick. On the whole, as astounding as it might seem, thus far the cash outlay from Texas taxpayers came in at less than $20,000.[45] Using convict labor had proved cost effective.[46]

When the penitentiary welcomed its first prisoner, only the "most hardened criminals" were being sentenced to do hard time at Huntsville.[47] And they were white. Remembering that the Texas prison was receiving convicted criminals prior to the Civil War is apropos.[48] Though somewhat indelicate today, a mid nineteenth-century reality divided just who could be straight away punished by just who. Texas Court of Criminal Appeals Judge John W. Henderson, though perhaps clumsily, put reality to paper when he penned that prescribed payback for significant transgression was

> in the good old days when white men were honest and law abiding, and if a negro committed such an indiscretion as stealing his master's shote [*sic* shoat—a weaned pig], or burglarizing his smokehouse, and was accidentally detected in the act, he was forthwith taken in hand and soundly thrashed and admonished to do so no more, which he invariably promised, and this was generally the end of the matter.[49]

Assuredly the first prisoner at Huntsville was white, and he had committed a serious infraction, stealing one or more of someone's cows. Owning this distinction was William G. Sansom from Fayette County, who arrived at The Walls in October of 1849.[50] Earning the red ribbon, second place, was convicted murderer Stephen Turner from Jefferson County in the southeastern reaches of the Lone Star State on the Louisiana line. However, convict Turner did manage his blue ribbon spot in the prison history book. He was the first prisoner trying to escape that would be shot and killed by prison personnel legislatively charged with preventing such indiscretions.[51] Convict Steve Turner was, however, not the very first to manage a breakout. George A. Davis "shot and killed Edward W. Baston" on or about April 14, 1849, according to an early-day blurb in the *Huntsville Banner*.[52] Subsequent to tidy conviction he was without any fanfare imprisoned. A blip in the *Texas State Gazette* of October 20, 1849, noted: George A. Davis, sentenced to the penitentiary last term at Walker County for the killing of Edward W. Banton [?], has escaped."[53] Historically enumerating *all* of the successful and aborted escapes from the Texas Prison System would prove a monumental challenge—certainly not one attempted for this project.

There will be enough patterns to illustrate part of the difficulties facing prison personnel back then and today, a timeframe now touching three centuries. With durable one-sentence clarity a modern-era educator and expert hammers an outright core truth across the anvil of time with regards to punishment and prisons: "Correctional institutions are a kind of barometer of society's attitudes toward its offenders."[54] Certainly such astute reasoning is relevant for studying the ceaseless evolvement of forward-thinking correctional philosophies. The evolvement, however, was not overnight and was not blunder free.

Bearing in mind at least two key theoretical components of Texas penology is central for understanding the place and time. First, honest men worked hard near everyday and dishonest ne'er-do-wells hardly worked any day. Primarily for the early, mid, and late 1800s (really much later) Texas was in the main an agrarian society. Though perhaps bothersome for a smattering of agenda-driven chroniclers, the majority of Texas's population were not wealthy plantation owners or slaveholders. They were eking out a living by toiling in the field. Slogging and stumbling while breaking ground behind the gaseous rumps of imported Missouri mules was very wearisome work—but it was honorable work. Self-sufficiency and feeding one's family were built-in and culturally admirable traits. Likewise, young men raised on ranches were deft at saddling and riding their own horses, even those with a hump in their backs on frost nipping mornings. It was imperative those ranch boys learned the fine art of tattooing a catch-rope's loop around the horns, pitching slack to the cow critter's off side, turning obliquely and spurring hard away from the near side, tightening the rope and throwing the creature to the ground for branding or doctoring or robbing its manhood with a sharp blade. Calves still on the teat were roped by the neck or hind legs and dragged bawling toward the white-hot embers and red-hot irons, gluey slobber clinging to their milk-splashed gums. At the catch-pen it was stinky, an odorous world of real sweat, scorched hair, burnt hide, and cow shit.[55] For everyday folks—men and women—it was hard work from sunup to sundown, no whining. Illustratively, then, one old-time cowboy queried his former saddle-forking partner about new employment on a different ranch. The reply was witty, but right: "Well, it's a pretty good place. They feed twice a day—and it's dark both times!"

A deep-rooted work ethic, at the time, was near all-pervasive for a law-abiding populace. Therefore and, not surprisingly, wording of the enabling legislation giving birth to a Texas penitentiary stipulated that all—each and every—convict was to be kept suitably busy at some "useful labor."[56] Even a later nineteenth-century Superintendent for the New York State Prison would underscore the philosophy of working convicts:

Every man who enters prison, and can work in prison, was a laborer before he was sent to prison, or he was a drone and lived off other people. . . . Shall a man who has assailed society be made the guest of society in prison and a tax upon other men?[57]

One well-known Lone Star State prison administrator didn't hesitate to parrot public policy attitudes regarding the kept: "It was never intended that man should be idle. If he is physically able, he should be at work, both for the sake of his health and for the earning of his living, whether he is in prison or out of prison."[58] An extract from an early Texas Penal Code solidifies the prevailing mind-set about convicts working:

> **Hard labor intended**—Whenever the penalty, prescribed for an offense, is imprisonment for a term of years in the penitentiary, imprisonment to hard labor is intended.[59]

Nonetheless, as always the case, there were a few misfits and malefactors more inclined to misappropriate profit from the efforts of others or murderously settle grudges or forcefully steal petticoat purity. Some guys and gals are not nice. Especially in an earlier day, prisoners who had avoided work at all costs while in the free-world, persistently bitched and bellyached about having to labor behind the tall walls and high fences and in the row crop's vast fields. Robbers and burglars and thieves abhorred hard work. In not just a few of their irrational minds, taxpayers should and could give them—maybe even owed them—what others had worked from can to can't to come by, laboriously but honestly.[60] A genuine good man smartly steered clear of prison; a bona fide badman didn't! From the get-go prison inmates were expected to work hard for their room and board. Too, one and all were sure expected to behave. Idle hands and minds were the Devil's playthings.

Secondly, early prison administrators were wedded to the notion that protecting society from the criminals and the criminals from each other was an admirable goal, as well as meting out more severe punishment penalties for habitual smart asses, troublemakers, assaulters, agitators, and escape artists.[61]

"Most riots and mutinies inside prison walls are due to idleness and want of discipline. Bad food is sometimes blamed. But that is seldom the real cause. In most cases, firm discipline, fair treatment, and plenty of work to keep everybody busy will keep the riotously inclined out of mischief."[62]

Sometimes bad children were in need of a good spanking, maybe with a leather belt or a switch. Some prisoners—it was deemed— frequently needed a reminder on their backside, the pain of imprisonment and red welts, dire warning to other convicts with disobedience on their minds. In general, social philosophy was, at that time, not opposed to therapeutic corporal punishment. And Texas prison authorities employed a dandy—but surely not in the eyes of offending recipients of its physical wickedness. Rather benignly the disciplinary tool was referred to as the "Bat."[63] Nomenclature of the instrument was rudimentary: four inch wide three-ply leather straps plaited together, attached to a stout oak wood handle. Typically the offender was stripped and spread-eagled, held down for the punishment. Ostensibly a nineteenth-century Sharps .50 caliber had a "kick worse than a little Spanish jack" and when discharged would get meat at both ends.[64] The Bat was a hide-ripper too!

During its earliest uses behind the tall walls at Huntsville, the prescribed number of blistering strikes was preset at thirty-nine (later reduced to twenty). Such was not by mere chance, as explained by modern-era researchers and writers: "Ancient Jewish punishment demanded that the maximum number of lashes allowed per infraction was forty, given in multiples of three, effectively making the maximum number at thirty-nine. The one left off was to show 'compassion,' . . ."[65]

While defending use of the Bat to a Texas State Legislative Committee, a generally respected prison administrator cut to the nub: "Gentlemen, it's just like using spurs. You get on an old cow horse without spurs—and you can't head even a milking-pen cow; but when you've got your spurs on, the old horse will do the job. And you don't have to use the spurs, because all he needs is to know that the spurs are there. It's the same with us and the 'bat.' The record shows we seldom have to use it. But the boys all know that it is there."[66] Though behavior deterred cannot be conclusively measured—only acts not deterred are statistically authenticated—there is in most quarters an agreement regarding use of the Bat: "While the physical damage from use of the bat cannot be overstated, the

fact is that prison officials also used, very effectively, the psychological effects of the instrument to discipline inmates."[67] Few were the
convicts that could take the full complement of flogs before crying
loud for mercy: "But the hell-raiser fears nothing more than he fears
the 'bat.' When I was in charge, he got it. Generally, after five lashes,
the rebel raised his hand and cried, 'That's enough; I'll behave.'"[68]

Suffice to say that in the free-world by the 1850s not everyone
was behaving; some folks seemed hell-bent on pocketing their one-
way ticket to Huntsville, courtesy the Texas judiciary and impaneled
juries. And some, like a convict named Perry from Liberty in Liberty
County, imprisoned for murdering his wife, opted to jump. Writing
for the *Texas State Gazette* the newsman tersely closed Perry's chapter: "made an attempt to escape on Sunday evening, the 25th ult.,
but was shot and killed by one of the guards."[69] *Finis!* A different
newspaperman for another sheet, the *Gonzales Inquirer*, matter-
of-factly penned of the state's budding penitentiary, touting the in
vogue philosophy of keeping convicts busy: "This interesting edifice,
useful for teaching rogues within to amend, and those without to
beware . . . ," encapsulated public opinion regarding incarceration
but not about funds siphoned from public coffers.[70] A sentiment
somewhat echoed in an Austin paper's piece:

> We were never more agreeably surprised than in visiting the peni-
> tentiary at Huntsville. Instead of a weak, frail, brick work, almost
> ready to tumble down from its own weight, as common rumor has
> informed us, we found a splendid massive building, constructed of
> excellent material and strong and durable workmanship. . . . The
> convicts are employed at present with making brick to add to the
> new building. It is thought that brick sufficient will be made by fall
> to enclose a large lot with a wall of sufficient magnitude to guard
> prisoners through the day.[71]

Always strapped for taxpayers' cash, Lone Star State politicos
figured that convicts sitting on their duffs, idling away their days
and who knew what at night, were basically a distressing drain on
preciously scant funds. As the penitentiary population swelled, the

apt prison appropriation packages seemed to deflate. Was there a coherent cure for the obligatory penny-pinching at the Statehouse? Should not the inmates contribute to their own upkeep? Was it wrongheaded to presume—and persuade—that a self-sustaining institution could and would alleviate a hefty percentage of the state's financial woes? Honest and hardworking Texas taxpayers were footing the bill, weren't they? The state's fourth governor was Peter Hansborough Bell, a combat-tested veteran of the Battle of San Jacinto, a frontier-era Texas Ranger, and survivor of the Battle of Buena Vista during the Mexican War.[72] In his mind, he owned the elusive answer. Governor Bell sought $35,000 from the Texas Legislature to construct a textile mill behind the Huntsville penitentiary's above-ground fifteen-foot red brick periphery walls. Governor Bell addressed the Texas State Senate and House of Representatives on the ninth of November 1853. With regard to the textile mill, he said in part:

> The State Penitentiary was instituted as one of the adjuncts of the criminal code of the country, for the suppression of crime and the protection of the morals of society; and, to properly effect this, it appears to me that the reformation of the convict constitutes the only certain means whereby the object of its institution can be accomplished. From a close examination of the causes of crimes, and the experience to be derived from similar establishments in our sister States [Louisiana and Mississippi] and other points of the world, it will be found, that nothing has had a more beneficial effect on the morals and physical health of their unfortunate inmates than the habitual and steady occupancy of some mechanical pursuit [industry] which would afford them the certain prospect of an honest and respectable livelihood when they emerged from the walls of their prison. All other considerations should give place to these, or the intention of such institutions will be defeated, and the State as well as the individual, in reality, are losers. I will, therefore, only recommend that a cotton factory be established in the Penitentiary, which will employ half of the convict labor existing

there, and the other half to be distributed in mechanical pursuits [a wagon yard and cabinet shop], under such regulations as may be deemed most advisable; it will then be found, that the convicts will not sensibly interfere with, or affect the mechanical interest of the country, and that they will have the chance when they leave, of making themselves good and useful members of society.[73]

Processing cotton and wool—keeping convicts industrially occupied—it was argued could pay a twofold dividend. The penitentiary would earn self-sufficiency selling refined cloth on the open market and, by his calculation, the inmates would be advantaged with newfound skills, a real "contribution to their moral reformation."[74] Obviously the tone of Governor Bell's address, despite popular myth that no one was interested in inmates' wellbeing, demonstrates that though it may not have been their first priority, which was security, most Texans and most policy makers were not anti second-chance reformation.

Governor Peter Bell resigned the Texas governorship and accepted an unexpected vacancy in the U.S. Congress. Representative David S. Kaufman had died, but the money and mill would prove P.H. Bell's penitentiary legacy, despite the objections of new Governor Elisha Marshall Pease who at the time wanted to lease the entire prison to private contractors, lock, stock, and barrel—plus the prisoners who could make profiteers rich by way of their compelled labor.[75] Simply said, Governor Pease had other priorities, most noble and necessary: public education, railroad construction, education for Reservation Indians, freed up funds for the Austin State Hospital, the Texas School for the Deaf, and the Texas School for the Blind. In the end he wanted to "put the penitentiary on a self-sustaining basis. . . ."[76] Nonetheless, the Fifth Texas Legislature acted during March 1854 passing "An act to provide for the establishment of cotton and woolen factories in the Penitentiary. . . ."[77]

Another Texas penitentiary first was the 1854 shameful appearance of Elizabeth Huffman, tried and convicted for murdering her newborn.[78] In compliance with the 1848 Act to Establish a State

Penitentiary, Chapter 80, Section 12, "That the convicts of the different sexes shall at all times be kept separate and apart," inmate Huffman had a private room reserved, the prescribed check-out time a year later.[79] Increasingly, as time passed and the inmate population multiplied, penitentiary administrators soon became increasingly aware that every fair damsel wearing a skirt was not necessarily fair or honest or pure of heart.

By close of the first half of 1856 the textile mill was operational. An inventory would reveal that there were "40 looms with 896 spindles for cotton and 200 for wool." When ginning at full tilt, a yearend tally would show that the mill's capability could process cloth from 500 bales of cotton, and produce 6,000 pounds of wool per annum.[80] Economically, the end product was "much heavier and firmer than the same description of goods brought from the North . . . [and] will wear nearly twice as long as the common articles," similarly manufactured in that distant marketplace. Practically speaking then, a "true policy of the State is to fix a moderate price upon these goods, and have them sold on small commissions, at those prices, in different parts of the State, so that the people may have the benefit of the Penitentiary, which belongs to them and is supported by them. . . ."[81]

Despite the generalized impression handed out by a few latter-day scribes, the Huntsville Penitentiary was not off-limits to the public twenty-four-and-seven. An August 19, 1856, edition of the *Galveston News* amplifies: "A resolution of inquiry having been introduced in the Legislature regarding charges for admission into the Penitentiary, Gen. [John Slater] Besser replies, through the State *Gazette*, that the number of visitors was so great that additional guards were necessary, and consequently the Directors ordered a charge of 25 cents for each visitor. The money thus collected was duly accounted for, and Gen. Besser says the Directors of Penitentiaries in several other states charge for admission. . . ."[82]

For the most part the Huntsville facility was patterned and operated after what became known as the Auburn System, named after the Empire State's penologists' and the general populaces' theories about running their state penitentiary at Auburn, New York. Convicts were to work in the daytime behind tall walls and in the evening, in strict silence, and after their supper, catch their shut-eye in one-man cells.[83] Under the Auburn System's management philosophy, when inmates were kept separate at night and silent in the daylight, there was less opportunity for inmate interaction and little prospect of fashioning prisoner unity, factors that if not monitored closely could lead to riots and escapes.[84]

By 1857 even Governor Pease was bent toward conceding the truth: Operation of the textile mill inside the tall walls was a winner. Updating the Texas Legislature with regards to overall operation of the Huntsville penal facility the governor acknowledged, "that the cotton and woolen goods manufactured 'have found a ready sale and the results are encouraging.'"[85] Austin-based politicos and the public at large presumed that on its present course the penitentiary could become wholly self-sufficient in but short order, washing away prospects of financial drainage on the state's budget. That success, though somewhat unspoken, also seemed to validate penology philosophy trending at the time; making prisoners work served society well. Too, that industrious frame of mind would serve the convicts well, putting them on a more sound footing when reentered into the free-world. Folks outside the tall walls were expected to work; that was truly the American methodology—the Texas way—every day. Shouldn't the criminals? Or had they by setting a course of robbing and stealing earned a free pass?

As the ginning and spinning ramped up behind prison walls, outside things were unwinding. Conflict between North and South was looming. Hostilities erupted. Interestingly, those men then employed at Huntsville's bastille as prison guards were exempt from conscription into the Confederate Army.[86] Beating back requests from Confederate Army hierarchy that the Huntsville facility be turned into a military prison for captured Union soldiers, then-Governor Francis R. Lubbock thought the textile mill could best serve the Confederate cause. He was not wrong. "During the war period the state controlled penitentiary annually manufactured more than one and one-half million yards of cloth to supply the needs of Confederate soldiers in the field, to satisfy the soldiers' families at home, and to provide for the demands of the general [Southern] consumer."[87] In fact, the Texas prisoners couldn't keep up with need. To satisfy the genuine shortfall in manpower, convicts from Arkansas, Louisiana, and Missouri were imported and unceremoniously bivouacked behind steel-barred cubicles when not sweating—and no doubt swearing—producing bolt after bolt of rough and ready fabric that was turned into cotton sacking, sheeting, woolen hats and other woolen goods and issued to lacking Confederate soldiers "in the field and their often nearly destitute families at home."[88] The demand for the prison product was near insatiable:

> A private letter from Huntsville, dated June 10th, gives an account of an attempt to sack the Penitentiary. Some people seem to have a very strong desire to be placed under the control of Federal [Reconstruction] bayonets. The letter says about forty jayhawkers approached the town and demanded the cloth in the Penitentiary. Being met by about seventy-five armed citizens, they retired, reinforced and returned with about one hundred and twenty-five men. But the citizens were about five hundred strong by this time and ready for battle, and the baffled marauders gave it up and left. Good for the citizens of Huntsville.[89]

A later edition of the newspaper, no doubt with tongue in cheek, offhandedly editorialized that that the assailants on Huntsville "saw more chance of losing blood than getting cloth."[90] During the war years the Huntsville mill turned out 2,258,660 yards of cotton and 293,298 yards of wool, with a sale price value of $1,174,439.07. After deduction of expenses the state pocketed a handsome profit of $800,000, no little sum at the time.[91] Governor Lubbock chimed in again: "The institution has proven of incalculable benefit to the army. In the present condition of the country its importance rises to supreme magnitude."[92] Looking back, a modern scholar constructively weighs in with clarity: "That such an asset was readily available to the Confederate forces proved highly beneficial to their cause and, although certainly not a decisive factor in either victory or defeat, accounted for the alleviation of suffering both on the battlefield and at home."[93]

Coarse cloth wasn't the only byproduct of the Huntsville penitentiary. As would be expected, meanness was ever spooled and ready to unravel. Though the reasons are nebulous, bad blood existed between convicts Tom Bird and Donicio Villarreal. At a workshop, the former was stabbed in the stomach by the latter, inflicting a mortal wound. Running for the doorway Villarreal was accosted by another convict John Q.A. Jones, so he cut him too, quick and deep. Then, apparently having run amok, Villarreal sprinted across the prison yard and stuck the shank into the body of Sidney Sheppard, the Assistant Steward of the prison. Thereafter he attacked the penitentiary's Steward, Gus Sheppard, but was slightly wounded by gunfire from Gus's hastily fired handgun. That was not the last act for this behind the tall walls high-drama. Prison Superintendent Thomas Carothers closed the curtain on Villarreal's madness for keeps, killing him with a well-placed shot before he exited the institution's front gate.[94]

2

"Muzzle the guard"

WITH CESSATION OF THE HORRORS and the return of Texans from distant theaters of war, one might suppose all was just peachy on the home front, outside the tall walls and inside the state's penitentiary. Idyllic musing, but such was wrongheaded. Simply said, the Lone Star State was lawless and for the most part broke.[1] There were even rumors raging that there would be an attempt made "to capture and rob the penitentiary at Huntsville."[2] Reconstruction was at hand, but few ex-Confederates were bent toward being reconstructed.[3] Change is seldom easy! With an influx of retuning veterans and the population surge of former slaves—freedmen—the state's economy soon was in shambles, unable to keep up with institutional demands for precious public funds or prized public services.[4] The freedmen, generally speaking, were hurled into a capitalistic society heretofore foreign to them on a wage-working basis.[5] Some turned to crime. Not a few of the returning Confederates were imbued with open hostility. Some turned to crime. The convict population escalated. The balance in the state's coffers plunged. Desperate prisoners at Huntsville's Big House were yearning to somehow escape captivity, while pot-bellied and cigar-chomping legislators at the Statehouse sought to escape bankruptcy—somehow?

In many minds there was a ready fix: reduce penitentiary overcrowding and expenses by leasing convicts to private entities. Hypothetically that approach would, besides reducing acute economic woes, "remedy the ills of idleness and inactivity" which had befallen much of the prison population due to endemic overcrowding.[6] In theory and on paper the idea didn't seem outlandish, and so it came to be. Advertisements were placed in area newspapers with regards to submitting bids to lease inmates. At length, at a fee of $12.50 per month, per convict, private enterprise zealously picked up part of the public's expense. The Airline Railroad was allocated 100 prisoners, and the Brazos Branch Railroad's workforce was augmented by 150 inmates.[7] One hundred and eighty-one convicts were leased, under contract to the Houston and Texas Central Railroad.[8] Reconstruction Governor Edmund J. Davis saw both the good and the bad with that way out of the perennial problem:

> The convicts at work on the railroad are not an expense to the State, but the system is considered demoralizing to the convicts, and it clearly does not tend to that improvement of their mental and moral capacity which (after the protection of the public) is the main object of the Penitentiary System.[9]

Part of the bad was that working outside and not confined by tall walls with guard towers, the figurative gateway to the literal getaway was wide open. Making a break for liberty was, well, not all that complicated were one to bide his time, be watchful, and jump at the right moment. There were numerous, an "undue portion," of triumphant escapes.[10]

And not to be unexpected there were also a number of escape "attempts" wherein the convict was formally introduced to the lead balls from a guard's six-shooter or shotgun. Sometimes they died, sometimes they didn't. And, sometimes the circumstance surrounding the thunderous discharge of guards' weapons was, well, dubious. Enough so that those politicos at Austin and prison reform-minded folks were becoming more and more alarmed as newspaper headlines heralded a fresh shooting. There was a cascade of complaints—some justified—some not. Though there was, at the time, a hard bottom-line: Contracts were cancelled coinciding with predetermined renewal dates.[11] Convicts heretofore making roadbeds and swinging sledgehammers were returned to Huntsville, swamping and stretching the facility's already overburdened blueprint.[12] And, county sheriffs were arriving daily, dumping recently convicted prisoners into the mix—and pocketing a haulage fee. The Texas Prison System—if "system" is not an overreach—was a mess.

Adding to the hardships and misfortunes was an outbreak of the dreaded Yellow Fever, which left several Huntsville free-world citizens dead and jumped over the tall wall and into the prison. Between thirty and forty prisoners were contaminated by the scourge but thanks to the stellar work and "skillful nursing and unremitting attention" of concerned state-paid employees only two convicts perished before the epidemic was eradicated.[13] Advocates for building additional prisons were—in addition to other justifications—touting the unhealthy outbreak as a good reason for placing prisoners "beyond the reach of yellow fever."[14] History will bear witness, the majority of prison employees then or now, are just as ready to step forward saving lives as they are with confining and/or taking lives. Unfortunately, however, some convicts are never convinced that complying may be much preferable than an ill-advised and iffy getaway. A Galveston newspaper updated interested readers with the reality of making an impetuous break—noting that of the dozen prisoners who had made an escape from Huntsville, thus far the pursuing posse had killed two, and though the others were yet presumed to be alive, surrender taking precedent over headlong flight would not be imprudent—it would be smart.[15]

One particular Huntsville prisoner was relatively sharp and quick on the trigger. The annals of Wild West history would know Benjamin "Ben" Thompson as the genuine article with regards to Lone Star State gunmen and gamblers, even though he was born in England. The legendary Texas shootist found himself in receipt of a four-year prison sentence for shooting but not killing James Moore, his brother-in-law, at Austin. The sentencing entity had, of course at the time, been a dutiful federal Reconstruction-era Military Commission, but nevertheless the gutsy but unlucky Ben Thompson was to do his hard time at Huntsville, confined at hard labor, an unsympathetic diktat of the military tribunal. When the Texas political climate changed and the Democratic Party had regained control of all things political, the natural order of Texas doings was to grant Ben Thompson a free pass from the penitentiary. Likewise his spending time, two years, behind tall walls was no handicap, career wise. Ben Thompson landed the top spot with the city of Austin's police force. Thereafter was an electrifying chapter of Texas high-drama; he and the ever dangerous sometimes lawman/sometimes desperado John King Fisher died from gunshot wounds inside Jack Harris's Vaudeville Theater and Saloon at San Antonio.[16]

Seemingly undaunted by the previous adverse penitentiary leasing experiment, an idea was propounded that perhaps, just perhaps, turning the whole shootin'-match over to privateers would workout much better than a piecemeal approach.[17] Roll the dice!

The entire prison was formally leased to Ward, Dewey, (N. Patton), and Company of Galveston, effective 29 April 1871.[18] Subsequent to the compliance of contract stipulations regarding appraising and placing an agreed-to monetary value on prison property and posting the required performance bonds of at least $50,000 but not to exceed $100,000, the brass key-ring to the Big House was passed to Ward, Dewey, and Company on July 5, 1871. The multi-year lease would give the lessees unfettered access to "all lands, buildings, machinery, tools, and other property belonging to the prisonn. . . ." Too, the lessees were to assume all costs associated with running the prison, which naturally included subsistence and clothing and medical care for the convicts, as well as salaries and quarters for guards and other personnel.[19] All told, during the life of the lease, the clever lawmakers figured the State of Texas would be ahead by about $325,000.[20]

With respect to the marriage between Ward, Dewey, and Company and the State of Texas, the honeymoon was fantastic. Acknowledging that the Huntsville facility had no dining hall or chapel, and was short by a whopping number of cells, the lessees set to work in the spirit of doing right, which would not handicap their overall goal—turning a profit. Convicts were awed after the lessees constructed a dining hall, which would substitute as a chapel on Sundays, christened an infirmary, added forty cells, and constructed new industrial workshops. In slightly over a year's time, busy inmates were engaged in productively and profitably manufacturing numerous items: "high-quality wool and cotton garments, 'furniture, doors, sash, blinds, wagons, boots, and shoes,' all of which found a good market in Texas."[21] Problematically though, sheriffs kept showing up at the doorstep with new "fish" as the first-timers were labeled by the grim long-sentence convicts. There was no fat thumb in dike; the deluge was unstoppable. In an effort to staunch the flow and lessen the expenses and sickness and fractiousness of overcrowding inmates, the lessees began subleasing convicts to "planters, tanners, brickyards, and railroad contractors."[22]

Therein, in a nutshell, was the precursor for fiasco and failure. Prisoners widely scattered about in the subcontractors' out-of-the-way and out-of-sight work camps was not conducive to suitable management principles of penology—even then. It hadn't worked the first time around! The isolation was rife for abuse and brutality and denials.[23]

Although he was no longer employed as a guard by Ward, Dewey, and Company, the Georgia-born Samuel Wright assumed the posture of today's whistleblower, though he did it in Louisiana talking with the editorial staff for the *New Orleans Times*. Ex-guard Wright told newsmen that "the matter had been a weight upon his mind for months, and that he felt it a duty to his God to let the world know what those hapless creatures suffered." His allegations were explosive. He submitted a lengthy sworn statement outlining numerous examples of mismanagement and mistreatment, but herein only one—for illustrative purposes—will be cited:

> He [convict John Harris] was first put in the stocks, and while there was beaten on the head with clubs until covered with blood. Then he was taken out in an insensible condition, and when he partially recovered Bud Robinson [guard] snapped a pistol in his face. Sergeant Chitty, standing by, did not attempt to interfere. The snapping of capped and loaded pistols in the faces of convicts is an everyday occurrence. John Harris finally recovered and

stood up, when Robinson, Chitty and [corporal] Shaw commenced throwing burning embers from the fire into his face. The sufferer begged piteously to them to desist, but the sport (?) continued until 12 o'clock at night, when they whipped him, striking him between five and six hundred lashes. The prisoner then went into the hospital, and was sick nearly two months. I was a witness to this cruelty.[24]

Not surprisingly such vile allegations were picked up in the Texas press, most particularly the *Galveston Daily News*. Their position was simple and plainspoken: "The News deems it its duty to publish the whole matter, the good names and fame of the State of Texas being involved. If the charges proffered are false and groundless, it will be easy to show who this Samuel Wright is. If they are true, then the duty of the State authorities is plain. An investigation of the most rigid character should be made into the affairs of the penitentiary, and its results made known to the world. The lessees of that institution must disprove the horrible statement given to the public. . . . If the lessees can not disprove this matter, then it remains for the State authorities to take action."[25] Shortly thereafter another allegation of seriousness surfaced. According to a newspaper report, several female convicts had become pregnant and given birth while in the state's custody. Purportedly, if the tally is right, guards were the fathers of seventeen illegitimate children born to prisoners leased to a farm outside of Huntsville proper. And even at The Walls, according to one of the convicts, Amanda Blackman, the keepers had unfettered access to the quarters of female prisoners for illicit and/or nonconsensual trysts.[26] Stringent observance of prescribed protocols and prohibitions was—during this timeframe—checkered at best.

Even the politically appointed Penitentiary Board of Directors were forced by reality to acknowledge as much, noting that while rules and bylaws governed administering discipline on disobedient and unruly convicts, there were blind spots: "They are often, however, violated; and it has been impossible, so far, to compel a strict compliance with them, especially on the part of guards and sergeants away from the prison proper."[27]

Unfortunately when recounting this darker chapter of Lone Star penitentiary governance the blame for excessive maltreatment is almost always placed on the backs of guards—which no doubt in many cases is justly deserved. Herein there is no defense for misconduct. Clearheaded thinking, however, exposes the hard truth: Sometimes work camp convicts could be and were rattlesnake mean and downright dangerous. Guards' very lives depended on watchfulness and readiness. That's why they were armed—not for an angry bear but a badman or badmen. As indicated in the investigative report of Prison Inspector James Knox Polk "J.N.P" Campbell, three convicts in Matagorda County assaulted and killed a guard, and for that they each received twenty-five hide-shredding lashes with the "strap."[28] Illustratively for another blood-spattered episode, though somewhat out of chronology, Joe Epperson wouldn't be the last unlucky guard to give up the ghost while watching after convicts assigned to his dreary and austere outside work camp. At an East Texas coal camp near Alto, Cherokee County, Epperson was deliberately overpowered, disarmed, and fatally gunned down by three convicts who had "snatched a pistol away from another guard."[29]

Truthfully, as it unwinds, this chronicle will be chock-full of instances wherein the unfortunate prison employee's day ended pushing up daises, not eating cathead biscuits and black-eyed peas. It's easy to lose sight of the fact that penitentiaries house some folks—whatever their justifications and/or excuses—who have long before abandoned living life by society's or anybody else's rules. Regardless the syrupiness about gentleness and gratitude, it's a damn tough neighborhood behind those tall walls or inside those high fences—and was in those early day work camps too.

Candidly telling this phase of the story though does dictate leaving any whitewash in the pail. There were abuses at the work camps and some Texas prison guards were fanatically, it seemed, handing out harsh punishments for this or that rule infraction—or pure cussedness. Some prisoners were "placed naked in stocks, raised off the ground, and whipped cruelly." Moreover, convicts were not inclined to up the truth to investigators or inspectors for fear of finding themselves in the middle when examiners headed to the house—the Statehouse—to write and submit their critical reports to an ever inquisitive and politically susceptible bureaucracy.[30] Corporal punishment was yet in vogue. Resorting to use of the Bat was not officially outlawed. Not just a few Texans supposed convicts deserved whatever punishment was meted out. Others, however, began voicing—sometimes loudly—concern and compassion for the prisoners' plight. Newspaper editors and prison reformers were not shy.

That the honeymoon was over with Ward, Dewey, and Company is reflected in the mid-1870s investigative report of Prison Inspector J.N.P. Campbell, who noted that the relationship between the lessee and the State of Texas had soured. The litany of complaints was long and, in many cases, indefensible. Inspector Campbell found many of the prison buildings were in disrepair and that the roofs leaked horribly and individual cells were "dripping with water, and hence unfit to be occupied—yet convicts did sleep in them. The lessees have recently put on several thin coats of coal tar and sand, which has done some good, but the roofs still leak." The "engine house" was completely demolished when a boiler exploded. Glass window panes were broken and not replaced and wholly inferior brick was being used in prison construction and spotty repairs. With regards to the overall physical plant, Inspector Campbell's rundown was down and dirty but true: "This prison [The Walls] is very unsafe for the class of criminals now confined here. A strong, able-bodied man can work through any of the walls with a good pick in five minutes."[31]

Campbell's findings were not simply focused on tumbling down architecture and dampness and wintertime chilliness, but on the convict profiles as well. Of the 1,723 state prisoners at the time of his report, 443 were inside the tall walls, and the remaining were laboring in the outside camps per lease and/or sublease agreements. Those work camp convicts were busy swinging hoes and hammers and axes in agriculture and railroad and sawmill pursuits. By and large the 1,280 outside convicts were racially segregated: blacks working the farms and fields at the direction of "planters," whites toiling on the railroad and in wood camps or in the prison shops. None had it any too good, regardless of color or age. The oldest prisoner was sixty-nine years, the youngest a lad of eleven years, though two-thirds had left their twenty-fifth birthday celebration as but a remembrance of, perhaps, better days.[32]

Not unexpectedly escapes were rather routine and the convicts took off "primarily from the outside camps." There was, always had been, a few breaks from Huntsville's headquarters unit. Inspector Campbell's notion was that the lessees should suffer the blame for their cost-cutting and hiring practices:

> The escapes are principally from the outside camps, but few having escaped from the walls. This is caused by employing any man who will apply for a position as guard, and the great majority have had no experience. The price paid by the lessees is not sufficient to get good men, (they, however, have some good guards) and those employed have been badly paid. The wages promised, as a general thing, is twenty-five dollars per month. I have seen, at the outside camps, and about the prison, youths not over eighteen or nineteen years old, with a double-barrel gun in their hands, guarding convicts.[33]

Inspector Campbell, with regards to escapes from the outside camps, mentioned the effectiveness of having and maintaining a pack of tracking dogs: "From the camps at which the lessees, or their sergeants, keep a pack of blood-hounds, very few convicts escape, and if they do escape, they are soon caught by the assistance of those dogs."[34] Making use of the natural capacity of Bloodhounds (hereafter a generic term for all breeds of the prison's tracking dogs) was then, and would continue into the twenty-first century, as one facet in the Correctional Officers' toolkit.

Without riding a jaded horse to ground, the more Inspector Campbell and his Assistant Inspector, Henry K. White, inspected, the more discomfiture they suffered and discovered.[35] Many, many, prisoners were short-rationed with foodstuffs, insufficiently clothed, many without shoes, and the attention paid to the convicts' medical maladies and injuries ranged from nil to basically inadequate, despite the fact a paid physician was on staff. In short—especially at the outside camps—living conditions ratcheted several notches past atrociousness.

And for the story in hand it was growing increasingly tough for Ward, Dewey, and Company to turn a profit. Aside from the above cited crescendo of prisoner mistreatment allegations and a burgeoning prison population, a downtick in the overall economy was not playing to the lessees' favor. For a number of quantifiable factors the company's expenses were not matching projected income. From the pure profitability angle, Ward, Dewey, and Company were in a financial freefall. At Austin, inside the Chief Executive's office, the governor and his staff were becoming more and more worried. The State of Texas had a lot riding on the lease—profits and pride.

Laying bare that Ward, Dewey, and Company were on the downfall is easy; citing but a couple of typical instances should suffice. The chief engineer for the Overton & Henderson Railroad (two towns in East Texas), B.S. Wathen notified Inspector Campbell in writing, among other things, that the lease convicts working on his line were "entirely without supplies of any kind—suffering for the necessaries of life, and nothing here with which to provide it. The men are naked, and not one half a dozen pair of shoes within the entire camp. If you can do anything as Inspector this needs your *prompt* attention." After the letter, upon a personal and worrisome investigation at the railroad work camp, Inspector Campbell was updated by the guard in charge: "For fifteen days before the above letter was written, that officer informed me that he had to appeal to the citizens for assistance, and the convicts and guards were fed, as he expressed it, by '*charity*.' He had exchanged everything that was available for supplies before he appealed to the citizens for help. The men were badly clothed, and all were barefooted, and the bedding disgustingly filthy. . . ."[36]

In Walker County at the outside farm camps, living conditions for convicts was hardly any better—about the same—according to

one of the sergeants overseeing a squad of "thirty-five white convicts." His descriptiveness is bare-bones about bare feet: For a time
his limping and sore-footed prisoners were "without shoes for over
three months, and that he had to work them in picking cotton during
the cold weather. In the latter part of November, fifty white convicts were returned from these farms barefooted, full of vermin, and
their clothing 'tattered and torn.' Men returned to the walls would
be without shoes for some weeks, but in the main the convicts have
had shoes. Some have cloth shoes not suitable for winter. Only two
of the shops in the whole prison are warmed by stoves, and during
last winter some of the men had their feet frosted in the severe cold
weather."[37] Then Inspector Campbell pitched in the kicker:

> It has been most fortunate that this has been, so far, an unprec-
> edentedly mild winter, or there would have been great suffering
> among the Texas convicts.[38]

In the meantime, for convicts living behind the tall walls at
Huntsville, life was *not quite so bad* as for the inmates domiciled in the
widely scattered subleased work camps. There had even been a move
underfoot to seek appropriation for an in-house prison library at
The Walls, which came to fruition with ratification of a $500 budget
allocation. The bookshelves would be stocked with "moral and useful
books for the use and improvement of the convicts."[39] Surprisingly
attendance for Sunday religious services exceeded expectation.[40] At
the time, to reach those in need of any spiritual uplifting, the Prison
Chaplains were multi-denominational: a Presbyterian, a Campbellite,
a Baptist, and a Catholic Priest.[41] Though by any standard one would
probably prefer to be elsewhere, from the outset prison administrators did not forsake the possibility of prisoner reformation.
Unceremoniously it was generally accepted if the cheerless detainee
really had "a change of heart," he could actually and productively
turn his life around. If he didn't, and acted out or "bucked"—refused
to work—well, prison officialdom had contingency plans for corralling meanness and correcting misbehavior. One bad apple can rot
the barrel.

And in the free-world there were plenty of bad apples—and not just a few raiding Indians for Texans to deal with. For historical context, George Armstrong Custer's battle at the Little Bighorn was not yet in the book. In Texas blue-eyed desperadoes and native Spanish-speaking bandits and warriors painted for forays were threatening peacefulness on multiple fronts. So much so—on all counts—just the year before convicts were furnished library books to peruse in their *leisure* time, the focused Texas Legislators put hard words to paper, maybe clumsily, but nevertheless it was law:

> An Act to provide for the protection of the Frontier of the State of Texas against the invasion of hostile Indians, Mexicans, or other marauding or thieving parties.[42]

The legendary Frontier Battalion AKA Texas Rangers was born. By most reasoned accounts this demarcation point, 1874, was when being a Ranger equated to having a job, not just serving as a quasi militiaman. Subsequent to doing away with the very unpopular Texas State Police, the Rangers had been institutionalized, becoming the law-enforcing and Indian fighting arm of state government.[43] Hardly had the Frontier Battalion been birthed when the all too often news issued from Huntsville—four convicts cut their way through a wall with a pickaxe and three others jumped for freedom while being marched to their cells after supper in the dining hall.[44] Fortuitously the Texas Ranger's rich and lively history would, from then to now, auspiciously intertwine with that of the Texas Prison System's riveting and colorful story, the common denominator being those recalcitrant bad apples.

One of those unmanageable convicts assaulted a guard with an axe during an escape, hitting him in the head and nearly killing him. The convict was—after some effort—captured. "On being brought into prison he was so severely stocked by one of the lessees that, when he was taken out he fell, and it was feared he was dead, but, a good many buckets of water having been thrown on him, he revived." There, of course, is the back story. Fortunately the assaulted guard did not die; unfortunately, it was medically and journalistically predicted he would in an irrevocable outcome "be an imbecile the balance of his life."[45]

What was not balancing was the ledger book at Ward, Dewey, and Company—the gig, as the saying goes, was up. Although in large part taking exception to the in-depth scrutiny and findings, the lessees could read the tealeaves:

> Without making use of the pretence of seeking the interest of convicts, or zealous care for the revenue of the State, we can truly say that if the State can succeed better with this institution and its unfortunate inmates, both morally and financially than we have, none will welcome the achievement more heartily than. . . . Your obedient servants, Ward, Dewey & Co., *Lessees*.[46]

Prison Inspector Campbell's unswerving summation to the governor was not mush-mouthed: "Referring to the existing lease of Messrs. Ward, Dewey & Co., I have to state that its provisions are not complied with, which is well known to your Excellency. I do not deem it necessary to go into further details than what has already been said."[47] Lone Star State government was not then, nor is now, and odds-on never will be, altogether exempt from structuring dreadful commercial partnerships. Par business it would seem. Into the abyss of bad Texas deals did the pact with Ward, Dewey and Company go![48]

Had power-players at the Statehouse at last stumbled onto prison management commonsense? In a quick turnaround, the legislators "authorized and required" the state's Chief Executive to take absolute control of the penitentiary and convicts without delay, and then find a suitable lessee and enter into a new agreement—one with an end-cap not exceeding fifteen years.[49]

After an interim lease to Burnett and Kilpatrick of Galveston, which had been designed as a temporary measure from the outset, the lasting contractual nod after opening nine offers was awarded—the highest and best bidder—to Edward H. Cunningham from Guadalupe County (county seat Seguin) and L.A. Ellis, from Marion County (county seat Jefferson), both savvy businessmen with broad real-estate holdings, much of it agricultural land south and west of

Houston.[50] They were already well attuned to leasing convicts for their large-scale farming operations, as well as subleasing prisoners to "other landowners, small industries, and railroads."[51] Perhaps one cent had put them over the top during the bidding contest, perhaps not. At any rate Cunningham and Ellis would be paying $3.01 per capita per month for each convict, which in the cumulative was projected to generate $250,000 of revenue for Texas over the five-year lifetime of the lease.[52] The new lease was effective on the first day of January 1878.[53]

Already in certain respects, life for convicts inside The Walls was improving, thanks in large part to the previous efforts of interim lessees Burnett and Kilpatrick: "By hard work and close attention to business, everything connected with the State Prison has been brought into first class order. The different industries of the prison, which had been allowed to run down, have been renewed, and there is being made a large quantity of cotton and woolen goods in addition to furniture, wagons, etc. The culinary department has been replenished with a new and complete outfit. The convicts are better fed and cared for now than ever, several articles of diet having been added, never heretofore used, such as coffee, bacon, molasses, dried apples, rice, etc. The convicts have all been supplied with new suits and shoes, and everything has been done to make the administration a credit to the State, the Governor and the lessees."[54]

With forethought, new policies and procedures were in place for the new lessees. There would be accountability for recruiting and retaining and remunerating the guard force and other prison personnel—including salaries for the Prison Directors, Superintendent, Physician, and Chaplain. Salary dollars were paid straight into the state treasury, and Texas accountants would issue the checks to prison personnel—a much needed improvement from the earlier era where no little mystery could web around just who was being paid how much, for just what. It was supposed that this new pay policy would put the damper on lessees salting the guards' wages for working convicts harder and longer, squeezing every ounce of labor from their already skeletal frames. New hires for the guard staff were to be good men, honest and true—and dismissible upon written demand of the Superintendent or Penitentiary Directors.[55]

Ever-evolving—maybe slowly—nevertheless inching forward was a statutorily required effort to ensure that "as far as practicable, to the exaction of the penalty imposed by law on each convict, and to the protection, well being and humane treatment to which each convict is entitled at the hands of the state. . . ."[56] Furthermore, according to law:

> and no lease shall be made by which the control of the prisoners, except as to a reasonable amount of labor, shall pass from the state or its officers to the lessees; and the state shall, in all cases, and under all circumstances, retain the absolute control of the persons of the convicts, put them to or withdraw them from any kind of labor; station and remove them at or from any point inside or outside of the prison; make or change, at pleasure, all rules of the discipline and punishment of convicts; prescribe regulations for their food, clothing, nursing, instruction and guarding; and any leases made shall be subject to the reservation of these rights and powers on the part of the state, whether so stated in the lease or not; the object of these limitations being to prevent the state, under the guise of contract, from parting with the right to direct how, at anytime, and under all circumstances, convicts shall be lodged, fed, clothed, worked and treated; *provided*, that no convict shall be hired or leased to do any labor outside of prison walls, and detached from the prison, when there is sufficient room for their accommodation within the walls of the penitentiary or penitentiaries of the state, and their labor can be utilized within said prison. . . .[57]

Though sometimes skipped over in a few agenda-driven prison chronicles, even then it was recognized that nineteenth-century convicts were cut off from the world and their families. Therefore, a stipulation in the lease agreement was that each convict was to be provided with stationery and postage so he/she could mail one letter per week—to whomever, wherever.[58]

With a concentrated effort to guarantee compliance of lessees was the patronage appointment of three Prison Commissioners (Directors) at a salary of $2,000 per annum, to be paid quarterly. They were under statutory authority mandated to make periodic inspection tours at "the penitentiary and each place which convicts may be employed." Then they were to monthly, "make a full report to the governor upon all such matters as he may require, connected with the penitentiary and the management of the convicts, and discharge such other duties as may be required by the governor, or by law. . . ."[59] Now, too, subleasing prisoners was nixed, excepting with permission of the governor or his on-the-spot delegate.[60]

Part of those duties would, necessarily, be to formalize and adopt rules and regulations relating to the "control and management of the penitentiary and the convicts belonging thereto, as may be deemed best, not inconsistent with the laws prescribing the treatment and management of convicts. . . . and such rules and regulations shall be binding upon all officers of the penitentiary, guards, employees, hirers of convict labor, and all others in any way connected with the penitentiary, or the convicts within or without the walls. . . ."[61]

For the Lone Star State's Prison System there was a new sheriff in town: Thomas Jewett Goree, Superintendent. Alabama-born Goree, an 1853 student at Baylor University and then during 1858 at Independence earning "both his academic and his law degree," was book smart—but practical. He, too, had been a veteran scout and aide-de-camp during the Civil War, and later a Texas Prison Board member. In a different era, Goree could be characterized as the Real McCoy. Although nobody knew it at that time, later Superintendent Goree would be unarguably and nationally recognized as "one of the more distinguished prison officials in the country." Governor Richard B. Hubbard was certain that the new Resident Superintendent could and would honestly earn his $1,500 yearly salary, and also be able to "provide the right kind of enforcement of the regulations established by the legislature."[62] His calculation was not astray! Governor Hubbard, at least from a public sentiment viewpoint, was not bamboozled about the cellblock prison life, but neither was he heartless and absent compassion: "under the very large discretion I have, that then bad men are treated *humanely*; but that they shall perform 'hard labor'—without much chance of escape—if it is possible."[63]

Perhaps to his dismay however, Governor Hubbard could not have been pleased with the lessee's guard staff going on strike—the first in the state penitentiary's history. The dispute revolved around wages being initially withheld and then, lateness of distribution when paid. Reasoning of the lessees—at least in part—was carried in the *Galveston Weekly News*:

> Much complaint had been made about the wages due guards, and their strike, which was telegraphed to Austin to the Governor, and to the [*Galveston Weekly*] *News*. . . . The lessees deem it advisable to hold one month's pay back, as guards have arms belonging to the prison of the value of such pay, which they are under no compulsion to return when they conclude to leave.[64]

That said, by any standard Thomas Goree morphed into a professional penologist, progressively minded but not blinded by maudlin dreaminess concerning the hardcore truth: Sometimes some convicts were due their comeuppance for aggressive, treacherous, or overtly insolent conduct. By law there were punishments available. Recalcitrant prisoners could be subjected to solitary confinement, shackled in irons, and suffer the withdrawal of a host of privileges. They could not, however, be lashed with the Bat on a guard's whim, but such punishment was not outlawed once a Prison Director or the Resident Superintendent gave the okay.[65]

With regards to working convicts, Superintendent Goree was fair-minded and realistic, heartily believing in the traditional work ethic, it fitting hand and glove with his general philosophy: "It will not do to keep the convicts confined in idleness, for 'without work there can be no discipline, and without discipline there can be no reform.'" Quoting a penal expert of the time, Frederick Hill, Goree ascribed to his practical viewpoint: "The basis of all good systems of prison discipline must, in my opinion, be work—steady, active, honorable work."[66] Though it tends to kick the stuffing out of Old West romanticism and, perhaps overblown mythology, Superintendent Thomas Goree was not overly impressed with cowboys and the cowboy way:

> The prison population in the older Northern States differs very materially from that in the Southern States. There, the majority of men are white, and raised up with more or less idea of some trades, so that their convicts either enter the prison with trades, or can soon learn one, while here in Texas a large majority of our population have been raised on farms, or have spent the greater part of their lives on the prairies, marking and branding "mavericks," and they have but little idea of doing skilled work. . . .[67]

This time around—at least from outward appearances—convicts inside The Walls were, if they wanted to, able to attend Sunday School and work on their illiteracy through one of three classes in "primary reading." They, too, if well behaved could receive "good time credit" that would knock time off their original sentence. Conversely, misbehavior could wipe the slate clean, and more than likely prohibit any ideas with regard to commutation or clemency. And it was a surefire boneheaded stunt to mandatorily lose all good time for willing participation in a "mutiny, conspiracy, or escape attempt."[68]

But boneheaded folks there are. And some were, in the annals of Wild West folklore, notorious. Unquestionably, for the nineteenth-century one of the most well-known of the Texas prison inmates was desperado John Wesley Hardin, who had arrived at Huntsville under heavy Texas Ranger guard on October 5, 1878, while the prison was leased to Cunningham and Ellis.[69] Though the cuts on Hardin's notch-stick are numerous and somewhat legendary, his actual concrete record of man-killing gunfights is rather spotty if the niggling historic question is posed: Does a gunfight genuinely count as a gunfight if only one person does the shooting—or should that just be marked on the scorecard as a homicide? Gunplay and fair play are not necessarily synonymous. Wes Hardin's trail of dead bodies in the dirt is blood bright; traces of his real standup, standalone gunfights are pretty dim.[70] Comparatively smartly though, John

Wesley Hardin, Texas's premier Wild West shootist, was really adept
at fast scampering in the opposite direction when or if someone else
was holding the Aces—or an eared-back and wicked looking Colt's
six-shooter.[71]

> Hardin picked a quarrel with a young fellow [at Williams Ranch
> then in Brown County, now Mills County] named Eugene De
> Lartiegue. But De Lartiegue was too quick for the outlaw, he
> whipped out a sixshooter [sic], and threatened to kill Hardin.
> Hardin, who was pretty much of a bully, and had a jaundiced spine
> like all characters who continually seek fights when they think they
> have the drop on a man, backed down. He assured De Lartiegue
> that he had been jesting, and the matter ended there.[72]

Much later, during two separate dustups, one in faraway West
Texas and the other at a sin-town in southeastern New Mexico
Territory, John Wesley Hardin caught good sense and scooted
away from suffering a dose of severe lead poisoning. Of the latter situation it has been adroitly written: "At booming Eddy [now
Carlsbad, NM], Hardin's story made the newspapers too, and the
Phenix [correct spelling] crowd was no doubt a little amused, but
they knew their town hadn't lost its nerve. Many suspected that
the El Paso badman [Hardin] was due a seminar in proper barroom
etiquette. . . . John Wesley Hardin was back in Phenix, and while
there, he 'tried to work his El Paso game of picking up money from a
gambling table.' Not intimidated in the least by John Wesley's viper-
ous reputation, an unwavering [Richard Alonzo "Lon" Bass] Lon
Bass poked his cocked six-shooter into Hardin's face and demanded
he put the money back and he did! 'John Wesley only tarried in Eddy
between trains that day,' so a flabbergasted newspaperman [for the
Pecos Valley Argus] wrote."[73]

At any rate, John Wesley "Little Arkansas" Hardin found himself
a convicted felon with twenty-five years owed to the State of Texas
for fatally gunning down a Brown County Deputy Sheriff, Charles M.
Webb, at Comanche, the county-seat of Comanche County.[74] Fearing
lynch rope injustice, a stalwart squadron of Texas Rangers, headed

by N.O. Reynolds, were tagged for transporting the notorious murderer to the penitentiary. Nobody thought enough of the shackled desperado to risk their life liberating him in front of Texas Rangers' Colt's six-shooters and Winchesters. Hardin found, much to his displeasure, new accommodations at Huntsville.[75] Ironically, of sorts, convict John Wesley Hardin wasn't the only headliner who would call the Huntsville Penitentiary home.

Company D Texas Rangers had captured a young Comanche during the Big Saline fight and subsequent to orders from the governor as to what should and would be done with the frightened prisoner delivered Littlie Bull (So-no-ya-na) to Huntsville's state lockup. Naturally the news broke big and correspondents later visiting The Walls were fascinated: "The young Indian chief who is now in the hospital, looks like he would never take another scalp. He has consumption and cannot last long. Since he has been in prison he has learned to write a little, and with facilities would have been an educated scalp-lifter. He wanted to go to school for a long time, and his desire should have been gratified, as he is not a convict but a prisoner of war; and as the State restrains him of his liberties, it should have tried to civilize the young man so as to raise up a mediator. . . ." Little Bull died while imprisoned.[76]

Another Indian prisoner was in short supply of receiving any sympathy. For his part in the atrocities committed during a raid labeled the 1871 Warren Wagon Train Massacre, post civil courtroom conviction at Jacksboro (in Jack County) and, later, a parole revocation, the battle-hardened Kiowa Chief, Satanta AKA White Bear, was also marking time at the Huntsville prison:

> Satanta, the Kiowa chief, has been interviewed by all newspaper men who have visited the prison. He never breaks through the stolid reserve of the genuine aborigine, except when given a chew of tobacco. Then he smiles a smile as bright and pleasant as perhaps it would be even when lifting the scalp of a white squaw.[77]

Within a week of desperado Hardin's arrival at the penitentiary on the eleventh day of October 1878, "Satanta—sullen, bitter, and ill—committed suicide." He had solemnly "cut his chest and legs for the purpose of bleeding himself." Then he jumped to his death from an upper tier landing in the prison hospital.[78] John Wesley had blueprinted an escape plan too.

Hardin's venture wouldn't call for any high-flying antics. He and other hardened convicts would burrow underground like eager badgers to the armory then "get weapons and seize the prison."[79]Afterwards they would "liberate all who wished to go except the rape fiends."[80] Though the wannabe escapees had been desperately tunneling horizontally toward the sizable cache of state-owned shotguns and Winchesters, the Grand Scheme went south abruptly—other convicts snitched.[81] Their identity was not secret stuff, not according to John Wesley Hardin: "There were twelve of us doing the tunneling. Two told it to the authorities and 'on pressure' nine others owned up. I am certain two long-time men were pardoned, Bill Owens and Bill Terril from Waco, the latter having a twenty-five year sentence. I believe that three others got their time cut for the same reason—betraying the plot."[82] For his part in the interdicted conspiracy Wes Hardin was fitted with a ball and chain, and put into a "dark cell" for fifteen days, his diet consisting of but bread and water.[83] John Wesley Hardin, though somewhat physically emaciated after release from solitary confinement, was mentally tough, thoroughly incorrigible:

When they took me out of the dark cell, they put me to work in the factory. I was now "celling" with a lifetime man named John Williams and he was the turnkey on our row. He was with me on the tunneling scheme and had played traitor, although I was not aware of it.

I now conceived the plan of making keys to all the cells on our row, in which there were some eighteen or twenty cells all locked with padlocks. I soon had the keys ready and also had impressions of the keys to the outer gates of the prison and had made keys to them which worked well.

For some time I had been able to dispense with my ball and chain. I had cut the brads off that held the shackles together and had put on instead a bolt with a tap on it, which I could unscrew at will.

On the 26th of December I gave John Williams the keys to see if they would work and he said they worked like a charm. I intended on the night of the 26th to unlock my door and then all the other cells, muzzle the guard, unlock the main prison door and then gate after gate to freedom. I determined to resist all opposition and had two good six-shooters that a trusty had brought in to me for that purpose. That evening I was suddenly arrested and locked up. They searched me, found my keys and also the bolt in my shackles; in short, my cell mate had betrayed me and the game was up.[84]

At this point John Wesley Hardin was forced to undergo corporal punishment, a formally authorized flogging with the leather strap, thick harness leather attached to an eighteen-inch wooden handle. By calculated design the penalty was horribly painful but not life threatening.[85] It too was good newspaper copy: "John Wesley Hardin got unruly at Huntsville the other day, and the penitentiary authorities harnessed him up and administered a whipping."[86] Whether Hardin took the thrashing without a whimper as has been written or as a convict witness recalled that "his liver was as white as any milk you ever saw. . . . [another disciplinary whipping ?] and the second crack that hit him he yelled for mercy and commenced spilling briney [sic] tears all over the court" is neither here nor there,[87] although a couple of brief items are noteworthy. By any standard undergoing such rigorous punishment hurt like hell, extraordinarily excruciating, and John Wesley Hardin at times was known to shed tears, such as the fateful day he mortally gunned down Deputy Charles Webb at Comanche.[88]

Certainly not arising to a level of conclusiveness, it's been alleged that prisoner 7109 (Hardin) did manage to compromise or bribe a Huntsville prison employee, John C. Outlaw, to smuggle letters from behind the tall walls and mail them to his wife Jane.[89] Which seems kind of dubious since the state was supplying convicts with stationery and stamps.

Thankfully, many of the letters have survived the ravages of time—and as historic treasures they are revealing, perhaps a little too revealing, at least according to somewhat salacious supposition from two of the inmate's prominent modern-era biographers. One convinced writer postulates: "Now and then Hardin asked Jane to read between the lines. He once apologized for a long period between letters, quietly commenting, 'it was not on account of any unfaithfulness on my part,' but that he wished to spare her some 'disgraceful correspondence and something I cannot mention now.' He closed by writing, 'I hope it needs no more explanation.' Hardin was 'probably' referring to a series of homosexual acts involving him in prison. The behavior humiliated and disgraced him. Yet, though disgusted, he participated. He could not talk about it, could not defend it, and therefore could not write about it. At least a year went by without any letters to Jane. She probably learned of the practice through other sources: letters, comments by released prisoners, rumors. Even when she questioned him, he responded reluctantly, his letter revealing self-hate, a revulsion about discussing the subject, whatever it was."[90] Purportedly, there were later allegations that another high-profile criminal, John Dillinger, while imprisoned in Indiana's state lockup, at least temporarily engaged in a little same-sex dalliance.[91] Notwithstanding the absence of decisive evidence, this should be no real surprise. Some human behavior, in certain arenas, is quite likely. Libido and lust are a timeless phenomenon: Assuredly not craved sensations recently exposed by revisionists.

Sexuality and masculinity and machismo are dynamics of prison life reality. More fully addressing the subject at this point will be sidelined, other than to assert that there is situational homosexuality, and such predilections are just as applicable or real today as they were in the dour days of Huntsville prisoner 7109's theoretical celibacy— or lack thereof.[92] Whether in the free-world or imprisoned, humans are complex creatures. In fact, for his classic (within its discipline) and oft-cited *The Society of Captives: A Study of a Maximum Security Prison*, Emeritus Sociology Professor Gresham M. Sykes is explicitly unhesitant in laying bare naked truths: "And if an inmate has in fact engaged in homosexual behavior within the walls, not as a continuation of an habitual pattern but as a rare act of sexual deviance under the intolerable pressures of mounting physical desire, the psychological onslaughts on his ego image will be particularly acute."[93] John Wesley Hardin? The distinguished penologist continues the analysis: "a fairly large proportion of prisoners engage in homosexual behavior during their period of confinement. . . . for many of these prisoners who do engage in homosexual behavior, their sexual deviance is rare or sporadic rather than chronic. And. . . . as we have indicated before, much of the homosexuality which does occur in prison is not part of a life pattern existing before and after confinement; rather, it is a response to the peculiar rigors of imprisonment."[94]

3

"Afraid they will kill me"

AND THOUGH IT WOULD BE NICE were it not so, some of those rigors of imprisonment, especially in the outside work camps, were indefensible scenarios of heartless guards run amok, if they were true. According to certain allegations in Wood County (county seat Quitman) picked up and carried in an area newspaper, the *Wood County Flag*, convict wood-cutters working near Mineola, just above the Sabine River in the southwestern part of the East Texas county were being horrifically abused. The local newspaper editor characterized some of the guard force unflatteringly, asserting they were committing criminal acts running the gamut from gratuitous mistreatment and brutality to out-and-out murder.[1] Peeking in on but one of those suspected murders is insightful—on several fronts— the death of a white convict, Robert Johnson.

Robert Johnson was not a happy prisoner, vowing to anyone who would listen that it was a surefire bet he "would never serve his time out." He would risk the imposition of buckshot first. Therefore, as a matter of course, he was fitted with a "Spur" around his ankle, the medieval cast-iron device with a sharp seven-inch prong fore and aft which, in theory, would prevent him from running—at least very fast. In theory! By anyone's reckoning it was acknowledged that Johnson made a break for liberty, escaping from his work detail. Soon on the fervent chase were William Roe and a fellow employee, mounted and dutifully following a pair of tracking hounds. Unbelievably, it turned into an overnight pursuit and into an adjoining county. Finally, convict Johnson was run to ground, armed with a stout club keeping the dogs at bay and swearing he would never, ever surrender. After clubbing one of the dogs senseless, Robert Johnson lunged at William Roe's horse. The manhunters pulled their revolvers and put the prisoner down—for keeps. The scenario hardly ends with the mortal gunning down of an escaping Robert Johnson.[2]

The local Justice of the Peace, Dallas Lankford, was obligated to preside over an Inquest and, apparently he had questions—serious questions. Especially subsequent to hearing testimony of Wood County Deputy Sheriff Benjamin F. "Ben" Pegues regarding the "wounds in the head and from the powder burns," and he believed the pistols' muzzles were "placed near the head." Offering at the time what was taken as expert testimony regarding arresting procedures, Deputy Pegues said: "I don't think that with the assistance of one man and two dogs it would be necessary to take a man's life when he had no deadly weapons. I don't think it would be necessary, when he had nothing but a stick, to kill him. . . ." Apparently Judge Lankford concurred. The former pursuers were now prisoners—subject to prosecution.[3]

Briefly jumping out of chronological sync is necessary. With regards to Correctional Officers while actually interdicting an escape attempt, then or now, the use of force—even deadly force—is lawful.[4] Momentarily sustaining that timeline skip is relevant. Even now trainee Correctional Officers are reminded that while the indiscriminate use of firearms is prohibited and will not ever be tolerated, there is an uncompromising second admonishment: Equally, failure to use a firearm when "necessary and appropriate to prevent an escape or serious bodily injury to another person, staff fails to perform a primary responsibility." Falling down on one of the primary obligations of the keeper's job, interdicting escapes and preventing the loss of life or serious bodily injury to other convicts, prison personnel, or the general public, then, is likewise wholly unacceptable and could actually lead to varying degrees of disciplinary sanction—or even termination.[5]

In this instance it may be reported that Sergeant Jeff Kelly—who had been placed in charge of the prison camp subsequent to the forced removal of another sergeant for good cause—had his take, declaring that convict Johnson "was dangerous even with a club, and was to be shunned" because he boasted he would never serve all of his prison sentence.[6] That then can sometimes foster tricky legal questions for judges and/or juries to muddle through. In this instance, the verdict was irrevocable: "While acting as a guard to convicts on a construction train for the railroad he [Roe] killed a convict, for which he was tried and acquitted as in discharge of his duty."[7]

And although it necessitates momentarily staying off the proper timeline, Mr. William H. Roe would undergo other legal troubles revolving around a death: Jennie's, his wife. After guarding railroad construction crews, William Roe returned to Huntsville, working as a Walker County deputy under Sheriff W.D. Adair, afterwards returning to employment at the penitentiary. Thereafter he was duly elected as the town's marshal. As his term expired so too did wife Jennie. She had been poisoned with strychnine. Though the ins and outs make for a fine police drama with twists and turns, for now the bottom-line is but germane. The onetime deputy, prison employee and Huntsville city policeman was lawfully convicted of Murder, and after appellate court review, legally hanged.[8]

Back in sync and back in East Texas, other journalists picked up the mantel, citing examples in their neck of the woods where management and security of prisoners gave way to murder and mayhem—and mendacious denials. The hard truths were extraordinarily elusive. The governor ordered an investigation. Superintendent Thomas J. Goree caught the assignment, assisted by his number-two man, Assistant Superintendent Daniel M. Short.[9]

For three days in July 1879 the taking of sworn testimony and signing of written statements was not boding well for a few keepers of the kept, particularly Sergeant J.H. Randle. Though his harsh discipline and brutality was not too hotly disputed, in the end there was sufficient cause to earn him a pointed dismissal. Conversely the local prosecutor was stymied. There was an actual dearth of articulative Probable Cause, that necessary ingredient for furthering a criminal case. There were no eyewitnesses to any murders—if they had been murders—rather than shooting at escaping prisoners, which was legally justified at the time. Prison policy and procedures and protocols had been violated, but not necessarily criminal law as set forth in the Penal Code—and for the hoosegow or hangman's knot that's what really counted. Telling, possibly, was a general consensus that after Sergeant Randel's forced separation and replacement by the aforementioned Sergeant Jeff Kelly, conditions regarding treatment of prisoners "improved considerably." As but par business the bad employees and defiant inmates catch media attention, the good guards and rule-compliant convicts seldom warrant any notice at all. As newsworthy material, both are invisible and worthless. With this Wood County state of affairs the Texas Prison System's inmates may have been literally taking the hit, but penitentiary administrators and lessees had grossed the black-eye, a public relations thumping.[10]

The Texas Prison System's initiation of Death Row was a 1880s phenomenon, if Death Row was loosely defined. The condemned criminals suffering the extreme penalty would not be executed at The Walls, but those convicted in Walker County and sentenced to die would be domiciled therein until the Sheriff called for their presence. On the second day of July 1880 such was the fate of English A. Carter, twenty-two and white. He had been convicted of killing W.K. Spalding near Dodge, northeast of Huntsville. Sheriff J. Harrison made his call at the penitentiary, formally read the Death Warrant, and escorted Carter to the scaffold where—before a crowd of an estimated 4,000 spectators—the trap-door opened and imposition of the jury's sentence was finalized at the end of a rope. According to a newsy blurb in the *Brenham Weekly Banner*, "The hanging gives entire satisfaction, and the people feel that the majesty of the law has been fully vindicated."[11] And although it would come later, Hamp Wade, AKA Hamp Banks, who had been convicted of killing a fellow black man known only as "Smutty," was whiling away his time at The Walls until Sheriff T.A. Jones made the mandatory visit, removing the prisoner from what in essence was Death Row to the city's gallows. This time before a lesser crowd—just 2000—during a crisp fall afternoon at 2:14 the drop of twelve feet broke Hamp's neck and he was formally pronounced "extinct" thirteen minutes later.[12]

Yes, there was not yet a Death Chamber at The Walls in the nineteenth-century, but if English Carter and Hamp Wade could speak from the grave—they'd attest to a Death Row!

That was outside; inside the tall walls at Huntsville the convicts—most of them—were beehive busy. The institution was buzzing, as reflected in the *Biennial Reports of the Penitentiary Board and Superintendent of the Texas Sate Penitentiary at Huntsville, Texas,* for the early 1880s. In alphabetical order there were under the generalized heading of Productive: "Blacksmiths, Brickmasons, Brickyard hands, Cabinet makers, Chair makers, Carpenters, General laborers, Harness and saddle makers, Machinists, Millers, Painters, Shoemakers, Soap and dye makers, Tailors, Tanners, Teamsters, Weavers, [and] Wheelrights." For another category of inmates identified as Indispensable were: "In wood shops, Bookkeepers, Building tenders, Clerks, Cooks and bakers, Dining room waiters. In engine room, Gate keepers, General roustabouts, Hospital steward, Hospital nurses, Messengers, [and] Yard sweepers."[13]

Not all convicts were lucky enough to require hospitalization. And the scenario quickly highlighted herein merits a mention on two accounts: First, not every death of a state prisoner could be credited to the brutality and criminality of those fellows guarding lessees' scattered construction camps. Secondly, even then, litigious arguments and contested civil lawsuits could spring forth. Catharine Augusta "Kate" (Seaman) Moore, twenty-six, sought an adjudicated financial settlement regarding the untimely death of a prisoner, her husband, Spencer C. Moore. The Calhoun County (county seat Port Lavaca) cowboy was found guilty of acquiring cattle not his own. During nighttime hours in an East Texas "prison house," confined prisoners were gambling away their time playing cards. The players and onlookers, some "twelve or fifteen" were assembled on an upper-tier bunk. For whatever reason—good or bad—Spencer Moore vacated his assigned bunk and crawled into the bottom bunk "nearest the ground," and one below the betting and bluffing gamesters. The stage then was set for disaster: "the fastening of the bunk above him gave way, and the bunk fell on Spencer C. Moore, inflicting a wound from which he died." The widow Moore sought compensation for herself and three kiddos, alleging that there was "negligence in construction of the bunks, and in permitting the men thus to congregate upon it." Eventually winding its way to the Supreme Court of Texas due to unarguably complex legal issues, the high-court rendered its decision: "Cunningham and Ellis were not responsible either for the construction of the bunks or for the imprudent act of the convicts which occasioned the injury. It may be added that the uncontradicted testimony further shows, that, had it not been for the contributory fault of the deceased, he would not have been injured, and besides, according to the great weight of the evidence, the bunks were reasonably well constructed for the legitimate purpose for which they were made."[14] Nineteenth-century legal sparring between private attorneys hunting injunctions and dollars and lawyers representing the Texas Prison System, as will become patently clear, was in its embryonic stage. It would mushroom to maturity.

Though hardly known—or at least mentioned—outside historical circles, another part of those rigors of imprisonment was having a devastating impact on not just a few local communities, places such as Longview in Gregg County, Marshall in Harrison County, and Texarkana in Bowie County. These East Texas locales were home to some hornet-mad denizens. Those damn outside leased convicts were flooding the job market and knocking them out of work. The heavily forested piney woods—seemingly a limitless supply of timber—was fuel for some working folks' steady weekend paydays. They cut crossties for the Texas & Pacific Railroad and chopped cordwood for powering steam-engine locomotives.[15] Another competitor was, too, contributing to the high-level of civilian unemployment—the State of Texas—at least so thought a percentage of those lower economic and middle-class working folks—those guys and gals humping through the week from can to can't:

> Several of the papers of the interior express qualified approval of the remonstrance of the workingmen of Galveston against the use of convicts on the railroad. What to do with the great surplus of

unskilled convict labor is a troublesome question in other States as well as in Texas. In the older States not only are day laborers but skilled mechanics compelled to compete with the labor of the inmates of penitentiaries, and this is also the case in Texas so far as mechanical manufacturing operations are carried on in the State prison. Boot and shoe making, chairs and cabinet furniture, and other similar pursuits are carried on in the Huntsville penitentiary. . . . Of course all such operations conflict more or less with free labor; yet it can hardly be expected that criminals are to be supported in idleness at the expense of free laborers in general.[16]

There was talk of a new prison and more free-world competition for those admittedly scarce greenbacks. In a herculean effort to deal with prison overcrowding and to somewhat offset expenditures—and perhaps turn a profit—legislators through the appropriation process gave blessing to establish a second prison at Rusk, Cherokee County.[17] Pleasantly positioned between the Angelina River to the east, and the Neches River to the west, Rusk was juxtaposed perfectly for exploiting two of the county's natural resources—timber and iron. The new prison—under the contract lease system—understandably would be constructed utilizing convict labor and become commonly known as the East Texas Penitentiary. Since one of the primary purposes would be the refining of rich deposits—seemingly limitless—of iron ore, construction and installation of the necessary industrial machinery was outsourced to highly skilled private technicians. Obedient prisoners would provide the backbreaking labor. With 250 convicts repositioned to Rusk by 1880, construction was well underway.[18] Three years later the state's second full-scale prison was up and running—open for business.[19]

An intended prisoner for the emerging Rusk facility was up and running too! He would brook no overnight stay where the state was furnishing room and board and demanding relentless work. The wicked shootout near Flat Creek in Erath County had been humorless and horrendous. Two of Sheriff Richard T. "Dick" Long's deputies, Marion David Robertson and John T. Ross, both in their late twenties, had been senselessly slain during an arrest situation gone haywire.[20] Whether they were normally good guys or bad guys is immaterial. On this night the Holloway family—father and sons— were frantic shooters. There is even one report that the patriarch, John P. Holloway and his daughter, after John T. was wounded and down, "wrenched the pistol from Ross' hands and Holloway placed it against his side and shot him dead. . . ."[21] Cutting to the nub for this Wild West shootout is not difficult. James L. "Jim" Holloway, after indictment and trial, caught thirty-five years. The senior Holloway was found *Not Guilty* at trial and Jim Holloway's brother, John Russell "Russ," fearing lynch mob justice and leaving his wife and baby daughter in a lurch, lit out for parts he hoped would forever remain unknown—and they did until he voluntarily surrendered forty-eight years after-the-fact.[22]

After his initial visit to The Walls, where his physical description was put on the books, convict Jim Holloway was scheduled to do his hard time at Rusk. While being transported for his lodging there he made his derring-do escape, not with a Colt's six-shooter, but by simply slipping out of the handcuffs and his keeper's notice. Though Texas authorities did not forgive or forget about Jim Holloway, who now had assumed the name Walter Moore, and in time remarried and fathered eight children—they never could find him. A fatal heart attack requisitioned him while working his hardscrabble farm at East Cape Girardeau, Illinois.[23] Jim AKA Walter candidly beat the Texas Prison System, never crossing the penitentiary's threshold at Rusk.

Were a free-world visitor to step inside, he/she might have stood overawed with what they saw; the Rusk Penitentiary surpassed the Huntsville Penitentiary's capacity for housing convicts, 1000 divided into 500 two-man cells.[24] The outer perimeter brick wall, enclosing the seven-acre compound, was imposing: Standing twenty feet tall and more than two feet thick.[25] As opposed to The Walls' "legitimate capacity of only six hundred inmates," the Rusk Prison was thought to be an overcrowding safety-valve. Still, even with two facilities, there was an overabundance of convicts for every prisoner to have a semi-private room.[26]

Understandably, with the ever-steady influx of felons being imprisoned, administrative and custodial headaches multiplied. Superintendent Goree felt compelled to address some of these problem areas in a publicly and purposefully leaked letter to all Sergeants under his authority. The lengthy missive addressed numerous subtopics: prison housing, bedding and clothing, food and nutrition, convict health and humane treatment of the infirm, escapes, punishment, and the necessity for careful attention to the hiring of prison personnel. Particularly he admonished the Sergeants that they could "not be too particular in the selection of guards. Employ no one who is not sober and moral, and who is not indorsed by some known responsible party. Require the oath to be taken before placing a guard on duty. When you get a good guard, try and keep him. When you find one is becoming negligent and careless in the discharge of his duty, you had better get rid of him before such carelessness results in escapes, or attempt to escape, and probably death of a convict. Nine-tenths of the escapes result from carelessness on the part of guards."[27] Moreover Superintendent Goree reminded—with acuity—a bona fide and ageless prison truism:

> There would be but few escapes if the guard watched the convict as closely as the convict watches him.[28]

More than a hundred years later—if a time skip is permissible—sharp ground-level penitentiary scholars would reaffirm Superintendent Goree's observation regarding convicts' watchfulness: "Whether staff likes it or not, the critical eye of the inmate is a twenty-four hour companion."[29] Regarding punishment, Superintendent Goree's forewarning was not smoggy but crystal-clear: "A sergeant who whips a convict except by order of the board of directors, is guilty of an assault and battery. You have a right to stock a convict provided you permit him to stand flat-footed, but you violate the law when you raise his heels from the ground. If death should result from illegal punishment of any kind, the offense is simply murder. It is determined that convicts shall be punished legally or not at all. Make particular note of this fact. . . . Under no circumstances punish a convict before making a thorough investigation of the offense charged, and giving him an opportunity to be heard; then, if punishment be absolutely necessary, whatever the kind, let it be legal and legally inflicted, and however slight, it will have a far more salutary effect then the most cruel and severe punishment illegally inflicted."[30]

With the closing of Superintendent Thomas Goree's letter his overall objective of prison management was not obscured: "We are all officers of the state, having in our charge and power the criminals of the state. Theirs is a hard lot at best. Let us use our utmost endeavors to keep them securely, but at the same time to treat kindly and humanely these unfortunates."[31]

And though it obviously shines the spotlight on one day out of the many, no reading between the lines is necessary to grasp that *all* Correctional Officers were not horrid folks, *all* of the time. The *Galveston Weekly News* picked up on festive penitentiary doings from the *Rusk Observer*:

> The convicts at the penitentiary were given the freedom of the yard and buildings on Christmas day, and a sumptuous dinner was given them, consisting of twenty-five turkeys, five hogs and three beeves, and a few nic-nacks [*sic*] in proportion. They were given a fiddle, banjo and some other musical instruments, and they spent the day making much glee.[32]

There may have been brief periods of celebratory frivolities and relaxation but for politicos and prison managers the ever-burgeoning headcount of felons owing time to the State of Texas was stretching scant resources, manpower, and money, to the breaking point. Although it may now ring of inanity in certain political camps there was even talk of Texas, along with other states, creating penal colonies. Where? "Alaska is suggested as a proper place. Texas, should the colonization scheme be adopted, could very well afford to barter a large portion of her unsettled territory for a sufficient tract of land in Alaska to answer the purpose of a penal colony. . . . The suggestion at any rate is well worth public consideration."[33] The stopgap idea, of course as we know now, melted.

Recognizing a separate need, during 1883 the state bought the 1,900-acre Wynne Farm in Walker County, not too far from The Walls at Huntsville, for the Texas Prison System.[34] Primarily this farm unit—one of many in the years to come—would house older and disabled convicts, along with the inmates suffering other sustained health issues. Be that as it may, it soon became apparent those convicts tending to the Wynne Farm's gardens and fields and livestock and poultry barns were supporting themselves through those compulsory agricultural pursuits. And there was another plus, an abundant surplus of edibles and cotton at Wynne Farm was now carrying the Huntsville unit too. These more settled and less fractious convicts due to aging had opened legislators and prison administrators' eyes: Appropriately managed prison farms were genuine cost-cutters, and on occasion could actually be profitable investments for strapped taxpayers. Even if operating in the red, the large farm units would offset part of the state expenditures for keeping Texas convicts busy and away from the state's law-abiding general population. And that's what, in the end, a prison was supposed to do—then![35] For the time being though, for Texas legislators and penologists, prison farms were no panacea. Outside work camps were yet deemed an imperative for confining those doing time, ensuring they were kept busy—hopefully absent grisly hassles.[36]

Such, in the annals of Texas Prison history, would be a pipedream. During the last month of 1883 there was a major episode at the East Texas facility, "one of the most exciting scenes ever beheld at the Rusk penitentiary." Twelve maddened convicts jumped, armed with clubs, stones, and hatchets, and assaulted their keepers. Nearby Correctional Officers touched off charges from their twin-barreled scatterguns but—due to distances—the buckshot for the most part was ineffective. The long and the short of phase one is that the convicts managed to make it to the dense woods which they set afire to cover their retreat, but not before killing one of the state's best tracking dogs with a short-handled hatchet, and bloodily and unmercifully chopping two others into worthlessness. Over the course of the next several days, at least eight of the convicts were rounded up before newspaper editors moved on; waiting for the next headlining prison story. It was not long in coming.[37]

On 15 March 1884 near the East Texas Penitentiary, Dog Sergeant George W. Taylor was overseeing the return of squads of convicts from working in a coal camp to the main complex. Correctional Officer Charles Irby was carrying one squad, which included convicts T.W. Wallace, G.W. Miller, and John Kennedy. According to a newspaper citation, Kennedy was bad to the bone, having pitilessly poured "coal oil on the heads of two men and burning them to death" in Hill County. The outlaws overpowered Correctional Officer Irby, seizing his shotgun, a double-barreled twelve-gauge. Firing one barrel as a warning accented their grit for the getaway. Seeing the unfolding drama, another guard fired a round but was only able to put the bullet into Wallace's elbow—not even knocking him down. During the ensuing chasing, cussing and chaos—ignoring demands to halt—the trio of escapees made it into adjacent woods, out of sight but not out of mind. Rallying to the cause was the Assistant Superintendent Captain F.P. O'Brian, who was soon joined by Correctional Officers Hiram Newman, John J. Dial, Joe Summers, and Sergeant Taylor's son William, who was also on the payroll. Bloodhounds were soon on the scene, and shortly the convicts were cornered in a brushy creek-bed, but descending darkness was quickly embargoing eyesight and gun-sights. Unfortunately Sergeant Taylor was straddling a handsome grey horse, pleasant to ride but a mount easier to spot in the dark than a brown, bay, black, or even a sorrel. Cautiously approaching the baying dogs, Correctional Officer Newman, horseback, thought he had the escapees hemmed in: Keen to surrender. He was wrong! A sudden blast from the convict's filched scattergun punctuated his big-time blunder. He and his horse were wounded, luckily not mortally but damn scarily. Sergeant Taylor and Captain O'Brian returned fire with blazing six-shooters, ineffectively. With a second round fired from a two-barreled gun, Sergeant Taylor assumed the convicts were scrambling for a thorny switch if they really wanted a fight, yelling to his steadfast comrades: "Don't shoot anymore boys, they have no more loads and we will get them now!" Sergeant George Taylor was dumfounded and dead, buckshot tearing into his chest. The merciless yahoos had plenty of ammo, having had it smuggled to them prior to the prescheduled breakout. The widow Mollie Taylor cried. As far as spotty records reveal, Kennedy and Miller were not soon caught, but later, May 1885, fugitive T.W. Wallace was captured, tried, convicted, and sentenced to life imprisonment for offing Sergeant George W. Taylor.[38]

Another 1885 convict didn't catch a life sentence but, perhaps, Cornelius Gaines set a record. The black bigamist from Panola County in East Texas was convicted and sentenced to hard time—fifteen minutes. It was an outrageous circumvention of the law, according to the *Dallas Morning News* editorial writer: "It would not take many sentences such as this to bankrupt the State. The cash money paid the convict after serving his fifteen-minute term is certainly a great inducement for the worthless characters of the state to settle in Panola County and violate the law prohibiting bigamy."[39]

At the time T.W. Wallace caught his life sentence—or thereabouts—and the Panola County judge and/or jury evoked widespread ire, the State of Texas, recognizing the Wynne Farm's sound contribution to the Texas Prison System's ever-troubled bookkeeping short-falls, bet again. This time they purchased the Harlem Farm (later renamed Jester Unit), an up and operational 2,500 acre enterprise along Oyster Creek in Fort Bend County (county seat Richmond) southwest of burgeoning Houston. In the years to come, the State of Texas would be buying additional acreage—as it came on the market—adjacent to their Harlem Farm.[40]

Unquestionably working the East Texas and Gulf Coast state prison farmlands was strenuous and sweaty—hot for man and/or beast, convict or Correctional Officer. In one heat-related instance a state-owned harness-mule suffered sunstroke and was blinded. Another scenario figuratively scorched a Correctional Officer guarding prisoners at a sugar plantation worked with contracted convict labor. The unnamed Correctional Officer was fortunate, indeed—thanks to convicts Jack Clark and Charles Jones. When the officer slumped, fainted, and fell out, the two prisoners, both doing time for theft, rushed to his aid. Jones quickly grabbed his shotgun and held other convicts at bay, preventing a wholesale escape. The other convict, Clark, diligently "helped the guard out of his swoon."[41]

Ensnaring no little criticism in the ongoing Texas prison saga focused not on buckshot and breakouts, but centered on a bloodless brouhaha, though at the time an underlying potential for violence was not totally out of the picture. While weather was naturally cooling for most Texans during November 1881, the temperature at Austin had skyrocketed. The state Capitol had been ablaze for awhile, then but a valueless pile of smoldering ashes—a total loss. As already noted herein, the State of Texas was strapped. Though ready money-poor the Lone Star was land rich. There then was a way out of the hole for a new Capitol: trade land to someone for rebuilding. And so it came to pass, 3,050,000 acres in the Panhandle of Texas to the Capitol Freehold Land and Investment Company of England and its shareholders. They, then, transferred holdings to American investors, the Capitol Syndicate of Chicago, Illinois. In return for building Texans a brand-new Capitol, investors now with the gargantuan chunk of real-estate bordering the eastern boundary of New Mexico Territory, had birthed the legendary XIT Ranch, a colossal cow/calf and feeder setup of historic repute and epic campfire stories of cowboys and roundups and pitchin' broncs and wild wolf hunts.[42]

How does the real-estate trade affect the unfolding Texas Prison chronicle? The original creative blueprint had specified that the contractor "was to build the superstructure of limestone upon a base of two courses of granite."[43] Due to logistical issues with regards to a short-supply of Texas limestone and the understandable resultant out-of-state transportation expense of importing same, a shift was made to wholly capitalize on granite construction, taking advantage of the seemingly bottomless reserve at Burnet and Marble Falls, Burnet County, not too terribly far northwest of Austin. To benefit from the more-or-less free labor pool for staking a railroad line from the pink hued granite deposit to Austin, as well as quarrying the granite, it was decided that leased convicts, by the sweat of their brows and backbreaking labors could staunch free enterprise from hemorrhaging the state's tax dollars.[44]

Once again, it should not be surprising that certain segments of the free-world tradesmen working class were thoroughly incensed. They were working hard, everyday, while in their minds, desperadoes and outlaws would be sopping the gravy. Particularly, for the case in hand, the stonemasons and their representative labor organization the Granite Cutters' International Union were hellishly mad and vocal. As explained to their membership, the union's top-brass may have had a point:

> and have the contract for the Capitol Building to put on 200 granite cutters and 100 convicts about November 15, we consider that there is a vital principle involved in the matter, so we lay it before the union for instructions. If 200 granite cutters work with, and teach 100 convicts the trade the probability granite cutters and the number of convicts would be increased to 200, and in two years time there would be 300 convicts and no free granite cutters whatever employed on the job, for if free granite cutters learn the convicts the trade, after the first lot is taught they will be put to teach other convicts, and thus drive out free labor altogether, for we have been reliably informed that state officials of Texas have agreed to supply the contractors with 500 convicts. . . .[45]

Union workers in and around Austin were not happy, to put it mildly. The local chapter called a total boycott by their membership, and warned non-union folks to steer clear of Austin and forsake any ideas about working alongside convicts on the Capitol venture. They were serious. Perhaps dead serious! The contractor was wallowing in a quandary. American union members, honoring their Texas brethren, stood pat. If the massive job was to be completed it would be accomplished by convicts costing him $.65 per day, per head (payable to the state), but trained craftsman, which were absolutely necessary, would have to come from another quarter—from a "scab" labor pool. The contractor's solution was elementary, though in violation of the Contract Labor Law of 1885. Journeyman stonecutters from Scotland temporarily immigrated to the United States to do what their America counterparts would not do. After cajoling at New York, several Scotsmen dropped out, but others were not dissuaded from continuing to Austin with their skill-set and tools.[46]

Naturally such doings was big-time news nationally. The *Austin Statesmen* updated readers: "There are at present 200 convicts engaged in quarrying and 100 in cutting the stone. There are also 148 regularly paid stone-cutters, making 448 men now at work dressing the granite for use here in Austin. The convicts are behaving well. The stone-cutters are perfectly satisfied. The quarries seem to be alive with men. Huge stones are piled up in every direction."[47]

There is, as with most tales of historic significance, a hard and fast bottom-line. During a chilly February of 1888 the Goddess of Liberty—in a feat of engineering brilliance—was placed atop the Texas State Capitol Dome. On April 21, 1888, the doors were opened for inspection by the general public and they were undoubtedly impressed. Their Austin edifice was and would be the largest state capitol, second only to the U.S. Capitol at Washington, D.C.[48]

Also opening its doors during 1888 was the House of Corrections/State Reformatory. Long had Texas penologists and the general public been concerned with finding a morally suitable site for incarcerating incorrigible juveniles. There was unanimity and an emerging enlightenment philosophy with regards to housing vulnerable youths with hardened criminals. Although the below cited example is from a later timeframe and the prisoner—age wise—did technically qualify as an adult subject to imprisonment, the extract is illustrative and somewhat telling. During a legislative look-see of Texas prison doings, the chairman of the investigating committee interviewed an inmate kept at a Fort Bend County prison farm:

> A young, 17 year old prisoner was found nude in this cell in which there was not light and inadequate air. It was found that this young man had asked to be put there for protection from the other prisoners. The boy told us: "I asked to be protected from the other

prisoners because the other convicts were trying to abuse me in the form of sodomy. I came in from Huntsville and was put in a tank. Immediately I was approached by another convict who had a knife in his hand and asked if I was going to be good to him tonight, and I told him no. He said I would or I would be killed. . . . upon being brought back to this tank [after supper], I refused to go back in. The convict keeper of the cell then hit me in the eye with his fist and tried to drag me into the cell. It was then that I asked to be put in solitary confinement. I don't want any of those men abusing me and I am afraid they will kill me.[49]

Pointedly a 696-acre spot in Coryell County at Gatesville, the county seat, was surveyed and chosen for the juvenile facility. To be sure the new reformatory was an agricultural institution, and the boys sixteen and under were expected to work the fields and do chores but their lot was an improvement—they would not and could not be subjected to toiling labor at the behest of private parties trying to turn a profit. The man placed in charge was the Assistant Superintendent from The Walls at Huntsville, Benjamin Eustace "Ben" McCulloch, a Confederate veteran and nephew of the legendary Texas Ranger Ben McCulloch, the Civil War General who had perished in Arkansas at the Battle of Pea Ridge.[50]

Although it would prove an ongoing story for a number of years, a logistical nightmare of sorts bears mention. The main purpose of the East Texas Penitentiary, aside from custody and control of convicts, was the production of iron, a commodity it was thought would bring national and positive attention to the Lone Star State's mineral wealth and industrial wherewithal. The requisite furnaces were voracious. Already, by 1887, feeding the insatiable furnaces had ravaged eleven hundred acres of timber—and the fuel shortage was growing at mindboggling proportions: The furnaces, even if operating at "minimum efficiency" demanded a quantity of charcoal "equal to that produced from the wood of six acres of land per day, or from nearly two thousand acres per annum." Most certainly, by 1889 the fire-belching furnaces' appetite had not been sated.[51]

Likewise, just as the kilns were ever hungry, the hazards facing Correctional Officers were to be reckoned with—they, too, were ravenous. Aforementioned herein was the murderous demise of Correctional Officer Joe Epperson who had been gunned down at an East Texas Coal Camp by escaping convict James Roach, and two pals.

Another scenario uncorked on the thirtieth day of June 1890 at the Butterfield State Coal Camp, roughly sixteen miles south of Rusk. Correctional Officer Benjamin "Riley" Williamson was in charge of a six-convict work detail. Some of the circumstances are vague. The outcome is crystal clear. Williamson was killed, several bullet wounds to the head. "The convicts he was guarding had shot him and fled with his weapon," though they apparently already had more firepower. The husband and father of ten was buried in the Arnold Cemetery at Forest, in the far southern reaches of Cherokee County.[52]

There is more of the story, and it's not benign. On the day Correctional Officer Williamson went under, other convicts had escaped. Some were caught. Post murder scene investigation revealed a fired and disgruntled Texas Prison employee, Walter Freeman, had furnished weapons to the convicts that had murdered the unsuspecting Williamson. Freeman suffered an Indictment, but fled. Not too long thereafter he was apprehended at Little Rock, Arkansas, and returned to Texas to face the music, but once more he jumped bond and danced out of Texas. Later, he was arrested at Princeton, Kentucky, and returned to the Lone Star for trial concerning the murder of Correctional Officer Williamson, the charges having been whittled down to Inciting a Riot and Insurrection. Defendant Freeman was convicted at the courthouse and caught a nickel, plus one—six years in the Texas Penitentiary. His stay was short lived, literally: "he attempted escape and was shot by a guard."[53]

Back in sync with chronology, at that same Butterfield State Coal Camp, two weeks after Riley Williamson was mortally gunned down, Correctional Officer Jesse F. Goodwin caught his unlucky break at the hands of two murderous convicts. While others were working outside, Goodwin had been left behind, in charge of the camp's infirmary tent. Somehow one of the convict patients had possession of a revolver. The convict pointed his weapon at Goodwin and ordered him to hand over his six-shooter, which he refused to do. The convict quick shot him. Trying to escape the madness, Correctional Officer Goodwin, though wounded, bolted from the tent only to be perforated with buckshot in the lower extremities and hip by a "trusty" who had grabbed a shotgun, which proved not all trustys are trustworthy, a fact time and time again made perfectly clear—unfortunately. Two days later, July 14, 1890, Correctional Officer Goodwin, with his father and his sister at his bedside, slipped to the other side.[54]

Though a new century was dawning and but two years away, old-school treachery was yet alive and well at the Donovan Convict Farm, seven miles from Eagle Lake, Colorado County, one of the original twenty-three Texas counties. Working the night shift guarding convicts domiciled for the evening was fifty-two-year-old Correctional Officer H.D. Parsons. Cagily laid was the trap. A convict was feigning illness, and believably so, no doubt mimicking the proper symptoms per sly guidance from Dr. J.K. Miles, a fellow convict from Polk County (county seat Livingston) doing ten years hard time for having at least one too many wives. Called to the grated-window of a cell, the request for medication was made. Compassionately Officer Parsons momentarily left and soon returned from the pharmaceutical locker, placing medicine at the widow sill. Hardly could a coiled Diamondback have struck any faster or deadlier. A convict grabbed Officer Parsons, jerking him against the grating, while another reached through and grabbed the six-shooter in his belt. Absent hesitation and sans remorse, the Colt's hammer was eared back, the trigger pulled. There were no more heartbeats for Correctional Officer H.D. Parsons, husband and father of three.[55]

Then, accompanied by three fellow convicts, the sawbones sawed out. They were on the run, scampering fast ahead of Bloodhounds and prison personnel with blood in their eyes and itchy trigger-fingers. The outlaws made it to Scull Creek, site of a legendary battle with Karankawas from days long past, and disappeared, no doubt glad not to have been chewed and/or shot into little pieces. The following month, after trying to elude detection, Dr. Miles was taken into custody by Milam County Sheriff Robert "Bob" Todd and his resolute posse near Mayfield, a little northeast of Cameron, the county seat. The good Doctor Miles denied pulling the trigger capping H.D. Parsons life, and if spotty records are correct, he ultimately discharged from prison half a dozen years after the breakout.[56]

It's important to note that the use of Bloodhounds (and other breeds) was a particularly important component of each and every prison unit, especially the state-owned farms. In fact, George Oglesby, a Waco kennel-master, was sparking a most enviable record, so reported in the *Fort Worth Gazette*: "He has already one of the finest kennels of that breed in the United States. Increasing frequency of acts of violence and multiplied instances of stage and train robberies cause a demand for the class of animals named, which encourages Mr. Oglesby to hope that if the noble work shall proceed he may find his dog-ranch a better thing than an African ostrich farm. . . . Oglesby has had large experience as a deputy sheriff and penitentiary contractor in tracking prisoners, and says hounds are a necessity in Texas."[57]

Buoyed by the overall success of the Wynne and Harlem Farms, Texas legislators plunged again during 1899 purchasing the Clemens Farm, a 5,527-acre tract in southern Brazoria County suitably located between the Brazos and San Bernard Rivers before emptying into the Gulf of Mexico. Soon thereafter an adjacent plantation, the Lowood Plantation, was tucked into the Clemens Farm fold, notching that prison farm's acreage to a respectable 8,212 acres of some of the most fertile agricultural ground in the Lone Star State. For a morsel of general perspective, a later newspaper tabulation suggests that the Clemens State Prison Farm during one season would plant "1,785 acres to corn, 700 acres to cotton, 1,000 acres to maize, 3,902 total acres to field crops, 549 acres to food crops," and the balance of the 8,000-plus acre set up would be devoted to livestock production.[58] And that would not be factoring in the planting and production and harvesting and butchering tallies for the other Brazoria County prison farm units that would come on line post 1899. At the time—and well into a foreseeable future—working convicts hard and shooting for the stars of self-sufficiency was a lofty objective.

As but one sterling example, aside from delving into a peek at the Texas Prison System's large-scale agricultural undertakings—which would continue to spread—a succinct look inside The Walls is not inappropriate, specifically the wagon-yard and shop. "By the end of the decade the penitentiary wagon shop had developed a diversified line of wagons and related type vehicles which, under the name of Star State Works, were marketed throughout the state in direct competition with private manufacturers."[59] Quite naturally some free-world competitors were not necessarily championing products—no matter the quality—if convict labor was used to cut production cost and drive what they deemed as unfair pricing. From its earliest days producing but a few dozen wagons per year, after mechanization and advances in wood curing techniques, the Star State Works had jumped the output to several thousand wheeled vehicles per annum. Naturally such production figures kept the inmate blacksmiths, machinists, body makers, hand stitchers, trimmers, varnishers, and wheelwrighting craftsmen busy and, besides dollars, that was one of the purposes from the get-go: "to employ the convicts committed to his [Superintendent] charge at any kind of useful labor which may be deemed most profitable and useful to the state."[60] There were, too, those other duties for paid-men; retaining custody and control.

They certainly did not retain close custody and control of a convict from Washington County, Jack Sanders, a twenty-nine-year-old "negro" doing time for Assault to Murder. More than once Sanders escaped from the East Texas Penitentiary. Those scenarios, of course, are not unusual. The actions of Sanders for his last escape, however, were atypical for a fugitive on the dodge. He surreptitiously traveled to Austin and staked out the governor's mansion. When Governor Joseph Draper Sayers appeared he was buttonholed by Sanders, not with a shank or six-shooter in hand, but a woeful plea for a Pardon. No doubt flabbergasted Governor Sayers told Sanders he would look into his version of the shooting affray and his assertions of mean treatment while imprisoned at Rusk. The escapee was told to stay out of mischief overnight and report to Governor Sayers's office the following morning. Jack

Sanders did both and made his command appearance. He shook hand with Governor Sayers and pocketed his Pardon.[61]

Although generally overlooked or obscured, even before the century clock turned, prison administrators gave convicts an in-house nineteenth-century voice, publication of the semi-monthly *Prison Bulletin*. With tongue in cheek the witty and, apparently well-educated convict editor, postulated for the *Prison Bulletin's* maiden issue:

> Grammarians and criminals object to long sentences. A criminal sentence also comes under the head of "sintax," and the imperative mood predominates. It is punctuated by periods of time, and occasionally by bold dashes. The "lower case" sentences are often capital. These points of similarity may have been in the mind of the convict who escaped from an insecure penitentiary and left a note saying: "Excuse haste and a bad pen."[62]

And the following year, touting an 1898 Christmas celebration by the Prison Minstrel Club, the *Prison Bulletin*, "published by convicts in the Huntsville penitentiary" proclaimed that the program would be the "hottest time ever seen in the Old Homestead on Christmas afternoon and evening." Again, alleviating the day by day dreariness with a touch of convict humor, the editor asserted: "The Minstrels have this year secured the finest array of talent ever gotten together by the sheriffs of Texas, and several counties have spared no expense in furnishing us the best histrionic material they had."[63]

Though within today's climate of enlightened and health-oriented thinking it might seem mind-boggling, but the Texas Prison System, too, was furnishing convicts with another type of material: Tobacco. Superintendent L.A. Whatley in his comprehensive January 1899 report to Prison Commissioners was effusive and optimistic: "Tobacco for prison consumption has been raised at the Wynne farm, near Huntsville for the last six years. This has been so successful that last year a tobacco farm of the same class was instituted at Woodlawn, near Rusk prison. The tobacco from Woodlawn is shipped to Huntsville, being manufactured at this point, and the amount of tobacco produced on these farms forms a large proportion of the total quantity consumed in the penitentiary system." Touting such functional success, Superintendent Whatley cast his eye to the future, having the system expand and specialize production for the free-world marketplace. "It is with great gratification that I note here the birth of a new industry in the history of the Texas penitentiaries, 'the culture of Havana or cigar tobacco for sale.' A farm has been established at the Huntsville wood camp, about four miles from Huntsville, on the state railroad, for the purpose of raising this grade of tobacco. . . . There are now fifty acres at the wood camp farm devoted to the culture of this grade [Cuban] of tobacco. . . . The most sanguine expectations are entertained as to the future of this industry."[64]

For Correctional Officers, maintaining watchfulness and caution is always smart; otherwise a bad day might morph into a last day. There is, though, as will become apparent throughout this treatment, a corollary caveat with regards to convicts ever being on the lookout too. They can and sometimes do assault, maim, and from time to time kill each other. The phenomenon is not new, just a fact of life—and death—behind tall walls and high fences. Still, even while prisoners and paid-men were enjoying a good smoke, it was best if Correctional Officers didn't let smoke get into their eyes, blinding them to situational reality.

A late-nineteenth-century case is chillingly illustrative. According to a newspaper report, on or about the third day of January 1899, at the East Texas Penitentiary during an altercation between convicts, E.E. Davis, doing seventeen years, killed Andres Campos by battering and bloodying his cranium with a stick of hardwood.[65] According to available information, convict Davis was to sit tight in prison and suffer the filing of a homicide case. With regards to this senseless in-house homicide, though it would take a few months to unravel, Fate would wink and intervene—dramatically so! In the meantime Mother Nature dealt an arctic hand.

During the wee morning hours of February 13, 1899, it was bitterly and bitingly cold at Huntsville: A Blue Norther had blown in. Thermometers' mercury plunged to near subzero. Water pipes throughout the city were frozen, including those behind The Walls. It was most assuredly an inopportune time for a raging fire—but a raging fire there was. The conflagration was purely accidental—a defective flue in the schoolroom—but an inferno it turned out to be, altogether destroying the east and west cell buildings, the administrative offices, and the BOQ (Bachelor Officer's Quarters) and as well, all the "hydrants above ground were frozen and no water could be had for an hour after the alarm was sounded. . . ." Valiantly the sleeping off-duty Correctional Officers upon an awakened realization of what was hotly transpiring—disregarding their spare clothes and personal property stored in trunks—boldly clutched their weapons and hurried to thwart an across-the-board getaway of "some of the hardest criminals in the country." Not unexpectedly and, understandably so, convicts locked in their "houses" (individual cells) were madly clamoring for aid before being barbequed behind grill-work of their locked tight steel doors. Assistant Superintendent J.G. Smither, though he may have been shaken internally, did not let any trepidation of disaster engulf cool thinking and quick action. Methodically he assured the confined men that they would not be cremated if they but remained calm and closely followed his explicit instructions. Then, overseeing the systematic unlocking of cells, Smither with military precision marched 663 freezing convicts into the prison's yard: "The discipline was perfect and the officers and guards had such splendid control over the prisoners that not an accident is [was] recorded." There were no escapes—or attempted escapes. The chapel, hospital, industrial shops and dining hall were not destroyed—and almost within the hour the prisoners were served a hot breakfast and were back on the job—doing what Texas prisoners of the day were supposed to do—work![66]

When the flames had died and the smoke had dissipated and the obligatory headcount had cleared, the "grim walls of the burned penitentiary cell buildings tower[ed] aloft to the breeze looking like the ruins of some deserted castle."[67] The sacrifice made by Correctional Officers did not go unnoticed or unheralded, not by a hard-working and glove-wearing reporter for the *San Antonio Express*: "The single guards roomed upstairs near the offices, between the cell buildings, and being aroused shouldered their guns and went immediately to places where they could assist in holding the convicts. Many of them lost their trunks and other possessions, none stopping to look after their personal effects, which were lost."[68]

Someone else took notice too, the Huntsville convicts. With near unanimity the prisoners—at least for this episode—sang high praises for the Correctional Officer staff and several wrote "voluntary letters" of sincere appreciation regarding their being saved from a crispy destruction. They readily acknowledged that thanks to quick thinking and levelheadedness and humane concern they had been forthrightly "rescued on the occasion of the recent penitentiary fire."[69] Although battling with bureaucratic red-tape was customary, in this instance the state stepped up: "It was ordered the guards and other officials [who were] losers in the February fire be reimbursed." Unfortunately cranking out semi-monthly issues of the in-house *Prison Bulletin*, due to destruction of administrative offices was suspended.[70]

What was not suspended—and never is—behind tall walls and high fences are the personal rows between disgruntled convicts. Though it might somewhat skew traditional nice-guy thinking: "Jails and prisons, moreover, have a climate of violence which has no free-world counterpart. Inmates are terrorized by other inmates, and spend years in fear of harm. Some inmates request segregation, others lock themselves in, and some are hermits by choice. Many inmates injure themselves."[71] As a quick note, two carried by the *Dallas Morning News* during the spring of 1899 are but representative samples of the many:

> There was almost a fatal tragedy in the walls of the penitentiary to-day. A life convict cut John Cox, a prisoner, five times with a large dirk knife. It happened at noon. It is thought Cox will recover.[72]

Two months later:

A difficulty occurred within the walls of the penitentiary to-day between two boys employed as waiters in the dining-room. They had a fight over a trivial matter. One of them cut the other. One is in for horse theft and the other for burglary.[73]

For the above cited assaults noting that both involved sharp weapons designed for stabbing or slicing is empirically relevant, even though neither of these attacks was mortal and not all prison blood-letting is accomplished with taboo shanks and shivs.[74] At other times the in-house trading of insults and barbs and middle-finger gestures morphed into dustups more profound. During October 1899, convict Perry Waggoner, a black man, was doing life for previously murdering a fellow in Van Zandt County (county seat Canton) during a dispute over a paltry $.50 debt. Though he didn't have a six-shooter inside the Rusk penal institution, apparently convict Perry Waggoner owned a hair-trigger temper and a wicked looking wooden club. *Déjà vu*! Regardless, whatever the causation, the volcanic anger was genuine. An infuriated Perry Waggoner had taken open offense at something, voraciously but vehemently exclaiming: "No white man can run over me!" The aforementioned killer of Andres Campos, convict E.E. Davis, the now totally unsuspecting fellow from Ellis County, a "highway robber," did or did not do something, did or did not say something, but for this retelling it really is more-or-less moot. While unperturbed convict E.E. Davis sat "picking his teeth after dinner," the calculating Perry Waggoner bludgeoned him, braining him senseless and dead.[75]

Eyewitness testimony of Correctional Officer John McCaskill, was assuredly not helpful to the remorseless defendant: "Somewhere between 10 and 11 o'clock on October 20, 1899, my attention was called to two men who were near the lime house. One was sitting down with his back against the wall of the lime house, and the other was standing up in front of him with a stick in his hand. I saw the man who was sitting down rise up, and about the time he rose or as he rose up, the man who was standing with the stick in his hand, struck him with the stick once or twice and knocked him down, the man falling forward on his face; and after he fell, the man who had the stick struck him two licks."[76]

Convict Waggoner was tried and convicted of his second murder—and sentenced to climb thirteen steps. In accord with Texas law before imposition of the death penalty an examination by the appellate court was mandatory—and in Waggoner's case the review was undertaken with little fanfare and not too much legal wrangling. In sustaining the lower court's findings, the Texas Court of Criminal Appeals determined, in part: "So far as the record discloses, the assault made by appellant on deceased was unprovoked. Deceased was sitting down, and was unarmed. Appellant set upon him with a heavy bludgeon of wood, felled him to the ground with a single blow, and then continued to beat him over the head until his brains exuded from the wounds. . . . A careful inspection of the record falls [sic fails] to furnish us any reason for setting the verdict aside. No error appearing in the record, the judgment is affirmed."[77]

Most legal executions of the day were big doings and public and well attended. An on-scene scribe penning for the *San Antonio Express*, duly noted:

> The crowd is here by the hundreds and thousands. They began to come early and continued to pour in till 12 o'clock. Standing room on the sidewalks and streets was at a premium. They are here from the city, town, homes and the forks of the creek. That class of citizens seemed to be represented from the small boy and timid maiden to the wild hurrah crowd which is always conspicuous on such occasions.[78]

On the day of his execution, from atop the gallows Perry Waggoner had nothing to say, short of damnably cursing the hangman and the crowd of "some 5,000 people, mostly colored. . . ." so reported the *Dallas Morning News* three days after Perry Waggoner made the drop, breaking his neck and "dying without a struggle."[79]

Someone else was struggling to come up with answers, good answers. The Lone Star State's Chief Executive, Governor Joseph D. Sayers, was in a quandary—and it was a genuine doozy. He had, apparently, been bamboozled into signing an official Pardon for one of the Southwest's then most notorious outlaws, George Isaacs, an Indian Territory native who had been entangled in a backfired insurance scam wherein Sheriff Thomas T. "Tom" McGee was murdered at the depot (the Wells Fargo Office) in Canadian, Hemphill County, Texas, during a November 1894 shootout. Unluckily for him, Isaacs caught a life sentence and was imprisoned at the East Texas Penitentiary.[80] George was in a real penitentiary pickle; his only hope, aside from jumping and running and maybe getting gunned down by a deadeye Correctional Officer, was a Governor's Pardon. That was at best—in wild George Isaac's case—whistling Dixie in the wind. This was the Lone Star State! A place where, as a prominent historian for West Texas and Texas Panhandle doings, spot-on noted: "a lot of funny things can happen when it comes to the business of finagling pardons in the great state of Texas."[81] That George Isaacs walked out of the facility at Rusk was for the Texas Prison System an awkward truth, though genesis for the whopping blunder began at the Texas statehouse.

Earlier a slick shyster and forger, William J. Dent, who himself had been pardoned in more than one state, conned his way into a meeting with Governor Sayers at Austin. The purpose of the confab was a ruse all around. Dent, using an alias and claiming to be a representative of the Montana Cattle Company, was there, he said, to speak out against the granting of clemency or a pardon to an imprisoned fellow. It seems the good governor was hoodwinked, referring his genially acting visitor down the hall to the Secretary of State, D.H. Hardy, an office in the same structure built by Texas convict labor some years before. There the imposter gathered—by deception—valuable information regarding pardon paperwork and the sequential numberings for those documents. All had to be just right for the scheme to come off without a hitch. Too, he also by hook or crook obtained "an executive department letterhead and envelop, and used them in forwarding the forged pardon to the penitentiary," mailing the letter with a City of Austin postmark.[82] Not surprisingly then—following accepted protocol—upon receipt of a suitably signed (forged) pardon from Governor Sayers, penitentiary officialdom at Rusk opened the gate of freedom for George Isaacs. No doubt the liberated convict tendered a smile while bidding his keepers adieu, but to himself quietly laughed as he sauntered down the road of deception. And what became of the now free-spirited George Isaacs? Well, he didn't personally pay W.J. Dent the agreed to $10,000 and he didn't mail him the money from South America or Australia or Fiji. George Isaacs, as far as the Texas Prison System knew, simply fled to wherever.

Relatively speaking, the scam was short-lived. William J. Dent was on the lam somewhere. The aforesaid researcher and writer, a former prosecutor and defense lawyer, cleverly pegged fugitive Dent's undoing: "he was not very clever when it came to bamboozling girlfriends. At least not bamboozling them for very long. Apparently Dent's silver tongue had, at first, produced the desired amorous result. . . . Then, in the crimson glow of romance, the lovebirds migrated to Arizona, where, in the after glow, Dent's attention turned to other matters—or girlfriends."[83] Whatever he was as far as a career shyster and William J. Dent was a good one, the ever-traveling trickster, was scooped up by authorities at Tucson, Pima County, Arizona Territory.[84] Governor Sayers sought extradition, legally and without delay:

> Gov. Sayers this afternoon received a telegram from the Governor of Arizona informing him that his requisition will be honored for a man [Dent] now under arrest at Tucson. This is a very important arrest, as the prisoner is not only under indictment at Austin and Dallas for swindling, but is also the party who forged the pardon that enabled George Isaacs to leave the penitentiary. The Arizona man himself was liberated from the penitentiary last August and used his pardon to affect Isaacs release.[85]

4

"until his body be dead"

WITH TICK-TOCK OF CLOCKS HERALDING a brand-new century, the Texas Prison System's headcount sustained its unremitting upward spiral. Just as prior to 1900, so it seemed, there was always a real surplus of convicts and a bona fide shortage of cots—cells and bunks to be more fastidious. For those earliest years of the twentieth-century, however, one creation was not in short supply: Prison narratives and titillating exposés penned by those purportedly in the know, ex-convicts. Quite sensibly a modern-era academician reminds: "Our public discourse about prisons has been shaped more by the bitter accounts of ex-convicts than by the studied reflections of ex-prison workers."[1] Certainly it's true some of these so-called insider versions make for fantastic reads. They also demand in a few particular instances, a healthy spoonful of skepticism.

Whether the authors' actual agenda was virtuous or venomous might stand analysis or argument. Though crass it may seem, one common thread in several of these treatments is that they were written by recidivists, which is or should be, just a little revealing. Several sortings are herein cited as but cursory examples. Bill Mills, author of *25 Years Behind Prison Bars*, in that lost quarter of a century he referenced, had caught hard time in Texas prisons five times, and two penitentiary stints elsewhere. Former convict Beecher Deason, author of *Seven Years in Texas Prisons*, had in his résumé five separate periods of court-ordered confinement, one in Arkansas, and four with the State of Texas. Milton Paul "Milt" Good, author of *Twelve Years in a Texas Prison*, had a masterful touch for self-aggrandizement in his memoir but does declare the main purpose of writing was "a desire for financial reward." And, regarding his first prison sentence, well, he asserts that "the less said about this affair the better it will be for all concerned." In his mind, no doubt he was right. The little unspoken "affair" was when he and his hard-as-nails fall-partner, Hillary U. Loftis AKA Tom Ross, mercilessly executed two Texas and Southwestern Cattle Raisers Association Field Inspectors as they were casually sitting and visiting on a Sunday night in the tiny lobby of the Gaines Hotel at Seminole, Texas. Subsequent to the verdict of *Guilty* and a chained ride to Huntsville, convict Good managed a prison break, was captured and returned to The Walls, but later was caught again trying to tunnel under the tall wall for a free-world holiday. Post his discharge for all this, somewhat later Milt Good caught another exacting sentence to the Big House, thanks to his unseemly conviction for Theft Over $50 in Motley County. Yes, Milton Paul Good had plenty of book material in his portfolio of anemic justifications and lame excuses. And then there is the super evocative penmanship of Joseph L. "Joe" Wilkinson's *The Trans-Cedar Lynching and the Texas Penitentiary*, an account penned not by a repeat offender but an ex-convict not just bitter with his Lone Star State prison experience due to culpable connection to a triple lynching in Henderson County, but ostensibly mad at everyone else in the world, including Texas Rangers and some co-conspirators, who had not surprisingly "flipped," revealing what they were a party to and who was standing as ramrod.[2]

There's more, and it's certainly relevant. Ex-convict John Shotwell had plenty to say about prison mistreatment in his little 1909 tome, *A Victim of Revenge or Fourteen Years in Hell*. There shouldn't be much doubt that some of what Shotwell wrote was probably—in part—true. On the other hand, at least for one episode, it seems a touch of literary license does not square with the facts. For ensuring that the reader is well apprised of prison guards' propensity for gratuitous violence and sadism, the ex-prisoner turned penman cites the woeful tale of a young man repeatedly whipped for not being able to cut enough wood, fast enough. The frail young man's first custodial year netted him twenty-five disciplinary thrashings, thirty-nine lashes each and every time, so says Shotwell. Pulling from deep within, the tormented young man vowed to solemnly do his time, then return and kill the captain, the ogre responsible for his lacerated back and blistered bottom. The maltreated boy's revenge would be served cold and go down sweet. That's what ex-convict Shotwell hoped, that an unquestioning and gullible reader would ingest and digest.

John Shotwell does not give the unfortunate and abused lad a name. History knows the young convict as George Charles King, Jr. Subsequent to murders of family members—under dubious circumstances—the slender young man accepted farm laboring employment with E.R. Nelson near Mount Pleasant, Titus County. There, unremorsefully it seems, he stole a pair of mules from his employer. After arrest and trial, he caught six years at Rusk, detailed to a wood-cutting camp. While thus grueling and chopping amid the attacking mosquitoes and slithering Copperheads, convict George Charles King, Jr. "quickly recognized the routine of the prison pay-master always arriving by train to pay the guards and other employ-ees in cash. King began fantasizing of the day he would be released from prison and then rob the paymaster of the entire payroll."[3]

In due course, upon bidding the East Texas Penitentiary adieu, the sly ex-inmate began effecting his larcenous design, nonchalantly ordering "a false beard and mustache, and a .45 caliber pistol from Montgomery Ward and Mail Order Company." After receipt of the dis-guise and handgun, the wannabe robber picked his spot, an isolated stretch of track not too far from the depot at Wells, a small but pleas-ant settlement on the Cherokee County/Angelina County borderline. There he placed discarded and decaying railroad crossties across the track and took a position in the dense underbrush and waited.[4]

Unluckily that day, Dr. Alfred Faunton Drewry, a dentist, was onboard heading for Rusk to attend to the dental needs of convicts and Correctional Officers alike. Offering to help remove blockage on the track, Dr. Drewry detrained as George Charles King stepped from his lair, pistol in hand. Certainly, then he recognized the good dentist not the intended target, Captain N.M. Harrison, the prison "financial officer," and the mean fellow Shotwell asserts brutally flogged King thirty-nine lashes X twenty-five times, equaling 975 hide-peeling wallops. At any rate, Charles King did what bona fide armed robbers are predisposed to do, barking: "hands up, damn you, I want your money." What was the real upshot of the gunshots? "King removed from Dr. Drewry his pocket watch with a charm, five dollars in silver, three five dollar bills, with one of the bills having a missing corner, a pocket knife, and a twenty-three dollar check drawn from the First National Bank of Rusk. King shot Dr. Drewry several times, and Drewry died two days later from his wounds."[5]

As bad luck would have it for George Charles King, Jr., a reasonably short time later he was apprehended on an East Texas train while carrying Dr. Drewry's watch and chain, his pocket knife, and the five-dollar bill with the missing corner. For the prosecutor it was a slam dunk; the verdict of *Guilty* was soon followed by formal courtroom sentencing before the no-nonsense bench of District Judge James T. Polly: He was "to hang by the neck until his body be dead. . . ."

The Court of Criminal Appeals of Texas, after their review, upheld King's murder conviction and death sentence, particularly mentioning the defendant's motive:

> The testimony in this case is purely circumstantial, but it is so complete as to have convicted the defendant, by a chain of circumstances pointing to him as the guilty perpetrator of one of the most diabolical and coldblooded murders that has ever stained the annals of this state. The object of this murder appears to have been robbery, and it was planned for weeks before its consummation. On the part of the defendant it was well and skillfully planned, and all his movements conducted so as to avoid escape and detection. But withstanding this, the state was enabled to bring to bear an array of facts establishing to a moral certainty, and excluding every reasonable hypothesis consistent with the defendant's innocence, that the defendant, and he alone, was guilty of this crime. . . .[6]

And so the tragic little story ends. After consuming a pint of whiskey, steeling his nerves, the gallows' trapdoor opened and, per an old-time and oft repeated saying, George Charles King, Jr. was "jerked to Jesus."[7] Ex-convict John Shotwell's literary charge that poor little King was determined to avenge his mistreatment seems somewhat belied by fact—replaced by larceny in George Charles's head and heart. Too, a case of sheer mistaken identity flies in the face of commonsense. It fits well with Shotwell's intended narrative about prison guard brutality, but wonderment must append: How would King not recognize the evil brute who whipped him with the dreaded Bat near one thousand times? Shooting to death the good dentist was heartless and coldblooded. Putting any mealy mouthing aside, Dr. Drewry's homicide was but a senseless killing during an Armed Robbery—not sprouting from the poisonous ivy of revenge.

Too, quite interesting are discrepancies and similarities when these ex-convict authors give their versions of the same event or characterization of someone or of a geographical setting, details they could not have gained through first-person observations or participatory knowledge. After-the-fact collaboration and/or lifting supportive stories from others' book-bound reminisces or pure supposition about another's confinement experiences is in fact likely—as pointed out by one adroit compiler of these early-era prison narratives.[8]

From the above paragraphs, hopefully, the reader will not be misled. There is not herein any defense—nor should there be—of inhumane treatment or wanton brutality or excessive force inflicted on any arrestee, defendant, or inmate, inside or outside the penitentiary. The solitary warning is but this—prudence and commonsense is not to be forsaken. That there were examples of horrific mistreatment and cruelty, especially throughout the period convicts were leased to be profited from, is irrefutable. Shamefully some bad episodes are in the bank, the vault of veracity. U.S. Constitutional guarantees protect the inviolable right to free speech, ex-convicts included! So, in that first decade of the twentieth-century a few chose to put attitudes to paper. Although it might interfere with their narratives somewhat, perhaps it's fair to ponder why several of the above cited neophyte essayists kept repeatedly jumping the fence into prison, only to be bitten time and again by that same rabid pack of junkyard dogs—those evil guards?

During September 1900 something more ominous than any real wickedness or alleged malice of Texas prison personnel roiled across the Gulf of Mexico and into the Texas prison world. Mother Nature's wrath, though, would not be limited to taking a slap at penitentiary officialdom. She was mad! The hurricane, carrying wind gusts of plus-120 mph, hit Galveston with vengeance. Businesses and homes were demolished and the body count hovered at 6000 lost lives on the island. In the surrounding lowlands, another four to six thousand folks succumbed to her fury.[9]

With regards to the Fort Bend and Brazoria County state prison farms the demolished buildings paled in comparison with human tragedies: Twenty-three convicts and two Correctional Officers were killed, either drowned or crushed beneath collapsing structures.[10] Although it normally goes unreported today, the prisoners at Rusk voluntarily stepped up, pooling meager financial resources to aid the thousands of homeless displaced by the Category 4 hurricane.[11]

With the above compassionate convicts' contributions in mind, a broad-based conclusion is apt: Aside from their original conviction and sentence, all convicts were not bad to the bone. More than just a few were regretfully swallowing their dose of reformation, cured from repeating past errors of good judgment and commonsense. In prison talk, they had their hearts right.

Many of the then-employed 1903 Correctional Officers, and civilians with an eye cast toward obtaining such a job, probably thought that Governor Samuel Willis Tucker Lanham, the last Confederate veteran to serve as governor, and Prison Board Chairman L.M. Openheimer had lost their marbles. In the first instance, though it garnered enough support in the House and Senate to land on the Chief Executive's desk, Governor Lanham vetoed a bill that was then deemed to guarantee Correctional Officers a living wage, not less than $25 per month escalating to $30 per month after two years dependable service.[12] Chairman Openheimer, speaking for the

Prison Board, pitched in his two cents' worth, that part about in the future only hiring single men:

> My motive in issuing that order is clearly not understood by those who criticize it. . . . I was actuated solely by a humane spirit in issuing the order. It came to my notice that the guards now employed there who have families are unable to provide for them properly on the salary of $25 per month, which they receive. I gave instructions that none of the married men now employed should be discharged for that reason, but that none but single men hereafter receive positions of that kind.[13]

Needless to say the very public firestorm about matrimony fell by the wayside, while the issue of prison employees being unappreciated and underpaid is perennial. Of course, some were better than others, vying for professionalism in a day when prison work was thought menial at best, unnecessarily brutal at worst. There, too, was a firestorm onboard a locomotive inside The Walls, a bold escape attempt demonstrating the illusory plans swirling in some convicts' minds.

On the first day of February 1905, convicts W.C. (Othelius in another account) Wilson AKA Willis Jones, a "lifer" due to his conviction of Murder in Eastland County and his pal for the day, Addington Tippen, also pulling a life sentence for a Homicide in Anderson County, effected phase one of their plan. Little did he know it then, but when International and Great Northern Railway engineer Mallory chugged his engine inside The Walls—where he would "do the switching and bring out the freight cars," he would have unwanted passengers aboard: two cons who had fashioned sharpened shanks from the industrial shops' rasps. Engineer Mallory, upon realizing what was taking place, daringly bailed off the locomotive—leaving the train's fireman behind. The yahoos pulled the engine's throttle and the train "dashed out through the [prison's] gate," amidst the torrent of buckshot and bullets let fly by prison personnel, now clued to what was happening. Fireman Egbert, during the bedlam, jumped from the locomotive—luckily not stabbed by bad guys or shot by good guys.[14]

The engine was now in total control of neophyte trainmen, throttling down the spur tracks and onto the main line, headed for Phelps Station, southeast of Huntsville. Assistant Superintendent T.H. Brown, as would be expected, rode horseback at the head of a contingent of Bloodhounds and wound-up Correctional Officers racing down the railroad tracks in pursuit. Prior to reaching Cline's Switch, convict Wilson finally figured out how to apply the "air [brake]" and the locomotive came to a spark-spewing stop. However he could not detrain. He had been seriously wounded in the volley unleashed at The Walls. Though but slightly wounded, Tippen jumped and ran. The flight was short-lived. Well within an hour the baying Bloodhounds overtook him, and he was in the free-world no more. For that day an area newspaperman summed it succinctly: "The main-line train, due at Phelps from the south at 12:30 o'clock, came into Huntsville, bringing the passengers and pushing the stolen engine." At the prison hospital the twenty-two-year old Wilson died the next day, 2 February 1905.[15] What did not die then—and never has—is the ingenuity and imagination secreted in prisoners' bags of tricks.

To be sure, too, not all Correctional Officers were vile. That said, not all of them were necessarily spot-on handy with a Colt's six-shooter. Tragedy spit from the barrel of prison employee Jim Bell's revolver on 23 April 1906. The end result was not good; even though devious convicts had dealt the first hand, they were cheating. That morning 24 guards and 149 convicts were aboard the prison train operating between the iron ore deposits and the voracious smelter at the Rusk Penitentiary. Unbeknownst to the keepers, the kept had surreptitiously decoupled two rear cars. The engine was pulling away, but the prisoners weren't waving bye; they were breaking for the woods. As soon as the locomotive ground to stop—maybe even before—the guard force opened a blistering fire on the fleeing convicts with six-shooters and shotguns. The out-and-out bombardment was, indeed, spectacular but problematic—too many whizzing bullets and pellets misdirected. One hotfooting convict, a damnable cow thief and murderer from Navarro County, Oliver Woodard, fell to the ground never to rise again. Convict George Smally, with Burglary convictions in Bexar County and McLennan County, painfully caught "six or eight buckshot, none of which are [were] likely to prove fatal." Although wounded and his escape attempt foiled, the wounded Smally put the blame square on the backs of his fellow prisoners, not the prison staff: Telling his custodians and now captors, that if they—his cronies—"had done as they agreed to do, that a lot of us would have gotten away."[16] Truly, honor among thieves is shaky.

Unfortunately, during the noisy and chaotic mêlée two prison employees fell victim to bullets. William Jordon "Will" Lloyd's wound was slight; Joseph Faulkner "Joe" Wilkerson's was fatal. None of the convicts had guns, but all of the guard staff did. It did not take Justice of the Peace T.H. Findley long to conduct the Inquest and render his ruling—which, though sad, came as no shocker: The death was purely accidental; it had been guard Jim Bell's bullet that had killed Joe Wilkerson. The widow Lizzie Mae Jernigan Wilkerson and her four small children mourned at the gravesite services in the Cedar Hill Cemetery at Rusk. Whether or not Jim Bell was there or not goes unrecorded, but he was, at least for the short-go, unemployed. Prison administrators had relieved him of duty and paychecks.[17]

And that same year, 1906, a convict caught bad news from the Court of Criminal Appeals of Texas. His rather spurious arguments for avoiding the death penalty for killing another convict were—to say the least—unique but unconvincing. Earlier forty-six-year-old Henry Brown had murdered inmate Albert Taylor, beating him to death with a shovel. He was already serving a life sentence for killing George Thomas near Franklin, Robertson County. Though the details are blurred, Henry Brown was pulling another ninety-nine years for a second homicide. This he did not deny: "yes, I've killed some men before Taylor; that's what I'm in the penitentiary for."[18] Scheduled to pay the ultimate price for his prison murder, his reasoning to the higher court as cited by a newspaperman was "A Novel Claim." In a nutshell the argument was that the convicted Henry Brown could not—should not—be executed until he had served out his previously imposed sentences—life and ninety-nine years.[19] Addressing this argument the appellate court ruled: "We have not been cited to any authorities, nor are we aware of any provision of law, statutory or otherwise, that would prevent the trial and conviction of a convict for homicide, or for any other offense, committed while he was detained as a prisoner by virtue of his prior conviction. It would take very strong reason or authority, or an express statute, to show that the person confined in the penitentiary could not be tried and punished for the homicide of one of his fellow convicts."[20] The death sentence was affirmed, and Henry Brown was legally executed for murdering his fellow inmate—hanged at Hondo, the county seat of Medina County, on 30 November 1906.[21]

Spurred by successes elsewhere, penitentiary wheel-horses opted to continue with the farm expansion program. Particularly one land buy was a national press newsmaker, garnering coverage in such print sheets as Vicksburg's *The Daily Herald* and *The Daily Messenger* at Owensboro, Kentucky. And, too, the *Harrisburg Star-Independent* astutely noted that the State of Texas purchasing the Cunningham Plantation in Fort Bend County was not unwise, but smart: "The State will work the plantation by convict labor. The plantation is one of the best in the entire south." The Mississippi paper echoed soundness of the transaction: "By agreement entered into today the penitentiary system of the state buys 20,000 acres of sugar lands with all mules, implements, etc. . . .The purpose of this purchase is to work the state convicts, taking them out of competition with free labor in manufacturing industries."[22] Geographically the Fort Bend and Brazoria County region was ideal and, too, it legally comported with requirements stipulated by law, that newly purchased farms be located within 200 miles of Huntsville, prison headquarters. Resultantly, looking at a Texas roadmap, "shows the original units placed on a line from north of Huntsville on the Trinity River to Clemens on the Brazos."[23]

Unquestionably that year some convicts in Brazoria and Fort Bend Counties opted out of contributing their parts to cutting sugarcane, hoeing weeds in the cotton rows, or picking in the pea patch for their table fare. It wasn't a buck—refusal to work—but a bid for illegal liberation: Friday evening on the seventeenth day of July 1908, tragedy struck hard at the Clemens State Prison Farm in Brazoria County. It was a coordinated and mean-spirited insurrection, at least according to the Houston newspaper correspondent updating the *New York Times* editor:

Negro Convicts Kill Two

As the result of a preconcerted uprising on two of the State penal farms in South Texas two men are dead and six armed and desperate negro [*sic*] criminals are at large ready to slay at sight any of the men who are trailing them with bloodhounds. Farmers of the surrounding country have turned out and a man hunt is in progress.[24]

At the Clemens Farm, thirty-year-old Correctional Officer James R. Elliot had been taken unawares by convicts Will Westfall, Austin St. Louis, Joe Westly, and Will Dow. They weren't playing. Elliot was overpowered, disarmed, and savagely beat to death with a hoe, blood saturating the ground below his mutilated and lifeless body. The escaping yahoos, grabbing Officer Elliot's gun, fled toward the river bottoms, dreaming—hoping—it would wash any tell-tell scent into the Gulf of Mexico, as they tried to elude notice and avoid capture. Unluckily their paths crossed with that of free-world citizen George Johnson, a black farmer. They kidnapped him outright, then set about trying to determine his legitimate value as a hostage—or otherwise? Worthless he tallied for them! Fearing he would give their direction of travel away, escapee Austin St. Louis—*purportedly*—triggered Elliot's stolen gun, and George Johnson was no more walking the land of the living.[25]

Meanwhile in adjoining Fort Bend County (county seat Richmond) at the Dewalt Farm, "a squad of negro [*sic*] convicts. . . . rushed upon their guard, knocked him unconscious, and were making off when intercepted by other guards." With the exception of convicts Robert Ware and Will Howard, this gaggle of escapees was right quick taken into custody. Not surprisingly they began singing like the proverbial canary—songbirds—snitching a delightful melody for those steely-eyed Texans carrying six-shooters and shotguns—and not encumbered by sympathy. As can be reasonably imagined, after it was learned that Ware and Howard had most probably by prearrangement joined the Clemens' fugitives, the countryside was "in a state of terror."[26] Escaped convicts, then or now, have to steal to survive. The excitement would, in the big picture, be short-lived. The runaway convicts were recaptured, save for one.[27]

Escapee Austin St. Louis wasn't in a state of terror—or any degree of fear—he was just dead. His badly decomposing body had been fished from the Bernard River on Saturday, 25 July 1908, a little more than a week after the madness and murders. He was wearing the street clothes of the foully slain George Johnson and, too, Austin St. Louis had twenty-six dollars taken from the lifeless form of Correctional Officer James Elliot. At the legally mandated Inquest it was determined that he hadn't drowned but "died from gunshot wounds received during the escape."[28] Which begs the logical question, did prison personnel or private citizens pop the caps, or could his comrades in crime have opted to eliminate a slow-poke weighted by too much lead—and leaking too much blood?[29]

Chronologically, almost on the heels of the aforementioned breakout, another area escape, in the end, would net the undertakers quintuple billing expectations. Technically the 1909 breakout would not be from a Texas Prison System's farming unit, but rather Sheriff N.M. Gibson's Brazoria County jailhouse at Angleton. Though it would officially register as a jailbreak, the electrifying episode would affect the penitentiary on more than one front, and that warrants brief inclusion herein.

One of the two black escapees, Otto Cooper, twenty-nine, had been jailed for theft; the other, Charles Delaney, had been convicted of killing his son with an axe and was awaiting transfer to the care, custody, and control of the state for the rest of his natural life. Subsequent to slipping past a semi-blind jailer while hiding behind a trusty when the cell door opened, the two outlaws owned free-run of the Brazoria County calaboose. They confronted a now wide-eyed and wide-awake jailer, callously "choking him to unconsciousness." Delaney wanted to shoot the jailer with the deputy's own revolver, but Cooper demurred, claiming noise of the gunshot would end their plan before they even exited the jailhouse. Easily stealing the comatose deputy's six-shooter, the escapees then cabbaged onto the N.M. Gibson's rifle and shotgun racked in the sheriff's office, and fled. Outside, the desperadoes stole a pair of high-stepping horses harnessed to a fancy surrey—and were gone.[30]

At the time the standing state reward for capturing a convict on the loose was $25 and had been at that amount for a number of years. Correspondingly then—whether for want of money or wholly unselfish public service—citizens rallied to the cause, just as they had a short time before when Correctional Officer James Elliot and the ill-fated Gorge Johnson had been murdered. There is, too, a prison angle. Joining the manhunt was the Dog Sergeant from Clemens and his pack of tracking dogs.[31] This absolute cooperation between lawmen and the handlers of prison-owned hounds for manhunts has endured into the twenty-first century.[32]

Tallying the gruesome details of this jailbreak will be succinct, though in whole it makes for a fascinating sad tale. Rancher J.T. Hardin tried to apprehend the two fugitives during a nighttime confrontation—one fired the sheriff's pilfered shotgun and missed, the other shooting the sheriff's stolen Winchester did not. Mr. Hardin expired several hours later. During a separate scenario near Sandy Point north of Angleton, prominent Brazoria County citizen and rancher Armour Munson was mortally gunned down by one of Delaney's cousins, Steve Hays. During the tension, again at night, an unsuspecting hobo carrying clothes tied to a stick was accidently but fatally dropped on the railroad track, two citizens thinking he was armed, toting a rifle. Their utter shock and grief was real—but the outcome unchangeable. And that would be the case in the next gloomy chapter. Steve Hays, now on the lam for killing Mr. Munson, was overhauled by a posse and during an ensuing shootout killed a Negro volunteer deputy, Joe Nunn, the bullet tearing into his neck. For the next hand the wretched murderer drew short: "As Steve came out [of the brush] near a deputy, the deputy called to him to stop, instead he raised his gun, but the deputy beat him to the draw and shot him down, killing him instantly."[33] On the run and hungry Charles Delaney sought sanctuary with relatives, but they, tired of the whole damn mess, snitched—and the fugitive was caught hiding under a bed—right where lawmen were told he would be. As far as determined then—or now—the elusive Otto Cooper triumphantly eluded capture, though somewhat later he was fleetingly seen at Houston.[34]

That very same year, 1909, Correctional Officer John L. Wylie, thirty-nine, exemplified that prison work was inherently dangerous work—whether at the hands of a convict, or otherwise. John Wylie was stationed at the Steiner Valley State Convict Farm in Hill County (county seat Hillsboro) about halfway between Fort Worth and Waco. On the twenty-second day of April 1909, accompanied by two other officers, Wylie was hunting for escapee Joe Yates while mounted on a mule. Working along the Texas & Central Railroad tracks searching for the convict, Wylie's mule stumbled, lost its natural sure footing and fell. During the plummet John Wylie's shotgun accidently discharged with disastrous result—buckshot tearing a gaping and gory hole into his midsection. Though one comrade stayed giving him comfort and urging him to hang on, the other raced for the nearest residence to summon a doctor. By the time medical help was onsite death had already called. And, once more a prison employee's widow, Mary, cried.[35]

Whether other 1909 gals were crying, for the most part goes unspoken—in a general sense. The female convicts had now a penal institution of their own, the Goree Unit, on the southern outskirts of Huntsville. The property originally purchased and serving as a wood camp during 1900 had—over time—been duly and dutifully shaped into an edifice of simplistic attractiveness and secure practicality.[36] Heretofore, except for very limited capacity at The Walls, female convicts had been doing their time either at the Eastham Share Farm in Houston County or at the Calvert Coal Mining Camp in Robertson County. At either location the female prisoners were guarded by men—which gave rise to unfounded allegations and hardcore truths.[37] By at least one published account, favored male convicts "were admitted to their apartments at night." Accordingly, more than one "became pregnant" while incarcerated.[38] As indicated by testimony of several black female convicts, the nighttime goings-on were wicked: Purportedly some guards would use the gals for their own pleasure, sometimes a freebee, sometimes paying for services rendered, or sometimes settling the debt of debauchery with but a promise—someday, maybe clemency or a pardon would come their way.[39] And though it may seem tactless today, could at least some of those clandestine trysts been of a perfectly consensual nature, or were all coerced? Though one may wish it weren't so, the progressively enlightened formula of placing male guards overseeing female convicts or putting female guards watching after male convicts is now—always has been—for a few guys and gals an erotically alluring spicy recipe for mischief. Resultantly, though it might have been born in an era of unvarnished political correctness, opportunities for hormone-driven and to some extent predictable acts of misconduct now fertilize and cultivate conscientious penitentiary administrators' disciplinary headaches and heartburn.

As already highlighted with the devastating hurricane of 1900, Mother Nature—when she wanted to be—could be as nasty as any felon with assassination or free-world autonomy on his/her agenda of trickery and treachery. While diligently supervising and keeping tabs on a twenty-three-convict Hoe-Squad weeding cotton at the Imperial Farm (Central), Fort Bend County, thirty-two-year-old Correctional Officer Charles E. Claiborne was killed by blue lightning bolts eerily dancing along the ground. The freak electrical charges snaking between rows also killed unsuspecting convict Frank Dale, who had been standing twenty feet away.[40] Unluckily a similar incident had previously taken place on the western outskirts of Hill County. There, Correctional Officer G.W. McKnight and the convict he was overseeing succumbed to a sudden thunderstorm's donation of an abruptly cracking yellow current.[41]

Correctional Officer W.P. Sims was assigned to supervising prisoners at the lignite mines in Raines County in East Texas near Alba, straddling the county line with Wood County. The reverberations were not from overhead, but at ground level. Sims was fashioning explosive charges from the powder keg at hand. Mindless it now seems, he too was smoking a cigarette. The horrific blast likely wasn't even heard by a careless Mr. Sims, nor was felt the deafening explosion shredding earthly existence. Yes, whether attributed to devious convicts or simple accidents or rank foolhardiness, prison work can be unsafe—then or now![42]

And too, even during its nascent stages of operational development, as herein indicated, the Texas way of running its prisons and treating convicts was ever under scrutiny from some quarter, whether reform-minded societies or individuals, but always vocal critics. Though there would be many of either stripe, one duo merits mention. Working within The Walls and at Rusk was the prison chaplain, the Reverend Jacob Rite "Jake" Hodges. He was not at peace with himself with regards to how prisoners were disciplined. Preacher Hodges was and had come to be "a thorn in the side of prison administrators," and had been for quite sometime. He was, according to one account "easily influenced by the sorrowful stories convicts would relate to him of their treatment. . . ." Assuredly he was not muted, muzzled, or muffled. He teamed with and made his misgivings known to an up-and-coming journalist of two years, George Waverley Briggs, reporter for the widely-circulated *San Antonio Express*. The young writer was—not surprisingly—progressively psyched and saddled with unbridled enthusiasm. With approval from the editor, Briggs trotted off to and did drop in on prisons and work-camp sites scattered about East Texas and the state farms in Brazoria and Fort Bend Counties. His series of newspaper articles were not puff pieces, but highly reproachful of the way convicts were treated and their labor was exploited for private party interest—and, perhaps, most egregious from his standpoint, was the utter indifference with regards to reforming and remolding society's miscreants into patterns of moral and productive ex-prisoners upon eventual discharge. At first—from numerous politicos' perspectives—the passionate greenhorn correspondent was beating the proverbial dead horse, but Briggs' crusading efforts were unrelenting. Not just a few free-thinking folks were taking note—maybe there really was something "wrong and harmful" with what he was unearthing. The drumbeat was pounding for resolution—another legislative investigative committee was impaneled and went to doing the work, ferreting truth from fiction; proffering answers for questions heretofore unanswered.[43]

Unfortunately for Preacher Jake Hodges—and maybe somewhat luckily for others—Judge W.H. Gill, Chairman of the Penitentiary Board, asked for and received a resignation, publicly justifying the dismissal of Minister Hodges for not following prison rules and other agitations: "Chaplain Hodges had shown rather unusual activity through the press, and his energy in this direction is too well known to need comment. The former chaplain assumed to himself a vast variety of duties not properly coming within his province, and revealed an activity in certain directions which made the demand for resignation necessary."[44] To some of the allegations against him—not all alleged improprieties—ex-Chaplain Jacob Rite Hodges irritably responded: "I accept the arbitrary and contemptible treatment of these penitentiary officials. I will be heard from as to them a little later on. I am not half as scared as they think I am. I will lift the curtain some more when I get good and ready. I am down and out—downed and outed—but I am not dead, damned and delivered."[45]

Though laying aside intertwining chronological dates, at this point it bears mention that continued employment of the Bat as a method of maintaining convict discipline had spilled into the public arena of political discourse, even into the twentieth-century. In his campaigns for the state's governorship, Oscar Branch "Budweiser" Colquitt, so disparagingly nicknamed due to his anti-prohibitionist stance, outspokenly decried corporal punishment for the state's prisoners. Sometimes during fiery campaign rallies Colquitt would brandish a blood-stained Bat, declaring: "I have one of them with me which I will show you if you want to see it. It will lacerate the human flesh and draw the blood with every blow. The bat will cut the life's blood at every lick."[46] Later, as governor the reform-minded Colquitt suspended use of the Bat, but this brand of enlightenment did not survive—in the short go—his administration.

Metaphorically it would be akin to putting the whoa on a runaway horse with a snaffle-bit, not an immediate hock-bumping sliding stop, but thanks to legislative tinkering during August and September of 1910 the Lone Star State underwent a significant restructuring of the Texas Prison System. Since there were already signed contracts extant, the cessation of renting prisoners was not implemented overnight. By law it would end no later than the first day of January 1914, though, from a pragmatic perspective 1912 was the terminal year for leasing of convicts.[47] Thereafter, under no circumstances were outsiders to own say-so over prisoners' custody, control, or everyday jobs.[48] On occasion it's written that the lease period and working black convicts on state farms was an evident and intentional extension of slavery. Clearly, as will be seen, life and work on the farms for prisoners and/or Correctional Officers was not a bed of roses, but a leading scholar and expert on the leasing era—who is not shy about identifying prison maladministration issues—decidedly cuts to the bone: "There is little credible evidence to support the contention that long-term lease agreements with private parties represented an attempt to reestablish slavery in a somewhat altered form."[49] The State of Texas had—after a troublesome period of trial and error—finally been restored to total dominance over the penal institution and its state farms and its court convicted wards.[50]

One of those horrific errors suffocated other news stories of early September 1913. At the Harlem State Farm Camp No. 3 in Fort Bend County, a dozen black convicts "slow bucked" in the vast cotton fields. Consequently, since use of the Bat was now prohibited by edict of the governor, as punishment Harlem Farm Manager T. Calvin Blakely ordered that the prisoners be placed in the dark cell, a single 8x10-foot room blueprinted for solitary confinement. As soon learned, ventilation for the cubicle was several degrees past deplorable. Fresh air was precious. When the solitary cell's door was opened on the morning of the sixth but four convicts were alive—fortunate enough to have been big and bad enough to have elbowed others away from the tiny air vents—which they were passionately embracing while sucking air: "The four who escaped death did so by sheer brute force, fighting their smaller and weaker fellows away from the air vents."[51]

As expected, eight dead convicts was newsy. And though it might somehow disturb partisan detractors of the Texas Prison System, no effort was expended trying to bury reality in a hasty and clumsy cover-up. Quite the contrary seems to be the case. Even the Texas penitentiary's top-dog, Prison Commission Chairman Benjamin Elias "Ben" Cabell, an ex-U.S. Deputy Marshal, previously elected Dallas County Sheriff, and former City of Dallas Mayor, was advocating for transparency, saying in part: "that this regrettable tragedy was the result of ignorance and possibly indifference. . . . I have made every effort and I believe I have succeeded in having this affair given the fullest publicity. The press has been given free access to all possible sources of the facts. . . ."[52] After physicians called to the scene attested to the fact that the eight deceased prisoners had glumly expired due to an obvious "lack of oxygen" the wheels of legality began to turn—speedily. Miner Lafayette Woolley, Sheriff of Fort Bend County, swore to and signed a written Complaint formally charging penitentiary Sergeant Sydney Johnson "Sid" Wheeler and Correctional Officers S.M. Fain and R.H. Stewart with Negligent Homicide.[53] The three defendants were arrested, posted bond, and awaited their Preliminary Hearing with regards to the state's criminal charges.

Though the initial hearing was at a lower-level court, Judge F.M.O. Fenn was bound by law as set forth in the Penal Code and its intended and unintended technicalities. And as he stated, due to the "unusual character of the offense charged, I render my opinion upon the law and the facts in writing," which was not par business for non-Court of Record proceedings.[54] His legal findings based on fastidious fidelity to law, do not seem too farfetched:

> The undisputed evidence shows that the defendants were employees and placed the deceased convicts in a dark cell, which had been constructed under the direction of prison officials by workmen sent out from Huntsville for the purpose, to whom plans and specification had been furnished.
>
> It is further shown by uncontroverted evidence that the deaths with which defendants are charged were caused by a lack of oxygen in the air of the dark cell and that the defendants were not responsible for the manner in which the cells were constructed, the character of ventilation or the form of punishment prescribed by the prison rules and that they acted in the prosecution of a lawful object by lawful means within the meaning of Art. 1111, Penal Code.
>
> It is further provided by the Penal Code, Art. 1116, that in order to constitute the offense for which these men stand charged there must be an apparent danger of causing the death of the person killed or some other. The evidence wholly lacks that ingredient of the offense. These three men should not and cannot be charged with knowledge of an apparent danger growing out of atmospheric conditions or to the faulty construction of the cells by their superior officers, which rendered those conditions possible. . . . But the act was done in accordance with the prison rules by men who had no voice in the promulgation of those rules or in the method of punishment prescribed. While the tragedy is deplorable, no offense defined by law had been committed by these defendants and I therefore discharge them.[55]

Not surprisingly the regretful incident reenergized the debate regarding just how prisoners were to be disciplined. Some were again advocating for picking up the Bat and reinstituting corporal punishment. Others though, were championing solitary confinement as being more humane if accomplished thoughtfully and according to guidelines. Perhaps it was said somewhat artlessly but Prison Commissioner Robert W. Brahan, who was onsite with Chairman

Cabell for a formal investigation, steadfastly defended the concept of solitary confinement when deemed necessary: "We don't stop ocean liners because the Titanic sank." On the other hand, Prison Commissioner Louis W. Tittle thought use of the Bat according to rigid protocols was "more merciful."[56] Commissioner Tittle was— as is evident—somewhat conflicted and, perhaps, understandably so. Suggesting that "under ordinary conditions the dark cell is the safest mode of punishment, and better than the chains or even the bat, when it was used." Furthermore, he acknowledged that "greater care should, however, be exercised in putting prisoners in the dark cell."[57] As with the plethora of penological philosophies, seldom was there then or is there now an indisputable consensus with regards to prison and prisoner management practices.

Unfortunately the state could not/cannot dominate—or fix— what is in some convicts' heads or hearts. Then or now Correctional Officers are not readers of minds or Tarot cards, nor is the clairvoyant help of Gypsy fortune tellers in their repertoire for problem solving. Psychiatrists and psychologists and well-meaning professors—and plumbers—are all provably ill-equipped to unfailingly predict the future; as are the professional penologists and/or their conscientious correctional staffs.[58] As a twentieth-century convict writes and affirms trickery thrives in *some* convicts' consciousness, doggedly: "Prison life is different from anything you can imagine. Everyone is out to screw everyone else out of anything they can. Almost everyone has some kind of hustle going."[59]

Sadly, during 1916, Correctional Officer Walter Isaac Vandorn, twenty-nine, had fallen victim to prison reality. On the twelfth day of August he was in the middle of the routine lunchtime headcount before convicts at the Clemens State Farm returned to their work assignments. Out of nowhere it seemed, a rascally convict rushed him, ferociously driving a shank (improvised knife) into his chest. Walter Isaac staggered backwards, drawing his revolver as the Grim Reaper was beckoning, while his kill-crazed assailant was prepping for his next strike with cold steel. Correctional Officer Vandorn's bullet flew true, knocking the misguided attacker to the floor and extinguishing his running-lights forevermore. Unluckily, Vandorn staggered and stumbled and then lifelessly fell beside the dead convict, never understanding the whys and wherefores of his untimely demise.[60]

Although the persnickety historical exercise is doable, for the treatment in hand it's not deemed necessary to chronologically align the Texas purchases of plantation lands, converting the vast agricultural enterprises into state-owned prison farms. In a nutshell, particularly in the historically rich and agriculturally productive region southwest of Houston, the state's commendable goal of prison-wide self-sufficiency flourished: "New farms included the 6,747-acre Darrington Farm and the 7,428-acre Retrieve Plantation in Brazoria County. The state had also purchased Blue Ridge Farm (5,416 acres) in Fort Bend County," as well as the whopping 13,040 acres in Houston County, which was known throughout the state as the Eastham Prison Farm.[61] Aside from the commendable objective of self-sufficiency, another aim of the Texas Prison Farm enterprises was, while keeping convicts busy and out of trouble, they would not be engaged in manufacturing enterprises competing with the free-world marketplace and thus draw the ire of union officials and hard-scrabble everyday working folks trying to eke out a living post-World War I. And though they didn't know it at the time, the pre-Great Depression milieu was near. All told, by the dawn of 1921, in the name of the State of Texas the penitentiary system was steward of more than 81,000 acres and those real-estate holdings would continue to escalate.[62] As would American's unquenchable thirst for spirituous drink, now prohibited thanks to ratification of the Volstead Act, which supposedly was to make 1921 and years thereafter dry-dry-dry. Nationwide outside the tall walls and high fences the so-called Gangster Era was birthed. Behind the tall walls and high fences of 1921 not all was peaches and cream, peace and quiet.

During the spring of 1921 in what was generically tagged as a "mutiny," some forty prisoners jumped, and were on the dodge, hunted by men, tracked by dogs. They had made their break and stolen prison-owned six-shooters and shotguns. Convicts C.C. Mims, doing time for robbing the Oklahoma Cabaret at Ranger (in Eastland County) and killing Ralf Fitzgerald at a Fort Worth soft-drink stand, along with five convict cohorts, chose surrender over a skirmish with lawmen even though they were smartly armed with two of the state's scatterguns and four of the penitentiary's revolvers. Mims's fall-partner on the cabaret highjacking, snagging a quarter, was Dan Hamilton, also catching a stacked dime for robbing a West Texas poker game. Hamilton and his running partner of late, Ralph Thomas, from Waller County (county seat Hempstead), had tactically split from the mutinous throng, opting to outrun Bloodhounds on their own. The snap decision was doggone pigheaded. To avoid gnashing canines' teeth, the less than brilliant outlaws climbed a tree—as if that would deter or quiet the drooling and baying of man-hunting dogs. Their next tactical decision was also decidedly hare-brained. Instead of giving up when offered the chance, the screwballs pointed revolver muzzles at possemen below—"The officers fired on the two convicts. Both Hamilton and Thomas fell from the tree dead."[63] This big breakout—and there would be others—was, of course quite newsy:

> With the surrender of Ernest N. Kelly of Harris County, serving a double life term and with the killing of two of the convicts, the penitentiary warden, Saturday announced that there are only thirteen of the forty yet to be captured. As the territory for miles around the penitentiary has been closely watched, guards believe that more of the mutineers will be taken. . . .[64]

Upper level prison brass wasn't immunized from meanness. On the first day of September 1921 at The Walls, convicts Ernest R. Conner and Maximo Vega, AKA Manuel Mendoza AKA Francisco Padillo, AKA "The Chief," had at last sneakily orchestrated their sinister plot to escape—at all cost. They were not nice people, and it would be contemporaneously written that Vega, a Mexican-Indian, was the "worst convict in the penitentiary at Huntsville."[65] Such an assessment didn't seem farfetched. Serving a seven-year sentence for Burglary and Theft from El Paso County, Vega notched an unenviable record while ensconced behind those tall walls in Walker County: twenty lashes for an Attempted Escape; eighteen days solitary confinement for Mutinous Conduct; fourteen days solitary confinement for Interfering With Men in Solitary; twenty stinging lashes for Fighting, and punishment for interfering with convicts at the institution's shingle mill.[66] On paper convict Ernest Conner didn't appear quite so bad, doing but a deuce from Tarrant County (county seat Fort Worth) for Theft Over $50, but his next move would advance him to the big leagues of nastiness.[67]

Advantaging themselves of within-reach opportunity, the pair of conspiring misfits slipped behind Dewitt Frisby Oliver, forty-nine, a former State of Texas Pure Food Inspector, but now admirably Assistant Warden at The Walls. Jerking his head backwards they stabbed him in the neck, effectively incapacitating him, but not mortally. They then bound his hands. Thereafter the insensitive desperadoes "forced the prison officer to climb the penitentiary wall to a picket station, using Oliver as a shield from the guards' rifles. Under threat of death for Oliver the convicts obtained a rifle and pistol from Guard Foster, threw Oliver from the wall, breaking his leg, and forced Foster to jump to the prison yard. The convicts then jumped to the outer side of the prison wall, and after that seizing a horse from a woman headed for Houston."[68] Assistant Warden Dewitt Frisby Oliver died as a result of the visible wounds and unseen internal injuries while hospitalized.[69] Rank has privileges, but guarantees no indemnity from madness.

Imprudently, as it now seems, after abandoning or selling the horse, the brutish outlaws tromped through the swamps and woods, surfacing at Conroe in Montgomery County not too far south of Huntsville. There, dingy and dressed in "greasy overalls," sans any shirts, the ferocious pair boldly boarded the International & Great Northern Railway train destined for Houston. The good eye and commonsense of the alert conductor fostered a message to the Houston Police Department. When the escapees detrained they were handcuffed without incident. Maximo Vega dejectedly declared that he would have fought long and hard, but that he "didn't have enough ammunition," only five cartridges in the state's Winchester.[70] The return trip to Huntsville in chains was uneventful.

Behind the tall ivy-covered red-brick walls, prior to any trial for murdering Assistant Warden Oliver, The Chief was spread-eagled and suffered his twenty lashes—the maximum—from an employee employing the Bat, corporal punishment having been officially reinstated.[71] Then he was assigned to a wood-cutting crew. Apparently convict Vega was incorrigible through and through. When Field Boss R.J. Wilson dismounted for a stretch and maybe a quick plant-watering relief, Maximo made his break for liberty. Unluckily, Maximo Vega wasn't as fast on his feet as Wilson was with his trigger-finger: "Ten buckshot took effect and he was instantly killed." A Walker County Justice of the Peace ruled the death a clear-cut case of justifiable homicide.[72] Confirming that he really was no sweetheart either, Conner—subsequent to discharge from the Texas Prison System—would succumb to Tuberculosis inside the Missouri State Prison while doing life for a senseless killing, First Degree Murder.[73]

Some other condemned convicts would not be serving out their life sentences courtesy the trial and appellate courts and the ever-evolving Texas Prison System. For Texas penology a new day was at hand in 1923. Heretofore the punishment for capital offenses—if it be death—was carried out in counties where the offense was committed. The sheriff oversaw the executions from atop the gallows—sometimes publicly, sometimes outside but behind the calaboose courtyard's tall walls and sometimes even from inside the jailhouse after levering open an upstairs trapdoor apparatus. Partly in response to reform-minded prison progressivity and to some extent wanting to shrewdly curb the often-ghoulish spectacles associated with public hangings on the courthouse square—or worse—an extralegal lynching, the Thirty-Eighth Texas Legislature, Second Session, acted. Thereafter, ninety days post their adjournment 14 August 1923, individuals condemned to die in the name of the State of Texas would do so at Huntsville inside The Walls, securely strapped to the relatively newfangled electric-chair, theoretically a more humane way of extinguishing life.[74]

Thirty-four-year-old Nathan Lee, black, though assuredly he didn't relish the distinction, was the last person legally hanged in the Lone Star State. Perhaps somewhat ironically in light of all of Brazoria County's prison lore, Nathan Lee murdered John Spurgeon, a wealthy white farmer, after a spat revolving around leased land and short-shift monies from a second-rate cotton crop. Nathan Lee pointed his shotgun to the back of John Spurgeon's neck as he was walking through a wire gap in a fence, pulled the trigger and ended the argument—dumping the lifeless remains into a nearby ditch. Investigation was prompt and productive. Lee's apprehension was swift, as was the trial and death sentence before the court of distinguished District Court Judge Milam S. Munson. The Texas Court of Criminal Appeals upheld the conviction and wooden scaffolding was erected on the courthouse lawn at Angleton. On the thirty-first day of August 1923 at 11:20 a.m. before 100 spectators and after a last-minute admission of guilt, Nathan Lee dropped to his doom— and into the Texas history book.[75]

Photo Gallery

1

Illustrious architect Abner Hugh Cook designed and oversaw construction of the Texas Prison System's initial facility, The Walls at Huntsville, Walker County.

S. E. View, Texas Penitentiary, Huntsville, Tex.

Undergoing continuous construction during its earlier era, The Walls was built utilizing convict labor, pictured here in their distinctive "prison whites."

The Texas Prison System's first administration building. Repair of the tower clock would screen an escapee.

The Texas Prison System Superintendent's residence at Huntsville.

The Texas philosophy for safely keeping and reforming prisoners was simple: Everyone worked. Pictured here is the wagon shop at Huntsville.

Other convicts worked in the cabinet and furniture shops. These items are on display at the remarkable Texas Prison Museum (TPM) at Huntsville.

Contrary to popular belief it was not always all work and no play within in Texas Prison facilities. Here prisoners at Rusk vie for hits and homeruns.

Rusk Prison, Tex 106.

Increasing convict population resulted in the need for a second walled penitentiary at Rusk, Cherokee County, also commonly called The East Texas Penitentiary.

A 9000 Pound Wheel made at Rusk Prison Foundry, Rusk, Texas. Pub. by Odom & Moseley. 16890

The caption on this Rusk Penitentiary photo is self-explanatory.

Dinner at Huntsville Prison July 4th 1911

A festive Independence Day celebration outside the prison's tall Walls. Note a few convicts are wearing striped uniforms reserved for disciplinary problems and/or known escape risks.

Sentenced to prison subsequent to the horrific attack on a Texas wagon train, Satanta, a notable Kiowa, mutilated himself and then committed suicide, jumping to his death inside The Walls.

The Texas Prison's long-time and well-known Captain Joe Byrd at the first gravesite of Satanta.

The Prison Cemetery at Huntsville, first known as Peckerwood Hill—later respectfully renamed the Joe Byrd Memorial Cemetery.

Convicts, dressed in whites, working as a railway construction crew. Note shotgun toting guard on flatcar and his attendant "Dog Boys" and their pack of man-tracking hounds.

Thomas Jewett Goree. Although rudimentary by today's ever evolving standards, an enlightened approach to penology began taking shape under Goree's administration of Texas prisons.

Convicts and staff at Fort Bend County's Imperial State Farm (Central Unit), Camp No. 1, pose for the photographer. Note the little girl in the foreground, an employee's child, cuddling one of the Lone Star's tracking hounds.

An assemblage of early and latter-day prisoner restraints artfully exhibited at the TPM.

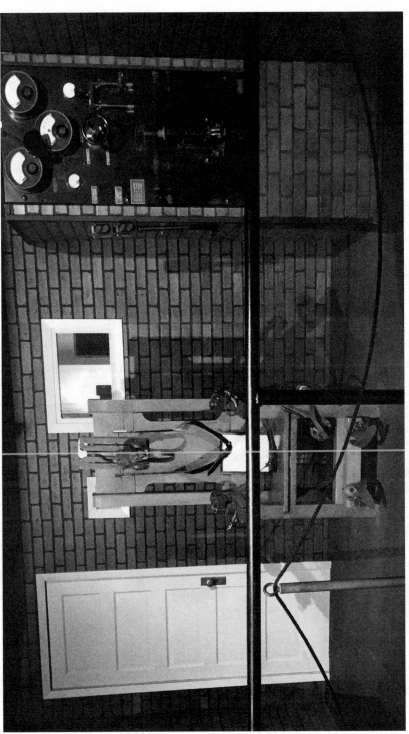

The State of Texas Electric Chair AKA Ole Sparky AKA Old Sparky and its necessary power source. Though now an antique, it remains a very popular attraction at the TPM.

One of East Texas's many prison camps, the legendary Eastham facility in the piney woods of Houston County just north of Huntsville.

Texas Prison Committeemen holding examples of "The Bat," a disciplinary tool not wholly outlawed until 1941.

The main Eastham Unit, a tough place for tough convicts to do time.

Bonnie Parker and Clyde Barrow engaged in horseplay for the cameraman. However when it came to murder and robbery and running from the law they played for keeps.

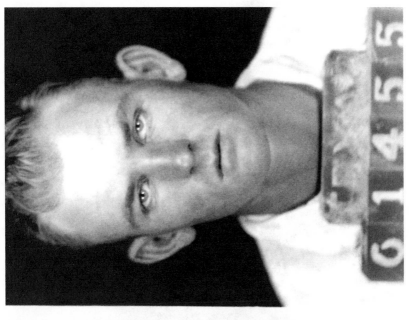
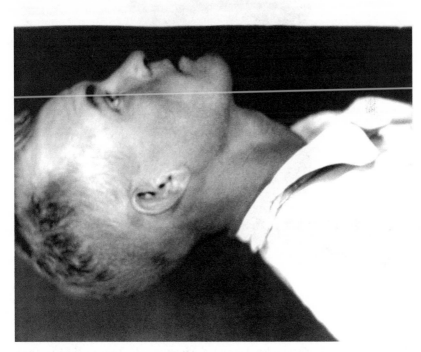

Joseph Conger "Joe" Palmer, one of the career outlaws freed during the infamous Eastham break and murder of Correctional Officer Crowson.

Major (name not rank) Joseph "Joe" Crowson, a Correctional Officer assigned to duty as a mounted High-Rider was coldly murdered during the infamous 16 January 1934 Eastham breakout blueprinted by Raymond and Floyd Hamilton, Bonnie Parker, and Clyde Barrow.

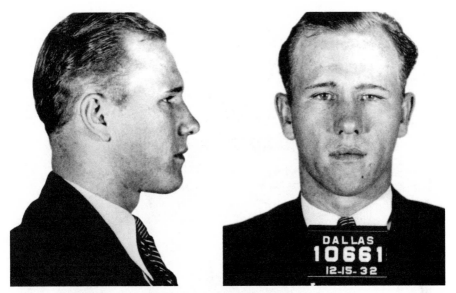

Raymond Elzie "Ray" Hamilton, another Eastham escapee. Though there was dispute as to just who fired the fatal shot ending Crowson's life, the state's Governor made his feelings known: "If Hamilton did not kill Crowson, it was due to his marksmanship not his intentions." After an escape from Death Row, both Palmer and Hamilton were recaptured and lawfully executed.

Correctional Officer (later Warden) Bobbie B. "Dub" Bullard maintained his cool and presence of mind during the 1934 blistering shootout at Eastham—preventing a wholesale escape—a fact duly noted in writing by the system's General Manager.

Bud Russell AKA Uncle Bud AKA One-Way Bud the Texas Prison System's noted Transfer Agent. Here Thompson Sub-machinegun in hand he stands by as chained convicts to-be are delivered to and offloaded outside The Walls. He was so well-known statewide that in the classic music-sheet piece "The Midnight Special" several vocal stanzas are name specific about Bud Russell and his infamous transfer vehicle Black Betty AKA Black Annie AKA The Goodbye Wagon.

WANTED
DEAD OR ALIVE

BONNIE & CLYDE
PARKER   BARROW

Wanted for Robbery, Murder, and other acts against the peace and dignity of the U. S.

Notify AUTHORITIES

That wicked cop-killing outlaws Bonnie Parker and Clyde Barrow had in policing lingo been "bought and paid for" is clearly evidenced by this handbill: Wanted—Dead or Alive!

Marshall Lee Simmons, headman of the Texas Prison System, had sharp words for the man he chose to hunt Bonnie and Clyde: "put them on the spot, know you are right—and then shoot everybody in sight."

5

"just like anybody's grandmother"

THE FOLLOWING YEAR AFTER NOT JUST A FEW unanticipated fits and starts regarding electrical manufacturing and technical installation issues, the execution stage was set. Subsequent to an unforeseen voluntary resignation by Warden R.F. Coleman due the fact he couldn't justify in his mind killing a person, albeit legally, at an institution where reformation should have been the eventual goal, a new day for the Lone Star was close: The State of Texas, the vacant electric chair AKA "Ole Sparky," and the next-door room generator were ready for business—and resultantly their very first sit-down client. Johnson County's former sheriff was tapped to do what Warden Coleman wouldn't. As the new Warden, Walter Monroe Miller was not necessarily chomping at the bit to flip the switch, but he had legally hanged men before and thought the electric chair was, in the end, more humane.[1]

Destiny and discomfiture collided at The Walls on the night of 8 February 1924. The very first Texas electrocution night, due to twists of fate and circumstances and earlier postponements and expired reprieves was not to be a singular affair. And, truthfully, it was not predesigned and premeditated to be an in-your-face macabre flaunting of the state's ultimate power. Nevertheless five condemned black men, all courtroom-convicted of Murder, were to meet their maker and a mortician, on the same night, one after the other: First up was

Charley Reynolds, twenty-seven, from Red River County; followed by Ewell Morris, twenty-three, convicted in a Liberty County killing; next was thirty-nine year old George Washington who had caught a death sentence for a double Murder in Newton County bordering the lowland Texas/Louisiana borderline; then came number four, Mark Matthews, fifty-eight, who had apparently been disenchanted with his wife, killing her with an axe while she slept in her Tyler County (county seat Woodville) bed; and last to take a seat that eventful night was nineteen-year-old Melvin Johnson who had shot and wounded his wife and, too, killed his wife's aunt, Lucinda Daniels.[2]

The following month, two black burglars and convicted cop killers, Blaine Dyer, thirty-six, and Ernest Lawson, thirty-nine, were electrocuted on the same night as result of murdering Dallas PD officers Johnnie C. "Hoot" Gibson and John Richard Crain, during separate 1923 springtime incidents but with the very same .38 caliber revolver. The very first Hispanic lawfully executed at Huntsville was Frank Cadena, thirty-five, who with aforethought shot and killed his sleeping sister-in-law lover, seventeen-year-old Pablita Jiminez, at San Antonio. Frank Cadena feared that Pablita was luring him away from his lawfully wed and then ailing but pregnant wife. The fourteenth legal execution in Texas at Huntsville touched a white man during April 1925. Sidney Welk, thirty-one, was in jailhouse custody awaiting his transfer to prison. He was to begin serving his forty-year stretch for shooting and killing Dallas Deputy Sheriff Tom Wood. During a thoroughly botched escape attempt at the Dallas County Jail, with a smuggled pistol, Welk murdered Assistant Night Jailer Willie Champion, and in due course caught an irreversible death sentence and a most uncomfortable seat between Ole Sparky's armrests.[3]

Also during 1925 two siblings were executed on the same night, the first of four such familial situations. Lorenzo Noel, twenty-five, and his twenty-three-year old brother Frank, had embroiled themselves in a murderous Dallas crime-spree. The short version is that the two black brothers armed with pistols would jump onto the running-boards of autos driven by a white man and, as a rule, one accompanied by a white lady. The Noels' criminal goals for the criminality were three-fold, robbery, murder, and rape. Alas, they succeeded—more than once. Competent investigative work by Sheriff Schuyler B. Marshall, Jr., and his deputies, and Dallas PD Detectives commanded by Captain Will Moffett, netted results—a string of indictments and confessions and the recovery of crucial and admissible evidence. Though the ensuing mob action and call out of the Texas National Guard and Texas Rangers makes for a spine-tingling story, the bottom-line is forthright: Lorenzo and Frank were found guilty in Criminal District Court No. 2 and awarded execution dates. Though it was inadvertent, their scheduled meeting with the Texas prison's executioner was set for a Sunday, which led to not just a little criticism by the citizens and within penological circles. Judge Charles A. Pippin, the trial judge, was miffed, publicly stating: "if the officials at Huntsville don't want to execute them on Sunday I'll go down and do it myself." In the end, the governor granted a five-day reprieve and the Noel brothers made their one-way trip to eternity on the third day of July 1925.[4]

Sam Phillips, thirty-three, owns Death House distinction. While doing twenty years for a homicide in Hill County, at the Imperial State Farm he engaged in shooting dice with fellow convict Jesse Davis, also a killer. Jesse Davis came up short, owing Sam Phillips $4.00. Davis, also, was either late or not inclined to settle his debt. Sam Phillips was not to be gypped out of his winnings. Too, he could ill-afford to lose face in a violent world of tough and distrustful men. Sam Phillips clubbed Jesse Davis to death, then rifled through his pockets and recovered 30 dimes, all that he could find. For this murder he caught a Capital Case. And though he would not be the very first convict executed for offing a fellow prisoner (see Perry Waggoner, 6 July 1900 and Henry Brown 30 November 1906), he would be the first convict suffering electrocution for an in-house—inmate on inmate—homicide.[5]

Forevermore—at least to date—policy and protocols about the Texas penitentiary Death Row and Death Chamber doings have intrigued and inflamed passions, all depending on whether societal groups are holding thumbs up or a thumbs down when queried about the rights and/or wrongs associated with Capital Punishment. Indeed, it's rich fodder for universal debate—and for journalists propounding the merits, or more likely the lack thereof. With newspapermen—newspaperpersons—the timeworn adage rings true: "If it bleeds it leads." So, generally speaking, the public is truly fascinated by convicts' shenanigans and sexuality and stabbings and scampering from custody and/or subverting control. It's true now, and was then in the early days of the twentieth-century.

Understandably, too, the reading public was moderately captivated by the doings at Goree, where women convicts were domiciled. According to one investigative reporter, this penal institution was "one of the most interesting units of the system." For it was there that all of the prisoners' clothing, system-wide, was manufactured:

> About two score negro [sic] and one white on the average are kept on this prison farm, where the population slowly changes. In the Texas prison system nearly all the convicts wear white straight pants and jackets. A few of the desperate ones, those particularly detested by fellow convicts, wear the black and white striped trousers. It is quite some job, the women prisoners say, to make the clothes for the 3,600 men who work on the fourteen farms and behind the walls in the different shops at Huntsville.[6]

The onsite newsman noted that for some of the heavier work, such as running the power plant and plowing, male trustys, both white and black, were dispatched for those duties. With regards to performing the actual day-by-day farm tasks, the reporter mentioned that some women really preferred working in the fields and tending the garden, especially those finding it difficult to adapt to sewing in the garment factory. He, too, remarked that occasionally the female convicts were disciplined—sometimes by lonesome stints of solitary confinement, sometimes by corporal punishment. Particularly highlighting for the August 5, 1926 article: "A negro [sic] woman recently was whipped because she tried to stab another negro and another who attacked the wife of the manager was whipped." Female convict Ellen Etheridge had been tagged and was called "406" because she was doing four stacked (consecutive) 100-year sentences for murdering four of her step-children and six years to boot for trying to kill the fifth. The scribe thought if appearances were taken at face value convict Ellen Etheridge could bamboozle the pitiably naive and clueless. "This woman is in her late fifties. Her hair is grey and she wears spectacles, just like anybody's grandmother." Furthermore, with regards to using the Bat, convict Ellen coolly chastened: "Yep, sometimes, but they deserve it. They are not whipped well as much as they ought to be. Some of these women are just naturally mean ones." Summing up about the trip to Goree and the unit's female population the engrossed *Corpus Christi Caller* correspondent closed out his human-interest piece: "Among these women prisoners are found murderers, forgers, drug addicts, bootleggers and thieves. Most of the negro [*sic*] women are forgers and thieves."[7] As this Texas Prison System narrative continues to unravel it will be revealed that some of these ladies—gals—were escape risks too!

During the same year, 1926, that a Gulf Coast newspaperman was writing of imprisoned women, belching gunfire erupted on the near-8,000-acre Ramsey Prison Farm (now Ramsey I, II, and III—17,000 acres) near Rosharon, northern Brazoria County. Fifty-nine-year-old husband and father Early Alabama Lott was supervising a work detail shucking and shelling corn—it was like any other breezy March day. That is until wild-eyed convict Colley Underwood, two months into his two-year sentence, decided to jump. In a heartbeat he overpowered the surprised Correctional Officer, fiercely disarming him. With Lott's revolver now in his hands, Underwood triggered two hot spiraling rounds into Early's heart, stepped into the stirrup of Lott's horse and fled at the gallop, desperately grabbing the apple (saddle horn) trying his best not to get dumped. Correctional Officer Lott was dead when he hit the ground. Colley Underwood's wild ride was short—he was overtaken and captured alive—not revengefully gunned down as one might have guessed. Ultimately the murderer caught 99 years for his cornfield madness, but that was of little consolation to three fatherless children and the widow Mary Atlas Armstrong Lott as they placed flowers at the gravesite in the Holland City Cemetery, Bell County.[8]

Other prison doings during 1926 were even more brazen, but just as deadly. The crime-scene for this Texas high-drama would be in Madison County at the Ferguson Prison Farm, adjacent to the Trinity River, southeast of Midway and just north of penitentiary headquarters at Huntsville. On the night of July 22, fifty-year-old Correctional Officer William M. "Will" Rader, a five-year veteran with the Texas Prison System, was on duty, having pulled the grave-yard shift—the sole watchman inside the picket station at the sleep-ing convicts' outmoded barracks. Another officer, John Kittlebank, was outside near the stock-pens patrolling the prison farm's rear-most outskirts. Though there were other employees at the detention facility, they were, at that time sound asleep, snoozing inside the guards' quarters. Seemingly out of nowhere "two automobiles, both large touring cars," eased onto the prison property, stopping right outside the barracks.[9] Then the gangsters bailed out—quietly—slip-ping inside with not a smidgen of resistance, it being such a preci-sion planned operation:

> Rader, according to convicts was sitting with his back to the door of the Wooden building. Without warning a heavy-set man, silently opened the side door and stepped into the little enclosure outside the barred prison [dormitory]. Before the guard became aware of the man's presence, the assassin, who wore a narrow black mask, leveled an automatic shotgun and fired three times. Rader slumped in his chair at the first shot, his body jerking as the other two charges struck him.[10]

Will Rader was a dead man falling! Others, however, were alive but afraid, while some of their roommates were drooling with antic-ipation—skipping into the free-world was on their near-term agen-da—a fact confirmed by a talkative and semi-trusted prisoner:

When the shooting began, the building-tender, Pat McCoy, a trusty, switched off all lights in the prisoners' quarters. The man who did the shooting called out the names of six prisoners and told them to strike matches and get ready to leave. He went directly to the keys to the inner compartments and opened the door to the prisoners' lockup.[11]

The raid ringleaders, by the best guess of Norman L. Speer, now Warden at The Walls, were two Bank Robbers, Harvey Ennis and Charles "Stoney" Frazier, who had escaped from the penitentiary two weeks earlier. The half-dozen freed desperadoes were classed as Known Offenders: George Dixon, doing a hard double dime for Armed Robbery from Bexar County; Charles Pryor, serving thirty years for Murder out of Red River County; Richard Naylor, two years for Burglary and Felony Theft from Fannin County; Alvin Ireland, twenty years for Bank Robbery out of Archer County; Robert Bernard, twenty years for Armed Robberies in Bexar and Guadalupe Counties; and C.R. Holland, unknown crime and community. And, though it doesn't speak too well of the felonious prisoners or Texas Prison System authorities at the time, according to a hurriedly penned newspaper piece, on separate occasions: "All of the convicts had previously escaped and had been recaptured."[12]

Not surprisingly the murder and breakout hurled Ferguson Unit personnel into action, two officers particularly catching public notice for nerve, the aforementioned John Kittlebank and Frank Dowlin, the latter being scheduled to have been the blood-spattered and now conclusively dead Will Rader's nighttime relief. Both emptied their revolvers at the fast fleeing getaway autos, but ineffectively, while the mobile outlaws were returning the horrific compliment in kind: "None of the other prisoners in the building attempted to escape believing the shooting outside of the building meant a pitched battle between guards and escaping men."[13] Quite naturally the excitement put state and local authorities in high gear, but mud from recent heavy and constant rains was hindering their forward pursuit. Conclusively, at long last, it was determined the felons had crossed the Trinity River via a ferry, their whereabouts but a good guess—possibly Crockett or Normangee (Madison/Leon County), maybe Waco—or somewhere else?[14]

While Will Rader, widowed twice and the father of nine, was being laid to rest in the cemetery at Midway, huddling Texas lawmen were mapping strategy at the highest level, though after the brainstorming session cards were being held close to the vest except for the fact that Texas Rangers were spearheading the investigation: "While no official statement was given out, it was indicated that Captain [Thomas Rufus "Tom"] Hickman and other rangers will begin work immediately in an effort not only to return the escaped convicts to prison, but to run down the others."[15] Captain Tom Hickman, it would subsequently be reported, theorized that the recently escaped prisoners were prime suspects in a rash of bank robberies then plaguing North Texas.[16] Though individual stories would play out over time, escapee Alvin Ireland, the Bank Robber from Archer County, was nabbed in the near-term at Pine Bluff, south of Little Rock, Arkansas, and, after the proper extradition paperwork was in place, returned to the Lone Star State.[17]

Somewhat embarrassingly close on the heels of the convicts escaping from the Ferguson Unit, Robert J. "Buck" Flanagan, Manager (Warden), at the Imperial State Prison Farm in Fort Bend County near Sugar Land (at times written as Sugarland) owned bad news. Twenty convicts had "sawed their way to liberty from a wooden barracks building," and were on the loose. None were suspected of being armed at the time, but who knew what the future held? Buck Flanagan was in the field, overseeing the chase with Bloodhounds, which proved effective. Ten escapees were apprehended the same Sunday night that they had flown the coop.[18]

A trio of El Paso County's murderous gangsters was also taking a forced 1926 hiatus, but at the Blue Ridge State Farm. Although the incidents had been separated by time, both involved the murders—bushwhacking—of city lawmen. Arnulfo "El Diablo" Valles, purported to be "one of the most dangerous gunmen in El Paso," shot and killed Special Officer Enrique "Yaqui" Rivera. Thereafter an alleged drug dealer, Salvador "The Buffalo" Jacquez, given up by his girlfriend, was taken into custody for mortally ambushing Detective Sergeant John "Jack" Coleman. Both defendants were condemned to death, but their sentences were commuted to life imprisonment. They were accompanied to prison by another El Paso owlhoot, Ysobel "Horseface" Murillo, pulling fifty years for Armed Robbery. During the month of October all three of these El Paso convicts bid Prison Farm Manager Dan J. Henderson *adiós*, escaping and presumably living out their remaining days in the sunshine, south of the Rio Grande/Río Bravo.[19]

Three other prisoners, Steve Howard from Liberty County (county seat Liberty), Willie Walker from Amory, Mississippi, and A.W. Jones from Cross Plains (in Callahan County), got wet but not in the Rio Grande/Río Bravo. And it would be historic. A.A. Davis, a minister of the gospel, was also a convict, doing time for Perjury with regards to an earlier "Klan flogging" in Williamson County (county seat Georgetown). In the presence of prison officials, trustys, free-world churchgoers and preacher Davis's wife, "with every eye moistened," the trio of souls to be saved were marched into the Trinity River and baptized. "This is [was] the first time in the history of the Texas prison system that one convict has baptized another while confined."[20]

The following month, during December 1927, four scheming convicts being transported via an automobile from the Eastham State Farm to The Walls made their play. They overpowered Correctional Officer Emmett Adam Appleton, twenty-six, grabbing his revolver during the madness. Not content with having the upper hand they beat him senseless with the state's six-shooter and then abandoned his still inert form. Luckily, a passerby "found Appleton still unconscious" and rushed him to the hospital—where for awhile it was touch and go. Recounting the manhunt and following the Bloodhounds is doable, but not necessary herein. There is an underbelly to this story and it belies the oft stereotypical portrayals of Correctional Officers.[21]

One of the escapees, George Miller, who had been pulling time from Runnels County for Burglary, managed his getaway to Tarrant

County. Diligently working criminal intelligence furnished by a snitch, Fort Worth PD Detectives Lewis and Weatherford, after a cautious stakeout, apprehended George Miller near the Rock Island Railroad crossing in the city's Riverside Section. He still had Appleton's revolver. For good detectives it was but routine work. The way they came into their hot clue, however, can be laid at the doorstep of that seriously hospitalized Correctional Officer—a previous act of compassion on his part. The detectives had received their information from an ex-convict, who told them of the purposed "rendezvous" between George Miller and a Fort Worth female—netting the arrest. Why had he squealed?

The ex-convict who gave the police the tip, said he was motivated through his friendship and gratitude to Emmett Appleton, the prison guard slugged by the escaping prisoners. He said Appleton had ridden nine miles through sleet and snow on a mule to get oranges and other fruit for him when he was sick while in the penitentiary.[22]

Not only did prison personnel have to be observant regarding devious escape plots cooked up by their custodial charges, but sometimes convicts' carelessness could also prove to be perilous. By this time in the ongoing saga of Texas penitentiary happenings the in-house Saturday night black-and-white movie was a highly anticipated bonus for those convicts not shutout due to misconduct the previous week and/or disciplinary lockdown in solitary confinement. The night of 28 July 1928 was no exception. The eager but quiet audience filing into the dining hall at the Blue Ridge State Prison Farm Camp No. 2 was happy to break a monotonousness cycle of hoeing and weeding and chopping under watchful eyes of armed horseback Bosses, the term "Boss" not then or now carrying derogatory connotation, merely descriptive jargon separating paid-men from prisoners.

All seemed well; the newsreel had run and the convicts were roiling in laughter while the follow-up cartoon played out on the portable movie screen in front of them. Near the projector and film canisters, however, one convict wasn't content with hassle-free hilarity. He wanted a smoke no matter the fact that while the movies were showing inside the dining hall, lighting up was strictly prohibited. In some minds rules are made to be broken, like this silly one. The devious convict "attempted to light a forbidden cigarette. The match broke and the blazing end fell into an open film container. A deafening explosion followed by a flash of livid flame. Laughter turned to cries of horror as the prisoners stampeded for the exit. Another blast came as a second film container exploded and flames swept through the frame structure. Twenty-three men who had been sitting between the projection machines and the door, and who were packed near the exit were burned horribly. Flames licked about their bodies and ignited their rough prison clothing as they shrieked, cursed, and prayed. So tightly was the rocking mass of tortured humanity pressed against the door it defied frantic efforts of guards to remove the lock. Men wept and shrieked for aid, but not a man could lift his arms to prevent the creeping flames from enveloping him."[23]

Courageously prison personnel managed to finally unbolt the exit door, one near hopelessly hemmed by pressing and panicky bodies. Correctional Officer J.H. Robinson was "knocked to the floor by the convicts, who trampled him injuring him internally in the mad haste to escape from the flames which quickly enveloped the frame building."[24] Momentarily chaos reigned. Unselfishly and quite gallantly, Correctional Officer C.D. Dunn—on duty outside the burning structure—"stopped the convicts with his drawn revolver and calmed them."[25] Immediately the prison staff began telephoning for physicians and ambulances, administering elemental first-aid. Soon other prison personnel, with revolvers in hand, stood by ensuring that the uninjured convicts didn't muster enough nerve for a "wholesale escape,"[26] though according to at least one newspaper report three convicts jumped, and were then on the loose being chased by Bloodhounds.[27] Others of the custodial staff, resourcefully and daringly, assisted by convicts, actually "formed bucket brigades and with wet sacks and blankets succeeded in confining the fire to the dining room after a strenuous effort."[28] The aftermath would measure tragic.

Texas newspaper headlines hotly branded fluctuating numbers into the general readerships' consciousness: "25 Convicts Badly Burned, Guard Nearly Killed. . . ." And, "Two Convicts Hurt in Blast Die at Houston." Ratcheting the known casualty numbers upwards the well-circulated *Corpus Christi Times* lamentably heralded: "Three Convicts Fatally Burned."[29] According to a succinct blip in the *Waxahachie Daily Light*, the three convict fatalities were William Key, L.B. Clinkscales, and Floyd Pinson.[30] Undeniably it was a huge catastrophe, one calling for an all-hands-on-deck, emergency response: "More than ten Houston ambulances went to the scene of the fire after being summoned by Fire Commander Allie Anderson, one of the first city officials to reach the prison farm. Five of the twenty of the most seriously burned convicts were loaded into the ambulances as fast as they reached the prison farm and were brought to a Houston hospital, first in an effort to save their lives. Little hope was entertained at either hospital [prison infirmary] however, of doing so."[31] Clearly it was a heartrending story. But as with many prison tales, there is a back story:

> Henry Revier, one of eight convicts being treated at a hospital for burns suffered in a fire which destroyed the dining hall of the Blue Ridge state prison July 28, escaped from the hospital at 1:30 a.m. today clad in pajamas. An automobile which had stood near the hospital two hours before the escape was missing and authorities thought Revier used it. Revier's feet were so sore from burns that physicians said it would be almost impossible for him to walk far. Revier escaped when his guard, A.W. Warren, left the ward for a few minutes to confer with attendants about the condition of George Hall most severely burned of the convicts.[32]

Correctional Officer Warren's compassion and concern—as would often be the case behind the tall walls and high fences—was but a display of weakness and inattentiveness and wholesale incompetence in the conniving mind of convalescing convict Henry Revier. A percentage of any prison population, though it may sound impolitic, devotes their mental energy and bodily efforts trying to outfox, outmaneuver, or misleadingly compromise their keepers, while those very same employees are charged with looking out for the convicts' well-being and reformation and are at the same time protecting them from each other—or trying to.

Even while watching an in-house movie, madness and murder lurked—as twenty-six-year-old Alton Crowson found out, though he wouldn't be around to speak of the stark details: The convict from China Spring in McLennan County was thoroughly engrossed in watching the film *The Escape of Tarzan* inside the Chapel at The Walls. Seemingly out of nowhere—at least according to other moviegoers—a sharpened file was thrust into Alton's neck, which prompted him to "suddenly got [get] up from his seat and fell [fall] in the aisle without saying a word." Dead! Not unexpectedly nobody saw nothing—at first. Though later, as the chance for personal benefit accrued and by the skillful interrogation of convicts by the Warden, well, hardened prisoner Homer Jack Turney, a Houston area Armed Robber and returned parole violator bought more prison time: A life sentence.[33] At the Big House dark-time can be dangerous-time.

The month that flames engulfed and snuffed the lives from unfortunate and panic-stricken convicts, Dog Sergeant Joseph Henry "Joe" Ward, thirty-one, was on duty in Fort Bend County at the Imperial State Farm Number II. Sergeant Ward—like everyone else at the prison farm save two—was wholly unawares of a cunning manipulation. After "catching the chain" bound for the penitentiary Raymond E. Hall, who had caught ninety-nine years for a Wichita County holdup, met a young first offender, Raymond Tucker, due to be a guest of the State of Texas for one year for a liquor law violation when they arrived at Imperial. The kettle for cooking up a scam was atop the sizzling coals. The crafty older Raymond induced the gullible younger Raymond to switch identities, trading "names and papers." Factoring time for good behavior, if he could maintain his cool, Raymond E. Hall would be erroneously discharged under the wrong name having served no more than a year. Of course there was the downside. Once the plot boiled out of the pot, Raymond Tucker would admit to the sham, accept his disciplinary punishment, and he, too, would shortly skate into the free-world. Trouble was, Raymond E. Hall was mean and impatient. Field work between turn-rows was not his forte.[34]

Hearing gunshots Sergeant Ward raced to the aid of a fellow Correctional Officer Jim Jeeter (sometimes Geter) who, after leaning over from his saddle to hand a convict a file, had been disarmed of his revolver and shotgun, and was galloping a fast retreat after being ordered "to getaway quick."[35] Two of the eight wannabe escapees were fast peppering shots in his direction as he spurred for distance and safety. Lamentably, Dog Sergeant Joe Ward, though courageous, overrode disaster. Convicts Raymond E. Hall, and R.R. Carter—one or the other—blasted him out of the saddle with a gut-shot of buckshot; then the other ran over to the de-horsed Sergeant and fired revolver rounds into his throat as he writhed in excruciating pain, gasping for air atop the pooling blood and plowed ground, dying in the dirt.[36] The Grim Reaper—wearing prison whites—had completed the dastardly deed. Correctional Officers Oscar Logins, L.E. McKinnon, and Jack Stiles had also been carrying hoe-squads that day but—unfortunately—were too far away to help maintain custody of their white-clad wards.[37] Penitentiary employees, local lawmen and a throng of area citizens swelled the posse to 150, augmented by the sniffing skillfulness of thirty-five Bloodhounds. During the resultant manhunt, though all escapees were chased and eventually apprehended, it was not without costs: During a shootout the flitting convicts—with prison owned guns and two shotguns and a rifle stolen from the home of a hard-working "negro trapper"—artfully managed to inflict serious but nonfatal gunshot wounds on Fort Bend County Deputies Frank T. Bell and Tom Davis. Their partner at the time, Deputy R.L. Wheaton, survived this shootout unscathed. Nevertheless the irreversible outcome was real, another prison employee fatality.[38] What was also very real was, now, the viability of an electrifying embrace by Ole Sparky. Ray Tucker was in way over his head—treading troubled waters—he right fast confessed to the skullduggery of swapping names.

Sergeant Joe Ward's wife, unfortunately, had preceded him in death, so at the McAdams Cemetery in Crabbs Prairie northwest of Huntsville he was mourned by his only son and parents—and a sizable crowd of Texas Prison System cohorts. The record is not exactly clear whether convicts Hall and Carter lied and cried, but after they were eventually captured and convicted they caught life sentences.[39]

Though herein it but merits a quick sidebar, murderer Raymond E. Hall excelled on two fronts, each at opposite ends of the spectrum. For much of his prison life he was thoroughly incorrigible, an assaultive escape risk with a reasonably thick dossier of disciplinary infractions and punishments: He was treacherous, not a man to turn one's back on. On the lighter side he was—provably—a talented poet and songwriter and singer, counting the Father of Country Music, Jimmie Rodgers, as a personal friend and confidant. Rightfully acknowledging that Raymond E. Hall's criminal transgressions were in many instances "unforgivable," a most gifted performer and devoted music historian hypothesizes with nonpartisan acuity: "Raymond Hall's creative contributions from his Texas prison cell represent something of a missing link for why the prison song is one of country music's defining themes."[40] Another of those defining themes of the kept and their keepers is unauthorized departure—escape.

On September 19, 1928, at The Walls, three convicts were being supervised by Correctional Officer A.F. Harris. Their mission was in the institution's clock tower. There they were tasked with repairing, resetting, and cleaning the big clock. The convicts, J.C. Parker, James Gillespie, and Styne Weatherred, had timed their move with precision. They suddenly "pounced" on Harris, "and before he could make an outcry had him tied and gagged. One convict stripped him of his clothing, which the prisoner then draped about himself, and lining up his companions ahead of him in the fashion of a guard and his prisoners, the trio marched out." Quite successfully the trio found themselves in the free-world and quite successfully they commandeered an automobile from Mr. C. L. Phillips and at high-speed left Huntsville in the rearview mirror. Their whereabouts were unknown.[41]

Well, their free-world vacation was unknown until 1 December 1928. And according to newspaper accounts that day would mark a Texas prison record. Penal authorities received a telegram that fugitive Gillespie was being held in Fort Bend, Indiana. "A few minutes later they received another stating that Weatherred and Parker were being held in St. Louis." That three convicts had escaped on the same day was not unusual, but that they were all retaken in two separate states on the same day was remarkable. They would all be picked up and returned to The Walls on the same day, too.[42] As the reader will see as this Texas Prison narrative unfolds, more than seventy years later mean convicts would again overpower their keepers, donning their clothing for an out-of-state trip after their in-state murder.

In the meantime and back on the timeline, a couple of other convicts caught more than they bargained for. And strikingly it taps into a hardcore truth: In penitentiary settings cordial smiles and/or submissively tendered requests might—on occasion—stand as but smokescreens for dangerous deception. Lee and Willie Davis, convicted of Armed Robbery in Jefferson County at Beaumont and suffering lengthy sentences, were plotting an escape from the Retrieve State Prison Farm in Brazoria County. Coldhearted meanness was on their upcoming 29 September 1928 agenda. As anticipated that fall day, the conniving convicts were working within the Number 10 Hoe Squad being supervised by fifty-two-year-old Sydney Albert Syms and W. J. Sealy. Though it was but a ruse, the convicts, feigning dryness, politely asked for a thirst-quenching drink. When given the okay they approached the water bucket and instead of benignly accepting consideration, jumped nearby Correctional Officer Syms with lightning speed, vigorously grabbing his revolver and shotgun. During the ensuing life or death struggle Syms was shot in the abdomen with his own revolver, in the hands of the twenty-one-year-old Lee Davis.[43] Once more, a Texas Prison System employee had made the ultimate sacrifice, dying on the spot. Correctional Officer Sealy was too far removed—with the other eight convicts—to effectively thwart the spine-chilling escape. The free-world break for Lee and Willie Davis was, by any analysis, really short-lived. They were recaptured the following day.[44] Correctional Officer Syms, interred at the Peach Creek Cemetery southeast of Bryan in Brazos County, was survived by his wife Rena and their seven children, plus one child from an earlier marriage. Doomed convicts Lee and Willie Davis did not survive. Subsequent to trial wherein both Prison System employees and prisoners testified, Lee and Willie caught Murder convictions and death sentences. Following the lengthy appellate process, at Huntsville behind the tall red brick walls, the Warden somberly oversaw execution by electrocution of Lee Davis. In a somewhat macabre twist, nineteen-year-old Willie Davis didn't take his seat in the electric chair, succumbing to tuberculosis at the Wynne Unit while awaiting his turn.[45]

The same year that Correctional Officer Syms went under, proposed legislation was being floated—perhaps as a trial balloon, perhaps not. At any rate it is reflective about squirmy issues relating to Capital Punishment and a state trading the hangman's noose for the executioner's electrical voltage four years earlier. In what can only be classed as bizarre, State Representative Roy Daniel of Wichita Falls was set to offer an amendment to "the Texas law prescribing the procedure in electrocution of persons condemned to death. . . ." According to Daniel, if they wanted to, friends and/or relatives of the electrocuted defendant could be given the opportunity to "resuscitate the victim after penitentiary physicians have given pronouncement of death." In his mind and—maybe a few constituents' too—since the deceased defendants were to undergo embalming post their execution, it would only be just and wise. His logic was simple in the extreme, based on "a belief that it is 'inhumane' to kill persons with embalming fluid in the possible event they are not dead from the electric shocks. If the electric chair does not kill the condemned, it should be abolished," so said the legislator from the Red River Country.[46]

By now the picture may be coming into focus. Sometimes convicts kill their keepers and sometimes they kill each other. David Rutherford, forty-eight, was serving hard time at the Ramsey State Farm for murdering Coleman County Deputy Sheriff Joseph Henry

"Joe" Griffith, sixty-four, at Santa Anna. Somehow for some reason convict J.K. Edwards, pulling but three years for Felony Theft
at Rockwall, Rockwall County, had a beef with Rutherford. The two
went at it in the Ramsey kitchen, and convict Edwards was the victor—his wielding of the knife put Rutherford first in the hospital
and then in the graveyard.[47]

Some folks, outside folks but well-intentioned, were undertaking a stab at reform. One of the active and vocal and most progressive was the Texas Committee on Prisons and Prison Labor (CPPL).
Their heartfelt recommendations were many—and not particularly
outlandish—such as classifying and segregating prisoners according
to age and offense, increasing educational and recreational opportunities, and prohibiting corporal punishment—those dreaded and
blood-drawing whippings with the Bat, as well as prompt "establishment of a parole board and the adoption of a modern probation
system." However, one recommendation was perfectly easy to propose, but most difficult to bring about: Centralizing the Texas Prison
System. Though the pros and cons were arguable, in the overall big
picture Texans and their politicians were not inclined to divest themselves of state-owned prison farms, replacing near 80,000 acres with
a "new penal colony near Austin." Although such a drastic proposition wouldn't be classed as an out and out dead letter, figuratively—
if results are the benchmark—the idea fell on deaf ears. What wasn't
disapproved was the earlier Texas Constitutional Amendment
restructuring the prison system, abolishing the three-person Board
of Prison Commissioners and replacing them with a nine-member
Texas Prison Board, unsalaried, supposedly freeing the institution of
certain irregularities and abuses: "Voters overwhelmingly approved
the amendment, undoubtedly recalling prison scandals from the
previous year when legislative investigators uncovered widespread
beatings and whippings, prison-operated whiskey stills, alteration of
financial records, and conflicts of interest involving a prison commissioner who sold supplies to the system in violation of state law."[48]

With support from several outside reform groups and even from
the Texas Prison Board, a philosophy of investing convicts with a

sense of democracy—allowing them some say so about their own affairs—had somewhat taken hold during the first trimester of the twentieth-century. Candidly, though, such liberalism with regards to penology was not new, but times had changed. Early on—near the last quarter of the nineteenth-century—commentators were reflecting on the true purpose and benefit of incarceration as a crime control measure. Some folks, even then, acknowledged its twofold rationale: Protection of society in general and reformation of the criminally inclined. Neglect on either count would be injurious to the public at large, as well as detrimental for the prisoner's prospect of turning his/her life around for the better. Brainy thinkers were, even in 1873, advocating for a Commutation Law because it would "inspire the convict with hope and thereby stimulate him to industry, good conduct, and cultivation of virtuous principles and habits, it gives a credit of time served on good behavior and in a measure places the pardoning power in the convict's own hands."[49] More progressively during the administration of Governor Daniel James "Dan" Moody, Jr., 1927-1931, reformers were touting that were prisoners denied the hope of some type of early release, "convicts lacked incentive to cooperate with prison authorities" and that a sensible and well-managed parole system could be the fountainhead for a "vital instrument for rehabilitation as well as a deterrent to prisoner escapes."[50]

Convicts at The Walls birthed the Prison Welfare League (PWL). The embryonic association would sponsor educational classes for prisoners utilizing convict teachers, as well as actively promoting entertainment and recreational activities designed to tamp down the profound frustration attendant to monotonous routines of institutional living. With forethought the infant outfit, in an effort to "acquaint the outside world with the worth and earnestness of many of the inmates," chose a communication instrument to echo their feelings. The Prison Welfare League's lasting legacy was anchored in their founding of an in-house monthly newspaper, The Echo, with the first pages unfolding for the November 1928 edition.[51]

December of 1928 may have closed, but according to newspaper accounts the month had "reached a high mark of sixty-five" escapes from the state's prison farms, although fifty-eight convicts, including escapees from previous months, had been recaptured and tabulated for the month's end report to Governor Dan Moody.[52] When the morning sun peeked over the eastern horizon that first day of January 1929 it shone down on a Texas penitentiary population of 4,561: 3,715 convicts divided among the state-owned prison farms, 817 prisoners ensconced behind the tall walls at Huntsville, and 29 troubled wards locked away at the Rusk facility, then serving as the state's asylum for the criminally insane.[53]

Three convicts—perhaps—would have found like company at Rusk, but they were inside The Walls—deep inside that night of 1 April 1929: April Fools' Day. They were "long-term" prisoners, courthouse convicted of highjacking corporate banks and innocent folks with guns. They had ingeniously burrowed below concrete in the facility's engine room—a labor of many weeks—and had hollowed out a cubicle five feet deep and six feet long to serve as their launch pad for tunneling under the prison's exterior wall—no matter how long it took. They all had plenty of time—at least ninety-nine years. Unfortunately for them, all three were in the hole during an ordered tally and, not surprisingly, the headcount didn't clear. Searching for the missing convicts was, besides being somewhat embarrassing for The Walls headman, then Warden Eugene Flowers "E.F" Harrell, a former Texas Ranger and Paris, Texas, Chief of Police succeeding the aforementioned Norman L. Speer who had resigned due his queasiness about Death Chamber doings, consumed twenty-eight hours. Then, luckily the yahoos were found tightly huddled below floor level, sweating, swearing, and saddled with knowledge that their hard work had come to naught.[54]

That not all convicts were black-hearted is illustrated by their charity when Warden Harrell became seriously ill with influenza. Kneeling at the Chapel inside The Walls, a group of convicts "prayed for the warden's recovery." Later, scraping together what little wherewithal they had, the concerned prisoners presented Warden Harrell "a silver loving cup" with an engraved inscription: "To our friend and warden, E.F. Harrell. From the boys, 1929."[55]

One of the boys—so to speak—an escapee, had no intention of spending any more nights behind the tall walls at Huntsville. Twice convicted of murder—in Lubbock and Taylor Counties—Hillary U. Loftis AKA Tom Ross AKA Charles Gannon had in the long-run turned out to be a much better fugitive than his murdering fall-partner Milt Good. Subsequent to his "mugging" a Correctional Officer four years earlier during the Texas prison break, now using the Gannon name, Hillary accepted cowboy employment for the Frye Cattle Company's Rimrock Division on the Blackfoot Indian Reservation not too far from Browning, Glacier County, Montana. Thereafter he was embroiled in a quarrel with the foreman, Ralph Hayward, howling: "I have a gun and I have a notion to kill you; in fact I am going to do so." And he did, shooting him six times. Realizing he was doomed to be hanged in Montana or returned to Texas, Hillary Loftis sat down on his bunk and scribbled his suicide note about what had just happened: "This fellow is a new man in the cow business. He may be all right among Dagoes but not among cow punchers. Good bye to the world."[56] Bang!

That same spring other Texas convicts opted for ill-gained liberty and, in this instance the fairer sex wasn't playing fair. Corinne Parish, Norma Pierce, and Marcie Barber put their heads together and formed a trio. Their 1929 Goree Unit ensemble was not created for crooning the latest hit-parade favorites; they were entertaining other ideas. Corinne, a scheming Forger from Tarrant County, Norma, an Armed Robber also from Tarrant County, and Marcie, a convicted Murderer from Hutchison County in the Texas Panhandle, chose to harmonize their way out of prison with a hot poker heated in their cast-iron stove. The three women "burned the woodwork away from the base of the bars on their window and let themselves to the ground with knotted blankets." Although good luck held during their nighttime decent via a colorful makeshift rope, their flight fizzled shortly thereafter. When the routine headcount failed to clear, the escape came to light. Even though it was night, Correctional Officers had commenced cutting for sign in the most logical of places: the roadway between Huntsville and Houston. The weary women had traipsed but less than three hours before they were trapped—then trudged back into their house away from home.[57]

At Goree it was not only girls gone bad that needed the eagle eye—men worked there too. Four convicts from The Walls had been dispatched to work on a water-well at Goree, under the watchful eye of Correctional Officer Arthur Thompson. Two of the convicts jumped, making a run for it. Correctional Officer Thompson fired his service revolver, which in turn alerted the mounted Boss, Tom Smith. The pair of fast scampering convicts, Jack Turnipseed, pulling four years from Grayson County for Assault, and W.C. Folsom doing an unbendable nickel from El Paso County for Highway Robbery were soon "headed off" by Boss Smith and ordered to return to the well and rejoin their toiling comrades. Convict Turnipseed complied; convict Folsom demurred. By this time Dog Sergeant Harold Augusta "Gus" Gray, thirty-seven, was onsite, demanding that Folsom do as ordered. Rather than doing as told Folsom began cursing, allowing that he didn't have to do anything as he advanced closer and closer and closer to Sergeant Gray. Though commanded to halt, Folsom continued toward Boss Gray with blood in his eye—epitaphs spewing from his lips. At a distance of three feet, Boss Gray did what he had to do, shoot till the convict stopped. The first bullet struck Folsom in the neck, the second in his chest. Folsom fell. Within but minutes Convict W.C. Folsom gave up the ghost. Upon closer inspection it was found "that Folsom was carrying a handful of loose tobacco, and [it was] said he probably intended to throw it in Gray's eyes and make another dash for freedom."[58] As herein already emphasized and will be made again and again apparent as these pages turn, in the prison setting—especially outside the tall walls and high fences—proximity is perilous.

During May 1929 technological change vaulted atop the red bricks surrounding The Walls: Telephones were installed not only inside the offices, but in the picket towers as well:

> As warden, Harrell is in charge of all that goes on within the walls. Operators working in eight-hour shifts will be on duty at the switchboard day and night. Each picket, stationed on top of the

walls, which are 18 feet high, and each one in the picket stands that surround the 10-acre site, will be required to report by phone every 30 minutes. At any time the operators will be able to ring the picket for a report. It is believed the telephone not only will be of service in keeping the pickets alert but also will be of valuable assistance in case of an attempted delivery of inmates. . . .[59]

Synchronizing his escape plan from The Walls perfectly, tush-hog convict Ed Crowder, convicted of robbing the Citizens State Bank of Houston, made news. His and a companion's breakout from a "concrete solitary cell," one that was supposedly escape-proof, and the prearranged placement of a ladder to scale the prison's tall perimeter wall, had not only the zealous newshounds baying but Prison Board Members as well, barking with barnyard innuendo.[60] Particularly, one member, Henry Cohen, publicly and disdainfully declared that, regrettably, the Huntsville Penitentiary was as "unsafe as a chicken coop." Another disgruntled member of the Texas Prison Board, J.B.H. Holderby, was and had been engaged in an investigation relative to "an alleged ring operating to affect the release of prisoners from the penitentiary." Their conference with Governor Moody was less than complimentary about institutional management.[61] Again highlighting the interplay between state governmental agencies, Texas Ranger Captain Tom Hickman was looking into the allegations of wrongdoing, the falsifying of convict release dates by some trustys and/or prison employees. With regards to escapee Crowder, he would be recaptured, but the career criminal's wild nightlife inside the state's Big House would spark legend and controversy and death.

Timing is important and for the beleaguered Texas Prison System an inopportune incident at the Clemens State Prison Farm in southern Brazoria County seemed to confirm Henry Cohen's chicken coop contention: Forty-three treacherous convicts had bolted after kidnapping and taking hostage three Correctional Officers, Emmett Moore, Virgil Cook, and "Red" Cash. According to Clemens Farm Manager (or Warden) Captain W.M. Hickman, two so-called trustys had shown their true colors, smuggling two handguns to the breakout's ringleaders, thieves Joe Williams and Robert Massey who "had received permission to go to the hospital ward for medicine." Once again calculated nefariousness had been cloaked behind the Correctional Officer's genially bending to a convicts' artificially hyped health needs. His kindness was not at all reciprocated. Now armed with pistols, the outlaws were "enabled to overpower the guards." Of the Clemens Farm population, 150 convicts opted to stay put, not risking discipline or death. The others, some carrying wicked-looking shanks, chose a free-world leave of absence. Seeking concealment, the escapees disregarded coherent thinking and made for the bottomlands between the Bernard and Brazos Rivers, which an onsite newspaper writer characterized as "the river jungle lands." Not at all surprisingly, and would over time become the norm for many Lone Star prison breaks, Texas Rangers were notified and according to the newspaper account Rangers Wheaton (Jerome B. "Rome" Wheatley) and (C.O.) Moore were commanding the efforts to recapture those desperadoes now being stabbed by mosquitoes and chased by Bloodhounds. Expectedly the prison staff and Texas Rangers were willingly joined by Brazoria County Sheriff John Wesley "Walkin' John" McKinney and his posse of resolute deputies. Realistically, the escapees were somewhat hemmed in by topography, the lowlands being surrounded by officers "stationed at intervals in a circle and all heavily armed," sculpting a cordon of cold steel and hot lead. The recapture tactic was straightforward:

> The guards are stationed in pairs. One goes into the surrounding bush and the other stands guard with gun ready to get the drop on a convict if he is "flushed."

During an on-the-spot interview with a Correctional Officer, the raring to go reporter was updated with optimism: "They lie low during the day. When the shadows begin to fall they come out of the bushes and try to make their way out of the swamps. Then is when we'll nab them."

All so soon, relatively speaking, two of those now miserable convicts, Tom Nichols, doing a dozen years for a Limestone County

Homicide, and J.L. Hailey, pulling time for a McLennan County Forgery conviction, were nabbed: Joe Roaden, a Correctional Officer assigned to guard a section of railroad tracks, sketches specifics. Noting that while so posted he "saw two men come out of the woods. 'I called to them to stop.' They kept running and I fired, dropping both." Their free-world holiday had been cut short: "We didn't try to run, boss," they said, "as they lay in the bottom of a wagon, groaning and smoking cigarettes, while they waited for an ambulance to come for them," and remove them to a Houston hospital. An escapee from El Paso, a Forger, wasn't in need of a doctor, but rather the services of a mortician: He had drowned in the San Bernard River while trying to elude capture.

One of the recaptured convicts, E.O. Hazelwood, maintained a defiant and threatening attitude, seemingly falling short of owning a rehabilitative personality, taunting: "We beat you three times before you got us. . . . I'll make it yet, and next time I'm going to be prepared for the same kind of treatment you guards give." Perhaps Convict Hazelwood knew hard times were in store, especially after hearing remarks of Captain Hickman with regards to the alleged betrayal of trust by the trustys: "If we back up our suspicions we will whip them or place them in solitary confinement."

Thankfully, during the confusion and chasing, the three hostages eyed opportunity for their getaway—and took it! By and large, though strategically separated into smaller groups to avoid detection, the escapees were eventually rounded up. Of course, such a newsy and thrilling story about the Texas Prison System and its reluctant residents was not spawning favorable publicity—though it made for helluva good copy.[62]

Not all convicts wanted to jump. In and of itself that does not mean they were real nice guys. Two in particular cooked up a plot—a murder plot. Completely unawares that his grave on the Ferguson State Farm, behind the "milking barn," had already been excavated, Clarence Harwell, twenty-eight, pulling a deuce from Haskell County for Forgery, was utterly clueless. Two nineteen-year-olds, Alton F. Breeding, a Cow Thief from Wilbarger County, and J.D. Echols, a

Burglar from Comanche County, had both caught two years. On the night of October 7, 1929, Harwell climbed into his bunk and went to sleep—permanently. The two teenaged boys had beaten him to death with "a heavy iron bar," and then buried him. Other convicts in the tank remained mum. When the headcount didn't clear, prison authorities quite naturally surmised that Clarence Harwell had—somehow—escaped. Several days elapsed. Apparently someone couldn't hold it in any longer or wanted to make a trade for something, and Captain (Warden) W.R. Crane zeroed in on young Echols and Breeding, separating them for the interrogation. A successful and time-proven strategy it was. The boys confessed and directed Captain Crane to the shallow gravesite. What was the convicts' motive? Well, Harwell had previously said something unbecoming about one of the killer's mother during a dispute, one revolving around in-house "Narcotics."[63]

Illicitly possessing and trafficking in mind-altering substances inside penitentiaries is not a new pastime for convicts. As but handy examples, on 30 March 1930 at the Wynne State Farm, it was noticed that several of the prisoners were "acting strangely like drunkards." Upon closer inspection it was determined that they were, indeed, inebriated—smashed. Correctional Officer John Osborn Jacks, fifty-three, after an investigative raid of the "tuberculosis department," discovered that secreted in the attic were four gallons of liquid—an odorous concoction of "potato peelings, yeast and left overs" from the prisoners' meals—fermenting in medicine bottles and jugs overhead. The homemade brew was potent enough to get one "soused." Also during the course of Correctional Officer Jacks's search he found "a quantity of narcotic pills which had been stolen from the medical room and passed among the prisoners."[64] And though it would be a few months into the future, another incident indicates convicts—at least some convicts—want for a liquid induced buzz. Several prisoners became violently ill and blinded at The Walls and one, twenty-three-year-old Ernest Hamilton, died after on the sly imbibing soda-water mixed with embalming fluid stolen from the prison's morgue.[65] Wrongheaded would be any thought that there was no drug culture—inside or outside prisons—during the 1930s. One convict inside The Walls was "aspiring to court the heavenly muse here in the penitentiary with the aid of marijuana cigarettes. . . . Several 'suspects' were brought into the 'bull ring' of the prison and when they found out the purpose of their detention, one dropped a tobacco sack on the floor, hoping it would remain unnoticed. . . . It contained four 'weeds' wrapped in brown cigarette papers. . . . Along with the cigarettes a sharp hypodermic needle which one of the doctors here pronounced 'a good one' [was found]. Meanwhile there's a convict somewhere on the yard who is probably vociferously cursing the luck—or alertness, if you will—of the prison officials who robbed him of another joy ride on a marijuana roll-your-own." During that same month, in mail sent to a prisoner, it was discovered that concealed in the cardboard backing of a writing tablet was a suspicious white powder: Heroin.[66] And later that same year it was discovered that several "convicts [were] peddling the weed [marijuana] in the prison yard." One of the dealers was Richard Young, who after being caught admitted that he "got four tobacco sacks of the marijuana from a negro [sic] driver of one of the wagons outside the walls."[67]

Illicit substances and the trafficking thereof would have 1930s far-reaching tentacles, in this instance down into fertile Brazoria County on the Ramsey, Clemens, Retrieve, and Darrington State Prison Farms. It seems that if the newspapers were spot on, a contract physician for the Prison System had a lucrative side-business aside from suturing lacerations and mending broken bones and passing out headache powder. At any rate, the Bureau of Narcotic's headman for Texas, Louisiana, and Mississippi, Joseph Bell, thought so. The good—maybe bad—medical doctor was "arrested by federal narcotic bureau agents who for several weeks have been investigating reports of narcotics being circulated in the prison system. Undercover agents it was alleged had met the doctor on a back road near the Ramsey State Farm." At the Initial Appearance before United States Commissioner W.F. Carothers, after professing his innocence and waiving the Preliminary Hearing, the defendant posted his $1,500 bond and prescribed himself a better day in tomorrow's free-world.[68]

Murdering and hiding a body on prison grounds and brewing beer and pilfering pills and gulping down embalming fluid and smoking dope and smuggling heroin in the mail and selling morphine to narcs were truly newsworthy stories, but on perhaps a higher plain there were other big doings about the state's penitentiary.

Generating not just a little widespread interest in political and statewide administrative governmental circles was the appointment of Marshall Lee Simmons as General Manager of the Texas Prison System. He had succeeded Acting General Manager W.A. Paddock, who was an interim appointment, filling administrative shoes vacated by General Manager W.H. Mead's resignation. By and large Lee Simmons, an ex-sheriff of Grayson County, Manager of the City of Sherman's Chamber of Commerce, an agriculturalist and prosperous businessman, was an exceptionally well-known Texas personality. The lean and lanky Lee Simmons was, too, a veteran—and survivor—of more than one gunplay.[69] On a personal level he was friends with Hollywood's puffed silver-screen Western movie idol Tom Mix and the bona fide cowboy, humorist and, perhaps, the most dexterous trick-roper to have ever awed spectators, Will Rogers. Marshall Lee Simmons knew governors too. Subsequent to serving on a Governor's penitentiary investigative committee and as a member of the Texas Prison Board, Lee Simmons—after some factual or feigned reluctance—picked up title as General Manager of the Texas Prison System on March 25, 1930.[70]

Lee Simmons had a prison management philosophy and it was not mush-mouthed, but straightforward, though not universally appreciated and not without detractors:

> In dealing with men most of whom came to be behind walls and bars because they could not discipline themselves, I had to make it perfectly clear to everybody that I could and would discipline them, if occasion arose. Prompt and certain punishment has a justice of its own, and I believe in it. . . . I do not belittle the methods of

correction advocated by the modern sciences, and I have made use of them, but I am a firm believer nonetheless in corporal punishment—in the home, in the schoolroom, in the reformatory, in the penitentiary. . . . Of course, I do not claim to have all the answers to these prison mutinies and outbreaks which continue to plague our penitentiaries. But, right or wrong, in the Texas Prison System we whipped our hardened criminals, when other means of persuasion failed. . . . And while love and kindness, sympathy and tender care are proper requisites for developing character in the home, the rod is needed. I have no doubt about that. Discipline of like sort is needed also in the schoolroom and in the prison. It has one great advantage: It works. . . . Excessive indulgence by the parents and misguided kindness go a long way, I believe, toward filling up our reformatories and penitentiaries. A little of the rod, rightly and sternly applied in childhood, I am convinced, would have saved many a grown man the pains of a prison sentence later on. In all my early school days I never knew of a pupil's being sent home for correction. Nobody was expelled from school. The teacher handled such problems with vigor and dispatch—and discipline did the job.[71]

While General Manager Simmons was not opposed to corporal punishment, he despised the practice of solitary confinement as a method of maintaining order inside the tall walls or on the prison farms, underscoring it as "inhuman and should not be tolerated. . . . I say that it is inhuman to place a man in solitary for thirty, sixty, or ninety days. In some cases the troublemakers are confined in isolation for years. It was never intended that man should be idle. If he is physically able, he should be at work, both for the sake of his health and for the earning of his living, whether he is in prison or out of prison. . . . The real objective of a prison sentence is, or should be, reformation. Surely it ought not to be merely punishment. . . . A prison official, whether he be guard, warden, or head of the system, should have patience and use it. He should study and know the individual prisoner. You cannot use the same method of discipline with all convicts, any more than you can deal with all children or all pupils alike. There is a wide difference in temperaments. . . . a knowledge of human nature is so important in prison management. . . . After every warning has failed, after every attempt at guidance has been rejected, corporal punishment should be used, but used for disciplinary purposes only."[72]

One who knew Lee Simmons chimed in with admiration but not sentimentality: "He still demanded a day's work out of each prisoner, but this work was in support of the prison itself and to improve conditions within the prison. He was concerned with their recreation after work and on weekends, and he set up schooling to improve prisoner's chance of becoming an employable citizen after his sentence had been served. He was 'old school' in his demands for a good day's work from every man, but he was ahead of his time in the Southwest for providing opportunities for inmates to make something of themselves through work and education. . . . But to expect that escapes would stop would be a mistake. The hatred for confinement or forced labor and the toughness of the men who were incarcerated combined to make the prison guard's life a hazardous one. These prisoners were hard men in the hardest of times."[73]

General Manager Lee Simmons did not hesitate too long before making some personnel adjustments. He asked for and received the resignation of Warden E.F. Harrell. There was no animosity associated with the change. Simply said, according to Simmons, he wanted someone at the post that was "more of a business man at the head of the prison. Harrell is a fine fellow, has a fine record as an officer and a ranger, and there has been no friction between us. It does not follow that a good officer is necessarily a good business man. I want it emphatically understood that he was not let out nor discharged. He merely resigned so that a person with more business knowledge could take over the large affairs of the prison."[74] Though not exactly disputing the reasoning behind the General Manager's decision, ex-Warden Harrell told an inquiring journalist that he really didn't want to give up the position, but "the general manager of the prison system was apparently dissatisfied with my services and I knew the climax had come. I deemed it best that I resign. The general manager and I could not agree on several points in the management of the prison. . . . I enjoyed my work and would have liked to continue in the capacity of warden. I have no grudge against anyone, and I wish the present administration the greatest success in the management of the prison."[75]

Particularly the newspaperman poked some reality at the readership—maybe: "During his two years as warden Harrell did not have a prison break, a mutiny or so much as a single prisoner who would not work, his friends pointed out. There was not a fire in the prison during his tenure and only two men were whipped, they after the present general manager, Lee Simmons, assumed office."[76] Furthermore—and it might be telling—"Although nearly 20 condemned men were executed the two years he was warden, Harrell did not throw the switch on one nor witness any of the executions."[77]

Lee Simmons was not through. "After 16 years of service as chaplain of the Texas penitentiary, Rev. W.E. Miller, 65—white-haired minister has been discharged to make room for a younger man. Mr. Miller said he had received a letter from the general manager of the prison system, praising him for his services, but saying that a younger man would replace him."[78] Then, Lee Simmons's reasoning did not raise an eyebrow! Now, probably indignation!

To refill behind E.F. Harrell, Lee Simmons chose Walter W. Waid, former Sheriff of Hunt County (county seat Greenville) and an ex-City Marshal of Wolfe City to replace Acting Warden R.H. Baughn, who had been temporarily holding down the fort at The Walls.[79] During his tenure in the offices of sheriff and city marshal, Walter W. Waid "conducted an ice, coal and bottling company and was successful in its operation for 26 years. He also bought and shipped cattle. It was not by 'six-gun' and flying bullets that Waid made his record. Before he entered public life he had equipped himself with a business knowledge that helped him when he entered upon his duties as sheriff."[80] Lee Simmons now had his businessman in place.

Commonly it seems, with much shock-value intended, it is emphasized that sometimes on the Texas State Prison Farms convicts resorted to self-mutilation to avoid working. Indeed, it's true! Finding a way out of hard work by chopping off a finger or toe, or even a hand or foot, or purposefully severing a heel-tendon was a tactic of choice for some convicts. With regards to convicts employing this expedient, two items—subjective and objective—might merit mention. There really should be no surprise, by consequence of courthouse conviction many—though it may sound callous—had already demonstrated honest work was not on their personal agendas, but robbery, burglary, thievery and forgery were—if one could get away with it—perfectly okay. And, too, such decisive disfigurement was not unique to Texas prisoners. Particularly two scholars noted: "The practice of self-mutilation by prisoners is an old one. Records show that it was prevalent in the hulks at Chatham Dock in England and in French Guiana." As the authors capably and insightfully reveal the practice was not a Texas phenomenon, but in the nineteenth and twentieth centuries was taking place at prison communities in other states as well.[81]

Sometimes the mutilation was unarguably real—but in a certain sense perhaps misleading by design. At least so asserted a talkative convict:

> A bunch of convicts would decide that the next morning a certain number would cut their heel strings. They drew straws to see who would cut. If you got the short straw you either cut your heel string or got killed. None of the tough guys ever cut theirs. They made the weaklings draw straws.[82]

General Manager Lee Simmons elaborates on this type of occurrence and his methodology for realistically putting the kibosh on such inanity: "For example, we had an epidemic of maiming on one of our prison farms. Men would cut the heel tendon to escape work—or even chop off a foot. I went down to look things over. I told the men who so injured themselves that they would not be transferred to the prison hospital but that they would be treated by the prison physician right there on the farm and that as soon as their wounds were healed, they would be put back to work, every last man of them, right there on the farm. Then I turned to the guards and said: 'Bring them more axes, boys.' The newspapers printed that."[83] And as would be expected within certain circles—folks genuinely advocating for prison reform—the offhand remark was ill-advised and ill-timed, a firestorm headline for editorial opportunism. What some of those 1930s journalists failed then to print—as do some contemporary chroniclers—there is an underside to Simmons's threat. "What they didn't print was that I got the guards off to themselves and told them privately to keep those axes out of sight for a while. We stopped the self-maiming epidemic right then and there."[84] Any empty notion, then or now, championing the premise that General Manager Lee Simmons would have actually passed out axes so convicts could permanently injure themselves is, to be kind, ludicrous.

During another 1930s spate of heel-stringing at the Retrieve State Farm, Texas Rangers were dispatched to try to determine if the mutilations were inflicted because of the kept being brutalized by the keepers, or were they exacting injuries—that would heal—just to avoid work. Captain Fred McDaniel and Private William Hale Kirby, subsequent to an onsite investigation were forced to report, that to their best knowledge the acts of self-hurt were designed to give the convicts a respite from toiling in the fields.[85]

Another example of somewhat backwards thinking was exhibited by convict Ennis Brock, thirty-five, a four-time Texas recidivist and two-time federal recidivist. Back in Texas he was doing a life sentence as a habitual criminal—the Big Bitch. At the Eastham State Farm convict Brock was tired of the field work. He preferred, if he could get his way, the so-called leisurely life awarded those in the prison hospital at The Walls. His methodology for getting from one place to the other was radical. He purposely found a rattler, "and fought it until the snake bit him on the thumb." Not unsurprisingly fellow convicts had observed the sparring with the serpent and had notified the Field Boss, who in turn notified the camp physician. "There the thumb was lanced and treated and Brock was sent back to his hoeing. His condition is [was] not serous since the bite was treated so quickly. Asked why he did it he told the captain he 'just wanted to see how it felt.' He also admitted a longing for the Huntsville 'walls' hospital and a ceiling fan, instead of the hot sun on the farm."[86]

The hard fact that convicts would do themselves damage was, again, made more than clear to General Manager Lee Simmons. Bill Smith AKA Roy Miller AKA Joyce Shepard had committed one Murder and escaped prison in Arizona. He was on the run in the Lone Star State. Near Roby at the southern edge of the Texas Panhandle, he coldheartedly murdered Fisher County Sheriff Robert Jefferson "Bob" Smith and Deputy Jake C. Owens subsequent to his arrest, while being transported to jail. He and his fall-partner, Lloyd Conaster, were later recaptured, and ultimately the man with many aliases was sentenced to die while strapped to Ole Sparky. By any man's standard Bill Smith was "hard to handle" and prison personnel forewent stripping him to make note of scars, marks, and/or tattoos. He too began feigning insanity. Finally, after two psychiatric examinations and sanity hearings, mean Bill had an irrevocable date with destiny and electricity. Cognizant of what was in store, Smith told fellow Death Row prisoners that he no longer believed that "this crazy business will work this time." While waiting on Death Row the condemned fellow was busy. Working a small nail loose from a ventilator in his cell was but part of the job. Using the concrete floor of his house as a whetstone—a very common penitentiary practice—he sharpened the metal point. Then he gouged out his eyes, one at a time. Purportedly he later remarked to a clergyman: "if the eye offendeth thee, pluck it out. It is better for a part of the body to die than be cast into hell." Which certainly begs the question, were the head-doctors right or wrong? General Manager Lee Simmons noted that the mutilation had been immediately discovered and that the convict had "blinded himself" during a "maniacal spree." Nevertheless, Simmons granted reporters an interview, and Bill Smith submitted after ordering and receiving a generous helping of ice-crème. Afterwards, he absolved his fall-partner of any wrongdoings, freely admitted to the homicides, and marched to the Death Chamber, slyly remaking to fellow convicts as he passed by: "Boys, I'm not going to have a tear in my eyes when I go over the road."

And he didn't—but he did leave something behind in his house—"the bone from a T-bone steak, whetted to a sharp edge. . . ." A push-dagger of sorts.[87]

A couple of Texas convicts at the Ferguson State Farm were armed with cutting and stabbing instruments and bad attitudes—at least toward each other. Volmer Gus Tinney, doing a quarter's worth from Wilson County for Armed Robbery and Elmer Lee Butler, a Building Tender, pulling but four years from Johnson County for Assault to Murder, were at each others' throats regarding something: "The fight started on a top bunk in the cell building and the two clinched, falling to the floor. Scrambling apart they drew dirks and lunged at each other. Tinney's knife pierced Butler's heart, killing him instantly. Tinney received some deep wounds in his abdomen, dying later in the prison hospital . . . Prison officials said they did not know what the fight was about."[88] In the convict world cold steel and hot tempers spark trouble.

Two other fellows had real bad luck during mid-year of 1930 too, and both had Texas Ranger and penitentiary connections, one a past employee, the other yet on the job. In the first instance, fifty-year-old Thomas Benjamin "Tom" Stowe, a former Ranger in Company B at San Antonio, had a brand-new home at The Walls. He had been convicted at Victoria in Victoria County—catching a life sentence—for "the slaying of Alvin Marshall." According to the newspaper account, ex-Ranger Tom Stowe arrived at Huntsville sans wearing the customary handcuffs or chained by the neck to another convict.[89] There is no indemnity keeping cops from becoming convicts.

The second scenario is sad, one involving Sergeant Manuel T. "Lone Wolf" Gonzaullas, Company B, Texas Rangers. At the time, 1930, it was, "among the duties of Rangers to escort condemned men from the scene of a trial to the Texas prison at Huntsville for execution."[90] During nighttime hours on July 30, Sergeant Gonzaullas and Texas Ranger Bob Goss were transporting Jesse Lee Washington, twenty-one, to Huntsville. The black prisoner had been convicted of beating to death Mrs. Henry Vaughn near Shamrock in Wheeler County. Subsequent to his courthouse conviction and death sentence before the bench of District Judge E.W. Ewing (at Miami, Roberts County on a Change of Venue), and a demonstrated commitment by local authorities and Texas Rangers to prevent lynch-mob injustice, Jesse Lee had been shackled for the long auto trip to Walker County.[91] Behind the wheel, according to the newspaper recap, was Sergeant Gonzaullas, Ranger Goss riding shotgun, the cuffed prisoner in the backseat. Roughly five miles northwest of Vernon in Wilbarger County, tragedy rolled into the picture in the form of a twelve-year-old "riding a scooter on the highway." Of course, the collision was accidental but the innocent youngster was "instantly killed." Lone Wolf would say to a journalist that he had tried, that "every effort was made to avoid hitting" the child, but his maneuvering, in the end, had fatefully been futile.[92] Though heart-stricken but dutifully the Texas Rangers, after awhile, continued with their auto trip to the Piney Woods Country. There on 12 September 1930, inside the Death Chamber and as the sixty-second convict to take the hot seat, Jesse Lee Washington was executed.[93]

Three other convicts fell out—dead—in the fields picking cotton: Jimmie Arnold and Herbert Davis, white, at Clemens and Zeb Daniels, black, at the Ramsey State Farm. "Mr. Simmons revealed that four other prisoners at Clemens farm had had to 'fall out' on account of the excessive heat," and were undergoing treatment at the prison hospital. With regards to the deaths at Clemens the General Manager laid that off to "heat prostration" and not to being overworked. He did, and probably had no choice, pledge to make a thorough investigation. He had taken other action too: Sending a letter to the managers of all the State Prison Farms instructing the custodial staff "not to overwork the men in the excessive heat and to allow them longer lunch periods and to work later in the evenings." Furthermore it was noted: "There is an ever-increasing number of prisoners being sent to the farms from the 'walls,' new men just admitted, and these men for the most part have been confined in jails for long periods and are not capable of stepping in and doing hard work at first."[94] That said, the "Fish" would be broken in slowly, but hard work for convicts with their Aggies still there would be. In Texas, prisoners worked![95]

Lee Simmons could be damn tough but fair and firm when necessary. He, too, had a softer side. Lus Arcos had killed three men: Joe Barrientes and his two grown sons, Joe and Ellfonso, in Medina County on Christmas Day 1928. Sentenced to pay the ultimate price, Lus Arcos, a most polite and well-groomed convict, had but one request from his last house—he wanted to be entertained with a concert. General Manager Lee Simmons granted his wish, having the prison orchestra take their musical instruments and play on Death Row. From 9 o'clock to 10 o'clock in the evening of 7 November 1930, "the death house was filled with the sounds of waltzes and fox trots." Thereafter the musicians returned to their cells, and Lus Arcos traveled to the hereafter—wherever.[96]

There was not and should not have been an ounce of sympathy or kindness for another convict. But, by and large *most* prison folks—despite sensationalized myth—have good hearts. At Fort Worth the six-year-old son of a prisoner confined inside The Walls was hastily admitted to St. Joseph's Hospital. The child's flammable Halloween costume had accidently caught fire, burning the child terribly. Sadly the boy's condition was deteriorating, according to physicians, worsening by the hour. Thoughtfully, citizens knowing that the poor lad's daddy was locked away at Huntsville, apprised prison authorities of the sad state of affairs. Was there any compassion to be had from keepers of the kept? Yes, although it would necessitate a drain on manpower, Texas Prison System officialdom would act for the boy and the dad—at once! Prison Transfer Agent E.E. Cato was gladly tasked with escorting the convict to the brick-streets of Cow Town for what might be the very last opportunity to say goodbye to his tragically and severely burned boy-child. Wardens and Correctional Officers and staff have children, too! Calculatingly, at the hospital via a rear entrance, the unappreciative convict eluded Agent Cato. Traced to the hotel operated by the shameful prisoner's wife in the 100 block of East Tenth Street, it seemed that latching on to the convict was but a done deal—until he "plunged through the wire screen of the window to freedom." Then the wily but ungrateful fugitive entered a trap door on an adjoining roof and made his escape through a pool hall.[97] Sometimes humanity's products are downright sorry! Correctional Officers, as already mentioned, have not crystal balls—some pleasantly smiling convicts can be dangerous; some frowning and scowling convicts can be harmless; misreadings can prove disastrous.

Shortly—Thanksgiving Eve—there was more mortification playing for prison folks—gunfire! A truck packed with twenty-seven convicts was returning to The Walls after their wood cutting chore. Riding on the vehicle's running boards—or fenders in other reports—were Dog Sergeant Fred Oliver Ross, forty-five, "the best fighter in the Texas prison system and one of the deadliest shots at the prison," and on the opposite side rode Correctional Officer Leonard E. Osburn, forty-six, a sure-enough scrapping dynamo in a tight place. Such positioning was but par business for these routine prisoner movements. A trusty was driving the truck and a follow-up "touring car" was driven by Correctional Officer Bud Barnes. On cue, about eight miles outside Huntsville, at 4:45 p.m. four desperate convicts made their play for a getaway. Armed with a dirk, twenty-year-old Houstonian Tony "Two Timer" Corona, doing 290 years for as many as 25 Armed Robberies, and Thomas Riley "Tom" Shook, the former Chief of Police at Electra in Wilbarger County convicted of Murder, jumped Boss Ross, grappling with him, trying to grab his holstered pistol. At the exact same time, armed with an improvised shank, J. Wheeler McCulley, twenty-five, pulling hard time for Burglaries in Tarrant and Van Zandt Counties, and thirty-year-old Argyle Etheridge Guyton, AKA Jimmy Talley, also serving time from Wilbarger County but for Armed Robbery, assaulted Boss Osburn. Understandably, the truck braked to a stop as bar-ditch scuffles were waxing hot. The struggle for firepower was intense. The driver jumped out, admonishing his non-paying passengers "to stay on the truck or you'll get killed." Trying to take sudden and unplanned advantage of the turmoil, Jim Long, "a lifer," made a break for the pine trees, but was chased down by white trusty J.W. Morris and a reliable black trusty, James "Jim" Mitchell, returning him to the truck. For a moment it was helter-skelter. Ross was overpowered and disarmed. Osburn was bested and made a hostage. Bailing out of his car with a shotgun in hand Boss Barnes was ready for war. He cut loose, wounding convict Shook in the arm, a pellet or two also striking and slightly wounding Boss Ross. Unarmed—but free of entanglement—Boss Ross literally limped over to Boss Barnes and borrowed his state revolver. Then with grit, guts, and gumption Boss Ross engaged McCulley and Corona in a six-shooter collision, dodging bullets but killing both sledgehammer dead. Argyle Etheridge Guyton gave up—right fast! Convict Shook was rushed to the hospital, his arm amputated, but he survived. During a post incident interview, Boss Ross declared that in the twelve years that he had been guarding prisoners he had never lost a man. Too, he light-heartedly bantered, "I'm right proud to have been shot by Bud Barnes. It would have been o.k. with me if he'd killed me, just so he got Shook." When notified of her son Two Timer's death, so nicknamed because he always pulled two robberies on the same night to confuse Houston city policemen, the mother's message from McAlister, Oklahoma, was undeniably plainspoken: "I expected him to go that way. I am glad he was killed instantly and did not suffer. I do not hold any hard feelings toward any person in Texas." Per instructions of his distraught mama, outlaw Tony Corona was buried at Huntsville, in the prison cemetery, colloquially known as Peckerwood Hill.

Quite appropriately as soon as he was notified of the spellbinding situation General Manager Lee Simmons, accompanied by Justice of the Peace R.J. Camp, made an onsite appearance. Not unexpectedly the Inquest ruling was in favor of the Correctional Officers: Justifiable Homicides. In fact, Simmons was "enthusiastic in praise of both the guards and the trustys. J.W. Morris, Arthur Dennis and Matthew King, white, and Jim Mitchell, negro [sic], were the trustys who assisted the guards. Their warning was given credit for preventing a general break for freedom, which in the melee might have been successful." When broached about any change in policy, Lee Simmons was noticeably adamant: No, the outside work would continue when and where as needed. Most assuredly Lee Simmons and his loyal security staff ran the prison, not the convicts. In the meantime, however, "as a reward for their assistance in preventing a break for liberty" General Manager Lee Simmons would permit the trustys—with the concurrence of Governor Dan Moody—ninety-day furloughs. In a rather poignant declination the black convict, Jim Mitchell, begged off, frankly saying he had no place to go, supplementing his remarks with: "The penitentiary is a good enough place for me."[98]

Although for some enlightened folks it might ring of hollow insensitivity—resorting to the rod—factually, if taking the word of Lee Simmons is okay, the prison population escalated during his tenure, although the number of times corporal punishment was officially administered and the numerical frequency of escapes plunged.[99] For the General Manager it was proffered that "neither severe discipline nor lax discipline would be able to keep order. . . ." Lee Simmons's practical streak was entrenched: "A convict knows what a convict is entitled to expect as a fair, square deal. If he gets it, he can be handled—to his advantage and to the advantage of the public, whose protection is the first object of his removal from circulation."[100]

6

"Only themselves to blame"

ALTHOUGH AS A MATTER OF CUSTOMARY hiring practices, the employment of female Correctional Officers was years into the future—there were some early exceptions if there was actually a piece-work payment for handcuffing and hauling a skirt-wearing fugitive back to Texas. A mention in the *Dallas Morning News* is reasonably clear:

> Ethel Russell, 23, daughter of Bud Russell State penitentiary agent demonstrated she was a chip off the old block when she arrived in Fort Worth Tuesday in charge of an escaped woman convict, Clarice Barker, under sentence for murder. Miss Russell brought the prisoner under an eight-year sentence from Borger, from Kansas City. After turning the woman over to Tarrant County Jailer Frank Anderson, she left for her home in Blum.[1]

Nineteen-hundred and thirty-one would not be a good year for Ike Gray. Though the native of Indiana had been sent to a Texas Prison as result of a property crime in Wise County, north of Fort Worth, he jumped and was on the lam. That is, until he caught more time and was imprisoned for three years in the federal lockup at Leavenworth, Kansas. Thereafter he was returned to Texas, making up for owed time, working as a cook at the Central State Farm. Although Ike Gray, now thirty-two, may have had greasy cooking oil on his hands, he had wanderlust in his blood. He walked off the job, answering "the call of the road." Naturally the sched-uled headcount did not clear—and the hunt was on. Fortunately two Correctional Officers in an automobile, N.L. Hidalgo and E.T. Searcy, spotted escapee Gray near the highway headed for Houston. Unfortunately for Gray, he failed to halt when ordered to do so by Hidalgo. Instead, he started running. The mistake in judgment was fatal. At the Inquest, Correctional Officer Hidalgo advised Justice of the Peace G.T. Pike: "He was walking along the highway and when we approached he started running. We speeded up our car and shouted for him to stop. When he ran faster I shot three times with my .45 caliber automatic. He fell and was dead when we picked him up. All three shots had hit him in the back."[2] Bending to the desire to escape is definitely not smart in the first instance, but actually trying to outrun an officer's bullets is past foolhardy. In the prison world ways of transgressors can be hard.

And sometimes those transgressions of a personal nature are handled personally. Hugh D. "Hop Toe" Butler, pulling ninety-nine years for the "torch murder" of Roy Hawthorne at Fort Worth, had a beef with Johnny H. Pringle doing a quarter for his homicidal mis-adventure—killing and robbing James Harney, a taxi-driver—also in Tarrant County. Inside the dining room at The Walls, both men were seated at the table and then Hop Toe "suddenly jumped to his feet and cut Pringle's throat with a razor. Then he threw the weapon under the table. Pringle staggered to the door, crying, 'He cut me!' There he col-lapsed. Luckily, in the end, the cutter and the cuttee survived.[3]

Keepers of the kept must remain wary at all times. They are inca-pable of mind-reading. Sometimes duplicitous convicts have by blood or marriage duplicitous relatives, in-laws that are outlaws. Convicts Jack Perry and Jim Rye AKA Merriman advantaged themselves of such kinship. Inside the Retrieve State Prison Farm dormitory they were armed, one carrying a .32 caliber revolver, the other with a Colt Model 1911 .45 caliber semiautomatic pistol that had been smuggled inside the institution by a prisoner's sister. James Bostic "Jim" Sneed, a thirty-nine-year-old Correctional Officer, was on picket duty that night of 6 July 1931. At 10:15 p.m. the aforementioned desperadoes approached Jim Sneed, drew their shooters and demanded he fork over keys that would unlock their plans for a free-world future. Correctional Officer Sneed, maybe foolishly, but nevertheless bravely, went for his gun rather than yielding his keys. Four gunshots echoed throughout the building, four bullets tearing into Jim Sneed's body, both convicts having unleashed two rounds. Correctional Officer Sneed's death was near instant, but heroic. He had stumbled and fallen—knowingly— outside the picket door, the prized keys wholly beyond the convicts' reach. The murderers' options now were but few. Taking other prisoners hostage under some whacky death threat would net nothing— prison personnel would not bend to that silliness. Prisoners and/or Correctional Officers as hostages—even if it seems awful—were by design expendable. The real-time choices were but two—suicide or surrender. Perry and Rye opted for the latter, and had more hard time stacked atop their original sentences.[4] They had also forfeited, in a metaphoric sense, their tickets to the very first Texas Prison Rodeo.

Unarguably one of the lasting legacies, among several, of General Manager Lee Simmons was the Texas Prison Rodeo (TPR), although Texas convicts had competed with each other riding rough stock and racing horses at the Eastham State Farm as early as Thanksgiving 1919.[5] And, too, interagency travel for entertainment purposes preceded the TPR's first Grand Entry. The Warden (Captain) at the Clemens State Farm, W.M. Hickman, as early as January 1931 took his Jubilee Entertainers and the unit's ten-piece band, "the best show troupe he had ever had," on a within-the-system tour. On a given day they were to appear first at the Goree Women's Farm, then at the Wynne Unit north of Huntsville, and that evening inside The Walls.[6] The intrinsic value of a little leisure time distraction from the rigors of imprisonment had long been a part of the institution's penology schema. While Lee Simmons did make his contribution as one of the classic TPR's founding fathers, as a knowledgeable academician rightly registers, he didn't do it by himself. The inaugural 1931 TPR was also the communal effort of four more fellows: the aforementioned Warden at The Walls, Walter W. Waid; R.O. McFarling, Prison Livestock Supervisor; Albert Ray Moore, the Texas Prison System's

Welfare Director; and Reece Lockett, a rodeo star and Hollywood stuntman in his own right and, later pertinent to this chronicle, Supervisor of the Texas Prison Parole Board. Too, Lockett was, after returning from his West Coast sojourn, a Texas ranchman, rodeo judge, sometimes stock-contractor, and a multi-decade elected local politician at Brenham in Washington County west of Huntsville, which naturally morphed into his long-time handle as the Cowboy Mayor of South Texas.[7]

The half-century saga of the TPR spawns—besides meaningful historical insights into the Texas Prison System's evolution—a helluva good story, one now finally preserved for posterity. With that in mind, leapfrogging exacting chronological sequence is crucial and, hopefully, okay. From inception, the TPR continued to outgrow its figurative britches and the available seats in the bleachers that awestruck spectators were clamoring for. The Sunday afternoon performances during the month of October were sold-out affairs, each year surpassing sales receipts of the previous fall's shows. Simply suggesting that the concept of having a full-scale rodeo arena adjacent to The Walls and of having convict cowboys riding rough stock and roping wild cow creatures was a crowd-pleaser would be a whopping understatement.

During the off season—the eleven other months—hardly could building crews keep up with the blueprinted plans for expanding seating capacity for the upcoming October. It was a frenzy of measuring and sawing and hammering and nailing. Purely from a builder's or contractor's perspective the construction angle—and angles— makes for an astonishing story within itself. From the townsmen's viewpoint—especially merchants and vendors—Huntsville was on the map, at least during TPR season. Souvenirs were peddled and purchased. The downtown parade was lively. Colorful clowns strutted and stumbled—and smiled big regardless the greasepaint. Parking spaces for spectators were at a premium. Pedestrians making their way to The Walls were crowed shoulder to shoulder, inching along at a snail's pace but enjoying every wide-eyed minute in a carnival environ foreign to anywhere else in the state. Even the great granddaddy State Fair of Texas at Dallas could not boast of prison bands and drill squads and glee club convicts decked in their best Sunday whites hawking rodeo programs—outside The Walls—of course under the watchful eyes of armed keepers in starched and pressed uniforms. Who could resist looking up, trying to catch a glimpse of that grim-faced fellow with a rifle looking down from corner watchtowers—surveying anybody and everybody?[8]

Preceding the TPR's slated Sunday performances also saw a flurry of activity—good activity—behind The Walls. There in the Shoe and Harness Shop several convict craftsmen engaged in building special bronc saddles and bareback riggings—under exacting standards set by the National Rodeo Association. Though not just a few of the imprisoned fellows had played unfair in the free-world, in the TPR's dirt arena everyone—cowboys and livestock—was to get "an even break." Quite expectedly then, these artisans also hewed cowhides into cowboy boots, chaps (leggins'), and hand-tooled spur-straps, items not common to the prison participants' otherwise sparse inventory of personal property. After all, TPR was being hawked and sold as an authentic—real deal—Wild & Woolly Western Show.[9]

In fairly short order the annual TPR was propelled into the psyches of a nationwide audience. Entertainment journalists and newsreel crews followed celebrity—and during its multiyear run the TPR attracted bona fide headliners. Though this listing is certainly incomplete, over the years it's suggestive of how magnetic and how lucrative was the draw for celebrities to make a personal appearance or perform at the TPR, personalities such as: Tom Mix, Fess Parker, James Arness, Dale Robertson, Steve McQueen, Guy Madison, Richard Boone, Robert Culp, John Wayne, Ernest Tubb, Red Foley, Roy Acuff, Rex Allen, Johnny Cash, Johnny Horton, Ray Price, Faron Young, Mickey Mantle, Willie Mays, Dizzy Dean, Dan Blocker, Chuck Connors, Tommy Sands, Ricky Nelson, Jimmie Rodgers, Bo Diddley, Frankie Avalon, Neil Sedaka, The Crewcuts, Molly Bee, Anita Bryant, Jerry Lee Lewis, Red Steagall, Merle Haggard, Loretta Lynn, Buck Owens, Sonny James, Hank Thompson, Willie Nelson, George Strait, Charley McLain, Gene Watson, The Judds, and Moe Bandy tends to showcase the overall premise.[10] The TPR was really big doings—the star-studded lineup confirmed that much. One celebrity, however, bowed out—she apparently didn't want to get her coiffed hair wet and "make a fool of myself." According to a critical piece in the *Dallas Morning News* somewhat disdainfully comparing entertainer Gene Kelly's performance in *Singing in the Rain*, and Tanya Tucker's backing out of her scheduled Sunday afternoon gig because it was drizzling: "The announcement that Tucker had refused to sing was met by boos from 13,000 rain-soaked spectators, who otherwise cheered convict riders as they competed for prize money in various events."[11]

Oh yes, there too was Juanita Dale Slusher AKA Candy Barr, the exotic and erotic Dallas nightclub stripper who had landed in the penitentiary due to a Possession of Marijuana conviction. Singing as well as dancing (appropriately clothed), Candy Barr boogied into the hearts of applauding critics in the grandstands and enthralled newscasters and print reporters covering the TPR fanfare. When Candy Barr was slinking and singing and sizzling on the TPR's makeshift platform—generally speaking—"she would match or outperform other big name attractions."[12] While domiciled at the crimson-hued Goree Women's Unit at Huntsville's edge, Candy Barr would light-heartedly quip: "Just what I always wanted—a big red brick home."[13] At the rodeo—in the arena with microphone in hand—knowing how they were compulsory attired, Candy would gesture to the wire-meshed grandstands where convict spectators sat, teasingly proclaiming: "Remember, all good guys wear white."[14] The laughter and ovation was thunderous! And even after Candy Barr gained free-world status she would return for encore performances at the TPR—wooing lonesome inmates and wowing the toe-tapping outsiders inside for an unforgettable Sunday afternoon.[15]

While there was a palpable make-believe ambiance associated with movie and television stars, Country & Western crooners, governors and politicos, and sports personalities—and a shapely dynamite stripper—down in the TPR's bucking-chutes it was real. The bareback horses were sidewinder quick, the stoutly built saddle-broncs were four-legged pile drivers, and the cross-bred bulls—at the nod of a hat and swing of a gate—bolted into the arena as would-be widow

makers. In fact, a pair of prized prison bucking broncs was characterized by their names: Hell's Angel and Death Dealer.[16] Here nothing
was phony! And here, too, not everyone was walking or riding the
straight and narrow.

According to a Houston newspaper story, convict cowboy Buster
Bishop was a "Rodeo Star." The newsy article noted that Buster
Bishop, twenty-eight, a cowboy from Midland ensconced in prison
for seven years for five cases of Theft, was "a hard-riding first-place
winner in many events in convict rodeos held here [Huntsville] for
the past three years." He, too, had not lost sticky fingers. Captain
(Warden) R.H. Baughn of the Wynne State Farm soon noticed a
prison saddle had gone missing. After investigation it was found
secreted in the house of two free-world blacks, who were taken
into custody and confined in the Walker County jail. Buster Bishop
copped to Warden Waid, and instead of his nearing release date,
"he lost his trusty job and was placed in stripes. Now he will have to
serve out his term."[17]

All participating cowboys were convicts. They had auditioned
against each other for a chance to convert another day into a Sunday
payday—legit loot and real glory went to winners. Aside from
event monies, the overall rodeo champion for the season—The Top
Hand—would be awarded immeasurable esteem from participating and grandstand witnessing convicts, as well as winning a fancily
engraved gold and silver belt buckle.

There were, too, novelty acts and non-typical rodeo doings such
as snagging a Bull-Durham sack stuffed with money from between
the horns of a Brahman Bull with blood in his eyes or wrestling with
a wild mare, quickly squeezing a teat for that smidgen of measurable
milk into a pop bottle before other competitors could put their liquid
white gold across the finish-line.

In addition to the riding and roping and wrangling there were
myriad other duties associated with each performance of the TPR—
and convicts jumped at the chance to break the daily routine of penitentiary life and pitch in—helping with this arena chore or that.
Thankful prisoners from the outlying farm units were trucked into

Huntsville—caged and under strict guard—so that they, too, could be spectators to the frivolity and fun of a wild and woolly Western afternoon—that is, if they weren't suffering disciplinary sanctions for previous bad conduct. Expectedly security was tight, but two wannabe free-world yahoos—with a stroke of good luck—managed to mingle with the civilian crowd. An accomplice had stashed everyday duds beneath the grandstands and quite cleverly the convicts doffed themselves in a change of clothes. Shortly thereafter a Correctional Officer espied them exiting from beneath the grandstand and, thinking they were sneaking into the rodeo without a ticket, promptly showed them to the main entrance and "threw them out."[18] That evening the headcount didn't tally—but embarrassment did.

During another incident five convicts showed their appreciation for being trucked to the TPR. After the Sunday performance, while being transported through Houston in the 3900 block of North Main, and after finding a weak spot in their rolling enclosure, they bolted. Three were directly recaptured. Floyd Brown "Dago" Seay, a multi convicted felon, was pulling fifty years for an Armed Robbery in Walker County, and Noble Guthrie, doing twenty for Robbery in Armstrong County above the Palo Duro Canyon at Claude, had avoided immediate capture. Guthrie had already pulled time in Oklahoma for felony Theft. Relatively speaking their flight was short. Dago Seay was apprehended at Kansas City, Missouri, and Noble Guthrie's fleeting good fortune ran out at Alamogordo, New Mexico. Back in Texas custody, good luck failed to hold. At the Retrieve State Farm while returning from the field Dago was fatally stabbed from behind by convict Louis "Buddy" Saddler. Afterwards during another boneheaded break for the free-world, Noble Guthrie would be incurably gunned down by Correctional Officer G.R. Thompson during an escape.[19] Later during a return trip from the TPR to the Central State Farm, convicts Manuel Ward, twenty-seven, and E.M. McCoin, twenty-four, jumped ship: The duo "had filed a hole in a heavy wire enclosure on a tarpaulin-covered trailer." Their timing had been awkward, to say the least; McCoin was crushed to death falling under the vehicle's wheels. Ward did get away for awhile—but it was amid a flurry of gunfire from Correctional Officers riding in the cab, while behind the wheel, sat a "convict driver."[20] Noticeably, these breaks for liberty came after the TPR Sunday performance, not before. Watching, then running was the preferred tactic. Many, if not most, convicts, however, thought the TPR was wonderful diversion.

At least one prisoner at Houston, W.W. Barbee, yet outside The Walls was figuratively spurring hard to get his convict number before that last Sunday in October. Indicted and charged with Robbery and Forgery, "he sent word to the district attorney he wanted to plead guilty so he could get to the penitentiary before the rodeo ended." Deferentially standing before the bench of District Court Judge Langston G. Kink, the pleading Barbee had his wish granted, by the court: "I'm going to make it possible for you to see several of these rodeos. Seven years." [21]

Female prisoners from the women's unit were also regularly scheduled and shuffled visitors for the TPR performances. There a melodic ensemble, the Goree Girls, was always a runaway hit with the enthused crowd. In fact, many of those other imprisoned gals voluntarily participated in what was then a popular county-fair or picnic type event, the Greased Pig Race.

While history of the TPR is rich and its full story has been told truthfully by a prominent and professional authority as herein cited in endnotes, on occasion others seem inclined to baselessly interject agenda-driven remarks into the captivating narrative. Political correctness is not always correct. One does not have to search long in the realm of prison or correctional literature to find the ineptly tossed but missed loop of preconceived aspersions about the TPR. And though it's been penned that it was somewhat racially insensitive to have black female convicts from the Goree Unit participate in an event as demeaning as a Greased Pig Race—facts deflate innuendo. Of the several known and widely published images of the TPR Sunday afternoon Greased Pig Race a handy magnifying glass or corrective spectacles are not needed to observe the multi-ethnicity of the participants: black, white, and brown. In this instance the proof isn't in the puddin'—it's in the photographs. Likewise

some of the male yearend TPR Top Hand honors were awarded to
cowboys of color, such as Will Hodge (1935), Sim Hodge (1936),
John Parker (1945), Cruz Davila (1957, 1960), and Willie Craig
(1976). There is another tied-hard-and-fast fact, the convict cowboy winning the most Top Hand tributes before the TPR closed for
keeps in 1986 was a black man, O'Neal Browning. O'Neal chalked
up seven such envied Top Hand victories (1950, 1954, 1956, 1958,
1962, 1968, and 1973).[22] Legit cowboys understand: In the dusty
rodeo arenas all competitors bleed red and white are the broken
bones. Though rodeo arena fatalities are rare, the risk is always
there, part of the game. Convict H.P. Rich, pulling four years from
Galveston County, may have pulled his rigging too tight—or not
tight enough: "He was thrown from a steer and suffered fatal injuries."[23] Pseudo intellectuals seldom toe stirrups and top broncs or
with a gloved-hand heat resin while tightening the plaited bull-
ropes—much less chase any slippery swine.

Far from The Walls at Huntsville there was a hue and cry to stage
a TPR extravaganza in Dallas—at the State Fair grounds. Subsequent
to addressing the issues of convict security and transporting convicts
into the free-world, there was an okay to proceed with the highly
anticipated event. Advance ticket sales were more than brisk, one lady
making a request for fifty. With a cadre of 150 convicts—some rough
stock riders and steer ropers—and others serving as kitchen workers
to handle food preparation and delivery, the Grand Entry at Dallas was
good to go. The necessary caravan would understandably be accompanied by steely-eyed THP Troopers, Texas Rangers, as well as the
attendant Correctional Officer delegation. Interestingly, according to
the TPR's most knowledgeable researcher and consummate chronicler,
Texas roping steers were "too big and antisocial," at least so said Rodeo
Director Albert Moore. Therefore a smaller genealogical strain—
sometimes commonly referred to as Cracker Cattle—were gathered
in Florida and removed to Dallas. The crowd-pleasing eight-night run
came off absent a hitch or escape or a fistfight. Dallas citizens and
their neighbors had opened their wallets and purses to the tune of
$118,391, with an 80 percent cut going to the "prisoner education and

recreation fund." All and all the TPR at Dallas was graded a whopping success. It too marked TPR history: It would be the one and only time the event was staged at a free-world city, outside of Huntsville.[24]

Most assuredly forty-five-year-old convict Ed "Perchmouth" Stanton didn't consider that TPR participants—black, white, or brown—were being exploited. Whether or not Stanton was a bona fide cowboy is lost to history. What is not misplaced is that he was a genuine outlaw and a veteran of shootouts in Texas and New Mexico wherein lawmen made the ultimate sacrifice. For a short time Pearchmouth Stanton ran and robbed with a North Texas desper-ado of infamous fame, Raymond Elzie Hamilton.[25] While on the run from a jailbreak at Lubbock, Texas, after stealing sub-machineguns, Stanton and his partner, Glen Hunsucker, ambushed area lawmen on the Nalda Ranch, east of Corona in Lincoln County in the Land of Enchantment. Chief Deputy Tom Jones was killed, as was desperado Hunsucker. Perchmouth Stanton made good his getaway for only a little while. After he was apprehended authorities extradited him back to the Lone Star State and into Death Row—he having already been courtroom convicted of murdering forty-nine-year-old Swisher County Sheriff John C. Moseley at Tulia in the sparsely populated Panhandle and stealing his repeating rifle and revolver. Perchmouth Stanton was blasé. A killer through and through, ambling toward the Death Chamber "chewing on a matchstick" decreeing: "Boys, I've been wrong all my life, but I'm right now." Stanton's only genuine regret—nothing about robbing folks or killing lawmen—was that he never had a chance to fork the saddle of a pitchin' bronc, riding for an October Sunday TPR show. Perchmouth Stanton did, however, take a seat on Ole Sparky and rode it to the end.[26]

During the 1930s the aforementioned Albert Moore was chas-ing free-world aspirants, with a tongue-in-cheek tease: "Manager Albert Moore of the Texas Prison Tigers today appealed to all Texas criminals who can pitch, play first base or cavort in the outfield and pound the pellet to surrender immediately to the nearest peace offi-cer." Moore was concerned and was in dire need of "another good pitcher, a first baseman and a gardener who can swat the horsehide at a healthy clip." What would a team member get in return? Well, they would receive "three square meals a day and a 'flop' [a bed], a clean white denim suit for everyday wear, and a pretty red uniform to play in on Sundays. Plenty of guards will be available to keep away such disturbing elements as big league scouts, guys who want to make a touch [borrow something] and pop bottle barrages from the bleachers."[27] Voluntary free-world applicants were in short supply.

Quite entertainingly a 1930s baseball game between Texas Prison Tigers and Oklahoma Prison Outlaws was being touted as the "Underworld Series." The rivalry was rich. Already the Tigers had—with approval of the Prison Board—traveled to Houston for a baseball contest with a free-world team. While on the road, so to speak, the Tigers successfully triumphed in a double-header over the Brenham Sun Oilers.[28]

Some prisoners, however, had other forms of gamesmanship in mind. Convicts were tireless and served as good reminders that watchfulness is an enduring challenge for Correctional Officers— way back then, as well as today. Though the valuation seems insignificant now, in 1932 a hard 25¢ quarter was meaningful. Not unexpectedly then it should come as no shocker that convicts at The Walls, in the metal shop, had improvised a counterfeiting machine, one capable of turning out near perfect "pewter quarters." Discovered during the semi-monthly "shakedown," the then-Warden, Walter Waid, sardonically quipped that he guessed "there were some dishonest men in the state penitentiary." Federal authorities at Houston were notified.[29] Shortly thereafter, a different quintet of convicts had meanness in their hearts and ingeniousness on their minds. Again, inside the machine shop at The Walls during a routine sweep for contraband Correctional Officers found something very, very, disturbing, "homemade guns [zip guns]." The crude shooters had been fashioned from "ordinary plumbing supplies," one being a "five-barrel gun designed to fire 12-gauge shotgun shells. The other two were pistols, also built to fire 12-gauge shells." These were not look alike or dummy guns meant to scare or bluff prison staff during a break for freedom. These deadly gadgets were clearly the Real

McCoy, proven by the fact that "each weapon was tested by prison officials and was found capable of discharging shells."[30] The zip gun threat was no joking matter. Though out of chronological sync, that assertion was again brought home to Correctional Officers and lawmen during the next decade. Two dodgy convicts, Horace Posey and Jack Williams, AKA Texas Jack, jumped the Eastham State Farm and when apprehended by Dallas City Detectives they were armed with "homemade shotguns secretly fashioned from gas pipe and put together in the penitentiary. . . . The crude guns they carried, loaded with 12-gauge shotgun shells, were fashioned from pipe, plow handles, leather and rubber. A leather strap, cleverly arranged with rubber bands, served as a trigger."[31]

Soon, the in-house counterfeiters had upped their illegally minted product. Inflation! It was no longer quarters but now half-dollars. Noting that the fakeries "come out about the time of the rodeo" and that "the coins were of a quality which showed they were made by an expert counterfeiter," Warden Waid, again wryly noted: "Well, boys, this is dishonest—crooked! I'll have the law on whoever is responsible." And he surely did, seeking professional outside help. He contacted Secret Service Agent Leo J. Williams of Dallas and U.S. Postal Inspector C.W.B. Long. Their secret investigation netted results, focusing on the prison hospital, "the only place where plaster of paris for making molds could be obtained." Thereafter the investigation took them straight to the Eastham State Farm where three-time recidivist George Droddy resided. Quite interestingly Agents Williams and Long learned:

> [Droddy] had broken his arm in the prison rodeo and had while in the prison hospital stolen sufficient plaster of paris to make six molds, two of which proved good. . . . The other four molds had been destroyed by Droddy. He was getting his metal out of the machine shops. He had a ladle, facilities for melting the metal and making the casts.[32]

Following the seizure of physical evidence and taking incriminating statements, the federal authorities advised that the entire matter would be turned over to the United States Attorney at Houston, "as Huntsville is in that district."[33] Battling wits with convicts is tiresome, but they were ingenious beyond belief and not just a few were consummate whittlers.

For sure, convict tricksters could fashion what looked like a handgun and try to bluff their way out of custody, as would condemned killer Augustus Dwight Beard, twenty-seven. The Death Row convict had already killed a man in North Carolina. The "strapping former [college] football player," had for that crime, been sentenced to death—later commuted to life, and had escaped before fleeing into Texas piling up a string of Armed Robberies in Dallas/Fort Worth. While on the dodge in the Lone Star State, during a robbery in Oak Cliff (in South Dallas), he murdered former Dallas PD Detective John Rush Roberts, for which he was sentenced to die. On Death Row with some time to kill before being killed, Dwight Beard deftly carved on a bar of soap—transforming it into a damn good facsimile of a real gun. With the very scary-looking shooterless shooter, convict Beard forced Correctional Officer T.W. Arnold to remove his civilian clothes, which he then slipped into. Slyly, however, Arnold had managed to secret a most necessary prison door-key and Augustus Dwight Beard's grandiose scheme for cheating the state out of an execution was foiled. Ole Sparky, in the end, was not defrauded; Beard was executed. As so often is the case, what one convict does illicitly affects the lives of others—as a rule negatively. The administrative remedy was immediate and clear; it was ordered that individual bars of soap would no longer be allowed in convicts' houses: they could lather up in the gang-shower and, when done with their bathing, leave the soap there.[34]

Somewhat later prison officials were bowled over when they discovered a "Time Bomb" inside The Walls: "It was a piece of pipe about eight inches long, wired to four flashlight batteries and rigged to a clock. The pipe was rigged to a clock. . . . Small holes were bored in each [end] cap. Wires ran through the holes to small metal plate inside and connected to the batteries to complete the circuit."[35]

Inside the tall walls and behind the high fences ingenuity is limitlessness, but not necessarily spot on effectual.

Occasionally, if the convict's word is taken at face-value, resorting to building a weapon to injure or kill or mess with a Correctional Officer's mind was not necessary, not on certain scattered prison farms. "Sometimes the guards would decide to search the tanks. We would bring water moccasins and rattlesnakes to the tank and put them in the lockers and cabinets. After several guards had been bitten, they were leery about shaking [us] down."[36]

Herein it's but fair to report, though it might be a touch troublesome for agenda-driven revisionists. Working for the *Beaumont Enterprise*, the Police Reporter interviewed a number of ex-convicts and those still imprisoned. His findings were and would not be surprising to long-time prison personnel:

> Practically to the man these fellows maintain that those who get whipped have only themselves to blame. They've tried to get away with something they knew was against the rules, maybe only against the rules of the prison, and maybe against the rules of the state and society in general. The cons and exes, with only a minority taking exception, say that a man in the penitentiary makes his own conditions. If a fellow wants to behave and shorten his stretch by good behavior, the prison keepers are anxious to help him. If he tries to run the whole works and get away with murder (literally or figuratively) the prison is going to be hard on him. It is apparent that the guards will have riot after riot and prison break after prison break—with the loss of many lives involved—if they allow the prisoners to run the place as they choose.[37]

As already herein highlighted, the Eastham State Prison Farm was inhabited by some of the toughest of the tough, baddest of the bad. Especially convicts and prison personnel and newsmen tagged Eastham the "Little Alcatraz."[38] Chaste history does confirm that such characterization is not hyperbole. Of the several wicked villains at Eastham on 15 October 1932, three grabbed the headlines: H.G. Daniels, Buchanan Sloan, and Charley "Chuck" Wilson, all serving time for Armed Robbery. Correctional Officer John Robert Hinson, already past sixty years, was that day horseback, carrying a Hoe-Squad. Suddenly he was knocked senseless and spilled from his saddle. Then while stumbling and struggling to regain his footing, using their long-handled tools, the aforementioned convicts viciously beat Hinson into unconsciousness and fled, taking the state's revolver and shotgun with them. Speaking well of the remaining Hoe-Squad convicts, they carefully conveyed John Robert back to Eastham headquarters for removal to an area hospital. Not unexpectedly a posse and tracking dogs were soon onsite. That evening, about 8:00 p.m. the manhunt and dog hunt for Chuck Wilson came to an end. When cornered he spurned orders to surrender. Correctional Officer John Cothorn shot him—mortally.[39] The following day, near Madisonville, Sloan and Daniels were run to ground and taken into custody, still in possession of Correctional Officer Hinson's weapons. And this, the safe return of convicts, seems in some way to mitigate the innuendo driven into some Texas prison narratives, many times unsupported by hard facts and/or admissible evidence, that callous Correctional Officers more-often-than-not murdered convicts in the river bottoms, rather than returning them to unit headquarters. Misconduct is wrong! But not everyone misbehaved! Even with attentive care at the Huntsville Hospital, Hinson's severe and unprovoked beating had been more than his body and age could withstand. He died on 3 November 1932, a Thursday, survived by his wife Ellie Smith Hinson and two of their children.[40]

With perverse spirit the Texas State Prison Board ginned-up some bad holiday news for employees. They would suffer an across-the-board 20 percent salary reduction. Rather anemically it was proffered: "We recognize the valuable services and long hours given by the employees of the system and this action is taken solely as an economy and emergency measure. The board members and general manager hereby voluntarily agree to a like reduction in their respective per diem and salary."[41] Merry Christmas!

The following year, 1933, a newspaper heralded a Texas prison first: "When the huge steel doors clanged shut behind [Norman L.]

Speer." He had returned to The Walls front gate and stepped inside to "don the garb of a convict."[42] Subsequent to his earlier-cited 1928 resignation as Warden at The Walls, Speer, during the two-year election cycles, had been three times elected Walker County Sheriff. Without resorting to non-penitentiary business Sheriff Speer found himself the subject of a successful criminal investigation revolving around financial affairs—and rightly or wrongly caught three years to do. He resigned his county post, and his wife Lela Mae Speer was appointed to fill his yet unexpired term.[43] Apparently the ex-Warden and ex-Sheriff harbored no rancor with prison officialdom. As a "good sport" he went through the booking procedures—fingerprinting and photographing—publicly proclaiming that he for sure intended to be "a good convict."[44] Quite interestingly, at the time M.D. Seay, son of Ed L. Seay, an Assistant Manager at one of the Ramsey Camps, was growing up on state-owned property. He knew and made observations about the former Warden and Sheriff—living as a convict:

> Since he was a former prison official and sheriff it was considered unsafe for him to be confined with other inmates. He was sent to the Ramsey Farm to work as a stock man trusty. There were several white trusties at the Ramsey at that time. They lived in a bunkhouse located near the site where the big barn had been located before it burned. These men were not locked up at night and ate their meals at a table set up especially for them in the guards [sic] dining room. The former warden was somewhere between fifty and sixty years old and had not ridden a horse in many years, yet he was required to ride the pasture ten to twelve hours every day but never complained. He was sore and stiff for a week or two but soon became accustomed to riding. It was amazing how quickly this man adjusted to life as a convict. He was polite to everyone and never spoke unless he was spoken to first. He kept his dignity but was never offensive. I like this man and admired the way he handled himself.[45]

And it's but fair to make mention, before he pulled a full year wearing prison-issued whites and riding the Texas Prison range, the indomitable Governor Ma Ferguson granted the forty-nine year-old Norman L. Speer a Full Pardon, due to his "clear prison record and [he] has been an exemplary prisoner during his incarceration."[46] Perhaps in this instance the compassion was but just—if according to a newspaper report the bookkeeping misunderstanding was widespread. During a purposeful but selective statewide audit the accounting of and fee system collections had been mismanaged in as many as thirty-two Sheriff's offices. N.L. Speer, of that crowd, was the only one to suffer an indictment and the resulting penitentiary time. The ex-Sheriff and former ex-convict had always—from the get-go—asserted his innocence due to an absence of mens rea (criminal intent).[47] Somewhat bolstering his claim, Norman L. Speer later served as the Sergeant at Arms for the Texas State Senate at Austin.[48]

Lamentably, perhaps, two convicts confined at two separate places didn't opt to wait out the governor for their chance at a pardon. Their 1930s miscalculated escapade would end with the same fate for both. At the Ferguson State Farm, a black convict, Dave Ladd, forty-two, a Forger from Chambers County (county seat Anahuac), jumped mean. Subsequent to taking a water break, Ladd was ordered back to work on the line. Apparently Ladd had other plans. Grabbing a hoe Ladd laid into the Dog Sergeant, P.N. Long. Whether his intentions were just striking his keeper or killing him is and would be irreverent. For that instant it was do or die and Dog Sergeant Long chose to live, drawing his revolver and putting a round in Ladd's head, killing him where he stood. Justifiable Homicide—by the book! On that very same summer day at the Ramsey State Farm, thirty-year-old Juan Lopez, doing 100 years hard time for an Assault to Rape in Bexar County, opted to quit the farm. Juan stole a state-owned horse and an axe, riding away—with any luck unnoticed. It was a mistake, a big mistake. Correctional Officers and the Dog Sergeant with Bloodhounds were soon on the chase. They found where Juan had chopped his way through one fence and then at a second fence—evidently cautious of wasting too much time—Lopez shed the stolen horse, continuing his flight afoot. After covering three more miles, the escapee was overhauled and yet while running was commanded to halt. He ignored the voice command, as well as the succeeding two warning shots. The third shot carried no disregarded warning. The revolver round connected, "a pistol wound to the brain."[49] Though it might seem insensitive—a footrace with a bullet has a predictable winner.

Regardless of the prisoner, the prison business is the people's business and the people's business takes no holidays—then or now. During the decade's first year, General Manager Lee Simmons noted that at The Wall's shoe-shop, eighty industrious convicts had manufactured 30,000 pairs of shoes. The newspaper reporter penned with delight: ". . . Simmons is wearing a pair that has the appearance of a neat job. The shoes are used by convicts and inmates of state institutions. This saves the State from paying out hard cash for shoes."[50] By May of 1933 there was even bigger and better economic news for the Texas Prison System—the License Plate business. Heretofore the fabrication of Texas auto tags had been contracted with outside and out-of-state vendors at a cost of $105,000 annually. And, irony of ironies, some of those license plates may have actually been manufactured behind the tall walls of other state's penitentiaries. Heavy thinkers at the Texas Statehouse had passed a bill mandating that license plates be manufactured in Texas—and furthermore with regards to that ever touchy issue of interfering with free-world markets, it was duly noted: "In this particular instance, the prison system will not be competing with any existing Texas firm, for the state always has gone afield for its plates. . . . Machinery will be installed in the Texas penitentiary and the convicts will do the work."[51] All so soon, in 1937, it would be reported that just for the License Plate Factory the Texas prison industry was consuming "900 tons of steel, 8,000 gallons of background enamels and approximately 8,500 pounds of numeral coating inks" packaged in "35,000 cartons weighing 20 tons; 1800 reams of glassine paper for envelopes, weighing 13½ tons; 65,000 craft envelopes, weighing more than a ton, and five tons of newsprint used between the pairs of license plates after they are packed." Shortly (in 1939, it will be reported that if the prison-manufactured license plates of the season were laid end to end, "they'd make a path almost entirely across the state at its widest part, or, to put it into miles, something like 720 miles of plates. . . . There will be no waste. . . . prison trucks are rumbling over Texas roads delivering the license plates to the 254 counties. All deliveries will be made this way."[52] And as but a quick sidebar, years later it will be reported that the TDC License Plate factory successfully—during a bidding process—won contracts to manufacture auto tags for Kentucky and Illinois.[53] Though it might sound somewhat trite—the business of making license plates is big business.

Unquestionably for prison settings, protection and pecuniary headaches measure as migraine, perpetually so. Logistical nightmares are driven home by just rattling off the fare for another holiday feast inside The Walls: "The dinner menu consists of 140 gobblers from the Eastham farm, 1000 pounds of dressing—about a pound to the man—100 gallons of gravy, 50 gallons of fruit salad, 72 gallons of cranberry sauce, 40 gallons of creamed corn with pimentos; 1200 quarters of cherry pie, 2400 cups of coffee, 240 loaves of white bread and 36 dozen stalks of celery."[54]

Yet one must never forget, although atypical—family members of personnel at The Walls or living on the State Prison farms could be at risk: "A negro [sic] convict at Clemens State Farm near here [Brazoria] was captured by other convicts late Thursday after he had attempted to assault the wife of one of the guards. The convict, a trusty, armed with a large butcher knife, threatened the woman. She fought him off and screamed. Her cries and those of her children attracted the attention of several other negro trusties who rushed to her aid and disarmed the assailant." The attacker caught the next chain to Huntsville, perhaps as a precautionary measure for his own good.[55] The fact that other convicts had overpowered and disarmed the would-be rapist is salient evidence men who have in the past gone wrong can do right.

Naturally other convicts were not attuned to doing right. At the Central State Farm, a prisoner from Northeast Texas (in Leonard, Fannin County), James W. Dovell, twenty-four, had been working, weeding, and sweating in the gargantuan cotton fields flanking a Gulf Coast convict from Anahuac in Chambers County, James Earl "Jas' Broussard, Jr., twenty-nine, doing a nickel for Armed Robbery. Stopping at the turn-row for a drink of water, for some undisclosed reason Dovell swung his Aggie from overhead and began chopping at the utterly dismayed Broussard, which is somewhat surprising since Jas had proven experience in the boxing rings at Houston and was a U.S. Army veteran. The Field Boss hollered for Dovell to cease and desist, but was flatly ignored. Repeatedly swinging the hoe, the berserk convict continued with his unchecked madness. Smartly keeping his distance, the Field Boss did what he had to do. He put a revolver round into Dovell. The stupidity stopped. James W. Dovell died on the turn-row. Unfortunately, Jas Broussard lingered in the hospital; then died of a "Fracture of the Skull, Sub-Temporal Decompression."[56] Outside on open ground the Field Bosses and convicts were both hoeing a tough row, the former figuratively, the latter literally.

Texas Prison Farms, aside from the administrative buildings and dormitories, were not closed off from the world by high boundary fences topped with razor-wire, but were open and adjoining private acreage and public rivers. Smuggling contraband onto prison lands—stashing it at the unit's edge—was child's play. For a few untrustworthy trustys it was a perfect setup. For the right price—and it varied—be it real green money, mind-altering drugs, clandestine sex, prohibited pornography, or store-bought liquor, what was sneakily ditched at the state property's perimeter could readily find its way into evil hands. Correctional Officer J.R. McCall, a three-year veteran with the Texas Prison System, learned the hard way at the Central Farm Unit near Sugar Land. During the wee morning hours convict Beaumont King, doing a nickel and dime, began whining he was in desperate need of medicine. The convict's reputation did not leave one to believe that he was really very dangerous or too much of an escape risk. There could even be reasonable argument that Beaumont King had really been duped, led astray by experienced convicts needing an upfront man to jump first, taking the real dicey chance. At any rate a 9mm German Luger had ended up in his hands, a pistol that had earlier been concealed in a stuffed cotton sack. Of course Correctional Officer McCall knew naught. He humanely stepped forward to aid convict Beaumont King with whatever medical malady, getting too close, to his detriment. King shoved the business end of the pistol into McCall's chest and a bullet spit forth. Accident? Conspiracy? Purposeful? Of course it really mattered not a damn whit to Correctional Officer J.R. McCall. As he was staggering in pain and collapsing, he drew his holstered handgun and put a round between Beaumont's lungs. Both men were hospitalized. Ultimately King was released back into the Central Unit's mainline population. Correctional Officer J.R. McCall was unfortunately released to an undertaker, dying on 27 August 1933. Compassion can prove costly—particularly in penitentiary settings![57]

And, wayward juveniles can be deadly too. At Gatesville, inside the blacksmith shop at the State Reformatory, sometimes benignly referred to as the State Juvenile Training School, four teens jumped. Viciously the beardless gangsters buried an axe blade—repeatedly—in the head of William Jackson "Will" Leonard, forty-eight, a State of Texas employee for the previous fourteen years. Stealing Leonard's auto, a black sedan, the murderous boy thugs were phantoms. While they were on the run, with his loving wife Lea at graveside, Will Leonard was laid to rest in the Turnersville Cemetery, at Turnersville, Coryell County. Later the stolen car was found abandoned near Meridian, Bosque County.[58] The boys, unfortunately for them in the big picture, were later apprehended and subsequent to sentencing by an unsympathetic jury imprisoned.[59]

Simply for broad-spectrum perspective, peeking in on the Texas Prison System's rather extensive land holdings in the 1930s is interesting as well as informative. According to an official survey conducted by the State of Texas Reclamation Department, not factoring in The Walls in downtown Huntsville and the adjacent penitentiary cemetery, Peckerwood Hill (now the Joe Byrd Cemetery), the state prison farm's acreage tallied at:[60]

Blue Ridge	4,505.48
Central	5,202.88
Clemens	8,115.91
Darrington	6,770.13
Eastham	12,969.66
Ferguson	4,344.20
Goree	966.88
Harlem	5,656.65
Prison Dairy	92.77
Ramsey	15,088.58
Retrieve	7,454.62
Wynne	1,912.59

7

"Put them on the spot"

REAL-ESTATE COMPUTATIONS ASIDE, the sixteenth day of January 1934 would mark heartbreak, again, for the Texas Prison System. It would prove a seminal installment of criminality: One nurturing gruesome headlines, deathly electrical currents, and a lethal barrage of buckshot and bullets, which would necessitate closing the lids on five caskets.

Eastham Prison Farm, Camp No. 1 would provide the wretched backdrop. The weirdly wired cop-killer Clyde Chestnut Barrow and two of his cohorts in crime, the undeniably incorrigible blue-eyed Bonnie Parker and just-released ex-convict James "Jimmy" Mullins AKA James Kinley AKA James Miller AKA James Muller AKA Jimmy LaMont, forty-eight, an eight-time dope-addicted recidivist, would figuratively and then literally pull the nasty conspiracy's trigger, setting the high-drama in play. It would be Clyde Barrow's third visit to Eastham. The first was as a state prisoner where and when he may or may not have been brutally and repeatedly sodomized by the afore-mentioned Ed Crowder and where he may or may not have murdered convict Crowder with a pipe-wrench in revenge for such an uninvited up close and personal penetration.[1] The second trip to Eastman was as a free-wheeling fast-driving bandit when Clyde drove Jimmy Mullins and Floyd Hamilton to the prison farm so they could conceal a rubber inner-tube inside a culvert near a turn-row. From there an under-handed trustee, Fred Yost, would retrieve the two Colt 1911 .45s and extra loaded magazines from their stretchy packaging, smuggling the pistols inside the dormitory—and into the waiting hands, as it turned out, of outlaw Joseph Conger "Joe" Palmer, spending his precious quarter for Armed Robbery. Also in the heinous mix for an at-all-cost breakout was the previously mentioned Raymond Elzie "Ray" Hamilton, Floyd's younger brother, who was downcast and dejectedly pulling more than 250 years hard-time for some of his felonies, including a suspected Murder in Central Texas.[2]

Clyde Barrow, accompanied by Bonnie Parker and Jimmy Mullins, made his third trip to Eastham on the rather foggy and misty morning of 16 January 1934, the preplanned day for the big-time breakout. Secreting themselves in the screening timber, Clyde and Jimmy, armed with Browning Automatic Rifles (BARs), waited for prison Hoe-Squads and their keepers to march into view. Bonnie had remained with the getaway car on the very secluded Calhoun Ferry Road. Unbeknownst for sure to the liberators, two other convicts, killer Hilton Bybee and highjacker Henry Methvin, wanted in and would jump too. Carrying Joe Palmer's assigned Hoe-Squad (gathering and stacking wood this day) was the mounted Correctional Officer Olin Bozeman, who had not incorrectly noticed that Ray Hamilton had sneakily maneuvered himself into his work crew, where he definitely wasn't supposed to be. Assuming the position of what today is known as a mounted High-Rider, but then the "long-arm man" or "backfield man," and armed with a .38 caliber revolver and a repeating .30-30 rifle, was a thirty-three-year-old former barber from Lovelady, east of the Trinity River and just up the road from the Eastham Prison Farm, Houston County, Major (name not rank) Joseph "Joe" Crowson.[3] According to General Manager Lee Simmons the young man from Lovelady had been so selected because he was "highly trustworthy," was really an excellent marksman, as well as possessing praiseworthy personality traits of "discretion and courage." Then or now at Texas penitentiaries the High-Rider's duty is clear, as then explained by Lee Simmons:

> It was to be his business to be around on the edges of the area
> where convicts were working, especially when the group was near
> standing timber or when opportunity for escape was better than

common. The backfield man was not assigned to guard any particular squad. He had no duty except to stay well clear of the convicts and to be in the background ready with his Winchester in case of any excitement. The prisoners seldom knew precisely where he was, and this uncertainty had its value in keeping the bad men under effective control.[4]

By anyone's take the morning's haze lent its eeriness to the stage of the day's upcoming tragedy. Understandably Correctional Officer Bozeman was facing a dilemma of sorts; he had a convict not assigned to his Hoe-Squad, Raymond Hamilton. Bozeman signaled for Crowson to join him for a confab—the misaligned headcount would be easy to fix. Unfortunately, Correctional Officer Crowson forewent adhering to accepted protocol, reining and nudging his mount too close to Boss Bozeman's Hoe-Squad. The opportunity for incapacitating the only rifleman—the one who could really thwart an escape—presented, Joe Palmer took advantage of Joe Crowson's slip-up. A Colt 1911 .45 barked and spit and Correctional Officer Crowson spun in the saddle, gut shot! With grit Correctional Officer Crowson—reeling in pain—managed to stay topside and trotted back to Camp 1 headquarters to sound the alarm.

In the meantime, back in the foggy field, it turned even more Western. Boss Bozeman and escapee Joe Palmer were trading shots. Boss Bozeman's revolver's round creased Palmer's temple, and Joe Palmer's .45 bullet struck the Correctional Officer's saddle scabbard and shotgun then ricocheted into his hip—painfully disabling him from further gunplay. Purportedly, and self-servingly, convict Raymond Hamilton would later maintain that he had inadvertently thumbed the magazine release and the .45's clip in his pistol had fallen into the dirt at his feet. That would be then. Now, during the pandemonium of a genuine chaotic assault and prison break, the crescendo of sounds ratcheted as Clyde and Jimmy began laying down a horrific covering fire with their BARs while Bonnie laid into the Ford's horn—the indicator to those running and ducking in the haze as to where the getaway car was parked.

With near 200 convicts in the squads scampering for cover and two or three keepers forsaking duty and hotfooting the opposite way, a daunting and dangerous task fell to another stand-your-ground Correctional Officer. Particularly, one of the convicts in one of the Hoe-Squads vividly remembered that day:

> Raymond Hamilton and Joe Palmer got the guns and began pouring lead into the guards. Major Clowson [sic], a guard, was mortally wounded. Hamilton, Palmer, Henry Methvin, and Hilton Bybee escaped with Bonnie and Clyde. Several of the guards were wounded and several ran. B.B. Bullard made the inmates in the squad lie on the ground and he fired at Clyde, Hamilton, and the others. We were all trying to find a hole to get in or someway to protect ourselves. We didn't know what was happening.[5]

Unmistakably the gutsy Correctional Officer's true heroism and display of raw courage did not go unrecognized, not by Lee Simmons:

> Two of the guards lost their nerve and fled. But guard [Bobbie aka Dub] Bullard stood fast, shotgun at the ready, roaring out to the squad men to the right and left of him to lie down in their tracks. The first man to raise his head, he shouted, would have it blown clear off his shoulders. The heads stayed down. Had it not been for Bullard, there is no telling what might have happened.[6]

What did happen was that half a dozen dodgy yahoos plus one, Barrow, Parker, Mullins, Hamilton, Palmer, Methvin, and Bybee, piled into the Ford coupe and were now on the run, gone!

James B. "Jim" French, a twenty-four-year-old convict with numerous felonies typed on his rap-sheet and earlier stints of imprisonment in Oklahoma and Texas, was not a part of the initial breakout plan. French simply took advantage of the machinegun mayhem and disappeared into the Trinity River's bottomland labyrinth of thorns, tangles, and treacherous undercurrents. Simply stated Jim French got lost—but the state's Bloodhounds didn't. The paid Dog Sergeant and his convict Dog Boys put the skids on French's flight before he had gone too terribly far.

Joe Crowson had gone, too—to the hospital at Huntsville. His physical prognosis was not good, but his mental anguish was worse. He knew he had blundered, and when Lee Simmons visited him at bedside, Crowson apologized: "don't think hard of me. I know I didn't carry out your instructions. I'm sorry."[7] Simmons's first retort—on the whole—was questionably sincere, "Don't bother about it . . . I'm for you." The bottom half, however, was pure and plain, hard and heartless: "Those fellows had their day; we'll have ours. I promise you I won't let them get away with it." He didn't speak the words to the lingering but obviously dying man, but Lee Simmons was not pleased with Eastham's High-Rider: "Crowson's duty was to stay away from the prison gang at work and never to go near them at any time. He was a crack shot with both revolver and Winchester. Had he kept his post on the edge of the timber, things would have turned out differently, I have no doubt. . . . If Crowson had been where he belonged when the break occurred, however, some men might have been killed, but I don't believe any of them would have got away. . . ."[8] What was slipping away was Major Joseph Crowson's earthly existence, the bullet tearing through his intestines in several places and pneumonia that had set in were more than he could endure and he didn't. Joseph Crowson passed to the other side on 27 January 1934. He was respectfully and peacefully laid to rest at Lovelady in the Evergreen Cemetery.[9] General Manager Lee Simmons, however, was not at rest—peacefully or otherwise—he was damn mad and damn determined.

For starters he fired the Correctional Officers who had fled rather than fight—or at least stood pat and assured that their Hoe-Squads didn't take flight. He was adamant. For future Texas prison work they were blacklisted. Undeniably Lee Simmons was somewhat personally embarrassed by the daytime raid on Eastham. He was more cognizant, however, of the need for putting the check on what he genuinely interpreted as an unprecedented assault on institutional government: "The killings of our guards involved a fundamental principal of justice. Also they constituted a fundamental hazard to our whole system of prison management. If such murders could be committed with impunity, we would have to change our whole manner of handling convicts in the field. . . . The Eastham farm raid was the first of its kind. . . . It is true that the fortitude of guard Bullard did keep nearby prisoners from getting away, but that couldn't be hoped for in the future, if machine-gun raids became common affairs. So I made my plans for retribution on those responsible for the Eastham affair."[10]

And he knew—as did everyone else—including newspapermen, just who was responsible.[11] Though he has earned censure from armchair critics—with regards to some things justifiably so—Lee Simmons knew the dirty ins and outs of dealing with convicts and ex-convicts, their proclivity for cutting deals in their self-interest. He well-knew that absent an out-and-out fluke, apprehending the murderous outlaws would call for putting "somebody on the ground," a not oblique reference to the governor granting clemency or a pardon to a snitch. Betrayal is not an uncommon commodity in the underworld. Already coming out of the woodwork, as is typical, Lee Simmons "was being approached by several of Barrow's former associates, both in the penitentiary and on the outside, who were offering to help put Clyde and Bonnie on the spot."[12]

One in particular—and not surprisingly—after he split from the escapees was Jimmy Mullins. According to Lee Simmons, "Mullin[s] was already in trouble again, having stolen some guns and ammunition from a federal armory. Thus he was sure of imprisonment again, either by Uncle Sam or by the state of Texas. Mullin[s] didn't like to work, and he had already had a taste of labor as it is required on the Eastham Farm. Accordingly he struck a bargain with us: if we would let him serve his next term at the federal prison, instead of at Eastham Farm, he would tell us what he knew about the break. We figured we needed help in the form of information more than Mullin[s] needed a choice of prisons, so we agreed."[13]

General Manager Simmons was proactive—he wanted someone to hunt the liable outlaws, not continually come up a day late and a dollar short, chasing after them following their latest heist or next reprehensible homicide. Not surprisingly for this manhunt his thinking turned to fellows who had made good names for themselves while serving the state as Texas Rangers. One well-known outlaw, Ralph Fults, said General Manager Lee Simmons had a short-list in mind: The aforementioned Manuel Terrazas "Lone Wolf" Gonzaullas, Thomas Rufus "Tom" Hickman, along with Francis Augustus "Frank" Hamer, and future captain Fred L. McDaniel.[14] Although it might tend to deflate legend, at that time Lee Simmons, by his own words, was a bit conflicted: "[Prison] Board members asked me who this person would be, and I answered that I did not yet know but that when I made up my mind I did not intend that they or anybody else should know who he was. I had my eye on one or two former Ranger captains. I weighed my choice strictly on the basis of who could be the best man for the job. Barrow was a desperado with no regard for human life, a man who despised the law and hated all peace officers. Whoever stopped Clyde Barrow would do so at the risk of his life."[15]

Once he had the okay from the Prison Board to hire a Special Escape Investigator for the Texas Prison System and the concurrence of Texas Governor Miriam Amanda "Ma" Ferguson regarding cutting secret deals with outlaws and who he would hire, Lee Simmons put ex-Ranger Frank Hamer on the penitentiary payroll at $180 per month and per diem.[16] Clyde Barrow and Bonnie Parker had already validated—and would soon do so again—that they absolutely had no regard for human life, excepting theirs. In policing lingo they were "Bought and Paid For," meaning their criminality and string of killings was so atrocious and they were so poisonously dangerous that shooting first—protecting oneself—was not unwise and would likely stand up in court anywhere, anytime. With that in mind, Lee Simmons's parting words to prison employee Frank Hamer should not be a maudlin shocker: "Captain, it is foolish for me to try to tell you anything; but in my judgment, the thing for you to do is put them on the spot, know you are right—and then shoot everybody in sight."[17]

Although the day-by-day intricacies and interviews during the manhunt are retrievable, having been revived and reprinted for what seems innumerable books and articles and documentaries, for the treatment in hand a skeletal remark or two will suffice. That it was smart to get in the first lick when approaching Clyde and Bonnie and their thieving pals was piercingly amplified on Easter Sunday, 1 April 1934. Northeast of Fort Worth, near Grapevine in Tarrant County, two Texas Highway Department motorcycle patrolmen, Edward Bryan "Ed" Wheeler, twenty-six, and twenty-two-year-old rookie lawman Holloway Daniel "H.D." Murphy, were cold-bloodedly murdered as they dismounted their bikes thinking of assisting the stranded motorists with car trouble. They lay dead in the dirt—Bonnie and Clyde and Henry Methvin burned rubber for parts unknown: maybe Oklahoma, Arkansas, Missouri—or Louisiana?

Though the grist is there for grinding out a showstopper story, for this rendering quickly moving to the bottom-line and finish-line will suffice. Due to General Manager Lee Simmons acting as the conduit for deal-making between the governor and a desperado and his family, and the surreptitiousness of a Louisiana sheriff in knowing the right go-between to put wrong people in the cross-hairs of cold-hearted deception, the deadly endgame starts taking shape.[18] Mix in a half-dozen Texas and Louisiana legitimate triggermen and the last breaths of murderous misfits are numbered.

On the morning of 23 May 1934, not too far from Gibsland, Bienville Parish, northwestern Louisiana, Sheriff Henderson Jordan and his deputy Prentiss Oakley were covertly holding an ambuscade line with four hardened and committed lawmen from the Lone Star State: Dallas County Deputies Ted Hinton and Bob Alcorn, former Texas Ranger but then working for the Texas Highway Department, Benjamin Maney Gault, and the Texas Prison System's Special Escape Investigator Frank Hamer, who was carrying a THD commission but was drawing his state paycheck siphoning from Simmons's prison budget.[19] And as planned when Clyde braked the rolling tan Ford to a sudden stop and while Bonnie was frowning and querying why, the heretofore hidden lawmen stood up, fast unleashing hellfire—discharging auto-loading rifles, a machinegun, and shotguns. For Mr. Barrow and Miss Parker, the fusillade was fatal.

While it's conclusively acknowledged that the concealed lawmen fired the first—and only shots—other dynamics merit attention. With six lawmen simultaneously letting loose with the blistering barrage of bullets—all fast squeezing triggers—crediting any single individual with killing Bonnie or Clyde or Bonnie and Clyde flies in the face of intellectual logic or country-boy commonsense.[20] Aside from the categorical advantage of opening the encounter with utter surprise—shock and awe—the shooters' closeness to their targets was key to ensuring safety and success. The actual distance between Clyde's and Bonnie's death car and the posse's tactically situated blind was twenty-five to thirty feet—a classroom's dimensions—direct hits during a machinegun and buckshot volley were surefire. The short gap between shooters and scoundrels guaranteed at least a few bullets would tear into their targets. Of course the reverse is true: at that short distance lawmen were, too, standing in the jaws of death. First shots were vital for survival. The smartly planned feat was openly confirmed by Special Escape Investigator Frank Hamer: "we had constructed a blind from pine branches within about twenty-five or thirty feet of the point where the car would stop."[21] Mincing words was not in Frank Hamer's makeup, telling an impatient newspaper reporter for the *St. Louis Post-Dispatch* during an impromptu telephone interview: "Sure, I can tell you what happened this morning. We just shot the devil out of them, that's all. That's all there was to it. We just laid a trap for them. A steel trap. You know, Bessemer steel, like gun barrels are made of. I hate to bust a cap on a woman, especially when she was sitting down. However, if it wouldn't have been her, it would have been us."[22]

With regards to another chancy lawman's preplanned Winchester and six-shooter scenario, nearly a half-century earlier, 1889, Rangers John Reynolds Hughes, Bazzell Lamar Outlaw, and Calvin Grant Aten laid a trap for the notorious Odle brothers, Will and Alvin, at the east foot of Bullhead Mountain, Edwards County (county seat Rocksprings). Long after the shooting stopped and the outlaw brothers were pushing up daises, an aging and somberly musing Cal Aten wrote to his brother Austin Ira Aten, by then a former Ranger and sheriff in two Texas Counties, Fort Bend and Castro: "I am responsible for [missing word] but you will understand that it pertains to the time the Odle boys were assassinated. That is all it was just plain legal assassination. However, there would have been someone else assassinated if we hadn't got the first shots."[23] Thirsting to survive is timeless.

Although there is a "rest of the story" with regards to the generalized Clyde and Bonnie narrative, for the purposes of this treatment—the saga of the Texas Prison System—being short-stopped by too much collateral detail is inappropriate and certainly unnecessary. The bad Eastham escapees of 16 January 1934—Joe Crowson's murderers—were finally run to ground and caged. The sly deal for Henry putting Clyde and Bonnie "on the spot" was honored in the Lone Star State. However the Sooner State wanted—and got—their piece of Methvin. He caught a life sentence at their penitentiary after the Oklahoma Court of Appeals washed away his execution date for offing Constable Carl (Cal) Campbell at Commerce, Ottawa County. As mentioned earlier Jim French was rounded up—lost and miserable—shortly after his failed getaway. Fugitive Hilton Bybee—subsequent to looting a National Guard Armory of sixty-three Colt 1911 .45s at Jacksboro in Jack County—gave up the ghost during a rip-roaring gunplay at Monticello in Drew County, Arkansas. And talkative Jimmy Mullins was snitching for dollars and leniency to General Manager Lee Simmons and for Dallas area lawmen—local, state, and federal. Not surprisingly the boneheaded Mullins during a pathetic Armed Robbery threatened to blow folks to smithereens with nitroglycerin, which in fact was really turpentine. His ensuing twenty-five-year trip to the Wynne State Farm near pretty Huntsville town punctuated Jimmy's foolhardiness.[24]

The manhunt for the Eastham Prison Farm escapees had, of course, been joined by many law enforcing agencies—Raymond Hamilton and Joe Palmer were on the loose. Short and snappily listing some of the Texas Rangers involved in the ongoing hunt serves to illustrate the close and ongoing interdepartmental relationship between the Texas Prison administrators and the Rangers: Captains Dennis Estill Hamer (Frank's brother), Harry T. Odneal, and E.H. Hammond. Also in on the pursuit were Texas Ranger Sergeant

Joseph "Joe" Osaba and Texas Ranger Privates James J. "Jim" Shown, Joe H. Brannon, and Winburne Reese Todd.[25]

In northeast Texas near Howe, south of Sherman in Grayson County, Raymond Hamilton topped a hill and the lawmen's roadblock was unavoidable and his undoing, which he realized at once. Stopping and exiting the vehicle before it collided with squad cars, with his hands held high and a smirk, Raymond Hamilton quipped: "Don't shoot boys, I'm fresh out of guns, ammo, whiskey and women."[26] That left Joe Palmer on the dodge. Subsequent to a squalling and breathtaking car chase—involving three hostages—fugitive Joe Palmer was taken into custody at St. Joseph, Missouri.[27] Shortly thereafter, at Huntsville, Lee Simmons welcomed both outlaws to his bed and breakfast address, The Walls.

And for their part in the ongoing drama—and the ins and outs make for an interesting legal read—Ray Hamilton and Joe Palmer were destined for the Death Chamber for killing High-Rider Joe Crowson, despite the fact Raymond was yelping he hadn't fired his pistol having inadvertently disengaged the clip from the .45 pistol's magazine-well. There would be, as might be expected, conflicting witness testimony with that defense tactic—whether accurate or perjured—and Joe Palmer really did try to take the fall for Raymond Hamilton's participation in the murder. District Judge S.W. Dean had had an earful: "Joe, you have had a fair trial. . . . It is not up to you to say whether Hamilton is guilty or not guilty. It doesn't matter which one of you killed Major Crowson. You were both shooting at him and therefore were equally guilty."[28] Though Ray was crying for post-conviction leniency, Governor James Burr V. "Jimmie" Allred wasn't buying the hog. The 1935 "Outstanding Young Man in America" was a staunch law and order man, a former District Attorney and Attorney General.[29] He was deaf to the whining excuse espoused by the condemned defendant, declaring: "The record shows that Raymond Hamilton planned and provided the weapons for a wholesale delivery from the prison farm which resulted in Crowson's murder. The record shows that both Hamilton and Palmer fired on two guards, that Guard Crowson was killed and Guard Bozeman seriously wounded. . . . If Hamilton did not kill Crowson, it was due to his marksmanship not his intentions."[30]

Pending their preset date with the executioner Joe Palmer and Raymond Hamilton were whiling away precious time on Death Row—evilness overriding contrition. For the short version it's only necessary to mention but a handful of other convicts also doing time at The Walls: William Jennings Bryan "Whitey" Walker, a first-rate gangster and second-rate fugitive, Eldridge Roy Johnson AKA Charlie Frazier, outlaw and escape artist supreme, Roy Alvin Johnson, a former promising ball player but now a convicted cop-killer, Herbert A. "Hub" Stanley, a "lifer," and another Death Row convict, bank robber and wounded veteran of police shootouts Irvin Newton "Blackie" Thompson, purportedly, at least according to a Texas Ranger Captain, "the meanest man he ever handled in Montgomery County."[31]

General Manager Lee Simmons would have another bad day on July 22, 1934, perhaps the "hardest jolt" he suffered throughout his entire penitentiary administration.[32] Or as a judicious researcher and adept writer wryly postulates: "the most dynamic and crow-eating escape in the history of the Texas Penal system."[33] Most of the involuntary residents were keenly watching and cheering for the convict baseball team, the Tigers, who were in a pitched campaign for hits and homeruns with a free-world team, the Humble Oilers from Brenham.[34] The winner would be irrelevant to those afore-named convicts, no matter what the scoreboard registered. With three smuggled Colt .45 autoloaders, courtesy a corrupt Correctional Officer, and prepositioned getaway automobiles with thrill-seeking and dishonest sisters (maybe?) behind the steering-wheels parked outside The Walls—the newsy "Death-Cell Break" kicked off in earnest.[35] When the sun went down that Sunday afternoon there were injured Correctional Officers, injured fellows bleeding real blood on their prison issued whites and stripes, plus one DRT convict. In spite of the high drama, three Death Row convicts were over the wall and inside the speeding getaway cars leaving Huntsville in a state of humiliation and a cloud of dust.

Understandably—facing cocked .45s—Correctional Officers Lee Brazil and Carey Burdeaux had been quickly rendered noncombatants. Scarily and uncomfortably that was not true for Correctional Officer H.E. George, who had been grazed by the bullet fired by a would-be escapee. Correctional Officer W.W. Roberts, who was in a tower picket, had observed convicts ascending the inside of the prison's tall wall on a filched institutional fire-house (a paint shop in other versions) ladder and quick jumping to the grass between the exterior wall and the sidewalk. He promptly phoned the front office sounding the general alarm, alerting staff that a firefight and escape was unfolding. Correctional Officer Ed Roberts from a distant picket tower had seen what was happening and shouldered his Winchester. One of Roberts's bullets had slammed into Charlie Frazier, toppling him to the prison yard's floor—inside the tall wall. Next to feel the hot sting of a true-blue Correctional Officer had been gangster Whitey Walker who caught a hot bullet to his side, a lung shot through and through, fired by W.W. Roberts. Whitey collapsed and died. Regaining his footing the wounded Frazier had tried for the ladder again, but was once more grounded, this time by three bullets—thoroughly incapacitated but not dead. Still not over the wall convict Roy Alvin Johnson had suffered a non-life threatening flesh wound and surrendered before adrenalin flooded and flushed maddened Correctional Officers' commonsense into the abyss of unreasonable force. Hub Stanley taking in the late July fireworks and his comrades spurting blood had taken cover fast, choosing to be a live Huntsville convict rather than a dead yearend Austin statistic. And though it necessitates a brief sidebar, later Hub Stanley would orchestrate another prison break, with J.C. Britton: rob a bank in the Texas Panhandle at Friona in Parmer County, shoot it out with Fort Worth police, and catch federal time in Leavenworth and Alcatraz, before being returned in chains to finish the term he owed the Lone Star State.[36]

Blackie Thompson, Raymond Hamilton, and Joe Palmer—all three Death Row convicts—had defied the Texas Prison System and the executioner. Lee Simmons was livid—for outlaws Palmer and Hamilton, it was their second escape in less than a year. Putting

out the word and keeping his ear to the ground, Lee Simmons
quickly received interesting intelligence with regards to one of his
Correctional Officers—vacationing in northeast Texas—and spending like a drunken sailor. With outside help and after accomplishing
several degrees of super sleuthing, General Manager Lee Simmons
and Warden Walter Waid and Welfare Director Albert Moore
knew who had spit on his oath, selling out. There was, as would be
expected, a big reckoning day in court: ex-Correctional Officer Jim
Patterson, forty-two, for his gun smuggling part in the breakout
caught hard-time, fifteen to do and not a smidgen of sympathy.[37]

The Death Row escapees, too, were short any empathy—
much less any lengthy free-world vacation. Near Amarillo, Blackie
Thompson, after the high-speed automobile chase and the high-cen-
tering of his radiator-spewing overheated auto, "bought the farm,"
dying in a blistering shootout with Panhandle policing personnel,
those letting loose with hellfire, popping caps with rifles and a
machinegun and handguns.[38]

Joe Palmer and Raymond Hamilton captured headlines as well
as the attention of more and more Lone Star Lawmen, including Captain Tom Hickman, Fred McDaniel, William Hale Kirby,
Stewart Stanley, and I.T. Reckley of the Texas Rangers.[39] The
manhunt was intensive and a thrilling newsmaker. Solid leads and
shaky leads were ubiquitous. Good fortune for bad men, however,
was playing out. Both hard-sought fugitives were finally arrested at
different places and at different times—albeit at very plain-spoken
commands and no-nonsense gunpoint. Joe Palmer was inglori-
ously captured at Paducah in McCracken County, Kentucky, tired,
broke, and hungry while catnapping under overhanging branches
of a tree.[40] Raymond Hamilton, at Fort Worth, awakened to find
himself scarily looking into what seemed large as the mouth of a
whiskey barrel—the gaping muzzle of Dallas County Chief Deputy
Bill Decker's autoloading Colt .45. Bill Decker and his boss, Sheriff
Smoot Schmid, and fellow Dallas deputies Ed Caster, Bryan Peck,
and the aforementioned Ted Hinton, accompanied by Tarrant
County Deputy Sheriff Carl Harmon and City Detective Chester

Reagan had, they hoped, at last put the kibosh on Hamilton's wayward enterprises—a crime spree of note.[41]

The outlaws had been—on separate dates—safely transported back behind The Walls at Huntsville where Ole Sparky awaited. And, once again, a quick pardon is asked of the reader for that leapfrogging narration with regards to one of the Texas Prison System's better known—at the time—personalities, Chief Transfer Agent Bud Russell, affectionately known by lawmen and desperadoes alike simply as "Uncle Bud." Though somewhat less flatteringly, sometimes Russell was fittingly characterized as "One-Way Bud."[42]

Before taking up employment with the state, the lean and lanky Bud Russell cowboyed on the famed Matador Ranch in Motley County for a couple of years, then moved back home to Blum where he served five years as a Hill County Constable. Bud Russell was boot-strap tough. Through the course of his near forty years with the Texas Prison System, Uncle Bud Russell transported 115,000 prisoners from county jails to Huntsville and between State Prison Farms. Purportedly, and it's believable, during the course of those duties it is estimated Bud Russell drove his specialized caged transport truck nicknamed Black Betty (also Black Annie) or rode the rails with convicts to-be between three and four million miles, positively equivalent to making several trips around the world.[43] By most everyone's account Bud Russell was quiet and respectful to all, but fearlessly recognized throughout Texas as one of those fellows best not to be "messed with." Though Uncle Bud was peaceful and unruffled he was always primed for business, arming himself with six-shooters, a sub-machinegun, brass-knuckles, and a blackjack.[44] The prisoners in his charge were leg shackled and each chained by the neck to another prisoner, which cultivated prison jargon that's yet used today: While being transported to or between numerous penitentiary units the sullen passengers are said to have "caught the chain." Bud Russell had a canned retort to those wild and woolly yahoos that thought they really were Billy badasses: "you're 40 years too late if you think you're tougher than I am."[45] Everyone, save one, believed Bud Russell: Of all the thousands of prisoners he moved, but one escaped. Bud Russell's quick pistol work put lead in the prisoner's ankle, subsequent to the outlaw's secretly hack-sawing through steel restraints and scampering for anonymity.[46] Unluckily for Bud, the escapee dashed into a milling civilian crowd where a follow-up shot might have risked injuring innocent bystanders. In a tight situation the gritty Transfer Agent was cucumber cool, unflustered, and levelheaded. Uncle Bud Russell holstered his six-shooter. At the time, thoroughly disgusted for allowing someone to get one over on him, Bud Russell sent a terse telegram to the General Manager: "Have lost my first prisoner. Am tendering my resignation." Lee Simmons replied, in jest: "Refuse to accept your resignation. Prefer to discharge you. Please go to hell."[47] Expectedly, the well-known and generally revered Texas Prison Transfer Agent kept his job. Later, however, he did in fact track down the wayward Carlos Brazil whose freedom had been only temporary, while hobbling on a wounded foot. Clearly statewide and, in fact, nationwide, the indefatigable Uncle Bud Russell was fodder for repeated human interest newspaper stories. In fact, Bud Russell was so familiar he was unmistakably memorialized in the first stanzas of the classic music-sheet piece *The Midnight Special*:

Let the Midnight Special shine her light on me,
Let the Midnight Special shine her ever-lovin' light on me.

"Here come Bud Russell." "How in the world do you know?"
Well he know him by his wagon and the chains he wo'.

Big pistol on his shoulder, big knife in his hand:
He comin' to carry you back to Sugarland.[48]

Uncle Bud Russell didn't deliver escaped murderer Palmer to Sugar Land, but to Huntsville where Fate unsmilingly waited behind The Walls—in the Death Chamber. On the tenth day of May 1935, going first, Joseph Conger Palmer took the "hot seat" and passed into whatever world was reserved for career thugs, even those pleading for a Higher Power to accept their bodies as atonement for past sins and more serious wrongdoings. That same night, Raymond Hamilton, recently converted to Catholicism, settled his fanny in for the "hot squat" and with electrifying sensations bid the land of the living goodbye.[49]

There was no deterrent value with the executions of Joe Palmer and Raymond Hamilton, not eighteen hours later at the Eastham State Farm. Convict Jack Peddy, subsequent to the stabbing mortality of prisoner Ernest Young by unknown hands during a 10 May 1935 brawl, jumped bad. As the incident was winding down—it was thought—Correctional Officer Thomas Stephens was surprisingly and forcefully grabbed from behind by Peddy. Stephens pulled his revolver trying to shoot Peddy, unsuccessfully as the convict had deflected the officer's arm. Peddy gained control of the revolver, fired four shots, wounding another prisoner and then turned his attention back to Tom Stephens, pistol-whipping him "until he was practically insensible." Upstairs in the guard's quarters, off-duty Correctional Officer Virgil "Verge" Welch, fifty-seven, had been asleep until awakened by the unholy commotion below. Courageously, revolver in hand, Verge Welch rushed to the sound of gunfire but was shot by Jack Peddy as he descended the staircase, incurring critical head injuries during the dreadful fall. By the time he tumbled to the first floor Verge Welch was dead.[50]

Eyeing opportunity for a general breakout, convict Peddy took the lead, breaking into the arms locker, taking an additional two revolvers, a double-barreled shotgun, and two lever-action Winchesters. Now reasonably well-armed, convicts Peddy, Sam Grant, Reese C. Tipton, and Harry Ludlow dashed across plowed ground making for the Trinity River's bottomland jungle. The pursuit was immediate and fast-paced and loud, Correctional Officers firing as they ran, ultimately fatally gunning down Peddy and capturing Tipton. Shortly thereafter, survived by his loving wife Gertrude Levert Hill Welch and five children, one of the older boys being a Correctional Officer at the time his father was coldly murdered, Virgil Welch was buried at the Hendrick Cemetery in Cherokee County.[51]

Shortly thereafter—speaking in months not years—The Texas Department of Public Safety came into being on 10 August 1935. Under the umbrella of the newly created institutional outfit was a reshuffling and reorganization of the Texas Rangers; the Texas Highway Department's law-enforcing element morphed into becoming the Texas Highway Patrol (THP), and the newly staffed Headquarters Division would oversee a fledgling Bureau of Identification and Records, a Communications Section, an Intelligence Branch, and the Educational Services subdivision. Realistically the so-called Gangster Era with its excess of bank robberies and business burglaries and senseless shootouts with lawmen and the incessant breaks from penitentiary confinement, had shifted statehouse legislators from a lackadaisical attitude to outraged public concern. Political convenience is no stalking stranger at state and national capitols—then or now. Most particularly did action follow the return and recommendations of Griffenhagen and Associates of Chicago, Illinois, which had been contracted to study Texas state government's overall management and its shortfalls.[52] The mention herein is obligatory. As already alluded to, the partnership between those charged with catching Penal Code wrongdoers and those charged with controlling and keeping them is an integral component of the state's system of Criminal Justice. And there was—and always will be—plenty of work for everyone.

8

"So he can better handle a shotgun"

THERE WOULD, HOWEVER, BE NO MORE PRISON WORK for Marshall Lee Simmons. In the face of mounting public criticism with regards to his reformation policies and continued use of the Bat as a method of discipline—which he supported—Simmons voluntarily tendered his resignation during November 1935,[1] soon thereafter accepting employment as Clerk of the U.S. Court, Eastern District of Texas.[2] Administratively there would be a succession of General Managers with varying degrees of successes and failures—it depends on who is grading.[3] Nevertheless, inside the cellblocks and on the vast state-owned prison farms, life for convicts and Correctional Officers was still hard—and always dangerous for the inattentive.

On the first day of June 1933, before Major Crowson had been assassinated, notorious outlaw Lucius M. "Luke" Trammell, Jr. murdered with bullets and car wheels Nolan County Deputy Sheriff John Harvey Lamkin, fifty-seven, during a West Texas burglary near Blackwell gone awry. Subsequently, after a shootout with lawmen wherein his brother Horace Starkweather "Doc" Trammell was killed, Luke saw the inside of the jailhouse, looking out through the steel bars. Exactly how he managed the homicide investigation is somewhat hazy, but Sheriff Jess D. Lambert (Lambeth?) saw to it—of course with prosecutorial aid of the district attorney—that Luke Trammell caught four-bits (fifty years) and was comfortably lodged at the Retrieve State Prison Farm for killing lawman Lamkin, with another 112 years stacked on top of that for other felonies in King, Motley, Nolan, Taylor, and Coleman Counties. At Retrieve the desperado teamed up with convict Forrest "Goodeye" Gibson, a multi-convicted burglar with three failed escape attempts already credited to his shameful string of persistent misadventures. Gibson's nickname was rightly earned during an in-house prison fight. His eye had been gouged out during the scrap, but he came out in first place, biting off the ear of his adversary who later died from the infected wound. Thereafter Goodeye Gibson, it was rumored, had the toxic bite of a rattlesnake. Over time Luke and Forrest held clandestine consultations of a nefarious nature. Moving forward, now, on the nineteenth day of June 1936, the conspiring convicts, accompanied by prisoner Terrell Beatrice "T.B." Atkinson, a "lifer" due to convic-·tion of the Habitual Criminal Statute, commonly referred to by Texas lawmen and desperados alike as the "Big Bitch," acted. They jumped tacky, overpowering Correctional Officer R.L. Steele, purloining his revolver and shotgun—and commandeering his saddle-horse as he brought up the rear of a deuced-up column of convicts. Then, horse-back, mean Luke Trammell armed with the state's shotgun, overtook Correctional Officer Felix Smith, a single man, forty-four-years-old and, for the moment totally oblivious to the madness that had just uncorked behind him, as he was riding at the head of the Hoe-Squads heading for the field. The shocking shotgun blast to his back was horrific and absolute, toppling him to the ground, another dead man falling.[4]

At the time of this Retrieve State Prison Farm murder, Captain Reuben W. "Rube" Conner was the official in charge, and noted for an on-scene newsman that Trammell was considered to be one of the worst and most dangerous criminals in the whole state of Texas. Consequent to taking to the field with other Correctional Officers, local lawmen, and a pack of Bloodhounds, Captain Conner came to the conclusion that escapee Atkinson had separated from the hard-running Trammell and Gibson who were at this time, as the saying goes, thicker than thieves.[5]

While Correctional Officer Smith was being returned to Smithville in Bastrop County for burial at the Oliver-Powell Cemetery, Luke Trammell and Forrest Gibson embarked on a three-state (Texas, Oklahoma, and New Mexico) crime spree, burglarizing and robbing and taking terrified hostages. On the lam in Texas the dog-tired duo hampered by mired roads finally pulled the stolen sedan over for a quick nap near Thornton, a few degrees and a few miles southwest of Groesbeck, the county-seat of Limestone County. Receiving word regarding the suspicious characters, Sheriff Willie Lee Adams gathered some gun-carrying helpmates and investigated. Trammell and Gibson were rudely awakened by lawmen's pistols and a sub-machinegun pointed at their heads and hearts. Though both hombres were armed with stolen pistols, they wilted. However, Trammell was not too overawed to talk, exclaiming: "It's a hell of a note to be caught by the law asleep with a gun in your hands."[6]

Perhaps there is rich irony, maybe outlaw Trammell was desirous of hearing a tune—or tunes—or national and international news. A radio had been placed on Death Row, a small creature comfort before condemned folks made their last walk.[7] Or maybe he knew the prison menu had been improved, especially after learning that an official position had been created and filled, a Dietitian.[8] Assuredly one convict, a four-time recidivist, Sam Weber, surmised that the 1930s Texas prison food was a vast improvement over what he had been fed in the 1890s.[9] And, as but a quick logistics sidebar, 82 percent of the food products set for the convicts' tables was "being produced within the system" at an estimated cost of less than seven cents per day per prisoner, and that too was welcome news for legislators and taxpayers.[10] There is a bottom-line for the hard crime story: Trammell, the confirmed triggerman in Correctional Officer Felix Smith's demise, afterward parked his heinie on Ole Sparky and was legally electrocuted after appellate contentions were exhausted.[11] Forrest Gibson was awarded sixty more years for his indubitable participation in the Retrieve prison break, but later during another escape attempt would be mortally gunned down by a sure-shooting Correctional

Officer, J.W Thomas, an incident starring big-name convicts of the day—a fact not missed by the media:

> Two convicts were killed and two were wounded when twen-
> ty-seven of the most vicious criminals in the vast Texas peniten-
> tiary system attempted to escape the Eastham prison farm late
> today. A guard atop the inmates' quarters picked off three of them
> as the group dashed from the building, and another guard slipped
> around the building and felled another. The others rushed back
> into the prison and guards quelled them quickly. The dead: Austin
> Avers, serving a sentence for participating in the death house
> escape in 1934 of the late Raymond Hamilton and Joe Palmer and
> others. Roy Thornton, husband of the late Bonnie Parker, notori-
> ous for her forays with Clyde Barrow, long the southwest's most
> hunted killer. Wounded: Forrest Gibson, one-eyed slayer serving a
> 60-year term for killing a prison guard in a break from the Retrieve
> prison farm last June. He was expected to die [and he did]. Clyde
> Thompson, young "thrill killer" from Eastland county, sentenced
> for slaying two brothers "just to see them kick." Thompson also
> killed another convict at the Retrieve farm. Thompson was shot in
> the shoulder and wounded slightly. The 27 prisoners, segregated
> because they are considered incorrigible and the most dangerous
> [in] Texas. J.M. Thomas, stationed atop the wing, saw Thornton
> first and killed him instantly. He then killed Avers, and shot Gibson
> three times. Another guard who had heard the shooting went to
> the other side of the building and shot Thompson.[12]

Awhile later T.B. Atkinson AKA T.R. Truman AKA E.R. Madden was captured in Canon City, Colorado, after his auto careened out of control, striking and killing an eleven-year-old newspaper boy, while fleeing apprehension after robbing a local café.[13] Atkinson did hard time—years—in the Colorado State Prison before being returned in handcuffs and leg-irons for his overdue welcome back at Huntsville.

Another mention of escapes warrants a brief note, namely because it involves long-time Texas Ranger Captain Hardy B. Purvis, Company A. Two black prisoners jumped from the Central

State Prison Farm near Sugar Land. They had stolen a car with a pistol inside and managed to make it into Cherokee County where they engaged in an exchange of shots with Constable Earl Pryor. Abandoning the auto, the pair fled into a field and began running for cover. Soon a posse under the command of Captain Purvis was onsite, "near Cornell Switch, two miles south of Wells in Angelina County [county seat Lufkin]," hunting for what Bloodhounds had failed to tree. The bottom-line is down-to-earth. One escapee was run to ground—pulled the pistol—and was mortally gunned down by a barrage of bullets. The other convict was later spotted, hotfooting across a peanut field near 200 yards away. The Ranger Captain's marksmanship was perfect: "Purvis dropped him with a bullet through the heart."[14]

Other convicts were faring much better, even those with major and minor medical problems. That progressiveness was brought to light by the investigative series penned by Alonzo Wasson for the *Dallas Morning News*. Aside from several other positive improvements, the writer noted the modernization of the hospital inside The Walls. This facility had "a full medical staff, including a dental surgeon, working under direction of Dr. W.B. Veazey, who is medical supervisor for the prison system. It is a three-story fireproof structure of 104 beds. There is a psychopathic unit in which all prisoners enter the prison system are put through psychological and psychiatric examination. The hospital is supplied with about all the facilities and equipment that are now used by physicians and surgeons."[15] Furthermore:

> All convicts enter the prison through the penitentiary at Huntsville, and when they are brought into that institution they are immediately made to undergo a clinical examination. Those found to need medical or surgical care are put under treatment and kept in the hospital until their condition warrants transfer to one or another of the farms. Only about 60 per cent of those examined are pronounced first-class as respects to health. Twenty-five per cent are syphilitic, and of this 25 per cent 8 per cent have

cerebrospinal syphilis. Another 10 per cent of the prisoners examined are found to have been treated for venereal diseases before
being brought to Huntsville. Crime and disease are oftener associated than not.[16]

Continuing with his assessment, the newspaperman noted that
in the most recent year for tabulated numbers (1935), at The Walls'
hospital, 2,113 cases had been treated and surgical operations topped
out at 784. Add in the 9000 dental treatments and the hospital staff
seemed quite busy, by any standard. Using these figures it was clear
to him: "Whatever may be said as to moral rehabilitation, physical
rehabilitation begins at once. In several ways the prison system is a
refuge for a large percentage of those who are taken into custody for
crime." With regards to that seemingly intangible and elusive mea-
surement of true rehabilitation, the scribe also noted that the library
inside The Walls contained 6,000 volumes. Of course many had been
donated by outside special interest groups—although a change was
underfoot: "But of late a great part of the additions [books] have
been bought with money taken from the amusement and recreation
fund. This is made up of receipts of the athletic contests which the
prisoners put on [TPR?], of the profits of the commissaries, patron-
ized mostly by prisoners themselves, and of the fees charged for
showing visitors through the penitentiary."[17] The Walls then, was
truly a bona fide slice of Texas real-estate where redemption could
begin—or for the ill-fated where Ole Sparky summoned its next sit-
down client.

An electrifying buzzing between condemned men's ears wasn't
the only humming emanating from behind The Walls. The powerhouse radio station at Fort Worth, WBAP, was broadcasting an
exceptionally popular program, *Thirty Minutes Behind the Walls*. The
Wednesday night radio show debuted on March 23, 1938—and due
to clear-channel capabilities from the get-go attracted fans "throughout most of North America." The live broadcast was a cornucopia of
musical and comedy entertainment, sprinkled with "human interest"
stories about men and women doing real time for committing real

crime.[18] As with the TPR there was a plethora of talent to draw from within the state's burgeoning prison population, smooth talkers, singers, musicians, and folksy humorists. Don Reid Jr., for decades affiliated with *The Huntsville Item* was, after personally witnessing 189 state-sanctioned executions, an outspoken anti-Death Penalty advocate. He, too, had a *Thirty Minutes Behind the Walls* linkage and a guarded personal secret: He was a convicted felon and had been an in-house correspondent for the prison *Echo*, penning news blips about musicians and melodies in one of his two regularly featured columns, "On the Down Beat: Looking IN on the Prison Orchestra." With regards to incarcerated and talented instrumentalists Don Reid Jr. knew them quite well. Before his return to the free-world and a lengthy career with the *Item*—he sat on the bandstand stool, picking up sticks as drummer for the prison orchestra.[19] Perhaps somewhat unbelievably now, during its heyday fan letters for the weekly broadcast received at the mail room measured in the thousands. Too, maybe surprising to some folks, the popular programs were open to the general public—and as seating permitted several hundred free-world spectators in the auditorium would provide live feedback to those cheerfully performing in front of the bandstand and behind the microphones.[20] Purportedly—and it's not pretend—*Thirty Minutes Behind the Walls* "had an estimated audience of five million listeners. . . . In honor of one early anniversary episode, the announcers challenged the audience to write and request that *Thirty Minutes* be extended to a full hour broadcast. They received 220,000 letters the following week in support of this proposal."[21] Gauging the program's free-world popularity is partly evidenced by the fact that if executions by happenstance were scheduled in conflict with the radio broadcast, the state's governor would step in granting a postponement, not of the radio program but of the convict's high-voltage surge to the hereafter.[22] As the cliché saying goes, "the show must go on," and for the penitentiary setting aside from high-jinks and hilarity and hillbilly music, well, there is a reoccurring theme. Not just a few convicts—not surprisingly—were dishonest, even musicians.

Woodrow W. Stansbury (or Stansberry), twenty-three, had lain down his instruments and was working unaccompanied in the visiting room at The Walls. Coincidently it was at that time the local tailor arrived with a freshly pressed blue serge suit and white hat, returning it to Warden Waid: "Stansbury, convincing himself that he had more use for the clothes than did the warden, discarded his convict uniform and donned Waid's suit, which was a perfect fit. Then he left the prison with a group of visitors. Guards at the gate thought he was one of them and passed him through." Or by another account: "The guard across the street thought he was a newspaper man." While in the free-world at Huntsville the escapee stole an automobile and headed southwest toward the Gulf Coast where he caught the attention of local officers, due to being passed out drunk. The Pied Piper, in the hulking form of Walker County Sheriff Claude L. Mitchell, hustled to Wharton and returned the wayward instrumentalist to The Walls.[23]

Sustaining once again that Houston County's Texas Prison System's Eastham Unit south of Weldon was home for some of the most desperate of the desperate is not too difficult. Sometime after morning light of 16 August 1938, Correctional Officer John R. Greer, a forty-one-year-old U.S. Army veteran, was carrying a Hoe-Squad from the secluded No. 2 Camp. As the trite saying goes, the day turned to hell-in-a-hand-basket, in a heartbeat! Thirteen brazen convicts jumped. Correctional Officer Starnes was nearby and his horse jumped too, pitching and kicking as two convicts tried to dethrone their horseback keeper. Luckily, Starnes stayed in the saddle, while two of the wannabe free-world fellows were pummeled into the turn-row by iron-clad hoofs and bad luck. At gunpoint Starnes convinced five of the escapees that the idiocy was over. Correctional Officer Greer's luck did not hold. Convict Jack Kinsley jumped Greer, holding him down while prisoner Leonard Smith repeatedly stabbed him in the stomach and groin with a jagged shank. Taking his revolver and shotgun, those two, accompanied by W.E. Garner, Elmer Charles "Chuck" Aaron, John Hendrix Frazier, Raymond Wilkerson, Roy King, and Frank Johnson, hit a high-lope for the Trinity River bottomlands.

That afternoon the scorecard was marked—convicts Kingsley and Aaron were shot and killed by possemen, and convict Garner was taken into custody. The next day's manhunt netted a body-count too: Convicts Wilkerson and Frazier were gunned down in the jungle flanked by the snaking river. Dog Sergeant Bob Parker asserted that the pair was shot and killed while they "were attempting to kill bloodhounds employed in the chase," and were doggedly resisting arrest. Unfortunately, the Houston County Sheriff, Archie L. Maples, was not yielding to that justification. The undaunted but concerned Sheriff "filed a charge of murder against Parker in Justice of the Peace D.D. Long's court, listing himself as chief witness." Herein was the rub for penitentiary officialdom. Houston County's top law-dog was—in his mind—not buying the hog:

> Maples said he was 200 yards away when the bloodhounds flushed Frazier and Wilkerson. There were some shots, and he ran toward the sound. Forty steps away he saw Frazier apparently seeking to surrender a moment before he was slain. . . .[24]

At his Initial Appearance before Judge Long, it was determined that Dog Sergeant Parker should be held without bail pending action of the next Houston County Grand Jury. Prison Board member, Dr. C.W. Butler, Jr., promised a thorough investigation into the affair.

A convict trusty operating the ferry separating Eastham Farm property from the Ferguson Farm acreage noticed two floating forms in the murky Trinity River, notifying Captain (Warden) James P. Hamilton, at Eastham. Escapees Smith's and Johnson's lungs weren't perforated with bullets and/or buckshot, but they did fill with the Trinity's wetness—they both drowned as hidden currents washed away their deliverance plot. Purportedly, a dirk fashioned from "a kitchen case knife" was found on Johnson's saturated body when fished from the river, and that was, by the best guesstimate, thought to be the murder weapon. The alleged ringleader was Will Evrette "W.E." Garner. He and his partner for the unwise two-day adventure, Roy King, were ultimately captured and returned to prison. Later, in February 1940, Convict W.E. Garner was already doing 100 years for "robbery of a Houston couple" and "also charged, but never tried, with wounding State Highway Patrolman C.H. Key shortly after the Houston robbery: ". . . Key was shot twice with his own pistol, taken from the holster, one leg wound resulting in an amputation later."

There were three outcomes as result of this horrifying scenario, two grounded in hard fact, one, perhaps, anecdotal. Sadly, on the twenty-seventh day of August, Greer, husband and father of two, died due to his irreparable and viciously inflicted stab wounds. Correctional Officer John R. Greer was peacefully laid to rest in the Weldon Cemetery. Secondly, Convict Garner was tried and convicted of offing Correctional Officer Greer, but only caught five years, and that time was to "run concurrently with previous robbery penalties."[25] And by this time it should not come as a surprise, years later Garner would receive a Full Pardon, be released from the penitentiary and live to the age of sixty-seven years. Lastly and ostensibly and, there's really no reason to doubt it, the horse Starnes had been riding that ill-fated day earned heroic status, not only during the breakout but in the TPR arena as well.[26] And what of Dog Sergeant Bob Parker's arrest? Though suggesting that the Houston County Grand Jury may have failed to return an Indictment is reasonable, although there is nothing conclusive herein to buttress that proposition.

The following month, September 1938, bad news punched forth again—and it was not boding well for the Texas Prison System. At the Ferguson State Farm near Midway in Madison County, a black convict, K.C. Morris, had undergone discipline: "placed in a cell four feet square on a bread and water diet for 11 consecutive days, then given '18 to 20' lashes and sent back to the field to work." Twelve hours later convict Morris collapsed and died. Prison Board members and much of the public was outraged:

No one can contend sensibly that convicts can be handled without punishment. Some measures are necessary to force a man who refused to work to do so. Solitary confinement, unless inhumanly conducted, bread-and-water diet, the lash under satisfactory conditions are penalties that may have to be applied in cases. But the combination of these punishments which Dr. Butler [C.W. Butler, Jr., Prison Board] charges were used, would quite probably kill the strongest man. The whip is used in the Texas prison system legally only under competent medical supervision. It is inconceivable that any competent doctor would permit whipping a man who had been on a bread-and-water diet for eleven days or allow him to be sent to work immediately after the diet period, whether he had been whipped or not.

The untimely and unfortunate and uncalled-for death of convict Morris was generating not just a little newspaper coverage and providing fuel for the camp seeking prison reform. Was the Bat really a legitimate and effective disciplinary tool? Investigations and change were in the air.[27]

Another event of Texas Prison System history did not happen in the arena next to The Walls, but at Goree, the women prisoners' facility. Though other confined gals during the penitentiary lease period—the work camp era—may have presented the world with precious gifts, the distinct honor, however, for this narrative will go to Tom Coleman, Jr. His mother, Rosa, forty-three, a "Houston negress" with a dime to do for Assault to Murder, brought baby Tom into the prison world on the second day of February 1939. The headlines were explicit: "First Baby Ever Born in Texas Penitentiary Paid Visit at Goree by Jurors." The touring Grand Jurors from Harris County were naturally spellbound but somewhat concerned. Their apprehension was put to rest when it was revealed that Rosa didn't want to raise the child in prison. Her mother, Tom's grandmother in the free-world, would assume those duties.[28]

Baby Tom may have been yet unable to crawl or pull himself up, but a passel of convicts from the Wynne Farm were stumbling and hobbling in what must have seemed comical if not so pathetic. An accomplice had secreted a pistol in the weeds they were hoeing/pulling. That in and of itself—by this time—should be no shocker. Nor should it seem overly strange they used the weapon and disarmed a Correctional Officer, fleeing via a stolen car. There is, though, a lesson to be had for prison personnel—even the harmless looking prisoners can muster big trouble. Arthur Louis Brown, serving a life sentence from Tarrant County as a Habitual Criminal, had but one arm. Another of the convicts, Dolph Tuck, a Burglar from Gregg County doing thirty-five years, had an artificial leg. Likewise, convict V.E. Cooper, pulling thirty-five years from Donley County for Forgery, had but one leg. None were blind, but Brown and Tuck did get blindsided in North Texas near Denison in Grayson County, surprised and taken into custody by Constable Ira Jessee. At Whiteright in the southwest section of the county, convict Cooper hobbling on his good leg surrendered to authorities, asserting that he had been taken against his will and finally had broken free of his captors.[29] Maybe so?

Another breakout, this time again at the always leaky Eastham Farm, did not go well for the Texas Prison System publicity wise, and was even more tormenting for Correctional Officer Robert Henry "Bobby" Hyde, III. Two convicts had jumped and Correctional Officer Hyde, accompanied by a fellow employee, was on the hunt at Rusk. During the roundabout pursuit Hyde and his cohort were successful with sacking up something—two pints of liquor from an area bootlegger. They, apparently, at least Correctional Officer Hyde, then became intoxicated. Without bogging the story down with miniscule details it may be reported as the night progressed Hyde confronted popular barber Charles Goodson, a World War I veteran, in the backyard of a private residence. Whether or not he thought Mr. Goodson was or was not an escaped convict is and was not material. Correctional Officer Hyde yanked out his revolver and killed Mr. Goodson, "a bullet piercing his heart." Hyde's employment at Eastham was irrelevant and the Cherokee County Sheriff, William Jesse "Bill" Brunt (later that year killed in the line of duty), and Precinct Constable C.E. Jay ensured that Justice of the Peace Ed Spinks would meet Bobby Hyde. Shortly the two escaped convicts were run to ground, one at Lovelady and the other at Crockett, and returned to Eastham—perhaps Hyde heard the good news from his jail cell. Normally the ceaselessly grinding wheels of justice turn excruciatingly slow—not in this case however. Within the month, after deliberating but three hours, the trial jury issued Bobby Hyde's comeuppance: "a life sentence in the penitentiary."[30] The Texas Court of Criminal Appeals, after reviewing the case, was not sympathetic, but was perceptibly plainspoken:

> This was a killing based upon a drunken carousal, with neither justification nor excuse in taking the life of a man who was unarmed and making no attack of any kind upon the appellant. . . . the only defense that appellant offered was intoxication at the time, his testimony showing that he remembered nothing of the transaction that took this man's life. . . . We find the charge to be admirably drawn, and possibly more favorable to appellant than he was entitled to, and under the circumstances presented to us we find no error shown in this record. . . . This judgment is therefore affirmed.[31]

Although judicially convicted of the homicide, it's but fair to mention that after a lengthy residence in prison Robert Henry Hyde, III was granted a Full Pardon for his criminal conduct on that chilly February night in 1939. The message to prison employees was clear—they were not immune to criminal prosecution just because they were chasing after escapees.

And even convicts with nary a thought about jumping into the free-world can generate havoc. Say, for instance, the 1939 mess emanating from the License Plate Factory. At the Potter County Tax Office it was all too soon discovered that their allotment of license plates had been "mismated." The two license plates, one designated for the front and one for the rear of automobiles were supposed to be the same. In this instance they weren't; they were out of numerical sync. All so soon maddened hordes of "disgruntled drivers" were returning the plates to befuddled county employees. History simply recorded the jumble as "the prank of some Texas penitentiary inmate."[32] That the Huntsville mischief came to light the first day of April might bear mentioning. Convicts, too, have a sense of humor.

The Prison Board, however, was humorless—vis-à-vis the dispensation of discipline. Their "revised and amplified code of regulations" was not mush mouthed:

> Punishment from now on must be limited to solitary confinement, loss of privileges, loss of commutation of overtime, reduction in grade, clothing in stripes, bread and water diet, standing on a barrel or stool for restricted intervals or whipping. . . . the medical department shall at no time use any drugs, vaccines or any form of appliance for the purpose of punishment.[33]

The argument over Capital Punishment was ginning for a full-court press, and the Anti-Dark Cell and Electric Chair League was drumming up support; urging folks to sign petitions and write letters to Texas legislators.[34] Candidly, it should also be noted that the Governor of Texas, Wilbert Lee "Pappy" O'Daniel, had had a sincere change of heart, and was now weighing into the Capital Punishment debate with gusto. For him, the possibility of executing an innocent man—or woman—was the philosophical game changer. "If the man has been put to death, it will have been too late to do anything about it. If he is in prison, the case can be reopened and new evidence received."[35] Whether his attitude about the subject was right or wrong, for prison personnel it was immaterial—or should have been! They were to do their jobs regardless of personal positions on this or that hot-button issue—or quit! With regards to the Governor's timing for making his remarks, well, it couldn't have been worse—not for Huntsville folks.

Four hardened convicts from The Walls jumped: Clifton Davidson, thirty-two, AKA George Miller, AKA Jack Moore, with a thirty-five-year sentence for Robbery in Dallas County; thirty-one-year-old Lloyd Leon Rayburn, AKA Lloyd Baker; twenty-four-year-old S.J. Whatley, Jr., a Burglar from Kaufman County; and Jack Cade, thirty, pulling his quarter's worth for Robberies in Harris and Dallas Counties. The October 1939 breakout was clever and a kick-starter for forthcoming high-drama. The quartet "dug out of the prison's rodeo ground stockade." Convict Cade opted to go his own way—he had twenty quarts of nitroglycerin stashed somewhere—stolen from a drilling firm at Kilgore in the southern reach of Gregg County. Escapee Cade was captured rather quickly in the Trinity River bottoms. "Police, whom Cade told where to find two ounces of the high explosive, fear he may use the remainder of the 20 quarts in future crimes."[36]

The other three escapees, looking for the fastest way out of nighttime Walker County, took advantage at first opportunity: They commandeered a car, kidnapping the occupants, four Huntsville High-School students, who had just returned from a football game. "Hurriedly they ordered the youths to let one of them under the wheel, and then started their wild trip through southeast Texas. In their flight the convicts stopped at Cold Springs [sic Coldspring, San Jacinto County], thirty-five miles southeast of Huntsville. . . ." There they "went into town and broke a lock on a filling station to get gas, then the window of a clothing store to get clothes."[37] Although the teenagers were not physically mistreated, the convicts were skirting around the East Texas towns "because officers would be looking for them." Who could have guessed what could have happened if run to ground? Finally the outlaws made it to Beaumont where they freed their hostages, stole another automobile belonging to R.C. Dawe—and disappeared.[38]

The released teens little realized it then, but they had been extremely fortunate. Within days, two of their three convict captors, Rayburn and Davidson, had been safely apprehended at Little Rock, Arkansas. And they weren't simply taken into custody as fugitives from a Texas prison break. The pair had attempted a holdup and during the course of that offense Sergeant Sigur Fosse of the United States Marine Corps was shot and killed. They then fled east toward the Mighty Mississippi. As good luck would have it they were caught by Arkansas State Police at West Memphis, Arkansas, and luckily this time too, a kidnapped victim, H.G. Harris, survived scared, but unscathed.[39] The debate raged hot—how should Rayburn and Davidson—if and when they were returned to the Lone Star State— after answering charges for the Arkansas homicide—be punished. Electrocuted? Solitary Confinement?

These were big doings in the arena of public policy opinions, too. Although in days of so-called twenty-first-century enlightenment one may ponder how whipping incorrigible convicts with the Bat lasted as long as it did, nevertheless such was legit punishment with administrative approval. From the outset of Texas prison doings in the mid-1800s the practice of presumably shaping behavior by employing the Bat to backsides and buttocks of incorrigibles had persisted. Conversely, spanking kids at home and administering "licks" to students with a wooden paddle in an Assistant Principal's office or the gymnasium lasted long past the mid-twentieth-century. Evolving standards do evolve, but slowly. Due to the clamoring and haranguing and pleadings of like-minded altruistic prison reform voices there would be change. The embittered cry for redressing an act of inhumanity was washing across the Lone Star State and, in this instance, politicians listened—finally. There should be little argument that Texas convicts, if they caught free-world headlines, would be more than happy: "Senate Votes Ban on Bat in State Prisons." The reading public was likewise informed: "The dreaded 'bat,' leather whip with which Texas penitentiary prisoners are sometimes punished, was on the way out today." As of 1941 corrective use of the Bat was formally and permanently suspended—in reality abolished. Although at least one Texas legislator had held out in opposition, publicly he was ruing its disuse: "If you pass this bill, those convicts will be thumbing their noses at us within two weeks."[40] Prison leadership would have to conjure other methods for punishing disobedient and unruly convicts, maintaining control of the institution. Now, the Bat was but a relic—a museum artifact.[41]

And apparently Frank Hamer's paycheck for expenses in running down the notorious duo was an antique—if it ever existed. At any rate, during the 1941 budget, approval of miscellaneous resolutions was what seems to be a long overdue claim for $1,075 as reimbursement. The line item was "to pay Frank Hamer, former ranger captain and peace officer, for his service in the capture of Clyde Barrow on May 23, 1934, the amount necessary for him to pay out in order to accomplish the task assigned to him by the manager of the prison system."[42]

What had not diminished were escapes and one particularly herein enumerated is not because it's a matter of reeling off another, but because of the players. The 1942 break from the Ferguson State Farm near Madisonville in Madison County was accomplished at the point of a gun. The telephone lines going into the Ferguson Farm were cut. Then, in a sedan, Gene Paul Norris and his malevolent helpmate rolled onto prison property and confronted Correctional Officer Tom Foster who was carrying a squad of convicts working on a farm building. He was disarmed and the seven convicts began piling into the stolen automobile—packed tightly to be sure—but inside nevertheless. It would be but a short ride to Buffalo in Leon County where they could carjack motorists and split up, fleeing in different directions. The mission for Gene Paul Norris was to free his older brother Thomas Nathan "Pete" Norris, one of the Southwest's most notorious outlaws.[43] And, according to the FBI, Pete Norris was Public Enemy Number One. The other six convicts were some of the hardest of the hard, but their vile stories warrant telling elsewhere. For now the short version regarding Gene Paul Norris is that he was eventually arrested for his part in freeing his wayward brother, and caught eight years. And the Court of Criminal Appeals gave him no relief. Nor was his brother Pete faring any too well after his North Texas arrest; the prison time he now owed measured in the hundreds of years, 400.[44]

Mentioning Gene Paul Norris is apt. History would soon know him as one of the most vicious and coldblooded killers traipsing across Texas and Oklahoma. Far and wide within the gangland world, conscienceless Gene Paul Norris, with his shotgun for hire, was well-established and unanimously feared. Portending that his string of murders and criminality would make such overrated fellows as John Wesley Hardin and Wyatt B.S. Earp look like weak stepsisters is not just resonant hyperbole. In fact, later a proficient and prolific journalist would catch a jailhouse interview with Gene Paul: "The first killer I ever interviewed was Gene Paul Norris, a notorious

badass in Fort Worth in the mid-fifties. . . . Norris was a high-profile player in what was known as the Dixie Mafia, and every news-
hound in town would have give his trench coat for an interview."[45]
Measuring murders is tricky—but for Norris the most often cited
figure is forty.[46] That very well may be close but for this prison saga
more of Gene Paul Norris later.[47]

And during this same general timeframe change was taking place
with regards to hiring Correctional Officers. Heretofore it had been
willy-nilly: "Time once was when a man could get a job at the Texas
prison system by merely being around when some other guard quit."
Now it was very different, and paperwork had to be completed and for
the times it was rather exacting: "You've got to set down on paper your
pedigree, so to speak. Apply to the prison service commission for work
and you'll have to fill out an application as long as the one they'd give
you before letting you coin silver dollars at the United States mint."
Members of the Prison Board were trying, and trying hard:

> The prison board, realizing that laxness in personnel often has had
> deleterious after-effects, has set about obtaining better men for
> the jobs it now has, realizing that will not only lessen troubles in
> the system, but that it also will increase chances of rehabilitating
> the convicts.

While physical agility was not specified or checked, an applicant
had to be at least sixty-six inches or taller "so he can better handle
a shotgun." Too, he had to be a citizen of the United States, submit
to fingerprinting, and "must be able to see and hear well and be in
good health, and between the ages of 25 and 55." There would be
written and practical tests measuring, or trying to: "Education and
character, educational attainment, observation, good citizenship,
wholesome attitude, and good common sense, marksmanship, farming ability. . . ." And of course there was an interview with regards
to gambling and/or drunkenness and/or arrests and/or convictions—and whether or not any relatives were either working for the
penitentiary or in the penitentiary serving time. Then, when it was
all over, a composite grade would be determined, and a numerical

placement would be made for the waiting list, containing as many as 1000 applicants on an approved register. Thereafter, according to the newspaperman, "if you're among the upperclassmen and have passed your exams with flying colors, you'll find yourself astride a horse, awkwardly waving a double-barreled shotgun loaded with buckshot and riding to the field behind a squad of some 15 convicts dressed in white. Praying, too, one won't run away before you've got the examination ink washed off your hands."[48] Admittedly, it was somewhat a rudimentary progression by today's standards—but it was a start. Newspaper announcements highlighted the timelines and deadlines for hopefuls to sign up for the examination, application forms being obtainable at U.S. Employment Service offices or at the Texas Prison System's headquarters at Huntsville.[49]

Photo Gallery

2

Poster for the very popular WBAP radio broadcast *Thirty Minutes Behind The Walls*, transmitted in front of an approving free-world audience, but inside the penitentiary at Huntsville.

Although seemingly at odds with a few agenda-driven accounts, at times The Walls seemed as open to public scrutiny as an amphitheater. Here a rapt audience from the free-world is in the auditorium enjoying a live Wednesday night WBAP radio broadcast of *Thirty Minutes Behind The Walls.*

Long has been the progression of manufacturing Texas motor vehicle license plates in prison, a viable industry. Here convicts are stamping out plates for 1960. Admittedly, as pointed out in the text, there is opportunity for a little mischief once and while—like April Fool's Day.

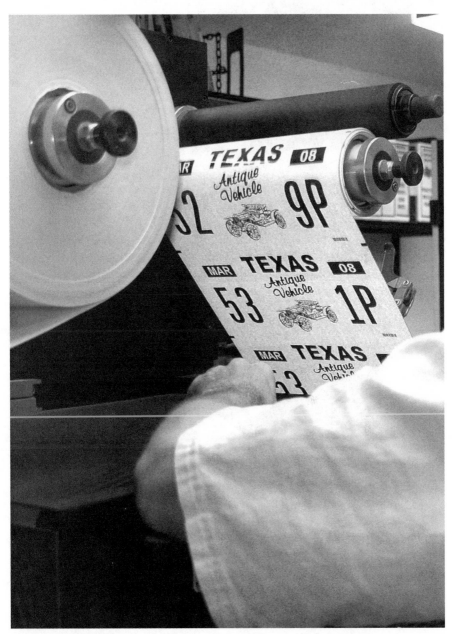

Though this photo may be out of strict chronological sync, it's illustrative of how TDCJ-CID must adapt to the latest technological development. Texas license plates and motor vehicle Safety Inspection Stickers are today, 2020, yet manufactured by State of Texas prisoners.

Prison employees and a convict are preparing to deliver vehicle license plates throughout the state of Texas, county by county.

Even though reformation is a notable and laudatory goal, not all convicts are like-minded. In this instance one opted on the sly to make a scary facsimile pistol from his Bible.

From an early time—relatively speaking—Texas Prison administrators have recognized the value of classroom education for its involuntary guests. Here a volunteer convict teacher is heading the class for his institutional companions.

That the Texas Prison Rodeo drew spectators surging the everyday Huntsville population is revealed in this Sunday afternoon in October photograph.

Clearly this is a wonderful aerial photograph depicting TPR drama unfolding in the adjacent arena, but also displaying the overall Walls complex. Note automobiles throughout; parking space was at a premium.

Juanita Dale Slusher AKA Juanita Dale Phillips AKA Candy Barr, a former exotic and erotic Dallas nightclub stripper and, later a convict, wows a TPR crowd—this time as an ex-convict belting out a tune with prison musician accompaniment.

This surrey with the fringe on top, now parked inside the TPM, would be the horse-drawn vehicle carrying headline performers into the arena for their entertaining engagement before excited convicts and enthusiastic free-world spectators.

Though he may or may not have made the eight qualifying seconds, quite literally this convict had his hands full during a Bull Ride—and at this point he best let go.

Top Hand convict Willie Craig preparing to take a seat, insert his hand in the bareback-riggin' and nod for the gate—as a cowboy he was the Real McCoy. That convict contestants wore stripes for the TPR is not an indication of errant conduct.

This snapshot in time reveals a convict cowboy is—at least for the moment—sitting tight during the Bareback event, but whether he made the qualifying buzzer is indeterminate.

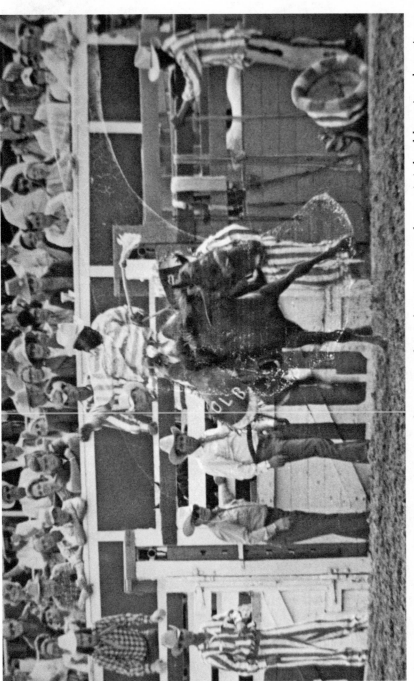

Multiple Top Hand winner O'Neal Browning, wearing his signature leggins', is sitting pretty, bronc rein in hand, boots in ox-bow stirrups, and free-hand stabilizing equilibrium.

Clearly this photograph depicts that female convicts from the Goree Unit vying for a win at the Texas Prison Rodeo greased-pig chase and capture are a multi-racial mix—as do several other images of the same event.

At the end of the Texas Prison Rodeo the blue-ribbon contender earned the Top Hand Buckle, a prize coveted by convict participants—a banking of esteem that would carry them another year.

There were no racial barriers preventing these two female convict Greased Pig contestants from cooperatively joining forces for this sacking. And, too, in the background both black and white cowboys are looking on, waiting their turn for an upcoming chance to earn glory and greenbacks riding rough stock or milking a wild mare or grabbing cash strung between a Brahma's horns. Cowboys and Cowgirls know well, everyone bleeds red in the arena.

THE ORIGINAL TEXAS

PRISON RODEO

DALLAS-JUNE 3-10, 1950

TOUGH VERSUS TOUGH
THE WILDEST RODEO IN THE WORLD

OFFICIAL 1950 SOUVENIR PROGRAM 50¢

The Texas Prison Rodeo was so very popular, performances were scheduled for Dallas, the only time the spellbinding show was held in a free-world setting. The 1950 *Souvenir Program* was purposely designed to promote the world's Wildest Rodeo and capture a smile.

Oscar Byron Ellis was recruited from Tennessee to give the Texas Prisons a systematic and overdue overhaul. His tenure improved living conditions for the convicts and working conditions for the Correctional Officers thanks to implementation of the five-phased Ellis Plan.

Although to some it might springboard mental images of another timeframe in Texas history, from the outset a Texas penal philosophy of self-sufficiency was ubiquitous: Everybody worked producing food and fiber or other commodities lessening the prison burden on taxpayers.

An observant mounted Field Boss had a much better platform for taking in what was around him; were convicts working as directed or was the passing of contraband and hatching of escape plans moved from the dormitories and cellblocks to the turn-rows?

Though sometimes omitted in agenda-driven accounts, a Field Boss overseeing a Hoe-Squad was exposed to the same environment and the same outside hours as the convicts—heat during a scorching summer and cold during the dead of winter. Here, slaking his thirst is well-known and well-respected Captain Billy Shipper, who later retired as a Major after 40-plus years of service.

One of the major changes during the O.B. Ellis administration was the introduction of mechanization such as tractors and scientific animal husbandry practices. Though farming and ranching progress was at hand, with the prison system's whopping acreage and legislative budget restraints, actual modernization would be years in the making.

Mr. Ellis was also progressively minded with regards to personnel matters. He forthrightly appointed Velda Quinn Dobbs to be the Warden at the Goree Unit, the first such position filled by a female in Texas Prison history.

Oscar Byron Ellis also was a believer in the betterment of convicts. Here a free-world teacher is scaling the opportunity for convicts to prepare for re-entry into the general population.

Zan E. Harrelson had a long-time career with Texas Prisons, serving as Warden at two of the toughest units, Retrieve in Brazoria County, and Eastham in Houston County.

The notoriously tough Retrieve Unit south of Angleton in Brazoria County, home to some of the nastiest and irredeemable convicts in the system—so said one of their brethren.

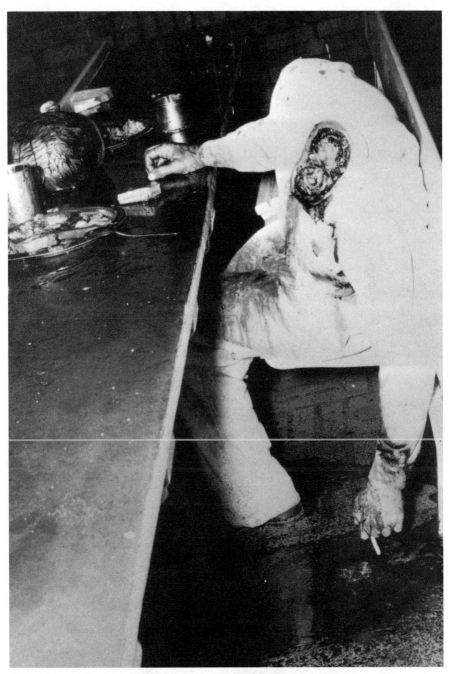

Though the photograph is gruesome, it's real. Subsequent to an argument between seven-time recidivist Ernest Cleve Jones and nastily disposed convict Clarence William Redwine, the former decapitated the latter in the Retrieve Unit's chow hall with a swipe from a sharpened cane knife.

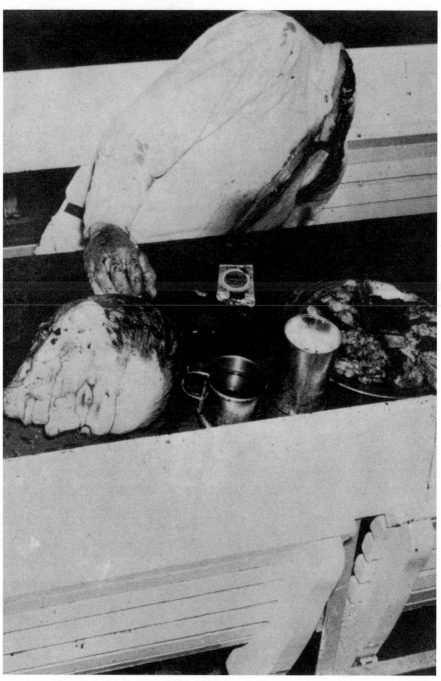

While Clarence William Redwine's torso remained upright after the assault, his severed head came to a rest on the table. Sometimes in prison revenge is best served quick and cold.

9

"Before He Whacks You"

ALTHOUGH IMPROBABLE WERE IT TO HAPPEN in today's climate of generational instant gratification, the Japanese attack at Pearl Harbor volcanically spurred Americans to the military's recruiting depots. Legion are the stories of voluntary enlistments by both men and women, some of the latter donning the civilian title of Rosie the Riveter, filling the workplace gap on the martial assembly lines as patriotic husbands and brothers and boyfriends and sisters boarded ships for overseas deployments. Some ladies learned to pilot airplanes, flying them from place to place in noncombat roles, freeing male military aviators to enter the Theaters of War. Demographically—in a general sense—it was all-hands-on-deck. And though it's generally underreported, a large number—1,500 to 2,000—zealous Texas convicts sought parole so they too could jump into the affray—and fight Japanese and Germans, or anyone else messing with the USA. Their patriotic volunteerism was generating a very interesting and very demanding public debate, prompting Chairman of the Texas Prison Board, Dr. Sidney M. Lister, to openly declare that he "hoped something can be worked out whereby a selected group could be paroled to join the armed forces for the duration of the war." After a caveat about not releasing dangerous criminals, he continued: "Of course, the offense that sent them to prison would also have a bearing on the matter and naturally their physical condition would play a big part." Editorial opinion was somewhat mixed: "Then there is the argument that, since the man on the production line behind the front is as valuable as the man on the firing line, the energy of the prison inmates could be more quickly converted to this type of war work than to active field service." Perhaps the proposal's real backbreaker came through the steadfast voice of Remy Ancelin, Vice-Chairman of the Fifth District of the Dallas American Legion and his jingoist cohorts. At an Adolphus Hotel meeting a resolution was passed putting them on record: They were unalterably "opposed to the release of any prisoner to the military."[1] Even if the strategy of paroling convicts into the U.S. Military had any bona fide merit, such was immaterial: It was a deadletter proposal on arrival. The secondary negative impact of WW II on the Texas Prison System, however, was conspicuous. The pool of Correctional Officers dwindled and, resultantly, the number of escapes increased.[2]

Highlighting but a trio of those WWII breakouts at one prison farm will suffice. At the Retrieve Unit, then predominately housing white recidivists, two convicts jumped on the twenty-first day of January 1943. Cleo Andrews, doing ninety-nine years for Armed Robberies in Upshur and Harrison Counties, and Robert Lacey, AKA Robert Lacey Cash, a lifer for a Dallas killing, slipped away from the farm's blacksmith shop making for parts they hoped would forevermore remain unknown. It was not Robert Lacey's first prison break; he had sneaked out during a 1938 TPR, and on other occasions as well.[3]

After stealing an automobile and handgun in Houston, the bad boys telephoned a good friend, running down their itinerary and asking for rifles, before they stepped heavy on the gas pedal, heading for East Texas. Confiding in their good friend an ex-convict was a bad investment. He speedily snitched to "Lone Wolf" Gonzaullas, by now Captain of Company B, Texas Rangers headquartered in Fair Park at Dallas. Knowing when and where the escapees would meet the informant to pick up the extra firepower and ammo, the Captain and Texas Rangers Dick Oldham, a native of Anderson County, and forty-one-year-old Robert Logan "Bob" Badgett, accompanied by multi-county lawmen, laid the trap. The stakeout, from the officers' outlook was a winner—though for desperadoes it was a loser. The shootout was conclusive. Escaped convicts Cash and Andrews both died that twenty-fifth day of January 1943, an extremely cold and stormy winter night on the Gilmer-Gladewater Highway.[4]

That same year, on April 18, again at the Retrieve Unit, Walter Henry LeMay, a four-time prison resident and C.M. Mershon, a multi-term convict, had skipped the headcount. They were, as the saying goes, "on the bricks," which meant they were running and hiding, robbing and stealing in the free-world. Their North Texas crime spree, umpteen major felonies, drew more than just a little attention from area lawmen. As many as fifty business burglaries was hot news. Their *Modus Operandi* (MO) was uncomplicated and mean. They would arrive at a small town "late at night, capture and bind the night watchman, and break into stores along the main street, taking merchandise and breaking knobs off safes for money." Soon on the manhunt were Captain Gonzaullas, and Company B Texas Rangers Robert Austin "Bob" Crowder, Tulley Elwyn Seay, thirty-six, and Vermont-born Norman Kemp Dixon, as well as some notable Dallas Policemen, such as Inspector J.W. "Will" Fritz, Leon Mash, and J.T. Luther. On 5 June 1943, working info supplied by a spy (snitch), a fixed surveillance was initiated on a specific address. The wait was brief—the car chase fast and harrowing, reaching speeds nearing 100 mph before the 1941 Mercury wrecked and the outlaws were put afoot. There were, by then, twenty squad cars at the scene, three aircraft overhead and a posse of ten horseback volunteers. The long and the short of it, is short. Within three hours the escapees were handcuffed and jailed. Skillfully, Texas Ranger Norm Dixon interrogated Mershon, extracting incriminating admissions about the pair's seven weeks of free-world outlawry. Shortly thereafter judges' gavels in several jurisdictions fell on cases involving LeMay and Mershon and they pocketed hard time measured in centuries, not decades. They caught the chain back to Huntsville.[5]

During another 1940s break from the Retrieve State Farm, convicts Jimmie Hudson, pulling a nickel from Jackson County

(county seat Edna) for Assault With Intent to Rape and Burglary, along with convicted burglars Oscar Abrams, doing five years from Dallas, and Joe Atkins, serving three years from Houston, had eluded detection, scampering into the Brazoria County free-world while they were supposedly hard working at the prison unit's "mule lot." An alarm was figuratively sounded and the mandatory manhunt was on. Correctional Officer George Rushing— alone—was posted on the east side of the Brazos River Bridge on State Highway 35, south of Angleton. Assistant Warden (Captain) B.W. Whitten, accompanied by Correctional Officer Gordon Robinson, along with civilian J.C. Young of the Dow Chemical Plant's Protection Department, scoured the Brazos River's tangled bottomlands. According to Warden (Captain) Joe Hines, their efforts paid off—Abrams and Atkins were recaptured. Escapee Hudson played a weak hand, coming up real short and real dead. Correctional Officer George Rushing noticed furtive shifting in the dark at 9:30 p.m., issuing his binding and unequivocal challenge: "Throw up your hands!" An area newsman offhandedly recorded the outcome: "When Hudson made a move toward his pocket Rushing fired his .38 automatic at him. Hudson turned and ran and Rushing leveled down on him, killing him with his second shot. . . . Angleton Funeral home took charge of the body pending word from relatives."[6]

As 1943 was drawing to a close three long-term convicts stepped up—and commendably so. They had learned through free-world newspaper reports that a twelve-year-old Houston lad had been horribly burned near a year earlier in a schoolroom stove accident, and that the boy was undergoing multiple skin grafts. Unfortunately, according the youngster's physician, the skin grafts "didn't take." Oscar Frazier, forty-three, an Armed Robber from Harris County doing ninety-nine years, thirty-two-year-old Lloyd Ranels pulling the Big Bitch, a life sentence as an Habitual Criminal, and William Garrett, thirty-three, doing ninety-nine for Burglary and Robbery, put their heads and hearts together. Choosing Frazier as their letter-writing spokesman, Texas Prison officialdom was notified and the missive was forwarded to the injured child's mother. The compassionate letter stated, in part:

> We have read where your young son needs skin for grafts. I and my fellow prisoners, Lloyd Ranels and William Garrett, are ready to furnish it and ask no favors. [signed *Oscar Frazier*]

Emmett Moore, now Warden at The Walls, assured the boy's mother and the newspaper writer that "he was sure the prison system would co-operate if possible and if a proper request was made."[7] In and of itself the above cited was a legit tearjerker and the convicts were sincere. Regrettably, some convicts learn well the art of deception—screening fraudulence behind the veil of heartrending tragedy.

Other convicts were anything but benevolent. At the Wynne State Farm, Correctional Officer George Tyrus Preston, fifty-seven, was dutifully sitting inside a picket cage pulling his shift that twentieth day of June 1944. Four convicts bolted for freedom: James McLemore, Eugene Padgett, W.M. Johnson, and forty-two-year-old Leonard Stockton, who was doing twenty years for an Armed Robbery in Palo Pinto County. Somehow, one way or the other, Convict Stockton was in possession of a pistol. He shot Correctional Officer Preston, mortally. Then the outlaws looted the facility's armory, making sure that each had firepower for their free-world flight. Within forty-eight hours Convicts Padgett and Johnson had been hard run to ground near Madisonville absent any gunfire; "worn out and ready to quit." They were returned to the Wynne lockup. The story would be different for Convicts Stockton and McLemore. During a vehicle chase and fast-running gunfight on Highway 62 between Buna (in Jasper County) and Mauriceville (in Orange County) local peace officers Freddie McWilliams and Asa Hickman finally managed to scoop up Convict McLemore after he wrecked the stolen car. Having lost the murder weapon in the sudden smashup, Convict Stockton had hotfooted—although on but one leg—away from the crash site. Rather proudly it would seem, the two fortunate lawmen turned "their prize" over to Sheriff Stanfield of Orange County, and DPS Highway Patrol Sergeant Chilcothe. Shortly thereafter—at night—two area rice farmers, Johnnie Womack and Oscar Breaux, espied Convict Stockton, afoot and acting suspiciously, so they made a citizens' arrest. The married George Tyrous Preston was peacefully lain to rest in the Lee Cemetery in Walker County. Ultimately, as the triggerman, Leonard Stockton was convicted of killing Correctional Officer Preston and sentenced to die, but a later clemency saved him from riding Ole Sparky's thunderbolt. He did not, however, wind up in the free-world, dying in prison on 12 December 1948.[8]

At about the same time, subsequent to an aborted escape from Eastham, career criminal Joe Werle, AKA the "Laughing Bandit, working off fifty-five years, admitted to authorities how he had pulled an illusory fast one over on them during a prior prison break, of which he had several. One was at Retrieve, where he and a companion, at Angleton, stole the Brazoria County Sheriff's automobile, fleeing until the gas tank was empty and then spending "four days of foodless, sleepless punishment" before being taken back into luckless custody. Back up to date, with free-world accomplices on his team, a man and woman, the conspiracy was put into effect. A phony telegram was sent to him—through prison officials, "saying his mother had been shot and had only five days to live." Included was a telephone number of his mother's hospital room. Selling the hog, according to Joe, was easy: "Boy, I broke down. You talk about an actor. They gave me money to call and this gal answered the phones and said she was the 'nurse' later the man wired, claiming to be the doctor and leaving his phone number. When the prison board called to check on the story, the 'nurse' answered and said the doctor was out. . . . The prison board approved a 10-day reprieve, and Governor Allred raised the time to 30 days. . . .[I] walked out of the prison with the official's permission— and mother didn't even have a headache." Unfortunately bad times were in store for Joe after this scam. Thinking that he was actually shooting at outlaw Floyd Hamilton, near Mexia in Limestone County, a Texas Ranger shot and wounded Joe Werle and it was he who needed hospitalization—not his mother.[9]

Another convict wasn't in need of a physician, but a mortician. Lee Smith and two other unnamed white convicts were on the yard at The Walls, provisionally transferred from Eastham to witness the October TPR. At the point of an improvised shank Smith approached and demanded that two black convicts, Dick Jennings and Earl McNear, fork over whatever they had, money and/or tobacco—or else! Excitement in the arena didn't compare to the rodeo on the yard. McNear stumbled over some loose lumber in the yard, falling down. But when he came up it was with a "piece of timber" in his hand. Protecting himself McNear clubbed Smith, and he fell to the ground—dead! The other two white convicts ran away.[10]

While the 1940s didn't play well for some convicts with free-world attainment on their agendas, the time period was not benign for Correctional Officers either. During November 1946 two convicts, trustys, at The Walls made their bid for more freedom and were chased by Correctional Officer Benjamin Franklin Larue, fifty-five. Unfortunately, as it turned out, he caught them. During the ensuing fight they hit him in the head, the injury proving as eternal as his manicured plot in the Lovelady Cemetery. Then, once again back at the Wynne State Farm on 29 June 1947, fifty-five-year-old Correctional Officer Guy Holman made the unanticipated but ultimate sacrifice. An enraged convict attacked him from behind with a shank, delivering the Grim Reaper's message: Prison work can be perilous work.[11]

Although he didn't catch the chain to get there, a new General Manager for the Texas Prison System rode an unstoppable whirlwind of admiration and adulation from Tennessee to Texas. Oscar Byron Ellis, forty-six, had been recruited by the Texas Prison Board after the pressured resignation of Douglas W. Stakes, who in light of a critical and comprehensive review of the Texas Prison System by an eminent outside-the-state penologist, consultant Austin MacCormick (from the reform camp, The Osborne Association), had concluded and caustically reported that the whole institution, statewide, was in sordid shape and massive correction was needed to put it in order— right now! With his nationally recognized penology expertise and a growing and glowing reputation in the Volunteer State, choosing O.B. Ellis had been a no-brainer. During their November 1947 Prison

Board meeting it had been decided to formally hand over the Texas Prison System's control to the Tennessee resident, if he would take the job.[12] Accepting the offer, Ellis picked up the penitentiary leadership reins in Texas on New Year's Day 1948.[13]

Hardly had General Manager Ellis been at the helm before tough Texas prison reality erupted. During a dreary and cold February morning at the Darrington State Prison Farm, after the count, convicts Cecil Chester Davis, John Tom Rawlings, and Harvey Lee Glass jumped. At the unit's laundry they had "slugged" and overpowered Correctional Officer B.E. Rollo and stolen his revolver. The timing had been unlucky for a Velasco (sixteen miles south of Angleton, four miles from the Gulf of Mexico) family, Mrs. R.L. Bailey and her children, John, old enough to drive, and teenaged Lula Frances. They were going to take a one-day holiday at Houston while Mr. Bailey pulled his regularly assigned shift at the Dow Chemical Plant near Freeport. On the road near Sandy Point, seeing a lone approaching automobile, the outlaws stepped into the roadway forcing the Baileys' vehicle to stop. In but a heartbeat—at the muzzle of the stolen weapon—the Baileys were kidnapped. The convicts crawled into the car and with a new white-suited chauffeur headed north at breakneck speed. In one sense it was fortunate—someone observed the hostage taking in-progress, reporting to authorities that they should be on the lookout for a "green two door sedan." Unfortunately the Baileys' automobile was "a black four-door model." By nighttime, after changing a tire and extricating themselves from a muddy back road the victims and the victimizers were in Coryell County at Gatesville. There the hostages were put afoot and the desperadoes stole another getaway ride. Recounting the experience to a reporter, Mrs. Bailey thanked her lucky stars that the family had not been harmed, but, in fact "they did suffer from the cold, no food, and too fast driving. . . ."[14] All's well that ends well—the Baileys returned to their home at Velasco and, later, the escapees were taken into custody.

Another episode of violence would be an unwelcome salutation to new General Manager Ellis, a mid-1948 breech of trust.

Twenty-seven-year-old James W. "Brazos" Morrow, a one-eyed giant of a man with a gregarious gift of gab, had already racked up prison time in Texas due to Tarrant County convictions for Armed Robbery and Burglary and Theft Over $50—plus hard time in Michigan for Burglary. Subsequent to a revocation of parole, Brazos Morrow was celled at The Walls where he shortly conned himself into the position of a trusty—a rather unusual trusty position to be sure. How or where he obtained the technical skill—if such is hard to master—is unsettled, but Brazos Morrow became a Motion Picture Projectionist. As such he traveled back and forth between the various prison locations showing nighttime and weekend black and white movies to convicts unable to sit in free-world theaters. With a fully stuffed bag of celluloid reels, sometimes he would remain at each unit for three or four weeks.[15]

While on a July 1948 stopover at the Blue Ridge State Farm fairly close to Missouri City (Harris County), twenty-odd miles southwest of Houston, Brazos Morrow became infatuated—or fell in love—with a pert redhead visiting another convict—a relative. The romance sparked and the motion picture man was thoroughly smitten—with but one thought on his mind. Further adult clarification is not obligatory, though it's implicitly understood. The lady of his dreams—and fantasies—stayed in Houston. Were he to sample and savor her pleasures it would be there, not at Blue Ridge. On the twelfth night of the month Brazos Morrow filched three of the state's revolvers and one of its Winchesters and on foot followed the Southern Pacific Railroad tracks northeast toward the metropolis stowing his pent-up desire.[16]

When about four miles from the city limits of Houston, the dog-tired Brazos Morrow came upon the West Junction Station, a telegraph locale for the railroad. Parked outside was a brand-new car. The shiny Chevrolet belonged to the telegrapher, Novita, a surprise birthday gift but the day before from her husband Theron Eldridge "Eddie" Shofner, thirty-one, a Harris County Deputy Sheriff assigned to bailiff a court.[17] Novita's shift would end at 2:00 a.m. and Eddie had driven to the station to follow his wife home—killing time the couple was inside playing cards. Outside, escapee Morrow discovered that the car key must be inside, and he would have it at any cost—coldblooded murder if necessary. And it was. Eddie went down, a bullet to the forehead, and Novita dodged two shots before Brazos skipped—bumping into Bernard Beaman, Novita's father who also worked for the Southern Pacific Railroad. He had come to relieve his daughter. The scuffle waxed hot and Morrow ultimately fled to a nearby field—hiding in the night shadows of a huge electrical grid complex. As dawn broke the next morning Texas Rangers and Harris County lawmen and Correctional Officers were Johnny-on-the-spot and thanks to an impatient pack of the state's Bloodhounds and a Dog Sergeant the murderer was put on the spot and taken into custody absent shots being fired.[18]

Ultimately sentenced to die strapped into Ole Sparky—which he did—Brazos Morrow's execution was marred—or made more interesting—by a stunning surprise. As the condemned man was being fastened to the electric chair and the hood placed over his head, a visibly distraught Correctional Officer bolted into the Death Chamber screaming that the state was the real murderer, trying to physically interdict the court's death order, in a tirade lambasting the imposition of Capital Punishment. He was physically restrained. The electrical switch was thrown. But certain Death House rituals and protocols were amended.[19]

While there was unfolding drama from time to time inside the tall walls and outside the high fences, the selection of General Manager O.B. Ellis to run the Texas Prison System had been a milestone event. A new day was at hand. Most prison scholars credit the new General Manager with a five-pronged methodology—something collectively known as the Ellis Plan:

1. Improve and repair existing physical plants; raising convicts' standard of living.
2. Reorganize and properly manage prison industries.
3. Upgrade prison farming operations: Mechanization and Diversification.

4. Readjust and revamp prisoner classification and rehabilitation programs.
5. Focus on higher recruiting standards and improved pay for employees.[20]

Clearly—though it would take time—Ellis through his honed managerial skills and agricultural expertise would began the transformation of the Texas Prison System, from perhaps one of the nation's worst to one of its best. And part of that agricultural expertise can be laid at the doorstep of Byron Frierson, who Ellis recruited to manage the Prison System's farm and ranch operations. A WWII veteran with a college education hard-earned from Texas A&M University, before accepting the penitentiary position Frierson had pulled down time as a county agricultural agent. In farming and ranching circles and at scattered Texas sale barns Frierson was—as the saying goes—legit![21] That said, his domain was yet a penitentiary—home to some bad men, capable of really doing bad things. Even before General Manager Oscar Byron Ellis could celebrate closure of one year on the tough Texas job—grotesque sensationalism sparked another deadly prison story.

Clarence William Redwine, thirty-eight, was a 1940s prisoner at Retrieve, serving five terms "ranging from 5 to 15 years for robbery by assault." Redwine had already served hard time in Kansas and also had to his credit a Dishonorable Discharge from the United States Navy. Purportedly, at Retrieve, convict Redwine was a predator, having pulled several stints in solitary confinement for vicious threats against other prisoners, as well as "attempted sex perversion." Whether or not convict Redwine wanted a piece of Ernest Cleve Jones, thirty-three, is somewhat factually nebulous. If he did he picked the wrong customer for a nonconsensual tryst. Convict Jones owned seven prior prison terms, two in Texas, four in Oklahoma, and one trip to the federal lockup at Leavenworth, Kansas. He, like Redwine, was no Angel. And, too, Ernest Jones had access—through his assignment in the kitchen—to a super wicked-looking cane-knife, one with a blade near two and half feet long, and four inches wide.[22]

Whether or not their difference spun on an axis of spurned sexual advances or, by another version, failure to extend $5.00 credit for another pint of pruno, the bottom-line is unaffected. Convicts Redwine and Jones were at odds, sworn enemies. The brouhaha spiraled hotter after Jones thrashed Redwine in a round of fisticuffs, purportedly apologizing profusely at the same time he was beating the daylights out of him. Clarence William Redwine promised revenge. Ernest Cleve Jones believed him. For these two, life at Retrieve had boiled down to basics: Whack the other guy before he whacked you.[23]

The calculating comeuppance was served cold. When Redwine sat down for supper in the dining hall, Jones approached from behind, cane-knife in hand. With one energized swipe Jones decapitated Redwine, his head rolling to a stop on the table, Clarence's torso remaining in the sitting position, blood jetting from the now headless neck. It weren't pretty! It was also no whodunit.

Jones copped to Warden I. K. Kelly, eventually catching a nickel tacked to an updated sentence. In the real world—and prison is the real world—fair fights are few.[24] That's why sage advice from old-time convicts to fish can be of life-saving worth, such as: Don't foolishly hogtie yourself when sitting on the toilet with both ankles trapped in dropped trousers—with haste before taking the throne, remove one leg to maintain ample freedom of movement in case of oncoming calamity at a most inopportune time.

An early 1950s blitzing predicament was fast coming on for worried wardens—a hurricane. They had weathered such storms in the past, but with the heavy concentration of farm units positioned along Texas's upper Gulf Coast this one was predicted by weathermen to be a doozie. Mother Nature's timing was discombobulated. The cotton crop, as much as 10,000 bales, had matured early and was ready to be picked—and the storm was on the way. As most convicts domiciled at the lower farms units were already scampering to complete or maintain other agricultural assignments—as well as pick cotton—the manpower shortfall could prove a disaster. Following notification of the looming threat, General Manager Ellis took unprecedented action. Anxiously he assembled convicts in the auditorium at The Walls; they were primarily working in the industrial shops, and not tied to producing food and fiber and fat cattle. At the mass meeting Ellis laid his cards on the table—he needed help lest the cotton crop be lost—any volunteers? "The 1,500 inmates in the auditorium agreed to help get the cotton picked." And that's what came to pass—the prisoners were trucked south in the nick of time and, with white shirttails billowing in the wind the cotton crop was saved.[25] Yes, the obliging convicts had stepped up! All's well that ends well—for a little while.

Another predicament there would be, this one inside The Walls, as there would be with many other prisons throughout the United States during the 1950s.[26] At Huntsville on the twelfth day of April 1955 a convict went on a "psychotic rampage," breaking sixty-three windows. The fuse had been lit. The next day after breakfast more than fifty convicts were turned out onto the recreational yard encircled by a high cyclone fence. At 10:00 a.m. they were ordered back inside—they bucked! They were given a second chance to voluntarily return to their houses (cells) and for a second time they stood pat—refusing to leave the yard. These convicts had already proven to be knotty disciplinary problems and resultantly were most of the time locked and fed inside their houses, excepting for the recreational respite. They, unlike most convicts, did not have job assignments. At the time, one of America's leading penologists (from the reform camp) was suggesting that penitentiary unrest could oftentimes be traced to two factors, "idleness inside the prison walls and politics outside." Furthermore, he theorized: "Caged, idle men are the dynamite of which prison explosions are made. Usually it is a small grievance, magnified by the ringleaders, that sets them off."[27] And therein lay underpinning for the Huntsville hubbub. It had surely been an administrative call, and the reasoning would not stand today, but this was 1955. Since these particular convicts didn't work at all, it was theorized their daily caloric intake should be and would be less than physically active working prisoners. They were fed breakfast and supper—nothing at noon. Therein was the actual gist of their come hell or high-water demand: Three meals a day, working or not. Back on the recreational yard, they were still refusing to move— and would not be stampeded. From that point forward the Warden apprised them that they were deemed to be in a state of mutiny and prison personnel would do what they had to do to enforce rules and maintain order.[28] Reasonable grievances might be sorted through and fixed—or adjusted—but an outright buck was unacceptable.

Inside the cellblock—in sympathy with those outside—"Water mains were broken, toilets were destroyed, and 76 windows were broken. . . ." For the short term a nausea-producing gas was employed to dampen the wherewithal of those unruly prisoners bent toward property destruction. It worked! For those inside, the gas was dissipating by the use of fans. For those outside the night air was turning rather chilly and uncomfortable, forty-eight degrees, and most convicts were covered only by their prison whites.[29]

General Manager O.B. Ellis—among his other strong administrative suits—cultivated a practicable working relationship with and understanding of the press corps. Not surprisingly the media appeared, reporters and photographers and television cameramen. A prison riot or near riot is always a damn good story—anywhere, anytime. The mere presence of print and photo and talking-head journalists was not missed by the uproarious convicts and never is. The Catch-22 for penitentiary administrators remains omnipresent: Deny the press access and suffer a very visible politicized and public-relations spanking or admit them and stand by while a few manipulative convicts nimbly play them like proverbial drums. Or, as an experienced journalist candidly conceded, if one is not open with media folks, well, they'll concoct their own story.[30] In this instance when news correspondents made the Huntsville scene, "it was just as if one had turned a hive of bees loose."[31] Absent a scared hostage the convicts really didn't own any bargaining chips: That is, until before the ravenous congregated press corps they threatened to start cutting their heel-tendons unless their demand was met: Three meals a day or blood on the menu for the evening news.

With really not too much to report on—just guys milling around in a prison yard—media folks began packing to leave, hunting elsewhere for a more gripping story. Several mutineers, realizing their audience was mobilizing and that they were leaking momentum, did cut their heel-strings to alarm salivating newshounds. Much to the cutting convicts' chagrin the self-mutilation did not come across as all that dramatic—a little blood and not too much pain.[32] By late in the afternoon of 14 April 1955, disheartened and with no more fight in their systems, the prisoners were ordered to remove their whites and stand for a necessary strip search, before being marched one at a time back into their houses with broken windows and a foul-smelling gaseous taint.[33] There they would continue to partake of but breakfast and supper—for the next thirty days in the lonesome and silent comfort of their individual houses, not in the drab but noisy dining hall. Not too much good comes from a buck!

Hardly any real time elapsed—two days—before incarcerated East Texas fellows revolted. In 1955, Texas Ranger Captain Robert A. "Bob" Crowder, fifty-four, was in command of Company B at Dallas.[34] As an ex-Marine, previous Dallas PD motorcycle policeman, and former Texas Highway Patrolman, the tall and lanky Crowder physically typified the persona, "One Riot, One Ranger." On 16 April 1955 he proved it. The unfortunate situation at Rusk, then housing inmates officially diagnosed and found to be criminally insane, was where ferocious bedlam had broken loose. *The Rusk Cherokeean* carried the bold-print Extra Edition headline: "State Hospital Patients Are Rioting on Maximum Security Ward in Rusk." The Texas DPS Director, Homer Garrison, Jr., telephoned Captain Crowder with a curt message: Get to Rusk and damn quick! The Ranger Captain— at breakneck speed in his brand-new 1955 Oldsmobile—covered the 120 miles in record time. Upon arrival, Captain Crowder found that inmate Ben Riley had been chosen spokesman for the other black patients/prisoners, many of which had armed themselves with scissors and ice-picks, and were holding several terrified civilian employees hostage. Though blood had already been spilled, Captain Crowder remained cool and calm. He would enter the Ward

6 and 7 sections alone, figuratively armed with but three things: "Commonsense in his brain, compassion in his heart, and ice-water in his veins. Literally, Captain Crowder carried two more things: cocked and locked semi-automatic Colt .45s in hand-carved holsters at each hip"[35]

Agitated black inmates, Crowder learned, were demanding that they be treated the same as white inmates, which didn't seem patently unreasonable to him. Captain Crowder skillfully defused the inmate's pent-up angst and stood by as they dropped their sharp weapons into a pile at the toes of his hand-stitched boots. Afterwards, when queried as to what he would have done had the mutiny turned Western, Captain Crowder was stoic, declaring: "I don't know what the story would have been. . . . but I know one thing, I had two .45s with eight shots in each of them, and that's about as far as I know."[36] As has been demonstrated, and will continue to be validated, the close working relationship between the state's custodians of the incarcerated and the state's Texas Rangers was/is solid.

Aside from the conventional miscues and missteps and mendaciousness sometimes associated with the daily lives of the kept and their keepers, one 1950s blunder was a humdinger. Ferdinand Waldo Demara, Jr., AKA Benjamin W. Jones, had landed employment with the prison, due in large part to his personal charisma marked by "courteous and charming manners." Of course the fact that Ben Jones also had a Ph.D. from the University of Texas had upped his hiring appeal; such a fellow would have a bright future with the Texas Prison System, by 1957 formally known as the Texas Department of Corrections (TDC). Ben Jones's entry-level position at the Wynne Unit had been that of lieutenant. About a month later he ascended in rank, and was issued captain's bars. Soon thereafter he was working out so well and displaying an ability to play well with others—prisoners and staff—Dr. Ben Jones was promoted to Assistant Warden at The Walls. He was specifically placed in administrative charge of more than 400 problem convicts in the Little Shamrock (mockingly named after Houston's plush Shamrock Hotel), those particular cellblocks reserved for hardcore "discipline cases, sexual deviants, psychotics, and prisoners in protective custody." What a godsend it was to have such a well-educated and highly competent penologist aboard.[37] Such good fortune was almost too good to be true.

And it wasn't. Casually thumbing pages from a back issue of *Life Magazine* a photograph caught the eye of an astonished convict. The article was about the wily misadventures of the Great Imposter, a fellow who had through the years fraudulently—but believably—assumed the roles of a surgeon with the Canadian Navy, a devoted Trappist Monk, as well as a cool-nerved State Trooper—and in line with his phony and doctored educational credentials, a studious college professor. Assistant Warden Ben Jones, to the convict's notion, bore a legit striking resemblance to the fellow pictured in the periodical piece. Were they not one and the same guy? The investigation commenced. The final conclusion—which came quickly—was almost beyond belief, but definitely true as reported FBI Special Agent Arthur Carter. During the interim timeframe the bogus Assistant Warden had disappeared—going undercover again—somewhere. Moviegoers may have been fumbling and spilling popcorn as they looked at then-Hollywood heartthrob Tony Curtis playing the slippery Demara in *The Great Imposter*, but it was TDC who had egg on its face.[38]

Though the hallmarks of the Oscar Byron Ellis administration are numerous—one in particular merits mention. The first female Warden of the Texas Prison System came into being under his direction. Recognizing her innate leadership abilities and, subsequent to her husband Frank McConnel Dobbs accepting another position within the system, Velda Quinn Dobbs, a native Texan (from Waller County), assumed the top job at Goree during 1954. And there, on state prison ground property is where she faithfully raised her two boys, Frank Quinn Dobbs and Ronald "Ronnie" Dean Dobbs, as well as progressively overseeing the wants and needs and security of her ensconced female charges. In the field of Texas corrections Velda Dobbs was a trendsetter, treading in deep water normally reserved for men.[39]

As but one thoughtful and trendy example Warden Dobbs gave the okay for prisoners at Goree—a prison first—to wear civilian attire: "dresses of their own design on special occasions" and during visitations. An inquisitive onsite journalist, Jim Brigance writing for the *Corpus Christi Times*, pinned and hemmed reality: "The female of the species, even when in captivity, cannot resist the subtle lure of a bright dress and a hair ribbon. . . . The overall effect is to create an atmosphere of help and rehabilitation rather than confinement and punishment." Warden Dobbs recognized reality: "It's really lifted spirits around here. It doesn't break down discipline and it makes a world of difference in the inmates' outlook." The theory behind the Warden's approach to penology was to make Goree as much as possible unlike the traditional penitentiary housing for male residents. Although Warden Dobbs contemplatively acknowledged that a few of her hardcore prisoners were beyond hope of rehabilitation, for the most part: "Some are really good people who just made a mistake. And some should probably never be released." Warden Dobbs was progressively cutting to the nub of actuality:

> We've had plenty who don't even know how to make up a bed. Who knows what the answer is? We want to create as good an environment here as possible so that when a woman leaves she will be equipped to keep herself out of trouble. It's not always easy. But something as simple as a checkered blouse and a colored skirt, where life is generally drab and white, may be the beginning to finding solutions.[40]

Was Warden Dobbs drowned in an ocean of discrimination and prejudice while breaking though the so-called glass ceiling? Emphatically not! Velda Dobbs continued her stellar management of the Goree Unit for near twenty years, before admirably retiring after twenty-two years with the prison system. In fact, in honorable recognition for her dedicated service to the State of Texas and TDC, the Education Center at Goree is named after the unstoppable and ground-breaking Velda Quinn Dobbs.[41]

Though he was now circulating in the free-world, the aforementioned outlaw Gene Paul Norris was living proof that not everyone underwent idealistic reformation by imprisonment. The stone-cold killer was—staying in character—always up to no good. He and two conspiring criminal cohorts, William Carl "Silent Bill" Humphrey and James E. Papworth had cooked up a devious and murderous scheme. Perhaps it might now register in some minds as ridiculous; nevertheless the plot was real—as real as it gets? These brazen thugs were going to rob the First National Bank at Fort Worth, and it was unlike most Tarrant County depositories. This bank was behind the high fences of the city's strategic bomber installation, the Carswell Air Force Base. The armored car delivering the monthly payroll for Air Force personnel—military and civilian—would put them on easy street, once it was off-loaded into their getaway vehicle. How would they gain entry to the base? Well, that was easy! They would murder a bank employee and her son in their home on Meandering Way and then, using her car with the appropriate windshield decal, drive to the base and be waved through along with traffic making up the morning rush to work. And although the dramatic story is worthy of an in-depth retelling, there is a bottom-line and herein that will have to suffice. The good guys got wind of the plot and at the end of a high-speed car chase and wreck near Springtown (in Parker County) Gene Paul Norris and Silent Bill Humphrey were fatal casualties of bullets fired by two Texas Ranger Captains, John J. "Johnny" Klevenhagen of Company A based in Houston, and J.E. "Jay" Banks, Company B at Dallas.[42] There are, whether inside or outside the tall walls and high fences, just some folks beyond redemption no matter the best intentions of the law-abiding public or penologists or peace officers. Meanwhile back at the ranch, on the prison farm units and inside The Walls, everyday work continued.

Too, during the 1950s era Oscar B. Ellis looked to modernizing equipment and fine-tuning personnel matters. Two-way radios were purchased "to facilitate communication between units and to assist in apprehension of escapees." An employee Credit Union was birthed and employees were enrolled in the Social Security structure. Correctional Officers were no longer allowed to be attired in civilian clothing of their choice; now they wore a distinctive uniform. And for the first time a Pre-Service Training School was established for new recruits.[43]

Quite interestingly one convict, Albert Race Sample, was doing some hard time on the Brazoria County prison farms during the 1950s and into the early 1970s. Subsequent to release and genuinely turning his life around for the better and, later, a Governor's Pardon, he penned his autobiography, *Racehoss: Big Emma's Boy*. Approvingly a writer for *The Chicago Times* praised the narrative, declaring it was "Brilliantly set down in street language" and the stories within were "worthy of Twain, Faulkner, and Lardner." Closer to home, an enthralled *Dallas Morning News* reviewer, speaking of Albert's "ear for how people talk," suggested that "Sample's book makes hell vivid." Within the cadre of progressive penologists and the prison reformist community, it is an oft-cited classic—with good reason. While imprisoned the author did witness first-hand some examples of prison personnel's apparent brutality and callous maltreatment. That makes the case—in some minds—for a blanket indictment of the prison staff. So, not surprisingly, sometimes devotees of penitentiary lore rely heavily—but selectively—on the wrongdoings and unprofessional conduct highlighted therein.

While once again reminding the reader that no excuse herein is being proffered for cruel and/or inhumane handling of the incarcerated, there is the backside to what author Sample wrote. Frequently obscured are the cherry-picked omissions, the carve-outs about interactions between convicts in some modern-era secondary narratives. A nonpartisan look at convicts and paid-men, spotlights that sometimes the befuddled Correctional Officers were dealing with violently inclined and—for lack of better and begin terminology—a weird lot. One of the convicts in Albert Sample's prison barracks snuck around during the dark nighttime hours, hunting for and sucking on other inmates' exposed toes. A convict assigned to the kitchen was adept at stealing pork-chops, bundling them in a dishrag and tying the pilfered goods to his scrotum to avoid detection, knowing routine pat-downs were not that personal. At least once—and who knows how many times undetected—that same kitchen worker was literally caught in the act having sexual intercourse with the on-purpose slit in a warm ham, one recently removed from the oven. Of that most convicts were thoroughly disgusted, not wishing to engage in oral sex by proxy.[44] One inadvertent mix-up between what was thought to be petroleum jelly—as a lubricant—and super-hot medicated balm produced a scorching surprise for a convict duo—for one where the sun don't shine, for the other where the sun shouldn't shine. Then there was another convict growing tired of being forced to masturbate and suck on the manhood of another, while everyone in the dimly lit dorm could watch—if that turned them on. The physically weaker of the two, with a sharp razorblade forestalled an ejaculation—the bloody and disconnected penis on the dirty floor—its former owner screaming in pain and disbelief at his loss.[45]

At the time the mixed-race Sample was at Retrieve State Farm, the unit was designated and segregated, reserved for, as Albert described them, the nastiest, most irredeemable black cons that were in the entire Texas penitentiary system. And, by his admission, Sample was not above cheating other convicts during card games when and if the opportunity for a sleight of hand presented.[46] Honesty didn't earn a ticket for a bunk at Retrieve. A vast majority of Retrieve's convicts had been to prison several times over, and were working on living out lengthy sentences the best they could, however and whenever. For one in-house settling of scores, the aggrieved convicts doused a sleeping fellow with lighter fluid, and while he slumbered flicked a lighted cigarette onto the bedclothes and onto the badass they wanted dead.[47] Fellow convicts weren't the only targets of opportunity in Albert Sample's tight world. When an outside squad was engaged in clearing land and cutting timber—swinging double-bit axes—if the prime chance came to deftly fell a tree on top of a mounted but distracted Boss, well, that was the cons' good luck and the luckless Boss and his horse's misfortune: So claimed Sample.[48] Albert Race Sample, perhaps, was spot on right, or perhaps not. Prior to the 1950s being put into the Texas prison's history book, Correctional Officer Charles Jesse Baker, forty-four, while carrying a timber cutting squad clearing land, was killed as result of a falling tree atop him.[49]

A youngster who lived the Retrieve State Farm, I.K. Kelley Jr., the Warden's son, recalled that some of the convicts at Retrieve "were the meanest, sorriest bunch in the prison system." Expressly he remembered an event from his boyhood:

> I remember one time of an incident involving two convicts. If I remember correctly, one was our cook. He was in the kitchen fixing dinner when he looked out the back window of the kitchen just in time to see a convict knock a guard off his horse near the lot. Seems the guard had a squad of convicts doing some kind of work there at the lot. (Horse and mule pens) They were fixing fences or something. Anyway after knocking the guard off his horse, the convict jumped on the horse and started toward our house. Our cook ran from the kitchen into the part of the house where Mom was and asked her where Caps pistol was, saying that there was [a] convict trying to escape. Seems Pop was gone from the farm that day on business. He usually left his pistol on the mantle above the fireplace in his and Mom's bedroom. I don't know if Mom got him the pistol or he knew where it was. He got the pistol and ran outside the house just as the escapee went past. The cook shot above the escapee's head. I guess the escapee decided things were against him, for he fell off the horse close to the Tarver's house. The Tarver's house was just across the road from our house. The convict surrendered to the cook. By that time some guards had shown up and took over. Well the cook had really not stopped to think of what he was doing. When it was over and he finally real- ized what he had done, Mom said he started shaking all over. What he had done could have cost him his life. For sure there was not anyway he could have gone back into the building with the other convicts. He would have been dead in just a short while. When Pop got back he took the cook to a safe place. Could have taken him to the jailhouse in Angleton. Needless to say he was granted a parole. We lost a good cook.[50]

As the 1960s kicked off, most Texans and not just a few convicts could see and were experiencing the benefits of forward thinking by Oscar Byron Ellis, now re-titled as the Director of TDC. He had already won well-deserved adulation from his professional penological peers when they hands-down elected him as President of the American Correctional Association. Yes, Texas had come a long way—as had the entire country—since first opening those cell-blocks at 1849 Huntsville. For the long-haul, the system's agricultural enterprises had blossomed—in the realm of profitability, proficiency, and productivity, under the sensible stewardship of O.B. Ellis. Sound tilling and drainage practices had increased the system's land usage, significantly in the "low lying acres of the Texas Gulf Coast." Thoughtful and tested breeding programs had bolstered livestock and egg production. As a practical matter it was feeding thousands of prisoners and cutting costs for the state's always strapped coffers. As TDC continued to strive for self-sufficiency, convicts noticed that their diet and medical care were much improved. So, too, were some of their available leisure time options: "Ellis introduced television sets into the cell blocks." For weekends convicts were entertained with Hollywood films—Technicolor—with an outcome that morale was conspicuously bettered. "He summarily fired brutal and corrupt convict guards and prison wardens, and to insure that qualified and competent personnel were hired to carry out his reforms, in 1958 he started (as previously noted) the first pre-service training program for Texas prison guards. Between 1948 and 1961 the annual starting salaries of guards almost tripled, and competent prison guards were rewarded by subsidized housing and other amenities such as barber and laundry services."[51]

To be sure emphasis wasn't only focused on the well-being of the keepers and the fattening of hogs or gathering of eggs or picking little green orbs in the pea-patch. Director O.B. Ellis was instrumental with developing—overseeing—that reformative curriculums and/or making sure free-world programs were available inside the tall walls and behind the high fences. Vocational training in a wide array of trades such as welding, carpentry, television repair, brick laying, and auto mechanics—to name but a few— was made accessible, as was more traditional type schooling. An educational syllabus leading to—if one wanted it and worked hard for it—walking across the stage and accepting GED recognition was in the cards for those with good behavior. There, too, was church and Alcoholics Anonymous. And, perhaps, at least at that time, a reasonably thoughtful realignment of prisoner classification was instituted that tilted toward rehabilitation, separating convicts by age and offense, prior criminal history and potential for reformation.[52] Unexpectedly during the last quarter of 1961 TDC Director Oscar Byron Ellis succumbed to a massive heart attack—but it would not be the only calamity that year.

Hurricane Carla was horrendous—a storm squalling across the Gulf during September 1961. The aforementioned lowlands in Fort Bend and Brazoria Counties, where several of the state's prison farms were located, was exceptionally fertile ground, but susceptible to ruthless flooding. Evacuations to higher and safer ground for both prisoners and the free-world population was at times called for—wind howling at unendurable decibels and water rising at insufferable rates. Convict Albert Race Sample was ensconced at Retrieve when Carla made her unladylike arrival. Subject to barely surviving a night of flooding in the dormitory styled "tanks," the morning light brought receding waters but through the drizzle also revealed an ungodly sight—snakes, scores of snakes.[53]

Townsmen at nearby Angleton sought help from Warden Zan E. Harrelson, the headman at Retrieve, a longtime Texas penitentiary employee salty as the Gulf of Mexico or maybe more so. At any rate, some frightened folks at High Island (in the Galveston/Chambers County region) were trapped in a church-house and unless some cuts were made at strategic places in levees and roadways, draining flood water to the sea, their predicament would become dire. At Retrieve several Hoe-Squads were turned out, loaded into wire-caged trucks and then transported for the sixty-minute ride to the High Island area and set to work—of course, under the watchful eyes of horseback Bosses.

Having to enter floodwaters and wade chest-deep to the spot where a drainage channel could be cut was unsettling for the convicts in and of itself. The unnerving was compounded by their sober realization that they were sharing murky water with slithering playmates—those with no shoulders. The snakes, as would be expected, were seeking any sanctuary for attachment, even the Hoe-Squads' one-eyed Aggies and the pommels and cantles of the Bosses' saddles. Any dry spot would do for the snakes. Scarily with the blades of their Aggies adjoining and turned downward the convicts began pushing water and snakes into an opening, somewhat herding the reptiles, according to Albert Race Sample, like South American gauchos. At last, after raging through that manmade cut the trashy water carried its scaly passengers toward the Gulf. At this juncture the wet and worn-down convicts were at last given a break. Volunteer workers associated with the Red Cross had noticed the prisoners' stellar performance and were soon handing them hot cups of coffee and glaze-covered doughnuts.[54] It would not be the last time Brazoria County prison farm inhabitants and the state's High-Riders dealt with high-water.

10

"guts, heart— and six rounds"

AFTER THE UNTIMELY DEMISE of O.B. Ellis, and an interim appointment of Jack F. Heard as Acting Director, Dr. George John Beto assumed the helm, steering TDC towards the transformational course set by his predecessor. Dr. Beto's credentials, in one sense, were rather odd for someone taking over as Director for the Texas Department of Corrections, he being an ordained Lutheran Minister and the President of Concordia Lutheran College at Austin, and later President of Concordia Theological Seminary at Springfield, Illinois, the position he was holding when Ellis had passed to the other side. On the other hand, his earlier appointment to the Texas Prison Board by Governor Allan Shivers, a post he had maintained for a half-dozen years, had served him and the Lone Star State's public well. George Beto had been, while a Board Member, an ardent and vocal supporter and energetic player helping Oscar B. Ellis transition TDC for the betterment of convicts and employees and Texas taxpayers. While in Illinois, Beto had become favorably acquainted and thoroughly impressed with one of America's leading penologists, Joseph E. Regan, Superintendent of the Land of Lincoln's legendary and damn tough Stateville Penitentiary. Although heavily involved with demanding theological pains as headman of the Seminary, Beto was also tapped by the Governor of Illinois, Otto Kerner, to participate in the state's correctional work. One of the several of those myriad duties was to travel abroad to England, France, Germany, Denmark, and Holland studying their methodologies for adequately dealing with and incarcerating criminals and safeguarding their societies.[1] Subsequent to the recruiting effort, when Dr. George John Beto formally accepted the leadership role for TDC on the first day of March 1962, Texans had not been capriciously hoodwinked. He came to the job with untiring enthusiasm and a down-to-earth attitude about what would be allowed behind those tall walls and high fences with regards to humane treatment, reformation, and discipline.

Convicts testing change is not an anomaly; it's routine, a sure-fire bet. With less than a week on the job Hispanic prisoners at the Harlem State Farm (now Jester Unit) bucked—sat down in the field and refused to work. Naturally, area Wardens hearing of the situation rushed to aid their TDC peer. The prisoners would not talk with anyone other than the newly installed Director. Expectedly with perhaps 300 convicts revolting—chiefly egged on by the No. 1 Hoe-Squad—the new sheriff in town, accompanied by the TDC Board's Hubert Hardison "Pete" Coffield, a powerhouse player in Texas penological doings, made his show at Harlem, prepared to listen. Seemingly the convicts had jumped half-cocked. Director Beto asked the men about their complaints but was "rebuffed" all around.[2] Bluffing with but a pair of deuces is not smart. Director Beto had to call their hand or lose control of TDC. News on the prison grapevine travels fast and its system-wide reach is not a hyperbolic myth.

Cutting to the nub is effortless, primarily by quoting Director George Beto's own words: "After I walked out there and attempted unsuccessfully to communicate with them, I went to the warden's office. . . . I recognized that this was a critical moment, so I put four or five of those wardens on horseback armed with wet rope . . . and instructed them to go out and put number one hoe squad to work. I told them to use whatever force was necessary. There was a flurry of excitement and then the number one hoe squad went to work in a hurry and the rest of the inmates followed."[3]

From a managerial perspective Director Beto's no-nonsense handling of the 1962 buck had its anticipated outcome. Except for one other buck at the Ferguson Unit that same year, during Beto's tenure as TDC Director any like upheaval was noticed—by its absence. And how far the legend actually reached might stand debate, but after that initial buck Director Beto was tagged by the convicts as the man with a Bat in one hand, a Bible in the other.[4] Of course, while there was no mass convict turmoil erupting, TDC was a multi-unit operation, housing many prisoners wanting to walk the straight and narrow, a moderate sampling of hopeless incorrigibles, and some committed to making a run for it—escape.

Perhaps it's not unfitting at this point to interject a remark or two that plays well into the history of the Texas Prison System— long before, during, and after the administrations of the generally well-respected Oscar Byron Ellis and George John Beto—the Building Tenders (BTs). The short version is uncomplicated. BTs were convicts expected to maintain order within their given cellblocks and dormitories and they were expected to keep officialdom updated with valuable prison intelligence matters—was there an impending buck, riot, or escape? Who cut who? Who raped who? Who was holding dope? Who in blue and gray was dishonest? In other words, they snitched to Bosses. Therein was the open secret; everyone knew who they were and what they were doing for their own self-interest.[5] Then, it should come as no shocker that some of the BTs were damn tough customers; type A personalities with ample psychosis to back their plays, psychologically or physically or deceptively. They ruled the roost. Not just a few guaranteed safety for Correctional Officers who were outnumbered by an ungodly ratio. Some were downright dangerous and mean. There would be no sane dispute in that quarter. In fact, while George Beto was walking and talking throughout the units, he recognized a particular BT—not approvingly either. In the good Director's mind this particular convict—if circumstances were right—"would rape a snake through a brick wall."[6] Beto had him stripped of his BT status.

The metaphoric fuel driving competent and successful criminal investigations, enlightened penitentiary management and, yes, even insightful journalism pieces may be summed up with but one word: Information. And within this framework of generalization a certain dichotomy erupts. Not just a few academic treatments disparage professional penologists—those actual folks with skin in the game—for developing and maintaining a network of informants behind the tall walls and high fences. Yet, oftentimes on the platforms of their published treatments is an upfront acknowledgment that they are themselves basing their theories and analytical findings on the words of convicts and correctional personnel, in most instances informants desirous of the pledged and granted anonymity; issuing pseudo-names and/or an identifying number in lieu of naming names is commonplace. Somehow and sometimes concealing sources is acceptable for their scholarly studies and hypothesis, but the on-the-ground correctional staff having their pool of secret operatives—snitches—is characterized as a truly wicked misuse of legal authority. Not unexpectedly now and again the broadcast and print media representative are more outspoken when ratcheting upwards their criticism of prison administrators utilizing confidential sources, while in the same piece or with the same breath they have cleaved unto themselves an indissoluble Constitutional right to protect the identities of clandestine folks whispering into their ear. Such ironies of irony are rich.

That prison staff could very well have a supportive stance with certain BTs, even if they were genuine hard-case outlaws in the freeworld, is exemplified by mentioning a late 1940s incident. Though he was a murdering hoodlum and a cop-killer, John Marion "Pete" McKenzie, while pulling his life sentence after his death sentence had been commuted, was a battle-scarred BT at The Walls. McKenzie had already killed one convict who had come at him with a two-by-four. Captain E.W. McCullar, sixty-four, had been summoned to the cell of an angry and assaultive Herman Lee "Humpy" Ross, a Galveston County convict awaiting an Appellate Court decision with regards to his death sentence for killing a luckless fellow, Guido Nasti, during a liquor store holdup. McKenzie followed McCullar to convict Ross's house. As soon as McCullar opened the cell-door Ross jumped out, attacking and slashing the Captain "across the face and arm" with a wickedly sharpened razor. The razor-wielding Ross had apparently slipped a mental gear—but that was of little consequence in a real time struggle for survival and, besides, not just a few Correctional Officers surmised that Humpy was, in fact, the meanest convict they'd ever come in contact with. BT McKenzie, though unarmed, in what was described as a "bare-handed fight against a razor armed convicted killer," connected with a powerful blow. The upheaval was catastrophic for Ross; he lost his footing and fell over "an iron railing of the third tier. . . ." The concussion was dramatic—Herman Lee Ross lingered and then recovered enough to die strapped to Ole Sparky, though the chair had to undergo modification due to his small physical stature despite his oversized streak of pure cussedness. McKenzie had been cut but his injury had not been life-threatening. Yep, the right BT at the right time at the right place could be an asset to a short-staffed workforce.[7] Captain McCullar thought so!

Dr. Beto was practical with regards to BTs and the convict in-house hierarchy: "Either you pick their [convicts'] leaders or they do."[8] Regardless warm and fuzzy niceties—or the lack thereof—George Beto was well aware that "there were liabilities with the system. Physical force was inherent in the system and violence could be used to resolve problems or enforce the rules."[9] Of course there was the flip side for BTs. Correctional Officers and Administrators could look the other way—and often did. BTs' cell doors were not normally locked. Shakedowns and searches for contraband in their houses was not really on anyone's near term agenda. Work assignments were not those requiring tough agricultural labor in an outside Hoe-Squad. Inside the facility, some BTs might have even had a stick to thump somebody or a shank to stick someone. For that earlier timeframe it was more-or-less common knowledge that BTs might actually be armed, such as the bloody brouhaha at Eastham's No. 2 camp: "[Jack] Rogers cut [Jimmy] Bostic slightly on the chin and the latter drew a knife, which building tenders were allowed to carry and stabbed Rogers once in the stomach [fatally]."[10] In their minds—and rightly or wrongly so—the BTs were walking a tightrope between the kept and the keepers. Upholding order is tricky business! And even though the BTs in most instances were tougher than a keg full of 16-penny nails, they assuredly weren't immune to being murdered inside the penitentiary: Well before the enlightened approach of Ellis and Beto, during the 1930s decade BT Hubert Woodall at Eastham was killed by convicts Pete Hennessey and Lacy Wingfield, but each caught only a cheap nickel for the in-house homicide.[11] Not too long thereafter BT Edd Ebbers, thirty-six, pulling fifty years, was bludgeoned and stabbed to death inside The Walls by recidivist convicts Johnnie Hall Gallups, then doing a 100 years for several Armed Robbery convictions and Jerry Lewis, working his way through eighteen years due to cases of Armed Robbery, Theft, and Burglary in East Texas.[12] Again at Eastham, BT Jack Havens, but twenty-four, pulling a slick quarter for Armed Robbery and Kidnapping from Tarrant, McLennan, and Parker Counties, went sound to sleep on the bunk in his house—forevermore. Convict Willard Scott, twenty-eight, from Refugio in Refugio County for Murder and Auto Theft and doing 101 years, buried a shank in the snoozing and snoring Havens. Scott was damn clear with his motive for offing Havens: He wasn't going to let BT Havens boss him around anymore.[13] For sure BTs weren't bulletproof, cut-proof, or indestructible supermen. Although now writing of this—the BT phenomena—it will garner much broader attention shortly herein when prevailing legal matters pick up an unexpected and unprecedented head of steam. Societal attitudes are ever evolving. But for now a salient truism is proffered for impartial reflection. And it will demand being mentioned again and—again—for it's germane for altogether understanding matters of place and time: During the reign of Mr. Ellis and Dr. Beto, when BTs were an unarguable apart of the Texas schema for managing and controlling its penitentiaries, not a single Correctional Officer or civilian staff member was murdered by a state convict—not one. From 1948 to 1972—not one![14]

At the Darrington Unit in hurricane-prone Brazoria County it wouldn't be slithering reptiles catching notice of fifty-year-old Warden Dub Bullard on 6 June 1963. No, he was horseback, fast following Bloodhounds chasing after a pair of escaping convicts, Robert

Emanuel Kirby and Billy D. Simmons. Perhaps he was thinking here we go again? Warden Bullard had, years before, been lauded for heroism during the 1934 Eastham break engineered by Clyde Barrow and Raymond Hamilton, brassily assisted by the auto-horn tootin' Bonnie Parker. Warden Bullard had steadily worked his way through the ranks but was not at all inclined to idle away time behind an administrative desk; downheartedly snarled in the Texas bureaucracy's never-ending red-tape. A newspaperman had noted that Warden Dub Bullard was a "man that quietly handled the toughest men in Texas." Before natural causes had overtaken Oscar Byron Ellis, he had characterized Dub Bullard as having "as much guts as any man I know wearing shoe leather."[15] By anyone's measure, Darrington Warden Dub Bullard was all man—all the time. E.L. Osborn, Livestock Supervisor at the adjoining Ramsey State Farm found Bullard's saddled horse, sans a rider, wandering the vast prison acreage. Of course, the intensive search for Warden Bullard was immediate. Unfortunately while his cognitive acumen had been yet whip-smart, his internal ticker had been flickering. The fatal heart attack had knocked him out of the saddle. Although there was little solace for the grieving widow, Beatrice, or Dub's son James Lee, as the husband and father was laid to rest at Huntsville in the Addicks Addition of the Oakwood Cemetery, knowing the two escapees had been captured brought a smidgen of comfort.[16]

Within but short-order Director Beto earned his nickname, "Walking George." Day or night, Saturday or Sunday, employees or convicts might look up and see an unannounced Director strolling through their prison unit, visiting with Correctional Officers and/or convicts, though an overt appearance of too much familiarity by actually shaking hands with the latter was a no-no. His concern for everyone was genuine. And though he wore eyeglasses, the lenses were not rose-colored. Whatever may be said of Director George Beto, good or bad, that he owned a superb knack for getting along with folks is indisputable: as his capable womb to tomb biographers make crystal-clear. Be they state or federal legislators, farmers and ranchers, oilmen, educators, lawyers, judges, businessmen, penologists, theologians—or journalists—one could normally get an audience with Director Beto, even mothers and dads of those doing time.[17]

In writing of his early-on experiences with TDC in general and Director Beto in particular, Professor Bruce Jackson is not inarticulate in describing the treatment awarded him when kicking off his 1964 research project identifying and detailing traditions of the convict work songs typified by black prisoners, as "White and Latin-American inmates do not sing these songs, nor do they have any body of metrically functional songs of their own used in similar fashion."[18]

On the first day of July 1964 Director George Beto welcomed Bruce Jackson to his office for a confab and to establish groundrules for the educator's probing research. There was no sparring. As Bruce Jackson explains, Beto was straightforward: "Abruptly, he asked me how I wanted to work. I said I would prefer to wander about the prisons, find people to talk with, then record and talk without interference from guards or wardens or anybody. He thought about that a moment, then said he thought that was a reasonable way to work. He picked up the phone and called Sidney Lanier, then warden at Ramsey Unit. Dr. Beto told Warden Lanier that I was coming down, that I might have some peculiar requests, but that I was to be granted every courtesy and not interfered with in any way. Which is just how it went. In all the years I did research in the TDC, whether I was studying folklore or homosexual behavior or criminalization patterns, the same courtesy and freedom were there for me. No one ever questioned any request for access of information—I was permitted to examine any files I wanted to examine, I could wander in the fields or cellblocks without having guards fritting about." Somewhat later Bruce Jackson told George Beto that at the time he was astonished with the freedom allowed him, and there was no atmosphere of secrecy, to which Beto replied: "How can we find out what we're doing wrong if we don't let people like you tell us?"[19] Admittedly, Bruce Jackson would not be a proponent for widespread incarceration for any demographic;

nevertheless he was favorably impressed with the openness of Director Beto's administration.

Perhaps unfortunately—at least by subjective degrees—many activists seem fascinated with myopically tying any and all agricultural field work accomplished at Texas prisons to be but a purposeful extension of abject slavery. Forcing convicts to work, however, was an almost universal practice of penology—no matter the state, no matter the demographic subset. Philosophically it was ubiquitous. Certainly in the State of Texas, which, indeed, had permitted discrimination and has a quantifiable Jim Crow past, the dirty and wearisome field work was not always racially reserved, despite what a few partisan purveyors push. During a 1929 examination of Fort Bend and Brazoria County farms by Texas Prison Commissioners—accompanied by newspaper correspondents—the diversity of convict Hoe-Squads was duly noted: "On all of the farms negroes [sic], white men and Mexicans were swinging hoes at a rather lively clip cutting weeds out of cotton and cane."[20] The newspaperman noted one squad of blacks "trudged along swinging their hoes in tempo and there was no appearance of sloth in their gait," while fellow convicts were setting the pace by singing work-songs in harmony. Furthermore it was dutifully reported: "Around 1,500 men are on the rolls of the three farms visited Thursday and all of the 440 on the Blue Ridge farm are Mexicans. White men predominate on the other two farms, though negro [sic] camps are located on all of them."[21] Decades later, appreciatively another journalist—as had industrious Bruce Jackson—enlisted the forbearance of Director Beto for his photographic essay during the late 1960s; sharp black and white images capturing convict life. During an extended period of fourteen months, camera in hand, the young journalist visited, without restriction, half-dozen Texas prison units, moving freely among them when and as he saw fit. While unquestionably striking, the photographs are also revealing—not just a few white convicts were assigned to the "Line" chopping and hoeing while Field Bosses and High-Riders sat tall in the saddle.[22]

At this time, unless there were believable and provable extenuating circumstances, new arrivals worked—and initially that work was in the vast agricultural fields. There was no shortage of weeds to be hoed, cotton to be picked, corn to gather, etc., etc., etc. Were one to behave and bend to the reality he was facing, after a period of time—usually measured in months—the compliant convict could earn assignment to a more cushy job: maybe the kitchen or dining hall or laundry or in one of the numerous industrial shops. As a pair of learned penologists remind, such a promotion "was not a right; it was a reward for his good conduct and attitude. If an inmate acted hesitant about his newly assigned job in the presence of a supervisor, the officer simply revoked the job and reassigned him to the field."[23]

Earlier, during the Great Depression, even some editorialists were championing working convicts in the field, advocating for what they deemed as but logical commonsense:

> The Texas prisons cannot afford to abandon the farm system, a large factor in the useful employment of Texas convicts. No prison system ought to guard against escapes by confining the inmates in cells and quitting all work. Merciful use of a lethal anesthetic would be better. Critics should not be too severe on harried management that has a far bigger job than is realized by most persons outside prison walls and their many problems.[24]

An illustrative example is not unfitting. Toward the end of Dr. Beto's TDC administrative tenure the agricultural statistics are apparently staggering. The prison system held title to 101,721 acres of real-estate; 50,000 acres of grazing land; and 40,000 devoted to food and fiber production. System-wide the convict cowboys and farm hands were overseeing 15,800 cattle (dairy and beef), 17,000 swine, 112,000 chickens, 3000 turkeys, 345 saddle horses, 290 brood mares, and 387 tracking dogs—and the mouthwatering farm-raised catfish numbered about 10,000. Aside from this enumeration, an annual total would come in revealing the farms produced about 819,000 dozen eggs, 83,500 lbs. of cheese, 4,000,000 lbs of spuds, 3,500 bales of cotton, and about one-half-million bushels of corn.[25] And though sometimes innocently omitted in generalized Texas Prison recaps, the sheer numbers of livestock—and tracking dogs—mandated that the State of Texas contract or subcontract the services of credentialed veterinarians; inoculations and pest control and tube worming and gelding the riding stock were ongoing but necessary duties constituting a heavy everyday workload for hypodermic and scalpel-wielding practitioners. Of course, that's discounting the nighttime call-outs spent with colicky horses and the number of breeches and expelled uteruses for first-calf heifers.[26]

Perchance at this point deviating from the chronological narrative with a brief sidebar is okay. Appreciating the precarious undertakings of those Field Bosses is fitting. Carrying an outside Hoe-Squad of ten to thirty convicts is/was not work for the faint-of-heart. There is to be sure, from appearances, an unmistakable semblance of romanticism festooned to horseback Field Bosses—men and women. After all, their day job is in the saddle, decked out in emblematic Western regalia: Stetson, cowboy boots, spurs, and a holstered revolver at the hip. Those accessories and accoutrements and a leathery complexion plentifully seasoned by brilliant sunlight and biting dust is but part of their persona—and story. Though indelicate, they relied on but "guts, heart—and six rounds."[27] The truth is irrefutable: Riding herd over cattle or convicts is risky. Some creatures have horns that can hook you; others have shanks that can gut you.

Ivory-tower theorists more often than not downgrade the mounted Field Bosses as but rural hayseeds, unable or unwilling to rise above horseback employment. Undeniably the majority—if any—do not have graduate degrees tucked into their saddlebags, but honesty and integrity and courage are not tangible traits. Evident, yes! Touchable, no! Too, nowadays it's somewhat fashionable with a political correctness spin to insinuate that the Field Boss was atop a horse in a calculated effort to cast off an aurora of superiority—sometimes racial superiority—looking down on pedestrian Hoe-Squads, omitting that not just a few Field Bosses, good Field Bosses, were men of color, black and brown, as well as white—some females too! Though in certain quarters it might be ignored, a respected scholar of hardcore correctional issues is spot on: "unless the inmates are working in broom corn, which is as high as a mounted man, [horseback] guards can easily see them at all times."[28] The truth is simple. Observing what's happening is better accomplished from elevation, rather than gawking, trying to haphazardly look around or through something or somebody. Blind spots are unsafe! Most metropolitan police departments have mounted officers. Ground-level observation is often very problematic. Even today in the parking lots of gigantic shopping malls, tall watchtowers serve as the surveillance platform for police personnel trying to interdict criminality—stealing from unattended cars or attacking heedless shoppers or pedophiles snatching kids.

In the wide-open spaces beyond tall walls and high fences conventional prison wisdom is valued, for it is there on the plowed ground and in the improved pastures that interactions between the keeper and the kept take on a whole new dimension. Showing any underlying weakness—losing control—can prove, as already herein documented, extraordinarily hazardous. There is, indeed, a wholly different and identifiable comparison that can be made between the methodologies of Correctional Officers assigned to the cellblocks and buildings and those Field Bosses carrying Hoe-Squads undertaking agricultural activities: "He [prisoner] is both highly visible and literally under the gun. Because the field operation emphasizes security and task completion, expectations of guards are clear and involve little negotiation."[29] In the field everyone works—or bucks.

> Fighting among inmates does not involve a direct test of the guard's authority. Escapes may be handled in an institutionalized manner, with bullets and dogs; they do not involve a direct, interpersonal confrontation between guards and inmates. Refusal to work, however, involves such a confrontation, one in which either the officer or the inmate will win. From the officer's point of view, the refusing inmate cannot be allowed to simply sit down and wait until quitting time when he can be tried for disobedience. This would be an inmate victory and perhaps the opening salvo of a strike. . . . To ensure that inmate refusals to work are few and

short-lived, the guard in the field cannot rely upon the authority of his uniform alone. He must add the weight of his personal authority. Indeed his success in this environment depends on how well he is able to dominate his squad and have his expectations met. He may do this by presenting such a tough, abrasive demeanor that his charges will produce because they believe that working for him is more acceptable than the consequences of not working. The field officer may also create in the minds of his squad considerable uncertainty about just what he might do. . . . [Field Bosses] try to style their behavior so that inmates will never doubt they can and will personally back up any directive.[30]

Perhaps an admittedly very crude but very honest example is apt, reminding that Hoe-Squads are not made up of adorable FFA boys and girls with agricultural aspirations in their career plans. An unsmiling and mean-dispositioned convict snarls at the mounted Field Boss: "What if we all get together and drag your mutherfucking ass off that goddamned horse and chop your ass to little pieces? I've already killed mutherfucking pricks a lot tougher you—on your best fucking day, asshole!" Was the prisoner mouthing or promising? Assuredly the vigilant Field Boss didn't admonish the convict with a lecture about the rude use of inappropriate language or dismount, offering to counsel with the testy convict about fixing any knotty personal problems. He didn't sheepishly call for help from a psychologist or social worker. Nor did the Field Boss proffer a gentle request: "Please continue with your work, pretty please." However, he did come back real fast in real time with real words. "Get your ass back to work and if you take one more shitty step toward me or my horse, I'll put a bullet right between your sorry ass eyes and radio for a damn pickup-truck to come out here and haul your stinking dead ass off the great State of Texas' dirt, try me, mutherfucker!" Though the salty rejoinder would not ring too nice from the witness stand, was his real time comeback wrong? Was he bluffing? In the end, and that's what really counts, the Field Boss didn't have to shoot anybody or call for a flatbed hearse.

And, too, if the convicts worked a full day in the field—from can to can't—they weren't hoeing on a milquetoast pledge to civilly quit, returning to quarters when the sun started to set. The horseback Field Boss kept the same hours. Likewise, especially in response to tempestuous assertions that convicts had to cruelly endure extremes of heat, wind, rain, and cold, it's but equitable to mention, if so, the dutiful Field Bosses and High-Riders and Dog Sergeants weren't back under roof by the warming fire playing Gin-Rummy. To be sure, there were a few tricks of the trade, as the mounted and armed Field Bosses worked hard at creating and upholding a tough-as-nails image, such as visibly drinking but ice-water in the dead of winter and steaming hot coffee during the scorching summer. When the temperature really dipped, an out-of-sight hand warmer in the jacket pocket guaranteed that a trigger-finger could launch a warning shot or a life-saving round if necessary. Fallaciously but believably salting a rough story about the killing or punishments of previous run-away convicts was but par business. Too, a competent and thinking and seasoned Field Boss carried his Hoe-Squad away from the unit on the trailers and then worked them afoot back towards the facilities' buildings—where if they decided to make a mad-dash for liberty, looking up they'd be running toward the prison facility rather than away from it. Gamesmanship in the harsh penitentiary setting is nothing new; it's time-tested and ubiquitous: Everybody plays—foxes outwitting foxes—or trying to.

George Beto was playing hard-ball, too, specifically to the good for ensconced convicts and strapped Texas taxpayers. Acknowledging that mechanization, while escalating TDC's farm and ranch production, was reducing the expenditure of man-hours, Dr. Beto turned to Austin. The Prison Made Goods Act was passed by the 58th Texas State Legislature: "It authorized the TDC to manufacture articles and compelled state agencies to purchase these materials, provided the quality and price were satisfactory. The purpose was to expand opportunities for inmate rehabilitation and generate additional savings for the state. . . . As the demand for agricultural work declined, the expansion of industrial activity was needed to provide work for the increasing number of prisoners. . . . New industries such as a broom and mop factory at the Ferguson Unit utilized the broom corn grown on the farms and fabrics from the textile mill. Then came a dental laboratory making false teeth, a coffee roasting plant, a tire recapping plant, a cardboard carton factory, and a detergent and wax factory. . . . the seven small and poorly equipped factories [of the past, license plate, canned goods for in-house consumption, etc.] had grown to twenty-two modern shops and factories providing training for 1,500 inmates and producing goods valued well in excess of six million dollars."[31]

To be blunt, George Beto believed in discipline—tomfoolery and lackadaisical attitudes were not a part of his game plan for sound prison management. Everyone was obedient. Everyone worked. And everyone absent an education went to school.[32] Short haircuts, clean shaven faces, and tidy whites with shirttails tucked in, were compulsory. An unkempt appearance and common sloppiness were not permitted—not for convicts, not for staff. His model was control and order. Disciplinary punishment for malefactors and the disrespectful was guaranteed. Convicts did as directed and that cultivated order, and everyone—everyone—was safer as a result.

Too, George Beto believed in education—even for convicts—maybe particularly for convicts. Under his administration the Windham School District was birthed—"the first school district in the whole United States with no geographical boundaries, designed solely to serve the primary, secondary, and vocational education needs of convicts in the Texas prison system."[33] And somewhat traveling the same road laid down by his predecessor in selecting Velda Quinn Dobbs for an executive position, Director Beto turned to a highly credentialed lady to serve as Superintendent of the new and accredited prison school district, Dr. Lane Murray.[34] Breaking from the past system, convicts would not be teaching other convicts in the prison classrooms. The Windham School District was formally endorsed by the state and the teachers were certified Texas free-world educators. Civilian men and women teachers went home at night—unless some unsavory something went haywire. Upon successful completion of their Windham schooling, convicts could stroll across a stage in front of their student peers with button-bustin' pride, receiving a legit High-School Diploma[35] College course work could follow. Free-world instructors were also available and on staff to teach vocational skills in a wide array of practical programs; "school bus repair, a tire recapping plant, garment manufacturing facilities, a dental laboratory, a license plate factory, and a number of computer data entry offices for conversion of state records to computer format, all of which were worked by convicts."[36] Other industrial and vocational opportunities would come on line and, herein, will be listed elsewhere.

One convict was working real hard, working his charm on a lady lawyer from New York. Fred Arispe Cruz, a Bexar County doper, was pulling a nickel and a dime for Armed Robbery.[37] In the vernacular of prison talk, Fred Cruz was a "writ-writer," a convict somewhat skilled in redressing his perceived wrongs through courts—rather than with the blade. Fred Cruz, to some extent a heavy thinker in some accounts, became the proverbial thorn in George Beto's side. The figurative wound festered more so after Cruz teamed up with a reform-minded lady, Frances T. Freeman Jalet, a highly educated and activist attorney for the Legal Aid and Defender Society of Travis County at Austin, the state's undisputed hotbed for liberally inclined theorists. Subsequent to a long-distance relationship with Cruz via stamped envelopes, Frances Jalet made the trip to Huntsville and conferred with convict Fred face to face at the tough Ellis Unit during October 1967. Shortly thereafter the divorced Jalet and mother of grown children became personally infatuated with Fred Cruz and professionally infatuated with the intricacies of prisoners' rights lawsuits.[38]

Metaphorically the floodgates had been flung wide open, and prison systems throughout the country were being deluged with litigious complaints filed by convicts. Analytically, some bore merit, others, however, were frivolous and asinine. For this short carve-out of the Texas Prison saga the bottom-line is relatively simple to plumb, though in a few of the retellings the actual practical end result is sometimes excessively amplified—occasionally awarded lopsided scale in the overall upshot of everyday TDC doings. That said, taken as a whole the narrative is emotive. In a nutshell convict Fred Cruz was successful—with the help of Jalet—in winning his lawsuit with regards to touchy legal issues regarding religious freedom, counseling other convicts about legal matters, and Solitary Confinement protocols—and assertions thereof. There was, too, another upside for him—and a provably wretched downside. Subsequent to his release from the Texas prison, Fred Arispe Cruz and Frances T. Freeman Jalet, across the Rio Grande/Río Bravo at the serene village of Colombia, Nuevo León, were legally united in matrimony, a shocker to print media outlets due to their ongoing attorney/client relationship, significant thirty-year age difference, and poles-apart levels of formal schooling: he an eighth grade dropout, her an Eastern educated and presumably sophisticated attorney. Later in the free-world the real-world troubles surfaced. Fred Cruz and Frances Jalet divorced—as do many couples. And after another marriage and fathering a precious girl-child, Fred Arispe Cruz at age forty-seven succumbed to a harrowing drug overdose—and died.[39]

Although George Beto—admittedly—lost his federal courtroom sparring with Frances Jalet (and her able lawyer helpmates) in the new nationwide era of federal court intervention into penitentiary doings, his reputation with penologists and politicians and the Texas general public—at least in most learned quarters—remained unsullied. To be sure, he had and has his philosophical and practical detractors well-grounded in the prison reformists' and particular journalistic camps, but on bona fide balance the scales do tilt in Dr. George John Beto's favor. He was president of the American Correctional Association and a "Distinguished Professor of Corrections at Sam Houston State University's Institute of Contemporary Corrections and Behavioral Sciences." No little tribute that would be, standing by itself. The actual physical plant, consisting of "106 offices and twenty-six classrooms, but also a courtroom [for mock trials, and sometimes a not mock trial], a crime laboratory, a 500-seat auditorium, and a hotel of ninety-eight rooms," was formally christened in honor of the esteemed theologian turned penologist and professor: The George J. Beto Criminal Justice Center.[40]

And it would be under George Beto's watch that a TDC barrier was broken, he hired the "first African-American correctional officers in the Texas Prison System."[41]

Although there seems a tendency—for some—in writing of Texas prison happenings to focus on the negative, more than a few public-spirited folks, not of the bleeding-heart variety, were tireless in their efforts to use TDC as the springboard for putting youthful probationers on the right path. As but one sterling and gold-plated example, the committed District Court Judge at Corpus Christi, Vernon D. Harville, and the go-gettin' and well-respected Nueces County District Attorney, William B. Mobley, Jr., took it upon themselves to ramrod a bold test for their community's wayward youthful but technically adult felony offenders. Accompanied by Chief Adult Probation Officer Jay Cazalas, Assistant District Attorney Paul Westergreen, and a reformed ex-convict Rick Brown, the assemblage of thirty young uneasy men—many of them lamentably characterized as problematic "backsliders"—then under the 105th District Court's supervision boarded a chartered bus bound for Huntsville.

The first stop was at the Diagnostic Center. And it was there that the temporary guests were reminded that TDC was "no country club." The former convict, Rick Brown, playing the impromptu part of a homeroom teacher, chided: Don't "be fooled by the pleasant surroundings on the outside. The deer and peacocks roaming around the grounds 'is for Mom and Daddy.' They see all that pretty stuff and they don't worry about their little boy—he has a nice brick home in the country." Prisons were real, and institutional life was not easy—but it was rule oriented and militarily structured. Respect to members of the staff and common courtesy was not optional. There, at Diagnostic, the probationers were introduced first-hand to the welcoming new fish received upon entering prison for their battery of tests and classification, where if their probation was revoked they would be stripped of clothing and herded into the gang shower. After the soaping and suds and rinsing they would be unceremoniously sprayed with disinfectant—and then asked to bend over for the ultimate inspection, that is subsequent to having oral cavities checked for any tidbit of contraband. Next they would be hustled into a barber chair where their heads would be shaved. Any facial hair would be pushed before the broom of a mean-looking trusty with tattoos, one with sinewy biceps jutting from his freshly pressed short-sleeved whites. This was not summer camp!

The next stop was at the Ferguson Unit. As the bus pulled up all the wide-eyed probationers noticed that outside the manicured grounds were Hoe-Squads—some convicts even on their hands and knees—"pulling crabgrass by hand" but always overseen by a mounted and armed Field Boss. The awestruck probationers—if they had any doubt—were apprised of the system-wide Texas philosophy about penitentiary residents, and it could be summed up in but three little words: "Labor is cheap." Clearly stated, with nearly 102,000 acres of rich farmland and pastures and numerous industrial shops and plentiful positions required just to maintain day to day operations, the undeniable fact was fast driven home: "There is [was] a job for everyone," like it or not—they'd have no say-so. Of course they could buck, but then it would be time in solitary where all light and sound would be shut out and they would receive but two slices of bread and all the water they could drink. Once, every third day they would get a "hot meal." After a while—if his heart was right—he could be reunited with the general population and expected to work when the morning Line turned out at the crack of dawn. The choice would be his.

On the return trip to Corpus Christi one probationer remarked: "I've been messing up, but not after today." Another chimed in: "I had never seen anything like it. I'd heard friends talk about it, but I had no idea what it was like up there." Though dead serious, another young man with tongue in cheek humor remarked: "I [now] know how good it feels to walk these streets," but he said he wouldn't mind going back for another visit, as long as it wasn't for an overnight stay.[42] Yes, DA Bill Mobley had his heart right—he and his cohorts were trying with vigor to keep the docket clear for murderers and robbers and rapists—not for first-offense probationers!

Tragedy speared through the TDC family once again—and it wasn't hurled by a convict; Mother Nature was the culprit. A writer of worthless checks, W.A. Johnson, thirty-five, hailing from De Kalb in Bowie County and pulling a nickel, had managed—somehow—to successfully make an appearance in the State of Oregon after his 1970 escape. Unsuccessfully it may be said his wanderings were transitory. He was captured and held for Texas authorities. Dispatched to make the long trip—post proper extradition—and return convict Johnson to the penitentiary unit northwest of Palestine in Anderson County were TDC pilots Major George Alan May, thirty-seven, and Major Robert Alexander "Bob" Arrington, thirty—both U.S. Military veterans. The first half of their flight in a twin-engine blue and white Beechcraft Queen Aire belonging to TDC was uneventful. With the handcuffed prisoner in tow the pilots stopped in Pueblo, Colorado, to rest and refuel. The next leg of their flight would take them to Amarillo, and then it would be home to Huntsville. On the morning of 17 September 1971, the TDC airplane departed the Pueblo airport—and vanished. An unusually severe and unanticipated snowstorm had dumped a quilt of white misery on southeastern Colorado, the earliest such covering since 1888 when record keeping began. The Colorado Civil Air Patrol closely coordinating with the Pueblo County Sheriff's Office—as soon as the weather cleared—began flying their search patterns. With good visibility the quest was short. The plane's wings had iced and it had crashed about twenty-five miles southeast of the airport, close to Fowler, Colorado. The airplane had been "demolished" and there were no survivors.[43] Major May was buried at Huntsville, survived by two children from a former marriage, and his wife Jacqueline Gayle, a bride of but two weeks. Major Arrington, buried at the Erwin Cemetery in his hometown, Navasota in Grimes County, left behind a wife, Myrtle Ann, and seven-year-old daughter, Melanie Ann.[44]

While the Grim Reaper continually stalked the cadre of prison employees, nationwide many convicts were by happenstance hitched to a strand of fortuitous good luck. Though the vote would be a split decision with one vote turning the tide, *Furman v. Georgia* was a landmark case before the United States Supreme Court. On the twenty-ninth day of June 1972 the ruling came down hard and unequivocal: Capital Punishment, as then administered, was declared Unconstitutional, an outright contravention of Eighth and Fourteenth Amendment guarantees promulgated by passage of the Bill of Rights. State-sanctioned executions were now verboten.[45] And what of those forty-seven Texas prisoners on Death Row awaiting their one-way trip through the Death Chamber's little green door? One and all, by executive action of Governor Price Daniel, had their death sentences converted to life imprisonment or ninety-nine years.[46] At the time there was no legislative statute on the books warranting Life Without Parole (LWP). Not all observant Texans—to be damn sure—were elated with the distinct possibility that someone sentenced to die for an atrocious act could be walking free-world streets, simply because someday the state's politically appointed Parole Board thought they had mentally mended their ways.

Such concerns were not boneheaded—not in the case of Kenneth Allen McDuff. The always niggling jump from an exacting chronology is necessary. At the time he received his free-pass from Ole Sparky, McDuff had been waiting his turn due to the 1966 sadistic murders of three Johnson/Tarrant County teenagers, Robert Brand, Marcus Dunnam, and Edna Louise Sullivan. McDuff, already a paroled ex-convict, was a predator—a monstrous predator. Though he would catch the ultimate sentence as result of conviction for but one of the murders (smart prosecutorial strategy, leaving cases in reserve) the triple homicide was gruesome—facts bringing tears to the eyes of some sickened jurors. The two boys had been coldly executed by point-blank gunshots. The unlucky young lady had been sexually assaulted. Not only raped according to the usual meaning— but viciously with a jagged broomstick as well. Then the broomstick was used, pressed against her neck, until she could breathe no more. Thereafter her body was discarded, dumped like garbage in an isolated field.[47]

Kenneth Allen McDuff's death sentence was commuted to a life sentence—and, incredibly, good-time credit could accrue as pages of the penitentiary's calendar turned. Therefore it should come as no shocker, but harebrained and unbelievable, that Kenneth Allen McDuff was paroled into the Texas free-world. Were one to suppose the ghoulish guy from Rosebud in Falls County had been chastened into behaving, well, over the next few years more gruesomely murdered and mercilessly dumped girls would erase foolishness of that notion.[48] Presently, Kenneth Allen McDuff will get his comeuppance, but not with Ole Sparky.

11

"Not dealing with Sunday School kids"

WARD JAMES "JIM" ESTELLE, FORTY-ONE, had been groomed for the job by George Beto and succeeded him as Director of the Texas Department of Correction during September of 1972. He did not step into Texas penology as a neophyte. Jim Estelle had worked in California at the state's legendary Folsom Prison. Later—as a Lieutenant—he was placed in charge of several prison camps in Northern California. At the pinnacle of his Golden State career Jim Estelle was charged with supervising all prison camp operations.[1] Afterwards, 1970, before coming to Texas as Assistant Director at Beto's behest, Jim Estelle had been Warden at the Montana State Penitentiary near Deer Lodge, southeast of Missoula and northwest of Butte.[2]

According to folks in the know, TDC Director Estelle had a basic two-pronged approach to prison management: "hold offenders securely, and make sure that they worked to defray the cost of their incarceration." Ellis and Beto would not find fault with that. Notably by the time Estelle assumed TDC command, escapes, attempted escapes, and in-house homicides were relatively rare, especially when compared to other state penitentiary systems. Particularly: "In Texas they do well all the things that prisons are supposed to do. They keep you in, they keep you busy, and they keep you from getting killed."[3] Even one of TDC's most vocal—and right—earlier critics had come around to recognizing the real state-of-affairs now. Austin MacCormick admitted that he had seen the Texas Prison System inch itself from one of the worst in the whole country to "its present position in the top half-dozen."[4]

David Resendez Ruiz certainly wouldn't pass out gold stars to TDC—he filed suit in 1972. The lawsuit *Ruiz v. Estelle* would soon make Texas history; marking the history of penology too!

David Resendez Ruiz was no choirboy—he was a convict. And, too, he was not a very nice convict. The recidivist had caught time at juvenile facilities prior to advancing into big league confinement in 1960. There he was imprisoned for Aggravated Robbery convictions—and, later a clear-cut parole revocation. During his brief seven-month sojourn in Ohio while on parole, he purportedly killed someone. Buckeye State legal authorities wanted him (later dismissed) for questioning when, if ever, he wound up his obligatory business with whittling off his court-imposed Texas sanctions. That, in one sense, seemed unlikely, primarily due to the fact while in Texas penitentiaries David R. Ruiz stabbed several other convicts, escaped and was nabbed, and also duly earned disciplinary residency in Solitary Confinement some fifteen times. And, that's not counting an awkward later Aggravated Perjury conviction for lying when he had taken an oath to tell the truth. Plumbing the authenticated depths of convict David Resendez Ruiz's actual creditability is not too taxing—though for a community of prison reform activists and passionate Civil Rights lawyers, even if well-intentioned, he has been anointed with folkloric status.[5] Conversely, and it's not outright unjust, some past and present prison employees—and others—rate David Ruiz as a quarrelsome convict intent on milking the judicial system to his egocentric benefit.

Was in fact, David Ruiz a brilliant legal mind? Or was his timing and filing venue the lucky break? David Ruiz's handwritten case was to be tried in the Eastern District of Texas, before the bench of the aforementioned Judge William Wayne Justice. Whatever he was, good or bad, biased or impartial, throughout East Texas—and elsewhere—it was generally understood, though not particularly liked, that William Wayne Justice was an activist judge. Liberal-minded political voices evangelistically touted him, while conservative political thinkers eternally damned him.[6]

East Texas bumper stickers were plainspoken: "Will Rogers never met William Wayne Justice!" Factually, as asserted by a seasoned journalist, with regards to *Ruiz v. Estelle*, the habitually controversial East Texas jurist "engineered the proceedings."[7] Of that there really is not too much argument, though predictably supporters defend his court actions and detractors decry them. Although it came afterward, Judge Justice may have tipped his hand inadvertently in much later legalese, when he unabashedly called the imprisoned Plaintiffs "a handful of brave prisoners."[8] At any rate, Judge Justice wedded other prisoners' filings into one, *Ruiz v. Estelle*, and awarded it judicially endorsed status as a class action lawsuit. Supplementary convict filings would be consolidated into *Ruiz v. Estelle* later, those of O. D. Johnson and (Ernesto) *Montana v. Beto*. That, as the saying goes was but the tip of the iceberg.[9]

Furthermore, Judge Justice ordered the United States Department of Justice (DOJ) to emerge as *amicus curiae* (friend of the court).[10] His reasoning for DOJ participation was not secret, though it topped the norm for a typical *amicus curiae* interest. According to Judge Justice, the DOJ should "investigate fully the facts alleged in the prisoners' complaints to participate in such civil action with the full rights of a party thereto, and to advise [the] Court at all stages of the proceedings as to any actions deemed appropriate by it."[11] Noticeably—at this point—it was more than perfectly clear that Judge Justice was, as two credentialed professionals candidly advise, "willing to extend his authority to the outer limits of his judgeship to ensure the *Ruiz* plaintiffs adequate representation."[12] Although it breaks down to simplicity in its purest mold, in essence Judge Justice was making the U.S. Government and the State of Texas "adversaries."[13] An *amicus curiae* in most litigation is named to lend a helping hand to the Court with regards to suggested solutions and/or worrisome investigative issues. However, in this instance Judge William Wayne Justice gave the federal government, through the DOJ, all inferred and conferred rights of a plaintiff suing the Texas Prison System.[14] And for his detractors—if that didn't tip his hand—other unloved judicial decisions kept stacking bricks atop the proverbial camel's back. He turned his eyes towards a setting sun California—San Francisco—to tap recruiting desires. Judge Justice personally recruited William Bennett Turner, perhaps the country's leading prisoner rights' lawyer, to serve as the plaintiffs' head attorney. Then there was that other kicker! Judge Justice allowed the plaintiffs to amend their original filings. They would forego seeking, any monetary damages at the time, only injunctive relief. With no dollars on the table there was no entitlement to have a jury hear the testimony, weigh the evidence, and render a rational verdict. Though certainly not addressing the litigation herein, a Retired U.S. District Judge and later Dean of the University of Texas at Dallas College of Law, the Honorable Royal Furgeson, is not vague about citizen input: "A decline in the jury trial is a decline in justice."[15] In their highly-acclaimed treatment two authors, one a former federal prosecutor and practicing attorney, the other a currently sitting Texas State District Court Judge, both recipients of honored recognition by the American Board of Trial Advocates, make more that clear their deep-seated respect for participatory government: ". . . we believe that the jury trial is an example of our constitutional democracy in action, and more significantly, an illustration of why democracy is important."[16] For the case at hand, *Ruiz v. Estelle*, the sole arbiter would be Judge William Wayne Justice: Like it or not! It would soon prove to be a textbook example of, as two learned authors observe, "A Lesson in Judicial Orchestration."[17]

Without too much doubt it might draw critical heat from the judiciary, but a long-time attorney for the Federal Bureau of Prisons—its former General Council—and a frequent lecturer in Correctional Law at the National Law Center, George Washington University, a recognized authority on penology, is not overly impressed with the executive talents of federal judges micromanaging prisons: "the underlying fact is that judges are in no way placed into their positions because of any expertise to manage. Federal judges—even if they are the best of the judicial lot—are appointed to their offices because of political connections, if not cronyism. Although they are carefully scrutinized in the appointment process and generally have outstanding experiences as lawyers, this experience is to my knowledge seldom evaluated as to managerial ability."[18]

At the Texas Statehouse some 63rd Legislature lawmakers were doing some tinkering too. House members, working with the Senate, ultimately passed into law HB 1056, generically dubbed the "Building Tender Bill."[19] Other than §3 which mainly was a housekeeping matter, HB 1056 was a two-pronged stab at righting what some thought as inherently wrong, and others thought a necessary implement in the toolkit for maintaining institutional safety in short-staffed prison units. Maybe, atypically, in this instance intentional gobbledygook was forsaken:

§ 1 An inmate in the custody of the Texas Department of Corrections or in any jail in this state may not act in a supervisory or administrative capacity over other inmates.

§ 2 An inmate in the custody of the Teas Department of Corrections or in any jail in this state may not administer disciplinary action over another inmate.[20]

While the legislative intent was crystal-clear, the inadvertent consequence of trying to reverse deep-rooted workplace custom overnight is beset with nightmarish reality. For the short-term, BTs were renamed SSIs (Support Service Inmates), though their in-house jobs and status remained the same—at least for awhile. And before this treatment is wrapped, there will be rather surprising examples of compliant convicts and confirmed prison gang members and a Death Row clergyman ruing the day a measure of in-house control was wrested away from Building Tenders—some Building Tenders! Easy answers for complex problems are elusive.

One of those complex problems turned ugly during mid-June 1973 at the Retrieve Unit, put down in history as the "Father's Day Incident" or the "Father's Day Massacre." The former label seems logically fitting, the latter an epic exaggeration. Regardless, the sweet corn was ripe and ready to harvest. Unseasonably drenching rains had delayed the process and, now, timing was critical if the corn was to be gathered and hauled to the prison cannery—lest it spoil in the field.[21] Therefore the Warden's command decision was easy to reach. Though normally there was no field work performed on Sundays, the Line would turn out on the Sabbath, work a half-day, and then be allowed to resume their normal routines of church services and/or visitations or other okayed activities. For their atypical Sunday work the convicts would be "compensated with time off for the time worked."[22] Although the Line numbered near 274 convicts scheduled for work, ten bucked. They refused to leave their cells, offering a myriad of unacceptable excuses. Quite naturally such an affront to authority was in the first instance cause for a disciplinary sanction for the slackers, and in the second instance—it could prove infectious, contaminating good order of the unit—maybe the overall prison system—if not forthwith nipped in the bud. The ten convicts would not be given a choice or time to waste. They must turn out for work. Director Jim Estelle was onboard with his on-the-ground employees, well attuned to hardcore reality: That if necessary, there was likelihood that an insubordinate convict's head might get thumped or his ass kicked. To be sure it was a Sunday, but the Retrieve Unit—in the big picture of twentieth-century doings—wasn't the backdrop for a Sunday School social where everyone was politely inclined because they were living by the Golden Rule: Not for the keepers nor the kept. It was prison! Everybody did as told! Everybody worked! Nobody bucked!

The ten recalcitrant convicts went to work, albeit with some bruises and battered bodies. Later allegations that the ten had to run a gauntlet of Correctional Officers armed with ax-handles and rubber hoses somewhat stretches the truth, at least according to someone that was there and did have to—admittedly—deliver a lick or two. The steadfast Correctional Officers were stationed at appropriate hallway entrances, so the ten intractable guys were easily funneled toward the proper building exit for the Field Force's outside gate, not allowed to run willy-nilly throughout the entire facility.

That could have proven catastrophic.[23] In the short run the insubordinate convicts went back to work. For the long haul, however, the episode sparked headlines and lawsuits.

A Federal Grand Jury, after hearing testimony and reviewing evidence, opted not to return any Criminal Indictments against any of the participating prison employees—zip! Apparently in their estimation the Correctional Officers had been put in an undesirable and untenable situation, but had acted in a lawful manner. In a companion civil case, however, with the trial judge as the sole arbiter—no jury—the judge did assess liability for three prison employees in the amount of $11,246.00 which was ultimately forked over by the State of Texas to settle the convicts' complaints about mistreatment. The real folks making out like Wild West bandits were the plaintiffs' (convicts') attorneys: The court awarded them $17,072.00 as remuneration for legal fees.[24] Rhetorically, one can only speculate as to how a jury, even a civil case trial jury, would have seen the disruptive matter. In that same hypothetical vein, idly wondering just how Judge William Wayne Justice characterized the following year's pathetic prison high-drama—while quite interesting and indicative—would in a very practical sense measure as meaningless. He unquestionably and unchecked wielded the big stick of supremacy. Courtroom optimism and naïve cell-block reality are worlds apart.

Not just a few days mark in-house tragedy. One day of penitentiary infamy seems to stand out more than others—24 July 1974—at least to this juncture in time and by news media attention. For the state's employees the morning sun peeking over The Walls heralded another hot day of close confinement—but for introspective convicts with their hearts right—a golden opportunity for educational enrichment and self-improvement, getting one's business straight. A trio of Spanish-speaking outlaws had other plans however, and they would ruin the day for everybody. Federico Gomez "Fred" Carrasco, the professed leader, a confirmed drug smuggling kingpin with numerous prison residencies in his past and a merciless killer, accompanied by fellow convicts Rudolfo Sauceda "Rudy" Dominguez Jr. and Ignacio Apodaca "Nacho" Cuevas, with ingeniously smuggled handguns and plenty of ammunition took hostages—prison personnel and prisoners alike. Like Carrasco, his two *amigos* were doing time as result of convictions for violence, Dominguez for Assault to Murder, and Cuevas for killing of an unarmed Rito Villalon with three shots "in the back of the head" in West Texas near Pecos. And as with Carrasco who had earlier escaped an austere Mexican calaboose, Cuevas broke jail in Reeves County but was later captured near Presidio. The plan and the guns were real. The *mal hombres* were no doubt desperate, but they were delusional too—supposing that pointing pistols at prison people would warrant throwing open the front gate. Hostages are not tickets to the free-world, then or now! What ostensibly began as a pure prison-break turned into the longest prison siege in modern history—or as a consummate journalist penned for his deftly researched treatment of the episode: *Eleven Days in Hell*.[25]

The first blood actually spilled during the outlaw's bid for freedom would be that of dedicated Correctional Officers—though both would be thankful their injuries were not life threatening. That was by mere chance and not any benevolence on the part of the mindless hostage-taking yahoos. Unarmed and responding to the first indication that something was amiss, Carrasco's gunfire interdicted the employees' loyal forward momentum. Sergeant Bruce Noviskie, suffered a bullet wound to his foot, while Lieutenant Wayne Scott, endured lacerations after "a bullet grazed his back and hit a concrete wall, spattering him with fragments."[26]

Understandably, word of bad doings inside The Walls, in today's vernacular, went viral. Company A Texas Ranger John Wesley Styles, a former West Texas Sheriff of Baylor County, but then assigned to Huntsville, was onsite within fifteen minutes, quickly notifying his headquarters commander at Houston, Captain James Frank "Pete" Rogers.[27] Rogers and Texas Ranger Sergeant John "Johnny" Krumnow, quickly set sail for Huntsville. Short-staffed prison personnel were scrambling, too. Armed Correctional Officers from nearby prison units were ordered to The Walls. Little sparks can ignite big fires in prison settings. Before too much time had elapsed, the prison personnel deployment in and around The Walls had nudged 110, exceeding the regular on-duty security staff by fifty, including tactically positioned sharpshooters atop the prison hospital.[28] Warden Howell Herbert "Hal" Husbands, a Rice University graduate, not only had to contend with the unfolding drama—trying to save employees' lives—but also had to manage the safety and security of those inmates wholly unaffiliated with the wickedness.[29] Straightforwardly, most prisoners, most of the time, are desirous of tranquility which is a byproduct of order and control: Stability shortstops stealing and stabbings and sexual assaults.

From an amicable Rotary Club luncheon at San Antonio, upon learning of the madness, Director Jim Estelle rushed to Huntsville via a state-owned airplane. Company B Texas Rangers from Garland (Dallas County), captained by G.W. Burks hurried to the location as did Resident Agent in Charge (RAC) of the FBI's Bryan Field Office in Brazos County, Robert E. "Bob" Wiatt, a fully "seasoned investigator with twenty-three years' experience and gunplay behind him."[30] Also racing to the scene of trouble was Winston Padgett, Agent for the Criminal Intelligence Division of the DPS.

And in short order (relatively speaking) media representatives from national networks and foreign news bureaus were calling Walker County—maybe not lovingly—their home away from home; wolfing down thick soda-fountain milkshakes and root-beer floats, and/or cheeseburgers from the Texas Café or pulled-pork sandwiches from Hailey's Barbeque. Fritos and potato chips and Hershey bars were in demand. Soon lawn chairs from area merchants for weary print media journalists and broadcasting newshounds and their technical staffs would be in short supply. As would be rain gear. An unusual summertime cloudburst from above washed across Huntsville with an unexpected four-inch deluge. City workers jumped to, using wood framing and a roof from vinyl, a makeshift shed was erected to protect soggy journalists and their moisture sensitive communications equipment and cables. Some reporters daring not to miss a fast breaking story chose to overnight on the lawn between the Admin building and The Walls, buying sleeping-bags and air-mattresses.

Unquestionably from their ravenous viewpoint it really was one helluva good story—good copy![31]

For Correctional Officers and their friends and families it was a ghastly nightmare unimaginable. Stomachs turned—some puked. Onsite lawmen and prison leadership were stymied—to a degree—not knowing exactly what they would do, but were categorically aware of what they couldn't and wouldn't do: Trade hostages for cost-free passes into the free-world. Though mentioned elsewhere within this narrative, upon engaging in employment with TDC all personnel were made aware, on page twenty-two of Rules and Regulations, and signed the document attesting that they clearly understood the inherent risks with the hardcore reality of earning paychecks behind tall walls and/or high fences, be they man or woman:

> In the event any officers or employees have been seized as hostages, no officer or employee on duty shall disregard, alter, modify or change in any manner, the prescribed duties, obligations or responsibilities of his position on demand by the prisoners, or pleas from the hostages, regardless of the consequences.

"There should be no difference in rules regarding male or female hostages. If a female should be taken hostage, her chances of safety are much greater within the prison walls with the warden and his staff than they would be if she were let out with a fear-crazed and pursued escapee. Furthermore, if everyone concerned, including the prisoners, understands that no difference will be given a woman hostage, the possibilities of such an occurrence are greatly diminished."[32]

A built-in conundrum, too, was that Fred Carrasco didn't shy away from gratuitous violence. It was purported—and believed—that on one homicidal night across the Rio Grande at Nuevo Laredo, he killed six men. Sitting on the top rung and maintaining a "heroin empire" is bloody business. Furthermore, he bragged that he had murdered "many men." Then he turned up the volume on his lack of remorse and conscience: "Killing is nothing to me."[33] Carrasco, Dominguez, and Cuevas, in a madcap brain-dead maneuver, had put themselves in an untenable spot and, at the same time, afforded criminal justice officialdom at Huntsville a nonnegotiable posture—at least for the big rodeo soon playing out before a world-wide audience.

For the short-go, however, a little gamesmanship on the part of policing and prison folks would buy precious time. So when the hostage takers asked that fancy clothes and new shoes be delivered to the education-center and library—where they were holed up—the demand was met. Sizes too small, ill-fitting street-clothes were the first to materialize—the exchanges ate hours. The befuddled outlaws asked for a television and one was forthwith rolled up the education center's three-tiered zigzag ramp, albeit it wouldn't work without cable installation—but that, too, would take time—precious time. The request for three AR-15 rifles and ammo was shelved. After asking for shop-made iron helmets—bulletproof—welders lit torches and fashioned heavy medieval-looking headgear. The paradox of putting a super weighty and burdensome helmet over one's head and at the same time cutting off peripheral vision had evidently not been factored into Fred Carrasco's ultimatum. His adversaries were not unhappy with this capitulation to his whim. Besides, as they knew, the iron helmet might actually stop a bullet, but the resounding gong inside the device would addle anyone—rendering them senseless.

Fred Carrasco's collection of bargaining chips—and that's how he saw the hostages—is revealing on at least two fronts: He looked for civilian employees, not security personnel to terrorize. The routine comings and goings of folks tending to reformative and/or rehabilitative undertakings, trying to better violators' lives once released back into the free-world, provided a target rich environment. With that in mind, enumerating that noncustodial staff and the peril they found themselves in is substantive. They were a cadre of the caring; educational and recreational administrators, librarians and teachers. They were not nameless, specifically taken as hostages were Elizabeth Yvonne "Von" Beseda, Anthony J. "Jack" Branch, Jr., Bertha Mae "Bert" Davis, Ann Fleming, Aline V. House, Glennon D. Johnson, Novella M. Pollard, Ronald Wayne "Ron" Robinson, Julia "Judy" Standley, and Linda Glass Woodman. And that's not taking into account the Catholic Priest officially assigned to The Walls, Father Joseph John O'Brian. In fact, the only Correctional Officer taken off-guard and captured was the unarmed Bobby G. Heard, twenty-seven, who was also a part-time student at nearby Sam Houston State University.[34]

From the get-go and through upfront negotiations, sixty-odd convict hostages had been freed, save four who volunteered to stay behind, Martin Quiroz, Florencio Vera, Henry Escamilla, and an Anglo, Stephen Ray Robertson. Those that remained did not escape questions about their motives and were walking a tightrope suspended over arenas of prosecution and/or punishment. Fred Carrasco knew convict hostages—though it sounds terrible—were completely valueless.[35] He also appreciated his architectural surroundings. Absent resorting to detailing the buildings' blueprint and though it wasn't by a purposeful plan—construction and all— Carrasco and cohorts occupied a formidable fortress. Penitentiaries' institutional design calls for keeping some folks locked within, which by correlation equates to keeping other folks locked out.

Though speculation is rife for exploitation, analytically firing ideas on three cylinders has not been inappropriate. Although it does seem highly unlikely, could the outlaws have entertained and executed the cockamamie escape plan absent a workable exit-strategy? Had someone in the free-world duped Fred Gomez Carrasco into taking a harebrained risk—hoping and/or knowing his chances were slim to none—in an effort to lastingly guarantee a kingpin's downfall? Or, could something wholly unforeseen—accident or circumstances—have embargoed an accomplice circling Huntsville's tree-lined streets waiting to spirit three mean and armed passengers to absenteeism? At any rate Fred Carrasco's team was stuck, under siege and unable to extricate.

There was a way out, however. At least he believed so. The demand that an armored-car be driven inside The Walls and parked in front of the education center and library complex's ramp was complied with, although those calling the shots knew without hesitation the borrowed Purolator Security truck would never pass back through the main entranceway carrying terrified hostages and the trio of career criminals capable of triggering mayhem outside the tall walls.

Fred Carrasco's plan—an amalgamation of ideas—for snaking down the zigzagging ramp to the armored-car without exposing himself to a sniper's bullet was uncomplicated. The frazzled convicts would inch along with hostages concealed inside a gigantic contraption with peep holes, fashioned from blackboards and cardboard and heavy books encircled by gobs of tape. It would be akin to the proverbial Trojan Horse. Supposedly the wannabe escapees would be able to see out, but the good guys couldn't see in—powerless to realize suitable target acquisition. Timing and method of movement was no under-wraps arrangement.

What was going on inside The Walls—logistically—was but half of the gargantuan problem. At the outset of Carrasco's boneheaded stunt the mainline population behind The Walls had been placed in at least a semi-lockdown status. They were not happy. Publication of the in-house *Echo* was suspended; the cellblocks were not air-conditioned and they were sweltering; they were being given Johnny Sacks in lieu of hot meals; time on the recreation yard was cancelled, as was their scheduled visitations with family or friends, sweethearts or sympathizers. No, though it's but speculative, there *might* have been a few lifers inside who—if handed a pistol—would have gladly capped Carrasco, ending a crisis so that normalcy would prevail.[36]

Indisputably, TDC Director Jim Estelle had inherited a handful of mess, to put it mildly. Thankfully, aside from the dedicated Correctional Officers inside, Estelle had the benefit of community and statewide support. Traffic and crowd control—and corralling the press—were not minor nuisances to contend with and could not be casually ignored. Huntsville Chief of Police Gail Burch and Fire Chief Jack King pledged and delivered unconditional backing. The Walker County Sheriff, W. Darrell White, added his department's expertise into the mix. Staff at the Huntsville Memorial Hospital was at the ready, constantly reviewing and updating multi-casualty game-plans. National Guard bomb technicians (EOD) were on standby. Further away Colonel Wilson E. "Pat" Speir, headman for the whole DPS, was overseeing that all of the department's assets would be available to Director Estelle when and if needed, be it helicopters or airplanes or portable communications or chemical munitions or an oversized assemblage of raring-to-go Texas Highway Patrolmen.[37]

Transition from a grounded fortress to a fortress with wheels was common knowledge between the kept and their keepers. The bad guys imagined their idea would work. The good guys couldn't let it!

During the evening of the eleventh trying day, 3 August 1974, Fred Carrasco ordered Father Joseph O'Brien into what law enforcing officialdom was now referring to as the Trojan Taco, facing backwards—he would serve as the down-ramp brakeman. Then half-dozen interior box trekkers, facing in the opposite direction, were paired and handcuffed together; Fred Carrasco and Von Beseda, Rudy Dominguez and Judy Standley, then Nacho Cuevas and Novella Pollard. Jerryrigging and twisting volleyball netting into a secure rope, the left-over hostages were fastened to the apparatus' mish-mash exterior, scarily serving as human shields. Slowly shuffling and wobbling toward the Purolator Security truck the ugly-duckling contrivance had evolved into a *piñata* of humanity's best and worst.[38]

At the siege's outset Director Jim Estelle had not greedily and grandiosely funneled all of the strategic and tactical planning to his desk—and his desk alone. Openly he sought the brainpower of others: Texas Ranger Captains Rogers and Burks, FBI Resident Agent Wiatt, Warden Husbands, along with TDC Assistant Directors Daniel V. "Red" McKaskle, and Jack Kyle. Collectively and colloquially these players would be and were known as the "Think Tank."[39] The consensus had been simple and upfront: Stop the Trojan Taco before it could reach the Purolator truck. How? At the right moment streaming water from high-pressure fire-hoses would knock over the container, bewildering the desperadoes to such an extent they would be overcome and debilitated as the hostages were being rescued.

Donning bullet-proof vests and protective helmets, Texas Ranger Captains Rogers and Burks, DPS Agent Padgett, RAC Wiatt—and other prison personnel and Texas Rangers—also armed with handguns—made ready to honor their oaths of office.[40] The time of truth had come. As the colossal carton moved down the ramp's incline, as planned it was deluged with a powerful jet of water momentarily. Unfortunately and abruptly a ruptured fire-hose depowered the stratagem's effectiveness. Hell broke loose in a hurry—gunfire from within: Assassination inside the soggy box, shots at officers slipping and sliding on the blood-washed ramp. Rangers Rogers and Burks and Agent Wiatt all took thumping hits to the torso but were—thankfully—saved by their protective vests.[41] Shots were "raging both out of and into the boxes' law-book-book armor. Dozens of shots were fired by both sides."[42]

Sucking courage from deep within, TDC Lieutenant Willard N. Stewart, Jr., amid the booming and bullets, and no doubt thunder-ous stream of excited expletives, subsequent to completion of his original assignment, rushed into the mêlée with but one thought in mind—saving lives. Deftly, Lieutenant Stewart began cutting the improvised rope anchoring outside hostages to the makeshift shell.[43] His plucky work paid its dividend: All of those hostages escaped death.

Regrettably, however, stunned prison personnel would mourn the loss of Von Beseda and Judy Standley. Carrasco's and Dominguez's ini-tial gunfire had been devastating and deadly, coldblooded executions. Tallying the other casualties is obligatory, but excepting for the seri-ous wounding of Father O'Brien, compassion is omitted: Carrasco ate the barrel of his smuggled revolver and died; Dominguez was killed by bullets fired by Winston Padgett. Nacho Cuevas was at the bottom of the pile, uninjured. His destiny would be delayed by seventeen years, when after multiple Texas Criminal Appeals Court reviews, "the state's pharmaceutical injection dispensed long overdue justice and eternal good behavior."[44]

Shortly, Ranger Captain G.W. Burks praised the Correctional Officers in general and one in particular: "While all of the shoot-ing was going on, a Department of Corrections guard—his name was Steward [sic: Stewart] or something like that—rushed out with a knife and cut the ropes which bound the hostages to the shield.

Somebody should give that fellow a medal. He risked his life—really risked it—to save the lives of those hostages."[45]

And just as soon as the shooting stopped—it seemed—the voracious press corps abandoned Huntsville—hightailing and hustling for the next story. Regrettably but not surprisingly they left in their wake a refuse field, at least according to the *Dallas Morning News*: "The only sign of violence was the litter strewn lawn area where the press had been camping out. Here prison trusties were quietly picking up cans, yards of discarded film, cards and broken lawn chairs."[46]

Naturally, a post-incident investigation was in order—particularly focused on how violent convicts inside The Walls acquired three handguns and several hundred rounds of ammunition? The answer was not long in coming. A trusty, with outside prison perimeter duties, had cleverly smuggled the firepower inside carved-out hollows of fresh cuts of meat and "tampered with and relabeled food tins." Already a six-time loser, for his part in this tragedy, Larry Hall caught another life sentence—eventually dying in prison at age fifty-seven.[47]

One offshoot of the sad tragedy which took the lives of Judy Standley and Von Beseda was a wakeup call: "For the fêted Texas Rangers—and DPS—the ugly situation at Huntsville had driven home an uncomfortable law-enforcing message. They were working on the deficit side of the ledger book." Company F Sergeant Jack Dean, at Waco, was handed the knotty assignment of organizationally formalizing, equipping, and overseeing the training of a Texas Ranger SWAT Team. Assuredly DPS did not want to get caught off-guard and unprepared should another horrifying incident take place at any one of a number of scattered TDC facilities. Once budgetary and training hurdles had been overcome—with backing from many generally well-respected politicos—Sergeant Dean stood for an impromptu press conference. No doubt TDC officialdom was all ears, and quite pleased with what newspaper folks penned: "Dean said that the Rangers would be trained to handle a situation like the Carrasco affair at Huntsville and sniper situations. He said they already do that job, and this would just create special Ranger units to be assigned when the problems arise." Furthermore and, emphatically, Sergeant Dean emphasized that the Texas Ranger SWAT Team would be there to help TDC and other law enforcing agencies—not "hamper or take over when a situational scenario turned hot."[48]

Subsequent to the Texas Legislature's effectively tweaking the state's Penal Code, as with other states, the U.S. Supreme Court ultimately allowed that if administered in accordance within sanctioned protocols, Capital Punishment would not be Unconstitutional. There was, however, no little statewide debate with regards as to how the ultimate penalty would be imposed and just who would be allowed to witness an execution at The Walls.

Director Estelle's policy was that only two national journalists could actually be in the Death Chamber observation room: one from the Texas writers for the Associated Press (AP) and one from United Press International (UPI). Both would be mandated to share their observations with other impatient reporters. Additional news media representatives would be permitted to observe the proceedings on a closed-circuit television. "No cameras or recording devices will be permitted in the death chamber or the room where other newsmen are watching the television screens." As would be anticipated, generally speaking the press corps was not pleased.[49]

With the climate of judicial intervention in prison business then underway, a federal court stepped in with regards to a suit filed by the PBS station at Dallas, KERA. Texas must allow TV crews to film executions—leaving it up to the stations' editors as to how much they would actually broadcast, so ruled U.S. District Court Judge William M. Taylor, Jr. Out of hand was the Judge's dismissal of the state's arguments that filming an execution would be "an offense to human dignity" and "distasteful" and/or "shocking." Judge Taylor reasoned that it was for the news media to decide "what governmental activities are sufficiently tasteful, dignified or acceptable to be reported."[50] The U.S. 5th Circuit Appellate Court quite understandably took a different tack; Death Chamber cameras were nixed.

With that court ruling as a backdrop, Texas legislators scrambled to find a substitute for doling out the Death Chamber's finality. And so it came to be. Lethal Injection replaced the necessity of "causing to pass through the body of the convict a current of electricity of sufficient intensity to cause death, and the application and continuance of such current through the body of such convict until he is dead." There would be a three-step injection procedure wherein the convict would painlessly be put to sleep—forevermore. In a sense it was but commonsense to lawmakers, some insisting on preventing a theatrical production blaring into citizens' living rooms, and to another it would be but an ever-evolving "technological progression from stoning, crucifixion, guillotining, [and] electrocution to drug injection."[51] For conscientious physicians it was an no-brainer: they could not knowingly introduce lethal drugs into an otherwise healthy person, a clear circumvention of their Hippocratic Oath.

Relatively quickly it was asserted that Ole Sparky would become a "museum piece." At least once Appellate Courts cleared any legal debris from the chosen pathway of the state issuing a ticket to the hereafter. Or would it? One of the niggling questions concerning TDC officials was rather elementary, but certainly in want of an answer: Should the condemned man or woman be killed sitting up "strapped to a chair or placed on a bed."[52] The first inclination was not to unglamorously send Ole Sparky to the ash heap of discarded relics. No, a condemned person could still sit upright between Ole Sparky's armrest, receiving their chemical comeuppance.[53] Not unexpectedly such symbolism was not being digested well by the vocal opponents of Capital Punishment.[54] TDC bending judiciously to public relations reality retired Ole Sparky, PIO Ron Taylor telling journalists: "The chair sits now in a storeroom. . . . the chair may go on display in a museum." With that sense of history is where Ole Sparky now resides.[55]

Director Jim Estelle followed in the progressive footsteps of predecessors Oscar Byron Ellis and Dr. George John Beto with regards to—for lack of better terminology—minority hiring practices. Ellis had appointed the very first female Texas Prison Warden, Velda Quinn Dobbs and Beto is credited with "hiring the first African-American correctional officers in the Texas prison system."[56] Estelle was actively recruiting minority group staff members, openly and with candor declaring that they would "have a real future with us [TDC]." Estelle noted that thus far, 1974, for day to day operations he had a black Assistant Warden, and also had "a significant number" of black and Hispanic supervisors at the various units to the grade of lieutenant, which he theoretically "compared as equal to responsibility of a Dallas police lieutenant." Additionally he had a two-pointed Affirmative Action Program, one headed by a black Captain and the other commanded by a Captain of Hispanic heritage.[57]

Regardless hiring tactics designed to be more inclusive, ground-level prison personnel and the Texas reading public were from time to time reminded that for at least a sampling of convicts, viciousness and venomousness stalked the cellblocks in a variety of variations. During one 1977 incident, convict Willie Smith had a beef over something with convict Freeman Chase. Revenge sometimes—it's been written—is sweeter if served cold. Not in this instance. Willie Smith doused Freeman Chase with Naphtha and ignited same. "Chase died from pneumonia and blood poisoning as a result of burns." As an upshot of the immolation Willie Smith caught a full-bore life sentence, a conviction upheld by the Texas Court of Criminal Appeals.[58] So, while untiringly corralling the relatively small but hardcore percentage of really mean convicts, Director Jim Estelle's administrative and personnel duties were ever at the forefront of his agenda: recognizing talent.

Acknowledging her intrinsic leadership qualities and levelheaded coolness during the nastiness with Carrasco and his cutthroats, former hostage Linda Woodman was recruited away from the Windham School District and selected as the Assistant Warden for the women's Goree Unit. At the time Goree was undergoing a major transition, being converted into an all-male facility. Federal Judge William Wayne Justice had arbitrarily ordered that the Texas Youth Council (TYC) cease holding juveniles in the Mountain View facility at Gatesville. Mountain View would be closed to kids, but opened for female convicts. Adhering to his fair-minded approach to prison business and wholly attuned to putting age discrimination by the wayside, Director Estelle selected Lucile Garrett Plane, already sixty, to serve as Warden at Mountain View.[59] And as but a quick sidebar, Linda Woodman would ultimately earn upward mobility status as a Warden, and both she and Lucile Plane would have Texas State Jail facilities named in their honor: The Lucile Plane State Jail Unit at Dayton in Liberty County and the Linda Woodman State Jail Unit at Gatesville.

Though she had no actual penal experience, newly named Warden Plane, at the time, was serving as Project Manager and Chief Probation Officer for a multi-county adult and juvenile probation outfit. Director Estelle's initial advice to Warden Plane with regards to accepting her newfound employment was simple. She should immediately do two things: establish a solid working relationship with the Coryell County Sheriff, C. Winfred "Windy" Cummings, and the Texas Ranger Captain whose company covered the Gatesville area, Robert K. "Bob" Mitchell. Lucile Plane became good friends with both. The Mountain View Warden remarked that she had been personally escorted to and sat alongside Captain Mitchell at a high-level Prison Board member's funeral. "And from that point on, I never had another problem with any of the male wardens. Bob enriched my reputation considerably by taking me down there."[60]

Transitioning prisoners from Goree to Gatesville also meant that Death Row for females would now be shifted from Walker County to Coryell County. Warden Plane's responsibilities, of course, amplified. With a touch of humor—a giggle of sorts—Lucile Plane highlighted an inadvertent reality associated with Judge Justice's strict order to quit housing juvenile males at Gatesville. She recalled: "Because when we got the Mountain View Unit, it had been a boys' facility and we had to make it, change it over to be a women's facility. And at one time, the *Dallas Morning News* had a picture of my [prison] laundry porch and there were 50 urinals on that porch. And it said, 'changing the plumbing facilities which are not conducive to female usage.'" Warden Plane, though compassionate and composed, was not blind to in-house truths about convicts—female convicts—always striving for the upper hand: "They'll beat you. . . . they can beat you every time. I always said if you could stay a half step behind them you were ahead of the game. . . . The women are sneaky. They yak all the time, they curse. . . . And uh they [fish] learned from the females when they got here more four-letter combinations of words than they ever heard in all their life. They never heard such language. The female inmates could put together more four-letter words than you'll ever hope to see."[61]

Subsequent to years of legal sparring during the Discovery Phase, the class-action lawsuit asserting that Texas prisons on many fronts were operating in an Unconstitutional manner and depriving prisoners of guaranteed rights was to be tried at Houston on a Change of Venue. And, though it's written in the main that TDC officialdom was bowled over upon learning that William Wayne Justice would yet be the presiding judge, a craftily manipulated legal maneuver, it shouldn't have come as any surprise. For whatever may be said of the judge, he was adept at marshaling the extensive weight of available federal resources to secure and implement his philosophical leanings, be it recruiting superb legal talent for the plaintiffs, utilizing investigative manpower of the DOJ—the Federal Bureau of Investigation—and dipping real deep into the seemingly bottomless well of U.S. taxpayers' dollars. State government coffers were for the most part inadequate, over the long haul, to sustain what was shaping up as a protracted fund-draining encounter. In not just a few gaming instances, some folks can find themselves money-whipped, a classic device wherein flush players overwhelm their less affluent adversaries, then rake the pot. As previously citied, for this legal skirmish there would be no impaneled jury. From the veritable outset it was evident that Judge William Wayne Justice intended, with gusto, to strike hard with his lifetime gavel: He would unapologetically hammer and forge brand-new worlds for the keepers and the kept. His trial court, wherever, was no champion of the status quo. That was fact. On the second day of October 1978 the trial began.

Weighing the pros and cons regarding judicial activism in prison reform sets in motion debatable subtopics—validity sometimes based solely on whose ox is being gored. Whether one is nose to the grindstone earning an honest living in the free-world or unwillingly sleeping on a thin mattress behind the tall walls and high fences, oftentimes defines where one plants one's flag. There are spirited advocates—sincere advocates—staked on both battlefronts. The legal wrangling before District Judge William Wayne Justice's provisional Harris County bench undeniably sparked collateral trouble.

In the concerted effort to demonstrate solidarity with the plaintiffs' litigation then underway at Houston, *Ruiz vs. Estelle*, not just a few Texas convicts ginned up a work stoppage, well aware the news media would hungrily devour the details. They were right! At the Ellis Unit just north of Huntsville "148 prisoners refused to eat, return to work or to go to their cells," and later they were joined by another assemblage of 260 convicts—running that grand tally to 408. At the Ramsey I Unit southwest of Houston, while they remained in their cells, 339 convicts refused to turn out for the Line or otherwise report to their assigned jobs. In Brazoria County at the Darrington Unit 209 prisoners joined the demonstration. Initially in the field these Hoe-Squad prisoners "began moving en masse toward guards." Three shotgun blasts—one in the air and two into the ground—checked their forward movement, but not without minor injuries: "one prisoner received a superficial thigh wound, and it definitely was caused by buckshot. . . . Two other men received superficial wounds, but it can't be determined whether they were caused by buckshot or ricocheting gravel." Darrington mutineers made their obstinate move more than perfectly clear: "We are in sympathy with the Ruiz case and with Judge Justice and we hope prison officials will not retaliate for this action."[62] Not unexpectedly it was not too long before convicts at the Ramsey II Unit, 200 strong, joined the throng of solidarity and, shortly at the Eastham Unit 130 supporters clad in prison whites followed suit.[63] Clearly these edgy opening acts—preliminary bouts—were but teases for the main event.

At the Coffield Unit in Anderson County, more than a hundred in-the-field convicts pitched their Aggies to the ground in defiance, sat down, and bucked. The uprising at Coffield was communicable. That afternoon as many as 1500 of Coffield's disgruntled felons barricaded themselves inside the cellblocks and began—it was rumored—manufacturing weapons from anything that would do: mop and/or broom handles, broken pieces of furniture, wire bucket handles, brush handles, etc., etc., etc. It goes without saying, that this armament only added to the contraband arsenal of shanks and sling-shots and spears and stones stuffed into socks. Property destruction was widespread at Coffield.[64]

At that juncture Director Estelle—in his mind—was compelled to dutifully take action, not idly stand by and watch pirates scuttle the ship: "It was necessary to use tear gas and riot batons to control the hostile inmates and return them to their cells. This action was completed in three hours. . . . 28 inmates were treated for minor injuries and six others were transferred to the Huntsville unit hospital.... One prison officer suffered a broken hand, two were cut by broken glass and 15 others were hurt by either scalding water poured on them by inmates or from foreign objects lodged in their eyes. All the guards have been treated or released."[65] A writer for the *Dallas Morning News*, based on Estelle's tally, somewhat expanded on particularizing the physiological trauma suffered by convicts sent to the infirmary: "All were treated for scalp wounds, and two were treated for additional injuries. One of the inmates received a collarbone fracture and the other suffered a broken shoulder blade. . . ."[66]

Bending to the urgent appeal from TDC officials, but apparently only after consultation and agreement with the lawyers for the plaintiffs and attorneys from the U.S. Justice Department, which should come as no bombshell, Judge Justice acquiesced and made a public statement, one ostensibly designed to calm troubled seas. However, it's noteworthy that he didn't condemn disobedience and destruction and dousing Correctional Officers with scalding water as acts that were fundamentally wrong in themselves, but only that "orderly progress of the trial could be impeded if violence and disruption continue. . . ."[67] In light of his sometime dogmatic qualities exhibited from the bench, Judge Justice's plea to the defiant convicts and their acts of destruction and violence—which again should come as no shocker—was, in a disheartening way, anemic: "It is my hope that they cease."[68] That hope, understandably, would be echoed by harried prison administrators and their front-line staffs—though they had to invest more than hopefulness!

And whether it measures as trying to leave an impression of the court's total impartiality in the pending lawsuit or rates more basically as skipping around taking any scary chances, the Honorable Judge Justice had no desire to—or at least he didn't—personally visit any of the state's prison facilities for a first-hand look at what he—and he alone—would decide to set right. ". . . Judge Justice's intervention might have been helped had he personally set foot inside of the prisons he was trying to reform. . . . As every serious student of correctional institutions knows, one can read all of the books, essays, operational manuals, post orders, and neatly typed depositions in the world and still have a less clear sense of how, and how well, a prison or jail operates than someone who has read none of this material but has spent a day or two observing operations and talking to inmates and staff, behind the walls. If you want to know whether cells are cramped, enter them; if you want to know whether food is decent, eat it; if you want to know whether the staff-to-inmate ratio is too low, sit in a cellblock and see how it runs; and so on."[69] Likewise, on-the-ground Correctional Officers, generally speaking, "have little regard for judicial opinions or operating procedures rendered by 'absentee authorities' whose familiarity with local problems may be suspect."[70] Judge Justice would build his reasoning and rationales from witness-stand testimony—much of it from convicts—and if anyone actually lied or committed Perjury, well, he could send them to prison!

The whole brouhaha in the mind of Director Estelle was simple: "I find little charity and less solace in bringing issues before a court that has no knowledge, direct or indirect, of what the real issues are and could care less that their personal social philosophy, finding its way into so-called law, jeopardizes not only our inmates' safety, but the safety of prison staff as well."[71] Director Estelle may have been out of step with progressively minded prison reformers, but he was not dancing by himself. Some big-time and well-respected newspaper editorial pieces were not espousing that convicts should be treated inhumanely or Unconstitutionally, but they were not necessarily being hoodwinked by prison reality:

> At the moment a class action suit on behalf of Texas prisoners is underway in Houston. In the lawsuit, it is being alleged that prisoners have suffered cruel and inhumane treatment. Meanwhile, back at some of the prison units, some inmates went on strike in sympathy with prisoners who brought the class action. . . . But the routes open to prisoners obviously can not be endless. After due process, they were adjudged to have committed crimes against society. And society has assigned them penalties, they must abide by certain rules.
>
> If cruel and inhumane treatment has been inflicted upon some of the prisoners, then they are getting their day in court. This is the purpose of their lawsuit in Houston. And certainly it is a day in court some of the prisoners never accorded to their crime victims. . . . Prison officials are not dealing with Sunday School kids. Prisoners are society's problem children. Some are beyond direction. Some can be rehabilitated. Others fall somewhere between these two extremes. Prison officials do not have an endless supply of money with which to build all of the prison units needed, staff them with superbly qualified people and meet every prisoner's need.
>
> What they do have is a system of mostly-modern units which are hard pressed in space and staff to keep pace with the rapidly-rising number of prisoners society keeps sending them to care for as they pay their debt to society and, yes, to rehabilitate if possible. What they have, too, is an abundance of land—Texas is more fortunate than most state prisons in this regard—which allows for an abundance of hard work. This way, the prisoners grow much of their own food. So they work hard but eat good.
>
> If some proof of wrongdoing comes from the Houston courtroom relative to treatment of prisoners, then Texans should begin a hue and cry which does not cease until corrective action is taken.

Meanwhile, though, Texans must stand firmly with prison officials who not only must go through class action suits and accompanying sitdown strikes but who, day in and day out, night in and night out must oversee 25,000 of society's worst.[72]

And not all of society's worst were imprisoned. Some were yet in the free-world as the idealistic and intrusive federal jurist from Tyler all too soon discovered. On the morning of 29 May 1979 at San Antonio in the driveway of his luxurious condominium, the Chateau Dijhon, United States District Judge John Howland "Maximum John" Wood, Jr. was assassinated. A sniper had triggered a round into his back. Within itself the true-crime story makes—and has made—for good reading.[73] How does this thriller play into the story at hand? Rather easily as it turns out. Ranger Captain Jack Dean, commanding Company D headquartered in the Alamo City was handed a clue—in a nutshell due to his most tactful cultivation of a confidential informant (CI). The alleged suspect for Judge Wood's premeditated slaying was entirely familiar to Jack Dean because of his involvement with two previous execution-type Texas homicides. Dutifully, DPS veteran Jack Dean turned the name Charles Voyde Harrelson over to the FBI, putting them on track to unravel the mysterious and ghastly and sensational murder.[74]

Enumerating all of Charles Voyde Harrelson's felony convictions is not herein mandatory; he was and could be classed as a recidivist. And as but a quick sidebar, Charles Harrelson's uncle, the aforementioned Warden Zan E. Harrelson, was within the large TDC community, rather well known. Courtroom convicted of offing Judge Wood and owing the federal government hard-time, Charles Harrelson also had a debt to pay Texas for other criminal offenses. That brings Charles Voyde Harrelson's proclivity for prison monkey-business full circle. While housed at the Eastham Unit north of Huntsville, rumor or gossip or fact came to the attention of authorities: Charles Harrelson was planning an escape and would be armed with a small—but naturally very dangerous—smuggled handgun.[75] According to the report of an inquiring newspaperman

one of Charles Voyde's defense attorneys disparaged any such suggestion: "Harrelson has spent 15 of the past 17 years in various
federal and state prisons. . . . There's never been any evidence he
ever tried to escape. It sounds to me like TDC is making something
out of nothing."[76]

Apparently the barrister was wholly unaware of facts from the
past, and he surely wasn't privy to what would unfold in the future.
With regards to the former, while in custody at Edinburg (in Hidalgo
County) awaiting trial for a coldblooded killing, Ranger Jack Dean
and local officers had searched and seized from Harrelson's cell a .25
caliber Beretta Jetfire which had been smuggled inside the lockup.
The tipster, as it turned out, was reliable—spot on right![77] With
regards to the assertion that Charles Voyde Harrelson had or was
about to have a pistol at Eastham is less than conclusive, though
circumstantially there might be a reasonable clue that he was trying desperately to arm himself. An astute and thorough Correctional
Officer discovered that inside one of Charles Harrelson's state-
issued brogans, the large heel had been hollowed out—or was being
hollowed out—a clear-cut indicator that Harrelson possessed or was
anticipating possession of contraband.[78] For a touch of rational perspective, a Freedom Arms (now North American Arms) .22 caliber
handgun is obviously lethal—but easy to conceal. Unquestionably
the loquacious lawyer speaking on behalf of his client could not predict the future, but later while kept as a federal prisoner at Atlanta,
Charles Voyde Harrelson was only halted by Correctional Officers
spraying gunfire in his direction while trying to gain free-world status on the far side of the institution's high security fence.[79] At least to
some degree this defaces earlier reporting that while imprisoned at
TDC the "Convicted Hit Man" was saying that he had "found religion
behind bars."[80] Perhaps, Harrelson figured his Deity's realm was outside not inside the wire. This clear-cut but blundered escape attempt
generated the uncompromising transfer of Charles Voyde Harrelson
to the BOP's Supermax facility at Florence (Freemont County),
Colorado, where the most incorrigible, dangerous, and high-profile
federal prisoners are still housed. And there, in the tightly controlled

Administrative Segregation institution, outlaw Charles Voyde Harrelson remained forevermore—at least until claimed by natural causes and an unsmiling undertaker.

By a long-shot Charles V. Harrelson wasn't the only *mal hombre* housed in a Texas prison. Some male convicts were not satisfied with spewing vitriolic words. Letting blood was on their near-term agendas. Death Row was not necessarily a safe spot. Prisoners there had little to lose once their legal appeals were exhausted and down the drain. Edward Lincoln King, thirty-six, a violent recidivist wanted for jumping bond for alleged Rape and Assault charges and also wanted for service of a Blue Warrant (Parole or Probation Revocation, no bail) was housed on Death Row due to his murdering a twenty-five-year-old Dallas PD Officer, a four-year veteran. King had earned such status following his Carjacking and Kidnapping of a female investigator, stealing her .38 Special, and after she successfully bailed out of her auto, taking two more scared ladies hostage. The car chase across Dallas was wild, but King wrecked, fleeing on foot. The footrace was joined by DPD Officer Leslie G. Lane, Jr. When Officer Lane began closing the distance, Edward King stopped, turned and shot Patrolman Lane in the side—twice. He died at the scene. Somewhat interestingly, Edward King had been the very first Dallas County defendant slated to die by imposition of a lethal injection.[81]

Enter into Death Row another recidivist, Anthony Pierce, twenty, convicted this time and sentenced to die for his participation in the Robbery-Murder at a Houston fast-food restaurant. Seeming from the best knowledge at hand, during one night Ed King threatened Tony Pierce with regards to one thing or another—who knows why? In Tony's mind there was but one thing to do: Whack King before he whacked him. A time-honored methodology for problem resolution in the Big House, but not necessarily one condoned by the letter of the law. And there's little doubt that other Death Row convicts championed such a way out the mess. At any rate, with a decidedly unusual shank—a pork chop bone—Pierce stabbed King in the left chest, inflicting a fatal wound measuring "about ½ to ¾ inch deep and ½ to ¾ wide." Pierce asserted that he didn't necessarily intend to kill King, but he was forced into stabbing him in what he deemed an especially logical act of self-protection. Taking everything into consideration, the astutely reasonable Walker County District Attorney charged Pierce with Involuntary Manslaughter and tacked three years onto his death sentence should his scheduled time on the Death Chamber's gurney fall by the wayside during appeals.[82] Understandably, then, as a matter of reactive policy TDCJ-ID kitchen workers began de-boning all meat served in the chow hall.[83]

Though there is no way to logically tie events together, convicts from Dallas County were not faring too well in Texas prisons. Shortly after Ed King was pushing up daisies, at the Ellis Unit, twenty-seven-year-old convict Earnest Alexander, doing a double dime for a Robbery in Dallas, was fatally stabbed twice in the back on his way to the Dining Hall by a convict wielding a "crude knife made of a tool." As the newspaperman rightly theorized, the death was result of two convicts "feuding," which is surely no understatement. The following month, October 1979, another unlucky convict from Dallas County was surprised—again at the Ellis Unit—in a dayroom. Carl Reed, thirty-one, pulling 200 years for Armed Robbery, didn't hear the pleasant-sounding jingle of the Popsicle Man's bell, but he crumpled to the grimy floor after his throat was "slashed with a makeshift knife": "Two razor blades sandwiched between ice cream sticks." Carl Reed bled out, the third Dallas County convict fatality within weeks. Purely a "coincidence" and not a "trend" although there being three Dallas fellows killed in prison within a matter of weeks, not months, was admittedly "a little out of the ordinary," so said Texas Prison spokesman Rick Hartley, Administrative Assistant to the Director.[84] Cutting to the nub is effortless, though in some quarters there is a tendency to downplay or someway downgrade the disconcerting reality: There was an uptick in Texas Prison violence.[85]

12

"An Unwilling pioneer"

ALTHOUGH THE ESCAPE WAS ENGINEERED from the Goree Unit before all of the female convicts had been transferred to the Gatesville facilities, the hard lesson for prison personnel is still not all of the world's gals are nice, daintily fashioned of Sugar and Spice. Some were characterized by TDC spokesman Rick Hartley as some "pretty rough little cookies." Chiefly, in this case he meant Sylvia Jean Brown, thirty-seven, Patricia Ann Watson, thirty-two, and Mary Lou Santellana, thirty, who were all pulling hard time for Harris County robberies. They were physically not very imposing, the tallest being but five foot and two inches, and the heaviest weighing only 135 lbs. but due to their crimes one and all were classed as "dangerous." Desiring an unauthorized jaunt into the free-world, during the wee morning hours the forenamed had opted to slyly unfasten an office window-unit air-conditioner and jump through the ground-level opening. Then they rather easily scaled Goree's perimeter security fence—and vanished. Understandably the routine nighttime head-count didn't clear. And the Bloodhounds could only track them to the I-45 Highway running between Houston and Dallas. Did they have an accomplice standing by with an automobile? Did they catch a ride on the freeway, hitchhiking? Texas Rangers and DPS Troopers were Johnny-on-the-spot, but for the moment they were foiled. The fleeing gals' whereabouts would, however, not go long unknown.

At Oklahoma City, Regina M. Raymond and her three-year-old son, Cameron, were threatened and kidnapped at a shopping center by three petite but tough talking women and, later, after a horrifying nine-hour ordeal released unharmed at the airport in Wichita, Kansas. FBI Agents quickly issued an APB (All Points Bulletin) for the gals who were by now unquestionably interstate fugitives. Thereafter a robbery at Enid, Oklahoma, pointed the finger of culpability at escapee Mary Lou Santellana, the prime suspect. In Pueblo, Colorado, at the Northside Shopping Center, another victim reported that she had been robbed at knife point and she furnished police with a sufficient eyewitness vehicle description, an auto earlier stolen in Oklahoma City. Shortly, a high-speed chase was underway, and adeptly the lead pursuing officer performed his skilled tactical maneuver, "by ramming their car as they were trying to avoid capture." Somewhat luckily and thankfully, no one, escapees or officers, was seriously injured. During the aftermath Pueblo PD Detective John Sheehan advised inquiring newshounds that bond had been set for the trio in the amount of $150,000 each, but "the suspects will not be released on bond if Texas authorities choose to extradite them." Correctional Officers and scholarly penologists presupposing petite gals with delicately painted lips and deftly sculpted eyebrows and polished nails is a precursor for harmlessness in the prison setting is—putting it mildly—a risky misstep. Prettiness can be illusory.[1]

While there seems to be a tendency in assorted academic and journalistic quarters, at least to some degree, for mitigating abhorrent conduct on the part of state prisoners, the world and Texas convicts took note of the mayhem and massacre unfolding south of historic Santa Fe, at the main New Mexico Penitentiary during February 1980. The bloodbath would be well beyond ghastly and gruesome and gut-wrenching, no matter how anyone sleeping in the free-world chooses to sidestep animalistic behavior. Practically speaking the pirates had wrested away control of the ship—and were dead-set on cannibalizing each other. There were gang-rapes, decapitations, castrations, disembowelments, and convicts killed by others holding blow-torches, besides the more or less customary and less sensational stabbings and cuttings and bludgeoning. Aside from the murderous actions of convicts offing thirty-three (or upwards?) of their own, wanton physical plant demolition registered in the millions of scarce taxpayer dollars. The stench of death and destruction was real. While there is no outright effort to absolve the rioting convicts of atrocious criminality and cruelty, as one might expect, the post-incident blame-game was kicked into high-gear. Preceding prison management styles and in-house protocols were—and should have been—scrutinized. On the other hand, how much understanding should be afforded to a convict capable of murders and disfigurements with a blow-torch? Is it meanness or madness to saw off another guy's head? Did degrees of judicial activism—nationwide—help set the stage for psychotic pandemonium? Rationally, that jury's yet deliberating.[2]

One does not long have to surmise about the measurable level of increasing violence within Texas prison units and the wholesale dangerousness Correctional Officers were daily facing as outside judicial forces tinkered with day-to-day operations. Unfortunately, at the Eastham Unit, on the first day of October 1980, the Grim Reaper knocked at the office door of Building Major Cephus DeWard Burson, fifty-eight, formerly of Alabama and an Auburn University graduate. Subsequent to two inmates fighting, the aggressor was escorted to Major Burson's office for a disciplinary query regarding the cause and justification or lack of justification thereof. There the convict was in no mood for quieting his agitation and he picked up a desk stapler and struck Correctional Officer Steve Shirley on the head. Resultantly and dutifully Major Burson "picked up a riot baton and attempted to stop the assault, but [Johnny R.] Johnson got control of the baton and started swinging it, hitting Burson, Shirley and Sgt. Allen Hughes." Immediately thereafter Major Burson began having chest pains and was rushed to the Huntsville Memorial Hospital but was DOA: The cause of death being officially recorded due to "Coronary occlusion, while on duty, during and/or following a scuffle."[3]

When exploring aspects of the prison subculture, the death of Major Burson is surely illuminating. One convict—a Texas Syndicate (Hispanic prison gang) member—seems to suggestively write with merriment regarding the Major's demise. On the other hand, a newspaper account may more accurately reflect a majority opinion of the Eastham prisoners: To assist the fallen Major's grieving family, concerned and compassionate convicts passed the hat, collecting $1,500 (from commissary accounts) as a memorial contribution. Not everyone behind tall walls and high fences is heartless. Major Burson was respectfully laid to rest in the Restwood Memorial Park Cemetery at Clute, Brazoria County. Major Burson's widow did not let the prisoners' heartfelt contribution go unnoticed or unappreciated. Jessie Merle (Gleason) Burson penned a respectful "Thank You" letter—which was prominently posted at Eastham.[4]

What was also posted throughout Texas prisons was the swiping and sweeping declaration by Judge William Wayne Justice: When measured in totality, according to the judge, TDC was institutionally Unconstitutional—a seedbed for Cruel and Unusual Punishment—and other abridgments of prisoners' inherent Civil Rights. The lengthy trial had consumed 159 days of testimony from 349 witnesses, and the federal court had received approximately 1,565 exhibits submitted into evidence.[5] There was no misunderstanding as to where the controversial judge came down on the class-action lawsuit. He was Deadeye Dick convinced and unapologetic:

> The trial of this action lasted longer than any prison case—and perhaps any civil rights case—in the history of American jurisprudence. In marked contrast to prison cases in other states, the defendant prison officials here have refused to concede that any aspect of their operations were unconstitutional, and vigorously contested the allegations of the inmate class on every issue. However, the evidence and the applicable law have demonstrated that constitutional infirmities pervade the TDC prison system.
>
> This memorandum opinion has, at some length, cited and summarized the evidence indicating the existence of these constitutional violations. But it is impossible for a written opinion to convey the pernicious conditions and the pain and degradation which ordinary inmates suffer within TDC prison walls—the

gruesome experiences of youthful first offenders forcibly raped; the cruel and justifiable fears of inmates, wondering when they will be called upon to defend the next violent assault; the sheer misery, the discomfort, the wholesale loss of privacy for prisoners housed with one, two, or three others in a forty-five foot cell or suffocatingly packed together in a crowded dormitory; the physical suffering and wretched psychological stress which must be endured by those sick or injured who cannot obtain adequate medical care; the sense of abject helplessness felt by inmates arbitrarily sent to solitary confinement or administrative segregation without proper opportunity to defend themselves or to argue their causes; the bitter frustration of inmates prevented from petitioning the courts and other government authorities for relief from perceived injustices.

For those who are incarcerated within the parameters of TDC, these conditions and experiences form the content and essence of daily existence. It is to these conditions that each inmate must wake every morning; it is with the painful knowledge of their existence that each inmate must try to sleep at night. But these iniquitous and distressing circumstances are prohibited by the great constitutional principles that no human being, regardless of how disfavored by society, shall be subjected to cruel and unusual punishment or be deprived of the due process of the law within the United States of America. Regrettably, state officials have not upheld their responsibility to enforce these principles. In the wake of their default, the United States Constitution must be enforced within the confines of TDC by court decree.[6]

Judge Justice's telling remark that some "youthful first offender [would be] forcibly raped [and] the cruel and justifiable fears of inmates, wondering when they will be called upon to defend the next violent assault" seems to comport with what in the building Correctional Officers and outside horseback Field Bosses already well knew: Some, assuredly not all, convicts can be downright mean and downright dangerous, despite their sometimes disarming demeanor and deceptive smiles. With a broad but accurate announcement it can be said that Judge Justice, subsequent to appointment of a Special Master and his staff of Monitors, assumed oversight of implementing gargantuan and costly changes for TDC—his version of a control model that would be long lasting. Delving deeply into prison administration practices and day to day prison operations, the freethinking jurist from Tyler methodically addressed nine issues of his, but not necessarily the convict plaintiffs', initially cited concerns. Each category was subdivided with exacting and spelled-out unyielding procedural details and demands: Overcrowding, Security and Supervision, Health Care, Discipline, Access to the Courts, Fire Safety, Sanitation, Work Safety and Hygiene, and Unit Size, Structure, and Location.[7] There was hardly any aspect of prison operations overlooked, forgotten, or ignored. Judge Justice had mapped the course for change, his hand on the throttle.

Perhaps two elements—at least two—cry for mention. During the trial both competing sides called qualified "expert" witnesses to support their beliefs and arguments. Such is par business. Naturally the experts are of divergent opinions and the weight and/or merit of their testimony is by and large graded by an attentive jury.[8] In *Ruiz v. Estelle* there was no jury. Judge Justice would pick and choose which experts did or did not proffer validity in harmony with his views. After-the-fact guesswork is valueless but interesting: Would a trial jury have reached the same end as the activist judge? Or, while exercising his authoritative prerogatives was he inclined to incorporate only what he wanted to hear, disregarding what he didn't personally hypothesize?

Perhaps there is somewhat of a reality check, a peek at applicable commonsense from one jury's perspective. The ever prolific convict writ-witin' David Ruiz—subsequent to being released and then returned to prison for another criminal violation—alleged that at the hands of eighteen Correctional Officers he had suffered retaliatory reprisals for the earlier *Ruiz v. Estelle* lawsuit. This time seeking monetary damages and not injunctive relief, the court impaneled a trial jury, Judge William Wayne Justice presiding.

Though but casually mentioned, if at all, the outcome was somewhat comedic. Guessing at the discomfiture of Judge Justice registers as but speculative, but juries do what juries do and the federal
judge was now not the sole arbiter. Subsequent to eight hours of
careful deliberation, sixteen of the defendants were found faultless. A pair of Correctional Officers were found to have "abused
their duties as prison employees." Quite insightfully a former Texas
Prison Warden, recaps, ponders, and posits:

> The federal jury, in a moment of supreme clarity, awarded David
> Ruiz $2.00 in damages for his suffering, one dollar from each
> officer. Judge Justice, accustomed to issuing decrees without the
> tempering influence of a jury, was no doubt disappointed by this
> two-dollar decision. In hindsight and in the interest of justice,
> the taxpayers of Texas may wonder just how much of their money
> could have been saved if only a jury could have heard the entire
> *Ruiz* litigation.[9]

Another thorny question—drawn from the hardcore law enforcing and penology perspective—is somewhat unanswerable but is
even more troubling. Judge Justice from the get-go had made known
that he would afford convict witnesses testifying on behalf of the
plaintiffs' protection from reprisals by TDC. On its face that doesn't
really seem farfetched, if one is predisposed to constantly impugn
the motives and actions of the Lone Star's prison personnel. Judge
Justice would, subsequent to their testimony should the convict witness so desire, transfer any prisoners straightaway out of any TDC-
controlled institutions and into a federal BOP facility—somewhere.
Though the question is rhetorical and remains so, could or would or
did any of the testifying Texas convicts take the witness stand with
an ulterior motive? Generally speaking—by most accounts—doing
time in a federal penitentiary is, from the convicts' perspective,
much easier than at state prisons. Hoodwinking a judge—or trying
to—for a convict already pulling a long stretch was cost-free: They
were already living in prison whether they told the full truth or not.
Realistically—and that's what counts—some outright perjury or

exaggeration was not unlikely. Did anyone testify solely to gain a transfer? ¿*Quién sabe?*

Rehashing in detail most of the changes wrought on TDC will not be tackled herein, chiefly due to the elementary fact that this treatment is a ground-level prison chronology and, even more importantly, *Ruiz v. Estelle* (and later styled *Ruiz* actions) has been written about extensively although scholars—unquestionably accomplished academicians—are time and again at odds with each others' findings. One only has to substantively review *Courts, Corrections, and the Constitution: The Impact of Judicial Intervention on Prisons and Jails*, to reel in the core truth: Not everyone agrees about everything regarding Judge William Wayne Justice's signature prison analysis.[10] The reader in want of more will have no problem.[11] Assuredly the Texas convict population would not have to look hard or very far. Though it would issue somewhat later, the final *Ruiz v. Estelle* settlement agreement was published in both English and Spanish for the Special Edition of *The Echo*, the Texas Prison newspaper.[12] Convicts gobbled up the news. It would have and did have meaningful significance for them. Maybe in not every instance a positive impact; nevertheless Judge Justice's ruling was the law. Unlike Las Vegas, what happened at Tyler didn't stay at Tyler.

Nearer to Huntsville, at the maximum-security Ellis Unit, on April 4, 1981, the Grim Reaper stalked Warden Wallace Melton Pack, fifty-five, a U.S. Army veteran, and the unit's fifty-year-old Farm Manager, Billy Max Moore, who had seen military service with the U.S. Navy. Both were killed. Billy Max Moore had been shot in the head with a .38 Special, expiring instantly. Wallace Melton Pack had been held down and drowned in a dirty ditch, one carrying but two or three feet of water. Aside from the general appalling news, Pack's untimely death would index in the Texas Prison history book as the first Warden killed in the line of duty. As would be expected, the collective TDC community was quite shocked—almost beyond belief.

Warden Wallace M. Pack, survived by his wife Faye and step-children, was peacefully interred in the Wheelock City Cemetery in Robertson County, not too far north of busy Bryan/College Station.

Billy Max Moore was removed to Troup, and buried in the Pinecrest Cemetery in Smith County, survived by his bride Lola, his two sons and her two children. Both funerals were well-attended—more than well-attended—by bereaving prison personnel, each knowing that they too were gingerly walking the tightrope suspended over arenas of possible deaths at the hands of a convict or convicts whether pre-planned or spontaneous.

Area lawmen such as Walker County Sheriff W. Darrell White's detective assigned to prison cases, Ted Pearce, and the Company A Texas Ranger based in Huntsville, the aforementioned John Wesley Styles, would conduct the initial criminal investigation.[13] Although the killing was a stunner it was no whodunit.

The killer was Eroy Edward "Weasel" Brown, thirty, a convict from Waco pulling a dozen years for an Aggravated Robbery with a Firearm at a Fort Worth Ramada Inn, and also owning two other stints in Texas prisons on his back trail.[14] Eroy Brown didn't dis-avow the killing of Pack and/or Moore. He was charged with Capital Murder. On the other hand, Eroy Brown insistently maintained that the dreadful double killing was nothing short of a reasonable act of self-preservation: Self-defense, a Justifiable Homicide under exist-ing Texas statutes.[15]

It was Brown's assertion that he had slain Pack and Moore because they intended to take him to the nearby Trinity River bot-toms and administer a severe beating—or worse—as unauthorized and/or extralegal penalty for his unacceptable behavior. As typical with criminal or civil lawsuits pitting convicts against Correctional Officers and/or prison staff, jurors will likely and did in this case hear two separate versions of the same—and for this testy wrangle—very sad story. The courtroom battle waxed hot. The prosecution and its list of witnesses staunchly affixed to the notion that convict Eroy Edward Brown had coldly murdered Billy Moore with the Warden's snubnose Smith & Wesson revolver, and then straddled Wallace Pack, pushing and holding his head beneath the shallow water till death stilled any further struggling. Eroy Brown had killed while trying to escape from prison, so the state theorized. For the state it was Murder—plain and simple. The witness list for the defense lawyers—including not just a few convicts—was taking the opposite approach. The defense premise was that Eroy Edward Brown had little or no choice: He could fight or die.[16]

For the particular case at hand an editorialist for the *Dallas Morning News* was championing arguments neither for the prosecution team or the defense lineup. The underlying theme was not masked by syrupy idealism:

> Too often public concern with criminals stops when offenders are shipped off to prison. Out of the limelight, prison guards and officials are the unsung heroes of the criminal justice system, however. They must deal daily with many of the most violent, mentally unbalanced people in our society. And corrections officials do so with little appreciation or understanding of their roles. . . . Critics often scoff at the rules and regulations in the prison system. But the measures are designed to assure the safety of everyone—inmate and officer alike—involved in the thankless process of corrections. . . . Our criminals who are out-of-sight, out-of-mind to most Texans are a daily reality to the men and women of TDC.[17]

The short version of the *State of Texas vs. Eroy Brown* may be encapsulated: He was tried at Galveston for killing Wallace Pack and the jury was unable to agree; District Court Judge Henry Dalehite had little option but to declare a *Mistrial*. Jury deliberations for Eroy Brown's second trial for killing Wallace Pack did not go well for the prosecution. A *Not Guilty* verdict favored the defendant. Within the framework of the Bill of Rights, he could not be tried again for killing Wallace Pack. For killing Billy Max Moore, Eroy Edward Brown would stand trial at Edinburg (in Hidalgo County), deep in the Rio Grande borderlands before District Judge Darrell H. Hester, aka "Hang 'Em High Hester," a WW II Navy veteran with service on destroyers in both the Atlantic and Pacific Theaters. At this trial—the last bite at the apple for the state—after hearing testimony and weighing admissible evidence, the jurors returned their verdict: *Not Guilty*.

Convict Eroy Brown was not convicted, and he could not undergo another trial for killing Farm Manager Billy Max Moore; guaranteed Double Jeopardy protections kicked in. According to one accomplished writer, some jurymen (or women) actually embraced the defendant.[18] For TDC employees—most of 'em—the jury's finding was a kick in the gut.[19]

Herein it's imperative to make mention of critical distinctions. All potential criminal defendants are covered with a blanket of presumed innocence. However, an aspect is frequently disregarded in generalized writings—perhaps honestly—about the destinies of criminal case defendants as handed down by Petit Juries (not Grand Juries) at closing of felony trials: They never return a verdict of *Innocent*. The burden of proof rests with the state government, and that inflexible standard of proof must rise to the level of belief Beyond a Reasonable Doubt. Texas criminal juries are chosen and delegated to render a unanimous decision and return the verdict to the trial court. And that verdict will clearly be either *Guilty* or *Not Guilty*. A *Guilty* verdict means the prosecuting attorney(s) proved the criminal case Beyond a Reasonable Doubt: A *Not Guilty* verdict is an uncontroverted result that the jury was not convinced Beyond a Reasonable Doubt, not that the defendant didn't commit the alleged crime, but rather that the required standard of proof was not met by prosecutors. So, the bottom-line is plain. A prosecuted person who did not commit the alleged crime may be found *Guilty* or *Not Guilty*. A prosecuted person who did commit the alleged crime may be found *Guilty* or *Not Guilty*. But in the courtroom no jury findings record that the defendant has been found *Innocent*.[20] When puzzled jurors cannot reach a unanimous verdict (a hung jury) the court may declare a *Mistrial*, and the defendant may be retried with an altogether different slate of jurors until a consensus is reached—or the state's attorney declines any further prosecution. From the practical penitentiary perspective, then, the staff becomes heir to the judge and/or jury's diktat. With regards to the case at hand, Eroy Edward Brown was adjudged *Not Guilty* of murdering Pack and Moore and that's the bottom-line, what counted! What also constitutes a bottom-line is that subsequent to Eroy Edward Brown's release from prison for the Armed Robbery at Fort Worth, he was involved in another robbery gone awry at Waco. This time around, his fourth adult felony conviction, Eroy Brown caught ninety years to do as a Habitual Criminal.[21]

Another resident Texas convict didn't catch a break. Charlie Brooks Jr. would, however, make his mark in history—a not enviable entry or as Warden Jim Willett wryly noted, he would be "an unwilling pioneer." Brooks a former federal convict at Leavenworth and a Texas prison recidivist, had been courthouse convicted of the Kidnapping and Murder of David Gregory in Tarrant County.[22] The killing had been gruesome, the victim having been gagged and bound with tape and wire, and then—in a motel room—shot in the head.[23] The forty-year-old Brooks was scheduled for a state sanctioned execution. Charlie Brooks would be the first prisoner in the United States to be executed via a lethal injection, and the very first prisoner to be executed in the Lone Star State since the Supreme Court had given an okay to reinstate Capital Punishment. On the seventh day of December 1982, Pearl Harbor Day, stringent Death Chamber protocols torpedoed Charlie Brooks' future—eternally![24]

Although the Texas juries would continue answering questions in the affirmative that fostered sentences of death, not all luckless Texas convicts would give up the ghost while strapped to the Death Chamber's gurney. Unfortunately but somewhat predictably, during the mid-1980s the in-house stabbing and murder rate for Texas convicts detonated. Theoretical arguments about prison business are not inappropriate, but sometimes peeling back the skin of commonsense cause and effect, while certainly revolting, is demonstrable. For this taste of prison reality the court's dismantling of the BTs—regardless the pros or cons—had devastating and measurable results, as well as coagulating puddles of senselessly spilt blood. Though court mandated to positively adjust upwards the Correctional Officer-to-convict ratio, the recruiting and hiring and training of thousands of new employees—despite good intentions and a real shortage of legislative appropriations—could not be accomplished overnight. Additional prison units couldn't be built fast enough. Convicts were sleeping in tents. Whether one chooses to tag Director Ward James Estelle, Jr. as an inflexible resistor of Judge Justice's complete and fastidious overhaul of TDC, or cast him in the role of an administrator pigeonholed in a position near impossible to manage, compliance with scores of mandated changes, is irrelevant. For this treatment, unsettled will remain practical critiques of the federal judge's wholesale intervention. There are, however, hard unbending truths. Throughout TDC's rank and file, Jim Estelle was generally revered, though his unequivocal legislative support was wavering. To a substantial extent it had been bitterly diluted in the state's chalice of poisonous politics: Estelle resigned on 7 October 1983.[25] Subsequent to the interim short-term appointment of Daniel V. "Red" McKaskle, the TDC top-spot opening was permanently filled by selection of Raymond T. Procunier, an experienced multi-state prison administrator known for his straightforward personality and an abounding vocabulary liberally salted with expletives. Director Procunier's second-in-command, TDC's Deputy Director, would also be a seasoned veteran of profound and profane prison business, Colonel Orson Lane McCotter, Commandant of the U.S. Army's Disciplinary Barracks at Fort Leavenworth, Kansas.[26] The timing of Procunier and McCotter accepting their new Texas jobs was inopportune. And whether it's attributed to a power vacuum or an authority deficiency or barefaced mismanagement is and, has been, arguable, though practically speaking for this storyline it's wholly irrelevant.

By 1984 TDC administrators had lost control of the ship; pirates were now in charge though they didn't sport three-cornered hats or have eye-patches or colorful parrots atop their shoulders. They did, however, have identifying tattoos and hand-signs and secret codes and an arsenal of stashed shanks, and in most cases, a rather well-recognized top-down hierarchy with a blood in, blood out, mentality. Prison Gangs—though TDC officialdom was loath to admit it for awhile, were now the buccaneers of Texas penitentiary dominance.[27]

A clear-headed and inquisitive AP journalist, Paul Recer, in his earlier piece about Texas prison overcrowding, penned, among other sharp yet troubling observations, a one-sentence fact: "Strength is the law among the lawless."[28] Likewise, Steve Blow, staff writer for the widely-circulated *Dallas Morning News* in a frightening article about surviving the prison experience was not wearing rose-colored glasses: "Stronger, meaner inmates prey on the weaker ones, threatening to beat them unless they are paid off—in money, sex, or both. . . . And prison wardens admit they are almost powerless to stop it."[29] There was even—at least in one case—a going rate for not suffering molestation or a beating. A physically or mentally weak convict could actually purchase a "written protection policy" from an enterprising and conscienceless tush-hog: A $49 per month payment would guarantee absolute security; a $29 fee would limit any physical injury to but lacerations and bruises.[30] Such assertions about inmate on inmate violence are not hyperbolic gibberish, as newsman Blow recorded subsequent to interviewing a prisoner:

> There was no way not to pay protection there without getting beaten or stabbed. They would just beat you over and over. You might get sent to the hospital, but when you came out, it would happen all over again.[31]

The in-house convict culture was ruthless, particularly at select units reserved for hard-cases. Unless one were willing and/or able to do battle or leave the tough and credible impression that he would not tolerate abuse, unaligned convicts would have to, in prison lingo, "catch a ride." That is, seeking and receiving protection from a stronger convict or hide beneath the wings of a prison gang. Either way it was not free. Whether riding with an individual or an identifiable gang the extortion toll was extracted, be it contraband green money, commissary goods, menial drudge work, and/or becoming a mean convict's punk—sexual slave—or in the case of a prison gang's overall domination and degradation, a pitiable pass-around prostitute.

Even convicts heretofore pulling their time sans a shank, in desperation for a modicum of self-protection, began arming themselves. During 1984 and 1985 with the BT control mechanism relegated to the past, there were 2,700 disciplinary cases written for convicts having weapons. Maybe—just maybe—some carried a concealed shank with good cause. During 1984 there were 25 convict homicides, in addition to the 404 stabbings and cuttings. At the near always troublesome and huge Coffield Unit alone, one in-house sweep for weapons turned up an astonishing 1000+ shanks, shivs, and sharpened steel-pointed rods capable of gutting, cutting, and sticking.[32] For short-staffed Correctional Officers other numbers were staggering and sickening, too. Just at the Coffield Unit during the first seven months of 1983, Correctional Officers were struck (assaulted) by convicts 38 times, though that gruesome tally had climbed to 168 during the equivalent reporting period for the following year.[33] Assaults on surprised Correctional Officers at but a single prison unit more than quadrupling was an eye-opener for many penologists and much of the appalled general public and most of the Texas mainline convict population who desired real safety and security. A 130-incident jump was and still is significant. Had tinkering with the tested idea of maintaining order eroded with the stroke of a judicial pen? Some bad consequences are not intended—nevertheless they can be real—as the practically experienced veterans of prison work well know. Just for the first three-quarters of the next year 237 convicts were sliced and diced or stuck, not counting the death toll that marked 27 Texas prison killings during 1985—a high-water mark.[34] Of course that's not counting the black-eyes and busted-lips suffered by convicts arguing over this or that; like whose radio was playing too loud or who was masturbating in the gang shower or who cut in line or just who insultingly gestured who with an in-your-face middle-finger salute. Not just a few overworked and underpaid Correctional Officers and more than several learned scholars linked the commonsense and quantifiable corollary with regards to the demise of the BT setup and the resultant typhoon of convict on convict and convict on staff violence: "For several *decades* [emphasis added], the Texas Department of Corrections was virtually free of inmate gang disruption. It is possible that this condition could be attributed to the introduction of the officially approved 'building tender' system. Under the supervision of prison officials, not only did building tenders effectively maintain order among inmates, but more importantly, they served as an intelligence network for prison officials."[35] Naiveté in the free-world is, by and large, safe. In prison it's dangerous! Although it might possibly have miffed a few so-called enlightened thinkers and/or reformers, one astute Texas journalist, Dick Reavis, was not bamboozled by asinine assumptions if they flew in the face of fact:

> In the days before the removal of the building tenders, inmate-on-inmate killings averaged fewer than three a year. If the building tenders were a gang, as the *Ruiz* plaintiffs alleged, they were a gang that stopped short of murder and even prevented murder. During their reign the murder rate in Texas prisons was lower than in most cities. It was safer to walk the hallways of prisons in Texas, where murderers abounded, than to walk the open streets of Houston. That's not true anymore. Our gang, the building tenders, has been replaced by new gangs, *their* gangs. . . .[36]

And perhaps at this point it's imperative to mention a relevant truth with regards to TDC's giving certain convicts BT status. Were one inclined to cherry-pick data regarding egregious and appalling and indefensible BT behavior the examples are there. Likewise there are instances where corrupt and disgraceful Correctional Officers jump the rails of integrity—and legality. There, too, is the surplus of illustrations—many cited herein—when non-BT convicts instigate, act out, or otherwise do stupid things. A reality check is incontrovertible, statistically and from the standpoint of commonsense. The majority of BTs did not stand victims in a commode, shock them with an electrical cord, and then viciously rape them while they screamed for mercy. Correctional Officers in the main did not smuggle dope, accept bribes, and/or beat convicts senseless in a fit of run-amok rage. The overwhelming numbers of mainline population convicts, though they might not have liked doing so, were generally rule-compliant and focused on release. Witnesses heard in the courtroom are those called by opposing sides—after all, winning is key. With regards to using BTs it is evident Judge Justice heard what he wanted to hear—and acted. Naturally, not everyone concerned concurred. Even a devoted Texas Prison Chaplain, Reverend Carroll Pickett, was not blinded to gritty penitentiary reality with regards to BTs, writing, in part:

> If problems arose, they [BTs] solved them. And, yes there were times when it was neither pretty nor subtle, but they were the men who saw to it that the convicts under their watch lived as close to a democratic lifestyle as prison would allow. . . . On occasion I was called to the hospital [*not the morgue*] when a badly beaten inmate was brought in from one of the other units. His jaw might be broken, teeth missing, ribs cracked—all in the name of the drastic discipline a building tender had deemed necessary. Almost without exception I would eventually learn that the injured inmate had sexually assaulted a younger prisoner, tried to kill a cell mate, thrown urine or feces on a passing guard, or stolen from others. . . . It was, I would learn, simply judged as the way by which order was kept in a disorderly society populated by men who recognized justice only at its most basic level. And, brutal though it might have been at times, it worked. It was an effective way of assuring that the Texas prisons were as nonviolent as possible. Fewer prisoners died at the hands of fellow inmates than in any prison in the country. . . . Old-timers insisted that discipline and calm were the product of the fear factor instituted by those who walked the halls of the cell blocks. In the idiom of the day, the building tenders—street-smart and themselves no strangers to violence—kept the lid on. But, in the wake of *Ruiz vs. Estelle*, the situation [had] changed drastically.[37]

Not surprisingly in that wake of violence churned by *Ruiz vs. Estelle*, newspaper reporters were energetically trawling for copy—and that sea-change within TDC's prisons was a good catch. Convicts would for the record lament the loss of BTs: "The increased violence among inmates has left some longing for the days when a tough inmate known as a building tender presided over each cellblock. The building tenders routinely beat inmates who crossed them or broke prison rules. . . . U.S. District Judge William Wayne Justice

outlawed the use of building tenders in his Ruiz vs. Estelle decision."
An unlucky convict, during one incident stabbed ten times, told the
inquiring journalists for the *Dallas Morning News*: "I think Ruiz did
some good with that case, but he did plenty wrong, too. . . . This
[getting stabbed] would have never happened before. The building
tender would have stopped it." Another convict chimed in: "Even
though you got harassed a little bit and the living conditions were
worse, it was a lot better before. . . . You could sit and do your time
with nothing to worry about. Now you've got to worry about the
other inmates and what they are going to do."[38] For his way of thinking a reflecting convict remarked, "that it would be nice to see the
day when building tenders kept order."[39]

Even a former Texas Syndicate gangster, who at one point was
highly critical and vocal about the physical power and influence of
BTs, had a practical change of attitude after surviving bloody intramural warfare with the Mexican Mafia. As a means of repressing the
runaway violence and anarchy plaguing the TDC Units, his cure was
to reinstate the BT system with certain caveats and giving the control and order model a restart.[40] That was the opinion of a prison
gang member, but TDC prison gang specialists concurred. As quoted
above it bears repeating: "For several decades, the Texas Department
of Corrections was virtually free of inmate gang disruption. It is possible that this condition could be attributed to the introduction of
the officially approved 'building tender' system. Under the supervision of prison officials, not only did building tenders effectively
maintain order among inmates, but more importantly, they served
as an intelligence network for prison officials. . . . As the 'building
tender' system began to fade away at the order of the *Ruiz* ruling"
the in-house turmoil and terror escalated.[41]

And though once before mentioned herein, it seems germane
to offhandedly reiterate that during the administrative reigns of
O.B. Ellis and George Beto, when BTs were primetime players, no
Correctional Officers were ferociously murdered by any uncontrol-
lable convicts. Regardless theorists' idyllic druthers, absent the
right measures of control and order in prison, folks—good and/or

bad—run the legit risk of incurably bleeding out on the highly polished cell-block floors or in the cramped storerooms or other locales screened by inadvertent blind spots.

Though uncompromisingly interconnecting the unprecedented spike in Texas prison mayhem and murder with the resignation of TDC Director Ray Procunier may be a stretch, nevertheless he was gone, replaced by his number-two man, Lane McCotter. After a series of same-day violence seemingly system-wide, Director McCotter was forced into taking action, which he did unapologetically. Those convicts classified as potentially murderous or violently incorrigible or confirmed or suspected members of STGs (Security Threat Groups, i.e. prison gangs) were assigned to Administrative Segregation blocs: lockdown twenty-three and seven, permitted non-cell activity to but shower and exercise—briefly—and even then under authoritarian close supervision. While graded by some armchair thinkers and theorists as extreme and excessive and cruel, there is now and was then a quantifiable upshot: It worked! Texas prison violence on the heretofore unparalleled scale nose-dived. Mainline convicts were now—by and large—much safer as were Correctional Officers and general staff. The wholesale killing and cutting had been curtailed, not to say, however, that the spilling of convict and Correctional Officer blood was, or would be eradicated. After all, it was yet prison! And despite society's wish for better, prisons house some pretty mean folks.

Even if the high-drama occurred somewhat later (before the century clock chimed again), the general reader might register surprise that convicts on Death Row—at the time—had as much move-about freedom as they did. At that time a number of Death Row convicts were classed as "work eligible" permitting them to leave their prison jobs as janitors and uniform tailors, and mingle on the recreation yard and in dayrooms, though at bedtime they were supposed to be serenely and securely tucked away in their houses. Prison officials on a Thanksgiving night received a wakeup call, literally and figuratively. Not since the days of the cop-killing Clyde and Bonnie had anyone made a triumphant break from Death Row, some sixty-odd years before.

After the holiday supper seven Death Row convicts chose to gamble; what did they have to lose? Howard Guidry convicted of a Murder for Hire scheme, Henry Dunn doing time for shooting a gay man nine times and leaving him in a gravel pit, Gustavo Garcia killed a liquor store clerk during an Aggravated (using a firearm) Robbery, James Clayton abducted and then killed a lady in Abilene, Eric Cathey was on Death Row for a Capital Crime in Harris County, Martin Gurule, had murdered two folks during an Aggravated Robbery at Corpus Christi, and Ponchai Wilkerson, who had triggered a round into a fellow's head during a Houston heist, had fashioned dummies for their cell bunk blankets to conceal during their absence and then did what escapees are supposed to do—try to leave the premises unnoticed. Under the cover of darkness the would-be free-world fellows did manage to peel through a recreation yard fence, climbed to the roof of a two-story building and laid low—assessing their odds for advancing their cause. They stripped to their undershorts—leaving their prison whites to be found later—coloring their underwear with dark felt-tip markers, making them hard to detect at night. They had all shucked down except for Martin Gurule, he having kept a pullover top and trousers, but both had been inked, too. Then they all jumped to the ground—hotfooting toward the first of two perimeter fences, then about seventy feet away. This time the outside Correctional Officers, though maybe fully stuffed with turkey, were eagle-eyed. The outlaws were literally in "No Man's Land," which was a demarcation point allowing picket tower officers to employ deadly force, which they did: Calling for a halt and popping eighteen to twenty rounds at the astonished convicts' feet, putting breaks on the Grand Plan. Six of the fellows opted to call it quits—throwing in the towel and throwing up their hands. Martin Gurule bet the farm, effectively scaling the first of two high fences and then the other—both crowned with razor-wire. Then he was gone!

Not surprisingly for Texas penitentiary officialdom it was an embarrassing state of affairs. The ensuing manhunt—with as many as 500 strategically placed Correctional Officers, DPS Troopers, Texas Rangers, and Walker County deputies—was a full-court press. The older Ellis Unit then housing Death Row, was a 1,700-acre unit flanked by dense pine forest and backed up to the sometimes languid and sometimes treacherous Trinity River and its snaky bottomlands. Clearly, as Prison PIO Larry Fitzgerald noted for the press: "Something broke down and allowed this to happen." A well-regarded and realistic professional Criminal Justice History educator, Professor Mitchel Roth, at Huntsville's other big-time institution, Sam Houston State University, added a somewhat soothing and practical note: "If it's 60 years between [Death Row] escapes, that's pretty good considering how many people have been on Death Row."[42]

Seven days later the lifeless remains of Martin Gurule were fished from Harmon Creek, a swollen side-stream of the Trinity, by two off-duty prison employees on a fishing excursion. Though they were surprised when they snagged the body, they were even more astonished on closer examination. Martin Gurule was clad in two pairs of underwear and his other clothing had been jam-packed with magazines and cardboard. And that explained the lack of a blood trail after Gurule had rolled across two fences capped with razor wire—the tightly packed paper products had served as his suit of not-shining armor. There, too, was that troubling downside for convict Gurule; trying to stay afloat while swimming the Trinity River tributaries while weighted with soggy cardboard and drenched stapled pages was a near impossible feat. It was more than the outfoxed convict could get done. Martin Gurule had gone under for keeps, sleeping with the catfish until hooked.[43] From escape to his ultimate finish-line, convict Gurule had traveled not quite three miles.[44] He did, however, in a way of sorts, prompt penitentiary leadership to rethink and remove Death Row to a more suitable and secure facility—the Polunsky Unit.

Although out of chronology, perhaps for an enhanced understanding of some Death Row doings and what Correctional Officers daily contend with is not inappropriate. Like the time Johnny Anderson stabbed Kenneth D. Dunn seven times with a fan guard—or another incident when Warren Eugene Bridge non-fatally stuck one convict after planting a crude bomb in another Death Row convict's cell.[45] Then there was the time when an elderly chaplain acceded to convict Juan Salvez Soria's appeal to pray and shake hands; he shouldn't have. When the clergyman reached though the food slot for that reassuring touch, the devious Soria in a flash encircled his wrist with a bed sheet, which he pulled excruciatingly tight—already having the other end anchored to the steel bunk in his cell. Then, Juan Soria began slicing the preacher's arm—trying to cut it off—with two razor blades. Luckily a Correctional Officer, after realizing what was happening, and with the use of tactical teargas saved life and limb of the trusting man of the cloth. A different Death Row convict, Monty Allen Delk, convicted of one shotgun murder and prime suspect in another, refused to shower and smeared himself with his own excrement and urine to such an extent even the other condemned prisoners were literally begging overworked Correctional Officers for relief from the overpowering stench.[46] With the right knowledge (not revealed herein), seemingly benign goods acquired from the prison's commissary storehouse, correctly proportioned, could be concocted into a dangerous and very combustible mixture. From that beginning a very crude but effective flame-thrower could be set for ignition. Barbequing another convict or a Correctional Officer was no anathema for some incorrigible prisoners. Michael Lee McBride, on Death Row due to a double Murder in Lubbock County, was desperately trying to acquire jalapeno seeds and a soft plastic toiletry lotion bottle so he could fashion a squirt gun and shoot someone or everyone in the eyes with the peppery concoction, just like a Spitting Cobra. Then, too, there was the revenge-minded Death Row convict slyly collecting Black Widow spiders so he could extract their venom, coat the tip of a spear with the poison—and then stab a Correctional Officer.[47] Farfetched? Hardly!

Some insensitive convicts—not necessarily just housed on Death Row—were selling HIV (Human Immunodeficiency Virus) infected blood to other prisoners. The craftily sharpened point of a shank or spear dipped in contaminated blood was a surefire killer—at least in some convicts' minds.[48] If tainted bodily fluids were not readily available, well, human feces was a never ending commodity, and as such could be liberally applied to a shank or a prison carpenter's nail and the resultant unhygienic so-called "Hard-Candy" could be driven deep into tissue—but not sweetly.[49] The ensuing death, hopefully, would not come quickly: Not for intended victims, be they an unwary Correctional Officer, a well-known enemy, or an unknown rival gang member simply murdered—well, just because!

In fact, the older brother of one of this treatment's authors, Sergeant Ronald J. "Ron" Alford (later Major at the Dalhart Unit, Hartley County), then a Correctional Officer supervisor working at the Diagnostic Unit at Huntsville, suffered an attack during a convict transfer from one unit to another. Curtis "Hard-Time" Weeks, whose escape-prone father Winifred Anthony "Wimpy" Weeks had also pulled penitentiary time, and his mother Panda who was a former exotic dancer and a then-current Houston area drug dealer, belligerently and purposefully spit his presumed HIV tainted saliva into the face of Sergeant Alford.[50]

During the irrational tirade wherein Weeks "tore a panel off of the door of the [prison] van and the headliner from the roof of the van. . . . [Weeks] said that he was 'going to take somebody with him when he went,' that he was 'medical now,' and that he was 'HIV-4' and that he was going to 'dog' the officers and that he was 'going to cut one of the boss' heads off." The spittle splashed across the lips, eyes, and nostrils of Sergeant Alford as Curtis Weeks was loudly and caustically declaring that he intended to kill the Texas penitentiary official and optimistically some of his damnable correctional colleagues as well.[51] The insolent deed was not simply graded as an abject case of stupidity—for ground-level prison personnel and officialdom it was much, much, more—and for that assessment, a state prosecutor concurred, more especially after reviewing such videotaped transgressions, which Weeks was unaware had been video-recorded when he broke belligerent.[52] In what proved to be a landmark criminal case, Curtis Weeks was criminally charged with Attempted Murder. Could pure saliva carry an infectious death? What if the disease carrier suffered Gingivitis— bleeding of the gums—and the spit was intermixed with the pathogen? Curtis Weeks, the spitting convict, had Gingivitis![53] Certainly, at that time, there was but rudimentary reliable data about the AIDS epidemic and its transmission, but in the courtroom for a moment a touch of levity issued from the witness stand. An animated defense attorney with a palpably disdainful tone asked Sergeant Alford if defendant Curtis Weeks had spit in a glass of water and he drank it, would he come down with AIDS? Sergeant Ron Alford, not having a good clue with regards to a scientific answer about infectious diseases, their pandemic diffusions and/or their debilitating consequences, simply parried with Texas country-boy commonsense logic: "Would you drink it?" The judge and jury smiled! Shortly, after returning their verdict of *Guilty*, the jury awarded Curtis "Hard-Time" Weeks more hard-time, a life sentence, the Big Bitch for his Habitual Criminal status. Whether or not he could have killed Sergeant Alford with spit was not as important as the fact he tried too—the criminal charge being Attempted Murder. The perpetually peeved Curtis Weeks caught the chain for one of Brazoria County's state-operated facilities.[54] Curtis Weeks remained defiant, continually spitting at, trying to bite, and cursing chaplains, nurses, fellow convicts, and his main nemesis, the Correctional Officer staff. Though stubborn as the proverbial mule, Weeks could not, however, beat the disease, and in the end succumbed to AIDS while undergoing medical treatment in the main prison hospital at Galveston.[55]

Death Row convict Ponchai Wilkerson was bad to the bone, having caught a death sentence for murdering Chung Myong Yi, during a Houston jewelry robbery, holding the murder gun but twelve inches from the decedent's head when he let the hammer drop. Ponchai was also thought to have committed several lucrative burglaries and, perhaps, "shot four other people in two separate drive-by shootings," and maybe even a separate Capital Murder, when "another store clerk [was] shot with a shotgun."[56] Fortunately for free-world folks, Ponchai Wilkerson's escape from Death Row, as previously mentioned, was abruptly foiled amid the nighttime blaze of Correctional Officers' gunfire.

Unfortunately though, aided by another Death Row convict, Howard Guidry, who also had tried for a Death Row getaway, Ponchai made a hostage of a female Correctional Officer at the Terrell Unit (now the Polunsky Unit) near Livingston in Polk County. Jeanette "Nettie" Bledsoe, fifty-seven, a three-year veteran of the unit, was the surprised prisoner when the security table was turned upside down. Both muscular convicts had been armed, one with a wicked looking makeshift knife with a 12- to 18-inch blade, the other with "a bean slot tool," the 24-inch metal implement used to open the feeding doors of single cells. Naturally, two aggressive male convicts had no trouble overpowering the Correctional Officer who tipped the scales at 125 lbs. and in her socks measured less than five and a half feet tall. Correctional Officer Bledsoe was shackled by the ankle to the bars of a cell. One would think the petite Jeanette Bledsoe was utterly terrified—and maybe she was internally—but to the hostage takers and for the outside world she remained calm, cool, and collected. To at least some degree her admirable and unruffled demeanor was contagious. She prayed with Wilkerson and Guidry, and they in turn "held up a shielding cloth and turned their backs" affording Correctional Officer Bledsoe privacy so she could inconspicuously answer nature's call. In a determined show of support the Correctional Officers on Jeanette's nighttime shift refused to go home; they symbolically stood with their respected comrade. One of Jeanette's grown sons, Biff, was also a Correctional Officer and, expectedly unhesitant, he joined the solidarity vigil for his mother. Texas Rangers were called to join with trained prison negotiators to hammer out a safe and reasonable resolution. Thereafter, Wilkerson and Guidry were allowed a controlled visit with sympathetic community activists wherein they listed their string of demands for changes in Texas prison policy, surrendered their weapons, and released Correctional Officer Bledsoe after the tense thirteen-hour standoff. The correctional community breathed a sigh of relief. Another son of Jeanette, John David, summed up the family's feeling about his mother being held hostage: "It could have been worse. Everybody in the family was just completely relieved. We had cried thinking what could have happened and then cried [tears of joy] that it didn't happen."[57]

Later, when the day of reckoning had finally arrived due to his Capital Murder conviction, Ponchai Wilkerson didn't cry but he was combative during his last walk from a holding cell to the Death Chamber. He fought and kicked but was finally overpowered. Then he was "bound to the gurney with additional restraint bands." With the state's needle in the underside of his forearm, as the lethal injection was beginning to take its effect Ponchai "spit out a universal handcuff and leg restraint key he had been holding in his mouth."[58] When and how he made such an acquisition was then, and is now, a Death Row cold case mystery.

What was not a Death Row mystery was who killed prisoner Maurice Andrews; that homicide was captured on videotape. The evilness that landed Jermarr Carlos Arnold AKA Troy Alexander on Texas Death Row was the Corpus Christi killing of Greenberg Jewelry Store employee Christine Marie Sanchez, twenty-one.[59] Fleeing the crime-scene with a bag of sparkly and expensive treasures, killer Arnold ended his cross-country flight in California. Whether he was running low on cash or just craved the thrill goes unrecorded, but Jermarr opted to rob a Los Angeles bank—and got caught.[60] He was promptly convicted and sent to the state's SUPERMAX facility, Pelican Bay. Even while held in the Security Housing Unit (SHU), Jermarr Carlos Arnold's conduct was not enviable. A California prison correctional employee would later tell a high-level TDCJ-ID official that at the time he was there, Jermarr Carlos Arnold was "the most dangerous man at Pelican Bay."[61] While a California prisoner, Jermarr was convicted of Possession of a Deadly Weapon, two counts of Assault with a Deadly Weapon, Possession of a Concealed Weapon, a second time for Possession of a Deadly Weapon, and charges of Aggravated Assault.[62] Previously, before his California imprisonment, Arnold could add Auto Theft and a string of as many as two dozen purported Rapes to his catalog of criminality.

Two items are worthy of mention. It seems Jermarr was aching to return to Texas. He began singing an oblique but teasing confessional tune. Never at rest, Texas Ranger Robert Garza, Jr. and Corpus Christ PD Investigator Paul Rivera traveled to California, finally zeroing in on Jermarr as a truly viable and credible suspect for the Gulf Coast homicide as Arnold continued to rattle.[63] Good detectives must ever be on guard. False confessions are not uncommon. Their sly staging encompasses a widespread gamut of nefarious calculations. Sometimes even Capital Murder convicts, once all their appeals are exhausted, take the blame for other pals on Death Row, letting them off the hook so to speak—or trying to! After obtaining an admissible confession and subsequent to the return trip to Texas, the hulking Jermarr Carlos Arnold was convicted of Capital Murder, sentenced to die and then housed on Death Row.[64]

Even cursory review of the appeal, *Arnold v. Texas*, 873 S.W.2d 27 (Tex.Crim.App 1993), highlights the typical sparring and perplexing differences of opinions proffered by expert witnesses—in this case psychiatrists, some asserting that the State of Texas should not execute an insane killer, others testifying that Jermarr was sane at the time he murdered Miss Sanchez. The dizzying campaign of competing "experts" in the courtroom—as in *Ruiz v. Estelle*—is timeless; each side putting on the witness stand only those who comport with their trial theory and strategies. A convict feigning a disturbed mind is not a new phenomenon: Often such bizarre behavior is designed to manipulate circumstances to their personal benefit, what is sometimes referred to in precautious psychological banter as a "secondary gain." And herein, under most conditions, front-line Correctional Officers have no dog in the hunt; they are not psychiatrists or psychologists or safe-space intellectuals or wannabes. For this case, in the end, the Texas Court of Criminal Appeals came down hard on the side of the prosecution: Jermarr knew right from wrong when he pulled the trigger. It was while housed on the Texas Death Row that Jermarr Carlos Arnold would validate the California prison employee's and California head-doctor's chilling personality assessment: He was, regardless of any mental abnormalities or absence thereof—metaphorically—dangerous as a coiled Diamondback.

Though condemned to die, Jermarr Carlos Arnold was not idle. Busily and sneakily, probably whetting it on the concrete floor, the beefy (230 lbs) and strong black convict ground and sharpened a point for a sizeable metal bolt he had purloined from somewhere. Though the cause of the dustup between Jermarr and convict Maurice Andrews—a double murderer—is hazy, the endgame scorecard isn't. On the recreation yard, which for Death Row was quite small, Jermarr caught Maurice in a tight headlock with one grasp and with the other arm, in a single but ghastly thrust, drove the bolt hard through Andrew's temple—Hard enough for the sharp point to exit on the other side! One prisoner fell dead as a cold-steel anvil to the bloody rec-yard floor, while the other convict danced in glee—perhaps promenading to the madcap music playing in his head.[65] Yes, Jermarr Carlos Arnold was a very dangerous man. Taking undue chances with convicts—any convict—was forbidden conduct for obedient and observant Correctional Officers. Sly smiles and soft-spoken words can be but a smokescreen for unfathomable meanness lurking within.

While waiting his turn on Death Row, the destined convict had an awakening: He found God. When judgment day arrived, Jermarr Carlos Arnold began singing "Amazing Grace" as the state's chemicals weakened his voice and—ultimately—extinguished his whispered hymn.[66]

Photo Gallery

3

Dr. George John Beto, a Lutheran Minister and Lutheran College President, picked up title as Director of the Texas Department of Corrections (TDC) on the first day of March 1962.

With an eye turned to convict reformation Dr. Beto brought an accredited school system to fruition for Texas prisons, the Windham School District. He selected Dr. Lane Murray, a highly accomplished lady educator to superintend the Windham School District.

Dr. Beto believed that control and order was the hallmark of effective and compassionate prison management and, ultimately, reformation of those that had succumbed to making poor decisions in the past. Part of that orderliness was maintained, in his mind, by good grooming and dress standards for both convicts and staff; haircuts were short, faces clean shaven, and shirttails tucked in. Sloppiness was not conducive to safety for the keepers or the kept. Positive change, morally, educationally, and/or spiritually could not take place in a helter-skelter atmosphere.

Though but a subjective analysis, this photograph is unquestionably suggestive of an effectual control and order model. Convicts and Field Bosses alike knew what was permissible—
and what wasn't. While it might shatter preconceptions, at this time all new prisoners went
to the field, white, black, or brown. With an eye to instilling the framework of a work ethic,
good conduct in the field earned reassignment to more cushy duty: the laundry, hospital,
dining hall, library or maintenance and industrial shops, or inside janitorial duties, etc.

A revered Field Boss by convicts and staff was Major Dick Andrews. He was fair but firm—and consistent, benchmarks for successfully and safely managing tough men under tough conditions.

Dr. Beto earned the nickname "Walking George" as day or night, weekend or holiday, he might appear for an impromptu session with convicts or staff—listening and visiting.

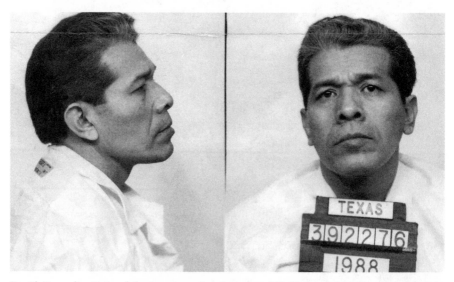

David Resendez Ruiz while in prison for Aggravated Robbery stabbed several convicts, escaped and was nabbed, and served as many as fifteen stints in Solitary Confinement for disciplinary infractions and intentional disobedience. While his handwritten writ may not have been an example of brilliant legal work, it did catch the eye of an activist federal judge and TDC was forevermore changed; some claim for the better, some posit not.

Ward James "Jim" Estelle, a career penologist, became Director of the Texas Department of Corrections upon Dr. Beto's resignation. Extraordinarily popular and well-thought of by rank and file prison employees, Jim Estelle, by luck of the draw, inherited near insurmountable administrative problems.

An iconic photograph of the storied Walls Unit's entrance. Inside, sometimes, misfortune and mayhem loomed. Few would be the Texans—native or otherwise—that could not identify this edifice at first glance.

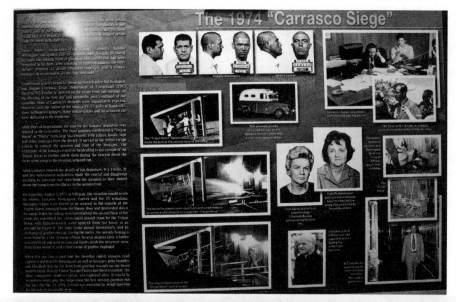

Although covered more fully in this text, the excellent storyboard at the TPM acquaints visitors with the murderous 1974 tragedy, *Eleven Days in Hell*, unfolding behind tall walls at Huntsville. Sorrowfully, two ladies, Julia Standley and Elizabeth Yvonne Besda, civilian employees, lost their lives. Two of the unrepentant murderous convicts, Federico Gomez "Fred" Carrasco and Rudolfo Sauceda "Rudy" Dominguez, Jr., were justifiably killed in an ensuing shootout. The third, Ignacio Apodaca "Nacho" Cuevas, was seventeen years later executed by lethal injection in the Texas Death Chamber.

On public display at the TPM are the three handguns smuggled into the prison by a certainly untrustworthy trusty.

tages held here

Von and commanity
are welded together

item

Bullet Proof Helmet

Three metal bullet proof helmets were made and delivered to Carrasco, per his demand. Upon receiving this helmet, Carrasco fired a round above the eye slot to insure that the helmet would stop a bullet. The additional two helmets are currently on display at other museums. One is at the Texas Ranger Museum in Waco. The other is on display at the Alcatraz East Crime Museum in Pigeon Forge, Tennessee.

Also exhibited at the TPM is one of the iron helmets built in the prison shop—but they didn't save outlaws Carrasco, a heroin smuggling kingpin, and Dominguez from paying the ultimate price for their meanness and delusionary scheme during the resultant gunplay.

Director Estelle chose Lucile G. Plane as a Warden when female convicts were transitioned from Huntsville to the Mountain View Unit at Gatesville, Coryell County.

Here a Prison Board Member, the esteemed Reverend C.A. Holliday, pleasurably chats with a Field Boss. The Holliday Unit, a 2000 plus convict facility, across Interstate Highway 45 from the TPM, was reverently named after this man of the cloth.

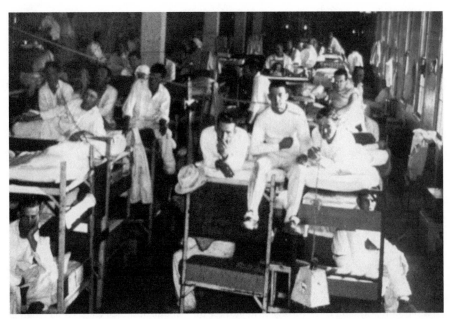

Taken at a time when racial segregation was in place at Texas prison units, this photo of white prisoners and the following image unquestionably reveal that overcrowding was a continuing headache not only for the convicts but for the staff trying to maintain secure order and protecting their charges from harming and/or preying upon each other.

Overcrowding of these black convicts in a dormitory setting, commonly referred to as a "tank," is not then nor would it be now conducive to maintaining effective security and acceptable order.

This simple photograph amplifies prison reality, the sheer staggering and secure movement of thousands—system wide—convicts daily, here for just one of three meals, is challenging.

Federal District Judge William Wayne Justice, fourth from left, after years of orchestrating the *Ruiz v. Estelle* lawsuit, finally opted to set foot in a Texas Prison. Although his micromanaging of the entire Texas Prison system may have met with approval in some camps, his detractors were many and vocal. The unintended consequences of several of his diktats are argued yet today.

Wallace Melton Pack, Warden at the Ellis Unit, unfortunately has distinction as the very first Warden to be killed by a convict.

Billy Max Moore, also killed at the Ellis Unit, served as the Farm Manager.

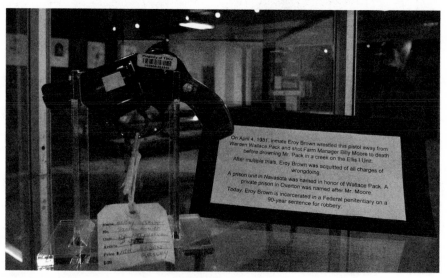

On April 4, 1981, inmate Eroy Brown wrestled this pistol away from Warden Wallace Pack and shot Farm Manager Billy Moore to death before drowning Mr. Pack in a creek on the Ellis I Unit.

After multiple trials, Eroy Brown was acquitted of all charges of wrongdoing.

A prison unit in Navasota was named in honor of Wallace Pack. A private prison in Overton was named after Mr. Moore.

Today, Eroy Brown is incarcerated in a Federal penitentiary on a 90-year sentence for robbery.

Warden Wallace Pack's .38 Special Smith & Wesson Bodyguard Model, the weapon a convict used to kill Mr. Moore before holding down and drowning Warden Pack.

Director Raymond Procunier, an experienced hand at running penitentiaries, was recruited to head-up the Lone Star's penitentiaries subsequent to the federal court's dismantlement of specific—and some argue effective—convict control measures and the exponential proliferation of upward spiraling prison gang violence and in-house homicides.

That overcrowding was a vexing problem for Texas Prison administrators is evidenced by this photograph. The barred cells on the left are designed to accommodate two convicts, but were then housing three—one on a pallet on the floor. Outside in the runs (hallways) bunk-beds were temporary homes to others. In the prison yard tents were homes for some. The prison population swelled at a faster rate than legislators could appropriate and new prison units could be built.

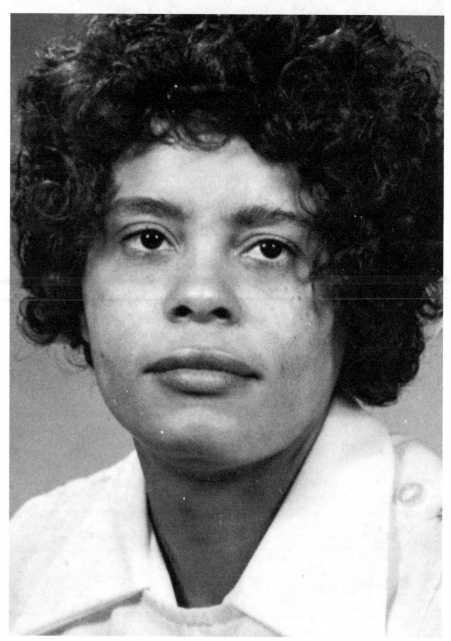

Already with successfully foiling an escape at the point of a state-issued shotgun under her career belt, Minnie Rene Houston was the first, but not the last, female Correctional Officer to die at the hands of an imprisoned convict.

Although they certainly were not lone-wolf examples, the plucky Sparkman brothers were Correctional Officers of the Real Deal stamp. From left to right, Paul, Emmitt, Kelley, and Chad.

Established during 1989 the Texas Prison Museum was at first downtown on the courthouse square, but later moved to its present location on the northern outskirts of Huntsville. Since moving to Interstate 45 the facility has brilliantly expanded in both size and scope. Outside, on the manicured grounds, stands the symbolic memorial, a respectful tribute to fallen officers and employees of Texas Prisons.

The TPM institution is truly marvelous from an artifact, exhibits, and research perspective but unlike other museum gift shops it is pleasingly incomparable. Many of the handcrafted items, especially jewelry and leather work—some quite unique and intricate—is due to the painstaking talents of convict artisans.

Murderous serial killer Kenneth Allen McDuff is at long last escorted to the Death Chamber.

A sanctioned peek from the witness room at the state's Death Chamber inside The Walls. In the State of Texas, imposition of Capital Punishment is accomplished by means of lethal injection.

An exhibit drawing much attention at the TPM is one displaying numerous items of contraband and/or examples of how they are concealed. Aside from the obvious homemade weapons, among other items of interest, note the hollowed-out roll of toilet tissue and the sharp dagger artfully concealed in a mallet's handle—and tattoo guns and brogans with concealed cavities, etc.

The potential for resorting to Deadly Force is omnipresent in the prison setting. At the TPM *some* of the Correctional Officers' preventative and defensive toolkit—past and present—is put on display, including firearms and delivery systems for chemical agents.

Still

The still is made from a metal milk can and copper tubing. It was found at the Wynne Unit, in the hay barn that is in the horse pasture, hidden in a hollowed out hay stack.

Once whisky was produced it [was put in] jugs and buried in the [grounds by] the chick[en coops.]

Also on exhibit at the TPM is an improvised Whiskey Still, one made from a Prison Farm milk-can and condensing coils. In most prisons yeast and/or fruit pilfered from the kitchen can result in a euphoric concoction or an appalling recipe for unchecked madness, riotous behavior—and sometimes the Grim Reaper's brew.

This cadre of stalwart and clean-shaven Correctional Officers—transfer personnel—posing before caged prison buses, Blue Birds with the prison emblem, are armed with an array of visible firepower and an unspoken but no-nonsense determination. They'll do to tie to!

The movement of thousands of convicts and the thousands of miles covered transporting them between more than a hundred units in but a single fiscal year ramps up statistics of mindboggling proportion. Amplified too, by doing it safely to the benefit of all—the prisoners and the public.

Although nowadays escapes from Texas Prison Units are not routine, they assuredly do happen. Here, on a very real manhunt, in the forefront is Doyle Caldwell working the tracking hounds.

Though but a picture-postcard, an overall essence of the Texas Prison history—from then to now—is captured in this splendid image. The narrative is rich—the legends and legacy are worthy of preservation.

One of the modern Prison Unit's highly polished runs—hallways. Note the enclosed picket station and crash gate halfway down the hallway. Convict movement is restricted to their deferentially walking between the wall and floors clearly painted line. When ordered to stop for some reason by a Correctional Officer, the convict is told to "catch the wall!"

13

"violent convicts commit violent acts"

RATHER AMUSINGLY—though that's not quite the proper word—there is coming from some free-world intellectual quarters an out-and-out condemnation of the policy wherein certain convicts are housed long-term in Administrative Segregation. These specialized wings of penitentiaries with what is commonly referred to as a general population are a proven and effectual strategy for interdicting violence, protecting Correctional Officers and convicts alike: Admittedly though, hardly is anything foolproof.[1] There is a distinction between imposing discipline with a fixed period of Solitary Confinement and the practice of indefinitely confining a convict in a cell, typically twenty-three and seven, the odd hours being legitimately dedicated for the prisoner's freedom to exercise or shower in a tightly controlled environment—oftentimes by himself/herself.

Sometimes the paradox seems quite rich. Not infrequently it's suggested that the way out of Administrative Segregation is to die, discharge, or debrief (snitch), disavowing gang affiliation and explaining an organizational chart prison gang hierarchy for prison staff, naming names, and fingering fellow gangsters, as well as identifying their felony crimes—inside or outside of Administrative Segregation. In many instances some well-meaning scholars postulate that the latter course, snitching, also might prove to be the gateway for getting oneself revengefully murdered for flipping, talking to the "Man." It does not require industrial strength logic to validate reality: If certain securely confined gangsters are indeed coldheartedly capable of stabbing, garroting, setting afire, or bludgeoning to death a fellow convict, cooperative informant, or institutional staff member, maybe that's why they are actually domiciled in Administrative Segregation in the first place!

Locking certain convicts within confines of an Administrative Segregation section—even long term—is not an abridgment of the prisoners' guaranteed Constitutional rights.[2] Though the challenge to the stringent control of prisoners dealt with the federal lockup at Marion, Illinois, at that time the highest security level of any federal penitentiary—the successor to Alcatraz—and intended to hold the most violent and dangerous prisoners in the entire federal system, the legal findings had far-reaching applicability. The U.S. 7th Circuit Appellate Court jurists had digested a hardcore litany of facts before rendering their decision, herein repeated only in part and with but a touch of added emphasis:

> There is no question that conditions in Marion deserve careful scrutiny, but they must be evaluated against the background of an extraordinary history of inmate violence and with proper regard for the limited competence of federal judges to micromanage prisons. . . . The defendants [prison officials] placed in the record a remarkable narrative of the violence that led up to the lockdown. We note a few highlights (some corroborated by decisions of this court). Two inmates, while exercising in the corridor outside their cells, garroted a third inmate, who was asleep in his cell with his head against the bars. . . . An inmate stabbed another inmate with a knife while they were exercising and was in turn stabbed by two inmates with knives on his way back to his cell. An inmate fired a zip gun (a homemade pistol) at another inmate and at a guard, wounding both. Inmates have attacked other inmates and guards with a homemade bomb, with a light bulb, with a padlock, with a sharpened pencil wielded as a knife, with a sharpened toothbrush, with feces, with a chair, with a mop wringer, with a home-made

mallet, and with a bucket of boiling water, as well as with the usual zip guns and shanks. (Shanks are homemade knives, often carved out of the legs of the steel beds in the cells. The steel beds have now been replaced by concrete blocks in an effort to prevent the manufacture of shanks.) A number of inmates were killed in these assaults, and in addition there were frequent riots and strikes by inmates, taking of guards as hostages, takeovers of cell blocks, and ingenious attempts to escape—once to the accompaniment of rifle fire directed at the prison from outside. One inmate managed to detonate a bomb in his cell.

In the climactic week that preceded the lockdown, two guards were murdered in similar incidents. In each a prisoner being escorted from his cell broke away from the three guards escorting him, thrust his handcuffed wrists (this was before the innovation of placing a box over the handcuffs) into an accomplice's cell, emerged sans handcuffs but holding a shank in his hand, and proceeded to attack the guards. In one of the incidents, another guard was crippled and the third was seriously injured. . . . Throughout this period, searches uncovered an astonishing quantity of knives, zip guns, and other contraband, including many homemade keys that fit handcuffs and others that fit doors in the prison Searches of body cavities, including the nose, the mouth, and the rectum, continue to turn up and impressive quantity and variety of contraband, including knives and hacksaw blades. . . . *Since the principal victims of murders and armed assaults in Marion penitentiary are inmates, the procedure that the plaintiffs describe as cruel and unusual punishment are the very procedures that are protecting them from murderous attacks by fellow prisoners. . . . Few inmates are assigned to Marion who do not have a substantial history of violence in prison; it is not likely that these wolves would have turned into sheep if Marion had been a gentler place.*[3]

And in California a U.S. District Judge, Thelton E. Henderson, in the case of *Madrid v. Gomez,* did find troubling questions regarding convict treatment. On the other hand, however, during the two decades of ongoing litigation and monitoring in this action, he was unable or unwilling to articulate an actionable finding that long-term close confinement (Administrative Segregation in Texas; SHU-Security Housing Unit in California) legally or Unconstitutionally collided with those convicts' Eighth Amendment protections against cruel and/or unusual punishment in the Golden State.[4] Expectedly, not everyone was elated. Subsequently, however, automatic SHU housing for an identifiable sub-prison population was tweaked: "Some states use administrative segregation to isolate suspected or known members of gangs or security threat groups. In wake of a recent settlement in California that will end the practice of send-ing gang members to supermax, it is unclear how other states with similar segregation policies will respond."[5] In a Lone Star State case, convict David Flores, Jr. contested, among other things, his classi-fication for Administrative Segregation placement. With regards to the issue at hand, the U.S. 5th Circuit Court of Appeals cut to the bone with two sentence clarity: "Flores argues that TDCJ-ID has improperly classified him as a member of a Security Threat Group [STG] in violation of his constitutional rights. A prisoner has no lib-erty interest in his custodial classification."[6]

Although it should come as no surprise, through years of ongo-ing research and legal compliance Texas prison administrators have with great care refined polices and procedures, rules and regulations, with regards to protecting employees and mainstream convicts from the predatory predilections of other prisoners—even if by necessity it manifests in authoritarian long-term close confinement. When fright-ened convicts and scared Correctional Officers acknowledge some folks among them can and do make exceptionally dangerous—some-times deadly—contributions to their workaday environment, practical wisdom overrides impractical idealism. Generally speaking, the courts have not been blind to that hardcore reality. Conversely, however, the cadre of critics, though unquestionably sincere in their philosophical bent, is vociferous. The irony of admitting that certain convicts are capable of premeditated and ruthless murders and rapes inside or out-side of prison, and in the next breath—or sentence—vilifying polices promulgated to insure someone's personal safety, is rich.[7] Admittedly there is no easy answer, as various practical and academic studies have aptly confirmed. As earlier highlighted herein, in the field of penology identifying a potentially troubling issue is easy for an array of sometimes self-proclaimed experts, though their actually tendering sound and safe fixes more often than not remains elusive. The tax for proffering a failed theory—especially with no skin in the game—is relatively cheap: Particularly in lieu of actually being held real-world accountable or disciplined for allowing lapses in good judgment to override proscribed actions. In what is an interesting and informative approach—and decidedly exploratory with regards to in-house prison bloodshed—a respected professor crosscuts to the unnerving nub: "The general conclusion of all this research are [is] that violent convicts commit violent acts. . . ."[8]

The thoughtful formalized and written Texas *Administrative Segregation Plan* when comprehensively reviewed seems to leave no weighty and troubling stone unturned. The multi-page document's Table of Contents alone is suggestive of attention to detail. The subchapters are Definitions, Placement Procedures, Review Procedures After Initial Placement, Conditions, Management Procedures, Recommendations for Release, Appeal Process, and Attachment A, "Administrative Segregation Reference Chart."[9] Peeking at just one, "Conditions" is somewhat indicative of the exhaustive subdividing and particularized fine points: Housing, Solid Outer Door, Cell Fixtures, Recreation, Visitation, Meals, Correspondence/Commissary, Property, Showering, In-Cell Programs, In-Cell Correspondence Courses, and, lastly, additional In-Cell Services. Broken-down step by step procedures—what's allowable and what's not—is for the Administrative Segregation convict and the like assigned Correctional Officer not unclear or even slightly ambiguous.[10] Rigorous compliance for either camp—officers or outlaws—is not discretionary. For the appropriate convicts, under the appropriate circumstances, as has been quantifiably and clear-headedly demonstrated, Administrative Segregation is literally a lifesaver. Placing a convict in Administrative Segregation is, indeed, serious business and Lone Star State executive prison decision makers take it seriously!

Even though it falls outside the Texas boundary line and in some respects tumbles past the Administrative Segregation topic, an experienced and learned Lone Star State professor references the unintended result of an Illinois convict's writ-writin' masterpiece. While trying to manipulate a court ruling to convicts' benefit, there was a tempestuous backfire. A federal court had ruled that convicts disciplined by being placed in Solitary Confinement could not be denied their acquisition of allowable commissary goods. Conversely, convicts as part of the general population could suffer a disciplinary suspension of commissary privileges as all or part of their punishment for infractions—big or little. The paradox is plain. Commissary items are valuable commodities to convicts. Therefore a number of conniving prisoners were shrewdly misbehaving and/or abruptly violating rules just so they would be punished by placement in Solitary Confinement: There they could, in peace and quiet, eat their candy and drink their soda pop, so guaranteed the federal court.[11]

With the unprecedented spike in prison violence, an eminent Brazoria County journalist, Marie Beth Jones, had earlier opted to interview, with a sincere pledge of anonymity, Correctional Officers' wives, preserving their first-hand 1980s perceptions. Extracting several comments from but one obviously disillusioned and exasperated Texas lady is sadly revealing on the one hand—and a little amusing on the other:

> In the kitchen, they issue knives to prisoners who work there, but the guards can't be armed. Not a gun or a billy club or anything. I mean here you have these prisoners all around you with great big kitchen knives, and the guard in charge of them doesn't have anything to protect himself with.
>
> Procunier [obviously before his voluntary resignation] has no idea what is going on. Surprise inspections are nothing but a bunch of hogwash. They always know beforehand that he's coming or that some other bigwig is . . . And the shakedowns. They're a joke, to.

They did random checks at one farm and had a stabbing in that wing less than two weeks later. . . . When they only check some wings, the prisoners give their weapons to their buddies to keep for them till after the inspection is over. Then they get the weapons back.

The prisoners' work schedule is a joke, too. They don't work if it is raining or if it's too cold or too hot. If they're there, they ought to have to work. Which of the rest of us get to lay off work when it's raining. . . . They have color TV, even cable. My family doesn't have cable. They were watching dirty movies until just a few weeks ago when Procunier said they couldn't watch them anymore.

They (guards) have to take a lot of abuse. Verbal all the time, of course. All kinds of insults. Anything they can think of to say. And every day there's an experience of some prisoners throwing things—they're really big on ink, and it's pretty hard to get it out of the clothes.

They're not supposed to have stuff like false eyelashes and T-shirts they can stretch into dresses and nail polish and makeup, but of course they do. Some of them even have false boobies.

My husband comes home and goes to bed. He talks in his sleep because of the pressure, he never did this before. I watch TV and hear them hollering on news programs about some poor prisoner having his rights violated, and I get mad. I mean I get really angry. My husband was in the military for a number of years before he took this job, and he never talked in his sleep then. He'd only been with TDC a few months before it started. It's the pressure. . . . You know something happened at work, but you don't know what. You understand that what I'm telling you is just the little bit my husband tells me. He doesn't tell much. He knows I'm so up-tight about it that he doesn't want to worry me more.

Sure we have grievances. My husband isn't safe. We're not guaranteed of anything. We're barely hanging on. They put their lives on the line every single day. And then all the bleeding hearts get a bunch of publicity about how the prisoners' rights are being violated. They've already proved that these guys are criminals. That's why they're behind bars. And what is Judge Justice saying?

That the prisons are overcrowded, so we'll turn them out early. That's just a joke. By the time you can turn around, those same people are back in prison again.

One I know of was back in a month. My God, they have no incentive to leave. They have everything right there. Free. Three meals a day and dessert—I can't afford to make dessert for my family.

Once you're promoted to sergeant, you don't even get time off to compensate for the extra time you work. Our last paycheck, a six percent raise went into effect, and we actually lost money because of insurance cost increases. . . . and the insurance doesn't cover anything except stubbing your toe on an elephant at midnight on Dec. 32.[12]

Underscoring the problematic fact that convicts are—or can be—an ingenious lot was also emphasized by one of the Correctional Officers' spouses being interviewed by Marie Beth Jones: "But it's scary, too, because they have such inventive minds. After all, most of the time they don't have anything to do except sit around and think of ways to get in trouble. Like one time, they didn't have any toilet seats for a long time because the prisoners were taking the seats and breaking them down and making knives out of the metal. And another time I heard they made a knife out of the aluminum vents. Those just made perfect knives."[13] Although it was penned by a former convict proffering a cautionary notification to his and future prison pals, the old saw is applicable to Correctional Officers as well, something it would, indeed, be wise to remember: "Everybody bleeds. Everybody dies. Anybody can kill."[14]

Perhaps at this point, digressing for a remark or two about convict ingeniousness is okay. Laying aside the clever making of dangerous weapons from near anything and concealing contraband near everywhere, confined minds are never at rest. Though seldom discussed in free-world circles, the efficacy of on the sly rummaging through trash should never be undervalued behind the tall walls and high fences: Discarded thin plastic bread sacks and sandwich bags can be and are often resorted to as handy substitutes for condoms which are not allowable commissary items. The juice from beets, if properly handled and applied can take the place of rouge and lipstick for effeminately bent male convicts. Clandestine manufactured tattoo guns can be motorized by disassembling such easily accessible items as electric shavers and appliances. The tiny protective piece of glued plastic at the very tip of a shoestring can be and has been manipulated to nimbly unlock steel handcuffs. Various mixtures—including urine—can produce invisible ink, perfect for forwarding messages about escape plans and murders and the business of smuggling contraband. Skillfully inserted lead from a pencil into an everyday electrical socket on the wall can spark flame, enough to light a forbidden cigarette—or set mattresses afire.

Not all of the convicts' heavy-duty thinking is focused on things of a material nature—there are mind games, too. Certainly one of the most common is the protection scam, a manipulative maneuver aimed to ensnare convicts and Correctional Officers alike. The scheme is simple. Two conniving convicts will assault or verbally challenge the intended victim, usually a fish or new boot. A third convict player will courageously jump into the physical or nasty verbal affray, momentarily interdicting any bad result, real or imagined. The shameful pair of mad-dogging troublemakers will wilt away mouthing, threatening, and shaking clinched fists, but giving prompt deference to the dauntless Lone Ranger who had ridden to the victim's rescue. For the intimidated and frightened convict the new savior will continue to offer his services as a protector—for a recurring price, be it taboo tobacco or candy or crackers or bluebags—or sex. When the knight in shining armor—prison whites—saves the Correctional Officer's bacon, quite naturally it would be hoped that the continuation of protection services would be or could be swapped for special favors or overlooking in-house infractions. Of course, the three scheming convict actors are in cahoots: All will share equally the spoils of Academy Award performances for the carefully crafted but fictitious cellblock dustup.[15]

Unfortunately what is not fictitious is the periodic corrupt and dishonorable prison employee. Temptation is a tempestuous mistress, alluring yet treacherous. And to the unqualified detriment and humiliation of the honest and hardworking security staff, it's the small percentage of misfits that generate headlines. As mentioned elsewhere within, whether convict or Correctional Officer, seldom do the keepers or the kept walking the principled path catch any notice. With thousands and thousands of Correctional Officers on the payroll, the anomaly is predictable and existent. The stale saying that one bad apple will rot the barrel is not necessarily 100 percent accurate while characterizing the general deportment and devotion of most Correctional Officers. However, now and again a putrid employee must be culled.

Certainly, as borne out time and time again, within the convict population there are not just a few champions at identifying, capitalizing, and exploiting employees' weaknesses. No matter how long it takes, they have plenty of time; sometimes a lifetime. Once an otherwise honest Correctional Officer is manipulated into handing over his/her integrity—even if ever so slight, the snowball of duplicity builds to avalanche proportion—that being the carefully crafted design. Those seemingly innocuous but small personal favors quickly morph into unlawful and unethical demands: comprise and comply or suffer the consequences.[16]

Whether for love or profit or fear or unvarnished naiveté on occasion, some paid prison folks have exercised—just like convicts— seemingly unspeakable and unfathomable methodologies for doing what they weren't supposed to do: Smuggling contraband inside, and carrying convicts' messages into the free-world. In their glorious wisdom the Board of Criminal Justice unanimously decreed that Texas prisons would be tobacco free; no hand-rolled or tailor-made smokes, no tins of Copenhagen and/or sissy Skoal, and not a pouch of Beechnut or Redman. Possession of tobacco in the free-world was certainly legal, but now a disciplinary infraction of bureaucracy's rules behind the tall walls and high fences. Overnight a black-market economy mushroomed. Correctional Officers with more piracy than scruples in their hearts could, literally, easily double their state salary smuggling inside what was not illegal outside; threats of free-world criminal prosecution were toothless. Sneakily smuggling tobacco products was—in point of fact—more profitable and much less risky than smuggling dope. On one occasion, according to a now retired Warden, an employee reporting for work was caught red-handed. He had more than fifty sacks of Bugler rolling tobacco under his clothing, strategically affixed to his body with gobs of tape.[17] Nevertheless, yet trafficking in illicit narcotics remained—and remains—a migraine headache for leadership prison personnel. Somewhat unbelievably— though not too much should really be surprising in a penitentiary— one Texas professional skidded off the track: At one prison unit the Drug and Alcohol Counselor was terminated for smuggling hooch onto the premises.[18] Technology, too, found its way into Texas prisons. A deceitfully dirty female Correctional Officer had slyly inserted a contraband cell-phone into her—well, very personal space—and cunningly "hooped" and "keistered" the slim battery charger and electrical cord. Another female employee, to avoid the metal detector when arriving at work, had worn two pair of socks and to the sole of her foot had taped a SIM Card—which in prison is almost as valuable as the prohibited cell-phone itself.[19] Thankfully for the good citizens of Texas and statistically verifiable, the vast majority—by a massive margin—of the state's effectual Correctional Officers consciously opt for honesty. Unlike their custodial charges, one of the prerequisites for spending workaday time at prisons is an absence of any felony convictions—whatsoever!

And herein it would seem a slight digression is appropriate, because from time to time it constitutes a genuine problem for penitentiary administrators and staff, from the tip-top to the very bottom of the pay-scale. As the reader is by now well familiar, much of the Texas prisons' whopping real-estate holdings are purposely positioned along or adjacent to the salty and breezy and tempestuous Texas Gulf Coast—Hurricane Country. When the practiced weatherman's or weatherwoman's forecast is gloomy and the free-world citizens are mandated to evacuate for higher and drier ground, prison folks cannot afford to be flippant with regards to their custodial charges—convicts warrant physical protection too—and therein is

spawned the logistical and security and sometimes terrifying nightmares of moving anxious prisoners to interior units for safekeeping.
Understandably it's not a simple play-like exercise. Security concerns
are of course paramount; that's to be expected. Escapes are painstak-
ingly guarded against as convicts are cuffed and chained and loaded
onto the Blue Birds (prison busses), that's a given, but just one of
the inherent problems. Evacuated prisoners will become transit residents at facilities already maxed-out population-wise. So the Gulf
Coast area convicts (except for violent security threats and genuine
gangsters) will be housed inside the receiving units' gymnasiums
and auditoriums and hallways, and they will have to have brought
their flimsy mattresses with them for the ride. Eighteen-wheelers
carrying fresh foodstuffs and canned-goods, as well as a host of
other necessities—toilet paper and underwear and soap and phar-
maceuticals—will undergo a preplanned but strategic system-wide
rerouting. Convict TCs (Travel Cards) will also be a part of the movement. Keeping up with just who is who is part of the plan, protocols
finely honed through decades of experience. The tests and tribulations of emptying seaside prisons and ballooning others with an
influx of temporary new faces with their own real and imagined personal problems can be absolutely mind-numbing but it's a real challenge, addressed by a skilled staff with real-world fixes. Mamas and
daddies, too, want to know where their convict kiddos are during a
bad storm—which really doesn't seem unreasonable.

Nevertheless—and it's almost comical in its artlessness—well
intentioned intellectuals with hard-fought-for academic credentials will sometimes stumble after forsaking what not just a few
less educated folks would categorize as everyday commonsense.
An easy example comes to mind and it's typical. At the unarguably
prestigious Stanford University, professors and their research staff
fashioned a pretend prison, "randomly assigning as either guards or
prisoners young men who were clinically normal and similar." The
clinical experiment was cancelled ahead of time, due to the fact that
"inmates" quickly assumed submissive and estranged postures, while
"guards" quickly morphed into pathologically flawed personalities,

"intoxicated" with dominance and authority. Even an ex-convict turned illustrious penologist, Professor John Irwin, wondered about the inherent validity of this methodology of experimentation, dutifully noting: "The volunteers were all naïve about prisons and knew that this was an experiment. They seemed to be attempting to imitate their distorted images of the guard and prisoner. The guards, for instance, wore the mirror sunglasses seen on a guard in a popular movie, *Cool Hand Luke*, that had been released two years earlier. The experiment may have created a very unique dynamic or been more like a hazing, in which young men attempt to make it difficult for pledges, but are not guided by well-established routines."[20] From the get-go the scholars and the subordinates absolutely knew that no throats would be cut, no spleen would be stabbed, no one would be doused with flammable liquids and set afire, and no ferocious gang rapes would occur, and no play-like convict would actually be cold-heartedly murdered while uncaring imitation Correctional Officers looked the other way. Nor would phony keepers of the sham kept strike anyone with a nightstick or spray them with real teargas. It was, no matter how well intended, a game from the outset. The fact that there was—for this exercise—no factor of fear is actually quite relevant. Cowboys & Indians is a child's fun game. Cops & Robbers is a child's fun game. Gritty life playing out behind penitentiaries' tall walls and high fences is not fun or hollow entertainment. The intrinsic value of make-believe is dubious—at best!

Another illustration is, likewise, at a minimum interesting. On the much broader plane, however, it's indicative of some college graduate-level naiveté when carrying out research in a world where many of the subjects under study have already demonstrated society's rules for moral, ethical, truth-telling, and lawful behavior are meaningless. For this idealistic academic assignment, the editing and publishing class, chose to—through a written questionnaire— explore the innermost feeling of Death Row convicts in order to ensure the outside world was aware of the humanity of those on the inside. One of the numerous responding Death Row convicts was Anthony Allen Shore, a transplanted Texan from South Dakota. To the inquiring college students Anthony Allen Shore lamented that he had not been a better father to his children, two daughters. Oh, regretful was he that when he had the chance in the free-world he frittered away the sacred responsibilities of parenthood. Were he awarded a second chance, a do-over at life—he wrote the graduate students—he would most certainly live life for his kiddos. Likable? Well, there was the part he omitted while cooking up chaste answers for the questionnaire. Perhaps the class would have been somewhat taken aback if they had been apprised that Anthony Allen Shore had been convicted of sexually molesting those two precious girl children. But that's but part of his story. Anthony Allen Shore was a serial killer: A tragic fellow real-world print journalists in Houston tagged the "Tourniquet Killer" due to his application of the ligature around the necks of his victims after sexually abusing them and then snuffing out their lives. A modicum of heartfelt deference warrants their mention by name: Murdered were teenager Laurie Tremblay, fourteen, Maria Del Carmen Estrada, twenty-one, sixteen-year-old Dana Sanchez, and Diana Rebollar, age nine. And that's not counting a fourteen-year-old schoolgirl he bound with electrical cord and cut off her panties with a knife, then raped her vaginally and anally before Lady Luck presented her the break to make a mad-dash from the clutches of a stalking sexual predator. The unfortunate lifeless girls—at least numbering four confirmed—lived their final seconds in abject horror as Anthony Allen Shore twisted the garrote— thankfully, perhaps, they were already dead when he callously dumped their bodies to decompose and decay. DNA put detectives on the right track and led to the undoing of Anthony Allen Shore. Yes, perhaps the real world needed know more about the true humanity of Death Row convict Anthony Allen Shore, and the thoroughly committed college folks would gladly provide the altruistic platform— but not necessarily one built atop the pillars of veracity.[21]

And as already alluded to, sometimes a manipulative Death Row convict might opt to let a fellow Death Row prisoner off the hook— so to speak—by proffering a false confession or by leaving a bogus impression. Such seemed to be the case with Anthony Allen Shore.

There was, apparently at one point after Anthony Allen Shore was scheduled to die, materials discovered in his prison house possibly linking him to the killing of Melissa Trotter in Montgomery County, a case-closed offense due to the Murder conviction of prisoner Larry Swearingen. Although the original execution date for Anthony Allen Shore was postponed and subsequently the Texas Ranger investigation cleared him of slaying Melissa Trotter, ultimately he reposed on the Death Chamber gurney. As he had earlier characterized it for the inquiring college class, on 18 January 2018 Anthony Allen Shore ascended the stairway to Neverland.[22]

Another respondent to the collegiate journalism scholars' querying probe was Death Row convict Rosendo Rodriguez III, a former Texas Tech University student and U.S. Marine Reservist. Articulate and complimentary with regards to the unfeigned friendliness and gregariousness of his fellow Death Row comrades, Rosendo Rodriguez III championed the cause for anti-Death Penalty advocates—which from his positioning is not surprising—avowing that everyone's life was worthy of salvation and deliverance. He, too, lamented that living life on Death Row was somewhat boring—"the general monotony of everyday rigmarole"—dismally supplementing the "stress and anxiety" he and his incarcerated associates were forced to tolerate. Whether the inquisitive graduate students prompting the survey did or did not know the nickname of Rosendo Rodriguez III goes unrecorded in their finished work-product. On the other hand some real-world and full-fledged journalists in the professional Texas press corps knew him as "The Suitcase Killer." You see, Rosendo Rodriguez III had murdered twenty-nine year-old Summer Lee Baldwin, five weeks pregnant, stuffed her into a suitcase he had purchased at Wal-Mart and pitched the whole shebang into the gargantuan Lubbock landfill. Earlier, at the same refuse station, the lifeless remains of Joanna Kathryn Rogers had been discovered, her temporary casket, too, a cheap suitcase. According to after-the-fact voluntary statements by Rosendo Rodriguez III, Lubbock Detectives and the persuasive District Attorney went forward with their Capital Murder case for the gruesome death of Miss Summer Lee Baldwin, the alleged crime occurring during the commission of an Aggravated Sexual Assault, which legally made it Death Chamber worthy. Though he copped to offing Joanna Kathryn Rogers, the State of Texas chose to prosecute for the homicide of Summer Lee Baldwin. With regards to her medically documented pregnancy and the lost life of the fetus, well, Rosendo Rodriguez III got a free pass for Murder in that particular instant; he didn't know Summer Lee Baldwin was with child and therefore could not have intended to kill the unborn, even if Texas law had defined the unborn as a person. Rosendo Rodriguez III, on the twenty-seventh day of March 2018 was everlastingly, at last, relieved of suffering anymore penitentiary-time rigmarole tedium. One respondent to the study, Christopher Chubasco Wilkins, federal prison time in his portfolio and who had admittedly Murdered three men, may or may not have shocked the harmless college questioners with his one sentence rejoinder for their theoretical aim of zeroing focus on Death Row convicts: "Some people just need killing." And the State of Texas killed him absent much fanfare.[23]

Classroom projects aside, perhaps measuring the humanity of those ensconced on Death Row has intrinsic value—at least for some folks. Though—in the real world—there are two sides to every coin. For this tome, perhaps someday or at some time nonaligned college students will somehow foresee the merit of polling Correctional Officers assigned to Death Row about their innermost humanity. ¿Quién sabe?

Marrying the specific causes for an absolute union is doable only in theory. The contributing dynamics were many. Within context of this treatment it might be suggested that one senseless event at Dallas and the out-and-out spike in Texas prison homicides moved some state legislators off high-center. At a definitely popular and somewhat trendy Italian eatery, Ianni's Restaurant & Club, a Moroccan immigrant wrought havoc with a smoking S&W 9mm. Abdelkrim Belachheb gunned down seven patrons, killing six. Catching the killer was not hard, although prosecuting him for Capital Murder was not possible. The deceased did not carry credentials as peace officers, firemen, or TDC employees, and the deaths did not occur during the commission of several predetermined felonies, and Abdelkrim Belachheb wasn't triggering rounds for money (a hit), nor was he escaping from a penal institution. Simply said, by a legality, there was no statute on the books designed for the wicked episode at hand, random multiple murders.[24] He could catch stacked life sentences (which he did) but riding into eternal dreamland courtesy the state's liquid chemical concoction would not do—lawfully. Legislators at Austin jumped rather quickly, revamping the Penal Code with emphasis on what elements constituted commission of Capital Murder.

Particularly as it relates to this Texas prison study, the revisions were specific and will be excised from the larger and presented herein for examination, but with no amplification or nuanced interpretation. They are self-explanatory.

Texas Penal Code, Title 5: Chapter 19, § 19.03:

§ 19.03 Capital Murder:

(a) A person commits an offense if he commits murder as defined under Section 19.02 (b)(I) and:

    (4) the person commits the murder while escaping or attempting to escape from a penal institution

    (5) the person, while incarcerated in a penal institution, murders another

        (A) Who is employed in the operation of the penal institution

    (6) the person:

        (A) while incarcerated for an offense under this section or Section 19.02 murders another

        (B) while serving a sentence of life imprisonment or a term of 99 years for an offense under Section 20.04, 221.021, or 29.03 murders another

Although Texas Governor Mark White, a Democrat, signed off on the new Capital Murder revisions during April 1985, at least one convict wasn't listening or reading—or giving a damn! The third day of June 1985 would be another dark day for prison employees. The first female Correctional Officer would be murdered by a convict. Certainly as readers will note, during the homicidal eleven-day Carrasco siege of 1974 dedicated female employees Julia Standley and Elizabeth Yvonne Beseda had been killed by wannabe escapees. However, these ladies were classified as civilians, not actually members of the security staff, though such technicality does not and should not depreciate their sacrifice.

That said, it may be dutifully reported that Minnie Rene Houston, forty-one, the widow of a deceased Correctional Officer, was on duty inside the dining hall at the Ellis I Unit, a Maximum Security facility also housing Death Row convicts. By then she may have heard some distressing news. Earlier that very day at the Coffield Unit near Tennessee Colony (in Anderson County), Correctional Officer George Billups had been stabbed by a convict as he was lining them up for the march to lunch. Fortuitously the forty-two-year-old Correctional Officer was not severely injured, thanks to a stroke of darn good luck. At any rate, Minnie Houston was supervising a squad of seven trustys that same evening and anticipated no trouble, else she would have intelligently summoned backup. Minnie's mettle had already been tested. Just the year before, she had shortstopped the escape of two Death Row convicts, Jewell Richard McGee and Kenneth Edward Gentry, already with one prison break under his belt. They were trying desperately to scale the perimeter's high fence. Acting alone Correctional Officer Houston climbed down from her elevated picket station, and leveled a scary looking .12-gauge pump shotgun at the wannabe be escapees. They were bewildered but returned to Death Row.[25] That was then, but now, close to 9:30 p.m. the horrifically stabbed body—eight to ten times—of Minnie Houston was found in an adjacent bathroom, soaked in blood. If the slaying was a whodunit, it wasn't for too very long. Somewhat unbelievably convict Ramon Mata, Jr., doing three dimes worth for a homicide in Pecos County, had after rummaging and finding Minnie's car-keys, sneaked outside and drove Minnie Houston's automobile to a prison picket outskirts checkpoint.

There he surrendered. The stunned prison officials quite naturally physically restrained Mata and, later, investigative authorities discovered the murder weapon in Minnie's vehicle—a bloody butcher knife with a razor sharp fifteen-inch blade. What motive could anyone have to slaughter the energetic and charismatic Minnie Houston? The brutal killer—though it seems warped—was not insistent on suppressing his innermost feelings. He was madly in love with the Correctional Officer so he murdered her, reasoning that if he couldn't have her—neither could anyone else. End of story!

Well, not quite. At Trinity, southwest of Groveton the county seat, the high-school auditorium filled to capacity with mourners, and an overflow crowd stood outside in sweltering Texas heat for Minnie Houston's memorial service. Predictably, many were the TDC personnel paying their respects, one and all realizing the precariousness of their chosen career field. Inside the Walker County Jail, defendant Ramon Mata sat—charged with Capital Murder. The Indictment came quickly—there were no issues concerning U.S. Constitutional rights to a speedy trial. Subsequent to a *Guilty* verdict by a deliberative jury at Madisonville on a Change of Venue, that same impaneled body unanimously voted for the legal qualifiers that would ensure that Mata should pay the supreme penalty. The Grim Reaper in Mata's case was impatient, the convict dying of natural causes at the TDC Hospital at Galveston. Aside from the loving memory of her surviving family, the endeared Correctional Officer was also memorialized permanently and publicly: The Region I training facility for new recruits was formally and fondly christened the Minnie R. Houston Academy, Huntsville.[26]

And though it might dip into a more-or-less mundane element of the otherwise compelling and exciting Texas Prison storyline, a brief highlighting of modern-era Correctional Officer training is imperative. It's revealing on several fronts. Strategically positioned throughout the Lone Star State are six Pre-Service Training Academies: Beeville in Bee County, Plainview in Hale County, Rosharon in

Brazoria County, Palestine in Anderson County, Gatesville in Coryell County, and Huntsville in Walker County. Long gone are the days when the new boots report for duty absent successful completion of reasonably intensive classroom course work and arduous on-the-ground practical exercises and agility tests. The wide-ranging curriculum is—or can be—mindboggling when examined on the whole. As would be anticipated, recruits are trained with the most updated techniques of securely restraining and moving prisoners, and the inherent job responsibilities of the associated institutional assignments guaranteeing security. Qualification with rifle, shotgun, and handgun are mandatory—application of Deadly Force is an acknowledged possibility. Likewise the proper and legal use of chemical agents demands a particularly focused bloc of instruction, as does the segment on how to protect oneself from an assaultive convict bent on outright cussedness or spontaneous outbursts. What to do and not do in a hostage situation are part of the instructors' comprehensive syllabus. And as would be but normal no little attention is given making sure tenderfoot Correctional Officers are familiarized with in-house rules and regulations, policies and procedures, Death Row protocols, emergency first-aid, "Infection Control, Blood Borne Pathogens," report writing, searching for contraband, court-imposed legalities, riot control, cunning convict manipulation scams, "Offender Rights," what constitutes unethical conduct—and, seemingly an *ad infinitum* index of subject material.

Then there are some of those other troubling topics, many of which have caused serious metaphorical headache and heartburn for a cadre of professional therapeutic practitioners, yet entry level Correctional Officers are thrust into an arena of perplexity and puzzlement. They are somehow expected to pre-identify disturbed convicts susceptible to taking their own or another's life and/or exploiting other convicts' projected weaknesses to gain pecuniary profit or varying degrees of physical pleasure. They must perceptively recognize and assess the psychological depth of their confined charges' "Mood/Personality/Psychotic Disorders," and competently manage "Mental Health Evaluation and Diagnosis," for prompt

referral to in-house psychiatrists or psychologists or convict classification specialists.[27] And therein is genesis for the all too common
blame game; sometimes after the convicts' behavior skids off the rails
of normalcy and/or acceptability, well, the ground-level Correctional
Officer should have seen the crisis coming and taken appropriate
steps to alleviate or interdict misfortune—in spite of a seminal fact,
the abstract mindreading staff were blindsided too. Too often the
case in the real world is that critical fact, using sterile terminology,
sometimes that upsetting stinky stuff rolls down hill. Since penitentiaries are but microcosms of the much broader society, the keepers,
at the bottom of the pecking order, bear the brunt of harsh criticism:
Not only justifiably so on occasion, but more often than not as sum
for political and/or philosophical expediency. As mentioned previously herein professionalism comes with training and experience—
and more training and more experience. Unquestionably for those
inclined to learn and persevere the rewards of a career in the Texas
prisons can provide a reasonably moderate monetary livelihood, but
somewhat more notably, the vocational platform for a psychologically fulfilling career choice.

14

"nothin' left to lose"

ALTHOUGH BY NECESSITY MUCH OF THE NARRATIVE about Texas prison units and its dedicated workforce may be steeped in tales of tragedy and judicial activism and enlightened rehabilitative tinkering, and some Death Chamber doings, the actual story—on the whole—is much broader. From the historical perspective the overall storyline is rich—a treasure worth safeguarding for future generations. With that philosophy entrenched in forward-thinking minds, a working coalition of then-current and retired Texas prison employees, highly credentialed educators at Sam Houston State University, and committed Huntsville area citizens, as well as a few public-spirited philanthropists, recognized a worthy cause. Collectively they stepped forward surrendering their precious time and opening their pocketbooks. On Huntsville's downtown square during 1989, the Texas Prison Museum (TPM) welcomed its first visitors. How could such a stellar museum exist absent public funding with taxpayer dollars? Well, with helpful donations from business houses and everyday citizens, a reasonable admission gate fee, and sales from the institution's well-stocked and capably managed gift shop, the lights remain on and the congenial staff continues to efficiently administer the duties entrusted to them. The TPM is self-sustaining. In fact, and it speaks well of interest and competence, the TPM metaphorically outgrew its little britches and in but a few short years moved to its present I-45 location on the northern outskirts of Huntsville. That's but half the story! With such a superb assemblage of artifacts dating from past to present exhibited with eye-catching appeal, the

TPM continually draws an enthusiastic throng of awestruck guests. The allure associated with prisons and prison business and prison personalities is a perpetual crowd pleaser. Not only are casual sightseers captivated by their tour through the facility, but writers and researchers are afforded opportunity to delve deeply into the professionally maintained archives. Actively reacting to the public challenge to prominently display even more interesting artifacts and enhance the museum experience, the TPM underwent a major expansion, recently adding an additional 5,000 square feet. From all indicators the future of the TPM is bright.[1]

Opening of the TPM chronologically coincided with a little Texas bureaucratic tinkering. During 1989, the TDC, the Texas Board of Pardons and Parole, and the Texas Adult Probation Commission were slated to merge into the Texas Department of Criminal Justice. Within that restructuring, what was once TDC is now TDCJ-CID, the Correctional Institutions Division, nominally referred to as the Institutional Division, headed by a Director, the top-dog in charge of overseeing policy implementation and day-to-day operations of all 100-plus Texas Prison units. As would be easily deduced, sitting atop the pinnacle of that organizational pyramid, by design, imparts to the executive colossal and somber responsibility.

Though the 1989 opening of TPM and the intended renaming and reshuffling of their outfit were events celebrated by many Correctional Officers, that same year another harrowing episode reminded them of prison job reality. Correctional Officer Lisa Cummings, accompanied by a work approved convict, a trusty driving the state's wrecker, were on the return trip to the Wynn Unit after picking up a disabled prison vehicle. Though the exact reason the prisoner, a multi-recidivist and then a lifer due to a Murder conviction in Liberty County, wigged-out is nebulous, what he did is not. According to prison spokesman David Nunnelee the robust would-be escapee grabbed Officer Cummings by "her hair and pulled her down on the seat. He did it again and was able to tie her hands with an elastic cord." Quite courageously Correctional Officer Cummings would not be a cooperative hostage. During her exertion to gain freedom, instability of the moving wrecker caused the towed vehicle to flip over. The trusty slammed on the brakes. Lisa Cummings, though almost an escapee from harm's way was trying to getaway but was overhauled by the convict, who "caught her and began hitting her again." Two passing motorists stopped, believing they had come up on an everyday traffic accident—which in a way they had—but they were caught totally by surprise. The prisoner no more fled in their pickup truck. While the convict was on the lam, Lisa Cummings was treated and, thankfully, released from the hospital with "bruises and minor abrasions." What happened next? Well, it seems the forty-nine-year-old convict began having serious second thoughts, although not exactly overnight. The following month the escapee telephoned prison authorities making arrangements to surrender before single-minded manhunters from the prison or Texas Rangers capped his free-world travels—one way or the other![2] Once more—and it's a sorrowfully recurring theme—not all trustys are 100 percent trustworthy, 100 percent of the time.

Not all Texas outlaws would attain preferential status as trustys. Two Death Row convicts were scheduled to die—and a concise recap of their criminality illustrates not the oft-cited Pains of Imprisonment, but rather the Pains of Employment: The day-by-day dealings with—in this case—a pair of society's worst. Really there were three, but as but par for such nefariousness one opted to flip, testifying for the state and against the interests of his, well, two supposed pals, Stephen Albert McCoy and James Emery Paster. At Houston the trio had Kidnapped and Raped and Murdered an eighteen-year-old stranded motorist, Cynthia Darlene Johnson, then residing at Conroe. To make certain they were leaving a dead body behind and not a living and breathing witness, James Emery Paster heartlessly and intentionally pounded a nail up one of her nostrils. Aside from the nauseating inhumanity and unchecked sexual lust, there was a back-story for Miss Johnson's demise. The three outlaws had been tied—one way or the other—to the contract killing of an unsuspecting Brown & Root machinist in Harris County, Robert Edward Howard, and in an unrelated offense, the Rape and stabbing

Murder of Diane Trevino Oliver, eighteen, near Channelview, a few miles east of Houston. The unfortunate Miss Johnson was executed, because they all agreed "that they would each kill someone in front of each other and thus seal their mutual trust in blood."[3] Grossly and quite particularly James Emery Paster, a sometimes lounge singer and Elvis impersonator, had also confessed to killing two other Houston area ladies, though prosecutors held those cases in reserve—they already had, hopefully, the goods on the reprehensible man local newspapers were not lovingly characterizing as "Satan Personified." While parked on Death Row the sometime "Heartbreak Hotel" and "Jailhouse Rock" crooning convict—along with another—lubricated themselves with greasy hair tonic and tried to escape through a vent. "Tried to" being the operative words. Absent a ripple Stephen Albert McCoy and James Emery Paster gave up the ghost inside the tall walls and behind the little green door at Huntsville, 24 May 1989 and 20 September 1989.[4]

Sounding positive notes about the new TPM, a wrecker driving escapee surrendering, and the open-case closure of grisly Harris County homicides, and what the future might hold was not mutually shared by everybody. Conjecturing what a majority of Correctional Officers thought about the upcoming execution of another Death Row resident is foolish absent a quantitative survey. Practically speaking, however, it's not outlandish to surmise that among most prison employees and not just a few prisoners James "Doom" Demouchette, a thirty-seven-year-old black convict, was not well-liked. For many folks—even a blood-relative—it seemed that Demouchette was the meanest man on Death Row. A description snappily proffered by a *Houston Chronicle* columnist backed up such a claim, suggesting that James Demouchette was beyond doubt the "most feared and dangerous man" on Death Row. Those deep-rooted fears were not unfounded.[5]

Without poking around profoundly into his biographical profile or total criminality, suffice to say what landed Demouchette on Death Row was the execution-style slaying of Scott Sorrell, nineteen, Assistant Manager at a Houston-area Pizza Hut and his roommate Robert White, twenty, who indeed were innocently at the very wrong place at the very wrong time. At the closed for the night eatery, the Manager, Geoff Hambrick, was also shot—saved from death only by assuming the persona of an opossum. Reportedly, subsequent to ransacking the back room, Demouchette, accompanied by his brother Christopher, noticed that Sorrell was yet hanging on, breathing—choking on his own blood—so James just "shot him a second time." James thought he would pop another round into face-down Geoff on the way out, but when he pulled the .38 Special revolver's trigger he found he had already milked his six-shooter dry.[6] Christopher, evidently after a sleepless night, voluntarily surrendered to authorities the next morning, gave a written statement, and soon thereafter James was taken into police custody.[7] In failing to kill Hambrick—the surviving eyewitness—James Demouchette categorically expressed no regret for the shootings, but was upset with himself for not eliminating the man that could finger him, coldly and arrogantly owning up to his blunt shortfall as: "the onliest mistake I ever made."[8] For his cooperation Christopher Demouchette caught a life sentence. James, the triggerman, was not as fortunate.

And it will be on Death Row where James Demouchette, absent a smidgen of contrition, cemented his reputation for unchecked nastiness and bloody volatility. Benignly referring to the in-house havoc Demouchette caused merely as disciplinary infractions would be folly. Not only is James Demouchette's conduct revealing about him personally, but it also pinpoints what dutiful Correctional Officers were forced to endure day in and day out, and in this instance for 5,529 maddening days.[9] In one episode, while being removed from his cell, according to an article in the *Corpus Christi Times*, Demouchette "attacked the employees with a two-pronged weapon made from metal removed from a shaving mirror," wounding and biting Lieutenants Jimmy Alford and Paul Pace, and Correctional Officer Mark Dawson. Taking into account the *Fort Worth Star-Telegram's* alarming report, other Correctional Officers' names are credited to Demouchette's in-house stabbing scorecard too: Charles

Agee and Scott Stoughton, both sometimes replacement football players for the Houston Oilers. On another occasion it was said mean James Demouchette "stabbed one of the most fearless guards to ever work the Ellis Unit—Major 'Big Jelly' Steele."[10]

James Demouchette did not simply reserve his meanness for the security staff; fellow convicts were fair game too. With an improvised fourteen-inch shank—a sharpened handle from a kitchen ladle—he attacked convict Johnny E. Swift, forty-two, who was doing 101 years hard-time for Murder With Malice. In the dayroom at the Ellis Unit, which was then yet home for Death Row, Demouchette began stabbing Swift. Swift fell to the floor and Demouchette straddled his flabbergasted target, weapon arcing in hand. A Correctional Sergeant boldly rushed to the dayroom door, demanding that James Demouchette surrender the shank. Demouchette demurred, icily spitting and snarling: "Nah, I ain't finished killing this nigger yet." Subsequent to stabbing Swift some more—sixteen times in the chest—the assaultive convict handed over the weapon, proudly declaring: "The son of a bitch is dead now." Swift had breathed his last, dying on the floor.[11] Demouchette caught a life sentence for this Capital Murder—stacked atop his death sentence, which was for the interim log-jammed in the appellate review process.[12]

Another act of James Demouchette's unchecked animalism was exhibited during a hideous episode with another Death Row prisoner, Kerry Max Cook, who would after more than two indescribable decades in prison, be legally and wholly exonerated for the Rape, Murder, and disfigurement of Linda Jo Edwards in East Texas at Tyler (in Smith County).[13] The horrors that frequently haunt prison life were not nightmares for anxious Kerry Max Cook; they were real! What follows is not for the squeamish, but it's real, disgustingly real and but another true-life example of mean convict James Demouchette's predilection for taking whatever he wanted, whenever he wanted it. Let it be a tawdry eye-opener for any naïve whiners. Eyeing brand-new prisoner Kerry Max Cook, Demouchette, flanked by hardened Death Row prisoners, and with a shank in his hand, frostily remarked that the new prisoner was an attractive MF, just like he had been told. The predatory Demouchette's license for lust was figurative, but his intentions were real. Absent hesitation or fear of being found out by prison personnel he ordered Cook to quickly shed his clothes, all of them, and while nude assume the position, breaking over like an over and under shotgun. Then he confidently moved behind the horrified victim. What then? A terrified Cook is explicit and vivid, recalling how James Demouchette placed that sharpened blade of the shank against his abdomen and then powerfully and brutally raped him. Other prisoners forwent coming to the rescue—that could have, in this case, proven suicidal. No one dared snitch. Aside from the emotional humiliation, Kerry Max Cook endured excruciating physical pain as Demouchette violently powered for release. Temporarily sexually sated the rapist openly declared that Kerry Max Cook was now his punk. Punctuating his declaration, Demouchette carved nicknames into Cook's buttocks. Then, Demouchette warned Cook that if he decided to snitch about what had taken place, well, "I'll kill you."[14]

Though repeating in detail each and every Disciplinary Offense Report in Demouchette's prison portfolio is, indeed, doable, it's not—at this point—actually necessary. The list is wide-ranging and very long and most violations are repetitive with a capital R, but herein mentioned but once for this admittedly abbreviated recap: Assaults With and Without Weapons, Failure to Work, Fighting, Using Indecent and Vulgar Language, Striking Officers, Threatening An Officer, Destroying State Property, Creating Disturbances, Possession of Weapons (multiple, multiple times), Possession of Tattooing Paraphernalia, Possession of Contraband, Use and Brewing of Alcoholic Beverages, Spitting on Officers, Throwing Urine on Officers, Throwing Urine on the Steam-Table, Burning Property in Cell, Throwing Food Trays, Threatening to "stick bitchass nurses," as well as Clogging Toilets and Flooding Cells.[15]

Though the humor is somewhat callous, James Demouchette didn't like squash or okra, punch or milk—and not surprisingly his Ellis Unit keepers didn't like him. So, on James Demouchette's very last day his desire for a grilled steak and baked potato was granted, but he had little choice about ingesting—intravenously—the state's chemical concoction.[16]

Another resident on Death Row was in a unique situation, but one of his very own doings. Unequivocally there was not a shard or splinter of sympathy for him coming from the ranks of Correctional Officers. Likewise, convicts all around—Death Row included—wholly reviled him. Robert Earl Carter was a former Correctional Officer and Robert Earl Carter was the murderer of a half-dozen folks, including little children ranging in age from nine to four years. After snuffing out their lives at Somerville (in Burleson County), Robert Earl Carter torched the deceased's house to cover the ghastly crime and destroy any evidentiary link. Purportedly—and there is no reason to doubt it—he even attended the victim's memorial service "wrapped in bandages for severe burns apparently suffered in the house fire." Without wasting word space, Carter was soon captured and convicted and caught the chain to Huntsville. Although he was implicating another person as the killer to cast suspicion elsewhere, naming Anthony Graves, Robert Carter confided in another convict, Kerry Max Cook, that when push came to shove and his ass was about to be dumped in the grease, firmly strapped to the Death Chamber's gurney, he would willingly confess and let the understandably worried Anthony Graves off the hook. Until then, loathed convict and dishonored former Correctional Officer Robert Earl Carter would hold his tongue. And then. . . . then came! After wolfing down a double-meat cheeseburger with French fries and absolving Anthony Graves for the Warden to hear, Robert Earl Carter was "ready to go home and be with his Lord." The State of Texas sent him on his way.[17]

A fellow who couldn't be sent on his way via the Death Chamber, legally, was a predatory convict serving two life sentences from a Lubbock court for Aggravated Sexual Assault and Aggravated Robbery. At the Robertson Unit in Jones County just northwest of Abilene, the outlaw proved he had not—at least at that time—been rehabilitated. During the late night headcount he viciously attacked a female Correctional Officer, manhandling her into his house—which he had rigged, in all probability, not to lock. With a wicked looking shank held to her throat, the unfortunate Correctional Officer was forced to submit to a Sexual Assault, repeatedly. Then, he surrendered: Handing over his eight-inch piece of sharpened steel and allowing another victim to suffer the physical and emotional trauma kin to such viciousness.[18] What would another long prison term mean to, a lifer? Apparently, not much!

And apparently some West Texas militants thought they were, too, immune from manmade laws and regulations propagated by the State of Texas. Long a festering thorn for Texas lawmen and peacefully inclined folks, members of the Republic of Texas (ROT) outfit, as they dubbed themselves, argued that Texas had been illegally annexed into the United States in 1845 and, therefore all 171,901,440 acres of what was now Lone Star State real-estate was yet a sovereign territory of the long bygone 1830s era. Resultantly, there was absolutely no need for them to acquire driver's licenses, state auto inspections stickers for their windshields, pay Texas taxes or anything else they perceived as forcing them into the cone of lawful compliance if they chose not to comply. After all, Texas was an independent country still, not a subdivision of another entity. Half-baked as it seemed, they were dead serious! Adding to those niggling illegal botherences, ROT revolutionists were filing bogus liens, all across the state. Unraveling a tangle of flippant filings was wearing thin—real thin at the Statehouse and county courthouses. On the whole such absurdity was really generating a perilous tight spot. The crescendo of a looming calamity was escalating, scarily so. Radically inclined ROT proponents fecklessly established an "Embassy" in faraway West Texas in the decidedly picturesque and historically rich Davis Mountains, not too very far removed from the county seat of Jeff Davis County, Fort Davis.[19] And how does such madness play into a narrative history about the Texas prisons and their committed security staff? Not only do TDCJ-ID personnel assume more than a cameo role, their involvement underscores their stellar working relationship with the Texas Rangers—and, in fact, all of DPS.

On 27 April 1997 the metaphorical pot boiled over. Three ROT radicals orchestrated and executed a boneheaded act, an impetuous Home Invasion directed at a couple living on the single roadway heading towards their compound, the ROT Embassy at the far end of the isolated lane. During the assault homeowner Joe Rowe was wounded by a gunshot to the left arm, with his bewildered and horrified wife Margaret witnessing the sheer idiocy in disbelief. Technically—from the ROT perspective—Mr. and Mrs. Rowe were now, "Prisoners of War."[20] Other ROT readied and armed adherents were further up the canyon at their headquarters—of sorts. A protracted siege had begun.

Jeff Davis County Sheriff Steve Bailey owned a different perspective; he saw it as an uncomplicated case of Aggravated Kidnapping and Attempted Capital Murder, though tactically he and his only full-time deputy needed assistance. Texas Ranger Captain Barry Caver, the Company E Commander then at Midland, got the call and quickly began organizing the onsite response. And it was massive: Texas Rangers and DPS Troopers, DPS SWAT Team, TP&W (Texas Parks & Wildlife) Game Wardens, U.S. Border Patrol Agents, Deputy U.S. Marshals, FBI Special Agents, U.S. Army EOD (Bomb Technicians) specialists, and U.S. Army Blackhawk helicopter pilots and crews lending air and logistical support. Roadblocks were promptly put in place to establish an area perimeter, designed to hem in the outlaws as well as preventing the arrival of any ROT reinforcements. Securing the outer limit also protected concerned area citizens and rubberneckers and the ever quickly on-the-spot press corps, always hunting for a good West Texas story about guns and guys gone awry. That more or less covered the asphalt and dirt roadways sealing off the ROT Embassy, which but amounted to "a 1950s model travel trailer that had been added onto with a little lean-to shack."[21]

While the Davis Mountains are alluring, they too are craggy and vast, spotted with steep inclines and rocky canyons and shielding scrub and tall pines—patrolled by mountain lions and rattlesnakes and, sometimes a bear, as well as other creatures that can bite or stick and sting. What if the outlaws opted to skirt the roadways and make a getaway navigating the rugged and remote backcountry? Well, such would be foolish. TDCJ-ID personnel were on the scene too, with their quite well-trained and competently handled teams of man-tracking dogs: Breaking for the brush might prove folly.

Since this is in actuality a Texas prison story, cutting to the nub is obligatory. Suffice to say due to the professionalism of approximately 300 lawmen and their support staff, and excellent on-the-ground cooperation of the United States Forest Service Incident Command System, coordinating and scheduling the manning of specific posts and "aptly rotating manpower, tribulations they had fine-tuned though years and years of frontline fighting wildfires," the multi-day siege was finally brought to an end. As a result of the levelheaded negotiations by Texas Ranger Captain Barry Caver with the ROT's main honcho Richard Lance McLaren, the once ROT "Ambassador" would in due time—after courthouse doings—owe TDCJ-ID a lengthy compulsory visit at one of its facilities, one with a tall wall or high fence.[22]

Although the endgame would register as somewhat passive on the frontend, the back-story would be anything but. Rather than surrender, two of the ROT fellows opted to slither through the backcountry, escaping to parts they forever hoped would remain unknown. One got away temporarily (apprehended later) but it was truly a horrible miscalculation for Michael Matson. And that part of the story can be snubbed succulently too. After shooting and hitting and killing one of TDCJ-ID's first-rate tracking dogs, Matson trained his rifle on an overhead DPS helicopter carrying Texas Ranger Gene Kea, who was armed with a state-issued Ruger .223 Mini-14. Stupidly, Mike Matson let loose on the whirlybird. Close in, atop the mountainous ground Texas Ranger Coy Smith laid down a covering fire for TDCJ-ID dog handlers, as did Texas Ranger Kea from the sky. Luckily, TDCJ-ID Field Lieutenant Joe Eric Pechacek, armed with a .270 caliber long-gun, finally had the clear shot that had eluded the two Texas Rangers. Lieutenant Pechacek brought Matson to the ground—sledgehammer dead. Dutifully he had taken an outlaw's life to save who knew how many others?[23] Due to steepness and ruggedness of the terrain, the National Guard rescue helicopter was unable to safely touch down. With a poignant twist, the slain tracking dog, Sugar Ray, was lifted overhead by the hydraulic cable rescue winch and into the circling helicopter's open bay just ahead of the dead desperado. Such, by design, was a touching tribute to the courageous canine, forfeiting its life in the line of duty.[24] All in all the ROT affair had once again proved a sterling example of inter- and intra-agency cooperation and determination.[25] Texas manhunts were no stranger to seasoned Dog Sergeants and their attendant trusty convict Dog Boys.

More than a hundred years earlier the reputation for effectiveness of the Texas prisons' hounds had garnered notice in a Rocky Mountain newspaper, the *Daily Enterprise* at Livingston, Montana, after a *Houston Post* correspondent visited with a Dog Sergeant, who said:

> Convicts will not leave when they know good hounds are on hand
> to catch them. . . . you can not hold convicts with shot-guns. It
> is the fear of the hounds that keeps them quiet. Desertion is use-
> less when recapture is a moral certainty, as is the case when good
> hounds are employed.[26]

And if a slight touch of hyperbole is allowed, some human hounds were doggedly hunting for the aforementioned monster Kenneth Allen McDuff, perhaps the very best—or worst—at that time example of the Texas Parole Board's signature screwup. Suspected—and good for—murdering and sexually assaulting several females, McDuff had fled the state and was for awhile working under an assumed name in Kansas City, Missouri, until diligently latched onto by lawmen and returned to the Lone Star State. There, according to one prison administrator who knew him, the only people who had to fear Kenneth Allen McDuff were schoolboys, little girls and old women, despite the fact he tried to project the sour persona of Billy Badass from Bitter Creek. He may have been a killer, but in legit prison speak he wasn't a man. Too, he wasn't any too successful in beating the raps. Thanks to the cooperative multi-agency efforts of Texas Rangers, the U.S. Marshals Service at Waco, a Western District Assistant United States Attorney, ATF Special Agents, city detectives and sheriff's deputies and, relevant for the book in hand, John Moriarty, Special Investigator, TDCJ, Kenneth McDuff's heartrending murderous days were kiboshed. He was first courthouse convicted of kidnapping and gutlessly killing twenty-two-year-old Melissa Ann Northrup, a nighttime Waco convenience store clerk, callously dumping her lifeless body in a Dallas County gravel pit. Score one for an outstanding and witty prosecutorial team from the McLennan County's DA's office. Round two was also won by on-the-ball lawyers representing the Travis County DA's office, earning another Capital Murder conviction for the Kidnapping and Murder of Colleen Reed, forcefully abducted from an Austin car-wash. Though it someway might ring as morbid, peace officers and prosecutors took delight in making history of sorts; Kenneth Allen McDuff would be the first paroled (the U.S. Supreme Court decision, *Furnan v. Georgia*) Death Row convict, again found *Guilty* and returned to a Death Row under revised and, now Constitutional, statutes. Thanksgiving of 1998 was fast approaching and Kenneth Allen McDuff did not have any turkey and dressing and cranberries reserved for his fun holiday repast. He wanted T-bone steaks, fried eggs, and French-fries—with a Coca-Cola. He was granted his last meal wish, but the State of Texas added its own chaser for that Coca-Cola, a pharmaceutical cocktail with an enduring aftertaste. Kenneth McDuff, at age fifty-two, went to wherever stone-cold killers go on that seventeenth day of November 1998.[27]

With reasonable certainty it may be suggested that most TDCJ-ID Correctional Officers and many convicts were in a seasonal upbeat mood regarding the forthcoming 1999 Christmas Holiday season; dawning of the twenty-first-century was at their doorstep. Of course the convicts in the William G. McConnell Unit at Beeville in Bee County in South Texas wouldn't be turned loose going door to door singing Christmas Carols in the free-world—they'd be celebrating behind the high-fence. And just because—in that same vein—most folks might take some time off to be with family and friends, the Correctional Officers would continue with their twenty-four and seven mission. The prison might be locked but it never shut down.

Daniel James Nagle, thirty-seven, no doubt was looking forward to at least spending part of the holidays with his wife, Crystal Anne, and their kiddos, Rebecca, Jonathon and Michael. As of mid-December he was working though, supervising convicts in a minimum security housing area, although the McConnell Unit domiciled convicts of all security levels. During the Friday afternoon of 17 December 1999 at about 3:45 the lifeless and bloody body of Daniel Nagle was found in a hallway, reposed in a fetal position—the obvious victim of a homicide, caused from eight stab wounds by a sharpened and piercing object. That much was obvious absent dissent. Evident too was the copy of a shredded disciplinary slip for a particular convict haphazardly strewn across the body and floor. Shortly it was noted that a sharpened cylindrical rod—about six to eight inches in length with tape and cloth wrapped around one end fashioning a nonslip handle—was found abandoned in the run not too far removed from dead Daniel James Nagle.

The in-house Murder of Daniel Nagle was—with an eerie respect—somewhat ironic. Just three weeks earlier, as President of the local chapter of the American Federation of State, County and Municipal Employees (AFSCME), Nagle had been on the steps of the Texas Capitol championing for better working conditions, higher salaries, and an increase in manpower for the woefully understaffed prison system. In fact he had decried that "someone would have to die" before the state legislators turned their attention to the shortage of Correctional Officers.

Back at the ranch, so to speak, the criminal investigation with regards to Nagle's death pressed forward until a likely suspect was identified. That convict was Robert Lynn Pruett, a twenty-year-old, doing ninety-nine years as a willing teenage accomplice to his father during a Harris County homicide. On the day in question Pruett had been escorted by a Correctional Officer to receive new footwear. Unhappily for convict Pruett that in-house trip coincided with the lunch hour. He missed the dining hall line, and instead was issued a Johnny-sack (paper-bag with a sandwich, fruit, etc.) in lieu of a steaming hot meal. With brown paper-bag in hand Pruett headed into the recreation quarter, but was reminded by Correctional Officer Nagle that food was not permitted there, a well-established prison rule. He would have to and should have consumed his lunch outside the recreation area. Robert Lynn Pruett was not happy and, perhaps, more unhappy after Daniel Nagle wrote him up for violating that regulation. It was later that same afternoon that the lifeless form of Correctional Officer Nagle was found.

During the post-incident investigation there were several convicts who asserted that they actually witnessed the crime—and others who testified that Pruett had forewarned that he would kill Nagle, while others remarked that after the death, a bloody Robert Lynn had been animated and jolly, even declaring that the Correctional Officer would never write him up again, never! On the other hand Pruett claimed that he was innocent and that the convict witnesses and the corrupt Correctional Officers were conspiring and lying to his detriment.

Robert Lynn Pruett at trial maintained his plea of innocence through his defense attorney yet still avowing that he had been "framed." And herein it's but fair to note, near anytime a convict testifies against the interest of a defendant, the defense declaration is proffered that prisoners always lie for their self-interest: a sweetened deal for shortened sentences or more privileges, etc. Conversely, the defense counsel argues that his/her client, also a convict, is always telling the truth—incapable of uttering any falsehoods. *Déjà vu!* Perhaps, somewhat analogous to Judge William Wayne Justice's obvious and occasional naiveté in the landmark *Ruiz* litigation? In this instance Robert Lynn Pruett was found *Guilty* of Capital Murder and was issued the ultimate sanction—to die by the state's lethal pharmaceutical injection. After the lengthy and fascinating exploration of legal issues during the appellate process was thoroughly exhausted, Pruett would die in the Death Chamber.[28]

In recent memory—though it's now been near twenty years— one of the most notorious prison breaks happened on the thirteenth day of December 2000. All so soon the escape would morph into a manhunt of gigantic proportion, at least one of the most intensive searches for fugitives in America's law enforcing history.[29] Seven proven violent and violently inclined convicts blueprinted and executed a daring escape from the TDCJ-ID's Connally Unit, a 2500-plus bed maximum-security facility employing 526 Correctional Officers located on State Highway 181 near Kenedy (in Karnes County), west of Victoria and southeast of San Antonio.

The conspiring convicts were George Angel Rivas, Jr., thirty, pulling seventeen stacked life sentences for Aggravated Kidnapping With a Deadly Weapon, Aggravated Kidnapping, Aggravated Robbery With a Deadly Weapon, Aggravated Robbery and Burglary of a Habitation; Michael Anthony Rodriguez, thirty-eight, a lifer due to his Capital Murder conviction for hiring a hit-man to off his wife in Bexar County for an insurance payout; Randy Ethan Halprin, thirty, doing a triple dime from Tarrant County for Injury to a Child/ Serious Bodily Injury With a Deadly Weapon; Donald Keith Newbury, thirty-eight, a three-time loser, pulling his ninety-nine years for Aggravated Robbery With a Deadly Weapon at Austin; Patrick Henry Murphy, Jr., thirty-nine, was chiseling away his half-century sentence for Aggravated Sexual Assault in Dallas County; Joseph Christopher Garcia, twenty-nine, had caught his hard fifty years for Murder With a Deadly Weapon in the Alamo City; and Larry James Harper, thirty-seven, owed the state his next fifty years due to several convictions, running concurrently, for Aggravated Sexual Assault and Aggravated Sexual Assault With a Deadly Weapon.[30]

Intricacies of the escape revealed that the planning had long been in the works, a detailed familiarity with the day-to-day routine of prison operations: work schedules, Correctional Officers' security post assignments, inclement weather adjustments, comings and goings of free-world contractors, etc. In short, who was where, when.

Without resorting to a play by play account inside the facility's Maintenance Department during lunch hour, the seven aforementioned outlaws began violently assaulting, one by one, and making worried hostages of taken aback civilian employees, flabbergasted

Correctional Officers, and even three unsuspecting convicts. They didn't say please, but had wielded and stricken victims with ax handles and pressed shanks into ears and to throats. When it was all said and done, these would-be escapees made prisoners of sixteen men, tightly binding and gagging them with plastic-ties and duct tape—and at least one pair of state-issued handcuffs. In some instances they had exchanged clothing, becoming convict chameleons.[31]

With the change in appearance and desperate boldness, the conspiring felons successfully carried out a radio/video repairman ruse, gaining access to an outside picket watchtower. There they acquired a portion of the Connally Unit's field-force firepower: a 12 gauge pump shotgun, a .223 caliber AR-15 Assault Rifle, and fourteen handguns, Smith & Wesson .357 Magnum revolvers, and several hundred rounds of assorted ammo. The ratio of guns to free-wheeling convicts now tallied at more than two apiece—a noteworthy computation: All were dangerous. Before they exited the back gate in a commandeered prison truck the escapees left scribbled messages behind foretelling the dire future, a figurative "Fuck You" to any speedy would-be pursuers.[32] One, with lyrics lifted from a Kris Kristofferson song, "Me and Bobby McGee," read: "Freedom's just another word for nothin' left to lose." The other had more threatening overtones: "You haven't heard the last of us yet!"[33]

Federal and State law enforcing entities were called into action, reflecting the intensity of the manhunt: A Task Force of TDCJ-ID Investigators, DPS Intelligence Unit Agents, DPS THP (Texas Highway Patrol), Texas Rangers, FBI Special Agents, U.S. Border Patrolmen, DOJ and ATF Special Agents, Deputy U.S. Marshals, and a significant multi-agency contribution from county sheriffs' offices and city police departments. Who they were hunting for was a given. Where the escapees had absconded to was the $64,000 question. Their whereabouts was wholly unknown. They could be anywhere. The breakout had quite naturally become hot fodder for the newspaper and broadcast crews. And this feeding frenzy, according to former Karnes County Sheriff Robert R. "Bobby" Mutz, focusing the media spotlight on the outlaws and their pursuit and televising their photos, was in fact more helpful than hurtful.[34] Nationwide the escapees were dubbed "The Texas Seven."[35]

Interestingly, the pure analytical work—not chasing leads in the field—was then and is now mindboggling. DPS CID Intelligence Agent H.L. "Hank" Whitman (later Chief of the Texas Rangers) pulled forty long days and forty near sleepless nights at the Command Center. The foundation for capitalizing on Agent Whitman's analytical acumen was in recognition of the cold reality: the Texas Seven were but individuals, each owning their own wasted life histories, regardless any failed rehabilitative reasoning and/or maudlin excuses. Somehow and somewhere, and it would be but only a matter of time, the Texas Seven would be run to ground—either together or splintered or as pathetic loners. And therein was the basis for CID Agent Whitman's analytic participation. Painstaking attention to case histories and social ties could yield a vast data bank if interpreted correctly. That said, finding them together or separately solved but half of the task before lawmen. How would each of the Texas Seven react when finally cornered? Therefore, for purely tactical reasons, Agent Hank Whitman also had to rate and rank the Texas Seven by strength of personality and pure cussed-ness—who was the dominant desperado? When the leader at the top of the pecking-order was tagged and bagged, who would take his place? What would that escapee bring to the table of badness? The breadth and depth of the nonstop intelligence gathering process is truly mind-blowing. At the time, circumspectly exploring genealog-ical family-trees and psychological predispositions and the violent convicts' personal predilections was super important from the ana-lytic angle, but the closeness or farness of any state or national bor-derlines was meaningless.[36] The brutal Texas Seven were phantoms. No one knew exactly where they were!

Lawmen did know, however, where they had been. Brandishing the state's stolen firearms the escapees had highjacked a Radio Shack in Pearland (Brazoria County), stealing money, walkie-talkies, and a police radio scanner. As would be expected, the robbers were not gentlemanly disposed. The store manager was particularly distraught by the iciness of the gang's evident leader, George Rivas: "I knew by the cold, hard look in his eye, that if anybody moved he wouldn't kill just one of us, he'd kill all of us."[37] Additionally the gangsters robbed a coastal area AutoZone Store, and yet later acquired uniforms that would pass as those of private security guards. Yet they were still ghosts.[38]

On Christmas Eve in the Dallas suburb of Irving, the Texas Seven struck again, unmercifully! They robbed an Oshman's Sporting Goods Store, holding terrified employees hostage while they gathered up winter clothing and $70,000 in cash. Then they turned their attention to the firm's firearms inventory—stuffing duffle bags full of guns and ammunition. That was inside. Outside, one of the Texas Seven, Patrick Henry Murphy, Jr. acted as the jigger (lookout), armed with a shotgun, AR-15 with 60 rounds, and a pair of .357 Magnum six-shooters and a walkie-talkie, all the while listening to the Pearland pilfered police radio scanner set to the right channel.[39] Unknown to the thieving outlaws, two unobserved eyewitnesses didn't know what was unfolding at the now closed and locked and dimly lit Oshman's Sporting Goods Store—except that something was amiss. One of them dialed 9-1-1.

A twenty-nine-year-old, five-year law enforcing veteran, Irving PD Patrolman Aubrey Wright Hawkins, husband and father, was dispatched to investigate. At the time the call seemed rather innocuous: Suspicious persons at the sporting goods store. Check it out. Listening to the scanner escapee Patrick Murphy was not surprised—alerting his comrades in crime that it was fixing to turn to hell in a hand-basket. On the other hand the dedicated Texas peace officer was dismayed and dead; eleven bullets had torn into his body as his squad car squared with the outlaws' getaway vehicles, one of which was the store managers' now stolen Ford Explorer. Then, callous George Rivas, driving the SUV, ran over the lifeless body of Aubrey Hawkins. The Texas Seven were, again, invisible but shameless spirits. Now they were even better armed and flush with cash—although their theft of heavy winter clothing was a not subtle indication they certainly weren't planning for an extended Caribbean Island vacation in swimsuits and cutoffs.[40]

So while the murderous and thieving yahoos were on the lam, doing damn well as they pleased, the all too typical sad story played out in their destructive wake. With his widow, Lori, and other close and extended family members, and peace officers from nearby and afar with black tape adorning their badges, reverently looking on, Police Officer Aubrey Wright Hawkins was peacefully interred in the Oak Grove Memorial Gardens at Irving.

Worried investigators worked tirelessly, exploring seemingly solid leads and even not just a few cockamamie supposed sightings of the killers—and that what's the Texas law declared they were: Killers. Under the *Law of Parties*, all participants in the criminality are equally festooned with culpability. In essence it translates with a commonsense point of view. In this instance, whether one or more were the triggermen, getaway drivers, or lookouts, the scales of justice equally weighed them all as murderers: For this high-drama, a Capital Murder.

Doubtlessly who turned out to be the most significant contributor to unraveling the nasty mess would not be lawmen, despite all their commendable and untiring exertions. True-crime television personality John Walsh had spotlighted the Texas Seven saga on his widely-viewed TV program *America's Most Wanted* four times. A sharp-eyed couple from Woodland Park, Colorado, northwest of Colorado Springs, subsequent to seeing the last segment, knew right where the Texas Seven were: The Coachlight RV Park, staying in a Pace-Arrow motor-coach. From all outward appearances the seven vacationers—if you will—outwardly manicured an overall impression that they were really pretty nice guys. Of course, such was an example of a self-serving flair for superlative acting. Once clued to the hot tip, lawmen surreptitiously confirmed that, indeed, the identities of the Pace-Arrow residents were dead-ringers for the slippery Texas Seven. Covert surveillance was initiated while the tactical plans for a takedown were being refined and manpower was positioned.

Recapping the next phase of Texas Seven's malicious misadventures and murder will for now be succinct. George A. Rivas, Jr., Joseph C. Garcia, and Michael A. Rodriguez were captured while fueling a gray Jeep Cherokee at a Woodland Park convenience store. Meanwhile back at the Coachlight RV Park, Randy E. Halprin, realizing he was outgunned and surrounded, surrendered. Larry J. Harper, inside the motor-home, opted for another way out of his big-time troubles. He placed the six-shooter's barrel to his chest and pulled the trigger: Suicide rather than submission. Relatively shortly, in the overall picture, escapees Donald K. Newbury and Patrick H. Murphy, Jr. finally capitulated to lawmen's demand that they give up, allowing officers to enter the moderately priced Colorado Springs motel room absent any kicked-in door and minus any echoing gunshots. The escaped convicts were all properly accounted for—and now the news-making Texas Six, after the necessary formality of resolving lawful extradition matters, would be returned to the Lone Star State—in cuffs and chains.[41]

The ensuing courthouse actions provide for a dissection of the fascinating panoply of legal maneuverings and settlement of several rather complex issues in the courtroom, but there is an end result—at least in part as of this 2019 writing. Eventually the six remaining members of the villainous Texas Seven would be issued tickets to Death Row, courtesy Capital Murder trials. Convicts Newbury, Rodriguez, Garcia, and alleged ringleader Rivas, would all pass to the other side at The Walls strapped to the Death Chamber's gurney, the state's potion ultimately working its lethality, just as juries had intended. Perhaps George Rivas's statement from the witness stand was quite apt about his mindset and future: "I wasn't going to be an old man dying in prison."[42] Prophetically, convict Rivas was but half-right: He wasn't an old man, but he did die in prison.[43] With regards to the fate of convicts Halprin and Murphy, at the time of this writing, both are housed on Death Row awaiting final adjudication of Appellate Courts.

While the foregoing events were unfolding, another horror story spit forth but was somewhat underreported—at least in the minds of Correctional Officers. At the Smith Unit, situated in Dawson County (county seat Lamesa) at the southern edge of the Llano Estacado, a malicious convict psychologically jumped sideways: He wittingly swallowed a small razor-sharp P-38 type can-opener. The convict, twenty-five, was pulling 140 years due to his involvement in an Auto Theft, Burglary, Sexual Assault, and the 1996 Rape of a forty-five-year-old female TDCJ-ID employee at the Telford Unit in far northeast Texas near New Boston in Bowie County, not too far west of Texarkana. He was not an amenable fellow; he was a dangerous hardcore convict. With regards to the present mindlessness herein highlighted, a hurried medical diagnosis indicated the high probability of internal bleeding. The physician ordered that the injured convict be transported to the hospital at Lubbock, specifically the University Medical Center. A pair of armed Correctional Officers—one male, one female—were the security team helping escort him to the hospital.[44]

Apparently the medical trip into the free-world was all part of the grand scheme, satisfying sexual yearnings. At the hospital the convict produced a facsimile pistol, one carefully crafted from "a hairbrush, a deodorant bottle, soap, and pages from a Bible. It was dyed black and had all the appearance of a real gun." Successfully bluffing the male and female security staff into abandoning the exam room and, then, after removing his shackles with a hidden handcuff key he took two female nurses hostage. If he ever owned good sense, it was now overpowered by primitive lust. During the ninety-minute game-plan and standoff he sexually abused both of the understandably shaken but utterly harmless medical caregivers. His innermost desires temporarily sated the convict meekly surrendered—and the University Medical Center tendered their ninety-day notice as stipulated by the seventy-two-million-dollar deal with TDCJ-ID, surrendering their multi-page health providing contract.[45] With regards to disciplining or punishing the nastily inclined violator, well, what more could really be done to a mean and compassionless convict on the short side of 140 years?

15

"die an outlaw's death"

ALTHOUGH THERE MIGHT BE ROOM FOR DISCUSSION about the prevalence of Aggravated Sexual Assaults (as opposed to consensual sex acts) taking place inside prisons, several dynamics merit mention regardless any well-meaning academic debate. First and foremost must be an acknowledgment of truth: Behind the tall walls and high fences sexual predators prowl, sometimes in packs and sometimes as lone wolves. Some of these wolves are not at all discriminatory; they hunt for prey of either gender. During the legislative session of 2003 the U.S. Congress, responding to public pressure advocacy groups, unanimously passed the Prison Rape Elimination Act (PREA).[1] Cognizant of reality unfolding around them in ever evolving times, TDCJ-ID earnestly jumped forward. Any allegation of Sexual Assault or Sexual Harassment lodged by a convict or Texas prison employee is taken most seriously and made a part of the composite yearend numbers for any alleged and/or any confirmed incidents. Not every state is that exacting. Nationally within these tabulations there can be variance. For some penal systems the reported offense is counted, but only after there is confirmation that a crime had actually been committed and that it was not a fictitious allegation made-up for the settling of scores by someone about something. Though it radically tends to skew the overall empirical numbers upwards, in Texas all such accusations are reported and worked into the tallied statistical equation. Texas PREA protocols are strict and demanding. System-wide no convict and no employee can hide under a threadbare blanket of feigned ignorance.[2]

The theoretical worth of some academic thinking with regards to Rape (any Sexual Assault) may or may not have merit for the college classroom, but in the free-world or in the penitentiary most solid solutions are fertilized by precedent and practicality, not necessarily by imperfect psychoanalysis and idealistic supposition. So, for the topic at hand, whether the perpetrator or perpetrators commit an act of Rape because they fit into neat categories such as the "Exploitative Rapists" or maybe a "Compensatory Rapists" or the "Displaced Anger Rapists" or even the "Sadistic Rapists" might measure as less than valueless to the victim.[3] Male or female victims of Aggravated Sexual Assault inside or outside of prisons are traumatized despite any intellectual personality labeling of the criminal attacker or attackers. Assuredly from the bottom-line perspective of TDCJ-ID, the whys that someone chooses to sexually exploit another person—violently or threateningly or profitably—is sufficient for a full-scale inquiry of the hard facts and collection of admissible evidence. And that comprehensive in-house investigation—often with outside Texas Ranger help—is initiated regardless any self-pitying pretexts and/or apologetic whining from the predator or his/her close at hand or faraway or purely theoretical therapist or any speculative sociologists. Sad to say, sometimes real world truths are downright ugly.

All TDCJ-ID prisoners are issued an *Offender Orientation Handbook*, and aside from the expected content about rules and regulations—the do's and don'ts—of penitentiary life, the constructive section regarding PREA is candid and graphic. For those not fluent in the English language, appropriate translation is provided. Additionally, as a part of their incoming familiarization with TDCJ-ID and its policies and procedures for addressing PREA issues, prisoners are mandated to view a professionally produced video.[4]

Employees of TDCJ-ID are not exempt from fastidious PREA training, but their tutelage is broader-based than that provided to convicts. Their blocks of pre-service instruction and ongoing Continuing Education curriculum address not only issues about how to prevent and/or report violations, but also taking the proper investigative and crime scene preservation steps as well. The 164-page *Correctional Officer Handbook* even enumerates—as a preventive step—possible psychological and obvious physiological character-istics that might tend to make a fish somewhat attractive for and somewhat susceptible to an egregious and aggressive Sexual Assault and/or pitiable sexual exploitation. Pre-identification is, indeed, a real worthwhile proactive measure.[5] The outlined and well-defined and after-the-fact PREA protocols are systematic and thorough: Ranging from securing professional medical and counseling and spir-itual help for sexually assaulted and/or sexually threatened victims, to identifying and interviewing and protecting potential witnesses.[6] In a nutshell all PREA investigations are approached from the per-spective that a very serious crime had taken place, not with skepti-cism that the allegations are intrinsically false on their face. Simply said, following facts and weighing evidence is the right course—and TDCJ-ID with regards to PREA is on the right track.

Sadly something else always on track in Texas prisons is the chance for a dangerous dustup. For whatever reasoning circulating in his brain—transferring to another job assignment is oft men-tioned—convict Travis Trevino Runnels, a twenty-six-year-old two-time recidivist, was doing seventy hard years for an Aggravated Robbery that took place in bustling Dallas County. He was agitated and aggressive, and his prison misconduct history reflected as much. Travis had previously been disciplined for drenching a Correctional Officer with urine; at a different time throwing a light bulb at an unsuspecting Correctional Officer. On a later occasion he threw feces at a Correctional Officer, an appalling act. In the idiom of prison speak it was colloquially called: "dressing up the Man."

At the Clements Unit in Potter County, he threatened to one keenly listening convict "that he was going to kill someone." To another prisoner, Travis predicted that he would be "shipped one way or another." He also remarked that he "planned to hold the boot-factory plant manager hostage in the office after the other correctional officers had left." Clearly—it would seem—big trouble was brewing.

Wholly unawares of the threats and looming thunderhead of aggression, thirty-eight-year-old Correctional Officer Stanley Allen Wiley, Supervisor of the facility's Boot and Shoe Factory, reported for duty that twenty-ninth day of January 2003. The gist of the story is gruesome but short. When Stanley Wiley arrived that morning, he was accosted by Runnels, apparently with blood on his mind and hatred in his heart. Correctional Officer Wiley didn't have a chance. The soon to be Murder defendant, with a knife in hand, simply "tilted Wiley's head back, and cut his throat." Then, taking a white rag, he wiped the blood from the knife, and went back to the "trimming tables" to await the next development. Another convict—seeing what had happened—queried Runnels about why he had viciously attacked Wiley. The answer was not incoherent: "It could have been any offender or inmate, you know as long as they was white."

Most correctly Stanley A. Wiley was white—and dead! At the hospital it was determined that the death cut "was a twenty-three centimeter long neck wound that transected the external carotid artery and the internal jugular vein and extended in depth to the spine." Meanwhile at the prison Travis Trevino Runnels told investigators: "I started boiling inside. It seems like my mind went on overload and I blanked out and started walking toward him. The next thing I know he was turning around looking at me with his hand on his throat with blood running down. I looked down at my hand and a knife was in it."

Sadly the TDJC-ID community—once again—mourned the loss of a coworker and friend. Correctional Officer Wiley was laid to rest in the Memorial Park Cemetery. Sometime later at Huntsville, Travis Trevino Runnels was lain to rest—for a little while—on the Death Chamber gurney inside The Walls: His repose was eternal. Though stunned and saddened, prison employees continued doing what they were paid to do—trying to protect society, themselves, and the convicts from harming each other. It was, always has been, and is a challenging practice for pocketing a paycheck.[7]

The following year would be bad, too! Although not classified as a Correctional Officer by job description, Ms. Rhonda L. Osborne,

thirty-three, performed important clerical duties at the aforementioned maximum-security Connally Unit. With a clean disciplinary
record inside the prison, convict Gary Laskowski, thirty-eight, was
beneficiary of a better work assignment; he was performing janitorial duties inside, no matter how damn hot or miserably cold it
was outside. Naturally such cushy labor meant that he would be
intermingling with Correctional Officers and civilian staff as they
went about their workaday duties. Whether or not Ms. Osborne
was aware of Laskowski's double convictions for Aggravated Sexual
Assault in Nueces County is not known. Unfortunately on the twenty-first day of October 2004 convict Gary—for whatever reason—in
an unguarded moment physically grabbed Ms. Osborne and dragged
her into a small storeroom. There, again, for whatever reason the
murderously assaultive convict strangled Rhonda Osborne to death.[8]
Shortly thereafter Laskowski killed himself, "by cutting his neck and
wrists with a sharp object." Convict grapevine speculation and runaway gossip, not unexpectedly, was rife that Laskowski's demise was
the result of prison employees' coldhearted and murderous revenge.
They were, quite expectedly, wrong! A TDCJ OIG and Texas Ranger
investigation, after careful analysis of evidence, concluded that the
tragedy was, indeed, a murder/suicide.[9]

Not unexpectedly, through challenging years of trial and error
and painstaking introspection, the Texas Department of Criminal
Justice has tweaked their formalized Mission Statement: "The mission of the Texas Department of Criminal Justice is to provide public
safety, promote change in offender behavior, reintegrate offenders
into society and assist victims of crime."[10]

Although it earns but short-shift appreciation in the majority of
academic and popular histories of the Lone Star State's penitentiaries
and overall administration of its penal system, today's official statement of purpose is packed with laudable goals of days long past. One
does not have to search too vigorously to spotlight early-on examples designed to better educate and improve the socialization and
employment prospects for convicts reentering the free-world. Many
of those creditable objectives—now touching three centuries—have

been mentioned thus far in this, admittedly, imperfect treatment. Trying to initiate positive change is seldom easy and most assuredly progressive thinking—ever evolving standards of human decency— is not a spanking new phenomenon. Likewise, one dynamic is applicable throughout the epic of Texas prison time: The foremost duty for the keepers of the kept, even today—in the enlightened twenty-first century—is set forth in the *Correctional Officers Handbook*:

> The primary responsibility of the Texas Department of Criminal Justice Correctional Institutions Division is to protect the citizens of Texas by maintaining custody and control of the offenders confined within the agency. Correctional personnel must make every effort to prevent offender escapes.[11]

Perhaps much to the chagrin of Judge William Wayne Justice's legacy vis-à-vis micromanaging Texas prisons, the Governor of Texas, Rick Perry, responding to citizens' outcry during 2005 signed into Lone Star law a LWP (Life Without Parole) statute. If Texans were a little queasy about killing convicts for their crimes, well, now they could just keep them locked up—forever! Naturally, there are two sides to this coin too. Certainly convicts locked away forevermore will be incapable of sparking any more free-world meanness; that's a given. On the other hand, as some academicians and administrators postulate, wholly removing the carrot from the end of the stick—cancelling a convict's hope—might produce in-house volatility. Fortunately, now perhaps in a somewhat sardonic thanks to the murderous "Bad Boy from Rosebud" the Texas parole laws and protocols now spin on an altogether different statutory axis: "parole for this and certain other offenses require a favorable vote from two-thirds of the entire eighteen-member Board of Pardons and Paroles, not a majority of a three-member panel like the one that released McDuff."[12] Criminal Justice—and its application—is ever evolving.

The convict with nothing to lose can be and sometimes is dangerous to other prisoners and/or staff. Practically speaking, be that as it may, the on-the-ground Correctional Officers are not awarded leeway to carry out their duties based on anyone's length of confinement. They are to treat everyone fair but firm, with consistency. Absent being able to maintain secure custody and reasonable control of convicted felons as sentenced by the courts, any and all other rehabilitative efforts—although definitely very well-meaning—ultimately and assuredly fall flat! Prison escapees, by their own furtive actions, give worldwide proof that they willingly choose to dodge reality and reliability—and forfeit any genuine respect. The dedicated and hard-working Correctional Officers, then, sometimes are truly the only safety valves plugging such perilous leakage from swamping a law-abiding society.

Sadly the morning of 24 September 2007 would once again mark tragedy for TDCJ-ID and once more confirms that in the scheming minds of some convicts, a Correctional Officer—man or woman—is fair game. At the Wynne Unit within Huntsville's city limits and adjacent to the incessantly busy I-45 Highway, Mounted Boss Joe Jeffcoat was carrying the No. 5 Hoe-Squad; one of four twenty-convict squads tending to agricultural chores. Particularly indentified will be two of the convicts under Boss Jeffcoat's watch. Convict Jerry Duane Martin, thirty-seven, was pulling fifty years at the Wynne Unit as a result of his involvement in a 1994 Collin County wild chase and shootout and standoff with North Texas lawmen. This was his second trip to the Texas penitentiary. Martin's coconspirator, also assigned to the No. 5 Hoe-Squad was forty-year-old John Ray Falk, Jr., a convict serving a life sentence due to a 1986 homicide conviction in Matagorda County (county seat Bay City). The Field Sergeant supervising the eighty-convict assemblage and other Bosses was Larry Grissom. And, then there was the ever vivacious and always adventurous fifty-nine-year-old Susan Louise Canfield, a seven-year TDCJ-ID veteran and a horsewoman of enviable and award-winning talent, armed with revolver and rifle, keeping the reasonable and predetermined distance as good High-Riders should do.

At 10:30 a.m. it turned Western in the onion patch. Convict Martin slyly masking his true intent, advised Boss Jeffcoat that he had accidently broken his wrist-watch, and asked if he would keep it for him until the Hoe-Squads returned to the Wynne Unit at noontime. Boss Jeffcoat acquiesced, allowing Martin to advance towards his horse, watch in hand. With his eyes and attention now focused on Martin—Boss Jeffcoat was unawares that convict Falk was sneaking up from the other side, until he heard a noise all too close. He turned his attention away from Martin and soon found himself battling to stay mounted as felon Falk was trying to push the toe of his boot out of the near-side stirrup. That split-second diversion allowed Martin to close the gap and grab the handle of Jeffcoat's holstered .357 Magnum revolver. Valiantly Boss Jeffcoat struggled to stay mounted and armed—but, in the end, was unsuccessful on both counts. During the fight for possession of the state's pistol, Martin was the winner—pitching the prize to Falk who knew who his target of opportunity next need be—that perceived "last line of defense," High-Rider Susan Canfield. Field Sergeant Grissom hollered for Boss Jeffcoat to get down, not to be standing upright in a field of fire—which, wisely, he did. Bullets were now flying.

The hottest fight was between courageous Canfield and frantic Falk, she ducking bullets and emptying her revolver, and then scrapping for balance to unsheathe the .223 caliber rifle in the saddle scabbard beneath her leg. The gyrations were vigorous, although Susan remained forking the saddle. With her revolver empty Falk closed the distance quick and with grit and meanness managed to wrest the rifle away from High-Rider Canfield. He then hotfooted to the nearby Huntsville City Service Center where Martin had luckily found the keys inside a municipal vehicle, a one-ton flat-bed pickup truck. Martin madly cranked the ignition and gunned the engine. Susan approached, fearlessly spurring Lucky toward sworn duty, not away from it—even though by this time she was wholly and helplessly unarmed except for her gutsy devotion to fellow Correctional Officers.

The only thing retarding the escape, getting the city truck out of the enclosed compound, was standing between the open cyclone-fenced gate and the revving engine. Susan Louise Canfield was committed—and brave. Jerry Duane Martin was callous and calculating, he popped the clutch, floor-boarded the accelerator and plowed into Correctional Officer Canfield and her horse. Susan was catapulted onto the truck's windshield and cab with a resounding thud, before she was involuntarily rag-doll vaulted to the concrete below, striking her head and closing her eyes for the solemn but now peaceful journey to the hereafter.

As if scripted for a thrilling action drama, Falk with Canfield's rifle in hand, leaped onto the truck and the getaway jumped into high-gear. Thrilling as the pursuit proved to be with exchanges of gunfire and commandeering an occupied red truck in a bank's drive-thru lane, a spinout on the busy Interstate, and chasing through the woods with Bloodhounds the manhunt ends— rather quickly. Falk was finally run to ground behind a Wal-Mart Discount Store—threw his hands up and surrendered: King's X! On the other hand, Martin's capture took a little longer—he having discarded all but his underwear in an effort to outwit the Bloodhounds, but in the end he was found sitting between branches of a tree, where tracking dogs couldn't reach and praying that lawmen's bullets wouldn't touch.

The news broke hard for TDCJ-ID. And even more so for Susan's husband, Charles, and their married daughter Kara Holub and son-in-law Allen, as well as living at home children Christian and Christepher—and grandchildren Trent and Jordon. At the Bernard G. Johnson Coliseum at Sam Houston State University, before hundreds of mourners, Chaplain Monty Montgomery eulogized the memorial service for Susan. Poignantly, Canfield would not be the last Correctional Officer to die at the hand of a convict—nor would she be the last prison system lady. Bubbly smiles and perky personalities were no indemnity from convict duplicity and treachery.

A window into Jerry Duane Martin's mindset is revealed in a letter to his brother, which is a part of the legal record. His justification for taking part in the killing of Correctional Canfield is not atypical—excuses are common—but might be vexing for some law-abiding free-world folks. With a light touch of editing for spelling, Martin wrote, in part:

> Well I'm sure by now that you have heard the news about my escape from the Wynne farm. I wasn't gone for more than a few hours until I was recaptured. There was a shootout with the police, a couple of high speed chases, and a death. You will never know the resolve, the desperate courage it took for me to wrestle an armed guard [Jeffcoat] off his horse—and take his gun away from him, while having three other armed guards on horses shooting at you. One of those three [Canfield] lost their life. . . . what other choice did I have? 25 years is a long-long time to do brother. I barely had 12 done and the next thirteen were overwhelming. I did only what was to be reasonably expected of me to do—win, lose or draw, I tried for freedom. I lost. I am a real outlaw brother. My prison record speaks of itself. Now I'm gonna die an outlaw's death.

Convicted killer Jerry Duane Martin was prophetic. He died an outlaw, executed by lethal injection after the Texas Court of Criminal Appeals sawed through a myriad of legal issues. Though it's now several years later, John Ray Falk, Jr. too has been scheduled to sufferer the ultimate penalty Texans had reserved for select folks with malice in their hearts and someone else's blood on their hands.[13] As of now (2019) he is housed on Death Row. Alas, the ever-gutsy Susan Canfield wouldn't be the last TDCJ-ID Correctional Officer to make that ultimate sacrifice in the twenty-first-century.

Thirty-four-year-old Correctional Officer Kellie "Big Pun" Peña, a seven year TDCJ-ID veteran and graduate of Wayland Baptist College, like his colleagues could not predict the future. Had he been so gifted and clairvoyant perhaps 19 August 2010 would have closed without any Texas Panhandle drama. Such wasn't in the cards. At the Neal Unit near Amarillo a convict bucked—refusing to exit his house as instructed. The intransigence was impermissible. After the verbal persuasion went for naught, a cell extraction was called for. Kellie Peña, accompanied by three cohorts, entered the convict's house to do what they had to do—temporarily evict him. During the ensuing struggle to restrain the convict, he "scrambled to his feet" and force-fully pushed Correctional Officer Peña to the floor. The pigheaded convict, as would be expected, was removed, but somewhat later and unexpectedly Kellie Peña was hospitalized—the hernia he suffered during the dustup required emergency surgery. The likable and well thought of Correctional Officer after the operation was transferred to a rehab facility for recuperation. Alas, while there several days later, 3 September, Kellie Peña suffered a massive and fatal heart attack—an unseen blood-clot the culprit.[14]

Though assuredly not 100 percent the case, the vast majority of convict on convict and convict on staff violence reveals an iden-tifiable perpetrator—a known culprit—a warm body warranting criminal prosecution—say, like the disagreeable prisoner men-tioned herein.

At the aforementioned Telford Unit in northeast Texas just below the Red River, with beds to accommodate 2,667 convicts and 675 Correctional Officers to oversee them, tragedy sprang forth on 15 July 2015. Correctional Officer II Timothy Allen Davison, for-ty-seven, no doubt presumed he would finish his assigned day shift and return home to Simms, south and slightly west of New Boston. Correctional Officer Davison—age wise was no rookie to life—but the divorced father of two had been with TDCJ-ID but eight months. Regrettably as he was escorting an Administration Segregation con-vict, Billy Joel Tracy, thirty-seven, from one secure area to another, the prisoner jumped tacky and began pummeling Correctional Officer Davison with the metal entry tool for opening the feeding slots in cell doors, which he had wrested away from his startled keeper. The unprovoked assault and resultant Murder were lastingly captured by a strategically placed and working surveillance camera—the reprehensible images preserved for posterity and prosecutors. This was, according to newspapers reports and prison records not the very first time that convict Tracy, a lifer, had assaulted Correctional Officers. At the Clements Unit near Amarillo on the twentieth day of November 2005, Billy Joel Tracy buried the blade of a shank into the back of Correctional Officer Katie Stanley—seven times! Then he unmercifully started stomping and kicking her in the head, before unsuccessfully attempting to pitch her over the third-tier railing. Thankfully she lived to testify. For this brutal assault Tracy caught forty-five years on top of his two life sentences plus twenty years for an Aggravated Assault and Kidnapping of a sixteen-year-old girl northeast of Dallas. Afterwards, while doing time at the previously mentioned Robertson Unit, Correctional Officer Brianlee Lomas was slashed with an in-house weapon fashioned from four razor blades, one cut dangerously near the victim's jugular. Thankfully he lived to testify. For this Aggravated Assault on a Correctional Officer convict Billy Joel Tracy bought another fifteen years hard time.[15]

The awful thumping that Correctional Officer Davison had suffered was severe, the bloodied injuries to his face and head not presenting a pretty sight. He was near unrecognizable as he was immediately transported to Christus St. Michael Hospital at Texarkana, where ER physicians and nurses had given it a mighty but unsuccessful try. Sorrowfully, once again a committed Correctional Officer had died. Billy Joel Tracy hasn't died—as of yet—though a Bowie County trial jury returned a verdict of *Guilty* and, shortly thereafter, sentenced him to pay the ultimate price by answering affirmatively questions about the likelihood of his future dangerousness.[16] As this is written (2019) the condemned convict is warily housed on Death Row at the Polunsky Unit.

That some hardened convicts can be blind to gender—with regards to Murder—was once again exposed northwest of Abilene in Jones County. Seven-year veteran Correctional Officer IV Marianne "Mari" (Vierra) Johnson, fifty-five, was conscientiously at her assigned post, the French Robertson Unit's kitchen that sixteenth day of July 2016. Though the categorical reason may be somewhat vague, the outcome is not. Around three o'clock in the wee morning hours the unconscious and unresponsive body of Officer Johnson was discovered in an adjacent storeroom. She was partially dressed and securely handcuffed to a stout metal fixture. CPR was to no avail. The obviously injured Correctional Officer was at once rushed to the Hendrick Medical Center at Abilene. Alas, Correctional Officer

Mari Johnson was DOA. Keeping with sound penitentiary protocols, Mari Johnson's death was treated—as would any deceased
Correctional Officer secured in tightened handcuffs—as a homicide;
a painstaking crime scene investigation and interrogations were initiated. Lending support to TDCJ-ID's Office of Inspector General
Investigator George Robinson, Jr. was another of the state's cracker-
jack lawmen, Texas Ranger Joshua Burson, Company C, stationed at
Abilene, company headquarters at Lubbock under the command of
Major Todd Snyder, later promoted to Assistant Chief of the Texas
Rangers. Also from Company C, meticulously handling evidentiary
duties relevant to the crime scene was Texas Ranger Danny Crawford,
now retired. The Medial Examiner ruled that Mari Johnson had
been brutally strangled and that she had as well suffered other internal injuries. Relatively shortly—three days later—the hard-working
and methodical sleuths had identified a viable suspect for the dreadful killing, Dillon Gage Compton, twenty-one, doing two-bits for an
Aggravated Sexual Assault of a Child out of Dallas County.[17]

For understandable security reasons convict Dillon Gage
Compton had been transferred from the Robertson Unit to the Allred
Unit near Wichita Falls. And it was there, during a videotaped interview, that he let his milk down (confessed) to killing Correctional
Officer Johnson, though he wasn't wholly truthful, upping incriminating inconsistencies immediately picked upon by Texas Ranger
Burson and OIG Investigator Robinson. Nevertheless the prosecut-
able case—from the admissible evidentiary standpoint—was solid
as concrete: Capital Murder charges were forthwith filed.[18]

Under the auspices of the Skyvue Funeral Home, the memorial
services were conducted at the First Baptist Church at Mansfield
(in Tarrant County). Peacefully, Mari Johnson the loving mother
of four and a devoted grandmother was laid to eternal rest. And
once again, aside from her near family, the TDCJ-ID correctional
community—statewide—mourned.[19]

Subsequent to the Grand Jury Indictment, Dillon Gage Compton
was officially prosecuted in the 259th District Court. The underpinning of his defense was that he and Correctional Officer Johnson

had been involved in an illicit affair—one that had gone on for quite some time. Naturally, according to Compton, he didn't intend to snuff the life out of Johnson, but only to choke her until she passed out so that he could get away before a unit employee found them together in the storeroom. In convict lingo he was trying to sell a hog. The jury wasn't buying! The scratch marks on his face, finger, and the steel shackles binding Correctional Officer Mari Johnson, and the fact the defendant didn't even know the murder victim's given-name despite their alleged long-term intimate involvement, apparently, were hard hurdles to overcome for any juror entertaining even a slight notion of acquittal. For their judicious take there was no question of Reasonable Doubt. Their verdict was *Guilty*. Their critical sentence was quick and absolute. Dillon Gage Compton caught the chain for Death Row and there, today (2019) at the storied Polunsky Unit he awaits his decisive date with destiny, whatever it may be.[20]

Certainly the untimely death of Correctional Officer Shana Renée Tedder, forty-one, cannot be labeled as a homicide—but it wasn't brought about by a freak accident either. Following an altercation—a confrontation with a female convict—in the Christina Melton Crain Unit at Gatesville, Officer Tedder complained of being short of breath. Shortly thereafter, while walking from one area to another, Shana Tedder unexpectedly collapsed. Paramedics were onsite quickly but their very best and first-rate professional efforts were futile. Correctional Officer Tedder had surrendered this life and was pronounced dead at the scene. Those who knew Shana were well aware that even a "Use of Force" conflict could not and would not have masked her normally "bubbly spirit and good sense of humor," so said a former Crain Unit co-worker, Sergeant Tanisha Woods, President of Local 3920 AFSCME. That clear-cut characterization was further cemented by the respectful remarks of the local chapter's Vice-President, Renee J. Rose: "She was always available to support her co-workers and was a dedicated, upbeat officer. . . . Her positive attitude was an inspiration to her co-workers and her union." Near unimaginable was the grief for Shana's daughter Tai, fifteen, and her step-daughter Precious Collins, thirteen, as well as her loving partner in life, Marjorie Collins. Once again family and friends and TDCJ-ID contemporaries would celebrate the life and mourn the on-duty loss of a devoted Correctional Officer as Shana Renée Tedder was peacefully laid to rest in her Bell County hometown at the Killeen City Cemetery.[21]

Though continually reeling off incidents wherein Correctional Officers and/or staff sacrificed their lives or suffered humiliation in the line of duty might ring of objectionable sensationalism, nevertheless, for this text the tales are true—and damn well illustrate the possible perils facing some of those folks selflessly doing what others turn down doing. And here too it's constructive to make the point: The blood and thunder aspects catch notice, interest, and readership, but there is a bottom-line truism. With thousands of dedicated Correctional Officers on the state's payroll the statistical chance—though it's never zero—of forfeiting one's life in the line of duty are exceptionally slight. But in many respects it's the spine-chilling and scary episodes that carry the narrative—even this one!

Supposing that as calendar pages unfold into the more enlightened milieu there is a cessation of the possibility of prison violence directed at Correctional Officers is intellectually imprudent. At the Ferguson Unit (in Madison County) a few miles up the road from Huntsville, on 13 November 2017, ugliness and criminality sprang forth from behind a schoolroom doorway. There, a twenty-five-year-old convict pulling thirteen years hard time for Burglary, had been secretly and lustfully lurking behind the door as other convict students, after completing assignments, exited the classroom. His textbook concealment, whether noticed or not by fellow prison pupils, went unreported to the dedicated female teacher. There were, at that time no classroom surveillance cameras and no Correctional Officers in close proximity. What happened next should not come as a surprise—even though it was premeditated evilness dressed in state-issued whites. The unsuspecting teacher was attacked, sexually assaulted, and then forsaken in the classroom to fend for herself physically and emotionally. Not surprisingly of course would be the fervent follow-up by OIG investigators and the formality of filing criminal charges of Aggravated Sexual Assault.[22]

Were one to surmise that 100 percent of the convicts housed at the Telford Unit had learned the underlying lesson issuing forth from the murderous assault on Correctional Officer Tim Davison they would be sorely mistaken. Convict Bryan Austin White, twenty-seven, was pulling a pair of concurrent twenty-five-year terms for Aggravated Robberies in Kaufman County, when he willingly bought more trouble—and hard time. During the first week of 2018 with an uncalled-for sucker-punch, he knocked the literal daylights out of Correctional Officer Kevin Squibb, rendering him unconscious with a concussion and in need of sutures for lacerations to his head. And as with the attack on Davison, Bryan White's striking Correctional Officer Squibb was captured on videotape—haunting evidence for any defendant trying to wiggle out of punishment.

Certainly the trial jury of nine women and three men were well aware of many details, including the fact mentioned by an astute and accomplished newspaper reporter that Kevin Squibb was a "man twice the age and half [the] stature" of the defendant. After the prosecution and defense rested and closing arguments were completed, attentive jurors retired for deliberation. They were out but thirty minutes. The verdict for an Aggravated Assault on a Public Servant was predictable: *Guilty!* In this instance the presiding Judge for the 102nd State District Court, Bobby Lockhart, was to decide what price Bryan Austin White would pay for his aggressive and violent misdeed. Though he could have caught more time, Judge Lockhart was not overly sympathetic: Forty-five years to serve, and that time stacked atop White's two concurrent Kaufman County sentences.[23]

What is not stacking up too favorably for TDCJ-ID is—apparently if newspaper reports and interviews are spot on—the wherewithal to keep the state's 104 prison units fully staffed. With the now (2019) booming Lone Star economy—especially in the oil and gas-rich Permian Basin of West Texas—the bottom-tier scale turnover rate for beginning Correctional Officers is, putting it mildly, dreadful:

After a 28% officer turnover rate and 14% vacancy figure raised red flags in late 2017, TDCJ Officials implemented a 12 % increase in starting pay and poured more than $9 million into $4,000-$5,000 hiring bonuses at a couple dozen particularly understaffed units. . . . Still by the end of 2018, turnover soared past 29%, and by April vacancy rates hit nearly 15%. . . . Initially, prison officials asked stare lawmakers for $169 million in extra funding for raised in the adult system. By the end of the legislative session, the agency ended up with half that—but was still enough to completely restructure the career ladder for more than 22,000 corrections officers.[24]

Although speaking of an earlier timeframe, a former Warden and now writer of prison lore and other relevant Brazoria County topics, captures part of the TDC-ID's recruiting dilemma in easy to read and easy to understand and, most importantly, insightful prose:

we received new officers every week. They would show up in groups of six or seven, in their new starched uniforms with the military creases all in place. I used to see them in the mornings waiting in the lobby outside the warden's office on their first day at work. It was customary for one of the sergeants to take them on a short unit tour before I invited them in for their orientation interview. Increasingly more and more of them didn't even make it through the tour. Sometimes, shortly after going through the control picket, and hearing the barred iron door to the main hallway slam shut behind them, panic would set in. In a moment of clarity, these wannabe correctional officers realized that not only were they locked inside of a place they couldn't get out of, but also discovered they were surrounded by convicted felons. After pleading with the sergeant to get back through the security door, they would go to the personnel office to turn in their I.D. cards and uniforms. When asked to give a reason for their abrupt termination of employment, most declined owing to the fact that they were in such a hurry to leave the unit, no doubt in search of a new, less ominous profession. . . . Many were so young they hadn't ever held a full time job. It was like holding school every-day. Sending some of those "kids" into a cellblock was like feed-ing Christians to the lions. Many of these bright-eyed new hires had no work ethic or sense of responsibility. The shift lieutenants complained of assigning new officers to post and then later finding them wandering around the building or playing checkers in some inmate's cell. Some were so scared they would come to work with knives hidden in their boots or under their uniforms. One young female came to work with a snub-nose .38-caliber revolver in her purse. . . . When asked why she brought the gun inside the unit she said, "I was scared." She was quickly advised that if she was that scared, she needed to find another way to make a living. Thankfully she agreed that working inside a male prison wasn't her calling and resigned. I hated to think about what could have happened if some convict had gotten hold of that gun.[25]

Although the episode didn't involve bullets, it comports with what the above cited troubled Warden discovered about an occasional new-hire. At the Ellis Unit—almost casually—a heavily tattooed Aryan Brotherhood member diffidently asked a new-boot Boss if he could just for a moment please borrow his lock-blade folding pocket knife—which at the time Correctional Officers were not actually prohibited from carrying. Foolishly the Boss—whether out of fear or timidity—acquiesced. Shortly thereafter the neophyte Boss asked the confirmed gangster to please return the knife and was told—unbelievably—no, he'd just keep it. Dismayed and scared the newbie Boss shrugged his shoulders and ambled down the run, weighing the wisdom of updating or not updating his shift Sergeant—which he opted, in the end, not to do. That inane decision provoked the deuc-ed-up fallout: The Aryan Brotherhood fellow killed a sworn enemy with the Buck knife, and the bewildered Boss was looking for a new employer.[26]

Exacerbating unending headaches for TDCJ-ID's office-bound executive administrators and the overworked front-line staff—some-what paradoxically—came to light as the completed manuscript for

Tall Walls and High Fences was submitted to the University of North Texas Press for publication: Coronavirus Disease 2019 (Covid-19), the unprecedented pandemic of 2020. Nightmarish consequences of the unforeseen state of affairs are easy to imagine, but at ground-level difficult to capably interdict, especially in a setting where protecting the public, TDCJ-ID employees, and prisoners is top priority while at the very same time not turning a blind eye toward security—keeping the kept where they are supposed to be in accord with courts' orders of confinement.

Understandably and appropriately, Texas prisons did not close down as the rest of the world was sidetracked by precautious reactions to the pandemic. Every day as they reported for duty thousands of Correctional Officers and civilian staff were screened for symptoms and elevated temperatures prior to entering facilities. Not just a few were sent home for temporary quarantine until absolute wellness was clearly indicated. Under such dire circumstances, complying with required security staff/prisoner ratios statewide was taxing. There is a finite personnel pool to draw from, no matter like-minded druthers that it be otherwise. Brand-new sanitization and sterilizing protocols were adopted and implemented. The system began manufacturing its own hand sanitizer—a necessary product but in short supply in the free-world. Within the system's industrial capabilities, the garment factories began producing surgical-type masks—20,000 per day—which all employees having contact with prisoners were mandated to don for their extended shifts.

Experienced prison employees well know changes in rules and regulations behind the tall walls and high fences can reap a devastating whirlwind. Most prisoners thoroughly dislike having daily routines interrupted. Nonetheless, for everyone's safety and well-being visitation by free-world family and friends was curtailed. Creating "social distance" zones within a penitentiary setting is challenging, particularly so when considering what was heretofore scheduled time in dining halls, recreation yards, and dayrooms. Movement between prison units was restricted, narrowed by necessity. In keeping with sound medical protocols an initial positive diagnosis for a prisoner required that he/she be totally isolated from other inmates until the malady ran its course—hopefully with minimal discomfiture for the afflicted person. For everyone's sake the free-world population was expected to exhibit unparalleled flexibility, suffering hardships while looking for light at the end of a metaphorical tunnel. Texas prisoners were not exempt. Most were not oblivious to the invisible lurking threat. Convicted felons no more want to acquire an infectious disease than non-lawbreakers.

Free-world folks might register surprise but seasoned prison personnel were not taken aback, though some newer hires might have naively supposed that in-place Grievance Procedures would have been the first stop for a few disgruntled convicts. While in the midst of the very real ongoing crisis, some prisoners opted to—with guidance from agreeable attorneys—file federal lawsuits alleging first one thing or another about supposed maltreatment. Whether or not any of the lawsuits have merit—in the final analysis—will be judgments made outside the tall walls and high fences by a black-robed District Court Judge wielding the gavel, or an Appellate Court overseeing the inherent wisdom or lack thereof in his/her decisions. As clearly spotlighted in this text, TDCJ-ID is no stranger to convict lawsuits.

Likewise, though there may have been a hiccup or two along the uncharted way, for getting a handle on Covid-19 and valiantly trying to protect prisoners and employees, TDCJ-ID in the authors' opinion warrant an A+ grade for effort and execution.

With that said, as herein previously highlighted, there are wonderful and widely varied meaningful career opportunities within TDCJ-ID. For those so inclined and willing to sacrifice on the front end—acquiring education and more education, experience and more experience, professionalizing—rewards on the back end are quite rich: Maybe not with overflowing buckets of greenbacks, but nevertheless rich with a sense of societal contribution and job satisfaction.[27]

There is—as with most hands-on Criminal Justice professions—an Oath of Allegiance, a solemn and serious pledge of workplace fidelity and *Tall Walls and High Fences* will close with that sworn to by TDCJ-ID Correctional Officers as they step into a new world:

> I do solemnly swear that I will faithfully execute the duties of a Correctional Professional for the great State of Texas. Through Courage, I will provide public safety. Through Commitment I will promote positive change in offender behavior. With Perseverance and Integrity, I will not be corrupted; I will not be manipulated; I will not be distracted from the agency's mission. I will adhere to the laws of the State of Texas and this agency's Code of Ethics. I will embrace our Core Values as I enforce the rules and regulation of the Texas Department of Criminal Justice. So Help Me.[28]

Appendix A
Fallen Heroes and Heroines

IN THE LINE OF DUTY MEMORIAM

Should there be any inadvertent omissions the authors apologize, deferentially kneeling—hats in hand.

James Monroe Butler	25 May 1882
George W. Taylor	15 March 1884
Israel S. Ewan	08 December 1887
Joe Epperson	29 April 1889
Benjamin Williamson	30 June 1890
Jesse F. Goodwin	14 July 1890
James Jackson	15 December 1890
H.D. Parsons	26 July 1898
Frank Miller	07 October 1899
Joseph P. "Joe" Wilkerson	23 April 1906
James Elliot	17 July 1908
John L. Wylie	22 April 1909
Charles E. Claiborne	09 August 1915
Walter Isaac Vandorn	12 August 1916
Dewitt Frisby Oliver	17 September 1921
Early Alabama Lott	27 March 1926
William M. "Will" Rader	22 July 1926
Deb Edward Long	02 February 1928
Henry Ward	27 July 1928
Sidney Albert Syms	29 September 1928
Tommy Mellie Starnes	11 June 1931
James B. "Jim" Sneed	06 July 1931
John Robert Hinson	03 November 1932
J.R. McCall	27 August 1933
Major Joseph Crowson	27 January 1934
Virgil "Verge" Welch	10 June 1935
Felix Smith	19 June 1936

George Washington Shiflett	08 December 1936
John Cleophus "Johnnie" Ford	04 October 1937
John R. Greer	27 August 1938
George Tyson Preston	20 June 1944
Benjamin Franklin Larue	22 November 1946
Guy Holman	29 June 1947
Charles Jesse Baker	21 July 1959
Bobbie B. "Dub" Bullard	06 June 1963
Robert Alexander Arrington	17 September 1971
George Alan May	17 September 1971
Nolan Buckhanan	14 June 1972
Julia "Judy" Standley	03 August 1974
Elizabeth Yvonne Beseda	03 August 1974
Edward Carter	31 May 1976
John B. Brown	18 July 1977
Cephus D. Burson	01 October 1980
Wallace Melton Pack	04 April 1981
Billy Max Moore	04 April 1981
Dalton B. Cawthray	05 January 1984
Robert A. Hunt	06 June 1984
Minnie Rene Houston	03 June 1985
Joe F. Gurney	12 August 1988
Sidney L. Lyons	19 November 1989
Stephen Glenn Stewart	07 January 1994
Timothy J. Parsley, Sr.	01 October 1996
Arthur B. Hanes, Jr.	14 November 1996
James Naum Dimanoff	14 October 1997
William Carl "Bill" Himstedt, Sr.	07 August 1998
Francisco F. Garza	31 May 1999
Wilmot Alfred Burnett	16 December 1999
Daniel James Nagle	17 December 1999
Stanley Allen Wiley	29 January 2003
John Murphy Bennett	17 July 2003
Rhonda L. Osborne	21 October 2004
Susan Louise Canfield	24 September 2007
Barbara Jean Leggett Shumate	13 June 2008
Ruben Hejl	19 May 2009
Kellie "Big Pun" Peña	03 September 2010
John T. Willhite	29 March 2011
Craig Allan Orrell	12 May 2011
Michael A. Jensen	02 June 2011
Phillip G. Hill	02 March 2012
Lorraine M. Quinn	10 May 2012

Jason A. Prosser	19 October 2012
Eligio R. Garcia, Jr.	14 January 2015
Christopher A. Davis	14 January 2015
Timothy A. Davison	15 July 2015
Mari Anne Johnson	16 July 2016
Shana Renée Tedder	09 June 2017

Appendix B

Talking the Talk

A PRISON GLOSSARY

Following is a small and, admittedly, incomplete listing of commonly used prison jargon:

AB Aryan Brotherhood (prison gang)

ABT Aryan Brotherhood of Texas (prison gang)

AC Aryan Circle (prison gang)

Ace-Deuce Good or best friend

Ad-Seg Administrative Segregation: Stringent cell confinement for security purposes

Aged Out Aging prisoner, one now with commonsense and an aversion to defiance

Aggie Long-handled hoe

All Day Life Sentence

Alice Baker Aryan Brotherhood (prison gang)

Amping Racing heartbeats

Archin' Male prisoners sculpting eyebrows to look like women

BA Barrio Azteca (prison gang)

Badge Correctional or Law Enforcement Officer

BATF Bureau of Alcohol, Tobacco, & Firearms (federal)

Bean Shoot Slot in cell door to accommodate food trays—and/or applying handcuffs

Beef Complaint or gripe

BGF Black Gorilla Family (prison gang)

Bid Times to prison and sentence ("His third bid was a dime for Burglary.")

Big Bitch Habitual Criminal Statute

Bitch Slap Striking someone with an open hand in lieu of a hard closed-fist punch

Black Box Hand Restraint Protector (protective device fitted over handcuffs)

Blind Location not normally observable by Correctional Officers or cameras

445

Blue Bag Four-ounce bag of Maxwell House coffee (a medium of exchange)

Blue Birds Prison busses with blue state emblem of Texas

Bonaroo Cleanest and best duds

Boneyard Institutional visiting area

Boof Contraband concealed in rectum

Boost Steal

Booster Antenna

BOP Bureau of Prisons (federal)

BOQ Bachelor Officers Quarters

Boss Correctional Officer—used by both offenders and staff—not derogatory

BOSS Chair Bodily Orifice Scanning System (chair for X-Ray type exam for contraband)

Boy-Girl Effeminate prisoner taking the female role in same-sex activity

Brick Carton of cigarettes

Broke Dick Elderly prisoner

Buck Refuse to do something

Building Tender (BT) Inmate with *quasi* authority over other prisoners

Bull-Dagger Female inmate assuming masculine role

Bullet One-year sentence

Bust a Cap Fire a gun

Bust a Cap in His Ass Shoot or shoot at a particular someone

Carry or Carrying Supervising convicts in their work assignments

Case Charged with violation of institutional rules

Cat Walk Overhead walkways between cell rows

Catch In Get to work

Catch Out Avoid work

Catch the Wall Instantly stop in hallway—against the wall—at direction of CO or to talk to CO

Cathead Large biscuit

Caught the Jesus Train Feigned or genuine rebirth as a Christian

CC Serving more than one sentence at same time—as opposed to stacked time

Cell Warrior Ready to fight until the cell door is opened

Cellie Cell mate

Chain Transportation to and from prison units

Chain Bag Orange mesh bag for carrying personal property when moved between units

Cheese Eater Snitch

Chester For Chester the Molester—a pedophile

Chock Illicitly distilled alcohol

CHOLO A conversational intermixing of English and Spanish words

Chow Food prepared at institutional kitchen

Chow Hall Institutional Dining Room

Chunking Throwing urine, feces, other bodily fluids, or food, at Correctional Officers

Click Up Affiliate with a gang

Clowning Belittling someone

CO Correctional Officer

Cold Shot Perception of unjust or unwarranted treatment/discipline

Commissary Institutionally sanctioned store

Convict Sense Ability to successfully survive within the convict subculture

COP Carry on Person—protective and debilitating chemical agents

Cop Out Admit to something

Count Routine tally of prisoners and there whereabouts

Crash Gate Strategically placed metal gates to isolate one area from another

Crawfish Back down

CRO Classification and Records Office

Crips & Bloods Black Prison Gangs

Cupcake Easily manipulated and/or male prisoner with feminine tendencies

DEA Drug Enforcement Administration (federal)

Deadline Fixed point of reference wherein crossing same allows COs to use Deadly Force

Debrief Dissociate from a validated prison gang and furnish relevant data to staff

Deck Package of cigarettes

Deuce Two-year prison sentence

Deuce it Up Walk abreast—in pairs

Dime Ten-year prison sentence

Dobie Biscuit

Dog Sergeant CO in charge of a unit's tracking dogs and Dog Boys (now, Kennel Sergeant)

Dog Boy Inmate assigned to care for tracking dogs (now, Kennel Attendant)

Donkey Dick Bologna

DPS Texas Department of Public Safety

Dress Up Chunking food, feces, urine, blood, vomit, etc., at Correctional Officer

Drive Up Brand-new prisoner and/or prison employee

Dropout Disassociate from prison gang—debrief to staff

Drop a Dime Snitch on someone

DRT Dead Right There

Dry-Cell Room with non-flushable toilet; used to recover keistered contraband

Dust Bull Durham tobacco

Ear Hustling Picking up small talk, gossip, future plans, and/or personal data about COs

Echo The Texas Department of Criminal Justice's offender newspaper

Eight Ball One-eighth of an ounce, typically referring to cocaine

EME Mexican Mafia (prison gang)

Fade the Heat Take the blame

Fall- Partner Fellow prisoner incarcerated for the same crime

FBI Federal Bureau of Investigation

FGM Former Gang Member

Field Boss Horseback CO overseeing squad of inmates outside prisons' wires or walls

Fish New prisoner or new Correctional Officer

Fishing Using improvised line to retrieve a kite

Flat Time Serving prison sentence day by day, no good time, no parole

Flip Turn informant

Flip Flopping Assuming both active and passive roles during homosexual activities

Flipping Tortillas Assuming both active and passive roles during homosexual activities

Food Loaf Compressed food to prevent chunking regular hot meals at COs

Free-World Outside the tall walls and high fences

Gassing Throwing feces, urine, spit, foodstuffs, etc. at CO

Gay for the Stay Interim homosexuality while imprisoned; chiefly a term used by female convicts

Gladiator School Units for first time offenders—young, foolish, ready to fight and show manhood

GP General Population

GRAD Gang Renouncement And Disassociation

Green Light Gang authorization to murder or take assaultive action

Green Money Actual U.S. Currency, as opposed to barter items from commissary

Grey Slave Correctional Officer

Grill see Crash Gate

Gunslinger Masturbates publicly within prison or in front of a specific female CO

Hack Correctional Officer (antiquated term)

Hard Candy Stabbing—sometimes with a purposefully unhygienic /contaminated shank

Has Heart Willing to fight or commit violence. Will not back-down

Head Running Talking too much and/or to the wrong person

Hermos de Pistoleros Prison Gang

High-Rider Outlying horseback CO with rifle watching over several Field Bosses and squads

Hit the Square Challenge to fight

Hoe Squad Group of convicts assigned to outside duties—supervised by a Field Boss

Hog Get something over on someone

Holding Possessing something (usually contraband)

Homeboy Convicts from same general neighborhoods in the free-world

Hooping Lubricating the rectum for insertion of contraband

Hot Seat Electric Chair

House Prisoner's assigned cell

HPL Hermanos Pistoleros Latinos (prison gang)

Hype-Kit Improvised needle and syringe

ICE Immigration and Customs Enforcement (federal)

In the Car Participation with others in some action, usually nefarious or illegal

In the Hat List of people inside or outside of prison subject to assassination by prison gang

Ink Tattoos

Institutionalized Unable or unwilling to function in the free-world, prefers prison life

Iron Pile Weight-lifting area

ITF Inmate Trust Fund

ITP Individualized Treatment Plan

Jack Book Erotic photographs and/or written text of sexually explicit nature

Jacket Convict's reputation, i.e., wearing a "snitch jacket." Also official rap sheet.

Jigger Lookout

Jocker Aggressive predator assuming male role for nonconsensual sexual acts

Johnny Ground Area where outside squads take their noontime meal and rest period

John Henry Noontime meal served to inmates in the field

Johnny Sack Sandwiches and fruit in a paper bag, served in the field or cell during lockdowns

Jonesing Initial stage of controlled substance withdrawal

Keister Rectum: Frequent hiding place for smuggling or storing contraband

Ketch In see Catch In

Killing Masturbating

Kite Illicit note passed from inmate to inmate. Can be note to CO from convict.

KOP Keep On Person (prescribed medications, medical items, identification card)

La Eme Mexican Mafia (prison gang)

Lay-In Excuse/Permission not to report to assigned work or programming activity

Lead Row Fastest working prisoner in an outside squad

Let His Milk Down Relaxed/Confessed

Line Force Convicts turned out for agricultural work under supervision of Field Boss

Lockdown Prisoners are locked in their cells

LWP Life Without Parole

Mad-Dog Stare/Glare at someone with a threatening and/or menacing expression

Mainline General Prison Population—as opposed to STG, PC, or medical placement

Man Correctional or Law Enforcement Officer

Mandingo Warriors Prison Gang

Mark Convict or Correctional Officer susceptible to being duped—buying a hog

Max Out Full discharge of prison sentence, no half-way house, no parole

MM Mexican Mafia (prison gang)

MEXIKANEMI Texas: Mexican Mafia

MO *Modus Operandi*

Monster HIV

Mud Coffee

Mules Smugglers

New Boot Rookie Correctional Officer

Nickel Five-year prison sentence

Ninga Turtles Cell Extraction Team and/or prison SORT personnel

Nuestro Carneles Prison Gang

ODR Officers Dining Room

OIG Office of Inspector General

OMG Outlaw Motorcycle Gang

On the Bricks The free-world

Overhaul Antiquated term for illicit physical abuse, more rigorous than a tune-up

Paid Man Correctional Officer or Jailer

Patch Gang insignia (can be a gang affiliation tattoo)

PC Protective Custody

Peckerwood Hill Prison cemetery at Huntsville (now The Joe Byrd Memorial Cemetery)

Peckerwoods Anglo (white) inmates

Pencil Whipped Repeated disciplinary write-ups

Picket Fixed location

Piddle Working on handicraft items; leather, jewelry, woodworking, etc.

Piddle Shop Particular work area with tools where certain inmates are privileged to piddle

Piece Gun

Pill Window Medical prescription dispensary (pharmacy)

PIP Point Incentive Program

Pirate Steal

Pouring it out, Boss In the field, asking for permission to urinate

PREA Prison Rape Elimination Act

Predator Preys on other prisoners for economic, sexual, or psychological gain

Prisneyland Penitentiary System and/or unit with a reputed tranquil environment

Prison Jewelry Handcuffs, leg-irons, belly-chains, etc.

PRM Partido Revolucionario Mexican (prison gang)

Prisonization Acquiring values, norms, and attitudes of the convict subculture

Programming Participation in self-betterment programs: school, AA, Toastmasters, etc.

Pruno Illicitly fermented alcohol

Punk A prisoner who easily bends to physical and/or psychological exploitation

Punk One who allows himself to be taken advantage of sexually (second meaning)

Queen Homosexual inmate; by choice assuming the female role in sexual activity

Rabbit Escape Risk

Rack To open or close

Rack-Up Locked in cells

RAPO Rapist

Ready-Mades Manufactured cigarettes, not hand rolled

Recreate Acting out, creating disturbance, assaulting CO—with intent to relive boredom

Red Heifer see, Bat

Red Whiskey Tax-paid spirits, not illicitly distilled, but not legally possessed in prison

RICO Racketeering Influence and Corrupt Organization (federal statute)

Ride Trade sex, items, or services, to inmate for protection from other inmates

Riding Bitch Riding behind the operator of a motorcycle

Ride the Lightening Electrocution in the state's electric chair (prior to lethal injection)

Road Dog Friend

Roscoe Gun

RU Raza Unida (prison gang)

Run Hallways

Run the Gears Stab in chest; then move shank up, down, back up—as if shifting gears

Run Warrior Brave Correctional Officer—until the cell door is opened

Running a Store Illicitly dealing in commissary or contraband items

SAFE Sexual Assault Forensic Examiner

SAFPF Substance Abuse Felony Punishment Facility

SANE Sexual Assault Nurse Examiner

Sap Improvised bludgeoning weapon, i.e., a padlock or rock in a sock

SAT State Approved Trustee

SCC State Classification Committee

Screw Correctional Officer (antiquated term)

Searcher's Desk Unit's Central Control Picket where routine convict traffic is monitored

Self Defense Family Prison Gang

Selling a Hog Getting something over on someone

Set Small group of convicts from same neighborhood (not necessarily a gang)

Shakedown Search for illicit materials, drugs, escape plans, and/or weapons, etc.

Shank Knife or other sticking weapon illicitly fashioned by an inmate

Shark Prisoner cruising for sexual outlet

Shitter Holdover term for solitary confinement, before punishment cells had toilets

Shiv Shank or sharpened weapon—contraband item

Short Nearing release date

Short Eyes Pedophile

Shot Incident or disciplinary report

Shot-Caller Gang member with authority to issue orders to others

SHU Security Housing Unit (Administrative Segregation)

Sissy Shank Razor blade inserted into melted end of toothbrush handle

Slow Buck Not actually refusing to work, but feigning hard work—Dragging one's feet.

Snap Smart; has good sense

Snitch Inform on other inmates' plans and activities or past crimes

Spread Generally, food items purchased at commissary but consumed in cell

Soak To pawn or hock an item

SORT Special Operations and Response Teams

Square Cigarette

Square Dude An honest person

SSI Support Services Inmate

Stacked Separated sentences. Must do time for one crime first, then start over with next

STG Security Threat Group

Stinger Narrow electrical heating rod placed in coffee cup or soup can, etc.

Store Inmate's personal items from commissary

Store Bought Legally manufactured in free-world, not improvised substitute

Swole Up Angry—mad—pouting—whining

SWP Tattoo—Supreme White Power

TABC Texas Alcohol Beverage Commission

Tag Gang insignia and/or tattoo

Tail Row Second best squad worker: others keep pace between Lead Row and Tail Row

Tailor Mades Free-world manufactured cigarettes—as oppose to hand rolled

Taking the Hot Squat Electrocution in the state's electric chair (prior to lethal injection)

Tango Prisoners of same race, from same town

Tank Penitentiary open housing or holding area—no individual cells—a dormitory

Tax Payments to gangs for okay to deal in illicit behaviors; drugs, tobacco, sex, etc.

TB Tango Blaster (prison gang)

TDC Texas Department of Corrections

TDCJ Texas Department of Criminal Justice

TDCJ-CID Texas Department of Criminal Justice—Correctional Institutions Division

TDCJ-ID Texas Department of Criminal Justice—Institutional Division (customary usage)

THP Texas Highway Patrol

Thump Therapy Correctional Officer illicitly striking a convict

Ticket Write up for rules violation

TMM Texas Mexican Mafia (prison gang)

The Brand Aryan Brotherhood (prison gang)

Tip Small—usually two or three—prisoners associating with each other (not a gang)

TM Texas Mafia (prison gang)

TPR Texas Prison Rodeo

Travel Card Convict's in-house prison history, accompanies him/her from unit to unit

Tripping Irrational behavior

TS Texas Syndicate (prison gang)

Tune-Up Antiquated term for unauthorized physical discipline action, minor in nature

Turn Key Person with capability of opening and closing, locking or unlocking entryways

Turnout Typically a convict forced into a nonconsensual sexual role

Tush Hog Exceptionally tough or mean prisoner

U.A. Urine Analysis

USA United States Attorney

USM United States Marshal

VOD Victim/Offender Dialogue

Whack Murder

White Shirt Non-Correctional Officer staff, i.e., councilors, teachers, nurses, etc.

White Whiskey Non tax paid, illicitly distilled

Wigged Out Oddball or irrational behavior

WISD Windham Independent School District

Wolf Sexually aggressive convict predator

Woodpile Areas where the Peckerwoods (Anglos) congregate

Writ-Writer Inmate challenging the institution through repeated legal filings; assists others

Yard Recreational area for general population prisoners

Yoke Strangulation

Yo-Yo Handheld weed cutting implement

Zigs Cigarette rolling papers

Zip Gun Crude device capable of discharging a fixed cartridge; typically a single-shot

Notes

Preface and Acknowledgments

1. Ben M. Crouch, ed., *The Keepers: Prison Guards and Contemporary Corrections*. For an interesting and insightful glance at this, the fictional movie phenomenon, see Chapter 4, "Prison Guards in America—The Inside Story," by Edgar May, pp. 111–137.

2. Jay Hyams, *The Life and Times of the Western Movie*, 190: "Thanks to the salesmanship of dime-novel authors and Wild West show promoters, the facts of the old West are inextricably blended with the legends of the old West, leaving filmmakers free to interpret the West according to their own lights. It is not surprising that the old West as seen through the eyes of the 1970s was the scene of urban blight, racism, sexism, imperialism, homosexuality, drug addiction, wanton violence, and loneliness. The only western heroes during the seventies were the mountain men in children's movies who got away from it all and befriended bears; everyone else out West was tainted, a progenitor, through degeneracy, of modern despair."

3. Roger Jay, "The Peoria Bummer," *Wild West*, August 2003; William B. Shillingberg, *Dodge City: The Early Years, 1872–1876*, 170; Leon Claire Metz, renowned nonfiction writer and past president of the Western Writers of America, postulates in *The Shooters*: "In truth, historians are not certain if Earp was a bona fide frontier Paladin, or a scoundrel with a clever biographer. Right now the evidence leans toward the latter assessment." See p. 270. The well-known and well-respected Frederick Nolan, *The Wild West: History, Myth and the Making of America*, frankly declares: "An almost forgotten relic of the old frontier. . . . Fueled first by books then movies, and later television, Wyatt Earp—a man who was never more than a deputy sheriff or an assistant marshal—was transformed into the most famous lawman of the frontier West. Controversy still swirls around his name and life. Was he a saint or sinner, a rugged frontiersman or a sly opportunists, a pimp and crooked gambler or an incorruptible lawman, a small time peace officer or a mendacious fabulist?" See p. 139. Lynn R. Bailey and Don Chaput, *Cochise County Stalwarts: A Who's Who of the Territorial Years*, Vol. 1: "Yet, in spite of the little time there, the Earps, Tombstone, and Cochise County have become linked forever in probably the most classic saga of gunfighters, frontier duels, and shootouts.

There is considerable irony here. Wyatt Earp, due to literature, movies, and television, has become the 'leader' of the Earps, but only in the Twentieth Century, not in history. And, irony of irony, Wyatt Earp, the most well-known shootist or gunfighter in America's past, was never in a man-on-man gunfight or duel. In fact, it cannot be demonstrated historically that Wyatt Earp ever killed a man. It is true that because of his presence (the famous shootout; the Tucson rail yard, etc.) certain dead bodies were found, but how they were killed and by whom has never been established with certainty. This is indeed a lamentable record for America's premier 'gunfighter,'" 114. Peter Brand, "10 Earp Vendetta Ride Myths." "The 1950s heroic myth of Wyatt and his men cleaning up the wild frontier was not popular in 1882. At the time, Earp and his men were not universally viewed as deputized lawman [sic] upholding the law, but rather as vigilantes carrying out personal vengeance. . . . As multiple posses dog their trail, Wyatt Earp and his handpicked avengers decide to make a run for safer climes and head out of Arizona Territory, following the Southern Pacific Railroad Tracks into New Mexico Territory." *True West*, April 2018, 36–37; Bob Boze Bell, "The Case Against Wyatt Earp." "March 1882, The Vendetta Ride: Wyatt Earp and his vendetta posse shot and killed an unarmed Florentino Cruz because Wyatt believed he was 'Indian Charlie,' the paid lookout in Morgan Earp's assassination. No proof that Florentino Cruz was, in fact, Indian Charlie has ever been found." *True West*, February 1999, 21; *The New Southwest & Grant County Herald*, April 22, 1882. For a cogent geographical and historical analysis of Wyatt Earp and cronies assuming phony names and slithering out of Arizona Territory and into New Mexico Territory ahead of authorities and in due course rendezvousing with organized crime figure Lou Blonger at Albuquerque, see Jan Devereaux's credible *Pistols, Petticoats, & Poker: The Real Lottie Deno, No Lies or Alibis*. 190–195.

4. The interested reader wishing to explore the nefariousness of this crime duo might wish to access Paul Schneider's *Bonnie and Clyde: The Lives Behind the Legend* and Jeff Guinn's *Go Down Together: The True, Untold Story of Bonnie and Clyde*. Also, John Neal Phillips, *Running with Bonnie and Clyde: The Ten Fast Years of Ralph Fults*; and see, John Boessenecker's *Texas Ranger: The Epic Life of Frank Hamer, The Man Who Killed Bonnie and Clyde*. And herein it is only fair—as with the Wyatt Earp gunplays—to mention that when multiple people are letting multiple bullets fly, absent competent ballistic comparisons, precisely knowing just who killed who is speculative, not conclusive; Bob Boze Bell for his piece in the January 2019 edition of *True West* places the number of lawmen killed by Bonnie and Clyde at nine. See p. 42.

5. Henry C. Parke, "The Man Who Redeemed the Hamer Name," *True West*, January 2019. This is a fascinating article in a popular magazine format, with regards to screenwriter John Fusco's "pledge to set the record straight on the takedown of Bonnie & Clyde," 46–47.

6. Robert M. Utley, "The Forgotten Hero," *True West*, April 2019: "Sheriff Henderson Jordan, however, was the true architect of the scheme [to put Clyde and Bonnie on the spot]. He located the hideout, received the offer of betrayal from Henry Methvin's emissary and organized the ambush. Hamer is entitled to credit for acting as a messenger to Governor Ferguson and for participating with the five others of the posse in gunning down the fugitives. He did not track down Bonnie and Clyde." See pp. 34–37.

7. Robert M. Utley, *Lone Star Lawmen: The Second Century Texas Rangers*, 162–163.

8. Tony Rafael, *The Mexican Mafia*, xiv-xv.

9. In his seminal analysis Professor James A. Inciardi, *Criminal Justice*, confirms: "Prison guards, more currently referred to as correctional custodial officers, work in a maligned profession. Guarding is considered a tainted occupation because people find the surveillance and repression that are characteristic of prison life to be repugnant. The popular media are in large part responsible for creating and sustaining this image. Contemporary cinema and television dramas have portrayed the correctional officer as evil and savage. Late-night TV movies such as *The Big House* (1930), *White Heat* (1949), *Inside the Walls of Folsom Prison* (1951), *Birdman of Alcatraz* (1962), *Cool Hand Luke* (1967), and *Chain Gang Women* (1971), to name but a few, have shown prison guards as bigoted, corrupt, brutal, and morally base. More recently, The Earle Owensby films of the 1970s and *Escape from Alcatraz* in 1978, have continued the tradition. Segments of the prison literature, particularly those that have appeared as emotional statements against the prison system—such as Eldridge Cleaver's *Soul on Ice* and George Jackson's *Soledad Brother*—have also presented the prison guard in a most negative way," p. 538. Though writing of the popularized champions of the Wild West era, Kent Ladd Steckmesser with analytical acuity in *The Western Hero in History and Legend* posits what may very well be moved over to the popular portrayals of prison personnel on the Silver Screen: "The historian's ruthless quest after truth frequently mars the beauty of a perfected legend. Such heartless destruction of cherished myths is quite unpopular in some quarters. . . . Yet the people also have a right to know whether they are reading fact or fiction, and the historian has a responsibility to draw the line which separates the two." See pp. 249–52.

10. John Irwin, *Prisons in Turmoil*, 128.

11. Jack Henry Abbott, *In the Belly of the Beast: Letters from Prison*, 7.

12. John E. Conklin, *Criminology*: "No more that 1 or 2 percent of all serious crimes lead to the imprisonment of an offender, but most people who commit many crimes eventually end up in jail or prison. Prison sentences probably deter some people from crime, but the certainty of punishment is low in the present-day United States." 462; Steve J. Martin and Sheldon Ekland-Olson, *Texas Prisons: The Walls Came Tumbling Down*. Within the Foreword

of this heavily detailed and learned legal analysis, Harry M. Whittington posits, among other comments, despite what many folks might presume, that it is but a small percentage of criminals that actually find residence behind the tall walls and high fences. See page ix. James R. Parrish, a former teacher in the Texas Prison System's Windham School District, cites an example in his attention-grabbing *Two-Headed Monster: Crime And Texas Prisons*, wherein one of his incarcerated students, a confirmed and self-declared "dope dealer" had been given three probated sentences before catching his first trip to prison. 7.

13. Rebecca Trammell, *Enforcing the Convict Code: Violence and Prison Culture*, 11. During a most insightful interview with retired TDCJ-ID Regional Director Tony O'Hare on 12 September 2019, any inane blanket assertion that Texas Correctional Officers might be "lazy" was lucidly dispelled by employment of unpretentious logic and simple arithmetic. Within the Lone Star State there are 104 TDCJ-ID units, housing some 140,000 convicts. As former upper-tier administrator O'Hare rightly points out, the sheer numbers of prisoners fosters mindboggling numbers. Three meals a day are prepared for those thousands of convicts and three times a day they undergo movement to and from dining halls. Just those three secure movements times 140, 000 computes to but part of the daily activities. Convicts must be "racked" several times per day for mandatory headcounts. They, too, must undergo movement in safety to work assignments and education classes and showering and recreation, and visitation etc. Yes, at least in Texas, tagging Correctional Officers as "lazy" is fallacious—even if done by a convict trying to con an academician. In a precise one sentence thrust Professor Lee H. Bowker in *Prison Victimization* cuts to the bone: "Many prisoners have attitudes toward correctional officers that are intensely negative—negative enough to support overt action against those whom they consider to be their oppressors." See p. 130.

14. John J. DiIulio, Jr., *Governing Prisons: A Comparative Study of Correctional Management*. This insightful and exceptionally well written exploration, as the title suggests, dissects the prison management philosophy utilized in three state correctional systems, Texas, Michigan, and California. The distinctions are enlightening.

15. Bruce Jackson, ed., *Wake Up Dead Man: Afro-American Worksongs from Texas Prisons*, 15.

16. Here the term "Big House" is used with its common connotation. Colloquially and conversationally the Big House is the prison. Although academicians sometimes make a distinction between the Big House and other custodial architectural or functional blueprints for incarceration of felons, herein the Big House and prison and penitentiary are analogous. For the more precise, perhaps, definition, the interested reader may wish to peruse Robert

Johnson's *Hard Time: Understanding and Reforming the Prison*, 40–46. Also see the first two chapters in Irwin's, *Prisons in Turmoil*.

17. Lon Bennett Glenn, *Texas Prisons: The Largest Hotel Chain In Texas*, 4; Ethan Hoffman and John A. McCoy, *Concrete Mama: Prison Profiles From Walla Walla*, 45.

18. Hans Toch, *Living in Prison: The Ecology of Survival*, 6.

19. Jorge Antonio Renaud, *Behind the Walls: A Guide for Families and Friends of Texas Prison Inmates*, xiii. Not surprisingly Glenn, *Texas Prisons*, regarding prisoners attempts to buy freedom with a knife to a hostage's throat, is crystal clear and, practically so, citing [or paraphrasing] the words posted at most Texas prisons:

> In the event any officers or employees have been seized as hostages, no officers or employees on duty shall disregard, alter, modify or change in any manner the prescribed duties, obligations, or responsibilities of their position on demand by the prisoners, or plea from the hostages, regardless of the consequences.

Not mincing words Glenn amplifies the message: "The ominous warning to all entering into TDC [now Texas Department of Criminal Justice, Correctional Institutions Division: TDCJ-CID, routinely referred to as simply the Institutional Division] units is a written-in-stone policy and means exactly what it says. There will be no exceptions granted. Inmates will not be released in exchange for hostages, not even if the hostages are the governor, the TDC director, the unit warden, visitors to the unit, or any group of male or female employees. Anyone who is contemplating entering a TDC unit for any reason, even to visit, should seriously consider the possible implications of the warning. Once inside a unit, it is too late," 195. Also see, Ruth Massingill and Ardyth Broadrick Sohn, *Prison City: Life with the Death Penalty in Huntsville, Texas*, 159, 161: This sign reads, "NO HOSTAGE WILL EXIT THIS FACILITY/ SECUESTRADOS NO SALDRAN DE ESTA FACILIDAD."

20. Mark S. Fleisher and Jessie L. Krienert, *The Myth of Prison Rape: Sexual Culture in American Prisons*. "Generally speaking, a lexicon provides as much cultural and social information as possible so that a careful study of a lexicon would be a partial ethnographic study of a culture or a specialized domain of behavior and meaning within a culture. A lexicon is more than a vocabulary list for common terms in a language. . . . A lexicon provides a broader cultural and semantic perspective on a language's terminology, which necessarily includes denotative and connotative meanings and variations in meanings. . . . A lexicon's words and expressions include those uttered by one, several, tens of dozens, or hundreds of inmates." See p. 141. During an insightful 15 October 2019 interview with Kathryn M. Lloyd, Sales Manager, Texas A&M University Press, and an authoritative specialist with regards to linguistics,

she confirmed the value and practical applications of recognizing subcultures' vocabularies and speech patterns.

21. Gary Brown, *Texas Gulag: The Chain Gang Years, 1875–1925*, quoting prisoner Bill Mill's *25 Years Behind Prison Bars*, 131.

22. Robert M. Bohm and Keith N. Haley, *Introduction to Criminal Justice.* "In many ways, an incarceration facility is like a miniature society within the larger society. Institutions have many of the same features as the wider society. . . . ," page 380. The massive logistical and mechanical problems faced by TDCJ personnel were brought to the forefront during a constructive and edifying personal 25 October 2019 interview with long-time TDCJ employee Richard Martin, a former Correctional Officer but now a Telecommunications Specialist charged with maintaining the systems' communications network throughout a gargantuan geographical territory and its multitude of individual Texas prison units. The technical issues and travel requirements of Mr. Martin's duties are mindboggling. At the same time he deals with technological problems, he can never turn a blind-eye to security matters. After all, he works in a prison setting where watchfulness is smart.

23. Ibid. The authors' nutshell definition of penology is: "The study of prison management and the treatment of offenders." See p. 352.

24. Austin MacCormick, "Behind Those Prison Riots," *Reader's Digest*, December 1953, 97–101.

25. Larry J. Siegel, *Criminology*, 581–582.

26. Renaud, *Behind the Walls*, 127.

27. Daniel Lockwood, *Prison Sexual Violence*, 33 and 38. Historian and writer Michael Koch, who retired after thirty-four years with the Oklahoma Department of Corrections, confirms, noting that some of the worse and most violent criminals in the prison system (cop killers, murderers, armed robbers), garner the lion's share of respect from their felonious comrades. Koch to Alexander, 8 November 2018.

28. William L. McWhorter, *Inmate Society: Legs, Half-Pants and Gunmen, A Study of Inmate Guards*, 83.

29. *Houston Chronicle*, November 15, 2017 and February 2, 2018, bylines Keri Blakinger.

30. *USA Today*, April 16, 2018; *The Kansas City Star*, April 16, 2018.

31. *David Ruiz et al, v. W.J. Estelle, Jr.* 503 F.Supp. 1265 (S.D.Tex. 1980). From the Memorandum Opinion as written by Chief Judge William Wayne Justice, Eastern District of Texas. Special note: The case had been transferred from Tyler and was tried at Houston.

32. Dick Reavis, "How They Ruined Our Prisons," *Texas Monthly*, May 1985; Albert Race Sample, *Racehoss: Big Emma's Boy*, himself at one-time a Texas penitentiary resident at the Retrieve Unit in Brazoria County, spotlights another

incident when fellow occupants doused someone with lighter fluid and ignited the combustible wetness with a tossed lit cigarette. See pp. 186–187.

33. *Dallas Morning News*, April 8, 1981.

34. Enumerations of some of the State of Texas prison employees killed in the line of duty may be accessed by reviewing Clifford R. Caldwell and Ron DeLord's two volume treatment, *Texas Lawmen: The Good and the Bad, 1835–1899* and *Texas Lawmen: More of the Good & the Bad, 1900–1940*. Also see, Program for The Thirteenth Biennial Texas Peace officers' Memorial Services, May 1–2, 2011, Texas State Capitol, Austin, Texas. And, Ronald G. DeLord, ed., *The Ultimate Sacrifice: Trials and Triumphs of the Texas Peace Officer*. Several of these horrific assaults and murders of correction employees will be covered reasonably extensively as this narrative unwinds. Supplementing that the prison setting can prove dangerous, is also easily confirmed by examining the similar workplace environment in the Land of Enchantment as catalogued by Don Bullis, *New Mexico's Finest: Peace Officers Killed in the Line of Duty, 1847–2010*, 4th ed. For a nationwide numerical snapshot of Correctional Officers assaulted or killed in the line of duty, see, Dan M. Reynolds, *On the Other Side of the Bars: Lessons Learned as a Prison Warden/Administrator*, 229.

35. Interview with Captain West Gilbreath, Criminal Investigation Division, University of North Texas Police Department, 4 April 2018. Early in his law enforcing career—as an eighteen-year-old—Captain Gilbreath was an entry-level Correctional Officer at the Retrieve Unit, Brazoria County. Some of his experiences and perceptions will be highlighted hereafter, as the text unfolds. In his current role as Criminal Investigation Commander at UNT PD, Captain Gilbreath noted that over the course of years he has investigated felony criminal violations whereas the perpetrators were professors—and thereafter filed charges on same resulting in custodial prison sentences. Captain Gilbreath advised that those felony investigations, indictments, and prison sentences included such felony criminal offenses as manufacture and delivery of methamphetamine; embezzlement of public funds; and on more than one instance wherein the college professors were imprisoned for "buying, trading, [and] downloading child pornography." College campuses are but a microcosm of the broader society, populated by the good and the bad. Captain West Gilbreath to Bob Alexander, 11 April 2018. The aforementioned Michael Koch clearly corroborates: Particularly highlighting that during his lengthy penitentiary career he professionally dealt with "an ex-mayor, a priest, and a sheriff from Missouri," all having been imprisoned upon felony convictions. Specifically, Mr. Koch commented that "They were all denied parole. The priest was eventually killed by other inmates while in the shower." Koch to Alexander, 8 November 2018.

36. Fleisher and Krienert, *The Myth of Prison Rape*, xiii.

37. Thomas E. Hogg, *Life and Adventures of Sam Bass: The Notorious Union Pacific and Texas Train Robber*. 68–69. The original copy of this treatment—on its face—is not identified by author. However, prominent Old West bibliophile Ramon F. Adams in *Burs Under the Saddle: A Second Look at Books and Histories of the West*, identifies the writer of an 1878 edition published by Dallas Commercial Steam Print as Thomas E. Hogg, "a member of one of the many posses which chased Bass all over Denton County," 252–253. Original of the 1878 edition courtesy the always helpful Tobin and Anne Armstrong Texas Ranger Research Center, Texas Ranger Hall of Fame & Museum (TRHF&M), Waco, Texas. Also see, Ramon F. Adams, *Six-Guns and Saddle Leather: A Bibliography of Books and Pamphlets on Western Outlaws and Gunmen*, entry 1001.

38. Renaud, *Behind the Walls*, 2.

Chapter 1: "Punishment of the refractory"

1. Charles H. Harris III and Louis R. Sadler, *The Texas Rangers in Transition: From Gunfighters to Criminal Investigators, 1921–1935*: "Texas also remained a violent place. You just never knew when you might run into somebody who needed killing. Disputes often ended in violence. . . ." 4; Richard Maxwell Brown, *No Duty to Retreat: Violence and Values in American History and Society*, 26; T.R. Fehrenbach, *Lone Star: A History of Texas and Texans*: "The old *code duello* brought across the Sabine fell into disuse, but the newer code of the West took its place. The informal, but no less bloody, duel in which the participants gave notice, drew, and shot it out. . . . was not recognized by the law as dueling, but as self-defense.. . . . It had the stamp of public approval, if a man went armed, he was expected to be able to defend himself." See p. 570.

2. Barry A. Crouch and Donaly E. Brice, *The Governor's Hounds: The Texas State Police, 1870–1873*, 76.

3. Chuck Parsons and Marianne E. Hall Little, *Captain L.H. McNelly, Texas Ranger: The Life and Times of a Fighting Man*, quoting the *Houston Daily Telegraph* of December 18, 1870, p. 72.

4. Henry W. Graber, *The Life Record of H.W. Graber: A Terry Texas Ranger, 1861–1862*, 333–334.

5. Gregg Cantrell, "Racial Violence and Reconstruction Politics in Texas, 1867–1868," *Southwestern Historical Quarterly*, January 1990. Author Cantrell rightly posits on p. 339: "One of the reasons that the nature of Reconstruction violence has eluded historians is that violence is difficult to quantify. Newspapers, even when objective, had access only to deeds that became known to their reporters and editors—probably a small and unrepresentative sample of the total violence in a region with a few cities and towns as Texas."

6. Crouch and Brice, *The Governor's Hounds*, 77; Roy R. Barkley and Mark F. Odintz, eds., *The Portable Handbook of Texas*. Contributor Ricky Floyd Dobbs identifies one of the arrested individuals as John McParrish, rather than John Parrish. See p. 944.

7. Ibid.

8. Carl H. Moneyhon, *Edmund J. Davis: Civil War General—Republican Leader—Reconstruction Governor*, 191; Sammy Tise, *Texas County Sheriffs*. "W.H. Stewart was appointed on March 1, 1869 by General Canby's Special Order #49; was elected December 3, 1869 and served until December 19, 1970 when he was removed by the District Judge. There were no reasons given for the removal." See p. 518.

9. For a modern-era biography of McNelly, see the awarding winning *Captain L.H. McNelly, Texas Ranger* by Parsons and Little.

10. Crouch and Brice, *The Governor's Hounds*, 79–80; June Rayfield Welch, *The Texas Courthouse Revisited*, 236.

11. *Galveston Daily News*, January 25, 1871.

12. Ibid., March 9, 1871. For this edition the aforementioned "dark room at the Penitentiary" seems to have undergone a tweaking—maybe significant, maybe not: Defense lawyer Maxey asserts ". . . I had good reason for believing and so expressed myself, before Outlaw, Parish, Wright and Parks were arrested that [Judge] Burnett and his coadjutor were plotting the destruction of these young men, and secret meetings had been held in a certain dark room in the precincts of Huntsville, by these conspirators, and against the life and liberty of my clients, and their destruction determined upon."

13. In *Message of Gov. Edmund J. Davis, With Documents in Relation to Lawlessness and Crime in Hill and Walker Counties* [Austin: J.G. Tracy, State Printer, 1871]. Courtesy Texas State Library and Archives [TSA], Austin, Texas. See pages 19–21, W.E. Horne, District Attorney, Thirtieth Judicial District, to Gov. E.J. Davis, 26 January 1871; Crouch and Brice, *The Governor's Hounds*, 79; Ed Blackburn, Jr., *Wanted: Historic County Jails Of Texas*, 341.

14. Ibid. "The prisoners in the meantime, who through aid of their friends outside and inside the court room, had concealed upon their persons at least two six-shooters each, and immediately began to fire upon the officers," 20; Kenneth W. Howell, ed., *Still the Arena of Civil War: Violence and Turmoil in Reconstruction Texas, 1865–1874*, 199: "Aided by 'friends outside and inside the court room,' each prisoner had concealed two six-shooters."

15. Crouch and Brice, *The Governor's Hounds*, 81; Carl H. Moneyhon, *Texas after the Civil War: The Struggle of Reconstruction*. "In this instance a preliminary hearing found probable cause for holding three young men arrested by the state police for the murder of a black man. When the judge ordered them held for trial, a shooting fray broke out. The young men had been armed by

friends, and they made their escape with their assistance and the refusal of local citizens to try to stop them." See p. 142.

16. *Message of Gov. Edmund J. Davis*, Horne to Davis as cited, TSA.

17. Ibid. Also see the exceptional work of Darren L. Ivey, *The Ranger Ideal: Texas Rangers in the Hall of Fame, 1874–1930*, Vol. 2, 74–75: "However, his [Nat Outlaw's] fellow prisoners escaped into the street and out of town with the aid of their armed associates."

18. Ibid., Burnett to Davis, 12 January 1871, 22–24, TSA. Graber's claims in *A Terry Texas Ranger*, that Texas State Police Captain McNelly only survived the courtroom shootout by dropping "between some benches, [and] pretending he was dead" seems somewhat farfetched, principally because he maintained custody of his prisoner, Nat Outlaw. See p. 334.

19. Ibid.

20. Crouch and Brice, *The Governor's Hounds*, 81.

21. *Message of Gov. Edmund J. Davis*, Judge J.R. Burnett to Governor Davis, 17 January 1871, pp. 24–25, TSA.

22. Ibid., Governor Davis to Judge Burnett, 20 January 1871, pp. 25, TSA.

23. Ibid.; Alwyn Barr, *Reconstruction to Reform: Texas Politics, 1876–1906*. "The Davis administration, which lasted four years, continuously suffered from political bickering. Democrats charged extravagance and gross abuse of power, especially in appointments, control of the state police, and declarations of martial law. Davis found himself plagued with a variety of difficult problems such as frontier protections, lawlessness, widespread refusal to pay taxes, and bitter political opposition," 8.

24. Ibid., Telegram: Governor Davis to Judge Burnett, 7 February 1871: "Martial law will be declared in Walker county, and cost assessed upon the people . . . ," 26, TSA.

25. Primary source documents relating to the Court Martial may be accessed in RG 401, 866–1, 866–2, 866–3, 866–4, 866–5, 866–6, and 866–7 the "Court Martial Proceedings vs. Nathaniel Outlaw," TSA.

26. *Galveston Tri-Weekly News*, March 29, 1871.

27. *Dallas Weekly Herald*, April 22, 1871.

28. Texas Department of Corrections (TDC), Treatment Directorate: Research and Development Division, *Texas Department of Corrections: A Brief History*, 3. Authors' copy courtesy Robert J. "Bob" Parker, TDCJ-ID Regional Director, Ret.; David M. Horton and Ryan Kellus Turner, *Lone Star Justice: A Comprehensive Overview, The Texas Criminal Justice System*, 211–212.

29. Lee Simmons, *Assignment Huntsville: Memoirs of a Texas Prison Official*, 50.

30. Bob Alexander, *Whiskey River Ranger: The Old West Life of Baz Outlaw*, 29; Blackburn, *Wanted*, 145; Bill Moore, "The Texas Calaboose," *Texas Co-op*

Power, June 2015, 29; James K. Greer, ed., *Buck Barry: Texas Ranger and Frontiersman*. Unapologetically, James B. "Buck" Barry, an early day sheriff of Navarro County, reflects on the place and times, remarking: "The county, as a part of the frontier, covered all the territory between the Brazos and the Trinity Rivers, west to New Mexico. Court was held in a log cabin. We had no jail, consequently, I had to chain the prisoners like so many pet bears inside a log cabin," 64.

31. Theresa Jach, *Huntsville Penitentiary*, 8; Marilyn D. McShane and Wesley Krause, *Community Corrections*: "Long ago, offending persons were often banished from their villages or countries. We now use prison as a type of symbolic banishment," 5.

32. Luke Gournay, *Texas Boundaries: Evolution of the State's Counties*, 53; Harry F. Estill, "The Old Town of Huntsville," *The Quarterly of the Texas State Historical Association*, April 1900. "What may be termed the first period of the history of Huntsville closes in 1846, when the new county of Walker was organized and Huntsville became a county seat," 269.

33. Ibid., 35–57.

34. A rather comprehensive yet succinct history of Texas Prisons as a system was prepared by the Management Services Department of TDCJ; Simmons, *Assignment Huntsville*, 50.

35. H.P.N. Gamel, comp., *The Laws of Texas*, vol. 3, 79–84; *Weekly Houston Telegraph*, March 30 and April 27, 1848; *Victoria Advocate*, May 4, 1848.

36. James Robertson Nowlin, "A Political History of the Texas Prison System, 1849–1957," Thesis: Trinity University, 1962, pp. 7–8. Another significant scholarly study which will merit later citations is R. Craig Copeland's outstanding 1980 Master of Arts Thesis for Sam Houston State University, "The Evolution of the Texas Department of Corrections."

37. Donald R. Walker, *Penology for Profit: A History of the Texas Prison System, 1867–1912*, 14; J. Keith Price and Susan Coleman, "Narrative of Neglect: Texas Prisons for Men," *East Texas Historical Journal*, October 2011, 46.

38. *Victoria Advocate*, August 3, 1848; *Clarksville Standard*, August 26, 1848; Typescript by Don Poston, "Leadership of the Texas Prison System." Author's copy courtesy Michael J. Bailey, Curator, Brazoria County Historical Museum (BCHM), Angleton, Texas.

39. Ibid.; Price and Coleman, "Narrative of Neglect: Texas Prisons for Men," 47; Thomas H. Kreneck for his contribution "Sam Houston," in the *Portable Handbook of Texas* has the former governor and hero of San Jacinto, moving to Huntsville during 1862, fourteen years after Huntsville was chosen as the state's prison site. See page 437.

40. *Weekly Houston-Telegraph*, April 27, 1848: "The editor of the Huntsville Banner recommends Huntsville as a suitable site for this institution."

41. Gammel, *The Laws of Texas*, vol. 3, 80: "The Penitentiary shall be built of substantial materials, and surrounded by a secure wall. . . ."; *Weekly Houston-Telegraph*, March 1, 1849.

42. Nowlin, "A Political History," 8; *The New Handbook of Texas*, Vol. 2, 302. Kenneth Hafertepe contributor.

43. *Weekly Houston-Telegraph*, January 24, 1850: "A wooden jail in the yard is the only place on the premises used for the safekeeping of convicts. . . ."; Jach, *Huntsville Penitentiary*, 12; Walker County Genealogical Society and Walker County Historical Commission, *Walker County, Texas: A History*, 17.

44. *Gonzales Inquirer*, July 16, 1853.

45. Nowlin, "A Political History," 8–9.

46. *Gonzales Inquirer*, September 17, 1853. "Estimating the work on the building, at usual prices, and the labor of the convicts prove, up to this time equal to the expenses of the establishment."

47. Nowlin, "A Political History," 9.

48. Chad R. Trulson and James W. Marquart, *First Available Cell: Desegregation of the Texas Prison System.* "Prior to 1865 and end of the Civil War, only the most serious white criminals were sent to the penitentiary. Blacks remained on slave plantations." xvi.

49. Nowlin, "A Political History," 10, quoting John H. Henderson, *The Lease System in Texas*, 2.

50. Jach, *Huntsville Penitentiary*, 8; *Texas State Gazette*, October 13, 1849.

51. Ibid. There may or may not be a touch of confusion regarding the name of the second imprisoned inmate. In *Wake Up Dead Man: Afro-American Worksongs from Texas Prisons*, collected and edited by author Bruce Jackson, quoting a 1968 Texas Department of Corrections publication, reports: "The second was Stephen Terry who was sentenced to ten years for murder. . . . Terry died of gunshot wounds while in prison. . . . ," 41–42; likewise, Horton and Turner, *Lone Star Justice*, enumerate Stephen Perry as the state's second prison inmate. 215.

52. Compilers Michael Kelsey, Nancy Graff Floyd, and Ginny Guinn Parsons, *Miscellaneous Texas Newspaper Abstracts—Deaths*, Volume I, quoting the *Huntsville Banner*. 170; *Texas State Gazette*, October 13, 1849.

53. Ibid. Quoting the *Texas State Gazette*, 1. Pragmatically, leaving room for a degree of clarification, prisoner Turner *might* have escaped his keepers before actually being imprisoned, though he was penitentiary bound.

54. Crouch, ed., *The Keepers*, 5. Also see, Bob Alexander, *Sheriff Harvey Whitehill: Silver City Stalwart*, 4: "A historical peek at a frontier communities' outlook regarding crime, criminals, and who they cooperatively entrusted to deal with the complexity, is illuminating. Probing a frontier locality's way of thinking, vis-à-vis its remedies aimed at negating social transgressions, and how the

neighborhood's lawmen were chosen, is revealing. It is a window into an area's overall frame of mind. Formulating an acceptable diagnosis for a town's moral temperament may be measured by inserting the thermometer squarely into the phenomenon of what behavior is endured and what misbehaviors are slated for obliteration. As the frontier shrunk so, too, did tolerance of conduct that just years before had been okay."

55. Bob Alexander, *Six-Shooters and Shifting Sands: The Wild West Life of Texas Ranger Captain Frank Jones*, 12–14

56. Nowlin, "A Political History," 8.

57. Billy M. Birmingham, "An Historical Account of the East Texas Prison System at Rusk." Master of Arts Thesis, 1979, Sam Houston State University, Huntsville, Texas, as contained in *Histories and Memories of Texas Prisons*, Complied by TDC Executive Services 1994. Quotation on p. 5. Authors' copy courtesy Robert J. "Bob" Parker, TDCJ-ID Regional Director, Ret.

58. Simmons, *Assignment Huntsville*, ix.

59. Sam A. Willson, ed., *Revised Penal Code and Code of Criminal Procedure of the State of Texas*. [St. Louis, MO: The Gilbert Book Co., 1888].

60. Norman Johnston, Leonard Savitz, and Marvin E. Wolfgang, eds., *The Sociology of Punishment & Correction*. As a contributor to this work noted social scientist Donald Clemmer in discussing "Prisonization" confirms that many convicts feel—or soon learns—a sense of entitlement. "Every man who enters the penitentiary undergoes prisonizaton to some extent. . . . This new conception [going to prison] results from mingling with other men and it places emphasis on the fact that the [prison] environment *should* administer him." 479–480.

61. Nowlin, "A Political History."

62. Simmons, *Assignment Huntsville*, x.

63. For an entire chapter devoted to the "Bat" see Gary Brown's *Texas Gulag: The Chain Gang Years, 1875–1925*. 34–42. Not unexpectedly any precise description of the Bat might vary from prison unit to prison unit. Practically speaking, however, minor variances in nomenclature did not interfere with its intended function and effectiveness.

64. Award winning author Rick Miller, quoting the *Corsicana Observer* of June 10, 1874 in his WWHA Best Book of the Year biography, *Texas Ranger John B. Jones and the Frontier Battalion, 1874–1881*. 41; *James B. Gillett, Six Years with the Texas Rangers, 1875–1881*, 4.

65. Chuck Parsons and Norman Wayne Brown, *A Lawless Breed: John Wesley Hardin, Texas Reconstruction, and Violence in the Wild West*, 273.

66. Simmons, *Assignment Huntsville*, x.

67. Brown, *Texas Gulag*, 35. Though actually not referencing use of the Bat in Texas, Marilyn D. McShane and Wesley Krause in *Community Corrections*

comment on punishment as a remedial methodology in the correctional tool-kit: "Deterrence by punishment means that the severity of the prospective punishment is strong enough to deter someone from ever committing that crime [or in this case, prison rule infractions]." See p. 6.

68. Simmons, *Assignment Huntsville*, x.

69. *Texas State Gazette*, October 11, 1851.

70. *Gonzales Inquirer*, July 16, 1853.

71. *Texas State Gazette*, July 19, 1851.

72. Barkley and Odintz, *The Portable Handbook of Texas*, Anne W. Hooker, contributor, 163; Frances T. Ingmire, *Texas Ranger Service Records*, Vol. 1: "Bell, Peter Hansbrough, Capt., Comm. Off: Taylor, Z., General, Organ: Mounted Texas Rangers, Enlist: Sept. 1845 in Corpus Christi, Disc. Dec. 1845, Ranger Muster Roll, Mexican, War." 12. Of a general interest may be the 1841 multi-page handwritten report of Bell, the then-Adjutant General of the State Militia, titled "Report of Col. P.H. Bell relative to Western difficulties, Oct. 4th 1841," in the TRHF&M.

73. *Gonzales Inquirer*, November 26, 1853. The edition of September 17, 1853, makes mention of the then prison industries: "Some few of the convicts are engaged in wagon making and cabinet work."

74. Walker, *Penology for Profit*, 16.

75. Ibid.

76. Barkley and Odintz, *The Portable Handbook of Texas*, Contributor Roger A. Griffin, 659.

77. *Gonzales Inquirer*, March 4, 1854.

78. Jach, *Huntsville Penitentiary*, 8.

79. Ibid.; Gammel, *The Laws of Texas, 1822–1897*, vol. 3, 84.

80. Walker, *Penology for Profit*, 16.

81. *Galveston News*, September 20, 1856.

82. Ibid., August 19, 1856; Reflective of a little later time period, John Mason Jeffrey writes of the Arizona Territorial Prison at Yuma and its interplay with area residents: "To help understand the phenomenon of the Arizona Territorial Prison we should keep in mind that the prison was really a community activity. The gates were open to the townspeople who came and went, selling merchandise and buying from the Bazaar, and visiting prisoners and guards. It was an operation in an amphitheater, as open to the public scrutiny as a fish bowl." See, *Adobe and Iron: The Story of the Arizona Territorial Prison*, 10.

83. Barkley and Odintz, *The Portable Handbook of Texas*, Contributor Paul M. Lucko, 682.

84. Irwin, *Prisons in Turmoil*, 202.

85. Nowlin, "A Political History," 19.

86. *Dallas Weekly Herald*, July 1, 1863.
87. Nowlin, "A Political History," 20. That the state penitentiary was not converted into a military prison during the Civil War does not necessarily mean that there were no Union prisoners domiciled therein. See, Price and Coleman, "Narrative of Neglect," 47–48: "The prison also supported the Confederacy by housing Union prisoners of war. One of these, the ships carpenter from a federal vessel captured at Galveston, built the coffin of the prisoners' frequent visitor, Sam Houston, who had left his office as governor of Texas rather than support secession."
88. Ibid., 21.
89. *Houston Tri-Weekly Telegraph*, June 14, 1965.
90. Ibid., June 19, 1965.
91. Walker, *Penology for Profit*, 17.
92. Nowlin, "A Political History," 21.
93. Ibid.
94. *Dallas Weekly Herald*, January 6, 1866.

Chapter 2: "Muzzle the guard"

1. Charles W. Ramsdell, "Texas from the Fall of the Confederacy to the Beginning of Reconstruction," *Quarterly of the Texas State Historical Association*, January 1908, 207.
2. Ibid.
3. Adalberto Aguirre, Jr. and Jonathan H. Turner, *American Ethnicity: The Dynamics and Consequences of Discrimination*, 70.
4. Walker, *Penology for Profit*. "The first decade or so following the end of the war brought lawlessness, a near collapse of the state's finances, and a weakening of state government to the point that, at times, it seemed almost incapable of maintaining any control at all." 18.
5. For this time period and the resultant turmoil, the attracted reader is referred to Moneyhon's *Texas After the Civil War: The Struggle of Reconstruction* and Howell's *Still the Arena of Civil War: Violence and Turmoil in Reconstruction Texas, 1865–1874*.
6. Nowlin, "A Political History," 25.
7. Walker, *Penology for Profit*, 21. Certainly the reader with a particular interest in this aspect of the Texas Prison story would be advised to review this cogent and exhaustive and well-written study. Also see, *Dallas Weekly Herald*, February 16, 1867.
8. Nowlin, "A Political History," 25–26.
9. Ibid., Quoting a report to the Texas Legislature by Governor Davis, 25–26.
10. Ibid.

11. Walker, *Penology for Profit*, 21.
12. Price and Coleman, "Narrative of Neglect," 48.
13. *Dallas Weekly Herald*, October 12, 1867.
14. Ibid., October 23, 1869.
15. *Galveston Tri-Weekly News*, June 14, 1869.
16. *Flake's Bulletin*, October 31, 1868. For Ben Thompson's tenure with the Austin PD see the commendable work of Doug Dukes, *Ben Thompson: Iron Marshal of Austin*. For Thompson's full-scale biography one must consult the wide-ranging multiyear research efforts by Bicknell as contained in *Ben Thompson: Portrait of a Gunfighter* by Thomas C. Bicknell and Chuck Parsons. A crisp history of the Vaudeville Theater and Saloon may be found in David Bowser's contribution for *Legendary Watering Holes: The Saloons That Made Texas Famous*, compiled and edited by Richard Selcer, 53–121. Also contained within *Legendary Watering Holes*, is the quite interesting and insightful piece by Byron Johnson, Director, TRHF&M, and Sharon Peregrine Johnson, "The Fine Art of Mixology," 43–51.
17. *Flake's Bulletin*, September 9, 1868.
18. Walker, *Penology for Profit*, 31.
19. Ibid., 30–31.
20. Ibid.
21. Ibid.
22. Nowlin, "A Political History," 29.
23. Ibid., 30: "Utilization of widely scattered convict camps in areas where prisoners had been sub-leased provided a situation extremely vulnerable to varied abuses."
24. Statement of Samuel Wright, printed in the *New Orleans Times*, and picked up by the *Galveston Daily News* of March 23, 1875.
25. Ibid. This news item was somewhat supplemented by the *Dallas Weekly Herald* of April 3, 1875.
26. *Dallas Daily Herald*, August 13, 1876.
27. *Report of the Board of Directors of the Texas State Penitentiary, to the Governor*, March 1876 (Houston: A.C. Gray, State Printer, 1876).
28. *Report of Condition of the Texas Penitentiary for the Years 1874-5-6* (Houston, A.C. Gray, State Printer, 1876). Submitted by Prison Inspector J.K.P. Campbell. Hereafter, Campbell—1876, p. 10. (BCHM); *Austin Weekly Democratic Statesman*, June 29, 1876.
29. *Galveston Daily News*, April 30, 1889. Purportedly the killer was James H. Roach, a convicted horse thief from Parker County; Caldwell and DeLord, *Texas Lawmen, The Good and the Bad, 1835–1899*, 359.
30. Walker, *Penology for Profit*, 34.
31. Campbell—1876. 4–6.

32. Ibid., 6–7. Mention of Inspector Campbell's focus on the Lake Jackson Convict Camp is also found in Joan Few's, *Sugar, Planters, Slaves, and Convicts*, 97–106.

33. Ibid., 8–9. At this point a relevant sidebar is highlighted, though not necessarily in proper chronology. Well-regarded researcher and talented writer of Old West nonfiction, David Johnson, in the 2019 release of *The Cornett-Whitley Gang: Violence Unleashed in Texas*, relates how a sadistic Texas outlaw, Braxton E. "Brack" Cornett, was imprisoned during the state's convict lease period. Not surprisingly Brack Cornett escaped. Somewhat interestingly though, later employing an alias of Bill McGinty (his grandfather's name), Cornett was employed as a guard for lease convicts working the railroad expansion. That is, until his true identity surfaced. See pp. 16–19.

34. Ibid.

35. For brief biographical sketch of Henry K. White, see John Henry Brown, *The Indian Wars and Pioneers of Texas*. For the text in hand, particularly 420: "In 1873 Mr. White moved to Ellis County; but, two years later, receiving from Governor Coke the appointment of superintendent of the penitentiary at Huntsville, he changed his residence to that place and lived there for three years." Actually he was not the Superintendent but one of three appointed State Prison Directors. Also see, Poston, "Leadership of the Texas Prison System: 1870–1883: Texas State Penitentiary Directors—1877–1878: JE. Shepard; H.K. White; I.T. Gaines," Penitentiary Director 1877–78. BCHM.

36. Campbell—1876. 17–18.

37. Ibid., 20.

38. Ibid.

39. Nowlin, "A Political History," 31.

40. Walker, *Penology for Profit*, 32.

41. Campbell—1876, 2.

42. Gammel, *The Laws of Texas*, vol. 8, 86.

43. Bob Alexander and Donaly E. Brice, *Texas Rangers: Lives, Legend, and Legacy*, 97–98. Asserting unpopularity of the Texas State Police at its demise is reflected in pages of the *Dallas Daily Herald* of April 22, 1873:

    The People of the State of Texas are to-day delivered of as infernal an engine of oppression as ever crushed any people beneath God's sunlight. The damnable Police Bill is ground beneath the heel of an indignant Legislature.

44. *San Antonio Express*, July 3, 1874.

45. Campbell—1876. 14–15.

46. *Report of the Lessees of the Texas State Penitentiary, April 1876* (Houston: Telegraph Steam Book and Job Print, 1876), 28.

47. Campbell—1876, 22: For infighting between lease partners refer to *Galveston Weekly News*, April 9, 1877.
48. Nowlin, "A Political History," 35–37.
49. John Sayles and Henry Sayles, Compilers, *Early Laws of Texas, General Laws from 1836 To 1879*, vol. 3, "That the governor be, and he is, authorized and required, at such time and in such manner as he may deem necessary or expedient, to take and resume, in behalf of the state, the possession, control and management of the penitentiary at Huntsville, and all the property and convicts belonging thereto, whether within or without the walls of said penitentiary. . . . Upon the resumption of the state penitentiary, under the provisions of this act, the governor is hereby authorized and required, as soon as possible, to lease the same by public advertisement, for such time, not to exceed fifteen years. . . ." See pp. 485–488.
50. J.S. Duncan, "Richard Bennett Hubbard and State Resumption of the Penitentiary, 1876–78," *Texana*, 47-55; *Galveston Weekly News*, April 2, 1877; Barkley and Odintz, *The Portable Handbook of Texas*, Contributor Paul M. Lucko, 682.
51. Price and Coleman, "Narrative of Neglect," 49.
52. Duncan, "Richard Bennett Hubbard and State Resumption of the Penitentiary, 1876–78." 53.
53. Walker, *Penology for Profit*, 49; *Dallas Daily Herald*, December 16, 1877.
54. *Austin Democratic Statesman*, June 21, 1877.
55. Walker, *Penology for Profit*, 49; Nowlin, "A Political History," pp. 40–41: "By an Act of March 24, 1879, the legislature required the lessees of the System to furnish the salaries of all officers and employees of the institution. The lessees paid the amount not directly to the individuals concerned, but rather deposited it in a special fund of the state treasury to be subsequently paid to the parties by the state."
56. Sayles and Sayles, *Early Laws of Texas*, vol. 3, 487.
57. Ibid.
58. Duncan, "Richard Bennett Hubbard and State Resumption of the Penitentiary, 1876–78," 53.
59. Sayles and Sayles, *Early Laws of Texas*, vol. 3, 487.
60. Ibid., 487–488: "The right to hire or operate convicts outside the prison walls is hereby expressly given; but this right shall be exercised only under such rules, and with respect to such class or classes of convicts, as the governor and commissioners may prescribe."
61. Ibid.
62. Duncan, "Richard Bennett Hubbard and State Resumption of the Penitentiary, 1876–1878." 49; *Dallas Daily Herald*, April 4, 1877; Walker, *Penology for Profit*, 147–148.

63. Ibid., 51; *Galveston Weekly News*, March 26, 1877.

64. *Galveston Weekly News*, December 10, 1877.

65. Nowlin, "A Political History." 42.

66. *Biennial Reports of the Directors and Superintendent of the Texas State Penitentiary*, December 1, 1878–October 31, 1880. 22–23.

67. Ibid.

68. Walker, *Penology for Profit*, 56.

69. Richard C. Marohn, *The Last Gunfighter: John Wesley Hardin*, 144.

70. Alexander and Brice, *Texas Rangers*, 126.

71. Ibid.

72. Tevis Clyde Smith, *Frontier's Generation: The Pioneer History of Brown County, With Sidelight on the Surrounding Territory*, 53.

73. Jan Devereaux's award-winning article, "Jagville," *Quarterly of the National Association for Outlaw and Lawman History, Inc.* March, 2004, 10.

74. Alexander and Brice, *Texas Rangers*, 126.

75. Chuck Parsons and Donaly E. Brice, *Texas Ranger N.O. Reynolds: The Intrepid*, 241–246.

76. *Galveston Weekly News*, December 10, 1877; Alexander, *Winchester Warriors: Texas Rangers of Company D, 1874–1901.* 72–73; A.J. Sowell, *Early Settlers and Indian Fighters of Southwest Texas*, 644; S.P Elkins, "Captured Indian." *Frontier Times*, March 1929. 245–246.

77. Ibid.

78. Dorman H. Winfrey and James M. Day, eds. *The Indian Papers of Texas and the Southwest, 1825–1916*, vol. 4, 366; Linda Lee Maxwell, "Satanta: Last of the Kiowa War Chiefs." *Texana*, Summer 1969, 125; *Brenham Southern Banner*, October 18, 1878; Barkley and Odintz, *The Portable Handbook of Texas*. Contributor Brian C. Hosmer confirms: "Demoralized over the prospect of spending the rest of his life in confinement, he [Satanta] committed suicide by jumping out of a window," 762. Regarding Satanta's suicide retired Texas Prison Warden and nonfiction author Lon Glenn, thankfully and insightfully, is more precise: "I suspect there has been a misunderstanding surrounding the circumstances of Satanta's death. The evidence does not support the premise that Satanta jumped out of a hospital window. Clearly, he committed suicide, but having {on several occasions} been inside the ole East Building—one used as a 'hospital' and now used for storage, I can say without fear of contradiction that Satanta did not jump out of any windows. Why? Because, the distance from the cellblock runs to the outer-wall windows is too far. The building is/ was designed as a multi-story cellblock with the cells configured on the interior of the building. The cells are ten to twelve away from the outer walls to reach a window by jumping. I suspect the confusion began when author Larry McMurtry decided to use the story of Satanta for his *Lonesome Dove* character,

Blue Duck. I suspect he used literary license for dramatic effect. Having Blue Duck jump out a window of the jail taking a deputy with him was quite dramatic, but I suspect the following account found on History.net is closer to reality. History.net, states, 'On October 11, 1878, he {Satanta} slashed his wrists. As he was taken to the second floor of the prison hospital, he jumped off the landing. The fall killed him. Satanta's descendants believe he was pushed off the landing. . . .' Note, I have also noted during my career, more than a few inmates have committed, or attempted to commit suicide by jumping or diving over the second or third tier railing of the cellblock runs. Most falls from those heights are fatal."

79. Marohn, *The Last Gunfighter*, 146; *Galveston Weekly News*, February 10, 1879.
80. John Wesley Hardin, *The Life of John Wesley Hardin As Written by Himself*. 128.
81. Ibid.; *Brenham Southern Banner*, December 27, 1868.
82. Ibid.; Parsons and Brown, *A Lawless Breed*, 269.
83. Ibid.
84. Ibid., 128–129.
85. *Brenham Southern Banner*, January 24, 1879.
86. *Austin Weekly Democratic Statesman*, January 29, 1880.
87. Marohn, *The Last Gunfighter*, 147.
88. *Hardin vs. The State of Texas*, No. 44, APP, 360 (1878); Alexander and Brice, *Texas Rangers*, 127.
89. Marohn, *The Last Gunfighter*, 145. According to the 1860 U.S. Census for Walker County, Texas, it appears that that John C. Outlaw [Jr. ?] was the brother of Nathaniel A. "Nat" Outlaw involved in the courthouse shootout with State Police Captain Leander McNelly. According to this same U.S. Census, Philip M. Outlaw, not living at home, was enumerated as a White/Male eighteen years of age, employed as a "Guard to Penitentiary." At the time desperado Hardin entered the prison at Huntsville, the younger [not the father] John C. Outlaw would have been twenty-four years old.
90. Metz, *John Wesley Hardin: Dark Angel of Texas*, 202; Marohn, *The Last Gunfighter*, a psychiatrist by profession weighs in: "Jane had not yet written to him [Hardin]. He later referred to 'something I cannot mention now' in another explanation of his failure to write. He felt humiliated because of something; perhaps from a suicide attempt or a homosexual act. . . . In a nineteenth-century prison, homosexual acts were not mentioned in their records although such behavior would have been considered an infraction and would have resulted in punishment. A suicide attempt would have also have been treated as a punishable infraction. In either case, John Wesley Hardin would have felt debased and disgraced." 150.
91. H. Jack Griswold, Mike Misenheimer, Art Powers, and Ed Tromanhauser, *An Eye for an Eye: Four Inmates on the Crime of American Prisons Today*, 162.

The authors aver that on 12 April 1930 John Dillinger was "written up" by Correctional Officers for then prohibited same sex activity.

92. Ethan Blue, *Doing Time in the Depression: Everyday Life in Texas and California*, for specific delineations between "situational" and "true" homosexuality, 128.

93. Gresham M. Sykes, *The Society of Captives: A Study of a Maximum Security Prison*, 71–72; also see, Vergil L. Williams and Mary Fish, *Convicts, Codes, and Contraband: The Prison Life of Men and Women* posit: "Most inmates who have homosexual relations in prison consider themselves to be heterosexual, and, for the most part, the inmates who abstain from homosexual relations take a philosophical view toward the activity around them. . . . In the value system of the inmate culture, the homosexual activity of the wolves, punks, and casual couples is considered to be situational, or behavior that is a direct response to imprisonment." See pp. 59, 63.

94. Ibid. Accordingly, esteemed Professor Leo Carroll in *Hacks, Blacks, and Cons: Race Relations in a Maximum Security Prison*, p. 78, impales hardcore truth: "If one were to judge the intensity of the deprivations of incarceration by the frequency of topics that arise in inmate conversation, sexual deprivation would top the list. . . . Heterosexual deprivation, then, is frustrating for the prisoner not merely because of the absence of this form of sexual release, but also because its absence is experienced as a severe threat to masculinity."

Chapter 3: "Afraid they will kill me"

1. Walker, *Penology for Profit*, 57.
2. *Galveston Weekly News*, July 10, 1879.
3. Ibid.
4. Texas Penal Code, Title 2, Chapter 9, Subchapter E, § 9.52: "The use of force to prevent the escape of an arrested person from custody is justifiable when the force could have been employed to effect the arrest under which the person is in custody, except that a guard employed by a correctional facility or a peace officer is justified in using any force, including deadly force, that he reasonably believes to be immediately necessary to prevent the escape of a person from the correctional facility."
5. TDCJ-ID, Correctional Training & Staff Development, *Pre-Service Training, Student Guide*, FY 2018, 363.
6. *Galveston Weekly News*, July 10, 1879.
7. *Dallas Morning News*, May 27, 1888, regarding Roe's execution; *Dallas Daily Herald*, December 17, 1880, contemporaneous to Roe's conviction.
8. [William] *Roe vs. State*, 8 S.W. 463 (Tex.App. 1888); Roe was executed at Anderson, Grimes County on a change of venue, see Gilbreath, *death on the gallows*, 157; Caldwell and DeLord, *Eternity at the End of a Rope*, 316.

9. Walker, *Penology for Profit*, 57. The prison officials for this investigation were accompanied and aided by Texas State Senator A.M. Buchanan.

10. Ibid., 58–62.

11. *Galveston Weekly News*, July 8, 1880; Gilbreath, *death on the gallows*, 344; *Brenham Weekly Banner*, July 8, 1880; Caldwell and DeLord, *Eternity at the End of a Rope*, 252.

12. *Fort Worth Daily Gazette*, October 16, 1887; *Dallas Morning News*, October 16, 1887; also see, Gilbreath, *death on the gallows*, as cited above, 345–346; Caldwell and DeLord, *Eternity at the End of a Rope*, 309–310.

13. *Biennial Reports of the Directors and Superintendent of the Texas State Penitentiary*, 1 November, 1880, to 31 October, 1882 (Austin: E.W. Swindells, State Printer, 1882), 37–38. Also see, Bruce A. Thomas, "Historical Analysis of the Texas Building Tender System" (Thesis: Master of Arts, 1987. Sam Houston State University, College of Criminal Justice, Huntsville, Texas).

14. *Cunningham & Ellis vs. Moore, et. al.*, 55 Tex.373 (Tex. 1881); *Dallas Weekly Herald*, November 3, 1881.

15. Walker, *Penology for Profit*, 57.

16. *Galveston Weekly News*, July 23, 1877.

17. *San Antonio Express*, July 21, 1875.

18. *Biennial Reports of the Directors and Superintendent of the Texas State Penitentiary*, 1 December 1878 to 31 October 1880 [Galveston, Texas: Printed at the News Book and Job Office, 1881]. Exhibit No. 25, Employment of Convict s In Outside Forces, reflects that 256 convicts were assigned to "Rusk prison const'n." 53.

19. Birmingham, "An Historical Account of the East Texas Prison System at Rusk." Birmingham's treatment of the penitentiary at Rusk is thorough, insightful, and interesting; Nowlin, "A Political History," 88–90.

20. Caldwell and DeLord, *Texas Lawmen: The Good and the Bad, 1835–1899*, 94.

21. To date the most in-depth recap of this affair is found in "Double Murder at the Prayer Meeting," a standalone chapter within researcher and writer James Pylant's, *Sins of the Pioneers: Crimes & Scandals in a Small Texas Town*, 114–121; *Fort Worth Daily Democrat*, April 8, 1879; Interview with Edward M. "Mike" Konczak, 10 April 2019.

22. *Abilene Reporter-News*, April 24, 1927. Remarkably, after 48 years as a fugitive, Russ Holloway at age seventy-two returned to Erath County and surrendered—the case was dismissed. Interview by Alexander with dedicated West Texas historian and researcher Mike Konczak, 12 December 2018.

23. Texas Convict and Conduct Register, J.L. Holloway, #7612; Pylant, *Sins of the Pioneers*, 120.

24. *Biennial Reports of the Directors And Superintendent of the Texas State Penitentiary*, December 1, 1878–October 31, 1880, 22.

25. *The New Handbook of Texas*, Vol. 5, 726. Paul M. Lucko, contributor.

26. Nowlin, "A Political History," 88–89.

27. *Galveston Weekly News*, April 22, 1880.

28. Ibid.

29. Bud Allen and Diana Bosta, *Games Criminals Play: How You Can Profit by Knowing Them*, 16.

30. *Galveston Weekly News*, April 22, 1880.

31. Ibid.

32. From the *Rusk Observer*, carried in the *Galveston Weekly News*, January 13, 1881.

33. *Galveston Weekly News*, May 13, 1880.

34. Ibid., May 31, 1883.

35. *Reports of the Superintendent and Financial Agent of the Texas State Penitentiaries. . . . For Two Years Ending October 31, 1884* (Austin: E.W. Swindells, State Printer, 1885). "Exhibit H, gives a statement of the Wynne farm for 1883 and 1884. This farm is situated about two and a half miles from Huntsville. . . . The tract of land contains something over nineteen hundred acres, and when bought, there was about nine hundred acres in cultivation, about half each being planted in corn and cotton. The crop was very nearly made. . . . The payments made by me for account of this farm were for stock, tools and permanent improvements, salaries of sergeant and guards, provisions for guards and convicts, etc. The value of horses and mules purchased is $830, and permanent improvements for the gin house, etc., $1,510.05 paid for by me and not properly chargeable to the crops of 1883 and 1884, as they are investments for future crops as well. The value of crops, etc., raised on the farm is given at market values. The place has been credited with the cotton raised and only for corn fed, fodder, wood, etc., sent to the prison at Huntsville; leaving corn and fodder, etc., sufficient to run the place. The cotton raised on the farm has been used for the manufacture of convict clothing and bedding, and for making lowells and duck, which we have sold. Vegetables have also been raised upon the farm for the use of the force there and for the feeding of guards and convicts at Huntsville prison. . . . ," 41; Barkley and Odintz, *The Portable Handbook of Texas*, Contributor Paul M. Lucko, 683; Walker, *Penology for Profit*, 97.

36. Nowlin, "A Political History." 88–90.

37. *Dallas Weekly Herald*, December 13, 1883; *Galveston Daily News*, December 17, 1883.

38. *Galveston Daily News*, March 17, 1884; [T.W.] *Wallace vs. State of Texas*, 20 Tex.App.360, (1886); Caldwell and DeLord, *Texas Lawmen: The Good and the Bad, 1835–1899*, 358–359; TDCJ *Line of Duty Deaths as of December 2017*, courtesy TPM, Huntsville, Texas; Poston, "Leadership of the Texas Prison

System," confirms the supervisor as Assistant Superintendent for the East Texas Penitentiary [Rusk] but spells his name as O'Brien, rather than O'Brian. [BCHM].

39. *Dallas Morning News*, November 15, 1885. See the *Houston Chronicle*, October 30, 1938, for other mentions of exceptionally short prison sentences, but none come in under fifteen minutes.

40. Barkley and Odintz, *The Portable Handbook of Texas*, Contributor Paul M. Lucko, 683. And see, Theresa R. Jach, "Harlem Prison Farm: A State Owned Plantation" (Master of Arts Thesis, University of Houston, 2001), 51: "Guards, with dogs, tracked escapees like any runaway slave."

41. *Brenham Southern Banner*, September 9, 1880; *Fort Worth Gazette*, May 24, 1887.

42. The classic work on the celebrated XIT Ranch is J. Evetts Haley's *The XIT Ranch of Texas, and the Early Days on the Llano Estacado*. Also see, Cordia Sloan Duke with Joe B. Frantz, *6000 Miles of Fence: Life on the XIT Ranch of Texas*; and Lewis Nordyke, *Cattle Empire: The Fabulous Story of the 300,000 Acre XIT*. Also BILL O'Neal's *Historic Ranches of the Old West*. Of particular note for someone interested in ex-Texas Rangers challenging cow thieves on the XIT's trouble-plagued Escarbada Division, see Bob Alexander's *Rawhide Ranger, Ira Aten: Enforcing Law on the Texas Frontier*.

43. Ruth Alice Allen, "The Capitol Boycott: A Study In Peaceful Labor Tactics." *Southwestern Historical Quarterly*, April 1939, 317.

44. Ibid., 318; and see, Barkley and Odintz, *The Portable Handbook of Texas*, Contributor William Elton Green, 207; in same also see 813, "One of the most spectacular strikes was the Capitol Boycott of 1885—a protest against the use of convict labor." Contributors Ruth A. Allen, George N. Green, and James V. Reese. Also see, *Temple Daily Telegram*, January 20, 2019, byline Brooke A. Lewis, *Houston Chronicle*: "Prisoners worked elsewhere in the state as well, even helping to construct the State Capitol in Austin after it burned down in 1881."

45. Ibid., Quoting the monthly circular for the Granite Cutters' International Union, September 1885.

46. Gary Brown, *Singin' a Lonesome Song: Texas Prison Tales*, 42–43.

47. Ibid., Quoting the *Austin Statesman* of January 31, 1886, 43. Also see, Sandra Fuller Allen, "The Iron Men: An Historical Review of the East Texas Penitentiary" (Master of Arts Thesis, Stephen F. Austin State University, 1982): "Thus the State saved abundantly on the project by using the prison facility," 230.

48. Ibid.

49. Nowlin, "A Political History," Quoting Texas State Senator Wardlow Lane, 155.

50. Poston, "Leadership of the Texas Prison System," BCHM; Roger Conger, ed., *The Texas Ranger Annual* 5, 9; Walker, *Penology for Profit*, 72, n.90. Readers interested in learning more about Ben McCulloch, would be well advised to review Darren L. Ivey's creditable *The Ranger Ideal: Texas Rangers in the Hall of Fame*, Vol. 1, and Thomas W. Cutrer's *Ben McCulloch and the Frontier Military Tradition*.

51. Nowlin, "A Political History," 95–96.

52. Caldwell and DeLord, *Texas Lawmen: The Good and the Bad, 1835–1899*, 360.

53. Ibid.; Birmingham, "An Historical Account of the East Texas Prison System at Rusk," 33–34.

54. Ibid., 361.

55. Ibid., 363–364.

56. Ibid.; "TDCJ Line of Duty Deaths as of December 2017," TPM; Gourney, *Texas Boundaries*, 31; Alexander and Brice, *Texas Rangers*, 5, 490 n. 18; Tise, *Texas County Sheriffs*, 375.

57. *Fort Worth Gazette*, October 11, 1889. For a more thorough glance at the utilizations of dogs and breed characteristics for tracking escaped convicts the interested reader is referred to Sitton, *Texas High Sheriffs*, Chapter 10, the contribution of Ira Raymond "Nig" Hoskins, Texas Prison System Dog Sergeant and later, the multi-term elected sheriff of Bastrop County. Also see Tise, *Texas County Sheriffs*, 32, and portrait photograph 36. Also see the *Houston Chronicle*, February 4, 1938, for an insightful glance at how the tracking dogs were trained.

58. Kenneth Reagans, Senior Warden, Clemens Unit, TDCJ, to Brazoria County Historical Museum, 21 September 2007, and booklet, *William C. Clemens Unit, Brazoria, Texas 1899–2007*, in BCHM. Not entirely dated 1968 in depth newsclip from *The Angleton Times*, highlighting history and agricultural production of Brazoria County's prison farms, state-owned land totaling in the aggregate 39,291 acres—at that time.

59. Don W. Hudson, "Quality Before Quantity," *Texas Correctional Industries* [TCI] *Newsletter*, October/November 1995, 13; also see *Austin Weekly Democratic Statesman*, May 8, 1890.

60. Ibid., 12–15.

61. Convict Register and Conduct Record, Jack Sanders; *Bryan Daily Eagle*, February 16, 1899.

62. *Brenham Southern Banner*, December 23, 1897; *Corpus Christi Caller*, May 13, 1898: "A man might not pick out a prison as a place to publish a paper, from choice, but it has its advantages, says the editor of the Huntsville (Texas) Prison Bulletin, which is published in the state penitentiary."

63. *Beeville Bee*, December 9, 1898.

64. Texas Prison Superintendent L.A. Whatley's summary report as reprinted in the January 9, 1899, edition of the *Dallas Morning News*.

65. *San Antonio Express*, January 3, 1899.

66. *Dallas Morning News*, February 14, 1899.

67. Ibid., February 15, 1899.

68. *San Antonio Express*, February 14, 1899.

69. *Dallas Morning News*, February 24, 1899.

70. *Houston Post*, July 19, 1899.

71. Hans Toch, *Police, Prisons, and the Problem of Violence*, 53.

72. *Dallas Morning News*, March 23, 1899.

73. Ibid., May 18, 1899. The remarks of Professor Diego Gambetta in *Codes of the Underworld: How Criminals Communicate*, with regards to inmates fighting among themselves are insightful. Though rightfully identifying the fact that convicts can and do fight over the acquisition of personal property and/or services, Gambetta goes further: "But perhaps the most common prelude to a violent conflict is a challenge issued by a settled inmate and designed to test a new entrant's mettle. There is evidence that new entrants, in prison or in new cells and wings, unless overtly and credibly menacing, are soon challenged by bullying, taunting, intimidation, insults, provocations, or overt invitations to fight. Sometimes the challenge is veiled under the mantle of a conflict over resources, including attempts to extract sexual favors." Picking up a quotation from Hans Toch, *Living in Prison: The Ecology of Survival*, Gambetta continues, "Aggressors and spectators seem concerned with his reactions or non-reaction to aggressive overtures. The man is on trial, and he is fatefully examined. The penalty for failure is accelerated victimization. If a man acquits himself fully, he ensures his immunity to attack. The test is manliness. The criterion is courage. Courage evidenced by willingness to fight and by the capacity for doing so." See pp. 98–99.

74. Sawyer F. Sylvester, John H. Reed, and David O. Nelson, *Prison Homicide*, 14: "Stabbing was the most common method of inflicting death. This reflects the fact that stabbing weapons are probably the most lethal weapons which are readily available to prisoners."

75. *Dallas Morning News*, June 9, 1900.

76. Ibid., February 15, 1900.

77. [Perry] *Wagoner vs. State of Texas*, 55 S.W. 491 (Tex.Crim. App 1900); *Houston Post*, December 15, 1899.

78. *San Antonio Express*, July 7, 1900.

79. Gilbreath, *death on the gallows*, 58–59; Clifford R. Caldwell and Ron DeLord, *Eternity at the End of a Rope: Executions, Lynchings and Vigilante Justice in Texas 1819–1923*, 426–427.

80. Frederick Nolan, *Tascosa: Its Life and Gaudy Times*, 152–154; Tise, *Texas County Sheriffs*, 251; Caldwell and DeLord, *Texas Lawmen: The Good & the Bad, 1835–1899*, 122–123.
81. Bill Neal, *Skullduggery, Secrets, And Murders: The 1894 Wells Fargo Scam That Backfired*, 117.
82. *San Antonio Express*, December 22, 1899.
83. Neal, *Skullduggery, Secrets, And Murders*, 126.
84. *Bryan Daily Eagle*, December 29, 1899.
85. *San Antonio Express*, December 21, 1899.

Chapter 4: "until his body be dead"

1. DiIulio, *Governing Prisons*, 165.
2. Certainly for coherent data and handiness of brief summaries for these prison memoirs, the reader would be well-advised to peruse Brown's captivating compilation in *Texas Gulag: The Chain Gang Years, 1875–1925*. For the murders of William Davis Allison and Horace Lorenzo Roberson at Seminole an interested reader might review Jan Devereaux's "Gentle Woman: Tough Medicine," *National Outlaw and Lawman History Association Quarterly*, April/June 2003. Also see, Bob Alexander, *Fearless Dave Allison: Border Lawman*. For Milt Good's second escape from The Walls see the *Beaumont Journal*, October 14, 1927, and the *Fort Worth Star-Telegram*, October 14, 1927. And, for Hill Loftis AKA Tom Ross, see James I. Fenton, "Tom Ross: Outlaw Stockman" (Master of Arts Thesis, University of Texas at El Paso, 1979). Regarding the triple-lynching in Henderson County, the reader would be well-advised to access *Yours to Command: The Life and Legend of Texas Ranger Captain Bill McDonald*, 171–185, by Harold J. Weiss, Jr. Also see, Caldwell and DeLord, *Eternity at the End of a Rope*, 415–416.
3. Gilbreath, *death on the gallows*, p. 57: "Although never proven or charged, citizens of Cookville [in Titus County] believe Charles King sexually assaulted his sister on December 11, 1888, and afterwards murdered his entire family."
4. Ibid. According to the story as carried by the *Galveston Daily News* of July 3, 1895, the ex-convict had been patient: "Upon being apprised of the shooting early on the morning of the 19th Sheriff Reagan and Deputy Dorough at once proceeded to the scene of the trouble. Upon examination they discovered a rendezvous made of brush and leaves about 200 yards from where the shooting occurred that had been occupied by some person seemingly for several days."
5. Ibid. An assertion that King killed the dentist thinking he was the captain that had abused him is a stretch too far—the dentist was robbed of his pocket possessions, face to face, up close and personal.

6. [George Charles] *King vs. State*, 29 S.W. 1086 (Tex.Crim.App. 1895).

7. Gilbreath, *death on the gallows*, 57–58.

8. Brown, *Texas Gulag*. For one particular example see, 51–53.

9. Barkley and Odintz, *Portable Handbook of Texas*, Contributor David G. McComb, 357.

10. Ibid.; Caldwell and DeLord, *Texas Lawmen: More of the Good & the Bad, 1900–1940*, report that one unnamed Correctional Officer perished in the Category 4 hurricane, while the *Fort Worth Register* of September 23, 1900, places the loss of prison personnel at two.

11. *Houston Post*, September 15, 1900. Also see Lon Glenn, "The Grand Surfside Hotel, 1891–1907," *Image*, no. 1, 2019, 20–23, for an insightful article regarding the 1900 hurricane's devastating destruction in Brazoria County.

12. Barkley and Odintz, *The Portable Handbook of Texas*, 511, contributor Lawrence A. Landis; Poston, "Leadership of the Texas Prison System," *Dallas Morning News*, March 25, 1903.

13. *Dallas Morning News*, March 29, 1903.

14. Ibid., February 2, 1905.

15. Ibid. Also see the edition of February 5, 1905.

16. *Liberty Vindicator*, April 27, 1906.

17. Caldwell and DeLord, *Texas Lawmen: More of the Good & the Bad*, 418–419.

18. Gilbreath, *death on the gallows*, 258.

19. *Fort Worth Star-Telegram*, May 24, 1906.

20. [Henry] *Brown vs. State of Texas*, 95 S.W. 1039 (Tex.Crim.App. 1906).

21. *Galveston Daily News*, December 1, 1906.

22. *The Daily Messenger*, January 26, 1908; *The Daily Herald*, January 24, 1908; and the *Harrisburg Star-Independent*, January 24, 1908.

23. *The Brazosport Facts*, May 13, 1985. Byline Jeff Brown.

24. *New York Times*, July 19, 1908.

25. Ibid.; *Galveston Daily News*, July 20, 1908; Caldwell and DeLord, *Texas Lawmen: More of the Good & the Bad*, 420: "Austin St. Louis, who was at the time about twenty-two years old, is credited with killing both Elliot and Johnson."

26. Ibid.

27. *Fort Worth Star-Telegram*, July 23, 1908.

28. Caldwell and DeLord, *Texas Lawmen: More of the Good & Bad*, 420–421.

29. Certainly Brazoria County Justice of the Peace B.P. Metgard had an informed opinion "after examining the negro [sic], found a pistol hole in his right side, and it is believed a guard shot him there last Saturday night when they had him surrounded in the Bernard bottoms a short distance from the Bernard River, the guards having shot at him nine times." See, *Dallas Morning News*, July 26, 1908.

30. Typescript: "Joe Jamison's Story of the Jailbreak of 1909," (BCHM).

31. Ibid.

32. For an interesting account relating to the experiences of a Texas Prison System's Dog Sergeant, see Sitton's *Texas High Sheriffs*, page 224, recounting the life and adventures of Ira Raymond "Nig" Hoskins: "I went out on call with my dogs lots of times. I got deputized under the Texas Rangers by them calling me, wanting to use me. . . . I went all over the state of Texas."

33. Jamison Typescript as cited; and see *Angleton Times*, September 24, 1909. For a quick but informative peek at this depressing misadventure, also see, *The Brazosport Facts*, November 17, 2003, byline Allison Pollan.

34. Ibid. Plausibly, Joseph "Pop" Jamison, several years later observed Otto Cooper at the City Market at Houston but the fugitive disappeared before police could be notified.

35. Caldwell and DeLord, *Texas Lawmen: More of the Good & the Bad*, 421; Program for Thirteenth Biennial Texas Peace Officers' Memorial Services, 1–2 May 2011, Austin, Texas.

36. Jane Howe Gregory, "Persistence and Irony in the Incarceration of Women in the Texas Penitentiary, 1907–1910," Master of Arts Thesis, Rice University, Houston, Texas, 1994, p. 1; Poston, "Leadership of the Texas Prison System," BCHM.

37. Walker, *Penology for Profit*, 135.

38. *Galveston Daily News*, March 23, 1875.

39. Walker, *Penology for Profit*, 135–136.

40. Caldwell and DeLord, *Texas Lawmen: More of the Good & the Bad,* 421. And see, *TDCJ Line of Duty Deaths as of December 2017*, TPM.

41. Ibid., 420. A twentieth-century Texas prison warden, speaking of his early days on the prison farms in Brazoria County, amplifies the legitimate worry of Field Bosses carrying a hoe squad when the heavens above are dancing with sparkly color. See, Lon Bennett Glenn, *Texas Prison Tales: The Largest Hotel Chain in Texas II.* "The electricity was so thick in the air you could smell it. If you've never been on horseback during a lightning storm, you don't truly understand the fear that Mother Nature is capable of burning into you soul." See p. 113.

42. Ibid.

43. Paul M. Lucko, "The Governor and the Bat: Prison Reform during the Oscar B. Colquitt Administration, 1911–1915," *Southwestern Historical Quarterly*, January 2003, 397–417; Walker, *Penology for Profit*, 183–185.

44. *Palestine Herald-Press*, December 26, 1908.

45. *Galveston Daily News*, December 27, 1908.

46. Lucko, "The Governor and the Bat," 408.

47. *The New Handbook of Texas*, vol. 2, 299, Donald R. Walker contributor.

48. Walker, *Penology for Profit*, 188.

49. Ibid., 191.

50. Martin and Ekland-Olson, *Texas Prisons*, 8.

51. *Dallas Morning News*, September 8, 1913; *The New Handbook of Texas*, vol. 3, 936, Stephen L. Hardin contributor.

52. Ibid., September 11, 1913; Rick Miller, *Tin Star Tales: Law and Disorder in Dallas County, Texas, 1846–1900*, 258. Citations to the noteworthy Ben Cabell are throughout this outstanding piece of long and overdue research by Miller; Tise, *Texas County Sheriffs*, 146.

53. Ibid., September 9, 1913; Tise, *Texas County Sheriffs*, 189. Also, *Cleburne Morning Review*, September 11, 1913.

54. David W. Neubauer, *America's Courts and the Criminal Justice System*, 486. Also, Horton and Turner, *Lone Star Justice*, for definition of a Court of Record, 368.

55. *Dallas Morning News*, September 11, 1913. Interestingly, but sadly, Correctional Officer Sid Wheeler would be murdered in Brazoria County, bludgeoned and shot to death with his own revolver. See, *Houston Chronicle*, August 16, 1937; Caldwell and DeLord, *Texas Lawmen: More of the Good & the Bad*, 432–433.

56. Ibid., September 9, 1913.

57. *El Paso Herald-Post*, September 9, 1913.

58. Sykes, *The Society of Captives*, 20.

59. Robert C. Cline, *From Rage to Redemption*, 89.

60. Caldwell and DeLord, *Texas Lawmen: More of the Good & the Bad*, 421–422.

61. Barkley and Odintz, *The Portable Handbook of Texas*, 683, Contributor Paul M. Lucko; James A. Creighton, *A Narrative History of Brazoria County, Texas*, 307–308. For a review of some of the early personalities—many of whom are historically significant—of this region the interested reader would be well-advised to consult Professor Paul N. Spellman's commendable *Old 300: Gone to Texas*, particularly Chapter 17, "The Brazoria Settlers," 338–360. The interested reader would also find Lon Bennett Glenn's historic overview of the Retrieve Prison Farm, in Chapter 3 of *Texas Prisons*, 48–75, both engaging and informative.

62. Ibid.

63. *Fort Worth Star-Telegram*, May 14, 1921.

64. Ibid.

65. *Victoria Advocate*, September 13, 1921.

66. Texas Convict and Conduct Register, #42953, Maximo Manuel Vega, aka Francisco Padillo.

67. Ibid., #46036, Ernest Conner.

68. Presentation Paper: Texas Department of Criminal Justice, Fallen Officers' Memorial Ceremony, 2017, courtesy TPM; Caldwell and DeLord, *Texas*

Lawmen: More of the Good & the Bad, 422–423; *Dallas Morning News*, September 2, 1921.

69. *Fort Worth Star-Telegram*, September 18, 1921.
70. *Port Arthur Daily News*, September 3, 1921.
71. Texas Convict and Conduct Register, #42953, Maximo Manuel Vega.
72. *Dallas Morning News*, September 14, 1921.
73. *Daily Capital News*, June 14, 1925.
74. Sandra E. Rogers, *Electrocutions in Texas 1924–1964*, 5. This interesting and informative cataloguing of Lone Star State sanctioned electrocutions reviews 361 executions with biographical and situational details; definitely a major historical contribution to a study of Capital Punishment in Texas. Author Rogers based on first-class research actually credits the Master Mechanic at The Walls, Robert "Bob" Storms, "in charge of all things electrical and mechanical" as being the employee supervising the crafting and installation of the electric chair. As a sidebar, more than a decade later Bob Storms sought and was granted a pass with sitting on jury, as he was opposed to the death penalty. See, *Houston Chronicle*, January 20, 1938.
75. Gilbreath, *death on the gallows*, 35; Lon Glenn, "Last Legal Hanging." *Image*, No.2, 2018. 33.

Chapter 5: "just like anybody's grandmother"

1. James W. Marquart, Sheldon Ekland-Olson, and Jonathan R. Sorensen, *The Rope, the Chair, & the Needle: Capital Punishment In Texas, 1923–1990*, 15; Although frequently referred to as "Old Sparky," oftentimes the contraption was also conferred with the title "Ole Sparky"—as but one example see the *Dallas Morning News* of January 25, 1974. Usage of either term would register as correct—the intended legal purpose and certifiable end results were equivalent; Tise, *Texas County Sheriffs*, 291. For an interesting sidebar, according to an area newspaper, an escape prone convict played a pivotal role in wiring the electric chair. See, the November 3, 1929 edition of the *Fort Worth Star-Telegram*: "An electrician by trade, he [Clarence Allen Puteney] designed and installed the electric chair now in use at the Texas penitentiary for the execution of condemned criminals, according to Warden E.F. Harrell [later named the Warden at The Walls]." When former prison employee Bob Storm was avoiding jury duty in a Capital Case, according to the January 20, 1938 edition of the *Houston Chronicle*, Storm stated that "he installed the electrical setup and 'hitched up' the chair." ¿Quién sabe? Rogers in her fascinating and thorough treatment, *Electrocutions in Texas*, notes Bob Storm's resignation as Master Mechanic, a vacancy filled by N.L. Boudreaux, who told a newspaper reporter that "it had taken him several weeks to connect the chair to the electrical apparatus and operating panel." See p. 8.

2. Rogers, *Electrocutions in Texas*, 5–11.

3. Ibid., 12–17; Caldwell and DeLord, *Texas Lawmen: More of the Good & the Bad*, 101–102.

4. Terry Baker, *Hangings and Lynchings In Dallas County, Texas 1853–1920*, 145–154; Rogers, *Electrocutions in Texas*, 19. The Texas Rangers involved were Captains Tom Hickman, Frank Hamer, and Sergeant J.B. Wheatley, see Boessenecker, *Texas Ranger: The Epic Life Of Frank Hamer*, 283–284; Harris and Sadler, *The Texas Ranger In Transition*, add Ranger P.F. Dyches to the action. 230–231; also, Marquart, Ekland-Olson, and Sorensen, *The Rope, the Chair, & the Needle*, 34.

5. Ibid. Sam Phillips was executed 14 May 1926. 24.

6. *Corpus Christi Caller*, August 5, 1926.

7. Ibid. For additional information regarding early day imprisonment of women the reader might wish to review Anne M. Butler's *Gendered Justice In The American West: Women Prisoners In Men's Penitentiaries*. In speaking of an earlier timeframe author Butler reports: "At the Eastham Camp, located twenty-three miles from the main prison, sixty-seven black women bunked in one house and three white women and one Mexican American woman shared quarters. The black women, much as their foremothers had in slavery, performed all the heavy field labor for the production of corn and cotton. Although the seventy-one women inmates no longer had random daily contact with all the male prisoners, men continued to supervise the camp and trusties worked there," 67. For additional data on female Ethridge and her crimes, see, Kelly E. McAdams, "A Social Study of the Women's Penitentiary of Texas." Master of Science Thesis, Texas A&M University, College Station, Texas, 1932, 132–133.

8. Caldwell and DeLord, *Texas Lawmen: More of the Good and the Bad*, 423.

9. *Corpus Christi Times*, July 22, 1926.

10. Ibid., July 23, 1926.

11. *Beaumont Enterprise*, July 23, 1926.

12. *Corpus Christi Times*, July 22, 1926.

13. *Beaumont Enterprise*, July 23, 1926.

14. *Corpus Christi Times*, July 22, 1926.

15. *Dallas Morning News*, July 24, 1926;Caldwell and DeLord, *Texas Lawmen: More of the Good and the Bad*, 424.

16. *Fort Worth Star-Telegram*, August 27, 1926.

17. Ibid., August 4, 1926.

18. *Dallas Morning News* August 17, 1926.

19. Samuel K. Dolan, *Cowboys and Gangsters: Stories of an Untamed Southwest*, 183–184; Caldwell and DeLord, *Texas Lawmen: More of the Good & the Bad*, 129–130.

20. *Dallas Morning News*, November 13, 1927.

21. Ibid., December 11, 1927.

22. Ibid., December 13, 1927.

23. *Corpus Christi Caller-Times*, July 30, 1928.

24. *Dallas Morning News*, July 29, 1928.

25. Ibid.

26. *Corpus Christi Caller-Times*, July 30, 1928. Purportedly two convicts did manage an escape during the pandemonium, while the Dallas paper puts the number at three.

27. *Dallas Morning News*, July 29, 1928.

28. *Corpus Christi Caller-Times*, July 30 1928.

29. Ibid.

30. *Waxahachie Daily Light*, July 30, 1928.

31. *Dallas Morning News*, July 29, 1928.

32. *Beaumont Journal*, August 11, 1928.

33. Ibid., May 24, 1937; *Corpus Christi Caller-Times*, May 24, 1937; *Dallas Morning News*, May 24, 1937; *Certificate of Death*, Alton Crowson, 23 May 1937; *Houston Chronicle*, June 25, 1937.

34. Caroline Gnagy, *Texas Jailhouse Music: A Prison Band History*, 99–100.

35. *Brownsville Herald*, July 28, 1928; *Dallas Morning News*, July 28, 1928.

36. *Corsicana Daily Sun*, July 28, 1928.

37. *Dallas Morning News*, December 7, 1928.

38. *The Sedalia Democrat*, July 29, 1928; Caldwell and DeLord, *Texas Lawmen: More of the Good & the Bad*, 424–425.

39. Ibid.; *Fort Worth Star-Telegram*, December 8, 1928; *Dallas Morning News*, December 6, 1928.

40. Gnagy, *Texas Jailhouse Music*, 104.

41. *Beaumont Enterprise*, September 20, 1928.

42. *Fort Worth Star-Telegram*, December 5, 1928; *Dallas Morning News*, December 5, 1928.

43. Caldwell and DeLord, *Texas Lawmen: More of the Good & the Bad*, 426. Correctly the authors note the various spellings used to identify the surnames of Sidney Albert: Syms, Symns, Symms, Sims, Simms; *Beaumont Journal*, August 22, 1930.

44. *Wichita Daily Times*, October 3, 1928.

45. Rogers, *Electrocutions in Texas*, 44; [Lee] *Davis vs. The State of Texas*. 25 S.W.2d 323 (Tex.Crim.App. 1930); Caldwell and DeLord, *Texas Lawmen: More of the Good & the Bad*, 426; *TDCJ Line of Duty Deaths as of December 2017*, TPM.

46. *Dallas Morning News*, January 19, 1928.

47. *Corpus Christi Times*, October 3, 1928; Caldwell and DeLord, *Texas Lawmen: More of the Good & the Bad*, 83,

48. Paul M. Lucko, "A Missed Opportunity: Texas Prison Reform during the Dan Moody Administration, 1927–1931," *Southwestern Historical Quarterly*, July 1992, 26–52.

49. *Austin Democratic Statesman*, May 1, 1873.

50. Lucko, "A Missed Opportunity," 47.

51. Ibid., 39–40.

52. *Dallas Morning News*, January 6, 1929.

53. Ibid.; Nowlin, "A Political History." As the author rightly advises, by an act of the Thirty-fifth Texas Legislature during a Special Session [1918], the penal facility at Rusk was converted "into an insane asylum for the incarceration of the Negro insane. . . ." 106.

54. *Dallas Morning News*, April 4, 1929; "Warden Speer for some time has felt a very great strain because of the necessity of officiating at the execution of condemned men." See, *Beaumont Enterprise*, April 5, 1928.

55. *Corpus Christi Caller-Times*, January 13, 1929.

56. *Cut Bank Pioneer Press*, February 8, 1929; Alexander, *Fearless Dave Allison*, 261; *Montana Statesman*, February 5, 1929; *The Cattleman*, March 1929. Certificates of Death, Gannon [Loftis] and Hayward, 3 February 1929. Courtesy Glacier County Clerk & Recorder.

57. *Dallas Morning News*, April 15, 1929.

58. *Corpus Christi Caller-Times*, November 15, 1928; *Fort Worth Star-Telegram*, November 15, 1928. By another report it was suggested that Folsom was doing time with regards to a conviction in Potter County [Amarillo].

59. *Fort Worth Star-Telegram*, May 19, 1929.

60. *Dallas Morning News*, May 7, 1929.

61. Ibid.; *Fort Worth Star-Telegram*, April 27, 1929.

62. Coverage of this prison break is a synthesis gleaned from several sources: The *Dallas Morning News*, June 21 and 22, 1929; Tise, *Texas County Sheriffs*, 55; Charles H. Harris, III, Frances E. Harris, and Louis R. Sadler, *Texas Ranger Biographies: Those Who Served, 1910–1921*, 401–402.

63. *Beaumont Enterprise*, October 8, 1929; Though with a primary focus on Mexico's female narco queenpins, educator and author Elaine Carey in *Women Drug Traffickers: Mules, Bosses, & Organized Crime*, most skillfully spotlights a north and south of the Rio Grande/Río Bravo reality: "In prison, men and women both sold and used drugs to gain power, to obtain privileges, and to make money. In both Mexico and the United States, family members of male inmates have played the role of sympathetic visitor but have also acted as fronts for the inmates' internal drug business by smuggling in supplies. As in the early 1900s, women passed drugs to their imprisoned men not only to help them assuage the slow passage of time, but also to allow them greater access to power within prison that drug possession provided." See p. 73.

64. Ibid., March 31, 1930.

65. *Fort Worth Star-Telegram*, July 2, 1931.

66. *Houston Chronicle*, April 23, 1936; for the discovery of heroin see the edition of April 3, 1936.

67. Ibid., July 21, 1936.

68. *The Freeport Facts*, February 2, 1939.

69. Light T. Cummins, "Bonnie & Clyde, The Barrow Gang & Lee Simmons," *Texoma Living!* March-April, 2010; *The New Handbook of Texas*, Vol. 5, 1052–1053. Brian Hart, contributor.

70. Simmons, *Assignment Huntsville*, 59; *Dallas Morning News*, March 25, 1930.

71. Ibid., vii-viii. As mentioned, most public officials have their detractors, and certainly this was and would be true for the Texas Prison System through its earliest history—and not abating even into the twenty-first century. As suggested earlier herein, armchair fixes are effortless to propose, but much more problematic to implement even if they seem to have merit—which some do and some don't. Particularly for critical assessment of Lee Simmons the interested reader may wish to peruse Paul M. Lucko, "Counteracting Reform: Lee Simmons and the Texas Prison System, 1930–1935," *East Texas Historical Journal* 30, no. 2 (1992), and the Epilogue in John Neal Phillips' *Running with Bonnie and Clyde*, 317–320.

72. Ibid., ix.

73. Ted Hinton, as told to Larry Grove, *AMBUSH: The Real Story of Bonnie and Clyde*, 117.

74. *Houston Chronicle*, June 20, 1930.

75. Ibid., June 21, 1930.

76. Ibid.

77. Ibid., June 20, 1930.

78. Ibid., January 17, 1931.

79. *Beaumont Enterprise*, August 5, 1930; Tise, *Texas County Sheriffs*, 274.

80. *Houston Chronicle*, August 8, 1930.

81. Harry Elmer Barnes and Negley K. Teeters, *New Horizons in Criminology*, 353.

82. TDC, *Texas Department of Corrections: 30 Years of Progress*, 22.

83. Simmons, *Assignment Huntsville*, x-xi. Also see, Umphrey, *The Meanest Man in Texas*: "Lee Simmons, general manager of TDC, was told of the self-mutilation problem on the farms. 'Give them more axes,' he was quoted as saying." 120.

84. Ibid.

85. Harris and Sadler, *The Texas Rangers in Transition*, 501–502.

86. *Houston Chronicle*, June 12, 1937.

87. *Corpus Christi Caller-Times*, October 17, 1930; Rogers, *Electrocution in Texas*, 46; Tise, *Texas County Sheriffs*, 184; Caldwell and DeLord, *Texas Lawmen: More of the Good & the Bad*, 134.

88. *Beaumont Journal*, September 18, 1930.

89. *Houston Chronicle*, June 6, 1930. Later, former Texas Ranger Stowe was given a reduced sentence clemency by Governor Ferguson and released from the penitentiary during 1936.

90. Robert W. Stephens, *Lone Wolf: The Story of Texas Ranger Captain M.T. Gonzaullas*, 39.

91. For additional details concerning the criminal offense and notable efforts expended to protect the defendant, see, Utley, *Lone Star Lawmen*, 133–134.

92. *Houston Chronicle*, July 30, 1930.

93. Rogers, *Electrocutions in Texas*, 45.

94. *Beaumont Enterprise*, August 22, 1930.

95. *Houston Chronicle*, November 12, 1931.

96. Rogers, *Electrocutions in Texas*, 47.

97. *Houston Chronicle*, November 13, 1930; *Fort Worth Star-Telegram*, November 14, 1930.

98. Coverage herein of the Thanksgiving Eve escape attempt and shootout is a synthesis of newspaper articles and genealogical data: See, *Houston Chronicle*, November 27 and 28, 1930; *Beaumont Enterprise*, November 27, 1930; *Beaumont Journal*, November 27, 1930; *Fort Worth Star-Telegram*, November 27 and 29, 1930; *Corpus Christi Caller-Times*, November 28, 1930; and the *Dallas Morning News*, January 1, 1931.

99. Simmons, *Assignment Huntsville*, ix.

100. Ibid., xi.

Chapter 6: "Only themselves to blame"

1. *Dallas Morning News*, February 4, 1931.

2. *Taylor Daily Press*, July 20, 1931; *San Antonio Express*, July 20, 1931; *Dallas Morning News*, July 20, 1931.

3. *Fort Worth Star-Telegram*, June 26, 1931.

4. Ibid.; *Houston Chronicle*, July 8 and 9, 1931; *Beaumont Journal*, July 27, 1931; DeLord, *The Ultimate Sacrifice*, 102; Caldwell and DeLord, *Texas Lawmen: More of the Good & the Bad*, 428; Simmons, *Assignment Huntsville*, 114; *TDCJ Line of Duty Deaths as of December 2017*, TPM.

5. *Lubbock Morning Avalanche*, November 27, 1919.

6. *The Freeport Facts*, January 9, 1931.

7. Thankfully now, though it's long overdue for those interested in the Texas Prison System's history and/or those fascinated by the legit saga of rodeo, an academic—though written in an easy to read style—work is Mitchel P. Roth's *Convict Cowboys: The Untold History of the Texas Prison Rodeo*. For citation to the TPR's founding as mentioned in this text, see pages 27–44.

8. Jach, *Huntsville Penitentiary*, 103–127.

9. Roth, *Convict Cowboys*, 93–94.

10. Ibid., Citation to celebrities throughout; 26 October 2019 interview with celebrated Western Entertainer and Television Personality Red Steagall. Mr. Steagall advised that performing at the TPR was a wonderful experience. Furthermore, as a sidebar, at the TPR two Texas Rangers were assigned as his protective escort.

11. *Dallas Morning News*, October 26, 1976.

12. Roth, *Convict Cowboys*, 243. For those desirous of exploring Candy Barr's criminal charges, see, *Juanita Dale Phillips vs. The State of Texas*, 328 S.W.2d 873 (Tex.Crim.App. 1959); Also, *Dallas Morning News*, October 14, 1959; and *Fort Worth Star-Telegram*, October 14 and December 4, 1959.

13. Ted Schwarz and Mardi Rustam, *Candy Barr: The Small-Town Texas Runaway Who Became a Darling of the Mob and the Queen of Las Vegas Burlesque*, 228.

14. Ibid., 245.

15. Roth, *Convict Cowboys*, again, citation to celebrities throughout—check index.

16. *Houston Chronicle*, September 11, 1937.

17. Ibid., November 10, 1937; Roth, in his splendid *Convict Cowboys*, p. 342, says of the prisoner: "Chute workers Vernon Thomas, Buster Bishop, and T.C. Corner spent between twenty-five and thirty years each preparing the cowboys for the most dangerous events."

18. *The New Handbook of Texas*, vol. 6, 391, Sylvia Whitman, contributor; *Wichita Falls Times*, October 15, 1970; *Corpus Christi Caller-Times*, December 3, 1972.

19. *Houston Chronicle*, October 26, 1936; *Fort Worth Star-Telegram*, December 17, 1936 and February 23, 1939; Rick Miller to Alexander and Alford, 3 April 2019; *Certificate of Death*, State of Texas, Floyd Seay.

20. *Beaumont Journal*, October 23, 1939.

21. *Beaumont Enterprise*, November 17, 1940.

22. Roth, *Convict Cowboys*, citations throughout. For an interesting biographical profile of O'Neal Browning, see Rev. Carroll Pickett and Carlton Stowers, *Within These Walls: Memoirs of a Death House Chaplain*, 163–169; Interview Fort Worth, Texas, 26 October 2019 with Teddy Weaver, Weaver Rodeo Company. Mr. Weaver stated the Weaver Rodeo Company put on the last TPR in 1985. Interestingly, black Top Hand convict cowboy John "Smoky" Parker worked for the Weaver family after his release from prison. Teddy Weaver advised that during his early childhood Parker often looked after him, assuming duties as a "babysitter," but always focused on teaching him the basic tradecraft skills of being a legit cowboy; Roth, *Convict Cowboys*, cites that Top Hand Parker was also nicknamed "Snake." See p.148.

23. *Dallas Morning News*, October 20, 1932.

24. Covered here—somewhat out of chronological sync—but for a generalized history the TPR at Dallas occurred during June 1950; *Texas Prison Museum*

Calendar for 2019, month of June; *Dallas Morning News*, March 8, April 27, and June 11, 1950; Roth, *Convict Cowboys*, 173–177.

25. Sid Underwood, *Depression Desperado: The Chronicle of Raymond Hamilton*, 143.

26. *Dallas Morning News*, May 24, 1934. "Sheriff's Slayer Will Go to Chair, High Court Rules: Rehearing Denied Perch Mouth Stanton in Killing of Officer"; Don Bullis, *New Mexico's Finest: Peace Officers Killed In the Line of Duty, 1847–2010*, 159; Rogers, *Electrocutions in Texas*, 66; Tise, *Texas County Sheriffs*, 482.

27. *Beaumont Enterprise*, February 10, 1936.

28. *Houston Chronicle*, March 14, 1936.

29. *Beaumont Journal*, April 2, 1932.

30. *Corpus Christi Caller-Times*, June 14, 1934.

31. *Dallas Morning News*, July 7, 1942.

32. Ibid., November 4, 1939.

33. Ibid., *Fort Worth Star-Telegram*, November 5, 1939.

34. *Beaumont Journal*, June 2, 1937; *Beaumont Enterprise*, June 2, 1937; Caldwell and DeLord, *Texas Lawmen: More of the Good and the Bad*, 107; Rogers, *Electrocutions in Texas*; *Corpus Christi Caller-Times*, June 3, 1937.

35. *Corpus Christi Times*, May 30, 1938.

36. TDC, *30 Years of Progress*, 21.

37. *Beaumont Enterprise*, March 30, 1936.

38. Lucko, "Counteracting Reform: Lee Simmons and the Texas Prison System, 1930–1935," 23; *Beaumont Journal*, September 6, 1938: "Eastham farm is the Alcatraz of the Texas prison system. The wing under study houses 25 of the state's most desperate criminals." During an insightful interview with former Warden Lon Bennett Glenn on 30 April 2019 at Angleton, he advised that due to the Retrieve (now Wayne Scott) Unit's geographical positioning in the Brazos and Bernard River country it, too, was sometimes referred to as the Little Alcatraz.

39. *Dallas Morning News*, October 20, 1932; *Galveston Daily News*, October 20, 1932; *Houston Chronicle*, November 4, 1932.

40. Caldwell and DeLord, *Texas Lawmen: More of the Good & the Bad*, 428–429.

41. *Fort Worth Star-Telegram*, December 20, 1932.

42. *Houston Chronicle*, July 26, 1933.

43. Ibid.; *Fort Worth Star-Telegram*, February 15, 1932; Tise, *Texas County Sheriffs*, 519.

44. Ibid.; *Dallas Morning News*, November 17, 1932.

45. Typescript. M.D. Seay, "Growing Up on The Big Ramsey: Memoirs of a Prison Brat," BCHM. That former prison employees, as prisoners, were subject to reprisals is real. For the time period see the *Houston Chronicle*, March 26, 1930: "Jess Randell, a former prison guard, was beaten severely by four convicts in the Texas penitentiary Tuesday night. 'The convicts first asked me if

I had any money and I told them I had none. They then asked me if I had ever guarded convicts and I told them I had. They said they were going to whip me for having been a guard.'"

46. *Houston Chronicle*, November 29, 1933; Rick Miller to Bob Alexander and Richard Alford, 6 March 2019.

47. Ibid., February 12, 1936; Joel Samaha, *Criminal Law*, 138: "*mens rea*—The mental element in a crime, including purpose, knowledge, recklessness, and negligence"; David W. Neubauer, *America's Courts and the Criminal Justice System*, 46: "Guilty intent (*mens rea*)—Mental state required for a crime."

48. Ibid., July 12, 1937.

49. *Beaumont Enterprise*, June 10, 1937; *Dallas Morning News*, June 10, 1937.

50. *Fort Worth Star-Telegram*, January 23, 1932.

51. *Corpus Christi Times*, May 30, 1933; *Forth Worth Star-Telegram*, June 6, 1934: "The State is installing $35,000 worth of machinery in the penitentiary for the purpose of manufacturing license plates for motor vehicles."

52. *Beaumont Enterprise*, December 26, 1937; *Houston Chronicle*, February 26, 1939.

53. *Dallas Morning News*, January 12, 1978.

54. *Beaumont Enterprise*, December 25, 1937.

55. *Houston Chronicle*, July 29, 1932.

56. *Beaumont Journal*, July 28, 1936; *Certificates of Death* for J.E. Broussard, Jr., and J.W. Dovell.

57. *Houston Chronicle*, July 29, 1932, August 28, 1933; Caldwell and DeLord, *Texas Lawmen: More of the Good & the Bad*, 428–429; *Dallas Morning News*, August 28, 1933; Phillips, *Running with Bonnie and Clyde*, 293. The author's take is somewhat different as to the death's details, and his reference to a "hated guard" stands unexplained—and undocumented. Perhaps the characterization had merit, then again, perhaps not.

58. *Dallas Morning News*, June 22, 1933; *Texas Certificate of Death* #26825, William Jackson Leonard, 21 June 1933.

59. *Beaumont Chronicle*, August 18, 1933.

60. Survey Map of Texas Prison Farms of the Texas Prison System, 1932–1934, by the State of Texas Reclamation Department, A.M. Vance, State Reclamation Engineer, R.J. McMahon, Surveyor. [BCHM].

Chapter 7: "Put them on the spot"

1. Patrick M. McConal, *Over the Wall: The Men Behind the 1934 Death House Escape*, 82–102; Schneider, *Bonnie and Clyde*, Guinn, *Go Down Together*, and Phillips, *Running with Bonnie and Clyde*, posit that Clyde Barrow was indeed the victim of sexual assault by Ed Crowder and in a jail-house conspiracy with a lifer, Barrow whacked Crowder while Aubrey Scalley took the blame claiming

self-defense. Boessenecker, *Texas Ranger: The Epic Life of Frank Hamer* discounts this scenario. The *Dallas Morning News* of October 31, 1931 covers the death of Crowder fairly extensively, naming his assailant as Aubrey Scalley, but does not mention Clyde Barrow. Also see, *Brownsville Herald*, October 30, 1931 and the *Amarillo Daily News,* October 31, 1931. Neither of these editions mention Clyde Barrow as being involved in the in-house prison murder. As well, during an interview with former Texas Prison Warden Lon Glenn (30 April 2019), he stated that after personally reviewing Barrow's prison record, that there was no indication of the little gangster ever killing anyone while incarcerated in the Texas Prison System, which should put the matter to bed. And as but a quick sidebar, sometimes it is written that Clyde Barrow's middle name was "Champion." Perhaps this might be traced to another Eastham convict that escaped, Clyde Champion Barrow, a twenty-year-old trusty doing two years for Auto Theft from Travis County. During February of 1941, this Clyde Barrow jumped, but was quickly apprehended and returned to Eastham. See, *Fort Worth Star-Telegram*, February 25, 1941. The Clyde Barrow and Bonnie Parker deaths in Louisiana, by this time, were already fused into the history books and folklore of Texas.

2. John Neal Phillips, "The Raid on Eastham," *American History*, October 2000, 55; T. Lindsay Baker, *Gangster Tour of Texas*, 18. Plausibly versions of this event vary, some placing recovery of the pistols from an outside woodpile.

3. This Eastham prison break is a synthesis of the sources enumerated in the endnotes above. More than once it is written that Correctional Officer Joe Crowson was twenty-four-years-old when murdered; however the DOB on his memorial headstone is 14 September 1900. Also see, Caldwell and DeLord, *Texas Lawmen: More of the Good & the Bad*, 430.

4. Simmons, *Assignment Huntsville*, 115.

5. TDC, *30 Years of Progress*, 21.

6. Simmons, *Assignment Huntsville*, 116; Correctional Officer Bullard's career and ascension in rank will be mentioned later herein.

7. Ibid., 117.

8. Ibid.; Simmons also wrote: "Every man makes mistakes. Crowson had simply made his last one."

9. Caldwell and DeLord, *Texas Lawmen: More of the Good & the Bad*, 430.

10. Simmons, *Assignment Huntsville*, 117–118; Underwood, *Depression Desperado*, name specifically asserts that Lee Simmons dismissed three Correctional Officers, B.S. Mathis, J.R. McCall, and Doc Robertson as "aftermath" of the Eastham Prison break. 45.

11. *Shreveport Times*, January 17, 1934.

12. For an interesting recap of some of the folks offering to snitch and put Clyde and Bonnie "on the spot," the interested reader may wish to review Schneider's *Bonnie and Clyde*, 320–324.

13. Simmons, *Assignment Huntsville*, 124; McConal, *Over the Wall*, 115.
14. Harris and Sadler, *The Texas Rangers in Transition*, 480; Phillips, *Running with Bonnie and Clyde*, 289.
15. Simmons, *Assignment Huntsville*, 126; James Randolph Ward, "The Texas Rangers, 1919–19035: A Study in Law Enforcement" (Master of Arts Thesis, Texas Christian University, Fort Worth, Texas, 1972), 224–225; Boessenecker, *Texas Ranger: The Epic Life of Frank Hamer* argues, for him, the improbability of Lee Simmons considering anyone other than Frank Hamer. See p. 496 n. 15.
16. Traveling Expense Account: Texas Prison System, for Frank Hamer, Investigator, February 15, 1934, to February 28, 1934. As a matter of general interest, selecting the random date of February 17, 1934, Frank Hamer's itemized expenses were: Lodging, $2.00, Breakfast at Scott's Café $.35, Lunch at the White Café $.55, and supper at the Colonial Café $.45 (TRHF&M); Guinn, *Go Down Together*, 254; Carol O'Keefe Wilson, *In the Governor's Shadow: The True Story of Ma and Pa Ferguson*, 204–205. For a chapter-length discussion of the Fergusons' questionable pardoning practices, see May Nelson Paulissen and Carl McQueary, *Miriam: Miriam Amanda Ferguson of Bell County, The Southern Belle Who Became the First Woman Governor of Texas*, 149–166.
17. Simmons, *Assignment Huntsville*, 128; John Boessenecker, "Frank Hamer vs. Bonnie and Clyde," *True West*, April 2019: "Hamer was appointed a special investigator for the Texas Prison System with orders to track down Bonnie and Clyde." See pp. 30–33.
18. Utley, "The Forgotten Hero," 37.
19. Stephen William Schuster, IV, "The Modernization of the Texas Rangers, 1930–1936," Master of Arts Thesis, Texas Christian University, Fort Worth, Texas, 1965, pp. 30–33. For an article-length profile of Maney Gault with photos, see John Fusco, "The Legendary Maney Gault," *True West*, April 2019, 38–41; VF-Maney Gault, TRHF&M.
20. Harris and Sadler, *The Texas Rangers In Transition*, 484; Karen Blumenthal, *Bonnie and Clyde: The Making of a Legend*, rightly confirms that Bonnie and Clyde, though guns were close at hand, never fired a shot during the Louisiana ambush. See p. 181. Rick Cartledge, "The Guns of Frank Hamer," in the Spring 1993 edition of *Oklahombres* asserts—with reasonable logic—that Frank Hamer besides being armed with a Remington Model 8 rifle, was also carrying a Colt 1911 chambered for .38 Super. See pp. 12–14.
21. Walter Prescott Webb, *The Texas Rangers: A Century of Frontier Defense*, 542. Though with good intentions Webb repeated Hamer's concocted tale about Clyde and Bonnie having a "mail box" which "lay on the ground near a large stump of a pine tree," which was wholly fictitious. Conversely, Hamer's intentions were good in providing Webb with the bogus story. He was, honorably, trying to protect the Methvin family's role as informants.

22. *Dallas Morning News*, May 24, 1934, quoting *St. Louis Post-Dispatch*; also see Bossenecker, *Texas Ranger, The Epic Life of Frank Hamer*, 437. For a cogent analysis somewhat deflating mythology associated with the "hype" about Frank Hamer's part in the deaths of Clyde and Bonnie, see Harris and Sadler, *The Texas Rangers in Transition*, 484; also, Blumenthal, *Bonnie and Clyde*, 186.

23. Calvin Grant Aten to Austin Ira Aten, 12 December 1936. Courtesy researcher and writer Robert W. Stephens; also see, Bob Alexander, *Whiskey River Ranger: The Old West Life of Baz Outlaw*. 147–156; and Bob Alexander, *Bad Company and Burnt Powder: Justice and Injustice in the Old Southwest*, 15–18.

24. McConal, *Over the Wall*, 114–115.

25. Underwood, *Depression Desperado*, 58, 7; Harris and Harris and Sadler, *Texas Ranger Biographies*; Kurt House, "Cold Steel and Warm Gold: Arms & Badges of Three Texas Ranger Captains." *The Texas Gun Collector*, Fall 2013. These named Rangers were what would become known as Ferguson Rangers, not all of which were incompetent, and not all of whom were admirable.

26. Ibid., 74.

27. Ibid., 122.

28. Ibid., 205.

29. Barkley and Odintz, *The Portable Handbook of Texas*, 120–121, contributor Floyd E. Ewing.

30. Rogers, *Electrocutions in Texas*, 71.

31. McConal, *Over the Wall*, 17, 114–115; James M. Day, *Captain Clint Peoples, Texas Ranger: Fifty Years A Lawman*, 37.

32. Simmons, *Assignment Huntsville*, 148.

33. McConal, *Over the Wall*, 141.

34. Underwood, *Depression Desperado*, 127; Jach, *Huntsville Penitentiary*, 92.

35. Day, *Captain Clint Peoples*, 38; Bartee Haile, *Texas Depression-Era Desperadoes*, unfortunately pens a fallacious but sometimes stereotypical characterization: "In those days, underpaid prison guards supplemented their meager income by smuggling contraband to convicts . . . ," 89. True, the criminality of some Correctional Officers was/is real; however, painting with too broad a brush mischaracterizes the vast majority of penitentiary employees, those with heads down, noses to the grindstone and unblemished honor and integrity in their back pockets.

36. *Dallas Morning News*, July 7, 1936.

37. Somewhat later there was considerable argument whether or not Patterson's three five-year sentences were stacked or running concurrently. See, *Dallas Morning News*, April 20, 1938, *Houston Chronicle*, November 6, 1938, and *Dallas Morning News*, November 15, 1938. Ultimately the decision was made: "Crooked Guard Must Serve Full 15 Years." See, *Dallas Morning News* November 11, 1939: "At a habeas corpus hearing in District Court, Judge King

ordered Patterson remanded to the custody of Warden W.W. Waid to complete the fifteen-year sentence given him Aug. 13, 1934."

38. Day, *Captain Clint Peoples*, 38; Texas Ranger Captain Clint Peoples purportedly said of Thompson's violent death: "Of the three successful escapees, only Blackie Thompson died in a manner befitting a hardened killer."

39. Underwood, *Depression Desperado*, 178, 188.

40. Ibid., 140.

41. Ibid., 197.

42. *Corpus Christi Caller-Times*, February 2, 1955.

43. *Fort Worth Star-Telegram*, May 26, 1944.

44. Jach, *Huntsville Penitentiary*, 48–49; Ethan Blue, *Doing Time in the Depression: Everyday Life in Texas and California Prisons*, p. 22, adds two gas guns to Bud Russell's armament.

45. Simmons, *Assignment Huntsville*, 184.

46. *Beaumont Journal*, August 11, 1931.

47. Simmons, *Assignment Huntsville*, 180.

48. Jackson, *Wake Up Dead Man*, 91–93; Jach, *Huntsville Penitentiary*, quotes another stanza version: "Well we know him by his wagon, and his forty-fo'." 48.

49. Rogers, *Electrocution in Texas*, 71–72. Quite interestingly esteemed authors Horton and Turner, *Lone Star Justice*, include a Death Chamber photograph of Raymond Hamilton strapped into Ole Sparky, the state's electric chair. See p. 268.

50. Caldwell and DeLord, *Texas Lawmen: More of the Good & the Bad*, 430–431.

51. Ibid. Also see, *Texas Department of Criminal Justice, Fallen Officers' Memorial Ceremony Program*, 2017, TPM.

52. Stephen William Schuster IV, "The Modernization of the Texas Rangers, 1930–1935" (Master of Arts Thesis, Texas Christian University, Fort Worth, Texas, 1965); James W. Robinson, *The DPS Story: History of the Development of the Department of Public Safety in Texas*, 3–12. Mitchel Roth's piece in the *East Texas Historical Journal* 35, 1997, "Bonnie and Clyde in Texas: The End of the Texas Outlaw Tradition," besides details about John Wesley Hardin's imprisonment and a comparative analysis of Wild West and Gangster Era outlaws, also insightfully includes remarks regarding the reasoning behind establishment of the Texas Department of Public Safety. See pp. 30–38.

Chapter 8: "So he can better handle a shotgun"

1. One critical assessment of Lee Simmons tenure with the Texas Prison System may be found in Paul M. Lucko's "Counteracting Reform: Lee Simmons and the Texas Prison System, 1930–1935," *East Texas Historical Journal*, 30, no. 2 (1992).

2. Horton and Turner, *Lone Star Justice*, 226; Price and Coleman, "Narrative of Neglect," 52.
3. Ibid. The three immediate General Managers following Simmons were, Dave R. Nelson, who died within two weeks of taking office, O.J.S. Ellingson, and Douglas W. Stakes.
4. This incident, as reported herein, is a synthesis of several sources and though there are minor discrepancies, the gist of the overall story remains unchanged. The interested reader should review, Rogers, *Electrocutions In Texas*, entry 148; Umphrey, *The Meanest Man in Texas*, 171–172; Caldwell and DeLord, *Texas Lawmen: More of the Good & the Bad*; Tise, *Texas County Sheriffs*; and Program for The Thirteenth Biennial Texas Peace Officers' Memorial Services, May 1–2, 2011.
5. *The Austin American*, June 20, 1936; *Fort Worth Star-Telegram*, June 22, 1936; Poston, "Leadership of the Texas Prison System," BCHM.
6. *Corpus Christi Times*, July 3, 1936.
7. *Houston Chronicle*, February 16, 1936.
8. *Fort Worth Star-Telegram*, February 10, 1936.
9. *Houston Chronicle*, March 12, 1936.
10. *Fort Worth Star-Telegram*, April 3, 1936.
11. [Luke] *Trammel vs. State of Texas*, 102 S.W.2d. 420 (Tex.Crim. App. 1937); *Houston Chronicle*, January 27, 1937; *Beaumont Journal*, March 10, 1937; *Corpus Christi Times*, August 20, 1937; Rogers, *Electrocutions in Texas*. 93.
12. *Beaumont Enterprise*, October 4, 1937; *Corpus Christi Times*, October 15, 1937; Also see Umphrey, *The Meanest Man* in Texas for additional commentary regarding this prison break. 180–190.
13. *Dallas Morning News*, July 6 and 23, 1936; *Fort Worth Stat-Telegram*, July 7 and 25, 1936; *Beaumont Journal*, July 6, 1936. Years later during a review of technical issues regarding his conviction under the Habitual Criminal Statue, T.B. Atkinson was formally discharged from custody per court order, see, *Ex-parte T.B. Atkinson vs. State*, 288 S.W.2d 89 (Tex.Crim.APP. 1956).
14. Stopka, *Partial List of Texas Ranger Company and Unit Commanders*. Hardy B. Purvis was Company A Captain from 1936 until 1956. 39, TRHF&M; VF-TRHF&M; *Houston Chronicle*, August 16, 1936; *Corpus Christi Caller-Times*, August 16, 1936.
15. *Dallas Morning News*, August 31, 1936.
16. Ibid.; certainly this health issue had not improved two years later. Texas Governor Allred noted: "During the past year, out of 2900 convicts received at the penitentiary 1300 were suffering from venereal diseases. . . ." "Some 850 of the 1300 were afflicted with syphilis. It takes over a year of treatment in the penitentiary to render this disease non-communicable. . . ." See, *Houston Chronicle*, December 20, 1938.

17. Ibid. In this three-part series the reporter also addresses educational matters within the system; For an informative and reasonably in-depth peek at the Prison Library, see, May 2, 1937 edition of the *Houston Chronicle*.

18. Gnagy, *Texas Jailhouse Music*, 77–82; Also see the pre-program tease for the very first broadcast as contained in the *Beaumont Enterprise*, March 20, 1938; And see the post broadcast remarks in the March 25, 1938 edition of the *Fort Worth Star-Telegram*.

19. Donna Reid Vann, *Dad, Man of Mystery*, 15–19. Don Reid's other column for the *Echo* was "Around the Yard."

20. Jach, *Huntsville Penitentiary*, 98–99. The author reports that as many as 400 free-world spectators would be in the audience for the weekly program—and inmates would provide them with a pre-broadcast show.

21. For a delightful and informative book-length treatment the interested reader should review *Texas Jailhouse Music: A Prison Band History* by Caroline Gnagy. With regards to an article-length piece the attracted reader would be advised to peruse Skip Hollandsworth's splendid "O Sister, Where Art Thou?" in the May 2003 edition of *Texas Monthly*; Blue, *Doing Time in the Depression*, devotes a chapter and his decided negative critical analysis to the radio program. See pp. 135–162.

22. *Dallas Morning News*, March 26, 1938. "Granting [Virgil] Terrell's plea not to be executed on the night of the broadcast, and on the recommendation of Warden W.W. Waid, Gov. James V. Allred stayed the execution twenty-four hours and reset it for April 1." Terrell had been convicted of Murder in Gregg County; Marquart, Ekland-Olson, and Sorensen, *The Rope, the Chair, and the Needle*, 35–36.

23. *Dallas Morning News*, April 20–21, 1938; *Houston Chronicle*, April 20, 1938.

24. Ibid., August 18, 1938.

25. Details of this prison break and resultant murder are a synthesis of several source materials: *Dallas Morning News*, August 18, 1938; *Houston Chronicle*, August 17 and 28, 1938; *Certificate of Death*, John R. Greer, 27 August 1938; *Corpus Christi Times*, February 16, 1940; Tise, *Texas County Sheriffs*, 268; and Poston, *Leadership of the Texas Prison System*.

26. Caldwell and DeLord, *Texas Lawmen: More of the Good & the Bad*, 433–434; Roth, *Convict Cowboys*, 94.

27. *Beaumont Journal*, September 29, 1938; *Houston Chronicle*, September 29, 1938; *Dallas Morning News*, September 30, 1938.

28. *Houston Chronicle*, February 3, 1939.

29. *Beaumont Journal*, March 23, 1939; *Beaumont Enterprise*, March 24, 1939.

30. Ibid., February 3, 1939; Tise, *Texas County Sheriffs*, 98; Caldwell and DeLord, *Texas Lawmen: More of the Good & the Bad*, 76–77; *Dallas Morning News*, February 4, 1939; *Beaumont Enterprise*, February 4, 1939; *Fort Worth Stat-Telegram*, February 26, 1939.

31. [Robert] *Hyde vs. The State of Texas*, 136 S,W,2d 850 (Tex.Crim.App. 1940). Also see, *Houston Chronicle*, January 11, 1940: "Life Sentence of Former Guard at Prison Is Upheld."

32. *Fort Worth Star-Telegram*, April 1, 1939.

33. *Dallas Morning News*, April 14, 1939.

34. *Houston Chronicle*, January 9, 1939; *Beaumont Enterprise*, February 10, 1939.

35. *Beaumont Journal*, September 8, 1939.

36. *Beaumont Enterprise*, October 1, 1939.

37. *Houston Chronicle*, October 1, 1939.

38. *Beaumont Enterprise*, October 1, 1939.

39. *Fort Worth Star-Telegram*, October 8, 1939.

40. Ibid., November 21, 1974, byline Carl Freund.

41. *Beaumont Journal*, April 30, 1941; Crouch and Marquart, *An Appeal to Justice*, 30; Lucko, "The Governor and the Bat," 203.

42. *Dallas Morning News*, June 19, 1941.

43. Bob Alexander, *Old Riot, New Ranger: Captain Jack Dean, Texas Ranger and U.S. Marshal*, 15.

44. [Gene Paul] *Norris vs. The State of Texas*, 175 S.W.2d 75 (Tex.Crim.App. 1943). *Dallas Morning News*, March 17, 1942; *Fort Worth-Star Telegram*, May 16, 1943 and October 28, 1943; *Beaumont Journal*, May 31, 1943 and February 24, 1943.

45. Gary Cartwright, "Talking to Killers," *Texas Monthly*, July 2002.

46. Stan Redding, "Top Gun of the Texas Rangers." *True Detective*, February 1963: ". . . for Texas police generally agree that Norris was responsible for upwards of forty slayings." 71–72.

47. For more regarding Gene Paul Norris the interested reader may wish to review Alexander and Brice, *Texas Rangers*, 370; Robert M. Utley, "Terminating Oklahoma's Smiling Killer," *Texas Ranger Dispatch*, no. 17 (Summer 2005); Ann Arnold, *Gamblers and Gangsters: Fort Worth's Jacksboro Highway in the 1940s and 1950s*, 155–161; and Douglas V. Meed, *Texas Ranger Johnny Klevenhagen*, citation to Gene Paul Norris throughout.

48. *Houston Chronicle*, January 26, 1940.

49. *Fort Worth Star-Telegram*, April 30, 1942.

Chapter: 9 "Before He Whacks You"

1. *Dallas Morning News*, August 2, 4, and 5, 1942.

2. Kemp Dixon, *Chasing Thugs, Nazis, and Reds: Texas Ranger Norman K. Dixon*, 85; Robinson, *The DPS Story*, p.23: "Due to the loss of experienced guards, the Texas Prison System suffered an unprecedented number of escapes from the state prison farms. . . ."

3. *Beaumont Enterprise*, October 18, 1938; *Dallas Morning News*, October 20, 1938 and January 22, 1943.

4. *The Gladewaters*, January 26, 1943; Brownson Malsch, *Lone Wolf: Captain M.T. Gonzaullas, The Only Texas Ranger Captain of Spanish Descent*, 145–148; Robert W. Stephens, *Lone Wolf: The Story of Texas Ranger Captain M.T. Gonzaullas*, 67–70; Alexander and Brice, *Texas Rangers*, 367–368; *Dallas Morning News*, January 26, 1943; Roger N. Conger, "Lone Wolf Gonzaullas: Courage with Composure," *Texas Ranger Annual* 4, 1985; VF, TRHF&M.

5. Dixon, *Chasing Thugs, Nazis, and Reds*, 116–117; *Dallas Morning News*, June 7, 1943; Malsch, *Lone Wolf*, 148–150; VF, TRHF&M.

6. *The Velasco World*, September 7, 1944.

7. *Dallas Morning News*, December 1, 1943.

8. *Certificate of Death*, George T. Preston, 20 June 1944; *Brownsville Herald*, June 28, 1944; *Beaumont Journal*, June 22, 1944; *TDCJ Line of Duty Deaths as of December 2017*, TPM; *Certificate of Death*, Leonard C. Stockton, 12 December 1948: "Inmate, Texas Prison System—Coronary Heart Disease."

9. *Fort Worth Star-Telegram*, November 19, 1943.

10. Ibid., October 30, 1941; *Dallas Morning News*, October 30, 1941.

11. TDCJ Fallen Officers' Memorial Ceremony Program, 2017, TPM.

12. TDC, *30 Years of Progress*, 24.

13. Horton and Turner, *Lone Star Justice*, 227–228.

14. *The Freeport Facts*, February 12, 1948.

15. Don Reid with John Gurwell, *Have a Seat, Please*, 175; Rogers, *Electrocutions in Texas*, 155.

16. Ibid.

17. DeLord, *The Ultimate Sacrifice*, 123.

18. Rogers, *Electrocutions in Texas*, 155; *Fort Worth Star-Telegram*, July 15, 1948; Reid, *Have a Seat Please*, 175.

19. Reid, *Have a Seat, Please*, 177; Texas Department of Criminal Justice, Correctional Institutions Division, *Death Row Plan*, 1–22, followed with and supplemented by multi-page appendices.

20. Horton and Turner, *Lone Star Justice*, 228; Crouch and Marquart, *An Appeal to Justice*, 32–33; Martin and Ekland-Olson, *Texas Prisons: The Walls Came Tumbling Down*, 19.

21. Copeland, "The Evolution of the Texas Department of Corrections." "One of Mr. Ellis' keys to success was that he surrounded himself with competent personnel." 105; Horton and Nielsen, *Walking George*, 123.

22. *Chicago Tribune*, December 15, 1948; *San Antonio Daily Express*, December 16, 1948; *Fort Worth Star-Telegram*, December 15 and 16, 1948.

23. Glenn, *Texas Prisons*, 65; TDC, *30 Years of Progress*, 20; TDC, *20 Years Of Progress, 1947–67: Texas Department of Corrections*, 98–99.

24. Ibid. The Cane-Knife used to decapitate Redwine is currently (in 2019) on display at the Brazoria Museum, Brazoria, Texas.

25. George Daniel Garza, "The Reforms of the Texas Prison System From 1948–1960" (Master of Arts Thesis, Sam Houston State Teachers College, 1961), 51–52; TDC, *Texas Department of Corrections: A Brief History*, 23.

26. Austin MacCormick, "Behind Those Prison Riots," *Readers Digest*, December 1953, 97–101.

27. Ibid., 98.

28. Lowell Mayrant, "The Mid-April, 1955, Riot in the Texas Prison System" (Thesis: Master of Arts, Sam Houston State Teachers College, 1955).

29. Ibid.

30. Michelle Lyons, *Death Row, The Final Minutes: My Life as an Execution Witness in America's Most Infamous Prison*, 36. Writer Lyons for the paperback edition of this book re-titled her work: *Death Row, Texas: Inside The Execution Chamber, Witnessing the Final Moments of the Condemned*. Somewhat paralleling this author's characterization, another writer admits that sometimes a journalist can stoop to smuggling contraband (in this instance marijuana) into the hands of an imprisoned inmate. See, Danny Lyon, *Like a Thief's Dream*, 58, 66, 82–83. Also see, Pickett and Stowers, *Within These Walls*, for another example of a news media person stepping to the wrong side of the ethical line: "In Ronald [Clark] O'Bryan's case, a reporter attempted entry by claiming to be a preacher. Word came that a woman had arrived at the prison, identifying herself as an ordained minister summoned to visit O'Bryan. She wore a clerical collar and carried a Bible. In truth, she was with a radio station and was turned away, cursing loudly as she was escorted out." See p. 203.

31. Mayrant, "The Mid-April, 1955, Riot in the Texas Prison System"; at this time, H. Emmett Moore was Warden; *Dallas Morning News*, April 14, 1955.

32. Ibid. Also, *Fort Worth Star-Telegram*, April 15, 1955: "Several times the convicts threatened to maim themselves by slashing their heel tendons. . . . earlier six of the men scratched their ankles with bits of glass but the condition of none was serious enough to cause hospitalization."

33. Ibid.; *Kerrville Daily Times*, April 15, 1955.

34. Christina Stopka, *Partial List of Texas Ranger Company and Unit Commanders*, 41, TRHF&M; Roger N. Conger, "Captain R.A. 'Bob' Crowder." *Texas Ranger Annual*, Vol. V [1986], 53; VF [TRHF&M].

35. *The Rusk Cherokeean*, April 16, 1955; *Dallas Morning News*, April 18, 1955; Alexander and Brice, *Texas Rangers*, 369–370; *The Longview Daily Review*, November 28, 1972; *Houston Chronicle* [Sunday Texas Magazine], February 9, 1969; *Brownsville Herald*, April 18, 1955.

36. Ben Proctor, *Just One Riot: Episodes of Texas Rangers in the 20th Century*, Chapter 6, 85–101, is wholly devoted to the "Rusk Hospital Riot"; also see,

Robert Nieman, "Captain Bob Crowder and the Rusk State Hospital Riot," *Texas Ranger Dispatch*, Spring 2001.

37. David M. Horton and George R. Nielsen, *Walking George: The Life of George John Beto and the Rise of the Modern Texas Prison System*, 71–73; Copeland, "The Evolution of the Texas Department of Corrections." "The first thing that Dr. Beto did that was contrary to the philosophies of Mr. Ellis was to phase out the Segregation Unit. . . .'the Shamrock,'" 241; *Dallas Morning News*, March 19, 1957: "Changing the name of the Texas Prison System to the Texas Department of Correction was approved. . . ."

38. Ibid.; *Corpus Christi Times*, December 24, 1955; *Dallas Morning News*, December 24, 1955.

39. Poston, *Leadership of the Texas Prison System*; Perkinson, *Texas Tough*, 231–232: "At Goree, the long-serving warden, Velma [sic Velda] Dobbs. . . ."; Also confirming that Mrs. Dobbs was in charge at Goree—and quite interesting—is the interplay between the Warden and headlining entertainer and nightclub stripper Candy Barr, as revealed by Schwarz and Rustam in *Candy Barr*, several indexed citations.

40. *Corpus Christi Times*, April 23, 1970.

41. Interview with Ronnie Dean Dobbs, Velda Dobbs' son, 19 April 2019; Upon the 1980 death of Velda Quinn Dobbs the headline was crystal clear: "First Female Warden Dies." See, *Dallas Morning News*, March 13, 1980.

42. Alexander and Brice, *Texas Rangers*, 370–373; Meed, *Texas Ranger Johnny Klevenhagen*, 173–186; Redding, "Top Gun of the Texas Rangers," 71–73; Utley, "Terminating Oklahoma's Smiling Killer"; *Dallas Morning News*, April 30 and May 3, 1957; Utley, *Lone Star Lawmen*, 210–214.

43. TDC, *30 Years of Progress*, 25–26; With regards to the correctional staff wearing uniforms, there might be room for a reasoned clarification—possibly. Reference to a 1950s switch from civilian attire to like uniforms would seem to be a system-wide innovation. According to at least one newspaper account, employees at The Walls were decked out in uniforms as early as the 1940s: "Guards are neatly uniformed and the inmates are encouraged to address them as 'Mr.' instead of 'Boss' or 'Chief.' Profanity has been outlawed, along with harsh treatment of prisoners. They are not to be coddled, but they are to be treated humanely." See, *Fort Worth Star-Telegram*, July 8, 1942.

44. Sample, *Racehoss*, 159–160. Albert Sample's learning experience in this situation, as he explained it, was clear-cut: "don't eat the fuckin ham." Somewhat regrettably, as mentioned in this text, Sample's contribution is significant—but best looked at in whole—rather than simply extracting only those incidents or episodes that further an agenda or preconceived notions.

45. Ibid., 167. For an honest, well-written, and realistic appraisal of some prison doings and a landmark civil case, see, Dick Reavis, "How They Ruined Our Prisons," *Texas Monthly*, May 1985: As but one pertinent example, "They

[Texas prisons] are places where men dissolve antihistamines in coffee to get high and where soft whole fruits are valued as aids to masturbation. . . ." With regards to in-house prison medications, writing for *The Huntsville Item's* June 16, 2000 edition Lyndol Wilkinson cogently and fascinatingly explains: "When controlled medication is administered, a person has to stand and watch the medication taken into the mouth, swallowed, and then inspect the cavity of the mouth, under the tongue and such, to be sure that the medication was actually swallowed by the individual for whom it is prescribed. Sure your eyes are rolling back in your heads now, wondering what the world has come to when a grown man has to be supervised while taking the very medication that allows him to function as normally as an individual can function while locked up 24–7 with only his like gender and those who watch over them. The reality is, some are drug abusers and would use the medication inappropriately. Others are weak and would have their medication taken from them if they weren't supervised while swallowing it. And, yet, others would sell any pill they could get to buy something that they wanted more than to have their blood pressure regulated." Watchfulness is the watchword in prison settings. For a later incident when a convict actually cut off his own penis, see Glenn, *Texas Prison Tales*, 187–188; Interview with former Warden Lon Bennett Glenn, 30 April 2019. For some other rather bizarre examples of convicts having amorous relationships with food products see Griswold, Misenheimer, Powers, and Tromanhauser (all Indiana penitentiary prisoners), authors of *An Eye for an Eye: Four Inmates on the Crime of American Prisons Today*, 163.

46. Ibid., 154. For those seeking to explore racial issues within the Lone Star State's correctional institutions from a scholarly point of view the reader should review *First Available Cell: Desegregation of the Texas Prison System* by Chad R. Trulson and James W. Marquart.

47. Ibid., 141 and 187.

48. Ibid., 171.

49. TDCJ Fallen Officers' Memorial Ceremony Program, 2017. Baker's untimely death happened at Eastham, TPM.

50. Typescript, I.K. Kelley, Jr. Courtesy, BCHM.

51. Horton and Turner, *Lone Star Justice*, 228–229.

52. Ibid.

53. Sample, *Racehoss*, 236.

54. Ibid., 239.

Chapter 10: "guts, heart—and six rounds"

1. Horton and Turner, *Lone Star Justice*, 230–232. An interested reader may also wish to peruse *Stateville: The Penitentiary in Mass Society*, by James B. Jacobs,

one of the classics of penology for the modern era whether one agrees or disagrees with Joseph E. Regan's philosophy or not.

2. Horton and Nielsen, *Walking George*, 111.
3. Ibid. The authors block the quotation from Craig R. Copeland's 1980 Sam Houston State University Masters Thesis, "The Evolution of the Texas Department of Corrections," 229.
4. Ibid., 112
5. A cogent characterization may be assessed by reviewing Chapter 4, "Co-optation of the Kept" in Crouch and Marquart's *An Appeal to Justice*, 85–116. The reader particularly interested in this aspect of the Control Model might also wish to peruse McWhorter's treatment—though not based on Texas prisons—*Inmate Society: Legs, Half-Pants and Gunmen, A Study of Inmate Guards*.
6. Horton and Nielsen, *Walking George*, 142; Alicia R. Deal, "A Preliminary Examination of Managerial Autonomy and Job Satisfaction Among Texas Wardens" (Master of Arts Thesis, Sam Houston State University, Huntsville, Texas, 2006), 38.
7. In addition to purportedly murdering an El Paso night-watchman, Pete McKenzie was convicted of killing Detective Samuel A. "Sam" Street, San Antonio PD, on 10 September 1927. See, Caldwell and DeLord, *Texas Lawmen: More of the Good & the Bad*, 318–319; *Fort Worth Star-Telegram*, August 23, 1949; *Dallas Morning News*, June 26, 1965; Rogers, *Electrocutions in Texas*, 173; *Dallas Morning News*, November 3, 1960.
8. Dilulio, *Governing Prisons*, 112.
9. Horton and Nielsen, *Walking George*, 142.
10. *Dallas Morning News*, November 16, 1938.
11. Ibid., January 20, 1937.
12. *Houston Chronicle*, February 13, 1937. *Certificate of Death*, Ed Ebbers, 12 February 1937; also see, Umphrey, *The Meanest Man in Texas*, who shares a slightly different version of Ebbers's murder. See pp. 177–178.
13. *Corpus Christi Times*, June 20, 1938.
14. *TDCJ Line of Duty Deaths as of December 2017*, TPM; Texas Department of Criminal Justice: Fallen Officers' Memorial Ceremony, 2017, TPM. Interview 6 April 2019 with Bill Stephens, Director of the Texas Department of Criminal Justice—Institutional Division, Ret.
15. *Corpus Christi Times*, June 7, 1963.
16. *Amarillo Globe Times*, June 7, 1963; *Fort Worth Star-Telegram*, June 11, 1963.
17. Copeland, "The Evolution of the Texas Department of Corrections." 230–231; Horton and Nielsen, *Walking George*, 112–120.
18. Jackson, *Wake Up Dead Man*, xv.
19. Ibid., xviii.

20. *Dallas Morning News*, August 2, 1929. Byline, Harry Benge Crozier.

21. Ibid.

22. Danny Lyon, *Conversations with the Dead*. A photographic album of prison life, stunning images throughout.

23. Crouch and Marquart, *An Appeal to Justice*, 67; Dilulio, *Governing Prisons*, 107–108: With emphasis added, "*Each* inmate spent his first six months in the prison working on the prison farms. Better jobs—in the industrial plants, kitchens, or elsewhere—awaited those who performed well." Johnson, *Hard Time*, p. 45, although not quite accurately, seems inclined to imply that toiling on the Texas prison farms was only reserved for black convicts.

24. *Dallas Morning News*, July 10, 1937.

25. Horton and Nielsen, *Walking George*, 124.

26. Interview with Dr. R. L. "Bob" Schwebel, DVM, 27 April 2019, Brazoria County, Texas.

27. Crouch and Marquart, *An Appeal to Justice*, 72. The quoted maxim, according to author Alford, himself a former Field Major, was/is a common saying among successful and seasoned Field Bosses. For an interesting and insightful newspaper article about TDCJ-ID horses, see *The Huntsville Item*, May 28, 2000, byline Michelle C. Lyons; Though a few writers, with varying degrees of commonsense it seems, sometimes decry the use of horses and dogs by TDCJ-ID personnel, these animals are valuable and practical assets—demonstrated by numerous law enforcement entities—whether it be defensive attack dogs, cadaver searching dogs, drug detections dogs, rescue dogs—and or quiet-natured saddle horses. During September 2019 TDCJ-ID dogs were used to track a disoriented elderly person lost in the twist and tangles of East Texas, safely retuning same to concerned family members.

28. Crouch, *The Keepers*, quotation on p. 211. Aside from the actual photographs depicting black, brown, and white Field Bosses, the hard facts were further confirmed through personal interviews with Former Director of TDJC—ID Bill Stevens, 1 May 2019, and former Texas Prison Wardens Arthur Velasquez, 29 April 2019, and Lon Bennett Glenn, 30 April 2019. Also 23 October 2019 interview with Lea Anne Kindle Ousley; now retired but a former horseback Field Boss with TDCJ-ID.

29. Ibid. For the anthology this chapter, "The Book vs. The Boot: Two Styles of Guarding in a Southern Prison," is most relevant and insightful, an unvarnished look at penitentiary reality by a well-regarded scholar. See pp. 220–221.

30. Ibid.

31. Horton and Nielsen, *Walking George*, 125–126.

32. Dilulio, *Governing Prisons*, 105.

33. Horton and Turner, *Lone Star Justice*, 233.

34. TDC, *30 Years of Progress*, 32.

35. Crouch and Marquart, *Appeal to Justice*, 67.

36. Copeland, "The Evolution of the Texas Department of Corrections," 249; Horton and Turner, *Lone Star Justice*, 233–234.

37. Horton and Nielsen, *Walking George*, 146; Perkinson, *Texas Tough*, 262–263.

38. Ethan Watters, "The Love Story That Upended the Prison," *Texas Monthly*, January 2019; Martin and Ekland-Olson, *Texas Prisons*, 30.

39. Ibid. Quite germane, Pickett, *Within These Walls*, mentions one of several frivolous convict-filed lawsuits: An example, given on page 147, would be when the convict's eggs were not scrambled to suit him. Also see the worthy treatment of David Skarbek, *The Social Order of the Underworld: How Prison Gangs Govern the American Penal System*, p. 64: "the number of legal suits filed against corrections officials increased from 219 in 1966 to nearly 10,000 annually by the late 1970s. By the mid-1980s, 45 states had some part of their correctional system under a court order." Not just a few in-house convict lawsuits are filed, not with the intent of redressing a wrong, but rather as a harassing tactic. Regardless the merit or lack thereof, taxpayers foot the bill while a bemused convict smirks with perverse delusions of self-grandeur.

40. Horton and Nielsen, *Walking George*, 153–157.

41. Horton and Turner, *Lone Star Justice*, 234.

42. *Corpus Christi Caller-Times*, April 25, 1971, byline Paul Slater.

43. *Navasota Examiner*, September 23, 1971; *Port Arthur News*, September 18, 1971; *Gazette Telegraph*, September 19, 1971; Texas Department of Criminal Justice: Fallen Officers' Memorial Ceremony Program, 2017.

44. Ibid., *TDCJ Line of Duty Deaths as of December 2017*, TPM.

45. Marquart, Ekland-Olson, and Sorensen, *The Rope, the Chair, & the Needle*, 129; *Dallas Morning News*, June 30, 1972.

46. Ibid., 123. The authors also address the situation regarding condemned prisoners in county jailhouses waiting to catch the chain to Huntsville; Crawford, *Texas Death Row: Executions in the Modern Era*, tallied the number of condemned prisoners on Death Row at forty-five and seven in county jails awaiting transfer to TDC. v.

47. Certainly the go-to treatment for the biography of this sordid serial killer is Gary M. Lavergne's captivating and chilling *Bad Boy From Rosebud: The Murderous Life of Kenneth Allen McDuff*. Lavergne's tally of inmates on Death Row in Texas at the time the U.S. Supreme Court upended state sanctioned executions registers as 127; 600 nationwide. See p. 52.

48. For following the trail of McDuff's post parole murders the interested reader is referred to the above citation; Too, it would be suggested to also peruse Gary Cartwright's chilling piece "Free to Kill," in the August 1992 edition of *Texas Monthly*. When appropriate for this text, time-wise, McDuff will reappear—for a little while.

Chapter 11: "Not dealing with Sunday School kids"

1. Martin and Ekland-Olson, *Texas Prisons*, 59.
2. Ibid.; *Beaumont Journal*, December 3, 1971; *Fort Worth Star-Telegram*, December 5, 1971; *Dallas Morning News*, March 2, 2972; *Corpus Christi Times*, September 14, 1972.
3. Ibid., 60, quoting Kevin Krajick, "They Keep You In, They Keep You Busy, and They Keep You from Getting Killed," *Corrections Magazine*, March 1978, 5.
4. Horton and Turner, *Lone Star Justice*, 234.
5. Reavis, "How They Ruined Our Prisons"; Crouch and Marquart, *An Appeal to Justice*, 122–123. According to the July 14, 1985, edition of *The Brazosport Facts*, "The Ohio officials dropped the old murder warrant."
6. Crouch and Marquart, *An Appeal to Justice*: "The judge even became something of a social pariah in his hometown of Tyler, Texas. To many his pro-underdog posture was too extreme; as one prison official put it he was a kamikaze liberal," 123.
7. Reavis, "How They Ruined Our Prisons."
8. Judge Justice's 11 December 1992 Memorandum Opinion, Civil Action No. H-78-987-CA, Houston Division of the Southern U.S. District of Texas, in the action styled *David Ruiz, et al., Plaintiffs, and the United States of America, Plaintiff-Intervenor vs. James A. Collins, et al., Defendants.*
9. Martin and Ekland-Olson, *Texas Prisons*, 92–93, 262, n. 35 and 36.
10. Crouch and Marquart, *An Appeal To Justice*, 123.
11. Martin and Ekland-Olson, *Texas Prisons*, 93.
12. Ibid.
13. Reavis, "How They Ruined Our Prisons."
14. Martin and Ekland-Olson, *Texas Prisons*, 92–93.
15. Thomas M. Melsheimer and Judge Craig Smith, *On the Jury Trial: Principles and Practices for Effective Advocacy*. From the Foreword by Retired U.S. District Judge Royal Furgeson, xi.
16. Ibid., 2. Thomas Melsheimer is the former federal prosecutor and Craig Smith is the State District Court Judge.
17. Martin and Ekland-Olson, *Texas Prisons*, 92.
18. Clair A. Cripe, "Courts, Corrections, and the Constitution: A Practitioner's View." In Dilulio, *Courts, Corrections, and the Constitution*, 268–286.
19. Martin and Ekland-Olson, *Texas Prisons*, xxiv.
20. H.B. 1056, 63rd Legislative Session, 1973; The current statute is found in § 500.01, Texas Government Code. The duties of and restrictions for SSIs post the landmark federal case are spelled out in detail within *Ruiz v. Estelle*, 679 F.2d 1115 (5th Cir. 1982), under the subheadings of "Orderly Functions, Clerk Functions, Field Service Worker Functions, and Turnkey Functions."
21. Crouch and Marquart, *An Appeal to Justice*, 117.

22. Glenn, *Texas Prisons*, 86–87.

23. Interview with Lon Glenn, 30 April 2019.

24. Ibid., and Glenn, *Texas Prisons*, 95.

25. William T. Harper, *Eleven Days in Hell: The 1974 Carrasco Prison Siege at Huntsville, Texas*. Certainly for the reader interested in a full-scale treatment of this incident Harper's product is seminal—and while the content is chilling from a real-life perspective, the narrative is a solidly researched page-turner. Harper also identifies convict Cuevas with the nickname "Iggy." Data regarding Cuevas' West Texas homicide conviction and escape is gleaned from the *Pecos Enterprise*, May 7–8, 1970, February 23, 1971, and June 11, 1971, byline Fran Lunday; Also see, [Ignacio] *Cuevas vs. State of Texas*. 467 S.W.D.2d 421 (Tex.Crim.App. 1971).

26. Ibid., 19–20; *Dallas Morning News*, July 26, 1974.

27. Alexander and Brice, *Texas Rangers*, 378; VF [TRHF&M].

28. Harper, *Eleven Days in Hell*, 37–39.

29. Ibid., 28. With regards to a ground-level Correctional Officer's perspective at the time, the attracted reader would be referred to the fascinating account in *Warden: Prison Life and Death from the Inside Out*, by Jim Willett and Ron Rozell. Jim Willett rose through the ranks, ultimately serving as Warden at The Walls. Subsequent to his official retirement Mr. Willett, assumed duties as Director of the captivating Texas Prison Museum at Huntsville, a post he held until 2018, turning over that institution's administrative reins to Bill Stephens, the former and now retired TDCJ-ID Director, who graciously penned the Foreword for this volume.

30. Alexander and Brice, *Texas Rangers*, 378. RAC Wiatt was, in fact, already in Huntsville.

31. Harper, *Eleven Days in Hell*; Mike Cox, *Stand-Off in Texas: "Just Call Me a Spokesman for DPS. . . ."*: "After nearly two weeks, the stand-off ended. . . ." 9; *Dallas Morning News*, July 31 and August 3, 1974.

32. *Beaumont Journal*, July 29, 1974; For generalized remarks regarding penitentiary employees being taken hostage, see Edwin J. Donovan, "Responding to the Prison Employee-Hostage as a Crime Victim," in *Correctional Officers: Power, Pressure and Responsibility*, edited by Julie N. Tucker, 17–24.

33. Procter, *Just One Riot*, 104–105. An interested reader also might choose to peruse Wilson McKinney's *Fred Carrasco: The Heroin Merchant* for supplemental data regarding this narco-kingpin. Also see, *Houston Chronicle*, August 3, 1984, bylines John Makeig and Frank Michel, for an edition looking back to ten years before: "As many as 150 people in Mexico and the United States may have died at the hands of the burly Carrasco, overseer of a San Antonio-based heroin syndicate that for years had operated between Mexico and Chicago. . . ."

34. Harper, *Eleven Days in Hell*, citations to individuals throughout. For a more-or-less behind the scenes recap with emphasis on families of the hostages, see Pickett and Stowers, *Within These Walls*, 1–20.

35. Proctor, *Just One Riot*, 109. Quite interestingly and poignant, during a 17 September 2019 interview with Pam Hobson, Judy Standley's daughter, she stated that throughout the trying ordeal it was her mother (a hostage) who through telephone calls kept the family's spirits boosted by consoling them, rather than casting an aura of fear, gloom, and hopelessness. Though perhaps using it as a measure of control, Carrasco allowed frequent telephone contact between hostages and their families. Likewise, on-the-ground TDC leadership briefed the families thrice daily—concerned with keeping them updated as much as possible without jeopardizing tactical plans. Though grief-stricken with the tragic end-result, Ms. Hobson did not harbor any rancor regarding TDC. She comes from a law enforcing background; her father, Troy Standley, was an esteemed FBI Special Agent and her husband, Bernie Hobson, is employed as a U.S. Department of Justice lawyer for the past forty years.

36. *Dallas Morning News*, July 29, July 30, and August 3, 1974.

37. Harper, *Eleven Days in Hell*, 282; *Dallas Morning News*, July 26, 1974: "And four military helicopters—one medical evacuation unit and three armored attack machines—were standing by at the small Huntsville airport." And in the edition of July 31, 1974: The Huntsville Hospital Administrator, James D. Stann, reported that the medical facility would "work with the prison hospital in the event the escape attempt by Carrasco has [had] a non-peaceful resolution. . . . The hospital will handle civilian casualties while the prison will handle prison and guard injuries. Severely injured people would be taken by Department of Public Safety helicopters to Houston. Although the hospital can handle severe car wrecks, it has never been on an emergency alert as it has been for the past eight days." Also see, W.J. Estelle, Jr. ed., *A Time to Forget. . . . And Remember*. In this 1975 post incident photo essay for TDC employees, Director Estelle highlights law enforcement and community support throughout the eleven-day crisis.

38. Ibid., 276–296; Alexander and Brice, *Texas Rangers*, 379.

39. Proctor, *Just One Riot*, 117; Harper, *Eleven Days in Hell*, 77. Certainly it's also fair to mention the contributions of Ron Taylor, TDC's Public Affairs Director, and Dr. Don Kirkpatrick, Assistant Director, "head of Treatment," though their areas of expertise were not necessarily in the realm of hardcore tactical operations.

40. Utley, *Lone Star Lawmen*, 274–275.

41. Ibid. Also see, Cox, *Time of the Rangers*, 299.

42. Harper, *Eleven Days in Hell*, 290. Authors for this narrative refrain from counting the number of gunshots.

43. *Dallas Morning News*, August 5, 1974: "Guard Saves 8 Hostages."

44. Alexander and Brice, *Texas Rangers*, 379; Crawford, *Texas Death Row*, 39; [Ignacio] *Cuevas vs. The State of Texas.* 742 S.W.2d 331 (Tex.Crim.App. 1987).

45. *Dallas Morning News* August 5, 1974.

46. Ibid.

47. Alexander and Brice, *Texas Rangers*, 379. Also see, the twenty-page written report of Warden Husbands, "The Escape Attempt of Inmates Fred Gomez Carrasco, #237163, Rudy Dominguez, #232414, Ignacio Cuevas, #218121," TRHF&M. And see, "Investigation of Attempted Escape at the Walls Unit of the Department of Corrections, Huntsville, Texas, on July 24, 1974. This Investigation Ordered By: The Honorable Governor Dolph Briscoe, Under the Direction of: Texas Ranger Captain J.F. [Pete] Rogers," TRHF&M.

48. For additional and detailed material regarding building a functioning and well-equipped Ranger SWAT Team, the interested reader might wish to review Bob Alexander's *Old Riot, New Ranger: Captain Jack Dean, Texas Ranger and U.S. Marshal*. For Jack Dean's citation to the Carrasco affair see, *Victoria Advocate*, July 14, 1975.

49. *Dallas Morning News*, November 23, 1976.

50. *Fort Worth Star-Telegram*, January 14, 1977.

51. Ibid., February 11, 1977.

52. *Dallas Morning News*, July 14, 1977.

53. Ibid., September 1, 1977.

54. *Corpus Christi Times*, September 6, 1977: "Must we recycle the electric chair?"; *Dallas Morning News*, October 20, 1977: "Lethal-injection law termed cruel."

55. *Dallas Morning News*, November 15, 1977. The state's electric chair, Ole Sparky, is now a museum artifact on display at the recently (2019) expanded and remodeled Texas Prison Museum, Huntsville, Texas, truly a first-rate historical institution documenting the evolution of the Lone Star State's prison saga and honoring the personnel who have made the ultimate sacrifice while so employed.

56. Poston, "Leadership of the Texas Prison System"; Interview with Ronald Dean Dobbs as previously cited; Horton and Turner, *Lone Star Justice*, 234.

57. *Dallas Morning News*, January 25, 1974.

58. Ibid., January 31, 1977.

59. Ibid., March 30 and June 1, 1975.

60. Transcript: Lucile Garrett Plane, TDCJ-ID Warden, Ret., interview by Nancy Ray, an Oral History project of the Texas Ranger Hall of Fame & Museum, Waco, Texas, 7 April 2009; Tise, *Texas County Sheriffs*, 132. For additional data regarding Texas Ranger Captain Robert K. Mitchell, see, Alexander, *Old Riot, New Ranger*; Eric J. Williams, *The Big House in A Small Town: Prisons, Communities, and Economics in Rural America*, emphasizes the relationships between prison unit administrators and local law enforcement officials. 108–112.

61. Ibid. With regards to Death Row for females, an interesting newspaper piece was published in the September 13, 2000, edition of the *Austin American Statesman*, an article focused on renovation. The reader in want of learning more about the prison life of a female Death Row convict might wish to peruse *Dateline Purgatory: Examining the Case That Sentenced Darlie Routier to Death* by Kathy Cruz. During an engaging and enlightening 26 October 2019 interview retired TDCJ Clinical Corrections Associate Brenda Martin revealed the best general philosophy of daily dealing with female convicts: Treat them as you would want to be treated. Though she did not welcome convicts into her circle of personal friends, she saw them as human beings worthy of fair but firm and consistent dealings.

62. Crouch and Marquart, *An Appeal to Justice*, 124; *Dallas Morning News*, October 7, 1978; *Fort Worth Star-Telegram*, October 8, 1978: "We are in sympathy with the Ruiz case. . . ."; *Corpus Christi Times*, October 9, 1978.

63. Martin and Ekland-Olson, *Texas Prisons*, 137–138.

64. *Corpus Christi Times*, October 18, 1978.

65. Ibid.

66. *Dallas Morning News*, October 19, 1978. Byline Donnis Baggett.

67. Martin and Ekland-Olson, *Texas Prisons*, 138–139.

68. Ibid.

69. John J. Dilulio, Jr., "Conclusion: What Judges Can Do to Improve Prisons and Jails." In, Dilulio, *Courts, Corrections, and the Constitution*, 287–322.

70. Crouch, ed. *The Keepers*, Chapter 7, "Screws vs. Thugs," by Anthony L. Guenther and Mary Quinn Guenther, 174.

71. Dilulio, "Conclusion: What Judges Can Do. . . .", Quoting the *Houston Post* of November 7, 1978.

72. *Fort Worth Star-Telegram*, October 11, 1978.

73. *Dallas Morning News*, May 30, 1979; Gary Cartwright, *Dirty Dealing: Drug Smuggling on the Mexican Border and the Assassination of a Federal Judge*; Alexander, *Old Riot, New Ranger*, 288–289.

74. Interview with Texas Ranger Captain and Western District United States Marshal, Ret., Jack O. Dean, 15 August 2017; Cox, *Time of The Rangers*, 306; Utley, *Lone Star Lawmen*, 278–279.

75. *Fort Worth Star-Telegram*, May 10, 1984, Byline Karen Hastings.

76. *Dallas Morning News*, May 10, 1984, Byline David McLemore.

77. DPS-PR (Progress Report), Texas Ranger Jack Dean, 8 May 1972, TRHF&M. Also see, Alexander, *Old Riot, New Ranger*, Chapter 8, "I located Harrelson's pistol," 204–228, 463 n. 12; Bobby Nieman, ed., "20th Century Shining Star: Captain Jack Dean, United States Marshal," *Texas Ranger Dispatch*, April 2008.

78. This particular prison work-shoe, with the hollowed-out concealment chamber is on exhibit at TPM.

79. *Desert News*, July 6, 1995; David Berg, *Run, Brother Run: A Memoir*, 218; Michael G. Santos, *INSIDE: Life Behind Bars in America*, 32.

80. *Fort Worth Star-Telegram*, December 30, 1984. Byline Jim Jones.

81. *Dallas Morning News*, August 29, 1979; DeLord, *The Ultimate Sacrifice*, 162.

82. Ibid.; *Beaumont Journal*, August 29, 1979; Marquart, Ekland-Olson, and Sorensen, *The Rope, the Chair, & the Needle*, 179–180; Regarding the death weapon being a chicken bone, see, Kerry Max Cook, *Chasing Justice: My Story of Freeing Myself After Two Decades on Death Row for a Crime I Didn't Commit*, 135–136, which tends to support the fact that newspaper coverage and prison officials were forced into admitting: "No weapon had been found as of late Tuesday afternoon, Hartley said. . . ." The authors do not quibble with Kerry Max Cook's assertion that the death weapon was a chicken bone; he was there—on Death Row—but the murder weapon mystery was later determined, according to a newspaper report, to be a pork-chop bone, a handy natural implement serving as a push-dagger of sorts.

83. *Dallas Morning News*, March 7, 1982.

84. *Beaumont Journal*, September 7, 1979; *Dallas Morning News*, October 6, 1979; *Fort Worth Star-Telegram*, October 7, 1979. The killing of Carl Reed is also covered in Martin and Ekland-Olson, *Texas Prisons*, 149. Their take on the motive for Reed's murder—which may or may not be correct—is that it revolved around the deceased's earlier testimony in the *Ruiz* lawsuit. *¿Quién sabe?*

85. *Dallas Morning News*, August 29, 1979: "[Edward] King's killing is the first on death row in recent history and the first in the correction department's 16–unit system in almost two years, according to [Rick] Hartley."

Chapter 12: "An Unwilling pioneer"

1. *Dallas Morning News*, December 22, 25, and 26, 1979; *Fort Worth Star-Telegram*, December 26, 1979. During a delightful and informative 21 September 2019 interview, former Correctional Officer Laura Greenwood, assigned to the Goree Unit during the 1970s, reiterated reality: Whether dealing with male or female convicts, watchfulness and fairness and consistency are important aspects of managing all convicts—protecting them as well as maintaining staff security being the primary goal of incarceration, then followed by the laudable and reformative programming. Anyone can be dangerous. Insecure settings are not conducive to rehabilitation.

2. Mark Colvin, with Foreword by Ben M. Crouch, *The Penitentiary In Crisis: From Accommodation To Riot In New Mexico*, approaches the 1980 New Mexico prison riot from an academic and historical baseline; Roger Morris, *The Devil's Butcher Shop: The New Mexico Prison Uprising*, tackles the subject with the skill of a well-seasoned print journalist; G. Hirliman, *The Hate Factory: A First-Hand*

Account of the 1980 Riot at the Penitentiary of New Mexico, proffers the remembrance of a convict that was there, W.G. Stone; For a chronological timeline of the murderous uprising, see the Santa Fe *New Mexican,* February 4, 1980. A thoughtful reader might choose to review these and other sources before reaching an unalterable cause and effect opinion. It is also but evenhanded to mention that the newsmaker 1971 New York riot at Attica had a higher body count, but only three convicts were killed by other convicts—far dissimilar to the disorder and death in New Mexico. Closer to home, the *Fort Worth Star-Telegram,* February 7, 1980, byline Lynna Williams, carried a story wherein a college social-work professor was inclined to indict the "U.S. correctional system itself. . . ."; Skarbek, *The Social Order,* 64.

3. *Del Rio News-Herald,* October 2, 1980; *Dallas Morning News,* October 2, 1980; Certificate of Death, Cepus DeWard Burson, 1 October 1980; *TDCJ Line of Duty Death as of December 2017,* TPM; DeLord, *The Ultimate Sacrifice,* 179.

4. *Dallas Morning News,* October 5, 1980: "Inmates Aid Family"; Bobby Delgado, *Gangs, Prisons, Parole: The Politics Behind Them,* 184–186.

5. *Ruiz v. Estelle,* 503 F. Supp. 1265 (S.D. Tex. 1980).

6. Ibid. For interesting assessment of attorney fees associated with this legal action, see *Ruiz v. Estelle,* 553 F.Supp. 567 (S.D.Tex. 1982).

7. Ibid.; Crouch and Marquart, *An Appeal to Justice,* 126–127.

8. For a cogent discussion of expert witnesses, see Melsheimer and Smith, *On the Jury Trial,* 125–137.

9. Glenn, *Texas Prisons,* 299.

10. Dilulio, ed., *Courts, Corrections, and the Constitution.* The reader interested in a comparative analysis of Judge Justice's ruling in *Ruiz v. Estelle,* will need to review John J. DiIulio's Chapter 2, "The Old Regime and the *Ruiz* Revolution: The Impact of Judicial Intervention on Texas Prisons," 51–72; Sheldon Ekland-Olson and Steve J. Martin's Chapter 3, "*Ruiz*: A Struggle Over Legitimacy," 73–93; and Chapter 4, "*Ruiz*: Intervention and Emergent Order in Texas Prisons," by Ben M. Crouch and James W. Marquart, 94–114. Not surprisingly these assessments are not necessarily harmonious, leaving the readers the option to choose what makes good sense to them.

11. Aside from the actual court documents, readers wishing to explore more about *Ruiz v. Estelle,* might access the aforementioned *An Appeal to Justice* by Crouch and Marquart; *Governing Prisons* by Dilulio, and Martin and Ekland-Olson, *Texas Prisons,* as well as "How They Ruined Our Prisons" by Reavis.

12. *The Echo,* Special Edition, Vol. 56, No. 3, May/June 1985.

13. *Texas Certificate of Death,* Wallace Melton Pack, 4 April 1981: "from asphyxia due to drowning (homicide), at the Ellis Unit prison farm." *Texas Certificate of Death,* Billy Max Moore, 4 April 1981: "from a gunshot wound to the head (homicide). . . ." *Fort Worth Star-Telegram,* April 5, 1981, byline Stan Jones;

Dallas Morning News, April 5, 1981, byline Nikki Finke Greenberg and Christi Harlan; Tise, *Texas County Sheriffs*, 38.

14. Michael Berryhill, *The Trials of Eroy Brown: The Murder Case That Shook the Texas Prison System*, 72–80. This treatment for someone interested in exploring further these killings would be suggested. Though, as with any hot-topic controversies—especially courtroom contests—it is the readers' responsibility to value or devalue any opinions and/or inferences. Interview with Art Velasquez, TDCJ-ID Warden, Ret., 29 April 2019.

15. *Dallas Morning News*, April 7, 1981. Byline Christi Harlan.

16. *Beaumont Journal*, April 7, 1981.

17. *Dallas Morning News*, April 8, 1981.

18. Berryhill, *The Trials of Eroy Brown*, 199; Short biographical profile of Judge Hester is courtesy researcher and writer extraordinaire Rick Miller, former lawman and retired County Attorney for Bell County [Belton].

19. Glenn, *Texas Prisons*, 142; Willet and Rozelle, *Warden*, 135 and 141.

20. David W. Neubauer, *America's Courts and the Criminal Justice System*, 33, 359.

21. Berryhill, *The Trials of Eroy Brown*, 207.

22. Willett and Rozelle, *Warden*, 138; Crawford, *Texas Death Row*, 1.

23. Marquart, Ekland-Olson, and Sorensen, *The Rope, the Chair & the Needle*, 148.

24. Horton and Turner, *Lone Star Justice*, 271; Also see, Pamela Colloff's piece, "The Witness" in the September 2014 edition of *Texas Monthly* and Dick Reavis's article "Charlie Brooks' Last Words," in *Texas Monthly*, February 1983.

25. *Dallas Morning News*, October 8 and 17, 1983; *Fort Worth Star-Telegram*, October 9, 1983; Copeland, "The Evolution of the Texas Department of Corrections," remarked: "Dr. George Beto realized that it was the guard that made the prison run smoothly." 231; Ward James Estelle was of a like mind—and Correctional Officers loved and respected him for it, reciprocating with the same and sincere and heartfelt personal and professional appreciation.

26. Ibid., May 22, 1984. Byline G. Robert Hillman; *Fort Worth Star-Telegram*, May 22, 1984. Byline Karen Hastings.

27. Juan Santana and Gabriel Morales, *Gangs in the Lone Star State*. Also, Morales, *La Familia—The Family: Prison Gangs in America*. Particularly with regards to Lone Star State prison gangs, see the characterizations of the Texas Syndicate, Mexikanemi (Texas Mexican Mafia), Barrio Azteca, Los Hermanos de Pistoleros Latinos, Raza Unida, Tango Orejon, Aryan Brotherhood of Texas, Texas Mafia, and OMGs (Outlaw Motorcycle Gang)] Bandidos, as well as Crips and Bloods for the short list. Also see, the October 4, 2005, edition of *Narcotics Digest Weekly*, "Gangs in the United States."

28. *Fort Worth Star-Telegram*, April 11, 1976. Byline Paul Recer; Copeland, "The Evolution of the Texas Department of Corrections." "Ever since the Texas

Prison System came into being, there has been a problem of the strong preying on the weak." See p. 108.

29. *Dallas Morning News*, September 30, 1984. Byline Steve Blow.

30. Crouch and Marquart, *An Appeal to Justice*, 189.

31. *Dallas Morning News*, September 30, 1984.

32. Crouch and Marquart, *An Appeal to Justice*, 195, 202. During one sweep at the Coffield Unit a search of two cellblocks uncovered 489 weapons—including 346 homemade knives, one of which measured a foot and half long. See, *Houston Post* July 21, 1984, byline Fred King.

33. *Dallas Morning News*, September 30, 1984. With several prison units in Brazoria County the cost to taxpayers for investigating and prosecuting convicts for in-house criminality skyrocketed. Sheriff Joe King and his command staff were required to make a statistical and financial accounting of expenditures of employees' time and monetary expenses associated with investigating felony offenses at TDCJ facilities, as was the District Attorney's Office. Interview with former Sheriff Joe King and former Brazoria County Assistant District Attorney Tom Selleck, 29 April 2019. Also see, related Brazoria County Sheriff's Office internal reports regarding same, nominally titled, "Break Down on Cases Worked by Brazoria County Sheriff's Department Identification, CID, and Patrol Divisions at the Texas Department of Corrections Units in Brazoria County," submitted by Chief Deputy James M. Hinton and Patrol Division Captain R.L. McCall.

34. Robert S. Fong, "A Comparative Study of the Organizational Aspects of Two Texas Prison Gangs: Texas Syndicate and Mexican Mafia" (Dissertation, College of Criminal Justice, Sam Houston State University, Huntsville, Texas, 1987).

35. Peter J. Benekos and Alida V. Merlo, eds., *Corrections: Dilemmas and Directions*, Chapter 4, "Prison Gang Dynamics: A Look Inside the Texas Department of Corrections," by Robert S. Fong, Ronald E. Vogel, and Salvador Buentello, 57–77. A cursory look at some prison gangs and Outlaw Motorcycle Gangs (OMGs) may be found in Michael Newton's *The Encyclopedia of GANGSTERS: A World Wide Guide to Organized Crime*, 109.

36. Reavis, "How They Ruined Our Prisons"; quite interestingly the U.S. 5th Circuit Appellate Court, in its 1982 review of *Ruiz v. Estelle* clearly noted the dearth of Texas prison murders: "Escapes are virtually unheard of and homicides are uncommon but there is excessive nonhomicidal violence. . . . all inmates are exposed to, and many are victimized by, the concomitants of unguarded, overcrowded cells and dormitories—the ever-present risk of assaults, rapes and other violence-for every day of their incarceration at TDC." See, *Ruiz v. Estelle*, 679 F2d 1115 (5th Cir. 1982). While not shying from widespread violence behind the tall walls and high fences of Texas prisons, the 5th Circuit Court also recognized reality: "The homicide rate at TDC is less than in many cities." Soon,

however, the in-house murder rate for Texas prison units would skyrocket—an irrefutable statistic—though the causative factors are yet fervently debated within academic circles—which is but par business for theoretical thinkers.

37. Pickett, with Stowers, *Within These Walls*, 141.

38. *Dallas Morning News*, September 30, 1984, byline Steve Blow. Another convict told a *Houston Chronicle* reporter for a May 28, 2000, piece: "in the old days, before federal control changed the system in 1981. . . . They [BTs] were charged with keeping the other prisoners under control, making it possible to run prisons with fewer guards. When the state was forced to stop using building tenders, there weren't enough guards to maintain the level of control. That is when gangs began to grow in number and strength. Prisoners formed or joined gangs for power or protection. Building tenders back then were better than the gangs now. . . ."

39. Ibid. Also see, the November 1985 edition of *Texas Research League Analysis*, 4.

40. Delgado, *Gangs, Prisons, Parole*, 408–409.

41. Fong, Vogel, and Buentello, "Prison Gang Dynamics," 63.

42. *Fort Worth Star-Telegram*, November 28, 1998; 24 September 2019 interview with Robert D. Garza, Jr., Texas Rangers, Ret.

43. Lyons, *Death Row*, 97.

44. Glenn, *Texas Prisons*, 325.

45. Crawford, *Texas Death Row*, 35, 83, and 183.

46. Lyons, *Death Row*, 141, 115–116; *Houston Chronicle*, June 10 and 11, 2000; *The Huntsville Item*, June 11, 2000, byline Michelle C. Lyons.

47. Ibid., 161; Crawford, *Texas Death Row*, 214. At the Telford Unit in northeast Texas, one convict, according to the *Texarkana Gazette*, put a mixture of feces and urine in a plastic squirt bottle and spewed it on an unsuspecting Correctional Officer. For this heinousness he caught a life sentence. See, the *Gazette* editions of August 31 and October 4, 2018, bylines Lynn LaRowe. Interview with Ronald J. Alford, former TDCJ-ID Major, 28 June 2019.

48. Delgado, *Gangs, Prisons, Parole*, 280.

49. Blatchford, *The Black Hand*, 124 and 305; Rafael, *The Mexican Mafia*, 123.

50. Interview with Ronald J. Alford, 28 June 2019; *New York Times*, August 31, 1992; Glenn, *Texas Prisons*, 301–303.

51. *Curtis Weeks v. The State of Texas*, 834 S.W.2d 559 (Tex.App—Eastland 1992); *Knoxville News-Sentinel*, August 27, 1988; *Morning Olympian*, August 27, 1988.

52. Alford interview as cited above; *Mobile Register*, August 27, 1988.

53. *Curtis Weeks v. The State of Texas*, as cited above: "Dr. Day testified that she was a member of the San Francisco General Hospital AIDS Committee, a member of the California Chancellor's AIDS Committee, and a member of the AIDS Task Force for the American Academy of Orthopedic Surgeons. . . . Dr. Day testified that appellant's [Curtis Week's] medical records show that he was

'HIV-4' a week before he spit on the officer. Dr. Day stated that the medical records showed that appellant had gingivitis and that, therefore, there was a much higher chance he had blood in his mouth and his saliva. In addition, the records showed that appellant had had nausea, vomiting, diarrhea, and fevers near the time of the incident, increasing the chances that appellant may have had lesions in his mouth or blood in his saliva. Dr. Day testified that it was possible that the complainant could contract HIV if appellant spit his saliva onto the complaint's face. If appellant's saliva entered the complaint's nose, the complaint's chance of contracting HIV would increase according to Dr. Day." Also see, *Weeks v. Collins*, 867 F.Supp. 544 (SD TX 1994) and *Weeks v. Scott*, 55F. 3d. 1059 (5th Cir. 1995).

54. Alford interview as cited above; *Baytown Sun*, November 6, 1989.

55. Glenn, *Texas Prisons*, 303.

56. For enumeration of the other felonies attributed to the Death Row defendant, see, *Ponchai Wilkerson v. The State of Texas*, 881 S.W.2d 321 (Tex.Crim.App. 1994). Also within this legal framework are the conclusions of a psychiatrist and a clinical psychologist who had testified for the defense during the punishment phase of Wilkerson's trial. Each proffered that—despite Ponchai's violent crime spree and the predictability of his acting out—those acts of criminality would not necessarily foretell or be indicative of his future dangerousness and/or his rehabilitative forecast. Of course, at the time of their testimony Ponchai Wilkerson had not yet participated in the failed escape attempt from Death Row, nor had he taken female Correctional Officer Jeanette Bledsoe hostage. The thoughtful reader may weigh the merit—or lack of merit—of their analysis. Certainly penologist Hans Toch, *Police, Prisons, and the Problem of Violence*, amplifies the disparity of thought bubbling forth from the psychological and psychiatric communities: "It is ironic that another group of psychiatrists concludes that 'Neither psychiatrists nor anyone else have reliably demonstrated an ability to predict future violence or 'dangerousness.' Neither has any special psychiatric 'expertise' in this area been established." 102, n.4.

57. *The Huntsville Item*, February 22 and 23 and March 26, 2000, bylines Michelle C. Lyons; *Fort Worth Star-Telegram*, February 22 and 23, 2000, byline for the latter edition Barry Shlachter; *Houston Chronicle*, February 23, 2000, bylines James Kimberly and Kathy Walt; *San Antonio Express News*, February 23 and 25, 2000, bylines Bill Hendricks; *Austin American-Statesman*, February 23, 2000, byline Mike Ward; *Dallas Morning News*, February 23, 2000, byline Diane Jennings and February 23, 2000, byline Pete Slover. The Texas Ranger participating with prison officials in the successful negotiations with convicts Wilkerson and Guidry was Captain Earl Pearson, Company A, later Senior Captain (Chief) of the Texas Rangers.

58. Crawford, *Texas Death Row*, 210; *Fort Worth Star-Telegram*, March 15, 2000: "Condemned killer spits out handcuff key, dies." Byline Michael Graczyk,

AP; *The Huntsville Item*, March 16, 2000, byline Michelle C. Lyons; *Houston Chronicle*, March 16, 2000, byline Bill Murphy.

59. [Jermarr] *Arnold v. The State of Texas*, 873 S.W.2d 27 (Tex.Crim.App. 1993); *Corpus Christi Times*, July 18 and 22, 1983.

60. Crawford, *Texas Death Row*, 258.

61. Interview with retired TDCJ-ID Regional Director Bob Parker, 16 July 2019. The authors have not, nor did Regional Director Parker, initiate any inquiry to determine if Arnold was incarcerated at the Pelican Bay facility. That he was a California prison inmate, however, is indisputable. Also see, Texas Attorney General Media Advisory: Jermarr Carlos Arnold. A Golden State psychiatrist (Dr. Sheppard) testified as an expert witness for the prosecution that Arnold, he believed, "was one of the most dangerous people he had come across." And he predicted that "Arnold would be an ongoing threat of physical harm to others, whether outside or inside prison."

62. TDCJ-ID Execution Report: Jermarr Arnold.

63. *Arnold v. Texas*, as cited.

64. 24 September 2019 interview with Robert D. Garza, Jr., Texas Rangers, Ret.; Crawford, *Texas Death Row*, 258.

65. *Fort Worth Star-Telegram*, April 6 and 7, 1995; United Press International [UPI], April 6, 1995, byline Wayne Sorge; *Orlando Sentinel*, April 7, 1995.

66. *El Paso Times*, December 20, 1990; Crawford, *Texas Death* Row, 258.

Chapter 13: "violent convicts commit violent acts"

1. With regards to this subject the reader may wish to study two of Gabriel C. "Gabe" Morales's informative works, *La Familia—The Family: Prison Gangs in America* and *The History of the Aryan Brotherhood*. Each volume is jam-packed with specifics and photographs of various convict gang members, many with representative and identifiable gang tattoos. Some inter-penitentiary "hits" are carried out while the convict murderer is being held in hypothetical close custody. Particularly, for a chilling account of two federal Correctional Officers, Merle Eugene Clutts and Robert F. Hoffman, Sr. being murdered within hours of each other by convicts Thomas "Terrible Tom" Silverstein and Clayton Fountain, respectively, at the federal lockup at Marion, Illinois, see Pete Early's *The Hot House: Life Inside Leavenworth Prison*, 227–241. Also see, Santos, *INSIDE*, 30–38.

2. John J. DiIulio, Jr., ed., *Courts, Corrections and the Constitution: The Impact of Judicial Intervention on Prisons and Jails*. Contributors Ben M. Crouch and James W. Marquart, "Ruiz: Intervention and Emergent Order in Texas Prisons": "Today, through perfectly constitutional means, TDC officials have placed in 'ad seg' thousands of prisoners whom officials have designated violence prone,

gang affiliated, or unwilling to follow prison routines. Prisoners can remain in segregation indefinitely. . . . ," 106 and 109.

3. The Constitutionality of Administrative Segregation was upheld in *Ronnie Bruscino v. Norman Carlson* (Director of Federal Prisons), 654 F.Supp.609 (S.D.Ill. 1987) and that lower court decision was affirmed by appellate review in *Ronnie Bruscino v. Norman Carlson*, 854 F.2d 162 (7th Cir. 1988). Quite interestingly and appropriately former TDCJ-ID Regional Director Bob Parker, confirmed (16 July 2019) that, indeed, a simple No. 2 lead pencil can be driven into eyes or a brain or a heart. His observation is based on bloody first-hand experience. And see, *Houston Chronicle*, January 17, 2000: "Inmate Stabs TDC Guard with Pencil"; *The Huntsville Item*, January 17, 2000, byline Michelle Lyons.

4. Keramet Reiter, *23/7: Pelican Bay Prison and the Rise of Long-Term Solitary Confinement*, 137.

5. Natasha A. Frost and Carlos E. Monteiro, "Administrative Segregation in U.S. Prisons Executive Summary," A paper prepared for the U.S. Department of Justice, National Institute of Justice, March 2016, p. 2.

6. [David] *Flores v. Livingston*, 405 Fed.App. 931 (5th Cir. 2010). Also see, [Robert King] *Wilkinson v. Austin*, 545 U.S. 209 (2005) and *Wilkerson v. Goodwin*, 744 F. 3d 845 (5th Cir 2014); [Marjan] *Rroku v. Cole*, 726 Fed.Appx. 201 (5th Cir. 2018).

7. The interested reader wishing to explore other academic viewpoints with regards to the practice of lawful Administrative Segregation and Supermax Penal Institutions may want to review Sharon Shalev, *SUPERMAX: Controlling risk through solitary confinement* [lower case correct] and/or Reiter, *23/7*. Whether or not the reader is swayed by the professors' interpretations is of course—as it should be—a call the individual reader is entitled to make— leveling their construal of commonsense or lack thereof into the equation. Perhaps for a contrasting appraisal—at least by some degree—the reader might also choose to examine James H. Bruton's assessment, *The Big House: Life Inside a Supermax Security Prison*. Author Bruton was actually Warden at a Supermax facility and brings forth a judicious balance regarding the welfare and humane treatment of dangerous convicts within the context of protecting society, protecting the convicts from each other and, perhaps most immediately important, protecting his custodial staff.

8. Mark S. Fleisher, *Warehousing Violence*, 197.

9. TDCJ-ID, *Administrative Segregation Plan*, 2012. For a look at Administrative Segregation guidelines at the federal level, the interested reader may wish to access the United States Bureau of Prisons (BOP), Program Statement 5270.07, "Inmate Discipline and Special Housing Units."

10. Ibid.

11. Crouch, *The Keepers*, 14–15.

12. Typescript: Marie Beth Jones, 24 August 1984 interview with unnamed wife of a Brazoria County Correctional Officer, BCHM.

13. Ibid. For convict ingenuity also see *Tom White: The Life of a Lawman* by Verdon R. Adams, where federal prisoners were stealing eggs from the kitchen wholesale and boiling them in the prison laundry's hot water so that they could have a "light snack" in their cells whenever they so desired. 138. Interestingly Tom White carried official commissions as a Texas Ranger and, later, a Special Agent with the FBI. Subsequent to his law enforcing service he was Warden at two federal penitentiaries, Leavenworth, Kansas, and La Tuna at El Paso.

14. Edward Bunker, *Education of a Felon*, 266. The author, a former convict, eventually became a celebrated writer of criminal doings, as well as an actor. For Quentin Tarantino's gritty portrayal of career criminals and killers in the movie *Reservoir Dogs* the part of Mr. Blue was played by Ed Bunker. See Rafael, *The Mexican Mafia*, 280.

15. TDCJ-ID, *Correctional Officer Handbook*, 21; TDCJ-ID, *Pre-Service Training Student Study Guide*, 224–231; Bowker, *Prison Victimization*, 61; Earley, *The Hot House*, 184–185; Correctional Officers also have to maintain constant vigilance so as not to be embroiled in an embarrassing and/or compromising off-duty scenario with a convict's wife or girlfriend, a not uncommon and devious ploy by the latter to ensnare the former.

16. For a most interesting example of the corruptive game designed to ensnare a Correctional Officer into illegality the reader may wish to peruse the brilliant piece in the August 1991 edition of *Texas Monthly*, "A Guard in Gangland," by Robert Draper. The story is sad in one sense, but altogether revealing in the other. Also see, Hoffman and McCoy, *Concrete Mama*, 66–67.

17. Glenn, *Texas Prisons*, 299–301. Quite interestingly, Jack M. Garner explores this issue in his 1995 Master of Science Thesis for Sam Houston State University, Huntsville, Texas, "The Impact of the New Tobacco-Free Policy in The Texas Department of Criminal Justice." Garner's findings are fascinating: "The respondents were asked, in their opinion, was the correctional officer's job easier, harder or experienced no change since the new [anti-tobacco] policy? It was the opinion of 68 percent of the Wardens and 62 percent of the staff and 63 percent of the inmates that the correctional officer's jobs had become more difficult." And, tellingly: "The Wardens, staff and inmates, by the results of the survey, believe that smuggling by inmates and staff had increased since the new tobacco-free policy went into effect. . . ." With regards to a black-market economy revolving around tobacco, the *Houston Chronicle* piece of May 28, 2000 is explicit: "a guard can bring in a couple packs of Bugler tobacco tucked in boot tops and sell it inside for 10 times what it cost at a store. . . . An inmate who buys a pack might turn around and sell individual cigarettes for as much as five stamps each. . . . Outlawing tobacco inside didn't stop the habit, but it did drive up the costs. . . . guards who

once might have smuggled in marijuana to supplement their pay now prefer dealing tobacco. . . . if a guard is caught peddling nicotine it could cost him his job, but if he is caught with marijuana it could mean doing some time." Also, interview with retired TDCJ-ID Warden Art Velasquez and Texas Ranger Tom Norsworthy, 26 September 2019.

18. Crouch and Marquart, *An Appeal to Justice*, 191.

19. Author Richard Alford's personal experience; Lyons, *Death Row*, too, makes note of convicts secreting cell-phones in their rectums. See p. 229. Also see, Skarbek, *The Social Order of the Underworld*: "More recently cell phones have become a serious contraband problem. Moreover, many inmates have SIM cards and simply rent phones from others," 22; Interview with Art Velasquez, TDCJ-ID Warden, Ret., and Texas Ranger Tom Norsworthy, 26 September 2019, Angleton, Texas.

20. Crouch, *The Keepers*, 93–94; Irwin, *Prisons in Turmoil*, 126; Bowker, *Prison Victimization*. 121–123.

21. Dana Allen, Regina Bouley, Paula Khalaf, James Ridgway, Haley Stoner, Daniel Stryker, and Cami Whitehead, eds., *Upon this chessboard of nights and days. . . . Voices From Texas Death Row*, 1, 132–133; [Anthony] *Shore v. State*, AP-75,049 (Tex.Crim.APP. 2007); *Fort Worth Star-Telegram*, October 29 and November 1, 2003; [Anthony] *Shore v. Stephens* [Director, TDCJ-ID], No. H-13-1898 (S.D. Tex. 2016).

22. Montgomery County District Attorney, 9th Judicial District, Brett W. Ligon to Kim K. Ogg, Harris County District Attorney, October 16, 2017; DA Brett Ligon to The Honorable Gregg Abbott, Governor of Texas, 16 October 2017; Media Advisory, Ken Paxton, Attorney General of Texas, 18 January 2018; *Houston Chronicle*, January 17, 2018, byline Keri Blakinger; Texas Death Row convict Larry Swearingen was lawfully executed 21 August 2019.

23. Allen, et al., *Voices from Texas Death Row*, 118–121, and 197; [Rosendo] *Rodriguez, III v. The State of Texas*, AP-75,901 (Tex.Crim.App. 2011); *Houston Chronicle*, February 22, 2018, byline Keri Blakinger; *Texas Tribune*, March 27, 2018, byline Jolie McCullough; [Christopher] *Wilkins v. William Stephens, Director, TDCJ-ID*, 560 Fed.Appx. 299 (5th Cir. 2014); [Christopher] *Wilkins v. Lorie Davis, Director, TDCJ-ID*, 832 F.3d 547 (5th Cir. 2016).

24. Gary M. Lavergne, *Worse Than Death: The Dallas Nightclub Murders and the Texas Multiple Murder Law*. Though this is exceptionally fascinating and skillfully penned nonfiction in its entirety, the pertinent legal issues are encapsulated in Chapter 14, "Dying by Littles," 220–238.

25. *Fort Worth Star-Telegram*, November 10, 1984; Crawford, *Texas Death Row*, 113; Gentry was lawfully executed 16 April 1997. For interesting perspectives with regards to the recruiting and employment of female Correctional Officers in close-contact convict assignments, see Lynn E. Zimmer, *Women Guarding Men*.

26. Once again a synthesis of sources narrates the murder of Minnie Rene Houston: *TDCJ Line of Duty Deaths as of December 2017*, TPM; *Kerrville Daily Times*, June 5, 1995; *Baytown Sun*, June 5, 1985; *Galveston Daily News*, June 5 and 19, 1985; July 24, 1985, February 10, 1986; *New Braunfels Herald Zeitung*, June 6, 1985; *Baytown Sun*, June 6, 1985; *The Seguin Gazette-Enterprise*, June 9, 1985; *Port Arthur News*, June 18, 1985; Program: Texas Department of Criminal Justice: Fallen Officers' Memorial Ceremony, 2017, TPM.

27. The 414–page TDCJ-ID *Pre-Service Training Student Study Guide*, FY 2018, is quite comprehensive dealing with a myriad of theoretical and practical correctional issues.

Chapter 14: "nothin' left to lose"

1. Interview with TPM Director Bill Stephens, 5 July 2019; Massingill and Sohn, *Prison City*, 30; Personal experience and observations of authors.
2. *Fort Worth Star-Telegram*, April 29 and May 16, 1989.
3. Crawford, *Texas Death Row*, 31–32; *McCoy v. Lynaugh*, 874 F.2d 954 (5th Cir. 1989).
4. *Galveston Daily News*, September 20, 1989; *Austin Daily Texan*, September 21, 1989; Marquart, Ekland-Olson, and Sorensen, *The Rope, the Chair, & the Needle*, 153; Crawford, *Texas Death Row*, 31–32.
5. Cook, *Chasing Justice*, 335; Jermnine Demouchette, *James Demouchette VS. The State of Texas: Texas's Meanest Death Row Inmate*. 3.
6. *James Demouchette vs. The State of Texas*, 591 S.W.2d 488 (Tex.Crim.App. 1979); *Fort Worth Star-Telegram*, September 22, 1992.
7. *Beaumont Journal*, October 18, 1976; Crawford, *Texas Death Row*, 52; *Dallas Morning News*, November 8, 1979.
8. Marquart, Ekland-Olson, and Sorensen, *The Rope, the Chair, & the Needle*, 180.
9. Crawford, *Texas Death Row*, 52.
10. *Corpus Christi Times*, July 27, 1979; *Fort Worth Star-Telegram*, January 8, 1988; Cook, *Chasing Justice*, 335. Major Steele's stab wound was not fatal.
11. Glenn, *Texas Prisons*, 218–219; Marquart, Ekland-Olson, and Sorensen, *The Rope, the Chair, & the Needle*, 180–181.
12. Ibid., Crawford, *Texas Death Row*, 52; Brian D. Price, *Meals to Die For*, 159.
13. Cook, *Chasing Justice*. Readers not overly familiar with the Criminal Justice System might wish to peruse this fascinating volume of the legal perils and pitfalls and, triumphs, of someone ultimately exonerated of the crime for which they were imprisoned. In that same vein, an interested reader might wish to review Michael Morton's *Getting Life: An Innocent Man's 25–Year Journey from Prison to Peace, A Memoir*.

14. Ibid., 122–123. Cook also writes that he was sexually assaulted by Death Row convict James Russell, who had murdered Thomas Robert Stearns, manager of a Radio Shack at Houston, who had previously testified against Russell on an Armed Robbery case where he caught fifty years. See p. 181; Crawford, *Texas Death Row*, 41; Russell was lawfully executed on 19 September 1991.

15. Glenn, *Texas Prisons,* 218, highlights some of James Demouchette's more volatile in-house criminality:

> Raped and stabbed a Harris County Jail inmate.
>
> Killed one other convict on death row at the Ellis I Unit.
>
> Beat and stabbed two other convicts.
>
> Stabbed at least four TDC officers.
>
> Threw lye in the face of another TDC officer
>
> Set fire to his cell twice.
>
> Destroyed a TV and commode with his hands.

Demouchette, *James Demouchette VS. The State of Texas*, supplements the writings about James by including copies of court documents and prison records. Jermnine Demouchette's candor—telling the truth about his brother—is commendable—but at the same time chilling. He writes in his Introduction, p. 3: "This book will take you into the mind of James Demouchette, Texas's meanest death row inmate. A rapist and murderer, he was an evil man, a beast bred from evil itself. . . . In his mind, before receiving a lethal injection, he said he would like to take the district attorneys, judges, warden, inmates, guards, and lawyers to the injection chamber with him. He would show them that he was James Demouchette, a real man who didn't give a shit about death or life in this world or the next. He would look into their eyes, and they would see Satan himself." Another recap of James Demouchette's prison misbehavior and maliciousness was carried by the *Fort Worth Star-Telegram*, September 22, 1992: "James Demouchette was dubbed the 'meanest man on Death Row'—he beat and raped a fellow inmate, stabbed two others, set fire to his cell, threw lye in a guard's face, stabbed two guards, slashed another and killed a fellow Death Row inmate. . . ."

16. Price, *Meals to Die For*, 159–160; Crawford, *Texas Death Row*: James Demouchette was legally executed on 22 September 1992, 160; *Fort Worth Star-Telegram*, September 22 and 23, 1992.

17. Ibid., 340–341; Cook, *Chasing Justice*, 259–260; Crawford, *Texas Death Row*, 218. Anthony Graves was later exonerated of any culpability in the gruesome crime.

18. Glenn, *Texas Prisons*, 328.

19. Alexander, *Old Riot, New Ranger*, 389–392.

20. Ibid.; also Cox, *Stand-Off in Texas*. Author Cox—at the time PIO for DPS—presents an insightful and timeline appropriate recap of this news-making West Texas event.
21. Bruce Glasrud and Harold J. Weiss, Jr., eds. *Tracking the Texas Rangers: The Twentieth Century*. For the chapter dealing with the ROT situation in West Texas refer to "Captain Barry Caver on The Republic of Texas Standoff," as contributed by Barry Caver with Robert Nieman, 204–237; Lorie Rubenser and Gloria Priddy, *Constables, Marshals, and More: Forgotten Offices in Texas Law Enforcement*, highlight the contribution of Texas Game Wardens to other law enforcing agencies due to their first-hand knowledge of geographical and, sometimes, remote areas. See p. 137.
22. Alexander and Brice, *Texas Rangers*, 389; Doyle Holdridge, *Working the Border: A Texas Ranger's Story*. 242.
23. Cox, *Stand-Off in Texas*, 202.
24. Holdridge, *Working the Border*, 244–245; the name of the slain prison dog comes from Cox, as cited above.
25. U.S. Marshals Service newsletter, *The Marshals MONITOR*, May-June 1997, quoting former Texas Ranger Captain Jack O. Dean, but then the United States Marshal for the Western District of Texas. 3.
26. Livingston, Montana, *Daily Enterprise*, September 17, 1884.
27. Interview with Lon Glenn, 30 April 2019; Lavergne, *Bad Boy from Rosebud*, 348–349; Cartwright, "Free to Kill," *Texas Monthly*, August 1992; Crawford, *Texas Death Row*, 161.
28. *Robert Lynn Pruett vs. The State of Texas*, No. AP—77, 037 (Tex.Crim.App. October 22, 2014); *Ex Parte Robert Lynn Pruett*, No. WR-62, 099–02 (Tex.Crim. App. December 10, 2014); *Robert Lynn Pruett vs. The State of Texas*, No. AP-77, 065 (Tex.Crim.App. April 5, 2017); *Victoria Advocate*, December 21, 1999; *San Antonio Express News*, December 22, 1999; *Corpus Christi Caller-Times*, December 18 and 23, 1999; *The Huntsville Item*, March 22, 2000, byline Michelle C. Lyons.
29. Alexander, *Old Riot, New Ranger*, 399. The U.S. Marshals Service Official Historian, David S. Turk, in his outstanding and long overdue treatment, *Forging the Star: The Official Modern History of the United States Marshals Service*, p. 338, confirms: "The Texas Seven case was one of the largest fugitive operations involving the U.S. Marshals in years. . . ."
30. Ibid., 400–401; TDCJ-ID, Serious Incident Review, 19 December 2000; Gary C. King, *The Texas 7: A True Story of Murder and a Daring Escape*. King particularizes the criminal histories of the seven escapees, 41–67.
31. TDCJ-ID Serious Incident Review, 19 December 2000.
32. Alexander, *Old Riot, New Ranger*, 400–401.
33. Ibid.; King, *The Texas 7*, 23.
34. Interview with former Karnes County Sheriff Bobby Mutz, 5 December 2017.

35. King, *The Texas 7*.

36. Interview with former Chief of the Texas Rangers, H.L. "Hank" Whitman, 18 November 2017.

37. *Orange Leader*, August 23, 2001.

38. Alexander, *Old Riot, New Ranger*, 403. Not unexpectedly the TDCJ-OIG conducted a full-scale investigation into the escape and a day by day chronological recap of activities by the multi-agency Task Force, as well as a breakdown of the escapees' daily activities—with recommendations for preventing and handling such situations in the future. OIG Report: *The Connally Unit Escape, December 13, 2000: A Chronology of the Fugitive Investigation*. In deference to respecting crucial security concerns, the proposed recommendations and/or future procedural issues are not particularized herein.

39. *Patrick Henry Murphy, Jr. v. The State of Texas*, No. AP-74, 851 (Court of Criminal Appeals of Texas, 2006); Also, *Ex Parte Patrick Henry Murphy, Jr. v. The State of Texas*, No. WR-63,549–01. (Court of Criminal Appeals of Texas, 2009).

40. *Joseph C. Garcia v. The State of Texas*, No. AP-74692 (Court of Criminal Appeals of Texas, 2005); King, *The Texas 7*, 84–91. True, Patrolman Hawkins only had fourteen months service with Irving PD—which may or may not have been considered rookie status—but as a licensed Texas Peace Officer he had also banked law enforcing service with the Kaufman PD (in Kaufman County east of Dallas) and, also, with the Tarrant County Hospital District, which certainly removed him from the general characterization as a rookie or trainee. In *U.S. Marshals: Inside America's Most Storied Law Enforcement Agency* the author, Mike Earpp (and David Fisher), a former Associate Director of Operations, further expands, writing: "They shot him [Aubrey Hawkins] eleven times—when he was on the ground, they lifted up his vest and shot him in the chest—then ran over his body with an SUV. It was more of an execution than a murder," 239.

41. *Houston Chronicle*, January 23, 2001, Byline John Henderson and John Williams; *Denver Post*, January 23, 2001, Byline, Erin Emery, Mike McPhee, and Kieran Nicholson; *Denver Post*, January 23, 2001, Byline Erin Emery; King, *Texas 7*, 166–179; U.S. Marshals Service Newsletter, *The Marshals MONITOR*, January-February 2001; Alexander, *Old Riot, New Ranger*, 405–406.

42. *Kerrville Daily Times*, August 29, 2001.

43. *Killeen Daily Herald*, December 5, 2018: "A member of the notorious 'Texas Seven' gang of escaped prisoners was executed Tuesday evening. . . . Joseph Garcia received a lethal injection at the state penitentiary in Huntsville for the December 2000 shooting death of 29–year-old Irving police Officer Aubrey Hawkins."

44. 27 July 2018 interview with William L. "Bill" Stephens, Director, TDCJ-ID, Ret.; Glenn, *Texas Prisons*, 328.

45. Glenn, *Texas Prisons*, 338.

Chapter 15: "die an outlaw's death"

1. Fleisher and Krienert, *The Myth of Prison Rape*, from the Foreword by James B. Jacobs, ix; Professor Lee H. Bowker in *Prisoner Subcultures* page 116, confirms what seasoned penologists know: "Prison rape, though perhaps less common than consensual homosexuality, is a major feature of all American prisons. Exposure to the possibility of rape, often by gangs of fellow prisoners, must be counted as one of the pains of imprisonment. . . ."
2. Prison Rape Elimination Act: TDCJ-ID procedures and protocols for timely reporting and investigating violations, §115.11 thru §115.89; Texas Department of Criminal Justice *Offender Orientation Handbook*, 26–31.
3. Conklin, *Criminology*, 169.
4. TDCJ-ID *Offender Orientation Handbook*, 26–31.
5. TDCJ-ID *Correctional Officer Handbook*, 6–7.
6. TDCJ-ID PREA Policies and Procedures §115.11 thru § 115.89 as cited; TDCJ-ID Pre-Service Study Guide Training Manual, 53–65.
7. *Travis Trevino Runnels vs. The State of Texas*, No. AP-75,318 (Tex.Crim.App. September 12, 2007); *Fort Worth Star-Telegram*, January 30, 2003; *Killeen Daily Herald*, June 19, 2018.
8. *TDCJ Line of Duty Deaths as of December 2017*; Lyons, *Death Row*, 192; Texas Department of Criminal Justice: Program: Fallen Officers' Memorial Ceremony, 2017.
9. *Fort Worth Star-Telegram*, October 23, 2004, and *Palestine Herald Press*.
10. TDCJ-ID, *Correctional Officer Handbook*, 2.
11. Ibid., 40–41.
12. Massingill and Sohn, *Prison City*, 198–199; Lavergne, *Bad Boy from Rosebud*, 327.
13. The information about the Murder of Correctional Officer Canfield is taken from a synthesis of sources. Many details of the criminality are drawn from several findings of the Texas Appellate Court System. See Direct Appeal, *Jerry Duane Martin vs. The State of Texas*; Cause No. 24,087, 278th District Court, Walker County (October 31, 2012); *Ex Parte* [John Ray] *Falk*, 449 S.W.3d 500 (Tex.App.—Waco 2014); Maurice Chammah, "Sitting in Legal Purgatory," *Texas Monthly*, December 3, 2013; *Houston Chronicle*, September 25, 2007; *Dallas Morning News*, September 27, 2007; *McKinney Courier-Gazette*, September 25, 2007.
14. Program: Thirteenth Biennial Texas Peace Officers' Memorial Services, May 1–2, 2011, Texas State Capitol, 62; *Plainview Daily Herald*, September 8, 2010; *Amarillo Globe-News*, September 14, 2010.
15. *TDCJ Line of Duty Deaths as of December 2017*; Program: Texas Department of Criminal Justice Fallen Officers' Memorial Ceremony, 2017. For excellent coverage of this Murder of a Correctional Officer and the assaultive history

of the defendant, as well as the hard-fought criminal trial, the interested reader should peruse the series of articles penned by Lynn LaRowe for the *Texarkana Gazette*; *Fort Worth Star-Telegram*, July 17, 2015: "Tracy had been housed in a single cell because he is classified as an administrative segregation inmate. . . ."

16. *TDCJ Line of Duty Deaths as of December 2017*; Program: Texas Department of Criminal Justice Fallen Officers' Memorial Ceremony, 2017; *Longview News-Journal*, July 16, 2015 and November 16, 2017; *Fort Worth Star-Telegram*, July 17, 2015; *Texarkana Gazette*, November 15, 2017.

17. *TDCJ Line of Duty Deaths as of December 2017*; Program, Texas Department of Criminal Justice Fallen Officers' Memorial Ceremony, 2017; Interview with Texas Ranger Joshua Burson, 8 July 2019.

18. Interview with Ranger Burson, as cited; *Brownsville Herald*, July 17, 2016.

19. *Fort Worth Star-Telegram*, July 20, 2016.

20. *Abilene Reporter News*, November 6, 2018. Byline Laura Gutschke.

21. *TDCJ Line of Duty Deaths as of December 2017*; *AFSCME* [American Federation of State, County & Municipal Employees] *Now*, Press Release, June 13, 2017; *Obituary Program*, Shana Tedder, Crawford-Bowers Funeral Home, Killeen, Texas.

22. *Longview News-Journal*, December 19, 2017.

23. *Texarkana Gazette*, August 31 and October 4, 2018, bylines Lynn LaRowe.

24. *Temple Daily Telegram*, June 30, 2019, picking up a story from the *Houston Chronicle*, byline Keri Blakinger; Near twenty years earlier Associated Press representative Michael Graczyk spotlighted the Correctional Officer shortage and retention crisis. See, *Houston Chronicle*, March 10, 2000.

25. Glenn, *Texas Prison Tales*, 245–246. For an insightful pre-service training approach for rookie Correctional Officers—thoughtfully mixing classroom and OJT segments—the interested reader may wish to peruse Professor Ben M. Crouch's piece in *Correctional Officers: Power, Pressure, and Responsibility*, "Maximizing the Effectiveness of Preservice Training," in the edition edited by Tucker as previously cited, 37–42.

26. Interview with former TDCJ-ID Regional Director Bob Parker, 16 July 2019.

27. Interview with Bill Stephens, former TDCJ-ID Director and, now, Director of TPM, 11 September 2019.

28. TDCJ—ID, *Correctional Officer Handbook*, 2.

Bibliography

Non-published sources—manuscripts, typescripts, theses, dissertations, tape recordings, official documents, courthouse records, appellate court decisions, tax rolls, petitions, correspondence, prison records, census records, licensing records, memorial registers, personal and telephonic interviews, etc.—are cited with specificity in chapter endnotes.

Books:

Abbott, Jack. *In the Belly of the Beast: Letters from Prison.* New York: Random House, 1981.

Adams, Ramon F. *Six-Guns and Saddle Leather: A Bibliography of Books and Pamphlets on Western Outlaws and Gunmen.* Mineola, NY: Dover Publications, 1998.

———. *Burs Under the Saddle: A Second Look at Books and Histories of the West.* 1964. Repr. Norman: University of Oklahoma Press, 1989.

Adams, Verdon R. *Tom White: The Life of a Lawman.* El Paso, TX: Texas Western Press, University of Texas at El Paso, 1972.

Aguirre, Jr. Adalberto, and Jonathan H. Turner. *American Ethnicity: The Dynamics and Consequences of Discrimination.* Boston, MA: McGraw Hill, 1998.

Alexander, Bob. *Old Riot, New Ranger: Captain Jack Dean, Texas Ranger and U.S Marshal.* Denton: University of North Texas Press, 2018.

———. and Donaly E. Brice. *Texas Rangers: Lives, Legend, and Legacy.* Denton: University of North Texas Press, 2017.

———. *Whiskey River Ranger: The Old West Life of Baz Outlaw.* Denton: University of North Texas Press, 2016.

———. *Six-Shooters and Shifting Sands: The Wild West Life of Texas Ranger Captain Frank Jones.* Denton: University of North Texas Press, 2015.

———. *Bad Company and Burnt Powder: Justice and Injustice in the Old Southwest.* Denton: University of North Texas Press, 2014.

———. *Rawhide Ranger, Ira Aten: Enforcing Law on the Texas Frontier.* Denton: University of North Texas Press, 2011.

———. *Fearless Dave Allison: Border Lawman.* Silver City, NM: High-Lonesome Books, 2003.

———. *Sheriff Harvey Whitehill: Silver City Stalwart.* Silver City, NM: High-Lonesome Books, 2005.

———. *Lawmen, Outlaws, and S.O.Bs.* 2 vols. Silver City, NM: High-Lonesome Books, 2004.

Allen, Bud, and Diana Bosta. *Games Criminals Play: How You Can Profit by Knowing Them.* 1981; repr., Sacramento, CA: Rae John Publishers, 2010.

Allen, Dana, and Regina Bouley, Paula Khalaf, James Ridgway, Haley Stoner, Daniel Stryker, and Cami Whitehead, eds. *Upon this Chessboard of Nights and Days: Voices from Texas Death Row.* Huntsville, TX: Texas Review Press, 2009.

Allen, Harry E., and Clifford E. Simonsen. *Corrections in America: An Introduction.* 9th ed. Upper Saddle River, NJ: Prentice-Hall, Inc., 2001.

Anderson, T. Carlos. *There Is a Balm in Huntsville: A True Story of Tragedy and Restoration from the Heart of the Texas Prison System.* Lancaster, PA: Walnut Street Books, 2018.

Arnold, Ann. *Gamblers and Gangsters: Fort Worth's Jacksboro Highway in the 1940s and 1950s.* Fort Worth, TX: Eakin Press, Imprint of Wild Horse Media Group, 1998.

Bailey, Lynn R., and Don Chaput. *Cochise County Stalwarts: A Who's Who of the Territorial Years.* Vol. 1. Tucson, AZ: Westernlore Press, 2000.

Baker, T. Lindsay. *Gangster Tour of Texas.* College Station: Texas A&M University Press, 2011.

Baker, Terry. *Hangings and Lynchings in Dallas County, Texas, 1853–1920.* Fort Worth, TX: Eakin Press, 2016.

Barkely, Roy R., and Mark F. Odintz, eds. *The Portable Handbook of Texas.* Austin: The Texas State Historical Association, 2000.

Barnes, Harry Elmer, and Negley K. Teeters. *New Horizons in Criminology.* Englewood Cliffs, NJ: Prentice-Hall, Inc., 1959.

Barr, Alwyn. *Reconstruction to Reform: Texas Politics, 1876–1906.* Austin: University of Texas Press, 1971.

Barrow, Blanche C., John Neal Phillips, ed., *My Life with Bonnie and Clyde.* Norman: University of Oklahoma Press, 2004.

Benekos, Peter J., and Alida V. Merio, eds. *Corrections: Dilemmas and Directions.* Cincinnati, OH: Anderson Publishing Company, 1992.

Berg, David. *Run, Brother, Run: A Memoir.* New York: Scribner, 2013.

Berryhill, Michael. *The Trials of Eroy Brown: The Murder Case That Shook the Texas Prison System.* Austin: University of Texas Press, 2011.

Bicknell, Thomas C., and Chuck Parsons. *Ben Thompson: Portrait of a Gunfighter.* Denton: University of North Texas Press, 2018.

Blackburn, Jr., Ed. *Wanted: Historic County Jails of Texas.* College Station: Texas A&M University Press, 2006.

Blatchford, Chris. *The Black Hand: The Bloody Rise and Redemption of "Boxer" Enriquez, A Mexican Mob Killer.* New York: Harper-Collins Publishers, 2009.

Blue, Ethan. *Doing Time in the Depression: Everyday Life in Texas and California Prisons.* New York: New York University Press, 2012.

Blumenthal, Karen. *Bonnie and Clyde: The Making of a Legend*. New York: Viking, an Imprint Penguin Random House, 2018.

Boessenecker, John. *Texas Ranger: The Epic Life of Frank Hamer, The Man Who Killed Bonnie and Clyde*. New York: Thomas Dunne Books, St. Martin's Press, 2016.

Bohm, Robert M., and Keith N. Haley. *Introduction to Criminal Justice*. New York: Glencoe/McGraw-Hill, 2002.

Bowker, Lee H. *Prison Victimization*. New York: Elsevier North Holland Inc., 1980.

———. *Prisoner Subcultures*. Lexington, MA: D.C. Heath and Company, 1977.

Brook, John Lee. *Blood In, Blood Out: The Violent Empire of the Aryan Brotherhood*. London, England: Headpress Book, 2011.

Brown, Gary. *Singin' a Lonesome Song: Texas Prison Tales*. Plano, TX: Republic of Texas Press, 2001.

———. *Texas Gulag: The Chain Gang Years*. Plano, TX: Republic of Texas Press, 2002.

Brown, John Henry. *Indian Wars and Pioneers of Texas*. Austin, TX: State House Press, 1988.

Brown, Richard M. *No Duty to Retreat: Violence and Values in American History and Society*. Norman: University of Oklahoma Press, 1994.

Bruton, James H. *The Big House: Life inside a Supermax Security Prison*. Stillwater, MN: Voyageur Press, 2004.

Bullis, Don. *New Mexico's Finest: Peace Officers Killed in the Line of Duty, 1847–2010*. Los Ranchos, NM: Rio Grande Books, 2010.

Bunker, Edward. *Education of a Felon*. New York: St. Martin's Press, 2000.

Butler, Anne M. *Gendered Justice in the American West: Women Prisoners in Men's Penitentiaries*. Chicago: University of Illinois, 1997.

Caldwell, Clifford R., and Ron DeLord. *Texas Lawmen: The Good and the Bad, 1835–1899*. Charleston, SC: The History Press, 2011.

———. and Ron DeLord. *Texas Lawmen: More of the Good & the Bad, 1900–1940*. Charleston, SC: The History Press, 2012.

———. and Ron DeLord. *Eternity at the End of a Rope: Executions, Lynchings and Vigilante Justice in Texas, 1819–1923*. Santa Fe, NM: Sunstone Press, 2015.

Carey, Elaine. *Women Drug Traffickers: Mules, Bosses, and Organized Crime*. Albuquerque: University of New Mexico Press, 2014.

Carroll, Leo. *Hacks, Blacks, and Cons: Race Relations in a Maximum Security Prison*. Lexington, MA: Lexington Books, D.C. Heath and Company, 1974.

Cartwright, Gary. *Dirty Dealing: Drug Smuggling on the Mexican Border and the Assassination of a Federal Judge*. El Paso, TX: Cinco Puntos Press, 1998.

Cline, Robert C. *From Rage to Redemption*. n.p. Self-Published, 2011.

Colvin, Mark. *The Penitentiary in Crisis: From Accommodation to Riot in New Mexico*. Albany: State University of New York Press, 1992.

Conklin, John E. *Criminology*. Needham Heights, MA: Allyn & Bacon, 1998.

Cook, Kerry Max. *Chasing Justice: My Story of Freeing Myself After Two Decades on Death Row for a Crime I Didn't Commit*. New York: Harper-Collins Publishers, 2007.

Cox, Mike. *Time of the Rangers: Texas Rangers from 1900 to the Present.* New York: Forge Books, 2009.

———. *Stand-Off in Texas: "Just Call Me a Spokesman for DPS. . . ."* Austin, TX: Eakin Press, 1998.

Crawford, Bill. *Texas Death Row: Executions in the Modern Era.* New York: Plume Books, by the Penguin Group, 2008.

Creighton, James A. *A Narrative History of Brazoria County, Texas.* Waco, TX: Brazoria County Historical Commission, 1975.

Crouch, Barry A., and Donaly E. Brice. *The Governor's Hounds: The Texas State Police, 1870–1873.* Austin: University of Texas Press, 2011.

Crouch, Ben M., and James Marquart. *An Appeal to Justice: Litigated Reform of Texas Prisons.* Austin: The University of Texas Press, 1989.

———. ed. *The Keepers: Prison Guards and Contemporary Corrections.* Springfield, IL: Charles C. Thomas, Publisher, 1980.

Cutrer, Thomas W. *Ben McCulloch and the Frontier Military Tradition.* Chapel Hill: The University of North Carolina Press, 1993.

Cruz, Kathy. *Dateline Purgatory: Examining the Case That Sentenced Darlie Routier to Death.* Fort Worth, TX: TCU Press, 2015.

Day, James M. *Captain Clint Peoples, Texas Ranger: Fifty Years a Lawman.* Waco, TX: Texian Press, 1980.

Del Carmen, Rolando. *Criminal Procedure: Law and Practice.* Belmont, CA: Wadsworth/Thomson Learning, 2004.

Delgado, Bobby. *Gangs, Prisoners, Parole: The Politics Behind Them.* n.p: Crown Oak Press, 2007.

DeLord, ed., Ron. *The Ultimate Sacrifice: Trials and Triumphs of the Texas Peace Officer, 1823–2000.* Austin, TX: Peace Officers Memorial Foundation, Inc., 2000.

Demouchette, Jermnine. *James Demouchette Vs. The State of Texas.* Tucson, AZ: Wheatmark, 2008.

Devereaux, Jan. *Pistols, Petticoats, and Poker: The Real Lottie Deno, No Lies or Alibis.* Silver City, NM: High-Lonesome Books, 2008

DiIulio, Jr., John J. *Governing Prisons: A Comparative Study of Correctional Management.* New York: The Free Press, A Division of Macmillan Publishing Co., 1987.

———, ed. *Courts, Corrections and the Constitution: The Impact of Judicial Intervention on Prisons and Jails.* New York: Oxford University Press, 1990.

Dixon, Kemp. *Chasing Thugs, Nazis, and Reds: Texas Ranger Norman K. Dixon.* College Station: Texas A&M University Press, 2015.

Dolan, Samuel K. *Cowboys and Gangsters: Stories of an Untamed Southwest.* Helena, MT: TWODOT, Rowman & Littlefield, 2016.

Duke, Cordia Sloan, with Joe B. Frantz. *6000 Miles of Fence: Life on the XIT Ranch of Texas.* Austin: University of Texas Press.

Dukes, Doug. *Ben Thompson: Iron Marshal of Austin*. Austin, TX: Self-Published, 2011.

Early, Pete. *The Hot House: Life Inside Leavenworth Prison*. New York: Bantam Books, 1993.

Earp, Mike, and David Fisher. *U.S. Marshal: Inside America's Most Storied Law Enforcement Agency*. New York: Harper Collins, 2014.

Estelle, Jr., ed., W.J. *A Time To Forget. . . . And Remember*. Huntsville, TX: Texas Department of Corrections, 1975.

Fehrenbach, T.R. *Lone Star: A History of Texas and the Texans*. New York: Macmillan Publishing Company, Inc., 1968.

Few, Joan. *Sugar, Planters, Slaves, and Convicts: The History and Archaeology of the Lake Jackson Plantation Brazoria County, Texas*. Gold Hill, CO: Few Publications, 2006.

Fleisher, Mark S. *Warehousing Violence*. Newbury Park, CA: Sage Publishing, Inc., 1989.

———. and Jessie L. Krienert. *The Myth of Prison Rape: Sexual Culture in American Prisons*. Lanham, MD: Rowman & Littlefield Publishers, Inc., 2009.

Fox, Vernon. *Introduction to Corrections*. Englewood Cliffs, NJ: Prentice-Hall, Inc., 1972.

Frost, H. Gordon, and John H. Jenkins. *"I'm Frank Hamer": The Life of a Texas Peace Officer*. Austin, TX: Pemberton Press, 1986.

Gambetta, Diego. *Codes of the Underworld: How Criminals Communicate*. Princeton, NJ: Princeton University Press, 2009.

Gammel, Hans Peter. *The Laws of Texas, 1822–1897*. 10 vols. Austin, TX: Gammel Books, 1898.

Graber, H.W. *The Life of H.W. Graber: Terry Texas Ranger, 1861–1865*. n.p: Self-published, 1916.

Gilbreath, West. *death on the gallows* [lower case correct]. *The Encyclopedia of Legal Hangings in Texas*. Fort Worth, TX: Wild Horse Press, 2017.

Gillett, James B. *Six Years with the Texas Rangers, 1875–1881*. New Haven, CT: Yale University Press, 1925.

Glasrud, Bruce, and Harold J. Weiss, Jr., eds. *Tracking the Texas Rangers: The Twentieth Century*. Denton: University of North Texas Press, 2013.

Glenn, Lon Bennett. *The Largest Hotel Chain in Texas: Texas Prisons*. Fort Worth, TX: Eakin Press, 2001.

———. *Texas Prison Tales: Largest Hotel Chain in Texas II*. n.p. Self-published, 2016.

Gnagy, Caroline. *Texas Jailhouse Music: A Prison Band History*. Charleston, SC: The History Press, 2016.

Good, Milt. *Twelve Years in a Texas Prison*. Amarillo, TX: Russell Stationery, 1935.

Gournay, Luke. *Texas Boundaries: Evolution of the State's Counties*. College Station: Texas A&M University Press, 1995.

Grann, David. *Killers of the Flower Moon: The Osage Murders and the Birth of the FBI.* New York: Doubleday, 2017.

Greer, James K., ed. *Buck Barry: Texas Ranger and Frontiersman.* Lincoln: University of Nebraska Press, 1978.

Griswold, H. Jack, and Mike Misenheimer, Art Powers and Ed Tromanhauser. *An Eye for an Eye: Four Inmates on the Crime of American Prisons Today.* New York: Holt, Rinehart and Winston, 1970.

Guinn, Jeff. *Go Down Together: The True, Untold Story of Bonnie and Clyde.* New York: Simon & Schuster, 2009.

Haile, Bartee. *Texas Depression-Era Desperadoes.* Charleston, SC: The History Press, 2014.

Haley, J. Evetts. *The XIT Ranch of Texas, and the Early Days on the Llano Estacado.* Norman: University of Oklahoma Press, 1967.

Hall, Joan Upton. *Just Visitin' Old Texas Jails.* Abilene, TX: State House Press [McMurry University], 2007.

Hallinan, Joseph T. *Going Up the River: Travels in a Prison Nation.* New York: Random House, 2001.

Hardin, John Wesley. *The Life of John Wesley Hardin as Written by Himself.* Norman: University of Oklahoma Press, 1977.

Harper, William T. *Eleven Days in Hell: The 1974 Carrasco Prison Siege at Huntsville, Texas.* Denton: The University of North Texas Press, 2004.

Harris III, Charles H., and Louis R. Sadler. *The Texas Rangers in Transition: From Gunfighters to Criminal Investigators, 1921–1935.* Albuquerque: The University of New Mexico Press, 2019.

———, Frances E. Harris and Louis R. Sadler. *Texas Rangers Biographies: Those Who Served, 1910–1921.* Norman: The University of Oklahoma Press, 2009.

Hassine, Victor, edited by Robert Johnson and Sonia Tabriz. *Life Without Parole: Living and Dying in Prison Today.* 5th ed. New York: Oxford University Press, 2011.

Herrera, Norma. *Last Words from Death Row: The Walls Unit.* LaVergne, TN: Nightengale Press, Lightning Source Inc., 2007.

Hinton, Ted, as told to Larry Grove. *AMBUSH: The Real Story of Bonnie and Clyde.* Austin, TX: Shoal Creek Publishers, Inc., 1979.

Hirliman, Georgelle. *The Hate Factory: A First-Hand Account of the 1980 Riot at the Penitentiary of New Mexico.* New York: iUniverse, Inc., 2005.

Hoffman, Ethan, and John A. McCoy. *Concrete Mama: Prison Profiles from Walla Walla.* Seattle: University of Washington Press, 2018. Originally published by University of Missouri Press, 1981.

Hogg, Thomas E. *Life and Adventures of Sam Bass: The Notorious Union Pacific and Texas Train Robber.* Dallas, TX: Dallas Commercial Steam Print, 1878.

Holdridge, Doyle. *Working the Border: A Texas Ranger's Story.* Dallas, TX: Atriad Press, LLC, 2009.

Horton, David M., and George R. Nielsen. *Walking George: The Life of George John Beto and the Rise of the Modern Texas Prison System*. Denton: The University of North Texas Press, 2005.

———. and Ryan Kellus Turner. *Lone Star Justice: A Comprehensive Overview, The Texas Criminal Justice System*. Austin, TX: Eakin Press, 1999.

Howell, Kenneth, ed. *Still the Arena of Civil War: Violence and Turmoil in Reconstruction Texas, 1865–1874*. Denton: University of North Texas Press, 2012.

Inciardi, James A. *Criminal Justice*. 5th ed. Fort Worth, TX: Harcourt Brace College Publishers, 1996.

Ingmire, Frances T. *Ranger Service Records, 1847–1900*. 6 vols. St. Louis, MO: Ingmire Publications, 1982.

Irwin, John. *Prisons in Turmoil*. Boston, MA: Little, Brown and Company, 1980.

Ivey, Darren L. *The Ranger Ideal: Texas Rangers in the Hall of Fame, 1823–1861*. Vol. 1. Denton: University of North Texas Press, 2017.

———. *The Ranger Ideal: Texas Rangers in the Hall of Fame, 1874–1930*. Vol. 2. Denton: University of North Texas Press, 2018.

———. *The Texas Rangers: A Registry and History*. Jefferson, N.C.: McFarland & Company, Inc., 2010.

Jach, Theresa. *Huntsville Penitentiary*. Charleston, SC: Arcadia Publishing, 2013.

Jackson, Bruce, ed. *Wake Up Dead Man: Afro-American Worksongs from Texas Prisons*. Cambridge, MA: Harvard University Press, 1972.

Jacobs, James B. *Stateville: The Penitentiary in Mass Society*. Chicago: The University of Chicago Press, 1977.

Johnson, David. *The Cornett-Whitley Gang: Violence Unleashed in Texas*. Denton: University of North Texas Press, 2019.

Johnson, Robert. *Hard Time: Understanding and Reforming the Prison*. Belmont, CA: Wadsworth/Thomson Learning, 2002.

———, and Hans Toch, eds., *The Pains of Imprisonment*. Beverly Hills, CA: Sage Publications, 1982.

Johnston, Robert, ed., with Leonard Savitz and Marvin E. Wolfgang. *The Sociology of Punishment and Correction*. New York: John Wiley and Sons, 1970.

Kelsey, Michael, and Nancy Graff Floyd and Ginny Guinn Parsons. *Miscellaneous Texas Newspaper Abstracts-Deaths*. Vols. 1 and 2. Bowie, MD: Heritage Books, Inc., 1995 and 1997.

King, Gary C. *The Texas 7: A True Story of Murder and a Daring Escape*. New York: St. Martin's Press, 2001.

Langohr, Glenn. *The Art of War: A Memoir of Life in Prison with the Mafia, Serial Killers, and Sex Offenders Who Get Stabbed*. n.p: Self-Published, 2013.

Lavergne, Gary M. *Worse Than Death: The Dallas Nightclub Murders and the Texas Multiple Murder Law*. Denton: University of North Texas Press, 2003.

———. *Bad Boy from Rosebud: The Murderous Life of Kenneth Allen McDuff*. Denton: University of North Texas Press, 1999.

Lockwood, Daniel. *Prison Sexual Violence*. New York: Elsevier North Holland, Inc., 1980.

Lombardo, Lucien X. *Guards Imprisoned: Correctional Officers at Work*. New York: Elsevier North Holland, Inc., 1981.

Lyon, Danny. *Like a Thief's Dream*. Brooklyn, NY: powerHouse Books, 2007.

———. *Conversations with the Dead*. 2nd ed. New York: Phaidon Press Limited, 2015.

Lyons, Michelle. *Death Row: The Final Minutes*. London: Blink Publishing, 2018.

McConal, Patrick M. *Over the Wall: The Men Behind The 1934 Death House Escape*. Fort Worth, TX: Eakin Press, Imprint of Wild Horse Media Group, 2000.

McKinney, Wilson. *Fred Carrasco: The Heroin Merchant*. Austin, TX: Heidelberg Publishing, Inc., 1975.

McShane, Marilyn D., and Wesley Krause. *Community Corrections*. New York: Macmillan Publishing Co., 1993.

McWhorter, Wm. L. *Inmate Society: Legs, Half-Pants and Gunmen: A Study of Inmate Guards*. Saratoga, CA: Century Twenty-One Publishing, 1981.

Malsch, Brownson. *Lone Wolf: Captain M.T. Gonzaullas*. Austin, TX: Shoal Creek Publishers Inc., 1980.

Marohn, Richard C. *The Last Gunfighter: John Wesley Hardin*. College Station, TX: Creative Publishing, 1995.

Marquart, James W., and Sheldon Ekland-Olson and Jonathan R. Sorensen. *The Rope, the Chair, and the Needle: Capital Punishment in Texas*. Austin: University of Texas Press, 1994.

Martin, Steve J., and Sheldon Ekland-Olson. *Texas Prisons: The Walls Came Tumbling Down*. Austin, TX: Texas Monthly Press, 1987.

Massingill, Ruth, and Ardyth Broadrick Sohn. *Prison City: Life with the Death Penalty in Huntsville, Texas*. New York: Peter Lang Publishing, Inc., 2007.

Meed, Douglas V. *Texas Ranger Johnny Klevenhagen*. Plano, TX: Republic of Texas Press, 2000.

Melsheimer, Thomas, and Judge Craig Smith. *On the Jury Trial: Principles and Practices for Effective Advocacy*. Denton: University of North Texas Press, 2017.

Metz, Leon Claire. *The Shooters*. El Paso, TX: Mangan Books, 1976.

———. *John Wesley Hardin: Dark Angel of Texas*. Norman: University of Oklahoma Press, 1996.

Miller, Rick. *Texas Ranger John B. Jones and the Frontier Battalion, 1874–1881*. Denton: University of North Texas Press, 2012.

———. *Tin Star Tales: Law and Disorder in Dallas County, Texas, 1846–1900*. Bloomington, IN: Archway Publishing, 2017.

Morales, Gabe. *The History of the Aryan Brotherhood*. Lexington, KY: Self-Published, 2018.

Morales, Gabriel C. *La Familia—The Family: Prison Gangs in America*. Lexington, KY: Self-Published, 2015.

Moneyhon, Carl H. *Texas After the Civil War: The Struggle of Reconstruction*. College Station: Texas A&M University Press, 2004.

———. *Edmund J. Davis: Civil War General, Republican Leader, Reconstruction Governor*. Fort Worth, TX: TCU Press, 2010.

Morris, Roger. *The Devil's Butcher Shop: The New Mexico Prison Uprising*. New York: Franklin Watts, 1983.

Morton, Michael. *Getting Life: An Innocent Man's 25–Year Journey from Prison to Peace*. New York: Simon & Schuster, 2015.

Neal, Bill. *Skullduggery, Secrets, and Murders: The 1894 Wells Fargo Scam That Backfired*. Lubbock: Texas Tech University Press, 2015.

Neubauer, David W. *America's Courts and the Criminal Justice System*. Belmont, CA: Wadsworth/Thomson Learning, 2002.

Newton, Michael. *The Encyclopedia of Gangsters: A Worldwide Guide to Organized Crime*. New York: Thunder's Mouth Press, 2007.

Nolan, Frederick. *The Wild West: History, Myth and the Making of America*. England: Chartwell Books, 2004.

———. *Tascosa: Its Life and Gaudy Times*. Lubbock: Texas Tech University Press, 2007.

Nordyke, Lewis. *Cattle Empire: The Fabulous Story of the 3,000,000 Acre XIT*. New York: William Morrow, 1949.

O'Neal, Bill   *Historic Ranches of the Old West*. Austin, TX: Eakin Press, 1997.

Paulissen, May N., and Carl McQueary. *Miriam: The Sothern Belle Who Became the First Woman Governor of Texas*. Austin, TX: Eakin Press, 1995.

Parrish, James R. *A Two-Headed Monster: Crime and Texas Prisons*. Austin, TX: Eakin Press, 1989.

Parsons, Chuck, and Norman Wayne Brown. *A Lawless Breed: John Wesley Hardin, Texas Reconstruction, and Violence in the Wild West*. Denton: University of North Texas Press, 2013.

———, and Donaly E. Brice. *Texas Ranger N.O. Reynolds: The Intrepid*. Honolulu, HI: Talei Publishers, Inc., 2005.

———, and Marianne E. Hall Little. *Captain L.H. McNelly, Texas Ranger: The Life And Times Of A Fighting Man*. Austin, TX: State House Press, 2001.

Perkinson, Robert *Texas Tough: The Rise of America's Prison Empire*. New York: Picador, Henry Holt and Co., 2010.

Phillips, John Neal. *Running with Bonnie and Clyde: The Ten Fast Years of Ralph Fults*. Norman: University of Oklahoma Press, 1996.

Pickett, Rev. Carroll, with Carlton Stowers. *Within These Walls: Memoirs of a Death House Chaplain*. New York: St. Martin's Press, 2002.

Price, Brian D. *Meals to Die For*. San Antonio, TX: Dyna-Paige Corporation, 2006.

Procter, Ben. *Just One Riot: Episodes of Texas Rangers in the 20th Century*. Austin, TX: Eakin Press, 1991.

Pylant, James. *Sins of the Pioneers: Crimes and Scandals in a Small Texas Town*. Stephenville, TX: Jacobus Books, 2011.

Rafael, Tony. *The Mexican Mafia*. New York: Encounter Books, 2009.

Reid, Don, with John Gurwell. *Have a Seat, Please*. Huntsville, TX: Texas Review Press, 2001. (initially published 1973 by Cordovan Press as *Eyewitness*).

Reiter, Keramet. *23/7: Pelican Bay Prison and the Rise of Long-Term Solitary Confinement*. New Haven, CT: Yale University Press, 2016.

Renaud, Jorge A. *Behind the Walls: A Guide for Families and Friends of Texas Prison Inmates*. Denton: University of North Texas Press, 2002.

Reynolds, Dan M. *On the Other Side of the Bars: Lessons Learned as a Prison Warden/ Administrator*. Mustang, OK: Tate Publishing & Enterprise, 2012.

Reynolds, Julia. *Blood in the Fields: Ten Years Inside California's Nuestra Familia Gang*. Chicago: Chicago Review Press, 2017.

Robinson, James W. *The DPS Story: History of the Development of the Department of Public Safety in Texas*. Austin: Texas Department of Public Safety, 1975.

Rogers, Sandra E. *Electrocutions in Texas: 1924–1964*. Huntsville, TX: The Texas Prison Museum, 2018.

Roth, Mitchel P. *Convict Cowboys: The Untold Story of the Texas Prison Rodeo*. Denton: University of North Texas Press, 2016.

Rubenser, Lorie, and Gloria Priddy. *Constables, Marshals, and More: Forgotten Offices in Texas Law Enforcement*. Denton: University of North Texas Press, 2011.

Samaha, Joel. *Criminal Law*. Belmont, CA: Wadsworth/Thomson Learning, 1999.

Sample, Albert Race. *Racehoss: Big Emma's Boy*. New York: Ballantine Books, 1984.

Santana, Juan, and Gabriel Morales. *Don't Mess with Texas! Gangs in the Lone Star State*. Lexington, KY: Self-Published, 2014.

Santos, Michael G. *Inside: Life Behind Bars in America*. New York: St. Martin's Griffin Publishing, 2007.

Sayles, John, ed., with Henry Sayles. *Early Laws of Texas: General Laws From 1836– 1879*. St. Louis, MO: The Gilbert Book Co., 1891.

Schillingberg, Wm. *Dodge City: The Early Years, 1872–1876*. Norman, OK: Arthur H. Clark and Company 2009.

Schneider, Paul. *Bonnie And Clyde: The Lives Behind the Legend*. New York: Henry Holt and Company, 2009.

Schwarz, Ted, and Mardi Rustam. *Candy Barr: The Small-Town Texas Runaway Who Became a Darling of the Mob and the Queen of Las Vegas Burlesque*. Lanham, MD: Taylor Trade Publishing, 2008.

Selcer, Richard, ed. *Legendary Watering Holes: The Saloons That Made Texas Famous*. College Station: Texas A&M University Press, 2004.

Shalev, Sharon. *SUPERMAX: Controlling Risk Through Solitary Confinement*. England: Willian Publishing, 2009.

Shannon, Elaine. *Desperados: Latin Drug Lords, U.S. Lawmen, and the War America Can't Win*. New York: Viking Penguin, Inc., 2004.

Siegel, Larry J. *Criminology*. Belmont, CA: Wadsworth/Thompson Learning, 2003.

Simmons, Lee. *Assignment Huntsville: Memoirs of a Texas Prison Official*. Austin: University of Texas Press, 1957.

Sitton, Thad. *Texas High Sheriffs*. Austin: Texas Monthly Press, 1988.

———. *The Texas Sheriff: Lord of the County Line*. Norman: University of Oklahoma Press, 2000.

Skarbek, David. *The Social Order of the Underworld: How Prison Gangs Govern the American Penal System*. New York: Oxford University Press, 2014.

Smith, Tevis Clyde. *Frontier's Generation: The Pioneer History of Brown County, With Sidelight on the Surrounding Territory*. Brownwood, TX: Self-published, 1980.

Sowell, A.J. *Early Settlers and Indian Fighters of Southwest Texas*. Austin, TX: State House Press, 1986. (A Facsimile Reproduction of the Original).

Spellman, Paul N. *Old 300: Gone to Texas*. Richmond, TX: Self-published, 2014.

———. *Captain J.A. Brooks: Texas Ranger*. Denton: University of North Texas Press, 2007.

———. *Captain John H. Rogers: Texas Ranger*. Denton: University of North Texas Press, 2003.

Steckmesser, Kent L. *The Western Hero in History and Legend*. Norman: University of Oklahoma Press, 1997.

Stephens, Robert W. *Lone Wolf: The Story of Texas Ranger Captain M.T. Gonzaullas*. Dallas, TX: Taylor Publishing, n.d.

Sykes, Gresham M. *The Society of Captives: A Study of a Maximum Security Prison*. Princeton, NJ: Princeton University Press, 2007.

Sylvester, Sawyer F., John H. Reed and David O. Nelson. *Prison Homicide*. New York: Spectrum Publications, Inc., 1977.

Tarpley, Fred. *1001 Texas Place Names*. Austin: University of Texas Press, 1980.

TDC. *30 Years of Progress*. Huntsville, TX: Texas Department of Corrections, 1977.

Thrapp, Dan L. *Encyclopedia of Frontier Biography*. 3 vols. Lincoln: University of Nebraska Press, 1988.

Tise, Sammy. *Texas County Sheriffs*. Hallettsville, TX: Tise Genealogical Research, 1989.

Toch, Hans. *Living in Prison: The Ecology of Survival*. New York: The Free Press, A Division of Macmillan Publishing Co., 1977.

———. *Police, Prisons, and the Problem of Violence*. Rockville, MD: National Institute of Mental Health—Center for Studies of Crime and Delinquency, 1977.

Trammell, Rebecca. *Enforcing the Convict Code: Violence and Prison Culture*. Boulder, CO: Lynne Rienner Publishers, 2012.

Trulson, Chad R., and James W. Marquart. *First Available Cell: Desegregation of the Texas Prison System*. Austin: University of Texas Press, 2009.

Tucker, ed., Julie N. *Correctional Officers: Power, Pressure and Responsibility*. College Park, MD: American Correctional Association, 1983.

Turk, David S. *Forging the Star: The Official Modern History of the United States Marshals Service*. Denton: University of North Texas Press, 2016.

Tyler, Ron, ed. *The New Handbook of Texas*. 6 vols. Austin: Texas State Historical Society, 1996.

Umphrey, Don. *The Meanest Man in Texas*. Dallas, TX: Quarry Press, 2007.

Underwood, Sid. *Depression Desperado: The Chronicle of Raymond Hamilton*. Austin, TX: Eakin Press, 1995.

Utley, Robert M. *Lone Star Lawmen: The Second Century of the Texas Rangers*. New York: Oxford University Press, 2007.

Van, Donna Reid. *Dad, Man of Mystery*. n.p. Silverfox Books, 2015.

Walker, Donald R. *Penology for Profit: A History of the Texas Prison System, 1867–1912*. College Station: Texas A&M University Press, 1988.

Webb, Walter P. *The Texas Rangers: A Century of Frontier Defense*. 1935, repr., Austin: University of Texas Press, 1965.

Weiss, Jr., Harold J. *Yours to Command: The Life and Legend of Texas Ranger Captain Bill McDonald*. Denton: University of North Texas Press, 2009.

Welch, June Rayfield. *The Texas Courthouse Revisited*. Waco, TX: Yellow Rose Press, Texian Press, 1984, 1990.

Willett, Jim, and Ron Rozelle. *Warden: Prison Life and Death from the Inside Out*. Houston, TX: Bright Sky Press, 2004.

Williams, Eric J. *The Big House in a Small Town*. Santa Barbara, CA: Praeger Books, 2011.

Williams, Vergil L., and Mary Fish. *Convicts, Codes, and Contraband: The Prison Life of Men and Women*. Cambridge, MA: Ballinger Publishing Company, 1974.

Willson, Sam A., ed. *Revised Penal Code and Code of Criminal Procedure of the State of Texas*. St. Louis, MO: The Gilbert Book Co., 1888.

Wilson, Carol. *In the Governor's Shadow: The True Story of Ma and Pa Ferguson*. Denton: University of North Texas Press, 2014.

Winfrey, Dorman H., and James M. Day, eds. *The Indian Papers of Texas and the Southwest, 1825–1916*. Vol. 4. Austin: Texas State Historical Association, 1995.

Zimmer, Lynn E. *Women Guarding Men*. Chicago: University of Chicago Press, 1986.

Periodicals:

Allen, Ruth Alice. "The Capitol Boycott: A Study in Peaceful Labor Tactics." *Southwestern Historical Quarterly*, April 1939.

Bell, Bob Boze. "Overkill! Bonnie and Clyde vs. Frank Hamer and His Posse." *True West*, January 2019.

———. "The Case Against Wyatt Earp." *True West*, February 1999.

Boessenecker, John. "Frank Hamer vs. Bonnie and Clyde." *True West*, April 2019.

Brand, Peter. "10 Earp Vendetta Ride Myths." *True West*, April 2018.

Burton, Jeff. "A Great Manhunt: Correspondence from 'W.B.S.'" *English Westerners Society Brand Book*, 1975–76.

Cantrell, Gregg. "Racial Violence and Reconstruction Politics in Texas, 1867–1868." *Southwestern Historical Quarterly*, January 1990.

Cartledge, Rick. "The Guns of Frank Hamer." *OklahombreS*, Spring 1993.

Cartwright, Gary. "Free to Kill. *Texas Monthly*, August 1992.

———. "Bad Girl of the Century." *Texas Monthly*, December 1999.

———. "Candy Barr." *Texas Monthly*, December 1976.

———. "Talking to Killers." *Texas Monthly*, July 2002.

Chammah, Maurice. "Sitting in Legal Purgatory." *Texas Monthly*, December 2013.

Colloff, Pamela. "The Witness." *Texas Monthly*, September 2014.

Conger, Roger, ed. "Ben McCulloch, 1811–1862." *The Texas Ranger Annual* 5 (1986).

———. "Lone Wolf Gonzaullas: Courage with Compassion." *Texas Ranger Annual IV*, 1985.

Cummins, Light T. "Bonnie and Clyde, The Barrow Gang and Lee Simmons." *Texhoma Living!* March-April 2010.

Devereaux, Jan. "Gentle Woman, Tough Medicine." *National Association for Outlaw and Lawman History Quarterly*, April-June 2003.

———. "Jagville." *National Association for Outlaw and Lawman History Quarterly*, January/March, 2004.

Draper, Robert. "The Great Texas Prison Mess." *Texas Monthly*, May 1996.

———. "A Guard in Gangland." *Texas Monthly*, July 1991.

Duncan, J.S. "Richard Bennett Hubbard and State Resumption of the Penitentiary, 1876–1878." *Texana* 12, no.1 (1974).

Eds. "Texas Prisons—A Continuing Crisis." *Texas Research League Analysis* 6, no. 11 (November 1985).

Estill, Harry. "The Old Town of Huntsville." *Quarterly of the Texas State Historical Association*, April 1900.

Fusco, John. "The Legendary Maney Gault." *True West*, April 2019.

Glenn, Lon. "Last Legal Hanging." *Image*, No. 2, 2018.

———. "The Grand Surfside Hotel, 1891–1907." *Image*, No. 1, 2019.

Hardy, Michael. "Blood and Sugar: Confronting Sugar Land's Forgotten History." *Texas Monthly*, January 2017.

Heimlich, Janet. "Brute Causes." *Texas Monthly*, November 1997.

Hollandsworth, Skip. "The Sting." *Texas Monthly*, May 2018.

———. "O Sister, Where Art Thou?" *Texas Monthly*, May 2003.

———. "Maximum Insecurity." *Teas Monthly*, March 2001.

Horton, Joel. "Texas Prison Units. . . . and Their Impact on Local Economies and Comparatives." *Texas Co-Op Power*, March 1992.

House, Kurt. "Cold Steel and Warm Gold: Arms & Badges of Three Texas Ranger Captains." *The Texas Gun Collector*, Fall 2013.

Hudson, Don W. "Quality Before Quantity." *TCI* [Texas Correctional Industries] *Newsletter*, October/November 1995.

Jay, Roger. "The Peoria Bummer—Wyatt Earp's Lost Year." *Wild West*, August 2003.

Jordan, Terry G. "A Century and a Half of Ethnic Change in Texas, 1836–1986." *Southwestern Historical Quarterly*, April 1986.

Korosec, Thomas. "The Death Row Inmate and His Cunning Bride." *D Magazine*, June 2011.

Lucko, Paul M. "A Missed Opportunity: Texas Prison Reform During the Dan Moody Administration." *Southwestern Historical Quarterly*, July 1992.

———. "Counteracting Reform: Lee Simmons and the Texas Prison System, 1931–1935." *East Texas Historical Journal* 3, no. 2 (1992).

———. "The Governor and the Bat: Prison Reform during the Oscar B. Colquitt Administration, 1911–1915." *Southwestern Historical Quarterly*, June 2003.

McCoy, Dara. "In the Shadow of Death." *Austin College Magazine*, September 2008.

MacCormick, Austin. "Behind Those Prison Riots." *Readers Digest*, December 1953.

Mattix, Rick. "The Confession of William Daniel Jones." *OklahombreS*, Fall 2001.

Maxwell, Linda Lee. "Last of the Kiowa War Chiefs." *Texana* 7, no. 2 (1969).

Moore, Bill. "The Texas Calaboose." *Texas Co-op Power*, June 2015.

NDIS [National Drug Intelligence Center]. *Narcotics Digest Weekly* 4, no. 5 (October 4, 2005).

Oyeniyi, Doyin. "The Exonerated." *Texas Monthly*, May 2018.

Parke, Henry C. "The Man Who Redeemed the Hamer Name." *True West*, January 2019.

Phillips, John Neal. "The Raid on Eastham." *American History*, October 2000.

Price, J. Keith and Susan Coleman. "Narrative of Neglect: Texas Prisons for Men." *East Texas Historical Journal* 49, no. 2 (2011).

Rakoczy, Lila. "Camp Logan Mutiny Revisited." *The Medallion*, Spring 2017.

Ramsdell, Charles W. "Texas from the Fall of the Confederacy to the Beginning of Reconstruction." *The Quarterly of the Texas State Historical Association*, January 1908.

Reavis, Dick. "How They Ruined Our Prisons." *Texas Monthly*, May 1985.

———. "Charlie Brooks' Last Words." *Texas Monthly*, February 1883.

Redding, Stan. "Top Gun of the Texas Rangers." *True Detective*. (double-length feature article), February 1963.

Reese, James V. "The Early History of Labor Organizations in Texas, 1838–1876. *Southwestern Historical Quarterly*, July 1968.

Richardson, Rupert N. "Edward M. House and the Governors." *Southwestern Historical Quarterly*, July 1957.

Robinson, Julia. "Texas: A Blues State." *Texas Co-Op Power*, March 2019.

Roth, Mitchel. "Bonnie and Clyde in Texas: The End of the Texas Outlaw Tradition." *East Texas Historical Journal*, 1997.

Rye, Dale A. "Understanding the Republic of Texas and Other Extremist Groups." *Criminal Law Update*, Summer 1996.

Smith, Ralph. "The Grange Movement in Texas, 1873–1900." *Southwestern Historical Quarterly*, April, 1939.

U.S. Marshals Service. *Marshals MONITOR* (newsletter) May-June, 2997; January–February 2001.

Utley, Robert M. "The Forgotten Hero." *True West*, April 2019.

———. "Terminating Oklahoma's Smiling Killer." *Texas Ranger Dispatch*, Summer 2005.

Watters, Ethan. "The Love Story That Upended the Prison." *Texas Monthly*, January 2019.

Newspapers:

Abilene Reporter-News
Amarillo Daily News
Amarillo Globe-News
Angleton Times
Arizona Republic
Atlanta Constitution
Austin American Statesman
Austin Weekly Democratic Statesman
Baytown Sun
Beaumont Enterprise
Beaumont Journal
Beeville Bee
Brazosport Facts
Brenham Southern Banner
Brenham Weekly Banner
Brownsville Herald
Bryan Daily Eagle
Chicago Tribune
Clarksville Standard
Corpus Christi Caller
Corpus Christi Caller-Times
Corpus Christi Times
Corsicana Daily Sun
Corsicana Observer
Cut Bank Pioneer Press
Daily Capitol News
Daily Messenger
Dallas Daily Herald
Dallas Morning News
Dallas Weekly Herald
Del Rio News-Herald
El Paso Herald-Post

Flake's Bulletin
Fort Bend Star
Fort Worth Daily Democrat
Fort Worth Gazette
Fort Worth Press
Fort Worth Star-Telegram
Fredericksburg Standard
Freeport Facts
Galveston Daily News
Galveston Weekly News
Gazette Telegraph [Colorado]
Gonzales Inquirer
Harrisburg Star-Independent
Houston Chronicle
Houston Post
Houston Tri-Weekly Telegraph
Huntsville Banner
Huntsville Item
Kerrville Daily Times
Killeen Daily Herald
Knoxville News-Sentinel
Liberty Vindicator
Longview Daily Review
Longview News-Journal
Los Angles Times
Lubbock Avalanche-Journal
Lubbock Evening Journal
Lubbock Morning Avalanche
McAllen Monitor
Mexia Weekly Herald
Mobile Register
Morning Olympian

Navasota Examiner
New Braunfels Herald Zeitung
New Orleans Times
New York Times
Orange Leader
Orlando Sentinel
Palestine Herald-Press
Pecos Enterprise
Pecos Valley Argus
Pittsburg Press
Plainview Daily Herald
Plainview Reporter-News
Port Arthur News
San Angelo Standard-Times
San Antonio Express
Seattle Post-Intelligencer
Sedalia Democrat
Seguin Gazette-Enterprise
Shreveport Times
Stephenville Empire
Taylor Daily Press

Temple Daily Telegram
Texarkana Gazette
Texas State Gazette
Texas Union
The Angleton Times
The Brazorian News
The Comanche Chief
The Daily Messenger
The Echo
The Gladewaters
The Hammond Times
The Longview Daily News
The Montana Statesman
The Rusk Cherokeean
The Velasco World
Vicksburg Daily Herald
Victoria Advocate
Waco News-Tribune
Waxahachie Daily Light
Weekly Houston Telegram
Wichita Falls Times

Index